T0281495

Lecture Notes in Computer Science   **14393**

Founding Editors

Gerhard Goos
Juris Hartmanis

The series Lecture Notes in Computer Science (LNCS), including its subseries Lecture Notes in Artificial Intelligence (LNAI) and Lecture Notes in Bioinformatics (LNBI), has established itself as a medium for the publication of new developments in computer science and information technology research, teaching, and education.

LNCS enjoys close cooperation with the computer science R & D community, the series counts many renowned academics among its volume editors and paper authors, and collaborates with prestigious societies. Its mission is to serve this international community by providing an invaluable service, mainly focused on the publication of conference and workshop proceedings and postproceedings. LNCS commenced publication in 1973.

M. Emre Celebi · Md Sirajus Salekin ·
Hyunwoo Kim · Shadi Albarqouni et al.
Editors

Medical Image Computing and Computer Assisted Intervention – MICCAI 2023 Workshops

ISIC 2023, Care-AI 2023, MedAGI 2023, DeCaF 2023
Held in Conjunction with MICCAI 2023
Vancouver, BC, Canada, October 8–12, 2023
Proceedings

Editors
M. Emre Celebi 🆔
University of Central Arkansas
Conway, AR, USA

Hyunwoo Kim 🆔
Korea University
Seoul, Korea (Republic of)

Md Sirajus Salekin
Amazon Development Center U.S. Inc.
Seattle, WA, USA

Shadi Albarqouni 🆔
University Hospital Bonn
Bonn, Germany

Additional Workshop Editors *see next page*

ISSN 0302-9743   ISSN 1611-3349 (electronic)
Lecture Notes in Computer Science
ISBN 978-3-031-47400-2   ISBN 978-3-031-47401-9 (eBook)
https://doi.org/10.1007/978-3-031-47401-9

This Springer imprint is published by the registered company Springer Nature Switzerland AG
The registered company address is: Gewerbestrasse 11, 6330 Cham, Switzerland

Paper in this product is recyclable.

Workshop Editors

Catarina Barata
Instituto Superior Técnico
Lisbon, Portugal

Philipp Tschandl
Medical University of Vienna
Vienna, Austria

Yuan Liu
Google (United States)
Palo Alto, CA, USA

Joshua Levy
Amazon (United States)
Cambridge, MA, USA

Annika Reinke
German Cancer Research Center
Heidelberg, Germany

Bennett Landman
Vanderbilt University
Brentwood, TN, USA

Yiqing Shen
Johns Hopkins University
Baltimore, MD, USA

Spyridon Bakas
University of Pennsylvania
Philadelphia, PA, USA

Chen Qin
Imperial College London
London, UK

Holger Roth
NVIDIA Corporation
Bethesda, MD, USA

Allan Halpern
Memorial Sloan Kettering Cancer Center
New York, NY, USA

Marc Combalia
Kenko AI
Barcelona, Spain

Ghada Zamzmi
National Institutes of Health
Bethesda, MD, USA

Huzefa Rangwala
Amazon (United States)
Fairfax, VI, USA

Diya Wynn
Amazon (United States)
Baltimore, WA, USA

Won-Ki Jeong
Korea University
Seoul, Korea (Republic of)

Zhongying Deng
University of Surrey
Guildford, UK

Xiaoxiao Li
University of British Columbia
Vancouver, Canada

Nicola Rieke
NVIDIA Corporation
Munich, Germany

Daguang Xu
NVIDIA Corporation
Santa Clara, CA, USA

ISIC Preface

The Eighth International Skin Imaging Collaboration (ISIC) Workshop on Skin Image Analysis was held at the Vancouver Convention Centre, Vancouver, British Columbia, Canada on October 12, 2023, in conjunction with the 26th International Conference on Medical Image Computing and Computer-Assisted Intervention (MICCAI).

The skin is the largest organ of the human body, and is the first area of a patient assessed by clinical staff. The skin delivers numerous insights into a patient's underlying health: for example, pale or blue skin suggests respiratory issues, unusually yellowish skin can signal hepatic issues, or certain rashes can be indicative of autoimmune issues. In addition, dermatological complaints are also among the most prevalent in primary care. Images of the skin are the most easily captured form of medical image in healthcare, and the domain shares qualities to standard computer vision datasets, serving as a natural bridge between standard computer vision tasks and medical applications. However, significant and unique challenges still exist in this domain. For example, there is remarkable visual similarity across disease conditions, and compared to other medical imaging domains, varying genetics, disease states, imaging equipment, and imaging conditions can significantly change the appearance of the skin, making localization and classification in this domain unsolved tasks.

This workshop served as a venue to facilitate advancements and knowledge dissemination in the field of skin image analysis, raising awareness and interest for these socially valuable tasks. Invited speakers included major influencers in computer vision and skin imaging, and authors of accepted papers.

Authors were asked to submit full-length manuscripts for double-blind peer review. A total of 31 submissions were received, and with a Program Committee composed of 22 experts in the field, reviewed by at least three reviewers. Based on the feedback and critiques, six of the best papers (19%) were selected for oral presentation at the workshop, and were included in the LNCS volume published by Springer.

We thank the authors for submitting their excellent work, our reviewers for their timely and detailed reviews, our invited speakers, and all our attendees. We sincerely hope that the efforts coming together to make this workshop possible will help advance the field and have a positive impact on health care worldwide.

October 2023

M. Emre Celebi
Catarina Barata
Allan Halpern
Philipp Tschandl
Marc Combalia
Yuan Liu

ISIC 2023 Organization

Proceedings Chair

M. Emre Celebi   University of Central Arkansas, USA

Steering Committee

Noel C. F. Codella   Microsoft, USA
Anthony Hoogs   Kitware, USA
Yun Liu   Google Health, USA
Dale Webster   Google Health, USA

Workshop Chairs

M. Emre Celebi   University of Central Arkansas, USA
Catarina Barata   Instituto Superior Técnico, Portugal
Allan Halpern   Memorial Sloan Kettering Cancer Center, USA
Philipp Tschandl   Medical University of Vienna, Austria
Marc Combalia   Kenko AI, Spain
Yuan Liu   Google Health, USA

Program Committee

Kumar Abhishek   Simon Fraser University, Canada
Euijoon Ahn   James Cook University, Australia
Sandra Avila   University of Campinas, Brazil
Nourhan Bayasi   University of British Columbia, Canada
Lei Bi   University of Sydney, Australia
Alceu Bissoto   University of Campinas, Brazil
Siyi Du   University of British Columbia, Canada
Ghassan Hamarneh   Simon Fraser University, Canada
Joanna Jaworek-Korjakowska   AGH University of Science and Technology, Poland
Jeremy Kawahara   Simon Fraser University, Canada
Jinman Kim   University of Sydney, Australia

Sinan Kockara	Rice University, USA
Kivanc Kose	Memorial Sloan Kettering Cancer Center, USA
Arezou Pakzad	Simon Fraser University, Canada
Eduardo Valle	University of Campinas, Brazil
Moi Hoon Yap	Manchester Metropolitan University, UK

Care-AI 2023 Preface

Over the past decade, Artificial Intelligence (AI) and Machine Learning (ML) have advanced many fields including finance, education, and healthcare. In healthcare, AI/ML has shown promising performance and efficiency in medical image analysis, computer-aided diagnosis, and computer-assisted intervention systems. However, there is a growing concern regarding the potential risks occurring as a result of poor design and development of AI applications. To address this pressing concern, responsible AI (RAI) has recently attracted increasing attention. RAI can be defined as the process of designing, implementing, and deploying AI algorithms that are fair, reliable, generalizable, explainable, robust, and secure. These principles and values are of paramount importance in high-stakes fields such as healthcare.

Given that biased AI models can cause adverse and life-altering consequences, the process of designing and developing AI solutions for healthcare should consider factors such as minority groups representation, biased benefits of stakeholders, technology misuse, among others. Another major factor that leads to bias in ML algorithms is their "black-box" nature, which makes it very difficult to detect discrimination as well as explain the "how" and "why" of clinical decisions. In addition to fairness and explainability, ML models that are applied in healthcare should be verified mathematically, evaluated comprehensively, and validated empirically to ensure consistent, generalizable, reliable, and robust performance under known and unknown (unexpected) conditions. Further, given that patient's data might contain sensitive information, AI-based healthcare applications should be designed to protect patient information, resist attacks, and comply with privacy laws that govern data collection, processing, and storage.

This was the first workshop proceeding on Clinically-Oriented and Responsible AI for Medical Data Analysis (Care-AI) at MICCAI, held on October 8, 2023 in Vancouver, Canada. In this workshop, we examined the technical and research progress towards accountable and responsible AI in medical image analysis, computer-aided diagnosis, and computer-assisted intervention systems. We received 9 full papers and 5 excellent papers were accepted. Each submission was reviewed by 3 reviewers and further assessed by the workshop's chairs. The workshop's reviewing process was double-blind.

We want to thank our Program Committee members, reviewers, keynote speakers, and authors who made this workshop successful. We are very grateful to the MICCAI committee for providing us with such a wonderful opportunity.

October 2023

Md Sirajus Salekin
Ghada Zamzmi
Joshua Levy
Huzefa Rangwala
Annika Reinke
Diya Wynn
Bennett Landman

Care-AI 2023 Organization

Proceedings Chair

M. Emre Celebi   University of Central Arkansas, USA

Workshop Chairs

Md Sirajus Salekin   Amazon, USA
Ghada Zamzmi   National Institutes of Health, USA
Joshua Levy   Amazon, USA
Huzefa Rangwala   Amazon, USA
Annika Reinke   German Cancer Research Center, Germany
Diya Wynn   Amazon, USA
Bennett Landman   Vanderbilt University, USA

Program Committee

Nkechinyere Agu   Amazon, USA
Jacqueline Hausmann   University of South Florida, USA
Nicholas Heller   University of Minnesota, USA
Md Imran Hossain   University of South Florida, USA
Weronika Hryniewska-Guzik Warsaw University of Technology, Poland
Dong Huo   University of Alberta, Canada
Rafsanjany Kushol   University of Alberta, Canada
Xiaoyang Liu   Amazon, USA
Hunter Morera   University of South Florida, USA
Rahul Paul   Food and Drug Administration, USA
Eike Petersen   Technical University of Denmark, Denmark
Sourya Sengupta   University of Illinois Urbana Champaign, USA
Elena Sizikova   Food and Drug Administration, USA

MedAGI 2023 Preface

The first International Workshop on Foundation Models for Medical Artificial General Intelligence (MedAGI) was held at the Vancouver Convention Centre, Vancouver, Canada on October 12, 2023, in conjunction with the 26th International Conference on Medical Image Computing and Computer-Assisted Intervention (MICCAI 2023).

In the context of medical image analysis, existing artificial intelligence (AI) solutions are carefully designed and evaluated upon one specific dataset, which is difficult to transfer to another task or handle datasets curated from different medical centers. However, data modalities and task formulation vary in real clinical practices across hospitals and institutions. This results in increasing attention towards a general model to tackle different medical scenarios. More precisely, a general AI model with excellent generalization ability for processing other medical image modalities to handle a variety of medical AI tasks is termed "general medical AI".

In computer vision and in the natural language processing domain, large-scale vision or language foundation models have shown amazing capabilities in visual recognition tasks, text-image generation, text-image retrieval, and high-level multi-modal multi-step reasoning. The outstanding generalization power of foundation models in new domains and tasks opens the door for zero-shot (or few-shot) visual recognition tasks: image classification, object detection, and segmentation. Despite the encouraging success in the computer vision domain, adopting foundation models in the medical domain is still in the early stage.

This workshop is dedicated to addressing the current medical AI systems and discussing opportunities for generalizing learning systems across multiple unseen tasks and domains.

This workshop accepted 23 full-length manuscripts and 13 extended abstracts, in total 32 submissions. Among them, the full-length manuscripts were peer-reviewed by at least two reviewers following a double-blind approach. The reviewers, as part of the Program Committee, were composed of 38 experts in medical image analysis. Based on their valuable reviews, 11 papers were accepted as oral presentation and 6 papers were accepted as poster presentation, to be published in the LNCS volume by Springer, and the authors were also invited to deliver oral presentations at the workshop. The extended abstracts were reviewed by two workshop chairs in a single-blind format but not included in the volume for publication.

We thank all the participants, including the authors, the reviewers, the invited speakers, and the attendees, for their valuable work and significant efforts, which contributed to the success of the workshop. We hope that this workshop will advance the development of general medical AI for multiple unseen tasks and domains.

October 2023

Won-Ki Jeong
Hyunwoo J. Kim
Yiqing Shen
Zhongying Deng

MedAGI 2023 Organization

Proceedings Chair

M. Emre Celebi   University of Central Arkansas, USA

Program Committee Chairs

Won-Ki Jeong   Korea University, Korea
Hyunwoo Kim   Korea University, Korea
Yiqing Shen   Johns Hopkins University, USA
Zhongying Deng   University of Surrey, UK

Program Committee

Edward Choi   KAIST, Korea
Junjun He   Shanghai AI Laboratory, China
Hoon Cho   Broad Institute of MIT and Harvard, USA
Donglai Wei   Boston College, USA
Jin Ye   Shanghai AI Laboratory, China
Jing Ke   Shanghai Jiao Tong University, China
Seong Jae Hwang   Yonsei University, Korea
Yun Gu   Shanghai Jiao Tong University, China
Weidao Chen   Beijing Infervision Technology, China
Xiaosong Wang   Shanghai AI Laboratory, China
Ruimao Zhang   Chinese University of Hong Kong, China
Jingchen Ma   Columbia University, USA
Yu Guang Wang   Shanghai Jiao Tong University, China
Jiancheng Yang   EPFL, Switzerland
Shunjun Wang   Hong Kong Polytechnic University, China
Xuebin Zheng   Fosun AITrox, China
Hongyu Zhou   Tsinghua University, China
Jong Hak Moon   KAIST, Korea
Hyungyung Lee   KAIST, Korea
Juan Caicedo   Broad Institute, USA
Seyoung Chun   Seoul National University, Korea
Seungryong Kim   Korea University, Korea
Jinkyu Kim   Korea University, Korea
Janghwan Choi   Ewha Womans University, Korea

Jintae Kwak	Korea University, Korea
Youngjung Uh	Yonsei University, Korea
Jaejun Yoo	UNIST, Korea
Changjae Oh	Queen Mary University of London, UK
Jiyoung Lee	NAVER AI Lab, France
Sangryung Jeon	University of Michigan, USA
Steve Lin	Microsoft Research Asia, China
Matteo Poggi	University of Bologna, Italy
Erfan Darzi	University of Groningen, The Netherlands
Wonhwa Kim	POSTECH, Korea

DeCaF 2023 Preface

Machine learning methodologies have exhibited the potential to bring about transformative effects across various applications and industries, leveraging extensive datasets to identify and comprehend patterns. A pivotal subject within contemporary scientific discourse pertains to the acquisition and utilization of data while upholding user privacy. The industrial utilization of machine learning and deep learning (DL) techniques has underscored the dual imperatives of sourcing user data from the relevant application domain to facilitate ongoing model enhancement and expose certain inadequacies in prevailing approaches concerning privacy preservation.

The need for innovative strategies in data acquisition, utilization, and management, coupled with the assurance of data privacy and security, has assumed paramount significance within the research community. Prevalent strategies predominantly rely on centralized data repositories housing sensitive information, often beyond direct user control. Within contexts demanding heightened privacy considerations, such as healthcare, wherein confidentiality takes precedence over functionality, strategies necessitating centralized data repositories prove suboptimal, potentially engendering substantial limitations on model development and application scope.

Additional privacy apprehensions stem from inherent mathematical underpinnings of machine learning paradigms, notably within DL methods. It has been evidenced that DL models may internalize segments of training data, potentially encompassing sensitive data within their parameters. Ongoing research endeavors are actively pursuing avenues to mitigate concerns arising from this phenomenon. Notably, these themes extend beyond the purview of distributed and collaborative learning techniques, yet they remain intrinsically linked to such approaches.

The 4th MICCAI Workshop on Distributed, Collaborative, and Federated (DeCaF 2023) aspired to stimulate scholarly discourse centered around comparative analysis, evaluation, and deliberation on methodological advancements and pragmatic concepts in machine learning, applied to scenarios wherein centralized databases are untenable for data storage. This includes instances where information privacy is of paramount concern, necessitating robust assurances pertaining to the extent and nature of private data exposure resulting from model training. Moreover, the workshop sought to address environments wherein the coordination, oversight, and direction of node clusters participating in a shared learning endeavor are indispensable.

During the fourth iteration of DeCaF, 10 submissions were subjected to rigorous consideration, ultimately culminating in the acceptance of 7 comprehensive papers for presentation following a double-blind peer review process. Each manuscript underwent meticulous assessment by no fewer than three independent reviewers, chosen to mitigate potential conflicts of interest and recent collaborative involvements. These reviewers were selected from a global cohort of preeminent experts within the field.

The final determinations concerning acceptance, conditional acceptance, or rejection were entrusted to area chairs, predicated upon the evaluative insights gleaned from the reviews, and these verdicts were final and irrevocable. In instances of conditional acceptance, authors were tasked with effecting substantive refinements and enhancements, aligning with reviewer feedback to bolster the scientific rigor and clarity of their manuscripts.

The double-blind review process, involving three dispassionate reviewers for each submission, coupled with the framework of conditional acceptance, alongside the oversight of meta-reviewers in the decision-making process, collectively safeguarded the scientific integrity and elevated the caliber of the contributions showcased during the third version of DeCaF. By extension, this commendable input has significantly enriched the MICCAI community, particularly the cohort of researchers engaged in distributed and collaborative learning pursuits.

Thus, it is incumbent upon us to express our gratitude to the authors for their valuable contributions and to extend our appreciation to the reviewers for their unwavering commitment and equitable evaluation of their peers' endeavors.

October 2023

Shadi Albarqouni
Spyridon Bakas
Xiaoxiao Li
Chen Qin
Nicola Rieke
Holger Roth
Daguang Xu

DeCaF 2023 Organization

Proceedings Chair

M. Emre Celebi   University of Central Arkansas, USA

Organizing Committee

Shadi Albarqouni   University of Bonn and Helmholtz AI, Germany
Spyridon Bakas   University of Pennsylvania, USA
Xiaoxiao Li   University of British Columbia, Canada
Chen Qin   Imperial College London, UK
Nicola Rieke   NVIDIA, Germany
Holger Roth   NVIDIA, USA
Daguang Xu   NVIDIA, USA

Outreach Committee

Manuela Bergau   University Hospital Bonn, Germany
Chun-Yin Huang   University of British Columbia, Canada

Contents

**Proceedings of the First International Workshop on Foundation
Models for Medical Artificial General Intelligence (MedAGI 2023)**

Proceedings of the Eighth International Skin Imaging Collaboration Workshop (ISIC 2023)

Continual-GEN: Continual Group Ensembling for Domain-agnostic Skin Lesion Classification

Nourhan Bayasi[1(✉)] , Siyi Du[1] , Ghassan Hamarneh[2] , and Rafeef Garbi[1]

[1] BiSICL, University of British Columbia, Vancouver, BC, Canada
{nourhanb,siyi,rafeef}@ece.ubc.ca
[2] Medical Image Analysis Lab, Simon Fraser University, Burnaby, BC, Canada
hamarneh@sfu.ca

Abstract. Designing deep learning (DL) models that adapt to new data without forgetting previously acquired knowledge is important in the medical field where data is generated daily, posing a challenge for model adaptation and knowledge retention. Continual learning (CL) enables models to learn continuously without forgetting, typically on a sequence of domains with known domain identities (e.g. source of data). In this work, we address a more challenging and practical CL scenario where information about the domain identity during training and inference is unavailable. We propose Continual-GEN, a novel forget-free, replay-free, and domain-agnostic subnetwork-based CL method for medical imaging with a focus on skin lesion classification. Continual-GEN proposes an ensemble of groups approach that decomposes the training data for each domain into groups of semantically similar clusters. Given two domains, Continual-GEN assesses the similarity between them based on the distance between their ensembles and assigns a separate subnetwork if the similarity score is low, otherwise updating the same subnetwork to learn both domains. At inference, Continual-GEN selects the best subnetwork using a distance-based metric for each test data, which is directly used for classification. Our quantitative experiments on four skin lesion datasets demonstrate the superiority of Continual-GEN over state-of-the-art CL methods, highlighting its potential for practical applications in medical imaging. Our code: https://github.com/nourhanb/Continual-GEN.

Keywords: Continual Learning · Domain-agnostic · Out-of-Distribution Detection · Skin Lesion Classification · Dermatology

1 Introduction

Deep learning (DL) models have emerged as powerful tools, surpassing human experts in certain cases, particularly in skin lesion classification [7]. However,

Supplementary Information The online version contains supplementary material available at https://doi.org/10.1007/978-3-031-47401-9_1.

M. E. Celebi et al. (Eds.): MICCAI 2023 Workshops, LNCS 14393, pp. 3–13, 2023.
https://doi.org/10.1007/978-3-031-47401-9_1

the conventional clinical practice of training DL models only once falls short of addressing the steady stream of medical data, where data is generated daily and often exhibits a domain shift arising from various factors such as diverse clinical practices, variations in clinical devices or diagnostic workflows, or differences in data populations [8,23]. Thus, there is a pressing need to design DL models that can effectively learn a stream of heterogeneous data and adeptly adapt to the substantial domain shift encountered across the different straining domains. The straightforward approach of fine-tuning DL models with either new lesions or heterogeneous data, without access to the initial training data, easily leads to overwriting of previously learned knowledge, resulting in *catastrophic forgetting*.

Continual learning (CL) [22] aims to enable DL models to adapt to changing environments and learn from new data while retaining previous knowledge. Replay-based methods [17,18] store a subset of data samples and replay them periodically to retain past domain information. However, these methods face challenges in medical domains due to data privacy policies that restrict unregulated data storage and transfer [24]. Regularization-based methods [2,16] impose restrictions on parameter updates to preserve prior knowledge while learning new domains. However, with the complex and heterogeneous medical data, the performance of these methods is significantly limited. Architecture-based methods [9] assign specialized architectural components for each domain, but encounter increased memory usage as new domains emerge. A promising recent approach has been developed that utilizes different subnetworks within a *fixed-size* dense network to learn the different domains [3,6,15]. Taking advantage of the over-parameterization of DL models, this subnetwork-based approach effectively addresses memory usage limitations in architecture-based methods by pruning unimportant weights, leading to optimized memory footprint and comparable or superior performance. However, existing CL methods face a crucial limitation in their practical deployment in dynamic real-world environments, particularly healthcare, due to the assumption of known data domain identities, such as the source of data or the specific device used for data generation. In practice, the anonymization process may erase domain identity information, making it infeasible to rely on such information during training or inference. As a consequence, current CL methods often underperform when evaluated in a domain-agnostic setup [19].

In this work, we introduce `Continual-GEN`, the first subnetwork-based CL approach for skin lesion classification that is not only forget-free and replay-free, but also domain-agnostic during training and inference. Specifically, we introduce a continual OOD detection method that is triggered when a domain shift occurs, allowing us to initialize a new subnetwork for learning the new domain during training. Our approach involves decomposing the semantic space for each training domain into distinct clusters with similar semantics, enabling the detection of new domains based on their distance to the clusters of previous domains. However, selecting an optimal number of clusters is challenging due to the complex heterogeneity of skin data. To this end, we introduce the novel ensemble of groups technique, which partitions the features into different groups,

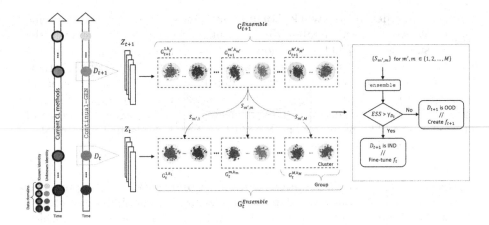

Fig. 1. Continual-GEN decomposes data into ensemble of M groups in the feature space, where the m-th group contains k_m clusters. To identify the similarity between two domains D_{t+1} and D_t, an ensemble similarity score ESS is calculated from the **ensemble** of all the minimum distances of each pair of groups, $\{(\mathbf{G}_{t+1}^{m',k_{m'}}, \mathbf{G}_t^{m,k_m})\}_{m',m=1}^M$. A large ESS score indicates higher similarity between the two domains, i.e., D_{t+1} is IND with respect to D_t and f_t is updated with D_{t+1}. Else, D_{t+1} is OOD and a new subnetwork f_{t+1} is initialized to learn D_{t+1}.

each with a different number of clusters. This approach enhances OOD detection reliability without the need for determining an optimal number of clusters. During inference, Continual-GEN utilizes a distance-based metric to select the most appropriate subnetwork for each test data, which is directly used for classification. Experimental results on four diverse skin image datasets provide strong evidence supporting the superiority of our method compared to others.

2   Continual-GEN

Preliminaries. We propose a CL framework where a network f, of a fixed size, learns T domains $D = \{D_1, \ldots, D_t, \ldots, D_T\}$ sequentially over time while retaining previously acquired knowledge. The t-th domain $D_t = \{(x_t^i, y_t^i)\}_{i=1}^{N_t}$ contains N_t tuples of input samples $x_i^t \in \mathcal{X}$ and their corresponding labels $y_i^t \in \mathcal{C}$. When encountering the t-th domain with unknown identity, the data from previous domains $\{D_i\}_{i=1}^{t-1}$ is either unavailable or restricted. Our objective is to identify an optimal domain-specific subnetwork f_t for D_t, which is only updated when encountering a new, in-distribution (IND) domain. Else, f_t remains frozen and a new subnetwork is created to learn the OOD domain. The network f should be deployable at any time and capable of extracting predictions using the best subnetwork without knowledge of the test image's specific identity.

Domain-specific Subnetwork Formation. After training f on a specific domain D_t, we utilize a culpability-based pruning technique [3] to identify the optimal subnetwork f_t. This technique involves pruning units with high culpability scores, effectively removing them as they are considered unimportant. Through this process, we ensure that the subnetwork f_t maintains performance comparable to the full network, while simultaneously creating room, i.e., preserving capacity, within the network f to effectively learn knowledge encountered in future domains. The pruning is performed based on a predefined pruning percentage p, which is set by the user.

Create a New or Update an Existing Subnetwork. When presented with a new batch of data, D_{t+1}, Continual-GEN assesses the similarity between D_{t+1} and each previously encountered domain $\{D_i\}_{i=1}^t$. This assessment, which includes three steps (I-III, below), determines whether the new data is IND with respect to any previous domain or OOD. In the case of IND, Continual-GEN reuses and updates the corresponding subnetwork, while for OOD, it creates a new subnetwork specifically for D_{t+1}. For notational simplicity, we illustrate the process using only the most recent domain, D_t.

I. Ensemble of Groups. Upon selecting the optimal subnetwork f_t for D_t, we extract the embedding features of D_t in the embedding space, denoted as $Z_t = \{\mathbf{z}_1, \mathbf{z}_2, ..., \mathbf{z}_N\}$. After that, as illustrated in Fig. 1, we partition Z_t into an ensemble of M groups, each with a different number of clusters, i.e.,

$$\mathbf{G}_t^{Ensemble} = [\mathbf{G}_t^{1,k_1}, ..., \mathbf{G}_t^{m,k_m}, ..., \mathbf{G}_t^{M,k_M}]$$

where $\mathbf{G}_t^{m,k_m}$ is the m-th group with k_m clusters. The mean and covariance of each cluster within each group in the ensemble are computed and stored, occupying only a few KBytes of memory.

II. ESS Score. To quantify the similarity between D_t and a new domain D_{t+1}, we form $\mathbf{G}_{t+1}^{Ensemble}$, which mirrors the configurations in $\mathbf{G}_t^{Ensemble}$, by performing a forward pass of D_{t+1} through the trained subnetwork f_t. Then, we measure the Mahalanobis distance between each cluster in a group in $\mathbf{G}_{t+1}^{Ensemble}$ to all the clusters in the mirroring group in $\mathbf{G}_t^{Ensemble}$. Then, for each pair of group configurations, e.g., $(\mathbf{G}_{t+1}^{m',k_{m'}}, \mathbf{G}_t^{m,k_m})$, we return the smallest Mahalanobis distance, $S_{m',m}$, representing the similarity score between the m'-th group in $\mathbf{G}_{t+1}^{Ensemble}$ and the m-th group in $\mathbf{G}_t^{Ensemble}$. As demonstrated in Fig. 1 (right), the total $2 \times M$ individual scores are then aggregated using an ensemble module, such as averaging in our implementation, yielding the final ensemble similarity score ESS as follows;

$$ESS = \texttt{ensemble}\{S_{m',m}\} \quad \text{for } m', m \in \{1, 2, ...M\}.$$

III. IND vs OOD Decision Making. If ESS exceeds a threshold value γ_{D_t}, indicating a higher degree of similarity between the two domains, f_t is updated with D_{t+1} and the mean and covariance values are recalculated and updated in memory. On the other hand, if ESS falls below γ_{D_t}, suggesting that D_{t+1} is OOD, a new subnetwork is initialized to learn D_{t+1} using the same culpability-based pruning technique. The mean and variance of all clusters and groups in $\mathbf{G}_{t+1}^{Ensemble}$ are calculated from the trained f_{t+1} and stored for future use. If ESS returns IND to multiple domains, we only fine-tune the subnetwork with the corresponding smallest ESS value. We refer the reader to Algorithm-1 in supplementary material for a summary of the training framework of Continual-GEN.

Domain-agnostic Inference. For a test image, a forward pass through all subnetworks is performed to calculate ESS with each domain. The subnetwork with the smallest score is selected and directly used to extract a prediction.

3   Experiments and Results

Datasets and Implementation Details. In our experimental setup, we consider a total of six sequentially presented domains that are constructed using four distinct skin lesion datasets: HAM10000 (HAM) [21] (partitioned into three domains as in [8]), Dermofit (DMF) [1], Derm7pt (D7P) [11], and MSK [10]. We use ResNet-152 as the backbone of network f. For each domain, we train it using the cross-entropy (CE) loss for 150 epochs with a constant learning rate of 1e-5 and a batch size of 16. We partition each domain into three sets: training (60%), validation (20%), and test (20%) sets. We balance all the training domains in PyTorch, and we resize the images to 224×224. To address domain order bias, we averaged the results across all 720 possible domain order combinations. We use p=80% pruning ratio when creating all the subnetworks. Each ensemble consists of $M=8$ groups, including one group formed using the Ground Truth (GT) clustering, which cluster features based on the known class labels, i.e., $k=GT$, and seven additional groups created by the Gaussian mixture model (GMM) clustering method, which models the features as a mixture of k Gaussian distributions in the embedding space ($k=1, 3, 5, 7, 10, 15$, and 20). We use averaging for the ensemble, and set γ_{D_t} at twice the mean of all clusters in $\mathbf{G}_t^{Ensemble}$.

Metrics. We evaluate the performance of our Continual-GEN using two metrics: 1) the widely-used accuracy of each domain after training all the domains: $ACC = \frac{1}{T}\sum_{t=1}^{T} a_{T,t}$, where $a_{T,t}$ is the test balanced accuracy of t-th domain after a model has learned all the T domains, and 2) the average accuracy computed over all domains, $AVG = \frac{1}{T}\sum_{t=1}^{T} ACC(t)$.

Comparison Against SOTA CL Methods. We compare Continual-GEN against several CL methods, including three subnetwork-based methods: CPN [3], PackNet [15] and CP&S [6], and two regularization-based methods: EWC [13] and LwF [14]. All the competitors require the availability of domain identity information, as they were not specifically designed for domain-agnostic

Table 1. Performance of `Continual-GEN` against baselines and SOTA CL methods on six skin lesion domains. '# of sub' indicates the total number of subnetworks in f.

Method	Test Sets Performance (ACC) %						Total AVG %	# of sub
	HAM-1	HAM-2	HAM-3	DMF	D7P	MSK		
Baselines								
JOINT	$90.72_{\pm 0.81}$	$91.43_{\pm 0.43}$	$89.65_{\pm 0.15}$	$84.07_{\pm 0.72}$	$88.65_{\pm 0.06}$	$84.21_{\pm 0.99}$	$\underline{88.12}_{\pm 0.52}$	-
SeqT	$40.38_{\pm 0.28}$	$42.06_{\pm 0.27}$	$41.84_{\pm 0.51}$	$44.97_{\pm 0.08}$	$44.52_{\pm 0.65}$	$40.78_{\pm 0.94}$	$42.43_{\pm 0.45}$	-
Competing CL Methods								
CPN	$84.36_{\pm 0.50}$	$83.37_{\pm 0.12}$	$82.63_{\pm 0.78}$	$76.54_{\pm 0.40}$	$80.46_{\pm 0.57}$	$70.11_{\pm 0.63}$	$79.58_{\pm 0.50}$	4
PackNet	$81.04_{\pm 0.35}$	$80.61_{\pm 0.29}$	$79.39_{\pm 0.81}$	$70.05_{\pm 1.02}$	$77.59_{\pm 0.46}$	$64.83_{\pm 0.59}$	$75.59_{\pm 0.42}$	4
CP&S	$80.47_{\pm 0.68}$	$79.51_{\pm 0.53}$	$78.84_{\pm 0.16}$	$71.18_{\pm 0.31}$	$78.55_{\pm 0.42}$	$69.91_{\pm 0.70}$	$76.41_{\pm 0.47}$	4
EWC	$44.15_{\pm 0.91}$	$44.98_{\pm 0.50}$	$43.25_{\pm 0.83}$	$56.34_{\pm 0.65}$	$46.08_{\pm 0.13}$	$43.12_{\pm 1.12}$	$46.32_{\pm 0.69}$	-
LwF	$53.28_{\pm 0.84}$	$54.22_{\pm 0.30}$	$53.01_{\pm 0.90}$	$59.62_{\pm 0.33}$	$47.50_{\pm 0.46}$	$45.14_{\pm 1.19}$	$52.13_{\pm 0.67}$	-
Proposed Method								
Ours	$\mathbf{85.78}_{\pm 0.20}$	$\mathbf{84.11}_{\pm 0.84}$	$\mathbf{85.41}_{\pm 0.71}$	$\mathbf{77.52}_{\pm 0.98}$	$\mathbf{81.73}_{\pm 0.30}$	$\mathbf{71.84}_{\pm 0.13}$	$\mathbf{81.07}_{\pm 0.50}$	5

scenarios. Additionally, we provide an upper bound performance (JOINT), which is obtained by the usual supervised fine-tuning on the data of all tasks jointly (assuming all available at one time), and a lower bound performance (SeqT), which simply performs sequential training without any countermeasure to forgetting. Our comprehensive evaluation, as summarized in Table 1, demonstrates the performance of `Continual-GEN`, surpassing other CL approaches across all domains. This superiority can be attributed to two key factors. Firstly, we address the potential issue of negative knowledge interference by identifying one HAM domain as OOD and assigning a separate subnetwork for it (the total number of subnetworks in f is 5 in `Continual-GEN` as opposed to 4 in alternative methods). Secondly, we use a culpability-based pruning technique to retain only the most relevant units for each domain, resulting in improved classification performance, even with the subnetworks in `Continual-GEN` having fewer parameters than those of other methods.

Comparison Against other Domain-agnostic Methods. To assess the effectiveness of the proposed OOD detection method in `Continual-GEN`, i.e., ensemble of groups, we compare it against alternative domain-agnostic learning techniques. In Method$-\mathcal{A}$, a new subnetwork is initialized when the accuracy on new domain drops below 10%. In Method$-\mathcal{B}$, the Gram distance [17] is used instead of the Mahalanobis distance for both training and inference. In Method$-\mathcal{C}$, domain shifts are detected by computing the Mahalanobis distance between features extracted after the first layer of Batch Normalization (BN) [9]. As demonstrated in Table 2, our proposed method outperforms the alternative approaches. The Gram distance (Method$-\mathcal{B}$) fails to accurately detect distribution shifts in skin datasets, and Methods$-\mathcal{A},\mathcal{C}$ are sensitive to hyperparameter choices, such as the 10% accuracy drop threshold in Method$-\mathcal{A}$ and the selection of the BN layer in Method$-\mathcal{C}$.

Table 2. Continual-GEN average performance with different OOD detection methods. '# of sub' indicates the total number of subnetworks in f.

Method	Continual-GEN			
	Ours	Method$-\mathcal{A}$	Method$-\mathcal{B}$	Method$-\mathcal{C}$
Total AVG %	$81.07_{\pm 0.50}$	$76.51_{\pm 0.38}$	$72.34_{\pm 0.18}$	$73.54_{\pm 0.62}$
# of sub	5	3	2	$6^\star$

$\star$ indicates that the pruning ratio was increased to 85% to accommodate more subnetworks.

Unraveling Cluster Quality for Skin Datasets. The quality of clusters in the embedding space is a fundamental aspect to the success of our method. Therefore, we conduct an extensive analysis to compare the quality of clusters generated by different clustering techniques and training methods, as follows:

Clustering Techniques: In addition to the GT and GMM clustering methods, we explore the use of k-means, which partitions the features into k clusters based on their similarity measured using the Euclidean distance in the embedding space. Although we considered other clustering methods, such as agglomerative clustering and DBSCAN, we found them to be less compatible and requiring careful hyperparameter tuning, such as selecting appropriate linking strategies for agglomerative clustering or determining the epsilon value for DBSCAN.

Training Methods: Besides the CE loss, we investigate the influence of contrastive learning approaches due to their demonstrated capability in OOD detection [20]. Specifically, we compare two approaches: supervised contrastive learning (Sup-Con) [12] and the unsupervised approach (SimCLR) [5].

Metrics for Cluster Quality: To evaluate the effectiveness of the different clustering and training approaches, we employ two metrics: Global separation (GS) and cluster purity (CP) [4]. GS quantifies the separability between clusters by evaluating the intra-cluster distances to the enter-cluster distances of the nearest neighboring cluster, whereas CP determines how many samples in a cluster belongs to the same class. Higher values of both metrics indicate higher quality of clusters. We refer the reader to [4] for equations of GS and CP.

Discussion of Results: By analyzing the results of applying the different clustering and training methods on the HAM-1 and DMF domains, as illustrated in Fig. 2, we can derive important observations about the quality of the generated clusters. The following key findings emerge from this analysis: 1) The three learning methods (CE, SupCon, SimCLR) exhibit comparable performance, with CE and SupCon showcasing slightly better results due to their supervised learning nature. 2) The quality of clusters generated by GMM outperforms k-means, particularly in terms of CP values. The higher purity values achieved by GMM reflect its capability to generate more internally homogeneous clusters, predominantly containing samples from the same class, suggesting its ability to capture the underlying data distribution of the skin more effectively. 3) The optimal

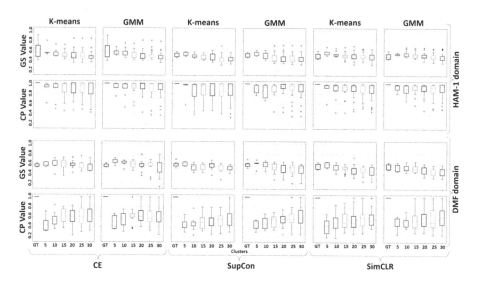

Fig. 2. Comparison of cluster quality for CE, SupCon, and SimCLR based on GS and CP on the HAM-1 and DMF domains. The evaluation process begins with the default GT clusters, followed by k-means or GMM with an increasing number of clusters.

number of clusters k cannot be easily determined, as the choice of it may not straightforwardly correspond to higher purity and separation. For instance, CE with $k = 5$ of GMM on the DMF dataset exhibits lower purity compared to that of $k = 10$, despite higher values of GS. These results demonstrate the challenge in selecting the ideal clustering technique and k value for skin-related analysis, further emphasizing the unique and effective nature of the proposed ensemble of groups method.

Ablation Study on the Impact of the Ensemble Size. We investigate the impact of the enemsble size (M) on the performance of Continual-GEN. Our findings demonstrate that utilizing a substantial number of diverse groups leads to improved average performance. Specifically, Continual-GEN achieves a performance of 75.34% and 79.34% for $M \in \{1, 2\}$ and $M \in \{3, 4, 5, 6\}$, respectively. With $M \in \{8, 9, 10, 11\}$, the performance further increases to 81.07%.

Ablation Study on the Impact of the ensemble Strategy. We investigate different ensembling strategies to compute the final ESS score: 1) Average (default) averages all distance scores, 2) Top averages the top q sorted scores, 3) Bottom averages the bottom q sorted scores, and 4) Trimmed Average averages remaining scores after removing top and bottom q sorted scores. Notably, the Top method identifies more domains as IND, which potentially led to decreased performance due to negative knowledge interference between domains, resulting in a reduction of 3.64% and 1.77% in performance with $q = 20$ and 40, respectively, compared to the default method (Average). On the other hand, the

Table 3. Continual-GEN average performance with different ensemble strategies. '# of sub' indicates the total number of subnetworks in f.

Strategy	Average	Top		Bottom		Trimmed Average	
		q=20	q=40	q=20	q=40	q=20	q=40
Total AVG %	81.07$\pm$0.50	77.43$\pm$0.62	79.3$\pm$0.48	74.94$\pm$0.66	81.07$\pm$0.50	81.07$\pm$0.50	81.07$\pm$0.50
# of sub	5	3	4	6*	5	5	5

⋆ indicates that the pruning ratio was increased to 85% to accommodate more subnetworks.

Trimmed Average method performs similarly to the default method, indicating that it detects the same IND and OOD domains.

4 Conclusion

We introduced Continual-GEN, a subnetwork-based CL approach for skin lesion classification. Our method supports sequential learning without forgetting and does not require domain identity information during training and inference. Continual-GEN decomposes the semantic space into groups, detecting domain shifts and assigning domain-specific subnetworks accordingly. Extensive experiments on diverse skin lesion datasets demonstrate its superior performance over SOTA CL methods and domain-agnostic learning techniques. Additionally, Continual-GEN ensures memory efficiency by avoiding network expansion and individual sample storage, crucial for maintaining patient privacy.

References

1. Ballerini, L., Fisher, R.B., Aldridge, B., Rees, J.: A color and texture based hierarchical K-NN approach to the classification of non-melanoma skin lesions. In: Celebi, M.E., Schaefer, G. (eds.) Color Medical Image Analysis, pp. 63–86. Springer, Dordrecht (2013). https://doi.org/10.1007/978-94-007-5389-1_4
2. Baweja, C., Glocker, B., Kamnitsas, K.: Towards continual learning in medical imaging. arXiv preprint arXiv:1811.02496 (2018)
3. Bayasi, N., Hamarneh, G., Garbi, R.: Culprit-Prune-Net: efficient continual sequential multi-domain learning with application to skin lesion classification. In: de Bruijne, M., et al. (eds.) MICCAI 2021. LNCS, vol. 12907, pp. 165–175. Springer, Cham (2021). https://doi.org/10.1007/978-3-030-87234-2_16
4. Bojchevski, A., Matkovic, Y., Günnemann, S.: Robust spectral clustering for noisy data: Modeling sparse corruptions improves latent embeddings. In: Proceedings of International Conference on Knowledge Discovery and Data Mining, pp. 737–746 (2017)
5. Chen, T., Kornblith, S., Norouzi, M., Hinton, G.: A simple framework for contrastive learning of visual representations. In: International Conference on Machine Learning, pp. 1597–1607 (2020)
6. Dekhovich, A., Tax, D.M.J., Sluiter, M.H.F., Bessa, M.A.: Continual prune-and-select: class-incremental learning with specialized subnetworks. Appl. Intell. **53**(14), 17849–17864 (2023). https://doi.org/10.1007/s10489-022-04441-z

7. Esteva, A., et al.: Dermatologist-level classification of skin cancer with deep neural networks. Nature **542**(7639), 115–118 (2017)
8. Fogelberg, K., Chamarthi, S., Maron, R.C., Niebling, J., Brinker, T.J.: Domain shifts in dermoscopic skin cancer datasets: Evaluation of essential limitations for clinical translation. New Biotechnol. **76**, 106–117 (2023)
9. González, C., Ranem, A., Othman, A., Mukhopadhyay, A.: Task-agnostic continual hippocampus segmentation for smooth population shifts. In: Kamnitsas, K., et al. (eds.) Domain Adaptation and Representation Transfer: 4th MICCAI Workshop, DART 2022, Held in Conjunction with MICCAI 2022, Singapore, September 22, 2022, Proceedings, pp. 108–118. Springer, Cham (2022). https://doi.org/10.1007/978-3-031-16852-9_11
10. Gutman, D., et al.: Skin lesion analysis toward melanoma detection: a challenge at the international symposium on biomedical imaging (ISBI) 2016, hosted by the international skin imaging collaboration (ISIC). arXiv:1605.01397 (2016)
11. Kawahara, J., Daneshvar, S., Argenziano, G., Hamarneh, G.: Seven-point checklist and skin lesion classification using multitask multimodal neural nets. IEEE J. Biomed. Health Inform. **23**(2), 538–546 (2018)
12. Khosla, P., et al.: Supervised contrastive learning. In: Advances in Neural Information Processing Systems, vol. 33, pp. 18661–18673 (2020)
13. Kirkpatrick, J., et al.: Overcoming catastrophic forgetting in neural networks. Proc. Natl. Acad. Sci. **114**(13), 3521–3526 (2017)
14. Li, Z., Hoiem, D.: Learning without forgetting. IEEE Trans. Pattern Anal. Mach. Intell. TPAMI **40**(12), 2935–2947 (2017)
15. Mallya, A., Lazebnik, S.: PackNet: Adding multiple tasks to a single network by iterative pruning. In: Proceedings of the IEEE Conference on Computer Vision and Pattern Recognition (CVPR), pp. 7765–7773 (2018)
16. Özgün, S., Rickmann, A.-M., Roy, A.G., Wachinger, C.: Importance driven continual learning for segmentation across domains. In: Liu, M., Yan, P., Lian, C., Cao, X. (eds.) Machine Learning in Medical Imaging: 11th International Workshop, MLMI 2020, Held in Conjunction with MICCAI 2020, Lima, Peru, October 4, 2020, Proceedings, pp. 423–433. Springer International Publishing, Cham (2020). https://doi.org/10.1007/978-3-030-59861-7_43
17. Perkonigg, M., et al.: Dynamic memory to alleviate catastrophic forgetting in continual learning with medical imaging. Nat. Commun. **12**(1), 5678 (2021)
18. Perkonigg, M., Hofmanninger, J., Langs, G.: Continual active learning for efficient adaptation of machine learning models to changing image acquisition. In: Feragen, A., Sommer, S., Schnabel, J., Nielsen, M. (eds.) IPMI 2021. LNCS, vol. 12729, pp. 649–660. Springer, Cham (2021). https://doi.org/10.1007/978-3-030-78191-0_50
19. Prabhu, A., Torr, P.H.S., Dokania, P.K.: GDumb: a simple approach that questions our progress in continual learning. In: Vedaldi, A., Bischof, H., Brox, T., Frahm, J.-M. (eds.) ECCV 2020. LNCS, vol. 12347, pp. 524–540. Springer, Cham (2020). https://doi.org/10.1007/978-3-030-58536-5_31
20. Sehwag, V., Chiang, M., Mittal, P.: SSD: a unified framework for self-supervised outlier detection. arXiv preprint arXiv:2103.12051 (2021)
21. Tschandl, P., Rosendahl, C., Kittler, H.: The HAM10000 dataset, a large collection of multi-source dermatoscopic images of common pigmented skin lesions. Sci. Data **5**(1), 1–9 (2018)
22. Wang, L., Zhang, X., Su, H., Zhu, J.: A comprehensive survey of continual learning: theory, method and application. arXiv preprint arXiv:2302.00487 (2023)

23. Wen, D., et al.: Characteristics of publicly available skin cancer image datasets: a systematic review. Lancet Digit. Health **4**(1), e64–e74 (2022)
24. Yoon, J., Jeong, W., Lee, G., Yang, E., Hwang, S.J.: Federated continual learning with weighted inter-client transfer. In: International Conference on Machine Learning, pp. 12073–12086 (2021)

Communication-Efficient Federated Skin Lesion Classification with Generalizable Dataset Distillation

Yuchen Tian[1], Jiacheng Wang[1], Yueming Jin[2], and Liansheng Wang[1(✉)]

[1] Department of Computer Science at School of Informatics, Xiamen University,
Xiamen 361005, China
`{tianyuchen,Jiachengw}@stu.xmu.edu.cn, lswang@xmu.edu.cn`
[2] Department of Biomedical Engineering and Department of Electrical and Computer
Engineering, National University of Singapore, Singapore 119276, Singapore
`ymjin@nus.edu.sg`

Abstract. Federated learning (FL) has recently been applied to skin lesion analysis, but the challenges of huge communication requirements and non-independent and identical distributions have not been fully addressed. The former problem arises from model parameter transfer between the server and clients, and the latter problem is due to differences in imaging protocols and operational customs. To reduce communication costs, dataset distillation methods have been adopted to distill thousands of real images into a few synthetic images (1 image per class) in each local client, which are then used to train a global model in the server. However, these methods often overlook the possible inter-client distribution drifts, limiting the performance of the global model. In this paper, we propose a generalizable dataset distillation-based federated learning (GDD-FL) framework to achieve communication-efficient federated skin lesion classification. Our framework includes the generalization dataset distillation (GDD) method, which explicitly models image features of the dataset into an uncertain Gaussian distribution and learns to produce synthetic images with features close to this distribution. The uncertainty in the mean and variance of the distribution enables the synthetic images to obtain diverse semantics and mitigate distribution drifts. Based on the GDD method, we further develop a communication-efficient FL framework that only needs to transmit a few synthesized images once for training a global model. We evaluate our approach on a large skin lesion classification dataset and compare it with existing dataset distillation methods and several powerful baselines. Our results show that our model consistently outperforms them, particularly in comparison to the classical FL method. All resources can be found at https://github.com/jcwang123/GDD-FL.

Keywords: Skin lesion classification · Dataset Distillation · Domain Generalization · Federated learning

---

Y. Tian and J. Wang — Contributed Equally.

M. E. Celebi et al. (Eds.): MICCAI 2023 Workshops, LNCS 14393, pp. 14–24, 2023.
https://doi.org/10.1007/978-3-031-47401-9_2

1   Introduction

Federated learning is an innovative approach to training deep learning models that allows for collaboration and sharing of knowledge without the need to centralize data. It involves transferring model parameters between different clients to improve model performance. Federated learning is particularly useful in clinical settings where privacy is of utmost importance, as it allows multiple healthcare providers to train models using their own data while keeping patient information secure. Recent studies have shown the potential of federated learning in predicting clinical outcomes [1,2,8,10,19].

However, federated learning methods require transmitting model parameters between the server and clients at each learning round [15], and the entire learning process typically involves hundreds of epochs. The resultant increase in communication costs has become one of the most significant challenges in federated learning. Moreover, some hospitals with strict privacy regulations do *not permit internet access*, rendering the communication-reliant federated learning methods infeasible. To address these challenges, previous studies have attempted to limit the number of communications to accelerate convergence and improve communication efficiency [4,6,14,17,21,29]. However, such methods still require tens of communications, and parameter transmission remains time-consuming and laborious in the era of large models. Synthesis-based methods are proposed to transfer the local images into synthetic images using GANs [18] and centralize them into the server for task learning, but GANs are hard to train and the generated synthetic images cost a lot of transmission loads. Recently, data distillation has been introduced in the federated learning domain [24]. This technique distills local datasets into a few synthetic images, typically fewer than ten, and sends these synthetic data to a global server for global training. As the transmission requires only one round of communication, and the synthetic data contains no original information, this method inherits the advantages of low communication costs and excellent privacy protection.

Nevertheless, the previous studies mainly discuss the usefulness of small datasets, i.e., handwritten digits. Whether the distilled image retains the abundant semantics for lesion classification is unknown and needed to be investigated. More importantly, this method adopts the oldest distillation algorithm and has not taken into account the distribution drifts among different clients. The drifts will lead to differing distributions of each synthetic dataset, and consequently, the global model trained on such distributed data may exhibit limited performance, which can impact the accuracy and robustness of the model in real-world settings. Solving distribution drifts is a significant challenge in the federated learning community and has been widely studied [3,12,13,16,25,26]. However, these strategies are primarily designed for parameter-communication methods, where the clients send their local model updates to the central server for aggregation. In contrast, data distillation aims to minimize the amount of communication by sending synthetic data instead of parameter updates. Therefore, these strategies may not be directly applicable to the data distillation approach.

In this paper, we propose a novel and generalizable data distillation-based federated learning (GDD-FL) framework to address the challenges of communication costs and distribution drifts in skin lesion classification. We first propose a generalizable data distillation (GDD) method that distills each client's local dataset into a small number of synthetic images and makes synthetic data from different sites located in similar distributions. It is achieved by approximating the possible Gaussian distribution of mean and variance values in one client's synthetic data and randomly sampling a new distribution to produce synthetic images. Unlike current data distillation methods that align synthetic images to a fixed distribution, our GDD method produces synthetic images with uncertain distribution so they obtain better diversity. Based on the GDD method, we further build a communication-efficient federated learning framework for skin lesion classification. In this process, each client applies the GDD method to distill its local dataset into a small synthetic dataset and sends it to the global server. The global server then trains a brand-new model using the gathered data. By minimizing the communication between clients and the server, our method reduces communication costs and improves privacy protection. We evaluate the performance of our method on the ISIC-2020 dataset in IID and Non-IID federated settings and compare it with the classical federated learning method and other data distillation methods. The experimental results demonstrate that our GDD-FL framework consistently outperforms other methods in terms of classification accuracy while reducing communication costs and protecting privacy. Our proposed framework has great potential for applications in real-world scenarios where large datasets are distributed across different clients with limited communication resources.

2   Method

In summary, we introduce the approximation of the uncertain distribution of a real dataset in Sect. 2.1, how to optimize learnable synthetic images in Sect. 2.2. and the communication-efficient federated learning framework in Sect. 2.3.

2.1   Generalizable Dataset Distillation

The goal of dataset distillation is to condense the large-scale training set $\mathcal{T} = \{(x_1, y_1), ..., (x_{|\mathcal{T}|}, y_{|\mathcal{T}|})\}$ with $|\mathcal{T}|$ image and label pairs into a small synthetic set $\mathcal{S} = \{(s_1, y_1), ..., (s_{|\mathcal{S}|}, y_{|\mathcal{S}|})\}$ with $|\mathcal{S}|$ synthetic image and label pairs so that models trained on each $\mathcal{T}$ and $\mathcal{S}$ obtain comparable performance on unseen testing data: $\mathbb{E}_{x \sim P_{\mathcal{D}}} \mathcal{L}(\Phi_{\theta^{\mathcal{T}}}(x), y) \simeq \mathbb{E}_{x \sim P_{\mathcal{D}}} \mathcal{L}(\Phi_{\theta^{\mathcal{S}}}(x), y)$, where $P_{\mathcal{D}}$ is the real data distribution, $\mathcal{L}$ is the loss function (i.e. cross-entropy loss). Φ is a task-specific deep neural network, i.e. ResNet-18, parameterized by θ, and $\Phi_{\theta^{\mathcal{T}}}$ and $\Phi_{\theta^{\mathcal{S}}}$ are the networks that are trained on $\mathcal{T}$ and $\mathcal{S}$ respectively. Similar to techniques [23,28], our goal is to synthesize data that approximates the distribution of the real training data, instead of selecting a representative subset of training samples as in [27,32]. The process has been visualized in Fig. 1.

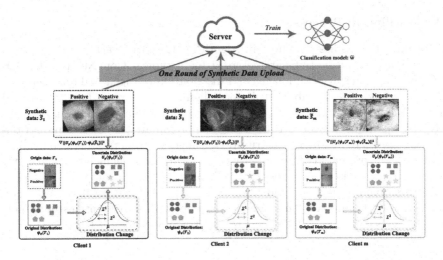

Fig. 1. Overall framework of the generalizable data distillation-based federated learning (GDD-FL). Unlike existing data distillation methods, GDD considers the possible distribution drifts inter-clients and proposes to change the target distribution with random deviations ($\sum$) so that the synthetic images' distribution can align the distributions of other clients.

To obtain a small dataset with similar semantics to the real dataset, we approximate the possible Gaussian distribution of real data and align the learnable synthetic data to the distribution. Typical data distillation methods adopt certain mean and variance values to determine the distribution. Instead, to simulate the possible client drift, we estimate the uncertainty of data distribution, and randomly sample new distributions. Specifically, the uncertainty of mean and variance values is estimated as:

$$\Sigma_\mu^2(x) = \frac{1}{|x|}\sum_{i=1}^{|x|}(\mu(x_i) - \mathbb{E}[\mu(x)])^2, \Sigma_\sigma^2(x) = \frac{1}{|x|}\sum_{i=1}^{|x|}(\sigma(x_i) - \mathbb{E}[\sigma(x)])^2, \quad (1)$$

where $\Sigma_\mu(x)$ and $\Sigma_\sigma(x)$ represent the uncertainty estimation of the feature mean μ and feature standard deviation σ, respectively.

After the estimation of possible client shifts, we randomly sample new feature statistics from the estimated distribution as $\hat{\mu}(x) \sim \mathcal{N}(\mu, \Sigma_\mu^2)$ and standard deviation $\hat{\sigma}(x) \sim \mathcal{N}(\sigma, \Sigma_\sigma^2)$ for the corresponding distribution:

$$\hat{\mu}(x) = \mu(x) + \epsilon_\mu \Sigma_\mu(x) \quad and \quad \hat{\sigma}(x) = \sigma(x) + \epsilon_\sigma \Sigma_\sigma, \quad (2)$$

where $\epsilon_\mu, \epsilon_\sigma \sim \mathcal{N}(\mathbf{0}, \mathbf{I})$. In the end, the feature after the simulated client shift is formed as: $\hat{x} = \hat{\mu}(x) \times \frac{x - \mu(x)}{\sigma(x)} + \hat{\sigma}(x)$. After the distribution change, we optimize the learnable synthetic images to obtain the same distribution with $\hat{x}$, where the details are introduced next.

2.2 Distillation Process

The training details are presented in Algorithm 1. During each learning epoch, we randomly sample initial parameters ϑ for a typical ConvNet [5], denoted as Ψ_ϑ, feeding the synthetic images and distribution-changed real data into the network to align the distribution. Before alignment, the read data is modified through the uncertain distribution change and Siamese augmentations. Specifically, the equations in Sect. 2.1 are used to approximate the uncertain distributions. We use U_p to denote the distribution change, where $p = 0.5$ is a controlling variable that represents the probability of performing the change to avoid introducing excessive noise. The differentiable Siamese augmentation [9] is denoted as $\mathcal{A}(\cdot)$, processing the real data and synthetic data respectively for better semantic alignment [30]. Finally, the optimization problem with uncertainty estimation is solved as: $\min_\mathcal{S} \mathbb{E}_{\substack{\vartheta \sim P_\vartheta \\ \omega \sim \Omega}} \| \frac{1}{|\mathcal{T}|} \sum_{i=1}^{|\mathcal{T}|} \psi_\vartheta(\mathcal{A}(U_p(x_i))) - \frac{1}{|\mathcal{S}|} \sum_{j=1}^{|\mathcal{S}|} \psi_\vartheta \mathcal{A}(s_j) \|^2$.

2.3 Communication-Efficient Federated Learning

Consider a federated learning task with m clients, the client k-th owns local dataset $\mathcal{T}_k$. We can obtain a set of synthetic datasets through our proposed GDD: $\widetilde{\mathcal{S}} = \{\widetilde{\mathcal{S}}_k | k = 1, 2, ..., m\}$. The server then collects all synthetic datasets from the local sites and uses the merged data $\widetilde{\mathcal{S}}$ to train a brand-new model from scratch. We consider a non-convex neural network objective in the server and train a machine learning model on $\widetilde{\mathcal{S}}$. For each iteration, we sample a mini-batch from the synthetic dataset, denoted as $(x, y) \in \widetilde{\mathcal{S}}$, and calculate the objective function $\mathcal{L}(x, y; w)$, where $\mathcal{L}$ represents the typical entropy loss. Note that the sampled mini-batch may contain synthetic images from multiple clients, which enhances feature diversity in each mini-batch. After optimizing for a total of E epochs, the parameter $\widetilde{w}$ is well-trained.

3 Experiment

3.1 Datasets and Evaluation Metrics

Datasets: For our experiments, we used the public skin lesion classification ISIC2020 [20] dataset provided by the International Skin Imaging Collaboration archive. The dataset contains a total of 33,126 samples in the public training set. Since the public test set is not available, we divided the training set into the train, validation, and test sets with 26,500, 3,312, and 3,314 samples.

Client Split: To simulate the federation, we used two types of splits, IID and Non-IID, as the prior work [11]. For IID federation, we randomly divided the train and validation sets into ten parts ($m = 10$) with equal numbers of positive and negative samples. For Non-IID federation, we used Dirichlet with $\alpha = 1$ to distribute local data. We evaluated the global model using the test set.

Algorithm 1. Process of Generalizable Data Distillation

Input: Training set $\mathcal{T}$
Output: Synthetic samples $\mathcal{S}$ for C classes
    function CLIENTDATASETDISTILLATION$(\mathcal{T})$
2:       Initialize $\mathcal{S}$ by sampling from random noise
       for *each iteration* **do**
4:          Sample $\vartheta \sim P_\vartheta$
          Sample mini-batch $B_c^{\mathcal{T}} \sim \mathcal{T}, B_c^{\mathcal{S}} \sim \mathcal{S}$ and augmentation $\mathcal{A}_c$ for every class c
6:          Compute $O_c^{\mathcal{T}} = \frac{1}{|B_c^{\mathcal{T}}|} \sum_{(x,y) \in B_c^{\mathcal{T}}} \Psi_\vartheta(\mathcal{A}_c(x))$ for every class c
          Compute $O_c^{\mathcal{S}} = \frac{1}{|B_c^{\mathcal{S}}|} \sum_{(s,y) \in B_c^{\mathcal{S}}} \Psi_\vartheta(\mathcal{A}_c(s))$ for every class c
8:          Compute $O_c^{\mathcal{U}} = \frac{1}{|B_c^{\mathcal{T}}|} \sum_{(x,y) \in B_c^{\mathcal{T}}} \Psi_\vartheta(\mathcal{A}_c(U_p(x))))$ for every class c
          Compute $\mathcal{L}_{\mathcal{S},\mathcal{T}} = \sum_{c=0}^{C-1} \|O_c^{\mathcal{T}} - O_c^{\mathcal{S}}\|^2$
10:       Compute $\mathcal{L}_{\mathcal{U}} = \sum_{c=0}^{C-1} \|O_c^{\mathcal{U}} - O_c^{\mathcal{S}}\|^2$
          Update $\mathcal{S} \leftarrow \mathcal{S} - \eta\nabla_{\mathcal{S}}(\mathcal{L}_{\mathcal{U}} + \mathcal{L}_{\mathcal{S},\mathcal{T}})$
12:     **end for**
       return $\mathcal{S}$ for C classes
14: **end function**

Evaluation Metrics: We used four widely adopted metrics, namely, Precision (P), Recall (R), F1 score, and AUC, to comprehensively evaluate the classification performance. Higher values indicate better classification performance.

3.2   Implementation Details

We use ResNet-18 [7] as the base classification model and a classical ConvNet [5] as the image feature extractor for data distillation training. To improve memory usage and computational efficiency, all images are resized to (224×224). During the distillation training, we use the SGD optimizer [22] with an initial learning rate of 1 for 300 epochs and set the batch size to 64. For training the classification model, we use the SGD optimizer with an initial learning rate of 0.01. The model is trained for 50 epochs using a batch size of 64.

3.3   Comparison of State-of-the-Arts

We mainly compare our method with the latest data distillation methods, namely DC [32], DSA [30], and DM [31]. Since these techniques have not been used in federated learning, we re-implement them in our settings. In addition, we compare the performance of the classical federated learning framework, FedAVG [15]. Furthermore, we demonstrate several centralized training results, where the "Upper Bound" refers to centralizing all data to train a classification model, and "R.S.@10" and "R.S.@100" denote randomly selecting 10/100 images per lesion class. Since the distillation method used in the prior work [24] is too old without novel designs, we focus on the latest distillation methods.

    The quantitative results are shown in Table 1. It is seen that GDD outperforms other distillation techniques consistently across all settings. Notably, the improvement is more significant when distilling the dataset into 10 images per class, as the diversity of synthetic images is progressively enhanced. Compared with FedAVG, the results in the IID setting show that data distillation-based methods still have room for improvement. However, data distillation-based methods have a significant advantage over FedAVG in terms of low communication costs. Moreover, GDD-FL shows a substantial improvement in the Non-IID setting for AUC scores, i.e., 5.88% and 6.37% for distilling 1/10 images per class.

Table 1. Comparison with latest data distillation methods on the ISIC-2020 dataset. "*" denotes the implementation on our federated setting.

Method		AUC	P	R	F1
Upper Bound		80.97 ± 2.12	97.23 ± 0.03	91.11 ± 2.36	94.07 ± 1.54
R.S.@10		56.86 ± 1.16	87.29 ± 0.19	59.63 ± 5.08	70.86 ± 3.99
R.S.@100		60.22 ± 2.70	87.67 ± 0.08	65.56 ± 3.53	75.02 ± 2.54
Transmit parameters: 12640 MB					
FedAVG (IID) [15]		75.33 ± 3.21	96.55 ± 0.34	80.12 ± 4.97	87.57 ± 3.13
FedAVG (Non-IID)		65.97 ± 4.17	83.22 ± 1.34	70.68 ± 6.26	76.44 ± 4.23
Transmit 1 image per class: 2.88 MB					
IID	DC* [32]	66.72 ± 2.98	96.71 ± 0.09	75.26 ± 5.23	84.56 ± 3.25
	DSA* [30]	64.43 ± 2.67	96.76 ± 0.09	74.35 ± 5.78	83.99 ± 3.56
	DM* [31]	68.82 ± 0.22	96.76 ± 0.09	74.35 ± 5.77	83.99 ± 3.56
	GDD-FL (Ours)	**71.76 ± 0.04**	**96.93 ± 0.11**	**78.55 ± 2.74**	**86.78 ± 0.04**
Non-IID	DC* [32]	65.18 ± 8.09	96.73 ± 0.04	72.50 ± 12.22	82.42 ± 8.58
	DSA* [30]	68.79 ± 0.88	96.70 ± 0.04	78.66 ± 2.93	86.73 ± 1.77
	DM* [31]	68.41 ± 0.17	96.60 ± 0.12	72.88 ± 0.56	83.08 ± 0.32
	GDD-FL (Ours)	**71.85 ± 1.75**	**97.17 ± 0.55**	**81.14 ± 3.28**	**88.41 ± 2.01**
Transmit 10 images per class: 28.81 MB					
IID	DC* [32]	66.79 ± 1.41	96.47 ± 0.03	78.21 ± 4.37	86.39 ± 2.35
	DSA* [30]	65.15 ± 3.03	96.69 ± 0.06	76.38 ± 4.67	85.34 ± 2.13
	DM* [31]	69.29 ± 2.35	96.58 ± 0.79	78.21 ± 5.73	86.43 ± 2.24
	GDD-FL (Ours)	**73.38 ± 1.50**	**96.79 ± 0.28**	**79.80 ± 10.68**	**87.48 ± 7.09**
Non-IID	DC* [32]	65.70 ± 2.47	96.83 ± 0.03	76.42 ± 4.13	85.42 ± 2.48
	DSA* [30]	69.99 ± 0.32	96.80 ± 0.02	79.40 ± 1.89	87.24 ± 3.75
	DM* [31]	69.07 ± 7.25	96.85 ± 0.73	76.75 ± 4.51	85.64 ± 3.28
	GDD-FL (Ours)	**73.34 ± 1.28**	**96.86 ± 0.34**	**81.37 ± 7.34**	**87.72 ± 10.73**

We also present the visualizations of our synthetic data in Fig. 2, where the first row shows negative samples and the second row shows positive samples. Each column represents the synthetic images distilled by a different client. We observed that the synthetic images underwent style changes based on the original dermoscopy images and contain more texture and style information useful for

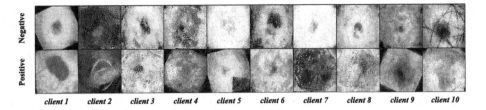

Fig. 2. Visualization of our synthetic images, including the positive and negative samples from ten distributed clients.

training a classification model. However, these semantics make the appearance abnormal from the human view, and therefore, it is hard to tell what these images exactly represent.

3.4 Detailed Analysis

Ablation Analysis: We also conduct an ablation study to evaluate the impact of our proposed distribution change. Results are shown in Table 1, where we compare the performance of GDD-FL to that of the baseline data distillation method, DM, and to the results of training a model with a randomly sampled subset of 10 or 100 images per class ("R.S.@10" and "R.S.@100"). The DM method is trained without distribution change. As seen from the table, when trained with the same number of samples, GDD-FL achieves significantly better AUC scores, with an improvement of nearly 6% over random sampling. Moreover, the comparison between DM and GDD-FL further confirms the effectiveness of our proposed distribution change. While the performance of DM drops slightly in the Non-IID setting, GDD-FL demonstrates stable performance across both IID and Non-IID settings. Notably, the significant improvement brought by GDD-FL suggests that the distribution change not only enhances generalization but also leads to more diverse semantics, thereby improving classification learning.

Computation Analysis: We further count the computational costs to make a comparison between GDD-FL and the traditional FedAVG. FedAVG trains the model in parallel for 1 h, requiring 16848 MB GPU. Our method involves distillation training at local sites (1.2 h, 9561 MB GPU) and classification training at the server (0.1 h, 16848 MB GPU). It indicates that our method minimizes communication resources while using similar computational resources.

Privacy Protection: GDD-FL condenses numerous real images into a smaller set of synthetic images. By treating the synthetic images as learnable variables and inputting them along with real images into a fixed network, we minimize the discrepancy between their feature outputs. This training aligns the synthetic images with the overall distribution of the real dataset, rather than specific individual images. We also apply random perturbations to the real distribution, reducing privacy risks. Consequently, the synthetic data doesn't contain precise personal information and is not part of the original dataset.

4 Conclusion

In this paper, we introduce a communication-efficient federated skin lesions classification framework using generalizable data distillation, named GDD-FL. Unlike current data distillation methods that align synthetic images to a fixed distribution, our GDD simulates the possible inter-client distribution drifts and produces synthetic images with better diversity and distribution alignment. The experimental results on the ISIC-2020 dataset demonstrate that our GDD-FL framework consistently outperforms other methods in terms of classification accuracy while reducing communication costs and protecting privacy.

References

1. Antunes, R.S., André da Costa, C., Küderle, A., Yari, I.A., Eskofier, B.: Federated learning for healthcare: systematic review and architecture proposal. ACM Trans. Intell. Syst. Technol. (TIST) **13**(4), 1–23 (2022)
2. Bdair, T., Navab, N., Albarqouni, S.: FedPerl: semi-supervised peer learning for skin lesion classification. In: de Bruijne, M., et al. (eds.) MICCAI 2021. LNCS, vol. 12903, pp. 336–346. Springer, Cham (2021). https://doi.org/10.1007/978-3-030-87199-4_32
3. Fallah, A., Mokhtari, A., Ozdaglar, A.: Personalized federated learning with theoretical guarantees: a model-agnostic meta-learning approach. Adv. Neural. Inf. Process. Syst. **33**, 3557–3568 (2020)
4. Gao, H., Xu, A., Huang, H.: On the convergence of communication-efficient local SGD for federated learning. In: Proceedings of the AAAI Conference on Artificial Intelligence, vol. 35, pp. 7510–7518 (2021)
5. Gidaris, S., Komodakis, N.: Dynamic few-shot visual learning without forgetting. In: Proceedings of the IEEE Conference on Computer Vision and Pattern Recognition, pp. 4367–4375 (2018)
6. Hamer, J., Mohri, M., Suresh, A.T.: FedBoost: a communication-efficient algorithm for federated learning. In: International Conference on Machine Learning, pp. 3973–3983. PMLR (2020)
7. He, K., Zhang, X., Ren, S., Sun, J.: Deep residual learning for image recognition. In: Proceedings of the IEEE Conference on Computer Vision and Pattern Recognition, pp. 770–778 (2016)
8. Hossen, M.N., Panneerselvam, V., Koundal, D., Ahmed, K., Bui, F.M., Ibrahim, S.M.: Federated machine learning for detection of skin diseases and enhancement of internet of medical things (IoMT) security. IEEE J. Biomed. Health Inform. **27**(2), 835–841 (2022)
9. Kingma, D.P., Welling, M.: Auto-encoding variational bayes. arXiv preprint arXiv:1312.6114 (2013)
10. Li, G., Togo, R., Ogawa, T., Haseyama, M.: Dataset distillation for medical dataset sharing. arXiv preprint arXiv:2209.14603 (2022)

11. Li, Q., Diao, Y., Chen, Q., He, B.: Federated learning on Non-IID data silos: An experimental study. In: 2022 IEEE 38th International Conference on Data Engineering (ICDE), pp. 965–978. IEEE (2022)
12. Li, T., Sahu, A.K., Zaheer, M., Sanjabi, M., Talwalkar, A., Smith, V.: Federated optimization in heterogeneous networks. Proc. Mach. Learn. Syst. **2**, 429–450 (2020)
13. Li, X., Jiang, M., Zhang, X., Kamp, M., Dou, Q.: FedBN: federated learning on Non-IID features via local batch normalization. arXiv preprint arXiv:2102.07623 (2021)
14. Malinovskiy, G., Kovalev, D., Gasanov, E., Condat, L., Richtarik, P.: From local SGD to local fixed-point methods for federated learning. In: International Conference on Machine Learning, pp. 6692–6701. PMLR (2020)
15. McMahan, B., Moore, E., Ramage, D., Hampson, S., y Arcas, B.A.: Communication-efficient learning of deep networks from decentralized data. In: Artificial Intelligence and Statistics, pp. 1273–1282. PMLR (2017)
16. Mu, X., et al.: FedProc: Prototypical contrastive federated learning on Non-IID data. Futur. Gener. Comput. Syst. **143**, 93–104 (2023)
17. Pathak, R., Wainwright, M.J.: FedSplit: an algorithmic framework for fast federated optimization. Adv. Neural. Inf. Process. Syst. **33**, 7057–7066 (2020)
18. Pennisi, M., et al.: Gan latent space manipulation and aggregation for federated learning in medical imaging. In: Distributed, Collaborative, and Federated Learning, and Affordable AI and Healthcare for Resource Diverse Global Health: Third MICCAI Workshop, DeCaF 2022, and Second MICCAI Workshop, FAIR 2022, Held in Conjunction with MICCAI 2022, Singapore, September 18 and 22, 2022, Proceedings, pp. 68–78. Springer (2022). https://doi.org/10.1007/978-3-031-18523-6_7
19. The future of digital health with federated learning. NPJ Digital Med. **3**(1), 119 (2020)
20. Rotemberg, V., et al.: A patient-centric dataset of images and metadata for identifying melanomas using clinical context. Sci. Data **8**(1), 34 (2021)
21. Rothchild, D., et al.: FetchSGD: communication-efficient federated learning with sketching. In: International Conference on Machine Learning, pp. 8253–8265. PMLR (2020)
22. Ruder, S.: An overview of gradient descent optimization algorithms. arXiv preprint arXiv:1609.04747 (2016)
23. Sener, O., Savarese, S.: Active learning for convolutional neural networks: a core-set approach. arXiv preprint arXiv:1708.00489 (2017)
24. Song, R., et al.: Federated learning via decentralized dataset distillation in resource-constrained edge environments. arXiv preprint arXiv:2208.11311 (2022)
25. Tan, Y., et al.: FedProto: federated prototype learning across heterogeneous clients. In: Proceedings of the AAAI Conference on Artificial Intelligence, vol. 36, pp. 8432–8440 (2022)
26. Wang, J., Jin, Y., Wang, L.: Personalizing federated medical image segmentation via local calibration. In: Avidan, S., Brostow, G., Cissé, M., Farinella, G.M., Hassner, T. (eds.) Computer Vision – ECCV 2022: 17th European Conference, Tel Aviv, Israel, October 23–27, 2022, Proceedings, Part XXI, pp. 456–472. Springer, Cham (2022). https://doi.org/10.1007/978-3-031-19803-8_27
27. Wang, T., Zhu, J.Y., Torralba, A., Efros, A.A.: Dataset distillation. arXiv preprint arXiv:1811.10959 (2018)
28. Welling, M.: Herding dynamical weights to learn. In: Proceedings of the 26th Annual International Conference on Machine Learning, pp. 1121–1128 (2009)

29. Yuan, H., Ma, T.: Federated accelerated stochastic gradient descent. Adv. Neural. Inf. Process. Syst. **33**, 5332–5344 (2020)
30. Zhao, B., Bilen, H.: Dataset condensation with differentiable siamese augmentation. In: International Conference on Machine Learning, pp. 12674–12685. PMLR (2021)
31. Zhao, B., Bilen, H.: Dataset condensation with distribution matching. In: Proceedings of the IEEE/CVF Winter Conference on Applications of Computer Vision, pp. 6514–6523 (2023)
32. Zhao, B., Mopuri, K.R., Bilen, H.: Dataset condensation with gradient matching. arXiv preprint arXiv:2006.05929 (2020)

AViT: Adapting Vision Transformers for Small Skin Lesion Segmentation Datasets

Siyi Du[1]([✉]) [iD], Nourhan Bayasi[1] [iD], Ghassan Hamarneh[2] [iD], and Rafeef Garbi[1] [iD]

[1] University of British Columbia, Vancouver, BC, Canada
{siyi,nourhanb,rafeef}@ece.ubc.ca
[2] Simon Fraser University, Burnaby, BC, Canada
hamarneh@sfu.ca

Abstract. Skin lesion segmentation (SLS) plays an important role in skin lesion analysis. Vision transformers (ViTs) are considered an auspicious solution for SLS, but they require more training data compared to convolutional neural networks (CNNs) due to their inherent parameter-heavy structure and lack of some inductive biases. To alleviate this issue, current approaches fine-tune pre-trained ViT backbones on SLS datasets, aiming to leverage the knowledge learned from a larger set of natural images to lower the amount of skin training data needed. However, fully fine-tuning all parameters of large backbones is computationally expensive and memory intensive. In this paper, we propose AViT, a novel efficient strategy to mitigate ViTs' data-hunger by transferring any pre-trained ViTs to the SLS task. Specifically, we integrate lightweight modules (adapters) within the transformer layers, which modulate the feature representation of a ViT without updating its pre-trained weights. In addition, we employ a shallow CNN as a prompt generator to create a prompt embedding from the input image, which grasps fine-grained information and CNN's inductive biases to guide the segmentation task on small datasets. Our quantitative experiments on 4 skin lesion datasets demonstrate that AViT achieves competitive, and at times superior, performance to SOTA but with significantly fewer trainable parameters. Our code is available at https://github.com/siyi-wind/AViT.

Keywords: Vision Transformer · Data-efficiency · Efficiency · Medical Image Segmentation · Dermatology

1 Introduction

Melanoma is the most common and dangerous skin malignancy estimated to cause 97,610 new cases and 7,990 deaths in 2023 the United States alone [32], yet early diagnosis and treatment are highly likely to cure it. Automated skin

Supplementary Information The online version contains supplementary material available at https://doi.org/10.1007/978-3-031-47401-9_3.

M. E. Celebi et al. (Eds.): MICCAI 2023 Workshops, LNCS 14393, pp. 25–36, 2023.
https://doi.org/10.1007/978-3-031-47401-9_3

lesion segmentation (SLS), which provides thorough qualitative and quantitative information such as location and border, is a challenging and fundamental operation in computer-aided diagnosis [30]. As a pre-processing step of diagnosis, it boosts the accuracy and robustness of classification by regularizing attention maps [40], offering the region of interest for wide-field images [4], or removing lesion-adjacent confounding artifacts [1,27]. On the other hand, SLS can serve as a simultaneously optimizing task for classification, enabling the models to obtain improved performance on both two tasks [39]. SLS is also essential for skin color fairness research [12], where the segmented non-lesion area is used to approximate skin tone [22]. Vision transformers (ViTs), with their inherent capability to model global image context through the self-attention mechanism, are a set of promising tools to tackle SLS [17]. Though ViTs have shown improved performance compared to traditional convolutional neural networks (CNNs) [24], they are more data-hungry than CNNs, i.e., need more training data, given the lack of some useful inductive biases like weight sharing and locality [35]. This poses a significant challenge in SLS due to the limited availability of training images, where datasets often contain only a few hundred [29] or thousand [8] samples.

To alleviate ViTs' data-hunger, previous SLS works incorporated some inductive biases through hierarchical architecture [5], local self-attention [34], or convolution layers [14]. Nevertheless, they trained the models from scratch and overlooked the potential benefits of pre-trained models and valuable information from other domains with abundant data. As transfer learning from ImageNet [9] has been demonstrated advantageous for skin lesion tasks [28], an increasingly popular and promising way is to deploy a large pre-trained ViT as the encoder, and then fine-tune the entire model [37,42]. Despite achieving better performance, these techniques that rely on transfer learning have two notable drawbacks. First, a robust ViT typically has plenty of parameters, e.g., ViT-Base (86 million (M)) [10] and Swin-Base (88M) [25], thus making the full fine-tuning strategy quite expensive in terms of computation and memory requirements, especially when dealing with multiple datasets, i.e., we need to store an entire model for each dataset. Second, updating all parameters of a large-scale pre-trained model (full fine-tuning) on smaller datasets is found to be unstable [31] and may instead undermine the model's generalizable representations [41].

The newer parameter-efficient fine-tuning (PEFT) has been proposed as an effective and efficient solution, which only tunes a small subset of the model's parameters. PEFT in computer vision can be divided into two main directions: 1) prompt tuning [2,21] and 2) adapter tuning [7,38,41]. The first direction uses soft (i.e., tunable) prompts: task-specific parameters introduced into the frozen pre-trained ViT backbone's input space and tuned throughout the task-learning process. For example, Jia et al. [21] utilized randomly initialized trainable parameters as soft prompts and prepended them to pre-trained ViT's input for downstream recognition tasks. The second direction uses adapters: trainable lightweight modules inserted into the transformer layers, to modify the hidden representation of the frozen ViT rendering it suitable for a specific task. These PEFT approaches have shown substantially increased efficiency with comparable, or even improved, performance compared to those of full fine-tuning on low-data regimes. Nonetheless, very few works have adapted PEFT to medical imaging. Wu et al. [38] employed adapters to steer the Segment Anything Model (SAM) [23], a promptable ViT-based foundation model trained using 1 billion masks, to medical image segmentation tasks without updating SAM's parameters. However, they require additional pre-training on medical imaging data prior to adaptation as well as hard prompts in the form of un-tunable information input, such as free-form text or a set of foreground/background points, which increases the computational cost and necessitates prior information collection.

To address ViTs' data-hunger while maintaining the model's efficiency, in this work, we propose AViT, a novel transfer learning strategy that adapts a pre-trained ViT backbone to small SLS datasets by using PEFT. We incorporate lightweight adapter modules into the transformer layers to modify the image representation and keep the pre-trained weights untouched. Furthermore, to enhance the information extraction, we introduce a shallow CNN network in parallel with ViT as a prompt generator to generate a prompt embedding from the input image. The prompt captures CNN's valuable inductive biases and fine-grained information, which guides AViT to achieve improved segmentation performance, particularly in scenarios with limited training data. By using ViT-Base as the ViT backbone, the number of tunable parameters of our AViT is 13.6M, which is only 13.7% of the total AViT's parameters.

Our contributions can be summarized as follows. (1) To the best of our knowledge, we are the first to introduce PEFT to directly mitigate ViTs' data-hunger in medical image segmentation. (2) We propose AViT, featuring adapters for transferring a pre-trained ViT to the SLS task and a prompt generator for enhancing information extraction. (3) The experimental results on 4 different public datasets indicate that AViT surpasses previous SOTA PEFT algorithms and ViT-based SLS models without pre-trained backbones (gains 2.91% and 2.32% on average IOU, respectively). Further, AViT achieves competitive, or even superior performance, to SOTA ViT-based SLS models with pre-trained backbones while having significantly fewer trainable parameters (13.6M vs. 143.5M).

2   Methodology

In skin lesion segmentation (SLS), the model is required to predict a segmentation map $Y \in \{0,1\}^{H \times W}$ that partitions lesion areas based on an RGB skin image $X \in \mathbb{R}^{H \times W \times 3}$. In Fig. 1-a, AViT applies a ViT backbone pre-trained on large natural image datasets to the downstream SLS task through adapters and a prompt generator and only optimizes a few parameters. We briefly describe the plain ViT backbone in Sect. 2.1 and discuss the details of AViT in Sect. 2.2.

2.1   Basic ViT

A plain ViT [10] backbone contains a patch embedding module and L transformer layers (Fig. 1-b). Given an image X, the patch embedding module first

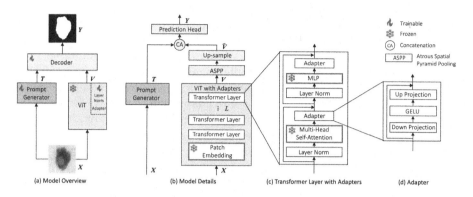

Fig. 1. Architecture of AViT: (a) Model overview with its prompt generator (a shallow CNN network), a large pre-trained ViT backbone with adapters, and a compact decoder. (b) Model details. (c) Details of a transformer layer with adapters. (d) Details of our adapters. During training, all modules in (b,c,d) contoured with blue borders are frozen, which encompasses 86.3% of AViT's parameters.

splits the image into N non-overlapping patches, then flattens and maps them to D-dimensional patch embeddings $x \in \mathbb{R}^{N \times D}$ through a linear projection, where $N = \frac{HW}{P^2}$ is the number of patches, and (P,P) is the patch size. The embedding sequence is then prepended with a learnable [class] token x_{class} to get $x_0 = [x_{class}; x] \in \mathbb{R}^{(N+1) \times D}$. To utilize the spatial prior, learnable position embeddings $E_{pos} \in \mathbb{R}^{(N+1) \times D}$, defined in [10], are added to x_0 to get $z_0 = x_0 + E_{pos}$, which is the input of the first transformer layer. Each transformer layer (Fig. 1-c without the adapters) comprises a multi-head self-attention module (MSA) and a multi-layer perceptron module (MLP), along with layer norm (LN). The output of the lth transformer layer $z_l \in \mathbb{R}^{(N+1) \times D}$ is:

$$z'_l = MSA(LN(z_{l-1})) + z_{l-1} \tag{1}$$

$$z_l = MLP(LN(z'_l)) + z'_l. \tag{2}$$

After getting the output of the final transformer layer z_L, we remove its [class] token and reshape it to a 2D feature representation $V \in \mathbb{R}^{\frac{H}{P} \times \frac{W}{P} \times D}$.

2.2   AViT

Given a pre-trained ViT backbone, we integrate adapters in each transformer layer to adjust the generated feature representation V adapted to skin images while leaving the weights of the backbone fixed. In addition, to enhance the information extraction, we employ a prompt generator in parallel, which is a shallow CNN network that produces a prompt embedding T based on the input image. Finally, a lightweight decoder combines V and T to predict a segmentation map. During training, we solely optimize the adapters, prompt generator, layer norm in the ViT backbone, and decoder, which collectively account for 13.7% of AViT's parameters. The details of these extensions are as follows.

Adapter Tuning: Similar to [20], we insert the adapter after MSA and MLP of each transformer layer (Fig. 1-c). The adapter (Fig. 1-d) contains two linear layers and a GELU function, which first projects the D-dimensional input into a smaller dimension $\frac{D}{r}$, where r is the reduction ratio, and projects it back to D dimension, i.e., $Adapter(input) = GELU(input \cdot \boldsymbol{W}_{down})\boldsymbol{W}_{up}$. $\boldsymbol{W}_{down} \in \mathbb{R}^{D \times \frac{D}{r}}$ and $\boldsymbol{W}_{down} \in \mathbb{R}^{\frac{D}{r} \times D}$. The output of lth transformer layer with adapters is:

$$\boldsymbol{z}'_l = Adapter(MSA(LN(\boldsymbol{z}_{l-1}))) + \boldsymbol{z}_{l-1} \tag{3}$$

$$\boldsymbol{z}_l = Adapter(MLP(LN(\boldsymbol{z}'_l))) + \boldsymbol{z}'_l. \tag{4}$$

Information Enhancement by Prompt Tuning: Inspired by the prompt tuning [13,21], we deploy soft prompts to extract more information from images and enrich the SLS task learning. Specifically, we utilize the first stage of a ResNet-34 (including 7 convolutional layers) as the prompt generator to automatically create a prompt embedding $\boldsymbol{T}$ from the input image. The prompt is hypothesized to grasp CNN's helpful inductive biases and fine-grained information, e.g., spatial details, boundaries, and texture, to facilitate AViT's segmentation ability despite the small training datasets. Our soft prompt produced by the network is more flexible, customized to each input image, and includes rich information, in contrast to previous soft prompts that are simple free tunable parameters and remain constant for all inputs. Moreover, it is worth noting that our prompt generator has only a small number of parameters (0.23M), which is different from previous hybrid models combining a ViT with a large CNN backbone, e.g., ResNet-34 (21.3M) [19,37] or ResNet-50 (23.5M) [36].

Lightweight Decoder: We incorporate a compact decoder for efficient prediction, as opposed to prior works that use complex decoding architectures involving multi-stage up-sampling, convolutional operations, and skip connections [18,37]. This choice is driven by the powerful and over-parameterized nature of large pre-trained ViT backbones, which have demonstrated strong transferability to downstream tasks [28]. As visualized in Fig. 1-b, after getting the feature representation $\boldsymbol{V}$ from the ViT backbone and the prompt embedding $\boldsymbol{T}$ from the prompt generator, we first pass $\boldsymbol{V}$ through the atrous spatial pyramid pooling module (ASPP) proposed in [6], which uses multiple parallel dilated convolutional layers with different dilation rates, to obtain a feature that extracts local information while capturing lesion context at different scales. After that, we up-sample the output feature of ASPP to get $\hat{\boldsymbol{V}}$, which has the same resolution as $\boldsymbol{T}$. Finally, $\hat{\boldsymbol{V}}$ is concatenated with $\boldsymbol{T}$ and sent to a projection head, which is formed by 3 convolutional layers connected by ReLU activation functions.

3   Experiments

Datasets and Evaluation Metrics: We evaluate our AViT on 4 public SLS databases collected from different sources: ISIC 2018 (ISIC) [8], Dermofit Image

Table 1. Skin lesion segmentation (SLS) results comparing BASE (AViT w/o both adapters and the prompt generator and is fully fine-tuned), AViT, and SOTA algorithms. We report the models' parameter count in millions (M). The 2nd column shows which pre-trained backbone the model used. R-34/50 represents ResNet-34/50.

Model	Pretrained backbone	#Total Param. (M) ↓	#Tuned Param. (M) ↓	GFL-OPs↓	Segmentation Results in Test Sets (%)									
					Dice ↑					IOU ↑				
					ISIC	DMF	SCD	PH2	Avg±std	ISIC	DMF	SCD	PH2	Avg±std
(a) Full Fine-tuned BASE & Proposed PEFT Method														
BASE	ViT-B	91.8×	91.8×	18.0	90.77	91.69	91.95	95.64	$92.51_{0.88}$	83.71	84.89	85.42	91.72	$86.43_{0.84}$
AViT	ViT-B	99.4 (13.6×)	13.6×	20.9	91.74	92.04	93.16	95.66	$93.15_{0.48}$	85.22	85.47	87.39	91.72	$87.45_{0.70}$
(b) PEFT Methods														
VPT	ViT-B	92.8 (7.0×)	7.0×	26.5	90.89	91.26	89.09	93.14	$91.10_{0.46}$	83.83	84.14	80.76	87.27	$84.00_{0.74}$
AdaptFormer	ViT-B	93.0 (7.2×)	7.2×	18.2	91.12	91.27	89.65	93.76	$91.45_{0.48}$	84.15	84.18	81.49	88.33	$84.54_{0.67}$
(c) SLS Methods w/o Pre-trained Backbones & Trained From Scratch														
SwinUnet	None	41.4×	41.4×	8.7	89.64	90.67	89.77	94.24	$91.08_{0.70}$	81.94	83.19	82.07	89.24	$84.11_{0.79}$
UNETR	None	87.7×	87.7×	20.2	89.60	90.53	88.13	93.92	$90.55_{0.87}$	81.86	83.02	79.96	88.68	$83.38_{1.24}$
UTNet	None	10.0×	10.0×	13.2	89.68	89.87	88.11	93.29	$90.23_{0.61}$	81.99	81.91	79.71	87.62	$82.81_{0.77}$
MedFormer	None	19.2×	19.2×	13.0	90.47	90.85	90.60	94.82	$91.68_{0.74}$	83.22	83.52	83.53	90.23	$85.13_{1.18}$
Swin UNETR	None	25.1×	25.1×	14.3	90.19	91.00	90.71	94.54	$91.61_{0.49}$	82.78	83.77	83.54	89.74	$84.96_{0.74}$
(d) SLS Methods w/ Pre-trained Backbones & Fully Fine-tuned														
H2Former	R-34	33.7×	33.7×	24.7	91.17	91.29	92.76	95.65	$92.72_{0.63}$	84.35	84.22	87.04	91.77	$86.85_{0.79}$
FAT-Net	R-34, DeiT-T	28.8×	28.8×	42.8	91.26	91.32	93.03	96.07	$92.92_{0.48}$	84.42	84.25	87.23	92.48	$87.10_{0.80}$
BAT	R-50	46.2×	46.2×	10.3	91.33	91.20	92.95	95.84	$92.83_{0.46}$	84.40	84.03	87.08	92.04	$86.89_{0.78}$
TransFuse	R-50, DeiT-B	143.5×	143.5×	63.4	91.73	91.96	94.11	96.18	$93.50_{0.87}$	85.22	85.33	89.03	92.69	$88.07_{0.47}$

Library (DMF) [3], Skin Cancer Detection (SCD) [16], and PH2 [29], which contain 2594, 1212, 206, and 200 skin images along with their segmentation maps, respectively. We perform 5-fold cross-validation and measure our model's segmentation performance using Dice and IOU metrics, computational cost at inference via gigaFLOPs (GFLOPs), and memory footprint via the number of needed parameters. Due to the table width restriction and the high number of columns, we only report the standard deviation (std) of average Dice and IOU in tables and provide the std for each dataset in the supplementary material.

Implementation Details: We resize the images to 224×224 and augment them by random scaling, shifting, rotation, flipping, Gaussian noise, and brightness and contrast changes. The ViT backbone of AViT is a ViT-B/16 [10], with a patch size of 16×16, pre-trained on ImageNet-21k. Similar to [41], the reduction ratio r of the adapters is 4. The output dimension of ASPP is 256. All models are deployed on a single TITAN V and trained using a combination of Dice and binary cross entropy loss [11,33] for 200 epochs with the AdamW optimizer [26], a batch size of 16, and an initial learning rate of 1×10^{-4}, which changes through a linear decay scheduler whose step size is 50 and decay factor $\gamma = 0.5$.

Comparing Against The Baseline (BASE): BASE is established by removing the adapters and the prompt generator of AViT and optimizing all the param-

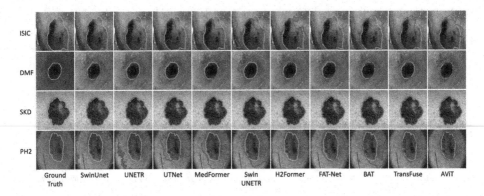

Fig. 2. Visual comparison with different SOTA methods. The green contours are the ground truth, and the red contours are the segmentation results. (Color figure online)

eters during training. In Table 1-a, AViT achieves superior performance compared to BASE, with average IOU and Dice improvements of 1.02% and 0.64%, respectively, while utilizing significantly fewer trainable parameters (13.6M vs. 91.8M). This suggests that BASE exhibits overfitting, and full fine-tuning is unsuitable for transferring knowledge to smaller skin datasets, whereas AViT effectively leverages the learnt knowledge and demonstrates strong generalization capability on the SLS task. When considering the memory requirements for the 4 datasets, BASE would require storing 4 entirely new models, resulting in a total of $91.8 \times 4 = 367.2$M parameters. On the contrary, AViT only needs to store the pre-trained ViT backbone once, resulting in reduced storage needs, i.e., $85.8 + 13.6 \times 4 = 140.2$M. As the number of domains increases, the memory savings offered by AViT compared to BASE will become even more pronounced.

Comparing Against State-of-the-Art (SOTA) Methods: We conduct experiments on SOTA PEFT and SLS approaches. We first reproduced VPT [21] that added learnable visual prompts in the input space and AdaptFormer [7] that introduced adapters in the transformer layers. We set the number of prompts in VPT to 100. In Table 1-b, AViT surpasses them across all datasets (gains 2.91% on average IOU over AdaptFormer), with comparable trainable parameters.

Additionally, we compare various ViT-based SLS algorithms and divide them into two groups. *Group 1* is models without pre-trained backbones and trained from scratch: SwinUnet [5], UNETR [18], UTNet [14], MedFormer [15], and Swin UNETR [34]. *Group 2* is models with pre-trained backbones and fully fine-tuned: H2Former [19], FAT-Net [37], BAT [36], and TransFuse [42]. H2Former and BAT used pre-trained ResNet but randomly initialized transformer modules. Table 1-c shows that AViT outperforms *Group 1* across all datasets by a large margin (increases average IOU of MedFormer by 2.32%), with comparable and even fewer trainable parameters (13.6M vs. 19.2M). Table 1-d illustrates that AViT

Table 2. Experiments using different pre-trained ViT backbones and ablation study of AViT. * means the pre-trained backbone is frozen throughout training. $^{-P}$ or $^{-A}$ represent not using the prompt generator or adapters in AViT.

Model	Pretrained backbone	#Total Param. (M)	#Tuned Param. (M)	GFL-OPs	Segmentation Results in Test Sets (%)									
					Dice ↑					IOU ↑				
					ISIC	DMF	SCD	PH2	Avg$_{\pm std}$	ISIC	DMF	SCD	PH2	Avg$_{\pm std}$
(a) Applicability to Various Pre-trained ViT Backbones														
BASE	Swin-B	63.8×	63.8×	15.6	91.63	91.70	92.71	95.88	92.98$_{0.37}$	85.05	84.89	86.60	92.13	87.17$_{0.61}$
AViT	Swin-B	68.9 (9.5×)	9.5×	18.3	91.54	91.73	93.60	95.68	93.14$_{0.39}$	84.90	84.94	88.12	91.77	87.43$_{0.64}$
BASE	Swin-L	139.8×	139.8×	32.3	91.64	91.69	92.93	95.83	93.02$_{0.25}$	85.08	84.86	86.97	92.04	87.24$_{0.43}$
AViT	Swin-L	151.1 (17.6×)	17.6×	36.3	91.56	91.91	93.74	96.07	93.32$_{0.31}$	84.93	85.24	88.38	92.47	87.76$_{0.50}$
BASE	ViT-L	311.2×	311.2×	61.2	91.37	91.76	93.23	95.86	93.06$_{0.29}$	84.60	84.99	87.52	92.09	87.30$_{0.47}$
AViT	ViT-L	336.9 (33.7×)	33.7×	67.7	91.54	91.77	93.48	95.73	93.13$_{0.48}$	84.88	85.01	87.94	91.85	87.42$_{0.79}$
BASE	DeiT-B	91.8×	91.8×	18.0	91.48	91.82	93.63	95.83	92.94$_{0.38}$	84.77	85.10	86.53	92.04	87.11$_{0.58}$
AViT	DeiT-B	99.4 (13.6×)	13.6×	20.9	91.70	91.85	93.67	95.97	93.30$_{0.31}$	85.14	85.17	88.22	92.30	87.71$_{0.51}$
(b) Ablation Study														
BASE*	ViT-B	91.8 (6.0×)	6.0×	18.0	87.18	89.23	86.24	90.17	88.20$_{0.46}$	77.92	80.81	76.27	82.30	79.33$_{0.65}$
AViT^{-P}	ViT-B	98.9 (13.2×)	13.2×	19.4	91.47	91.80	91.18	94.75	92.30$_{0.31}$	84.74	85.04	83.98	90.09	85.96$_{0.48}$
AViT^{-A}	ViT-B	92.3 (6.5×)	6.5×	19.5	90.87	91.00	89.09	93.87	91.21$_{0.83}$	83.78	83.72	81.18	88.53	84.30$_{1.19}$
AViT	ViT-B	99.4 (13.6×)	13.6×	20.9	91.74	92.04	93.16	95.66	93.15$_{0.42}$	85.22	85.47	87.39	91.72	87.45$_{0.70}$

achieves competitive or higher segmentation performance compared to *Group 2*, with fewer trainable parameters. For instance, AViT achieves a marginally lower average Dice compared to TransFuse (0.35% difference), yet its parameter count and computational complexity (GFLOPs) are 1/10 and 1/3 less than that of TransFuse, respectively. Figure 2 visualizes AViT's segmentation performance.

AViT on Different Pre-trained ViT Backbones: We conduct experiments using ViTs in varied sizes, structures, or training strategies, including ViT-L/16, Swin-B, Swin-L [25], and DeiT-B, as the pre-trained backbone. For Swin-B/L, we use the output of its 3rd stage as the encoded image feature, whose resolution is the same as ViT-B's output feature. DeiT-B and ViT-B have the same architecture but different training strategies. In Table 2-a, for each ViT backbone, AViT achieves competitive and even higher performance compared to fully fine-tuned BASE, but with substantially fewer parameters (trainable and total) for the 4 datasets, indicating the applicability of our method on different ViTs.

Ablation Study: To show the efficacy of our proposed components in Sect. 2.2, we freeze the parameters of BASE's pre-trained ViT to get BASE* and remove the adapters and prompt generator in AViT to get $AViT^{-A}$ and $AViT^{-P}$, respectively. In Table 2-b, BASE* attains average Dice and IOU of 88.20% and 79.33%, respectively. However, it still falls far behind fully fine-tuned BASE with 92.51% and 86.43% on average Dice and IOU, respectively. After adding adapters to BASE ($AViT^{-P}$), the average Dice and IOU increase by 4.10% and 6.63%, respectively; after adding a prompt generator to BASE ($AViT^{-A}$), the average Dice and IOU increase by 3.01% and 4.97%, respectively. Finally, AViT achieves the highest segmentation results and significantly outperforms BASE* (increases average Dice and IOU by 4.95% and 8.12%, respectively) with only 7.6M more trainable parameters. The above results reveal that our proposed mechanisms boost the segmentation performance, and a combination of both performs best.

4   Conclusion

We propose AViT, a new method to alleviate ViTs' data-hunger and apply it on small skin lesion segmentation (SLS) datasets by employing a pre-trained ViT backbone whilst keeping computation and storage memory costs very low via parameter-efficient fine-tuning (PEFT). Specifically, we integrate adapters into the transformer layers to modulate the backbone's image representation without updating its pre-trained weights and utilize a prompt generator to produce a prompt embedding, which captures CNNs' inductive biases and fine-grained information to guide AViT for segmenting skin images on limited data. Our experiments on 4 datasets illustrate that AViT outperforms other PEFT methods and achieves comparable or even superior performance to SOTA SLS approaches but with considerably fewer trainable and total parameters. Moreover, the experiments using different ViT backbones and an ablation study showcase the applicability of AViT and the effectiveness of AViT's components. Future work will focus on improving AViT's architecture so that it can achieve SOTA segmentation performance while retaining computation and memory efficiency.

References

1. Adegun, A., Viriri, S.: Deep learning techniques for skin lesion analysis and melanoma cancer detection: a survey of state-of-the-art. Artif. Intell. Rev. **54**, 811–841 (2021)
2. Bahng, H., Jahanian, A., et al.: Visual prompting: modifying pixel space to adapt pre-trained models. arXiv preprint arXiv:2203.17274 (2022)
3. Ballerini, L., Fisher, R.B., Aldridge, B., Rees, J.: A color and texture based hierarchical K-NN approach to the classification of non-melanoma skin lesions. In: Celebi, M.E., Schaefer, G. (eds.) Color Medical Image Analysis, pp. 63–86. Springer Netherlands, Dordrecht (2013). https://doi.org/10.1007/978-94-007-5389-1_4
4. Birkenfeld, J.S., Tucker-Schwartz, J.M., et al.: Computer-aided classification of suspicious pigmented lesions using wide-field images. Comput. Methods Programs Biomed. **195**, 105631 (2020)

5. Cao, H., et al.: Swin-Unet: Unet-Like Pure Transformer for Medical Image Segmentation. In: Karlinsky, L., Michaeli, T., Nishino, K. (eds.) Computer Vision – ECCV 2022 Workshops: Tel Aviv, Israel, October 23–27, 2022, Proceedings, Part III, pp. 205–218. Springer, Cham (2023). https://doi.org/10.1007/978-3-031-25066-8_9

6. Chen, L.C., Papandreou, G., et al.: DeepLab: semantic image segmentation with deep convolutional nets, atrous convolution, and fully connected CRFs. IEEE Trans. Pattern Anal. Mach. Intell. **40**(4), 834–848 (2017)

7. Chen, S., Ge, C., Tong, Z., Wang, J., Song, Y., et al.: AdaptFormer: adapting vision transformers for scalable visual recognition. In: NeurIPS 2022 (2022)

8. Codella, N., Rotemberg, V., Tschandl, P., Celebi, M.E., Dusza, S., et al.: Skin lesion analysis toward melanoma detection 2018: a challenge hosted by the international skin imaging collaboration (ISIC). arXiv preprint arXiv:1902.03368 (2019)

9. Deng, J., Dong, W., Socher, R., Li, L.J., Li, K., Fei-Fei, L.: ImageNet: a large-scale hierarchical image database. In: CVPR 2009, pp. 248–255. IEEE (2009)

10. Dosovitskiy, A., Beyer, L., Kolesnikov, A., et al.: An image is worth 16x16 words: transformers for image recognition at scale. In: ICLR 2020 (2020)

11. Du, S., Bayasi, N., Harmarneh, G., Garbi, R.: MDViT: multi-domain vision transformer for small medical image segmentation datasets. arXiv preprint arXiv:2307.02100 (2023)

12. Du, S., Hers, B., Bayasi, N., Hamarneh, G., Garbi, R.: FairDisCo: fairer AI in dermatology via disentanglement contrastive learning. In: Karlinsky, L., Michaeli, T., Nishino, K. (eds.) Computer Vision – ECCV 2022 Workshops: Tel Aviv, Israel, October 23–27, 2022, Proceedings, Part IV, pp. 185–202. Springer, Cham (2023). https://doi.org/10.1007/978-3-031-25069-9_13

13. Gao, Y., Shi, X., Zhu, Y., Wang, H., et al.: Visual prompt tuning for test-time domain adaptation. arXiv preprint arXiv:2210.04831 (2022)

14. Gao, Y., Zhou, M., Metaxas, D.N.: UTNet: a hybrid transformer architecture for medical image segmentation. In: de Bruijne, M., et al. (eds.) Medical Image Computing and Computer Assisted Intervention – MICCAI 2021: 24th International Conference, Strasbourg, France, September 27–October 1, 2021, Proceedings, Part III, pp. 61–71. Springer, Cham (2021). https://doi.org/10.1007/978-3-030-87199-4_6

15. Gao, Y., et al.: A data-scalable transformer for medical image segmentation: architecture, model efficiency, and benchmark. arXiv preprint arXiv:2203.00131 (2022)

16. Glaister, J., Amelard, R., Wong, A., Clausi, D.A.: MSIM: multistage illumination modeling of dermatological photographs for illumination-corrected skin lesion analysis. IEEE Trans. Biomed. Eng. **60**(7), 1873–1883 (2013)

17. Gulzar, Y., Khan, S.A.: Skin lesion segmentation based on vision transformers and convolutional neural networks-a comparative study. Appl. Sci. **12**(12), 5990 (2022)

18. Hatamizadeh, A., Tang, Y., Nath, V., Yang, D., et al.: UNETR: transformers for 3D medical image segmentation. In: WACV 2022, pp. 574–584 (2022)

19. He, A., Wang, K., et al.: H2Former: An efficient hierarchical hybrid transformer for medical image segmentation. IEEE Trans. Med. Imaging **42**, 2763–2775 (2023)

20. Houlsby, N., Giurgiu, A., Jastrzebski, S., Morrone, B., et al.: Parameter-efficient transfer learning for NLP. In: ICML 2019, pp. 2790–2799. PMLR (2019)

21. Jia, M., et al.: Visual prompt tuning. In: Avidan, S., Brostow, G., Cissé, M., Farinella, G.M., Hassner, T. (eds.) Computer Vision – ECCV 2022: 17th European Conference, Tel Aviv, Israel, October 23–27, 2022, Proceedings, Part XXXIII, pp. 709–727. Springer, Cham (2022). https://doi.org/10.1007/978-3-031-19827-4_41

22. Kinyanjui, N.M., et al.: Fairness of classifiers across skin tones in dermatology. In: Martel, A.L., et al. (eds.) Medical Image Computing and Computer Assisted Intervention – MICCAI 2020: 23rd International Conference, Lima, Peru, October 4–8, 2020, Proceedings, Part VI, pp. 320–329. Springer, Cham (2020). https://doi.org/10.1007/978-3-030-59725-2_31

23. Kirillov, A., et al.: Segment anything. arXiv preprint arXiv:2304.02643 (2023)

24. Li, J., Chen, J., Tang, Y., Wang, C., Landman, B.A., Zhou, S.K.: Transforming medical imaging with transformers? a comparative review of key properties, current progresses, and future perspectives. Medical image analysis p. 102762 (2023)

25. Liu, Z., Lin, Y., Cao, Y., Hu, H., et al.: Swin transformer: hierarchical vision transformer using shifted windows. In: ICCV 2021, pp. 10012–10022 (2021)

26. Loshchilov, I., Hutter, F.: Decoupled weight decay regularization. arXiv preprint arXiv:1711.05101 (2017)

27. Maron, R.C., Hekler, A., Krieghoff-Henning, E., Schmitt, M., et al.: Reducing the impact of confounding factors on skin cancer classification via image segmentation: technical model study. J. Med. Internet Res. **23**(3), e21695 (2021)

28. Matsoukas, C., Haslum, J.F., et al.: What makes transfer learning work for medical images: feature reuse & other factors. In: CVPR 2022. pp. 9225–9234 (2022)

29. Mendonça, T., Ferreira, P.M., et al.: PH 2-A dermoscopic image database for research and benchmarking. In: EMBC 2013, pp. 5437–5440. IEEE (2013)

30. Mirikharaji, Z., Abhishek, K., Bissoto, A., Barata, C., et al.: A survey on deep learning for skin lesion segmentation. Med. Image Anal. **88**, 102863 (2023)

31. Peters, M.E., Ruder, S., Smith, N.A.: To tune or not to tune? adapting pretrained representations to diverse tasks. ACL **2019**, 7 (2019)

32. Siegel, R.L., Miller, K.D., Wagle, N.S., Jemal, A.: Cancer statistics, 2023. CA: a cancer journal for clinicians 73(1), 17–48 (2023)

33. Taghanaki, S.A., Zheng, Y., Zhou, S.K., Georgescu, B., Sharma, P., Xu, D., et al.: Combo loss: handling input and output imbalance in multi-organ segmentation. Comput. Med. Imaging Graph. **75**, 24–33 (2019)

34. Tang, Y., Yang, D., Li, W., Roth, H.R., Landman, B., Xu, D., Nath, V., Hatamizadeh, A.: Self-supervised pre-training of swin transformers for 3D medical image analysis. In: CVPR 2022, pp. 20730–20740 (2022)

35. Touvron, H., Cord, M., Douze, M., Massa, F., Sablayrolles, A., Jégou, H.: Training data-efficient image transformers & distillation through attention. In: ICML 2021. pp. 10347–10357, PMLR (2021)

36. Wang, J., Wei, L., Wang, L., Zhou, Q., Zhu, L., Qin, J.: Boundary-aware transformers for skin lesion segmentation. In: de Bruijne, M., et al. (eds.) Medical Image Computing and Computer Assisted Intervention – MICCAI 2021: 24th International Conference, Strasbourg, France, September 27–October 1, 2021, Proceedings, Part I, pp. 206–216. Springer, Cham (2021). https://doi.org/10.1007/978-3-030-87193-2_20

37. Wu, H., Chen, S., et al.: FAT-Net: feature adaptive transformers for automated skin lesion segmentation. Med. Image Anal. **76**, 102327 (2022)

38. Wu, J., Fu, R., Fang, H., Liu, Y., Wang, Z., Xu, Y., Jin, Y., Arbel, T.: Medical SAM adapter: adapting segment anything model for medical image segmentation. arXiv preprint arXiv:2304.12620 (2023)

39. Xie, Y., Zhang, J., Xia, Y., Shen, C.: A mutual bootstrapping model for automated skin lesion segmentation and classification. IEEE Trans. Med. Imaging **39**(7), 2482–2493 (2020)

40. Yan, Y., Kawahara, J., Hamarneh, G.: Melanoma Recognition via Visual Attention. In: Chung, A.C.S., Gee, J.C., Yushkevich, P.A., Bao, S. (eds.) Information Processing in Medical Imaging: 26th International Conference, IPMI 2019, Hong Kong, China, June 2–7, 2019, Proceedings, pp. 793–804. Springer, Cham (2019). https://doi.org/10.1007/978-3-030-20351-1_62
41. Yang, T., Zhu, Y., Xie, Y., Zhang, A., Chen, C., Li, M.: AIM: adapting image models for efficient video action recognition. In: ICLR 2023 (2023)
42. Zhang, Y., Liu, H., Hu, Q.: TransFuse: fusing transformers and CNNs for medical image segmentation. In: de Bruijnede Bruijne, M., et al. (eds.) Medical Image Computing and Computer Assisted Intervention – MICCAI 2021: 24th International Conference, Strasbourg, France, September 27–October 1, 2021, Proceedings, Part I, pp. 14–24. Springer, Cham (2021). https://doi.org/10.1007/978-3-030-87193-2_2

Test-Time Selection for Robust Skin Lesion Analysis

Alceu Bissoto[1](✉), Catarina Barata[2], Eduardo Valle[3,4], and Sandra Avila[1]

[1] Recod.ai Lab, Institute of Computing, University of Campinas, Campinas, Brazil
alceubissoto@ic.unicamp.br, avilas@unicamp.br
[2] Institute for Systems and Robotics, Instituto Superior Técnico, Lisbon, Portugal
[3] School of Electrical and Computing Engineering, University of Campinas,
Campinas, Brazil
[4] Valeo.ai Paris, Paris, France

Abstract. Skin lesion analysis models are biased by artifacts placed during image acquisition, which influence model predictions despite carrying no clinical information. Solutions that address this problem by regularizing models to prevent learning those spurious features achieve only partial success, and existing test-time debiasing techniques are inappropriate for skin lesion analysis due to either making unrealistic assumptions on the distribution of test data or requiring laborious annotation from medical practitioners. We propose TTS (Test-Time Selection), a human-in-the-loop method that leverages positive (e.g., lesion area) and negative (e.g., artifacts) keypoints in test samples. TTS effectively steers models away from exploiting spurious artifact-related correlations without retraining, and with less annotation requirements. Our solution is robust to a varying availability of annotations, and different levels of bias. We showcase on the ISIC2019 dataset (for which we release a subset of annotated images) how our model could be deployed in the real-world for mitigating bias.

Keywords: Test-time Debiasing · Robust Skin Lesion Analysis · Deep Learning

1 Introduction

Spurious correlations between conspicuous image features and annotation labels are easy to learn, but since they have no actual predictive power they compromise the robustness of models. In medical image analysis, with datasets much smaller than the typical computer vision state-of-the-art, their effect is increased. In skin lesion analysis, one of the most studied confounders are artifacts produced during image acquisition (such as rulers, color patches, and ink markings). Even if the correlation of the presence of each artifact with the lesion diagnostic is small, the combined effect suffices to distract models from clinically-robust features [1,2,8]. Mitigating bias during training is an active research area, but methods still

© The Author(s), under exclusive license to Springer Nature Switzerland AG 2023
M. E. Celebi et al. (Eds.): MICCAI 2023 Workshops, LNCS 14393, pp. 37–46, 2023.
https://doi.org/10.1007/978-3-031-47401-9_4

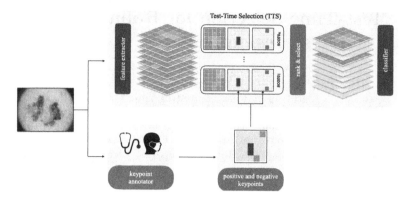

Fig. 1. Test-Time Selection (TTS). An annotator provides negative (background, arti-facts) and positive (lesion area) keypoints, used to rank and select activation units from the last layer of the pretrained feature extractor. Features related to negative keypoints are masked to zero.

struggle to surpass strong baselines [10]. A complementary solution is to change the inference procedure to mitigate biases during test [4]. For that, solutions have exploited test batch statistics for feature alignment [12,18]. However, test batch statistics heavily rely on the batch size (the bigger, the better) and on the homogeneity of the test distribution. For medical data, one attractive option is to exploit (few or quickly obtainable) extra annotations to infuse domain knowledge into the models' predictions, increasing model robustness and trust of medical practitioners [9].

In comparison to other medical fields, skin lesion analysis researchers have access to rich annotations to support this path. Besides high-quality images, there are available annotations regarding segmentation masks, dermoscopic attributes, the presence of artifacts, and other clinical information such as age, sex, and lesions' anatomical site. In particular, segmentation masks experience the most success, granting more robustness to classification. We build upon this success to create a solution that dependd on human-defined keypoints, which are far cheaper to annotate than lesion segmentation masks.

In this work, we propose TTS (Test-Time Selection), a method to incorporate human-defined points of interest into trained models to select robust features during test-time. In Fig. 1, we show a summary of our method. In more detail, we first gather human-selected keypoints of interest (positive and negative). Then, we rank the last layer activation units based on their affinity to the keypoints. Finally, we mute (set to zero) the 90% worst features, using only the remaining 10% for classification. There are no changes to the models' weights, making this procedure lightweight and easy to integrate in different pipelines.

Our method is compatible with the daily clinical routine to avoid overwhelming medical practitioners with the technology that is intended to assist them. The human intervention must be as quick and straightforward as possible while granting enough information to steer models away from spurious correlations. We show that we can improve robustness even from a single pair of positive and negative interest points that merely identify lesion and background, and achieve stronger results by using the location of artifacts.

We summarize our contributions as follows:

- We propose a method for test-time selection based on human-defined criteria that boosts the robustness of skin lesion analysis models[1].
- We show that our method is effective throughout different bias levels.
- We show that a single positive and negative interest point is sufficient to improve significantly models' robustness.
- We manually annotate the position of artifacts in skin lesion images and use these selected keypoints in our solution, further improving performance.

2   Related Work

Test-time debiasing can adapt deep learning to specific population characteristics and hospital procedures that differ from the original dataset. Most methods for test-time debiasing exploit statistics of the batch of test examples. Tent [18] (Test entropy minimization) proposes to update batch normalization weights and biases to minimize the entropy of the test batch. Similarly, T3A [12] (Test-Time Template Adjuster) maintains new class prototypes for the classification problem, which are updated with test samples, and finally used for grounding new predictions. Both approaches rely on two strong assumptions: that a large test batch is available during prediction, and that all test samples originate from the same distribution.

Those assumptions fail for medical scenarios, where diagnostics may be performed one by one, and populations attending a given center may be highly multimodal. To attempt to work in this more challenging scenario, SAR [13] (Sharpness-Aware and Reliable optimization scheme) proposes to perform entropy minimization updates considering samples that provide more stable gradients while finding a flat minimum that brings robustness regarding the noisy samples. Despite showing good performances in corrupted scenarios (e.g., ImageNet-C [11]), SAR is heavily dependent on the model's architecture, being inappropriate for models with batch normalization layers. In contrast with these methods, our solution does not use any test batch statistic, does not require training nor updates to the models' weights, and does not rely upon any particular architecture structure to improve performance.

Another approach is to change the network's inputs to remove biasing factors. NoiseCrop [3] showed considerable robustness improvements for skin lesion analysis by using skin segmentation masks to replace the inputs' backgrounds with a common Gaussian noise. Despite its benefits, NoiseCrop is hard to integrate into clinical practice as it depends on laborious segmentation masks annotated

---

[1] Code is available at https://github.com/alceubissoto/skin-tts.

Table 1. Comparison of TTS with state-of-the-art test-time debiasing.

	Tent [18]	T3A [12]	SAR [13]	NoiseCrop [3]	TTS (Ours)
Test-time only	✓	✓	✓	✓	✓
Human-in-the loop	✗	✗	✗	✓	✓
No parameter updates	✗	✗	✗	✓	✓
Robust to changing test statistics	✗	✗	✓	✓	✓
Architecture agnostic	✗	✓	✗	✓	✓
Few extra information required	–	–	–	✗	✓

by dermatologists. Also, NoiseCrop discards relevant information in the patient's healthy skin and introduces visual patterns that create a distribution shift of its own. Our solution does not suffer from these problems since our intervention takes place in feature space, and we show it is effective using very few keypoints. We summarize the differences between our method and the literature in Table 1.

3   Methodology

Previous works showed the potential of test-time debiasing, but depended on weight updates using test batches statistics [12,18] and architecture components [13]. We decided instead to use human feedback over positive and negative image keypoints to steer the models. We aimed at making the annotation procedure as effortless as possible, allowing to integrate the method into the clinical practice of skin lesion analysis. The resulting Test-Time Selection (TTS) is summarized in Fig. 1.

TTS: Test-Time Feature Selection. We assume access to a single test sample x, associated with a set of positive $K_p = \{kp_1, kp_2, ..., kp_p\}$ and negative $K_n = \{kn_1, kn_2, ..., kn_n\}$ human-selected keypoints on the image. The positive keypoints represents areas of the image that should receive more attention (e.g., the lesion area), while the negative points represent area of the image that should be ignored (e.g., the background, or spurious artifacts). We denote the feature extractor from a pretrained neural network by $f(\cdot)$, and the associated classifier by $g(\cdot)$.

   For each image x, the feature extractor generates a representation $f(x)$, which is upsampled to match the original image x size for test-time selection. For each channel c in $f(x)$, we extract the values corresponding to the coordinates specified by the keypoints and compute their sums $S_{p_c} = \sum_{k \in K_p} f(x)_c[k]$, and $S_{n_c} = \sum_{k \in K_n} f(x)_c[k]$, where $f(x)_c[k]$ denotes the value at the keypoint k for channel c of $f(x)$. We calculate a score S_c for each channel c as the difference between the sums of the representations at the positive and negative keypoints:

$$S_c = \alpha S_{p_c} - (1 - \alpha) S_{n_c}, \qquad (1)$$

where α controls the strength of the positive and negative factors. We use $\alpha = 0.4$ to give slightly more weight to the negative keypoints related to the sources of bias (i.e., artifacts) investigated in this work. If the keypoint annotation confidently locates positive or negative points of interest, α can be adjusted to give it more weight.

We use the scores to rank the channels with higher affinity to the input keypoints. We define a set T which consists of the indices corresponding to the top $\lambda\%$ scores in S_c, i.e., $T = \{c : S_c$ is among the top $\lambda\%$ of scores$\}$. In other words, λ controls how much information is muted. In general, we want to mute as much as possible to avoid using spurious correlations. In our setup, we keep only 10% of the original activation units. Next, we form a binary mask M with values m_c defined as: $m_c = 1$, if $c \in T$, or $m_c = 0$, if $c \notin T$.

Finally, the masked version of $f(x)$, denoted as $f'(x)$, is computed by $f(x)$: $f'(x) = f(x) \odot M$, where $\odot$ represents the element-wise multiplication. The masked feature map $f'(x)$ is the input for our neural network's classifier component $g(\cdot)$, which yields the final prediction. As such procedure happens individually for each dataset sample, different samples can use the activation units that best suit it, which we verified to be crucial for the effectiveness of this method.

Keypoints. We always assume having access to the same number of positive and negative keypoints (i.e., for 2 keypoints, we have one positive and one negative). We explore two options when selecting keypoints. The first option is more general and adaptable for most computer vision problems: Positive keypoints represent the foreground target object (e.g., lesion), while negative keypoints are placed in the background. To extract these keypoints we make use of skin lesion segmentation masks[2]. Using keypoints instead of the whole mask lessens the impact of mask disagreement (from annotators or segmentation models) in the final solution.

The second option uses domain knowledge to steer the model's prediction further: instead of sampling negative keypoints from the background, we restrict the points to the artifacts. The main benefit is allowing models to consider the skin areas around the lesion, which can provide clinically meaningful features. For that option, we manually annotate the samples on our test sets, adding negative keypoints on 4 types of artifacts: dark corners, rulers, ink markings, and patches. Other types artifacts (hair, gel bubbles, and gel borders) are hard to describe with few keypoints, and were not keypoint-annotated, but were used for trap set separation. This fine-grained annotation, allows us to boost the importance of negative keypoints by setting α to 0.2, for example.

Data and Experimental Setup. We employ the ISIC 2019 [6,7,16] dataset. The class labels are selected and grouped such that the task is always a binary classification of melanoma *vs.* benign (other, except for carcinomas). We removed from all analysis samples labeled basal cell carcinoma or squamous cell carcinoma. Train and test sets follow the "trap set" separation introduced by Bissoto

---

[2] We employ the ground-truth segmentation masks when available, and infer the segmentation with a deep learning model [5] when they are not.

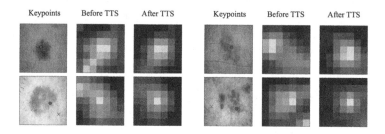

Fig. 2. Attention maps before and after our feature selection. Using a few keypoint annotations, TTS successfully reduces the importance of spurious features in the background, shifting the model's focus to the lesion.

et al. [2,3], that craft training and test sets where the correlations are amplified between artifacts and the malignancy of the skin lesion, at the same time that correlations in train and test are opposite. Trap sets follow a factor that controls the level of bias, from 0 (randomly selected sets) to 1 (highly biased). In detail, for each sample, the factor controls the probability of following the train-test separation suggested by the solver or assigning it randomly to an environment.

All our models consider Empirical Risk Minimization [17] as the training objective. Our baseline is doing test-time augmentation with 50 replicas, a standard in skin lesion analysis [14]. For a more realistic clinical setup, we always assume to have access to a single test image at each time. The results for TTS also perform test-time augmentation with 50 replicas, showing that our model can easily be combined with other test-time inference techniques. The pretrained models used for all the experiments were fine-tuned for 100 epochs with SGD with momentum, selecting the checkpoint based on validation performance[3]. Conventional data augmentation (e.g., vertical and horizontal shifts, color jitter) are used as training and testing. All results refer to the average of 5 runs (each with a different training/validation/test partition[4] and random seed).

4   Results

We show our main results in Table 2, comparing our solution with the state-of-the-art of test-time adaptation. All models are evaluated in trap sets, which create increasingly hard train and test partitions. On training, biases are amplified. On test, the correlations between artifacts and labels are shifted, punishing the models for using the biases amplified on training. The "training bias" controls the difficulty, being 1.0 as the hardest case. In this scenario, traditional trained models, even with test-time augmentation, abdicate from learning robust features and rely entirely on biases. Despite NoiseCrop [3] can highly improve the

---

[3] For choosing these models hyperparameters, we performed a grid-search over learning rate (values 0.00001, 0.0001, 0.001), and weight-decay (0.001, 0.01, 0.1, 1.0), for 2 runs on a validation set randomly split from the training set.

[4] Training/validation/test contains 60/10/30% of the total data.

Table 2. Main results and ablations (on number and annotation source of keypoints) for the hardest trap tests (training bias = 1.0). TTS achieves state-of-the-art performances while using very few annotated keypoints.

	Method	#Keypoints	Annotation	Alpha	AUC
baseline	Test-Time Aug	–	–	–	58.4 ±1.6
literature	T3A [12]	–	–	–	56.7 ±3.2
literature	Tent [18]	–	–	–	54.1 ±14.5
literature	NoiseCrop [3]	50,176	segm. mask	–	72.7 ±3.1
	TTS (ours)	40	artifacts	0.2	**75.0** ±1.1
ablation	TTS (ours)	2	segm. mask	0.4	68.2 ±1.5
ablation		10	segm. mask	0.4	71.6 ±2.2
ablation		20	segm. mask	0.4	72.9 ±2.4
ablation		40	segm. mask	0.4	73.3 ±2.6
ablation		100	segm. mask	0.4	73.9 ±2.5
ablation		2	artifacts	0.4	69.6 ±1.1
ablation		40	artifacts	0.4	73.3 ±0.9
ablation		2	artifacts	0.2	72.2 ±0.9

performance, it requires the whole segmentation mask, which is expensive to annotate and suffer from low inter-annotator agreement issues [15]. We show that TTS consistently surpasses baselines using very few annotated keypoints. By analyzing the attention maps before and after our procedure (Fig. 2), TTS successfully mitigates bias, diminishing the importance of artifacts. Also, its flexibility allows for better results once the annotated keypoints locate the artifacts biasing the solution (e.g., dark corners, rulers, ink markings, and patches).

Amount of Available Keypoints. We evaluate the effect of limiting the availability of keypoints. This is an essential experiment for assessing the method's clinical applicability. If it requires too many points to be effective, it may overwhelm clinical practitioners with annotating duties, which beats the purpose of using computer-assisted diagnosis systems. In Table 2, we show that our method can positively impact the robustness of pretrained models even in extreme conditions where a single negative and positive keypoint is annotated. Aside from the minimum impact in the clinical pipeline, it also shows to be robust to different annotators since the improvements are consistent by sampling positive and negative keypoints at random from segmentation masks.

Keypoint Annotation Granularity. The flexibility of using keypoints (instead of full segmentation masks) not only allows for easy inclusion in the daily clinical routine, but also allows for fine-grained concepts to be annotated without being time-consuming. In this experiment, we manually annotated the trap test sets with keypoints that locate 4 artifacts: dark corner, ruler, ink markings, and patches. With fine-grained annotations of artifacts to provide negative

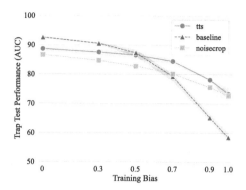

Fig. 3. Ablation of our TTS over different intensities of bias. TTS consistently out-performs NoiseCrop [3] across bias intensities while using a fraction of the extra-information available: NoiseCrop uses the whole segmentation mask, while in this example, we use 20 positive and 20 negative keypoints.

keypoints, we can increase negative keypoints importance by shrinking α, achieving our best result. We show our results in Table 2.

Using artifact-specific keypoints instead of background ones does not punish models for using the lesions' surrounding skin in the decision process, being beneficial for diagnosis classes such as actinic keratosis, where the skin itself provide clinically-meaningful information. This change further boosts previous gains both when 1 or 20 positive and negative points were available. Our method can be used in other scenarios, where not only negative but relevant positive information can be encouraged to be used by models, such as the presence of dermoscopic attributes.

Different Levels of Bias. We evaluate our solution over different levels of bias from trap sets. Trap sets allow a better assessment of models ability to generalize. As the training bias increases, the task becomes increasingly hard for the model, as correlations between artifacts and labels get harder to pass unnoticed. At the same time, the higher the bias factor, the better trap test does at punishing the model for exploiting spurious correlations. When the training bias is low, robust models are expected to achieve a worse result than unbounded ones, as exploiting spurious correlations is rewarded by evaluation metrics. However, even if we can not perfectly measure the bias reliance in intermediate bias, performing well in these situations is crucial since real-world scenarios might not present exaggerated biases. In Fig. 3, we show that our solution outperforms NoiseCrop across all bias factors. We hypothesize that NoiseCrop introduces a distribution shift when it replaces the inputs' background with noise. We avoid this shortcoming by intervening in the feature space instead of the pixel space, which proved robust to the sparsity induced by our procedure.

5 Conclusion

We propose a method for test-time debiasing of skin lesion analysis models, dealing with biases created by the presence of artifacts on the ISIC 2019 dataset. Our method select features during inference taking user-defined keypoints as a guide to mute activation units. We show that our method encourages the attention map focus more on lesions, translating to higher performance on biased scenarios. We show that our model is effective throughout different levels of bias even with single pair of annotated keypoints, thus allowing frugal human-in-the-loop learning. It benefits from fine-grained annotations, such as artifact locations, and is lightweight as it does not require training. In future works, we want to explore the possibility of keeping a memory bank of important previously annotated concepts to consider before each prediction. Muting features is a general principle, extensible to other data modalities, including text (e.g., from medical summaries), an idea that we would also like to explore in the future.

Acknowledgments. A. Bissoto is funded by FAPESP (2019/19619-7, 2022/09606-8). C. Barata is funded by the FCT projects LARSyS (UID/50009/2020), CEECIND/00326/2017, and Center for Responsible AI C645008882-00000055. S. Avila is funded by CNPq 315231/2020-3, FAPESP 2013/08293-7, 2020/09838-0, H.IAAC, Google LARA 2021 and AIR 2022.

References

1. Bissoto, A., Fornaciali, M., Valle, E., Avila, S.: (De)Constructing bias on skin lesion datasets. In: IEEE Conference on Computer Vision and Pattern Recognition Workshops (CVPRW) (2019)
2. Bissoto, A., Valle, E., Avila, S.: Debiasing skin lesion datasets and models? not so fast. In: IEEE Conference on Computer Vision and Pattern Recognition Workshops (CVPRW) (2020)
3. Bissoto, A., Barata, C., Valle, E., Avila, S.: Artifact-based domain generalization of skin lesion models. In: European Conference on Computer Vision Workshops (ECCVW) (2023)
4. Bissoto, A., Barata, C., Valle, E., Avila, S.: Even small correlation and diversity shifts pose dataset-bias issues. arXiv preprint arXiv:2305.05807 (2023)
5. Chen, L.-C., Zhu, Y., Papandreou, G., Schroff, F., Adam, H.: Encoder-decoder with Atrous separable convolution for semantic image segmentation. In: Ferrari, V., Hebert, M., Sminchisescu, C., Weiss, Y. (eds.) ECCV 2018. LNCS, vol. 11211, pp. 833–851. Springer, Cham (2018). https://doi.org/10.1007/978-3-030-01234-2_49
6. Codella, N.C., et al.: Skin lesion analysis toward melanoma detection: a challenge at the 2017 international symposium on biomedical imaging (isbi), hosted by the international skin imaging collaboration (isic). In: IEEE International Symposium on Biomedical Imaging (ISBI), pp. 168–172 (2018)
7. Combalia, M., et al.: Bcn20000: Dermoscopic lesions in the wild. arXiv:1908.02288 (2019)
8. Combalia, M., et al.: Validation of artificial intelligence prediction models for skin cancer diagnosis using dermoscopy images: the 2019 international skin imaging collaboration grand challenge. Lancet Digital Health 4(5) (2022)

9. Daneshjou, R., Barata, C., Betz-Stablein, B., Celebi, M.E., Codella, N., et al.: Checklist for evaluation of image-based artificial intelligence reports in dermatology: clear derm consensus guidelines from the international skin imaging collaboration artificial intelligence working group. JAMA Dermatology **158**(1) (2022)
10. Gulrajani, I., Lopez-Paz, D.: In search of lost domain generalization. In: International Conference on Learning Representations (ICLR) (2021)
11. Hendrycks, D., Dietterich, T.: Benchmarking neural network robustness to common corruptions and perturbations. In: International Conference on Learning Representations (ICLR) (2019)
12. Iwasawa, Y., Matsuo, Y.: Test-time classifier adjustment module for model-agnostic domain generalization. In: Advances in Neural Information Processing Systems (NeurIPS) (2021)
13. Niu, S., et al.: Towards stable test-time adaptation in dynamic wild world. In: Internetional Conference on Learning Representations (ICLR) (2023)
14. Perez, F., Vasconcelos, C., Avila, S., Valle, E.: Data augmentation for skin lesion analysis. OR 2.0 Context-Aware Operating Theaters, Computer Assisted Robotic Endoscopy, Clinical Image-Based Procedures, and Skin Image Analysis (2018)
15. Ribeiro, V., Avila, S., Valle, E.: Less is more: sample selection and label conditioning improve skin lesion segmentation. In: IEEE Conference on Computer Vision and Pattern Recognition Workshops (CVPRW) (2020)
16. Tschandl, P., Rosendahl, C., Kittler, H.: The ham10000 dataset, a large collection of multi-source dermatoscopic images of common pigmented skin lesions. Sci. Data **5**(1) (2018)
17. Vapnik, V.: Principles of risk minimization for learning theory. In: Advances in Neural Information Processing Systems (NeurIPS) (1992)
18. Wang, D., Shelhamer, E., Liu, S., Olshausen, B., Darrell, T.: Tent: fully test-time adaptation by entropy minimization. In: International Conference on Learning Representations (ICLR) (2021)

Global and Local Explanations for Skin Cancer Diagnosis Using Prototypes

Carlos Santiago$^{(\boxtimes)}$, Miguel Correia, Maria Rita Verdelho, Alceu Bissoto, and Catarina Barata

Institute for Systems and Robotics, Instituto Superior Técnico,Lisbon, Portugal
`carlos.santiago@tecnico.ulisboa.pt`

Abstract. Providing visual cues to justify the decisions of deep neural networks contributes significantly to increase their explainability. Typical strategies to provide explanations rely on saliency or attention maps that may not be easy to interpret. Moreover, the actual decision-making process is still a black-box. This paper proposes to overcome these limitations using class prototypes, both at the global (image-wide) and local (patch-based) levels. These associate images with the corresponding predictions by measuring similarity with learned image/patch descriptors. Our approach offers both global and local explanations for the decisions of the model, providing a clearer justification that resembles the human reasoning process. The proposed approach was applied to the diagnosis of skin lesions in dermoscopy images, outperforming not only black-box models, which offer no explanations, but also other state-of-the-art explainable approaches.

Keywords: Skin Cancer · Prototype Networks · CBIR · Explainable AI

1 Introduction

In the last years, the landscape of medical image analysis has been transformed, mainly due to the adoption of deep learning (DL). The field of skin image, in particular dermoscopy, is a clear example, where recent studies have shown that DL achieves similar or even superior performance to that of clinicians [6]. While most experiments were conducted in artificial settings, it is undeniable the collaborative value of AI [18]. Another lesson to be taken from these studies is that any AI model should incorporate mechanisms to explain its decisions,

C. Santiago—This work was supported by FCT projects LARSyS UIDB/50009/2020, 2022.07849.CEECIND, CEECIND/00326/201 and PRR projects PTSmartRetail C645440011-00000062 and Center for Responsible AI C645008882-00000055.

Supplementary Information The online version contains supplementary material available at https://doi.org/10.1007/978-3-031-47401-9_5.

increasing its safety and pedagogical value. As matter of fact, the incorporation of such mechanisms was recently recommended in a set of guidelines [5].

Explainable models can be divided into two main categories [20]: i) those that are intrinsically interpretable, being possible to understand the decision making process; and ii) those that resort to additional models to explain their output (post-hoc methods). Most works in dermoscopy fit in the latter. Methods like [7,10,18] use saliency maps (*e.g.*, Grad-CAM [15]) to visualize the regions of the image that contributed to the predictions of DL models. Other methods like LIME [11] have also been used [16]. While these approaches are quite visual, the actual decision process still lacks clarity.

Example-based approaches are based on the assessment of past cases to infer a diagnosis. One of the most popular approaches is content-based image retrieval (CBIR) [12,17]. This family of methods use the features of a DL model, usually trained for classification, to compute image distances, identifying dermoscopy images that are close in the latent space. However, there is no guarantee that the latent space is actually capturing lesion similarities. Moreover, the original classifier still comes short of being explainable. Finally, clinicians also screen the lesions for local structures that are hallmarks of each class. Adding a region-based reasoning to a diagnostic system may increase its complexity and often requires additional domain knowledge, such as annotations to identify clinically relevant structures [8]. Recent works in computer vision have overcome this issue using a prototypical part-based architecture called ProtoPNet [2], which is able to identify relevant region prototypes with minimum supervision. However, this method has been shown to underperform when compared with non-interpretable networks. Additionally, the learning process requires setting a trade-off between different loss terms. This is not trivial and leads to prototypes that lack diversity.

We propose a new model that easily integrates the best characteristics of CBIR and ProtoPNet, while simultaneously overcoming their limitations. The proposed approach learns: i) a set of global prototypes for each lesion class, thus

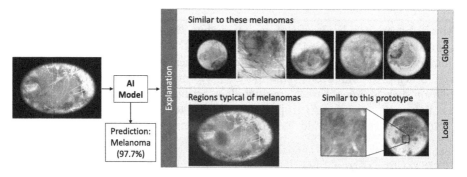

Fig. 1. The proposed method is able to justify its decisions using both image-level (global) explanations, obtained by retrieving the most similar training images for the predicted diagnosis, and patch-level (local) explanations that identify discriminative regions using heatmaps of similarity to local prototypes from training images.

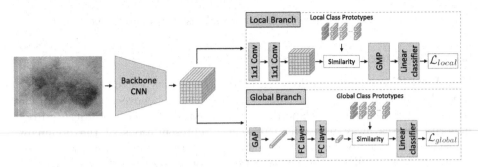

Fig. 2. Proposed approach - the method comprises two branches: i) a global branch that compares an input image with a set of class prototypes; and ii) a local branch, where regions of the input image are compared with local prototypes.

achieving a more interpretable classifier that predicts a diagnosis from similarities; and ii) local prototypes to perform an interpretable part-based classification. Both the global and local feature spaces can be used to perform CBIR, in order to identify class specific images or image patches that justify the decision, as shown in Fig. 1. We conduct extensive experiments to validate our approach using the ISIC 2019 dataset and various CNN backbones. Our results demonstrate that the proposed approach achieves competitive performances when compared to the black-box models and ProtoPNet-based approaches, while providing a more transparent classification.

2   Proposed Approach

Figure 2 shows the scheme of our proposal. A CNN backbone is used to extract a set of feature maps, F. Any CNN backbone can be used, as shown in our experimental results, where we compare several architectures. The feature maps are forwarded to the **global** and **local** branches. Each branch is responsible for estimating a probability vector $\hat{y} \in \mathbb{R}^C$, where C is the number of lesion classes. These estimates are obtained by computing a weighted average of the similarity between the latent vectors of the input image and learned class prototypes. The final classification is then the class with the highest probability obtained from averaging the two estimates.

The local branch identifies image patches that are specific of each class, while the global branch learns image-level representations of those classes. In both cases, the proposed approach is learning feature representations and simultaneously clustering them, ensuring that both local and global CBIR explanations can be provided.

To train the model, we combine the cross entropy losses for the global and local branches, $\mathcal{L}_{\text{global}}$ and $\mathcal{L}_{\text{local}}$, with a clustering loss, $\mathcal{L}_{\text{cluster}}$, that ensures the learned prototypes represent centroids of class-specific clusters. The final loss is

$$\mathcal{L} = \mathcal{L}_{\text{global}} + \mathcal{L}_{\text{local}} + \lambda \mathcal{L}_{\text{cluster}} \ , \tag{1}$$

where λ is a hyperparameter. Each individual loss term is detailed below.

2.1 Clustering

ProtoPNet [2] combines two loss terms to force prototypes to be near patches from the corresponding class. However, these losses behave poorly when the training set is severely imbalanced, as it will repeatedly push prototypes from minority classes away from the patch-level representations of the dominant classes, while seldomly pulling them towards the correct patches representations.

As such, we modified the learning process of all prototypes to ensure that they effectively capture clusters from their respective classes. Specifically, let $p_{c_k} \in \mathbb{R}^D$ define the prototype vector, of size D, corresponding to the k-th (global or local) prototype of class c. We adopt a mini-batch K-Means algorithm [14] to iteratively update the desired position, $\bar{f}_{c_k} \in \mathbb{R}^D$, of prototypes p_{c_k} according to

$$\bar{f}_{c_k} \longleftarrow (1 - \frac{1}{n_{c_k}})\bar{f}_{c_k} + \frac{1}{n_{c_k}}f_i \quad , \tag{2}$$

where f_i is the feature vector of sample i assigned to prototype p_{c_k}, and n_{c_k} is the current total number of samples that were assigned to p_{c_k}. Then, the clustering loss used to regularize the prototypes is given by

$$\mathcal{L}_{\text{cluster}} = \frac{1}{CK} \sum_{c=1}^{C} \sum_{k=1}^{K} \left\| \bar{f}_{c_k} - p_{c_k} \right\|_2 \quad , \tag{3}$$

where K is the number of prototypes per class. This loss term is applied to each branch, since each performs a similar tasks but either at a global (image) or local (patch) level. In the following sections, we will refer to global and local prototypes as $p_{c_k}^G$ and $p_{c_k}^L$, respectively.

2.2 Global Prototypes

The global branch aims to learn a set of K prototypes for each class, $\{p_{c_k}^G\}$, with $c = 1, \ldots, C$ and $k = 1, \ldots, K$. These prototypes are used to classify images based on the similarity of their image-level representations to the prototypes. To achieve this goal, the feature maps F computed by the CNN backbone are first combined using a global average pooling (GAP) layer, and then embedded into a smaller dimension latent space $f^G \in \mathbb{R}^{D^G}$ using two fully connected layers (see Fig. 2). The latent representation is compared to each prototype using the cosine similarity, $s(p_{c_k}^G, f^G)$. Then, we compute the probability of class c, $\hat{y}_c^G$, using a linear classifier with softmax

$$\hat{y}_c^G = \frac{e^{\sum_{k=1}^{K} w_{c_k} s(p_{c_k}^G, f^G)}}{\sum_{c'=1}^{C} e^{\sum_{k=1}^{K} w_{c'_k} s(p_{c'_k}^G, f^G)}} \quad , \tag{4}$$

where w_{c_k} is the weight given to the k-th prototype of class c. These weights are frozen and set to $w_{c_k} = \frac{1}{K}$ when training the prototypes and encoding layers, which means that each class score is given by an average of the similarities to the corresponding prototypes.

The prototypes are latent variables learned in an end-to-end fashion, together with the backbone layers. Given a batch of N samples, the global branch loss is

$$\mathcal{L}_{\text{global}} = -\sum_{i=1}^{N}\sum_{c=1}^{C} y_{i,c} \log(\hat{y}_{i,c}^{G}) \ , \tag{5}$$

where $y_{i,c}$ is the one-hot encoding of the ground-truth and $\hat{y}_{i,c}^{G}$ is given by (4).

2.3 Local Prototypes

The local branch performs a similar analysis to the global branch, but in a patch-wise way. First, instead of finding a latent representation for the entire image, the feature maps, F, extracted by the CNN backbone are transformed into a lower dimensional latent space through two 1×1 convolutional layers, as shown in Fig. 2. This results in a new feature maps, $F^{L} \in \mathbb{R}^{H \times W \times D^{L}}$, where the j-th pixel contains the latent representation of the corresponding patch in the input image, denoted by f_{j}^{L}. Then, we compute the cosine similarity between the local prototypes, $\{p_{c_k}^{L}\}$, with $c = 1,\ldots,C$ and $k = 1,\ldots,K$, and the latent representation of each patch, f_{j}^{L}, $j = 1,\ldots,H \times W$.

A global max pooling (GMP) is used to obtain a single vector with the similarity of each local prototype to the image. This vector is then fed to a linear classifier to obtain the final probabilities of each class c, $\hat{y}_{c}^{L}$, following a similar approach to (4). Finally, the classification loss for this branch is given by

$$\mathcal{L}_{\text{local}} = -\sum_{i=1}^{N}\sum_{c=1}^{C} y_{i,c} \log(\hat{y}_{i,c}^{L}) \ , \tag{6}$$

where $y_{i,c}$ is the one-hot encoding of the ground-truth and $\hat{y}_{i,c}^{L}$ is the predicted probability of class c for sample i.

2.4 Pruning and Final Classifier

Once the global and local prototypes have been learned, the final step of the training procedure is to tune the linear classifier, similarly to the training procedure described in [2]. For this last part, we freeze all the other parameters in the model, including the prototypes, and focus on improving the performance of the classifier by tuning the weight of each prototype. Specifically, the similarity vectors, given by the global and local branches, are concatenated into a single vector, $s \in \mathbb{R}^{T}$, where $T = 2CK$ is the total number of prototypes. Then, we build a weight matrix, $W \in \mathbb{R}^{C \times T}$, such that it initially computes exactly the same average used during the training of the prototypes – i.e., $w_{c,t} = \frac{1}{K}$ if the t-th prototype belongs to class c and $w_{c,t} = 0$ otherwise. The resulting matrix is used as initialization of a fully connected layer with no bias, which is then trained with the cross-entropy loss.

Since some of the learned prototypes may eventually be redundant, we also prune our model, discarding the less relevant prototypes. To achieve this, we rely on a binary mask, M, with the same dimensions of matrix W, that discards a prototype t by putting 0 on the t-th column of matrix M. As such, the class probabilities are obtained by first computing an element-wise multiplication of M and W, followed by the matrix product with the joint similarity vector, s. This prevents the discarded prototypes from contributing to the final prediction, similarly to a dropout strategy. As for the criteria for discarding prototypes, we chose a simple approach – if the same training sample was the nearest neighbour to multiple prototypes, we kept only the closest one.

2.5 Visual Explanations

The model's decisions are explained to clinical experts at two levels. On the global level, the representation f^G is used to perform CBIR, by comparing it with the representations of the training images associated with the closest class prototype. This process resembles the identification of past similar cases. On the local level, we show similarity heatmaps highlighting discriminative regions, along with the patch and image representing the corresponding prototype. Examples are shown in Fig. 1 and in supplementary material.

3 Experimental Setup

The proposed approach is trained and evaluated using the ISIC 2019 dermoscopy dataset [3, 4, 19][1], which contains 25,331 images for training and $C = 8$ classes, including 3 malignant ones. The dataset was normalized as proposed in [1] and split into training (80%) and validation (20%).

The proposed approach is assessed in five CNN architectures commonly used in dermoscopy image analysis: ResNet18, ResNet50, VGG16, DenseNet169, and Efficient-NetB3. For each of these architectures the following models are trained: i) baseline CNN with an 8-neuron fully connected layer for diagnosis; ii) global prototypes only; iii) local prototypes only; iv) joint prototypes; v) ProtoPNet [2]; and vi) ProtoTree [9], an improved version of ProtoPNet that assumes an hierarchical organization of the prototypes. For each method, we compute the following evaluation metrics: a) the balanced accuracy (BAcc), which corresponds to the average recall; b) the average F-1 score; and c) the overall accuracy (Acc).

We optimized the training all models to convey the best results. Regarding the hyperparameters of our approach, we tested different configurations of: i) the dimension of the global prototypes $D^G \in \{128, 256\}$; ii) the local prototypes depth $D^L \in \{128, 256\}$; iii) $\lambda \in \{10^{-3}, 10^{-2}, 10^{-1}\}$ (from (1)); and iv) whether to prune the prototypes in the end. We set the initial number of global and local prototypes per class K^G and K^L to 10, as used in ProtoPNet. Nevertheless, it is important to recall that after the pruning stage, the number of prototypes will be smaller and vary across classes.

All models were trained for a maximum of 100 epochs with early stopping. We set the batch size to $N = 50$ and use online data augmentation. Additionally, we use a curriculum-learning approach to modify the importance of each training sample [13], in order to deal with the severe class imbalance. The weights of the CNN backbones are initialized using models pre-trained on ImageNet and fine-tuned with learning rate of 10^{-5}, while for the fully connected and convolutional layers in the global and local branches we used 10^{-3}, and 10^{-2} for the prototypes. The final classifier were trained for 20 epochs with the same batch size and a learning rate of 10^{-2}. For ProtoPNet [2] and ProtoTree [9], we adopted the optimal training procedures described in their corresponding papers. The models were trained on a NVIDIA Titan Xp using Pytorch[2].

---

[1] Under CC BY-NC 4.0.
[2] https://github.com/cajosantiago/LocalGlobalPrototypes.

Table 1. Comparison of CNN backbones, without using pruning. Best results for each backbone in **bold**.

Model	Approach	Acc	BAcc	F1
VGG16	Baseline	76.2	60.3	63.2
	ProtoPNet [2]	73.4	58.9	57.7
	ProtoTree [9]	75.9	54.6	58.4
	Global	76.7	60.9	63.6
	Local	75.6	61.3	62.4
	Joint	**77.3**	**62.9**	**65.1**
ResNet18	Baseline	75.6	63.7	62.8
	ProtoPNet [2]	71.7	56.0	53.9
	ProtoTree [9]	**78.7**	58.9	61.9
	Global	76.0	63.2	**64.2**
	Local	73.5	61.5	61.0
	Joint	75.1	**64.8**	63.9
ResNet50	Baseline	76.7	64.4	65.0
	ProtoPNet [2]	71.9	49.3	50.5
	ProtoTree [9]	**81.5**	**68.3**	**71.0**
	Global	78.3	67.6	67.7
	Local	77.3	65.9	66.2
	Joint	77.7	66.2	67.5
EfficientNet	Baseline	82.3	73.1	74.0
	ProtoPNet [2]	64.2	46.0	44.1
	ProtoTree [9]	**84.2**	**74.1**	**76.5**
	Global	79.8	71.2	70.7
	Local	78.7	68.7	68.9
	Joint	82.8	73.1	74.7
DenseNet	Baseline	**83.1**	74.7	**75.5**
	ProtoPNet [2]	75.8	55.2	57.5
	ProtoTree [9]	78.6	66.0	66.0
	Global	82.7	74.3	74.1
	Local	80.9	72.1	71.9
	Joint	82.4	**75.0**	73.4

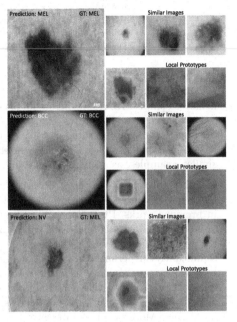

Fig. 3. Examples of predictions and corresponding CBIR explanations: global (top) and local (bottom).

4   Results

Table 1 shows the best experimental results for each CNN backbone, across all the evaluated methods (see the Supplementary Material for details on the best set of hyperparameters). Here we compare the results of our approach using a classifier without pruning, to make it more similar to the frameworks adopted in ProtoPNet and ProtoTree. In Table 2 we compare the results of our model with and without pruning. Figure 3 shows examples of the proposed approach at inference time (additional examples can be found in supplementary material).

Table 2. BAcc results without and with pruning prototypes in the final classifier.

Model	No Prunning			Prunning		
	Global	Local	Joint	Global	Local	Joint
VGG16	60.9	61.3	62.9	60.3	61.0	62.6
ResNet18	63.2	61.5	64.8	61.7	59.9	63.8
ResNet50	67.6	65.9	66.2	66.1	64.6	65.6
EfficientNetB3	71.2	68.7	73.1	69.7	66.8	72.4
DenseNet169	74.3	72.1	75.0	73.5	71.2	74.6

Global Prototypes vs Baseline: The approach based on global prototypes alone achieves competitive results across all backbones, outperforming the baseline into three out of the five architectures. This demonstrates that enforcing feature similarities between lesions of the same class does not affect the quality of the final classification. Additionally, it leads to more interpretable decisions that can be grounded in similar examples, as shown in Figs. 1 and 3.

Local Prototypes vs ProtoPNet/ProtoTree: ProtoPNet consistently exhibited lower performances when compared with all the other methods, as already reported in previous works. ProtoTree achieves better results than ProtoPNet, being the best approach for ResNet50 and EfficientNetB3. However, this method is very sensitive to the architecture, showing highly variable performances. The proposed local prototypes significantly outperform ProtoPNet, demonstrating the benefits of our training process. In particular, we achieve a better BAcc, since our approach handles class imbalance better than ProtoPNet. When compared with ProtoTree, our local prototypes seem to achieve more stable performances across backbones, being better in three of the five backbones. Moreover, it is interesting to observe that ProtoTree often shows a bigger gap between Acc and BAcc than our approach, suggesting that our model is also more robust to severe class imbalances than ProtoTree. Figs. 1 and 3 show some examples of the local prototypes and their matching regions.

Joint vs Single Models: The proposed framework allows the training of a single branch (global or local) as well as their integration into a joint model. When comparing the individual branches, it is clear that the global prototypes always outperforms the local ones. This is somewhat expect, as by resorting to a local analysis alone, we might be missing relevant context cues about the lesions. When the two branches are combined, we observe that this usually improves the performance, suggesting that both of them contain relevant and complementary information. The results in Figs1 and 3 were obtained using the joint model. These visualizations give us a better understanding of the model's behavior, including its incorrect decision (last example in Fig. 3).

Prototype pruning: Table 2 shows the results before and after pruning. Interestingly, while there is a small decrease in the performance of both branches and the combined model, the scores obtained are still competitive with other methods. Overall, these results suggest that there is some redundancy on the learned prototypes, with an average of 35% of prototypes being pruned.

5   Conclusions

This paper proposed a new approach for skin cancer diagnosis that simultaneously provides global and local explanations to support the decision. Our model integrates two interpretable classifiers based on global and local prototypes. An experimental evaluation using various CNN backbones demonstrates the potential of our approach and opens a new direction in the development of XAI in medical image analysis. In the future we plan to integrate a few annotations to regularize the training of the local prototypes, as well as incorporate this model into a user-experiment to assess the clinical value of the prototypes and incorporate medical knowledge in the system.

References

1. Barata, C., et al.: Improving dermoscopy image classification using color constancy. IEEE JBHI **19**, 1146–1152 (2015)
2. Chen, C., et al.: This looks like that: deep learning for interpretable image recognition. In: Advances in Neural Information Processing Systems 32 (2019)
3. Codella, N.C.F., et al.: Skin lesion analysis toward melanoma detection: a challenge at the 2017 international symposium on biomedical imaging (isbi), hosted by the international skin imaging collaboration (isic). In: 2018 IEEE 15th international symposium on biomedical imaging (ISBI 2018), pp. 168–172 (2018)
4. Combalia, M., et al.: Bcn20000: dermoscopic lesions in the wild. arXiv preprint arXiv:1908.02288 (2019)
5. Daneshjou, R., et al.: Checklist for evaluation of image-based artificial intelligence reports in dermatology: clear derm consensus guidelines from the international skin imaging collaboration artificial intelligence working group. JAMA Dermatol. **158**(1), 90–96 (2022)
6. Haggenmüller, S., et al.: Skin cancer classification via convolutional neural networks: systematic review of studies involving human experts. Eur. J. Cancer **156**, 202–216 (2021)
7. Jaworek-Korjakowska, J., et al.: Interpretability of a deep learning based approach for the classification of skin lesions into main anatomic body sites. Cancers **13**(23), 6048 (2021)
8. Kawahara, J.E.A.: Seven-point checklist and skin lesion classification using multitask multimodal neural nets. IEEE J. Biomed. Health Inform. **23**(2), 538–546 (2018)
9. Nauta, M., et al.: Neural prototype trees for interpretable fine-grained image recognition. In: Proceedings of the IEEE/CVF Conference on Computer Vision and Pattern Recognition, pp. 14933–14943 (2021)
10. Nunnari, F., et al.: On the overlap between grad-cam saliency maps and explainable visual features in skin cancer images. In: International Cross-Domain Conference for Machine Learning and Knowledge Extraction, pp. 241–253 (2021)
11. Ribeiro, M.T., et al.: Why should i trust you? explaining the predictions of any classifier. In: Proceedings of the 22nd ACM SIGKDD International Conference on Knowledge Discovery and Data Mining, pp. 1135–1144 (2016)
12. Sadeghi, M., et al.: Using content-based image retrieval of dermoscopic images for interpretation and education: a pilot study. Skin Res. Technol. **26**(4), 503–512 (2020)
13. Santiago, C., et al.: Low: Training deep neural networks by learning optimal sample weights. Pattern Recogn. **110**, 107585 (2021)
14. Sculley, D.: Web-scale k-means clustering. In: Proceedings of the 19th International Conference on World Wide Web, pp. 1177–1178 (2010)

15. Selvaraju, R.R., et al.: Grad-cam: visual explanations from deep networks via gradient-based localization. In: Proceedings of the IEEE International Conference on Computer Vision, pp. 618–626 (2017)

16. Stieler, F., et al.: Towards domain-specific explainable ai: model interpretation of a skin image classifier using a human approach. In: Proceedings of the IEEE/CVF Conference on Computer Vision and Pattern Recognition, pp. 1802–1809 (2021)

17. Tschandl, P., et al.: Diagnostic accuracy of content-based dermatoscopic image retrieval with deep classification features. Br. J. Dermatol. **181**(1), 155–165 (2019)

18. Tschandl, P., et al.: Human-computer collaboration for skin cancer recognition. Nat. Med. **26**(8), 1229–1234 (2020)

19. Tschandl, P., Rosendahl, C., Kittler, H.: The ham10000 dataset, a large collection of multi-source dermatoscopic images of common pigmented skin lesions. Sci. Data **5**(1), 1–9 (2018)

20. Van der Velden, B.H.M., et al.: Explainable artificial intelligence (XAI) in deep learning-based medical image analysis. Med. Image Anal., 102470 (2022)

Evidence-Driven Differential Diagnosis of Malignant Melanoma

Naren Akash R J$^{(\boxtimes)}$, Anirudh Kaushik, and Jayanthi Sivaswamy

Center for Visual Information Technology, International Institute of Information Technology Hyderabad, Hyderabad, India
naren.akash@research.iiit.ac.in
https://cvit.iiit.ac.in/mip/projects/meldd

Abstract. We present a modular and multi-level framework for the differential diagnosis of malignant melanoma. Our framework integrates contextual information and evidence at the lesion, patient, and population levels, enabling decision-making at each level. We introduce an anatomic-site aware masked transformer, which effectively models the patient context by considering all lesions in a patient, which can be variable in count, and their site of incidence. Additionally, we incorporate patient metadata via learnable demographics embeddings to capture population statistics. Through extensive experiments, we explore the influence of specific information on the decision-making process and examine the tradeoff in metrics when considering different types of information. Validation results using the SIIM-ISIC 2020 dataset indicate including the lesion context with location and metadata improves specificity by 17.15% and 7.14%, respectively, while enhancing balanced accuracy. The code is available at https://github.com/narenakash/meldd.

Keywords: Melanoma Diagnosis · Differential Recognition · Ugly Duckling Context · Patient Demographics · Evidence-Based Medicine

1 Introduction

Melanoma is the most invasive form of skin cancer with the highest mortality rate; its incidence is rising faster among other types of cancer and is projected to increase by 57% globally by 2040, leading to an estimated 68% rise in mortality [1]. When caught early, it has an increased survival rate and tends to have a better prognosis. However, melanoma is a complex and heterogeneous disease which makes accurate early recognition non-trivial and challenging. Melanoma can masquerade/appear as benign lesions and benign pigmented lesions can resemble melanoma, making diagnosis difficult even for skilled dermatologists [2].

A dermatologist's expertise to discriminate between benign moles/nevi and melanoma relies on the recognition of morphological features through the ABCD criteria [3], applying the 7-point checklist [4], overall pattern recognition and differential recognition of the ugly duckling nevi [5]. Most nevi in a patient tend

© The Author(s), under exclusive license to Springer Nature Switzerland AG 2023
M. E. Celebi et al. (Eds.): MICCAI 2023 Workshops, LNCS 14393, pp. 57–66, 2023.
https://doi.org/10.1007/978-3-031-47401-9_6

to be similar and can be grouped into a few clusters based on morphological similarity [6]. Any nevus that deviates from a consistent pattern within an individual is an outlier or an ugly duckling which is taken to be a suspicious lesion [7]. Dermatologists utilize an intra-patient lesion-focused as well as comparative analysis, recognising overall patterns to identify ugly ducklings before forming a provisional diagnosis [8]. This approach considers the characteristics of individual lesions while also taking into account the context of the patient's overall nevi distribution, leading to improved accuracy in identifying melanoma [9]. Furthermore, patient demographics, including age, sex, and anatomical site, are risk factors to consider in the differential diagnosis of melanoma [10]. Age-related susceptibility, anatomical site variations, and sex-specific characteristics contribute to the complexity of melanoma diagnosis.

Recent advances in deep learning techniques have led to an interest in the development of AI models for dermatology. The integration of AI systems into clinical workflows has the potential to improve the speed and accuracy of melanoma diagnosis, saving lives. Existing deep learning methods have reported good diagnostic accuracy in the classification of skin lesions. These use largely lesion-focused approaches and include the seven-point checklist [11], hierarchical structures [12], lesion segmentation [13], and ABCD-based medical representations [14]. Despite integrating clinical knowledge, most existing methods have not fully harnessed the potential of the clinician's comprehensive diagnostic process and strategy. While some approaches, such as CI-Net [15], incorporate zoom-observe-compare processes, they focus only on individual lesion characteristics. The UDTR framework [16] incorporates contextual information of lesions to model ugly ducklings but assumes a fixed number of contextual lesions. No attempt has been made by any approach so far to take into account a richer set of information that clinicians rely on for melanoma diagnosis [17]. These include lesion counts in a patient, which can be variable, lesion location in the body and patient demographic information. Further, existing models are essentially a black box, with no or limited explainability that too post facto on the basis of visualisation of activations and so on.

We wish to design a melanoma recognition solution that incorporates a rich set of information similar to the clinical practice. Our aim is to understand how the addition of specific information influences the decision-making process. An understanding of the sensitivity-specificity tradeoff when considering different types of information can make a method more transparent. This transparency can enable clinicians to critically evaluate the AI system's recommendations and ensure that decisions align with their clinical expertise and patient-specific circumstances. In this paper, we present a method for melanoma recognition with the following contributions:

- A modular, multi-level framework for evidence-based differential diagnosis of melanoma. This offers a solution to holistically integrate evidence at multiple levels (lesion, patient and population).

- A solution based on a masked transformer to utilize *variable-count* context lesions from a patient along with their anatomic location and metadata such as age and sex.
- Insights on the role of various information in melanoma recognition, based on validation results of the proposed approach on the 2020 SIIM-ISIC dataset.

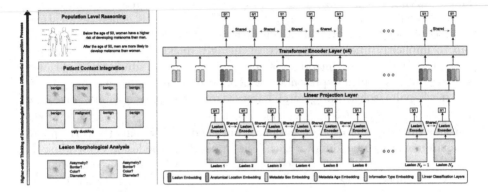

Fig. 1. The dermatologists' melanoma diagnostic reasoning process (left) and the pipeline of the proposed MelDD framework (right) inspired by the clinical process. Lesion features are extracted and grouped by patients first, and lesion anatomical site information and patient metadata are incorporated later for enhanced context.

2   Method

In our design, features are first extracted for each given lesion image (using a CNN) and are grouped patient-wise. The *context* of lesions within each patient is captured using a transformer encoder with masked self-attention. Age, sex, and anatomical site embeddings are included as *supporting evidence*, which along with lesion context, are fed into the classification layers to predict melanoma.

Modelling the Context of Patient's Skin Ecosystem: As per the ugly duckling criteria, in a patient, nevi which stand out from the rest are suspicious regardless of morphology. Conversely, lesions which are considered atypical in the absence of patient context may turn out to be normal within the context of a patient. Hence, contextual information is critical. Transformers have demonstrated a remarkable ability to analyze the global context in text, images and videos [19]. Stacked self-attention layers to model dense relations among input tokens allow transformers to capture context information at a patient level. This modelling is used in our design to capture ugly ducklings, if any. We denote the set of extracted (from a CNN) lesion features for a given patient p by the set $L_p = \{l_i^p\}_{i=1}^{N_p}$, where each $l_i^p \in L_p$ is obtained by passing the set X_p of lesions from the same patient through a ResNet101 finetuned on SIIM-ISIC 2020 dataset.

The dimensionality of each lesion feature is projected onto the dimension D of the transformer. Since the number of lesions per patient is variable, we employ masked self-attention with key padding [19] that applies padding to patients with fewer lesions to align them with N_{max}^p, the maximum number of lesions for any patient in the dataset and ignores padding tokens during processing.

Anatomical Site and Masked Self Attention: Different regions of the body exhibit varying levels of melanoma risk. Hence, the anatomical locations of a lesion can help in ruling out benign lesions. Self-attention [19] generates an attention map of the context utilizing all of the patient's lesions. We use this attention map to implicitly infer the presence of an ugly duckling. To further enhance contextual analysis, we introduce a learnable anatomic site matrix, denoted as $E^L \in \mathbb{R}^{D \times 7}$, which represents the general anatomic sites in our dataset: head/neck, palm/soles, oral/genital, lower extremity, upper extremity, torso, and an additional category for unknown locations. Let $A_p = \{a_i^p\}_{i=1}^{N_p} \in \mathbb{R}^{D \times N_p}$ be the anatomic site representation for patient p, obtained by retrieving the corresponding anatomic site embedding for each lesion from E^L. The lesion embedding L_p is added to the anatomic site embedding A_p, element-wise, to derive an enhanced contextual embedding $Q_p \in \mathbb{R}^{D \times N_p}$: $Q_p = L_p + A_p$. Embedding Q_p is utilized in masked self-attention, generating an attention map that captures *spatial, inter-lesion interactions* within the context of a patient. This integration enables the model to effectively learn the relationship between the anatomical context and individual lesion characteristics at the patient level.

Combining Patient Demographics for Differentials: Age and sex are risk factors for melanoma, as women have a higher incidence of diagnosis before the age of 50, while men have a higher rate after the age of 50. The incidence of melanoma increases progressively with advancing age, indicating a greater prevalence of melanoma development among individuals as they age [20]. Patients' sex and age information is generally part of the metadata. A learnable embedding $E^S \in \mathbb{R}^{D \times 2}$ is used to represent the male and female sexes. The transformer's trainable embeddings effectively capture and encode the dataset statistics. Positional encodings, incorporating sine and cosine functions, are employed to denote the patient's age through integer binning. The age, sex, and lesions are represented by learning three type embedding vectors, forming the trainable embedding matrix $E^M \in \mathbb{R}^{D \times 3}$, to distinguish one piece of information from another. These distinct type embedding vectors are then added element-wise to the corresponding age, sex, and contextual lesion embeddings, denoted as S_p, Y_p, and Q_p. The modified embeddings are then concatenated, capturing the combined information of age, sex, and lesions as input to subsequent stages.

Transformer Encoder for Melanoma Recognition: A multi-layer transformer encoder [19] is composed of a stack of encoder layers, each comprising multi-head self-attention, layer normalization (LN) and feed-forward neural networks (FFN). In the proposed framework, the combined patient representation $E^p = [S_p; Y_p; Q_p]$ undergoes encoding using a multi-layer transformer encoder.

Given input patient representation E_{l-1}^{p} at the lth layer,

$$Encoder(E_{l-1}^{p}) = E_{l}^{p} = FFN(LN(Attention(E_{l-1}^{p}))) + E_{l-1}^{p},$$

$$Attention = Softmax \left(\frac{E_{l-1}^{pQ} . E_{l-1}^{pK}}{\sqrt{D}} \right) E_{l-1}^{pV}.$$

The contextualized representation of the lesions E_{L}^{p} is sent to shared linear layers to perform melanoma recognition.

3 Experiments

3.1 Data

The 2020 SIIM-ISIC melanoma recognition dataset [21] was used for all our experiments. It includes 2,056 patients, among whom 428 individuals exhibit at least one melanoma, with an average of 1.36 melanomas per patient. The dataset comprises 33,126 dermoscopic images, including 584 histopathologically confirmed melanomas, as well as benign lesions that are considered melanoma mimickers such as nevi, atypical melanocytic proliferation, café-au-lait macule, lentigo NOS, lentigo simplex, solar lentigo, lichenoid keratosis, and seborrheic keratosis. Hence, the dataset is severely imbalanced, with melanomas accounting for only 1.8% of the samples. In addition to the image data, the dataset provides metadata pertaining to the approximate age of patients at the time of capture, their biological sex, and the general anatomical site of the lesion.

3.2 Experimental Settings

The dermoscopic skin lesion images were cropped to the maximum square from the centre and resized to 256 × 256. Our experimental setup involved a patient group stratified five-fold cross-validation without age and sex stratification. Each fold included a designated testing set, while the remaining data was split into 80% for training and 20% for validation. The evaluation on the challenge leaderboard is not conducted due to the unavailability of ground truth for the challenge test set, preventing analysis on our evaluation metrics. The ResNet101 [22] backbone pre-trained on SIIM-ISIC 2020 dataset to predict lesion-focused recognition was employed for transformer feature extraction. The transformer consisted of 4 layers with 4 MHSA heads, and the model dimension was set to $D = 64$. The training process utilized the Adam optimizer [23] with a learning rate of 8e−5, implemented in PyTorch [24]. It employed the weighted binary cross-entropy loss, based on the inverse of proportions, and was conducted on a single NVIDIA GeForce RTX-2080 Ti GPU. The training, incorporating early stopping, was limited to a maximum of 200 epochs with a batch size of 32.

Metrics: Many state-of-the-art models for SIIM-ISIC 2020 classification focus on optimizing the area under the ROC curve (AUC). However, this may be inappropriate since AUC is not clinically interpretable [25]. For instance, a recent work [15] reports a high AUC score but exhibits poor sensitivity, making it unsuitable for clinical use in melanoma recognition. Additionally, different methods can possess identical AUC values yet perform differently at clinically significant thresholds. To address these limitations, we opt to optimize the balanced accuracy (BACC) at the Youden's J index [26]. This may be more clinically meaningful for a small and imbalanced dataset with low melanoma prevalence (1.8%) such as SIIM-ISIC 2020 dataset. The operating point determines the cut-off value that minimizes the difference between sensitivity and specificity, better evaluating the clinical utility of diagnostic tests in melanoma recognition.

Table 1. Comparision of classification performance in melanoma recognition averaged across five-folds on SIIM-ISIC 2020 dataset: BACC: balanced accuracy, SN: sensitivity, SP: specificity at Youden's J statistic cut-off, and ROC AUC. (PC = patient context, VC = varying lesion count, L = anatomical location, M = metadata).

MelDD variants	PC	VC	L	M	BACC	SN	SP	AUC
V0 (Baseline)	✗	–	✗	✗	0.7649	**0.8867**	0.6431	0.8371
V1	✓	✓	✗	✗	0.7841	0.8679	0.7003	0.8558
V2	✓	✓	✓	✗	**0.7904**	0.8274	**0.7534**	**0.8612**
V3	✓	✓	✗	✓	0.7867	0.8843	0.6890	0.8544
V4	✓	✓	✓	✓	0.7793	0.8761	0.6825	0.8504
CI-Net [15]	✗	–	✗	✗	0.6200	0.3220	0.9180	0.9230
UDTR-L [16]	✓	✗	✗	✗	0.7564	0.7522	0.7605	0.8493
UDTR-Adapted	✓	✗	✗	✗	0.7094	0.7922	0.6266	0.7634
UDTR-Full [16]	✓	✗	✗	✗	0.8183	0.8164	0.8202	0.8964

Table 2. Performance improvement of the variants over the baseline (in percentage).

MelDD variants	PC	VC	L	M	BACC	SN	SP	AUC
V0	✗	–	✗	✗	0.7649	0.8867	0.6431	0.8371
V1	✓	✓	✗	✗	+2.51%	−2.12%	+8.89%	+2.23%
V2	✓	✓	✓	✗	**+3.33%**	−6.69%	**+17.15%**	**+2.88%**
V3	✓	✓	✗	✓	+2.85%	−0.27%	+7.14%	+2.07%
V4	✓	✓	✓	✓	+1.88%	−1.20%	+6.13%	+1.59%

4 Results and Discussion

We assess the contributions of the additional information in melanoma recognition using variants of our proposed MelDD framework. These results are presented in Table 1. Variant V0 (baseline) which solely considers the lesion has a

BACC of 76.49% and AUC of 83.71. This, however, is at a low specificity (SP) of 64.31%. Overall, from the figures in Table 1 and 2, it can be seen that the addition of information is beneficial as there is a consistent boost in all performance metrics except SN, relative to the baseline. This boost ranges from a modest 1.9% (in BACC for V4) to a significant 17.15% (in SP for V2). The degradation in SN ranges from 0.27% (for V3) to 6.7% (for V2). Including all (lesion, its context, location and metadata) information serves to boost the performance (of V4) by a minimum of 1.6% (AUC) and a maximum of 6% (SP) with a decrease in SN by less than 2%. Figure 2 illustrates patient case studies, demonstrating the impact of incorporating additional context and metadata on melanoma recognition.

The obtained results provide sufficient insights that can help in deciding which information is preferable for a specific use case. For instance, the combined knowledge of lesion source (which patient), its characteristics vis a vis other lesions of the patient (to help identify the ugly duckling) and where in the body it is located appears to be best for melanoma diagnosis with an optimal detection threshold, as seen in the figures for MelDD-V2. While balancing both SN and SP is crucial to ensure effective and reliable melanoma diagnosis, their relative importance varies based on priorities. A high SP value will be required to avoid overdiagnosis and needless biopsies. MelDD-V2 is a good choice to meet this requirement. If on the other hand, the application scenario is screening, a higher SN is preferable, and hence, simply using metadata instead of lesion location may be preferable as MelDD-V3 has a high SN and a marginally lower BACC and AUC. This suggests that patient sex and age do play a key role in improving SN. Intuitively, combining all information should be beneficial to performance which is not seen in the result in Table 1. When we examined the reason for this, we found that there was a sex-wise skew in the melanoma cases in the dataset. A sex-wise stratification in the data split for training/testing could be explored in the future to mitigate the effect of skew.

Finally, we compare the proposed method with the state-of-the-art (SOTA) frameworks, CI-Net [15], and UDTR [16]. There are some differences in the settings which may impact the comparison. For a start, the SOTA models utilize higher-resolution images compared to our work. UDTR is designed for a fixed number of lesions; it handles deviation in input through repeated sampling and uses contrastive learning and test-time augmentation techniques. However, repeated sampling in a transformer-based model can lead to overfitting, limited generalization, potential information loss, and difficulties in capturing complete patient context due to random selection and discarding of lesion instances. To ensure fairness, we introduce UDTR-Adapted as a baseline that aligns with our MedDD-V1 while considering a fixed number of lesions. Notably, MelDD-V1 outperforms (in terms of BACC) UTDR-L by 3.66% and UDTR-Adapted by 10.53% (see the lower part of Table 1). This highlights the significance of considering the complete patient context.

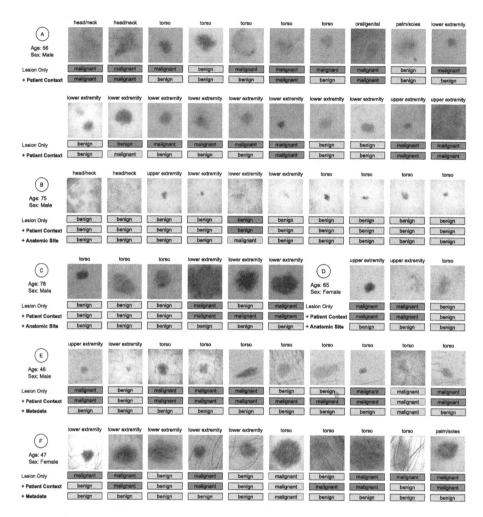

Fig. 2. Examples of malignant melanoma prediction changes with additional context and evidence information. Green/red boxes indicate correct/incorrect predictions, respectively. In Patient A, multiple atypical lesions reduce suspicion of malignancy in an additional atypical lesion, while a morphologically typical lesion distinct in the nevus landscape is considered suspicious. Patient B demonstrates how including anatomical location accurately detects an ugly duckling suspicious lesion by comparing it to other lesions in the same location to predict malignancy effectively. The examples of Patients C and D underscore how incorporating location information prevents the misclassification of benign lesions as malignant by considering the specific anatomical characteristics that differentiate suspicious lesions in different locations. Lastly, Patients E and F emphasize the importance of patient demographics to help the model correlate lesion characteristics with susceptibility to risk factors, avoiding misdiagnosis of benign lesions as malignant based on a better understanding of patient-specific factors. (Color figure online)

5   Conclusion

Inspired by the clinical diagnostic reasoning process where multiple sources of information are used for diagnosis, we present a modular, multi-level framework for differential diagnosis of malignant melanoma that integrates information at lesion, patient, and population levels. Since the number of lesions a patient may have is unknown, the proposed solution employs a masked transformer to seamlessly incorporate variable lesion counts, enabling flexible integration of patient context information in the decision-making process. Results show the differential roles played by additional information: the context and location information leads to a significant improvement in SP values with a marginal dip in SN, whereas metadata serves to restore SN value to that of the baseline model with a modest increase in SP value. Our results demonstrate that optimising BACC at Youden's J index aids in gaining good control over SP and SN variations. This is in contrast to the conventional approach of optimising AUC, which typically leads to a big tradeoff between SP and SN. Our solution offers a transparent decision support system for melanoma recognition, supporting clinicians in evidence-based decision-making.

References

1. Arnold, M., et al.: Global burden of cutaneous melanoma in 2020 and projections to 2040. JAMA Dermatol. **158**(5), 495–503 (2022)
2. Grant-Kels, J.M., et al.: The misdiagnosis of malignant melanoma. J. Am. Acad. Dermatol. **40**(4), 539–548 (1999)
3. Nachbar, F., et al.: The ABCD rule of dermatoscopy. high prospective value in the diagnosis of doubtful melanocytic skin lesions. J. Am. Acad. Dermatol. **30**(4), 551–559 (1994)
4. Argenziano, G., et al.: Epiluminescence microscopy for the diagnosis of doubtful melanocytic skin lesions: comparison of the ABCD Rule of dermatoscopy and a new 7-point checklist based on pattern analysis. Arch. Dermatol. **134**(12), 1563–1570 (1998)
5. Grob, J.J., et al.: The 'Ugly Duckling' Sign: identification of the common characteristics of Nevi in an Individual as a basis for melanoma screening. Arch. Dermatol. **134**(1), 103–104 (1998)
6. Wazaefi, Y., et al.: Evidence of a limited intra-individual diversity of nevi: intuitive perception of dominant clusters is a crucial step in the analysis of nevi by dermatologists. J. Investig. Dermatol. **133**(10), 2355–2361 (2013)
7. Gaudy-Marqueste, C., et al.: Ugly Duckling Sign as a major factor of efficiency in melanoma detection. JAMA Dermatol. **153**(4), 279–284 (2017)
8. Gachon, J., et al.: First prospective study of the recognition process of melanoma in dermatological practice. Arch. Dermatol. **141**(4), 434–438 (2005)
9. Jensen, J.D., et al.: The ABCDEF Rule: combining the "ABCDE Rule" and the "Ugly Duckling Sign" in an Effort to Improve Patient Self-Screening Examinations. J. Clin. Aesthetic Dermatol. **8**(2), 15 (2015)
10. Yuan, T., et al.: Race-, age-, and anatomic site-specific gender differences in cutaneous melanoma suggest differential mechanisms of early-and late-onset melanoma. Int. J. Environ. Res. Public Health **16**(6), 908 (2019)

11. Kawahara, J., et al.: Seven-point checklist and skin lesion classification using multitask multimodal neural nets. IEEE J. Biomed. Health Inform. **23**(2), 538–546 (2019)
12. Barata, C., et al.: Explainable skin lesion diagnosis using taxonomies. Pattern Recogn. **110**, 107413 (2021)
13. González-Díaz, I.: DermaKNet: incorporating the knowledge of dermatologists to convolutional neural networks for skin lesion diagnosis. IEEE J. Biomed. Health Inform. **23**(2), 547–559 (2019)
14. Yang, J., et al.: Clinical skin lesion diagnosis using representations inspired by dermatologist criteria. In: Proceedings of the IEEE Conference on Computer Vision and Pattern Recognition, pp. 1258–1266 (2018)
15. Liu, Z., et al.: CI-Net: clinical-inspired network for automated skin lesion recognition. IEEE Trans. Med. Imaging **42**(3), 619–632 (2023)
16. Yu, Z., et al.: End-to-End ugly duckling sign detection for melanoma identification with transformers. In: de Bruijne, M., et al. (eds.) MICCAI 2021. LNCS, vol. 12907, pp. 176–184. Springer, Cham (2021). https://doi.org/10.1007/978-3-030-87234-2_17
17. Marghboob, A.A., et al.: The complexity of diagnosing melanoma. J. Investig. Dermatol. **129**(1), 11–13 (2009)
18. Yan, Y., Kawahara, J., Hamarneh, G.: Melanoma recognition via visual attention. In: Chung, A.C.S., Gee, J.C., Yushkevich, P.A., Bao, S. (eds.) IPMI 2019. LNCS, vol. 11492, pp. 793–804. Springer, Cham (2019). https://doi.org/10.1007/978-3-030-20351-1_62
19. Vaswani, A., et al.: Attention is all you need. In: Advances in Neural Information Processing Systems, vol. 30 (2017)
20. Cancer.Net Melanoma Guide: Statistics by American Society of Clinical Oncology. https://www.cancer.net/cancer-types/melanoma.(Accessed 30 June 2023)
21. Rotemberg, V., et al.: A patient-centric dataset of images and metadata for identifying melanomas using clinical context. Sci. Data **8**(34) (2021)
22. He, K., et al.: deep residual learning for image recognition. In: Proceedings of the IEEE Conference on Computer Vision and Pattern Recognition, pp. 770–778 (2016)
23. Kingma, D.P., et al.: Adam: a method for stochastic optimization. arXiv preprint. arXiv:1412.6980 (2014)
24. Paszke, A., et al.: PyTorch: an imperative style, high-performance deep learning library. In: Advances in Neural Information Processing Systems, vol. 32 (2019)
25. Halligan, S., et al.: Disadvantages of using the area under the receiver operating characteristic curve to assess imaging tests: a discussion and proposal for an alternative approach. European Radiol. **25**(4) (2015)
26. Youden, W. J.: Index for Rating Diagnostic Tests. Cancer **3**(1) (1950)

Proceedings of the First Clinically-Oriented and Responsible AI for Medical Data Analysis (Care-AI 2023) Workshop

An Interpretable Machine Learning Model with Deep Learning-Based Imaging Biomarkers for Diagnosis of Alzheimer's Disease

Wenjie Kang[1(✉)], Bo Li[1], Janne M. Papma[2], Lize C. Jiskoot[2],
Peter Paul De Deyn[3], Geert Jan Biessels[4], Jurgen A.H. R. Claassen[5],
Huub A.M. Middelkoop[6,7], Wiesje M. van der Flier[8], Inez H.G.B. Ramakers[9],
Stefan Klein[1], Esther E. Bron[1],
and for the Alzheimer's Disease Neuroimaging Initiative,
and on behalf of the Parelsnoer Neurodegenerative Diseases study group

[1] Department of Radiology and Nuclear Medicine, Erasmus MC,
Rotterdam, The Netherlands
w.kang@erasmusmc.nl
[2] Department of Neurology, Erasmus MC, Rotterdam, The Netherlands
[3] Department of Neurology and Alzheimer Center, University Medical Center
Groningen, Groningen, The Netherlands
[4] Department of Neurology, UMC Utrecht Brain Center, University Medical Center
Utrecht, Utrecht, The Netherlands
[5] Radboud University Medical Center, Nijmegen, The Netherlands
[6] Department of Neurology & Neuropsychology, Leiden University Medical Center,
Leiden, The Netherlands
[7] Institute of Psychology, Health, Medical and Neuropsychology Unit, Leiden
University, Leiden, The Netherlands
[8] Amsterdam University Medical Center, location VUmc,
Amsterdam, The Netherlands
[9] Alzheimer Center Limburg, School for Mental Health and Neuroscience (MHeNS),
Maastricht University Medical Center, Maastricht, The Netherlands

Abstract. Machine learning methods have shown large potential for the automatic early diagnosis of Alzheimer's Disease (AD). However, some machine learning methods based on imaging data have poor interpretability because it is usually unclear how they make their decisions. Explainable Boosting Machines (EBMs) are interpretable machine learning models based on the statistical framework of generalized additive modeling, but have so far only been used for tabular data. Therefore, we propose a framework that combines the strength of EBM with high-dimensional imaging data using deep learning-based feature extraction. The proposed framework is interpretable because it provides the importance of each feature. We validated the proposed framework on the Alzheimer's Disease Neuroimaging Initiative (ADNI) dataset, achieving accuracy of 0.883 and area-under-the-curve (AUC) of 0.970 on AD and control classification. Furthermore, we validated the proposed framework on an external testing set, achieving accuracy of 0.778 and AUC of 0.887

© The Author(s), under exclusive license to Springer Nature Switzerland AG 2023
M. E. Celebi et al. (Eds.): MICCAI 2023 Workshops, LNCS 14393, pp. 69–78, 2023.
https://doi.org/10.1007/978-3-031-47401-9_7

on AD and subjective cognitive decline (SCD) classification. The proposed framework significantly outperformed an EBM model using volume biomarkers instead of deep learning-based features, as well as an end-to-end convolutional neural network (CNN) with optimized architecture.

Keywords: Alzheimer's disease · MRI · Convolutional neural network · Explainable boosting machine · Interpretable AI

Code availability: https://gitlab.com/radiology/neuro/wenjie-project

1 Introduction

Dementia is a major global health problem [20]. However, early and accurate diagnosis of AD (Alzheimer's Disease) is challenging [23]. Machine learning methods have shown large potential for early detection and prediction of AD because they can learn subtle patterns and capture slight tissue alterations in high-dimensional imaging data [6,24]. Nevertheless, those machine learning methods with high diagnostic performance, such as deep learning, are considered black boxes because of the poor interpretability of the predicted results [3]. On the other hand, intrinsically interpretable methods can provide explainable results but often have worse predictive performance as they cannot fully exploit the high-dimensional data [2]. To this end, to facilitate the translation of machine learning to clinical practice it is crucial to find an optimal tradeoff between the accuracy and interpretability.

To solve this problem, we built an interpretable machine learning framework that meanwhile makes use of high-dimensional imaging features. Recently, Explainable Boosting Machines (EBMs) [16] is a tree-based Generalized Additive Model (GAM) [13] which have shown comparable accuracy to the state-of-the-art conventional machine learning methods [19], and meanwhile provide the contribution to the final decision by each feature for interpretability. Currently, EBM takes as input only tabular data and have not been used with imaging data. By exploit high-dimensional biomarkers from imaging data, we expect the combination of EBM and deep learning techniques will contribute to a more interpretable and accurate prediction for AD diagnosis.

In this work, we propose a framework to extract high-dimensional features from brain MRIs, i.e., deep learning-based imaging biomarkers (DL-biomarkers), which is used by EBM for AD diagnosis. We designed a data-driven strategy to select the region of interest (ROI). Convolutional Neural Networks (CNNs) [15] were used to extract DL-biomarkers from whole brain MRI and ROIs. EBM trained with DL-biomarkers can give the importance of each DL-biomarker. For model validation, we compared the performance of the proposed model with an EBM that uses the volumes of brain regions (V-biomarkers) as input. We also compared the proposed model with a CNN with optimized architecture to investigate whether the proposed model maintains comparable diagnostic performance to black-box models.

2   Methods

2.1   Study Population

We used data from two studies. The first group of 855 participants was included from the Alzheimer's Disease Neuroimaging Initiative (ADNI). We included participants with T1-weighted (T1w) MRI scans available at the baseline timepoint from the ADNI1/GO/2 cohorts, consisting of 335 AD patients, and 520 control participants (CN). The second group of 336 participants was included from the Health-RI Parelsnoer Neurodegenerative Diseases Biobank (PND) [1], a collaborative biobanking initiative of the eight university medical centers in the Netherlands. We included participants at baseline timepoints, including 198 AD patients, and 138 participants with SCD.

2.2   Data Preprocessing

The T1w scans were preprocessed following the same pipeline as in [5]. After the construction of a dataset-specific template, we computed probabilistic gray matter (GM) maps with the unified tissue segmentation method from SPM8 [4]. Thereafter, the pre-processed GM maps were cropped to $150 \times 180 \times 150$ voxels to remove the background region.

2.3   Explainable Boosting Machine (EBM)

EBM is a subclass of GAMs which based on trees [8]. Given a dataset $D = \{(x_i, y_i)\}_1^N$, where for any subject $i \in [1, N]$, $x_i = (x_{i1}, ..., x_{in})$ is a feature vector with n features, and y_i is the label, EBM is of the form:

$$g(Y) = \beta + \sum f_j(X_j) + \sum f_{ij}(X_i, X_j),$$

where $g(.)$ is the link function that adapts the classification setting, X_j is the jth feature vector in the feature space, Y is the target class, and shape functions f_j and f_{ij} $(i \neq j)$ are gradient-boosted ensembles of bagged trees in EBM. As a subclass of GAM, EBMs prevent interaction effects from being learned. The ability to analyze features independently makes EBMs easy to reason about the contribution of each feature to the prediction [7]. EBMs include pairwise interaction terms $f_{ij}(X_i, X_j)$ [17], it finds all the possible pairs of interactions in the residuals and orders them by importance. A previous work using EBM have applied it to volumetrics in the task of predicting whether mild cognitive impaired (MCI) patients will convert to AD [22]. However, such features of regional volume are a crude summary of the high-resolution brain images, only part of the information presented in the images is included in the regional volume.

2.4   Proposed Extension

Here, we propose to use deep learning models to extract features (DL-biomarkers) from high-dimensional brain MRIs. The predicted results of CNNs for binary classification which are the probability of positive are used as the DL-biomarkers. For the full brain DL-biomarker, a CNN is trained in classification task that takes whole-brain images as input (Global CNN, Glo-CNN). For the regional DL-biomakers, lightweight CNNs are trained that take selected image patches as input (Local CNN, Loc-CNN). The architecture of our proposed EBM is shown in Fig 1. Each input image is handled by a shape function which is a trained CNN.

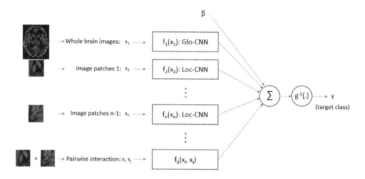

Fig. 1. Architecture of the proposed EBM using DL-biomarkers. Shape function f_{1-n} outputs a DL-biomarker for the whole brain or a brain region and f_{ij} outputs a pairwise DL-biomarker. Σ is the weighted sum of shape functions and $g^{-1}(.)$ is the activation function.

2.5   Extraction of the DL-Biomarkers

The architectures of the Glo-CNN and Loc-CNN are adapted from the state-of-the-art research [9,10]. We provide the details of the CNNs optimized for AD diagnosis in the supplement. The DL-biomarkers of the subjects in the testing set were predicted by trained CNNs. Loc-CNNs shared the same architecture but trained on different image patches. To select patches for brain regional features, we used an occlusion map strategy [21,25]. This method computes the impact on the output of the network by occluding a patch in the input image. The gap between the two outputs, therefore, shows quantitatively how much an image patch affects the decision-making of the deep learning model. Subject-level occlusion maps in testing set were summed into a group-level map, which was used for patch selection. Within the group-level occlusion map, total weight per patch was computed, and patches were ranked and selected according to the total weight. With the selected patches, Loc-CNNs were trained to predict the regional DL-biomarkers. The value of the DL-biomarkers indicates the probability of the subject being positive. We provide a flowchart of the extraction of DL-biomarkers in Fig. 2, and implementation details in Sect. 3.2.

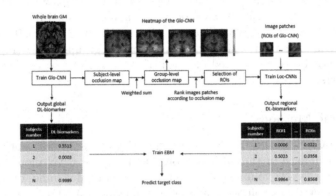

Fig. 2. The flowchart of the extraction of DL-biomarkers.

3 Experiments

3.1 Validation Study

We compared the proposed EBM using DL-biomarkers with two baseline methods: a CNN and an EBM using V-biomarkers, for AD-CN classification. For the validation on ADNI, AD and CN groups were split in a stratified way into an optimization set and a clean testing set (test_{split}) in a ratio of 9 : 1. Glo-CNNs and Loc-CNNs were trained in 5-fold cross-validation in the optimization set. Occlusion maps and imaging biomarkers for on the testing set of each fold (test_{cv}) were gathered. The models trained on ADNI were also validated on external testing set PND.

We used accuracy (ACC), sensitivity (SEN), specificity (SPE), and area-under-the-curve (AUC) as the performance metrics for binary classification. We validated the performance of the proposed CNN model separately. To test the performance of Glo-CNN on ADNI, AD and CN groups were randomly split for 10 iterations preserving relative class sizes. Confidence intervals (95%CIs) for the mean performance measures were calculated using the corrected resampled t-test [18]. For the validation of Glo-CNN on PND, we used ADNI as the training set and PND as the external testing set. 95%CIs were obtained based on bootstrap on testing set. For the validation of the proposed EBM and the two baseline methods, we trained models on the split optimization set on ADNI, and test the methods on the test_{split} and PND. 95%CIs were obtained based on bootstrap on the testing set.

3.2   EBM Using DL-Biomarkers

The Glo-CNN and Loc-CNN were compiled with a class balanced binary cross-entropy loss function. All CNN models used Adam optimizer [14]. The initial leaning rate was 5×10^{-4}. The group-level occlusion maps were obtained by the summation of the subject-levavel occlusion maps obtained from subjects in (test$_{cv}$) using trained Glo-CNNs. The occlusion patch has a size of 20^3. We chose the top 10 ROIs with a patch size of 30^3 based on the group-level occlusion map, and trained ten Loc-CNNs based on each of the ten ROIs to predict regional DL-biomarkers.

3.3   Baseline Methods

We used Glo-CNN as the baseline CNN model, because it was optimized for the best performance in the optimization set among all CNN models. For the baseline EBM, the GM volume (corrected by intra-cranial volume) of each brain region is considered as a volume biomarker (V-biomarkers) [11,12]. V-biomarkers were named after brain regions, with 'Total brain' indicating the GM volume of the whole brain. We chose the top 11 among 75 V-biomarkers with the smallest p-values between AD and CN groups in the optimization set. The EBMs based on DL-biomarkers and V-biomarkers included 11 biomarkers, and top-2 pairwise biomarkers. In addition, we took the average output of the Glo-CNN and Loc-CNNs as the output of a CNN ensemble model (Glo/Loc-CNN) which has the similar computational complexity as the EBM based on DL-biomarkers. We provide the performance of the Glo/Loc-CNN in the supplement.

4   Results

4.1   Glo-CNN and ROIs

We provide the details of the cross-validation results of Glo-CNN in the supplement. The model yielded an ACC of 0.880 (95%CI: 0.852-0.908) and an AUC of 0.944 (0.870-1.00) on the AD-CN task on ADNI. On the external PND test set, the model yielded an ACC of 0.789 (0.744-0.834) and an AUC of 0.872 (0.830-0.914) on the AD-SCD task.

The selected 10 ROIs based on the Glo-CNN are shown in Fig. 3 (a), the overlap of ROIs is demonstrated by colors. We name the selected ROIs after the overlapped brain regions. The location and name of ROIs in the coronal plane are shown in Fig. 3 (b).

4.2   Comparison Study

The performance of the methods on the ADNI dataset is shown in Fig. 4 (a). The accuracy and AUC of the proposed EBM using DL-biomarkers were significantly higher (p-value <0.01) than those of the EBM using V-biomarkers. The AUC of EBM using DL-biomarkers was significantly higher than Glo-CNN. The

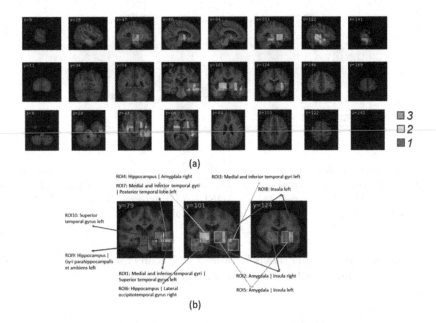

Fig. 3. (a) The location, and (b) the ID and name of the selected image patches.

performance of the methods on the external testing set PND is shown in Fig. 4
(b). The accuracy and AUC of EBM trained with DL-biomarkers were significantly higher than those of the EBM trained with V-biomarkers. The group-level
feature importance of EBMs trained with DL-biomarkers and V-biomarkers in
training set are reported in Fig. 5. The two pairwise biomarkers in the EBM
trained with DL-biomarkers are the combination of Total brain with ROI1, and
the combination of Total brain with ROI6. The feature importance shown in
Fig. 5 can show which brain regions highly affect the decision-making of EBMs.

5 Discussion and Conclusions

In this paper, we proposed a new EBM using high-dimensional imaging biomarkers predicted by CNNs for AD diagnosis, which used occlusion maps for region
selection. The proposed framework is more interpretable than black-box models because it provides the feature importance of all biomarkers. We compared
the performances among the proposed EBM using DL-biomarkers, the standard
EBM using V-biomarkers, and a CNN baseline. The results show that our proposed framework yielded higher classification performance than the other two
methods in the AD-CN task on the ADNI dataset. We suspect that the improved
performance is because DL-biomarkers are the predictions of Glo-CNN and Loc-
CNNs, which enables the encoding of high-dimensional features [4]. Furthermore,
the results of the EBM trained with DL-biomarkers yielded higher AUC than

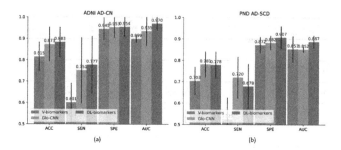

Fig. 4. The performance of the EBM trained with V-biomarkers (V-biomarkers; blue), Glo-CNN as the CNN baseline (Glo-CNN; orange), the EBM trained with DL-biomarkers (DL-biomarkers; red) (a) on ADNI (b) on external testing set PND. The error bars represent for the confidence intervals. (Color figure online)

the CNN model. We assume this is because EBM is an ensemble of models that extract complementary features from brain regions.

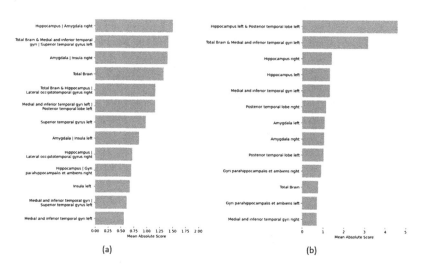

Fig. 5. The feature importance of (a) the proposed EBM using DL-biomarkers, and (b) EBM trained with V-biomarkers.

In conclusion, our proposed method achieved higher classification performance than the baseline models and allows for the interpretation of the brain features relevant to AD diagnosis based on imaging data. In future work, we intend to further explore the interpretability of the proposed method. We also intend to validate the generalization of our method. Further validation will include dementia prediction in MCI and diagnosis of other subtypes of dementia.

References

1. Aalten, P., et al.: The dutch parelsnoer institute-neurodegenerative diseases; methods, design and baseline results. BMC Neurol. **14**(1), 1–8 (2014)
2. Ahmad, M.A., Eckert, C., Teredesai, A.: Interpretable machine learning in healthcare. In: Proceedings of the 2018 ACM International Conference on Bioinformatics, Computational Biology, and Health Informatics, pp. 559–560 (2018)
3. Arrieta, A.B., et al.: Explainable artificial intelligence (xai): concepts, taxonomies, opportunities and challenges toward responsible ai. Informat. Fusion **58**, 82–115 (2020)
4. Ashburner, J., Friston, K.J.: Unified segmentation. Neuroimage **26**(3), 839–851 (2005)
5. Bron, E.E., et al.: Cross-cohort generalizability of deep and conventional machine learning for mri-based diagnosis and prediction of alzheimer's disease. NeuroImage: Clinical **31**, 102712 (2021)
6. Bron, E.E., et al.: Standardized evaluation of algorithms for computer-aided diagnosis of dementia based on structural mri: the caddementia challenge. Neuroimage **111**, 562–579 (2015)
7. Caruana, R., Lou, Y., Gehrke, J., Koch, P., Sturm, M., Elhadad, N.: Intelligible models for healthcare: Predicting pneumonia risk and hospital 30-day readmission. In: Proceedings of the 21th ACM SIGKDD International Conference on Knowledge Discovery and Data Mining, pp. 1721–1730 (2015)
8. Chang, C.H., Tan, S., Lengerich, B., Goldenberg, A., Caruana, R.: How interpretable and trustworthy are gams? In: Proceedings of the 27th ACM SIGKDD Conference on Knowledge Discovery & Data Mining, pp. 95–105 (2021)
9. Cui, R., Liu, M., Initiative, A.D.N., et al.: Rnn-based longitudinal analysis for diagnosis of alzheimer's disease. Comput. Med. Imaging Graph. **73**, 1–10 (2019)
10. Dyrba, M., et al.: Improving 3d convolutional neural network comprehensibility via interactive visualization of relevance maps: evaluation in alzheimer's disease. Alzheimer's Res. Therapy **13**(1), 1–18 (2021)
11. Gousias, I.S., et al.: Automatic segmentation of brain mris of 2-year-olds into 83 regions of interest. Neuroimage **40**(2), 672–684 (2008)
12. Hammers, A., et al.: Three-dimensional maximum probability atlas of the human brain, with particular reference to the temporal lobe. Hum. Brain Mapp. **19**(4), 224–247 (2003)
13. Hastie, T.J.: Generalized additive models. In: Statistical Models in S, pp. 249–307. Routledge (2017)
14. Kingma, D.P., Ba, J.: Adam: A method for stochastic optimization. arXiv preprint arXiv:1412.6980 (2014)
15. Krizhevsky, A., Sutskever, I., Hinton, G.E.: Imagenet classification with deep convolutional neural networks. Commun. ACM **60**(6), 84–90 (2017)
16. Lou, Y., Caruana, R., Gehrke, J.: Intelligible models for classification and regression. In: Proceedings of the 18th ACM SIGKDD International Conference on Knowledge Discovery and Data Mining, pp. 150–158 (2012)
17. Lou, Y., Caruana, R., Gehrke, J., Hooker, G.: Accurate intelligible models with pairwise interactions. In: Proceedings of the 19th ACM SIGKDD international Conference on Knowledge Discovery and Data Mining, pp. 623–631 (2013)
18. Nadeau, C., Bengio, Y.: Inference for the generalization error. In: Advances in Neural Information Processing Systems 12 (1999)

19. Nori, H., Jenkins, S., Koch, P., Caruana, R.: Interpretml: a unified framework for machine learning interpretability. arXiv preprint arXiv:1909.09223 (2019)
20. Prince, M.J., Wimo, A., Guerchet, M.M., Ali, G.C., Wu, Y.T., Prina, M.: World alzheimer report 2015-the global impact of dementia: An analysis of prevalence, incidence, cost and trends (2015)
21. Rieke, J., Eitel, F., Weygandt, M., Haynes, J.-D., Ritter, K.: Visualizing convolutional networks for MRI-based diagnosis of alzheimer's disease. In: Stoyanov, D., et al. (eds.) MLCN/DLF/IMIMIC -2018. LNCS, vol. 11038, pp. 24–31. Springer, Cham (2018). https://doi.org/10.1007/978-3-030-02628-8_3
22. Sarica, A., Quattrone, A., Quattrone, A.: Explainable boosting machine for predicting alzheimer's Disease from MRI hippocampal subfields. In: Mahmud, M., Kaiser, M.S., Vassanelli, S., Dai, Q., Zhong, N. (eds.) BI 2021. LNCS (LNAI), vol. 12960, pp. 341–350. Springer, Cham (2021). https://doi.org/10.1007/978-3-030-86993-9_31
23. Van Vliet, D., et al.: Time to diagnosis in young-onset dementia as compared with late-onset dementia. Psychol. Med. **43**(2), 423–432 (2013)
24. Wen, J., et al.: Convolutional neural networks for classification of alzheimer's disease: overview and reproducible evaluation. Med. Image Anal. **63**, 101694 (2020)
25. Zeiler, M.D., Fergus, R.: Visualizing and understanding convolutional networks. In: Fleet, D., Pajdla, T., Schiele, B., Tuytelaars, T. (eds.) ECCV 2014. LNCS, vol. 8689, pp. 818–833. Springer, Cham (2014). https://doi.org/10.1007/978-3-319-10590-1_53

Generating Chinese Radiology Reports from X-Ray Images: A Public Dataset and an X-ray-to-Reports Generation Method

Wen Tang[1], Chenhao Pei[1], Pengxin Yu[1], Huan Zhang[1], Xiangde Min[2], Cancan Chen[1], Han Kang[1], Weixin Xu[1], and Rongguo Zhang[1,3](✉)

[1] Infervision Medical Technology Co., Ltd., Beijing, China
zrongguo@infervision.com
[2] Department of Radiology, Tongji Hospital, Tongji Medical College, Huazhong University of Science and Technology, No. 1095 Jie Fang Avenue, Wuhan 430030, Hankou, People's Republic of China
[3] Academy for Multidisciplinary Studies, Beijing National Center for Applied Mathematics, Capital Normal University, Beijing 10048, China
zrongguo@cnu.edu.cn

Abstract. Deep learning methods have revolutionized medical image analysis, enabling tasks such as lesion classification, segmentation, and detection. However, these methods rely on annotations, posing a burden on healthcare professionals. In contrast, medical reports contain valuable information, leading to the emergence of Medical Reports Generation from Medical Images (MRGMI). Despite advancements, MRGMI predominantly focuses on English reports, lacking solutions for other languages. To address this and to generate responsible Chinese MRGMI model, we present a Chinese MRGMI dataset of over 40,000 Xray-image-report pairs, covering diverse diseases. We further provide 500 graph-node annotations of the reports and propose the CN-RadGraph model, extracting graph nodes from reports to, in a clinical-responsible way, evaluate our MRGMI model: Chinese X-ray-to-Reports Generation (CN-X2RG) model. Considering linguistic disparities, we enhance the SOTA method with prompt training, graph-based augmentation, and sentence shuffling. Our CN-X2RG model shows significant improvements over baselines. The dataset and code are publicly available, fostering clinical-responsible research and development.

Keywords: Radiology Reports Generation · Dataset · Xray

1 Introduction

Deep learning in medical image analysis has shown great success in tasks like lesion classification, organ segmentation, and lesion detection. However, its

---

First authors (W. Tang C. Pei—Are with the same degree of contribution, they are the co-first authors).

M. E. Celebi et al. (Eds.): MICCAI 2023 Workshops, LNCS 14393, pp. 79–88, 2023.
https://doi.org/10.1007/978-3-031-47401-9_8

reliance on annotated medical images poses a burden on healthcare workers. Alternatively, leveraging comprehensive medical reports can aid in Medical Reports Generation from Medical Images [9] (MRGMI), reducing reliance on annotations and maximizing clinical data for automated analysis.

While significant advancements have been made in MRGMI, the prevailing focus of most methods and datasets [4,10] lies on English-language reports. However, the critical need arises for MRGMI models and datasets in languages other than English due to the linguistic diversity and variations in report styles within the medical field. The translation of medical terminologies and the precise capture of nuanced language present substantial challenges, especially given the impact of report data on MRGMI models and the model's responsibility in medical practice. Therefore, for contexts like medical diagnosis, where errors are unacceptable, access to native medical report data and corresponding models becomes indispensable. Additionally, the development of comprehensive evaluation criteria is equally vital, encompassing not only the assessment of report generation similarity but also a heightened focus on key diseases within anatomies. High-quality evaluation metrics can contribute to designing and obtaining more reliable and secure MRGMI models.

To address the challenges above, this paper presents the Chinese Chest X-ray (CN-CXR) dataset, comprising 46,301 X-ray image-report pairs, covering a wide range of medical scenarios and diseases detectable through X-rays. Additionally, we provide 500 graph-node annotations for the corresponding Chinese reports. Leveraging this dataset, we propose the CN-RadGraph model, which extracts meaningful graph nodes from medical reports, serving as a crucial component in evaluating the performance of our MRGMI model, Chinese X-ray-to-Reports Generation (CN-X2RG). Both datasets provide the possibility to create responsible-Chinese-MRGMI. Thus, we also introduce enhancements to bridge the gap between English-based methods and the unique linguistic characteristics of the Chinese language. Extensive experiments demonstrate significant improvements over existing baselines, highlighting the effectiveness, relevance and clinical responsibility of our proposed enhancements.

2   Related Work

The task of MRGMI [9], has gained significant attention due to advancements in deep learning, natural language processing (NLP), and multimodal learning. In this review, we highlight key works that have contributed to the MRGMI field, and analyze the potential for enhancing their clinical responsibilities.

Datasets. The availability of suitable datasets plays a crucial role in advancing MRGMI research. Two widely used public datasets in MRGMI are the MIMIC-CXR [10] dataset and the IU X-Ray [4] dataset. However, these datasets only provide valuable resources for English-based MRGMI research, the availability of language-specific datasets is essential to cater to different linguistic contexts. For instance, the CX-CHR [11] dataset, a proprietary internal dataset, addresses the need for Chinese MRGMI research. In parallel efforts, Wang et al.

[16] have attempted to address the need for Chinese MRGMI research by translating English datasets into Chinese using ChatGPT. However, it should be noted that even ChatGPT struggles to precisely translate medical terminology, leading to a considerable gap between the translated reports and the authentic ones. The language of authentic reports is more written and standardized, which facilitates quick reading and comprehension. Therefore, it is irresponsible for clinical application to obtain data only by using language translation.

Considering the limitation of current Chinese datasets and to ensure responsibility of MRGMI model, we have collected a new dataset called CN-CXR. This dataset includes 46,301 X-ray images and their corresponding authentic reports, specifically focusing on the medical findings observed in the X-ray images. By providing a large-scale Chinese MRGMI dataset, we aim to facilitate research in this domain and encourage the development of language-specific MRGMI models.

Auxiliary Models. Auxiliary models play a vital role in enhancing the performance of MRGMI models. One notable auxiliary model is RadGraph [7], which extracts entities and relations from medical reports, thereby providing valuable structured information. By incorporating RadGraph into the MRGMI pipeline, researchers can benefit from its ability to provide semantic information during model training [18], as well as evaluate the performance of MRGMI models [8]. Both provide semantic specifications for model-generated reports to enforce accountability. There are also other model such as Clinical-BERT [1] and RadCLIP [5]. However, it is worth noting that most of the existing auxiliary models are primarily designed for English-based datasets, highlighting the need for language-specific auxiliary models for different linguistic contexts.

To address the language-specific nature of MRGMI, we extend the RadGraph approach to the Chinese domain and propose the CN-RadGraph model. Following a similar annotation process, we annotate entities and relations from 500 samples of our CN-CXR dataset. The CN-RadGraph model serves as a valuable resource for Chinese MRGMI research, offering structured information and evaluation capabilities specific to the Chinese language. This reinforces the clinical responsibility of our model.

MRGMI Models. Recent advancements in transformer models and multimodal learning have paved the way for the development of various MRGMI models. For instance, [3] and [13] leverage memory-driven Transformers to generate radiology reports. [2] utilizes a memory bank to enforce consistency between input image features, while [14] employs uncertainty and Kullback-Leibler similarity to maintain consistency between image and report features. Similarly, [20] incorporates a weakly supervised contrastive loss, and [8] utilizes contrastive learning and matching techniques to improve MRGMI performance. Furthermore, auxiliary models can help enhance report generation. Both [18] and [21] use RadGraph model to provide knowledge to their models.

In this paper, we present improvements to existing MRGMI model for our CN-CXR dataset. We utilize the MedCLIP [19] pretrained model as a prompt training feature and employ a memory-driven Transformer architecture for radiology report generation. The CN-RadGraph model assists by providing a classification auxiliary loss, guaranteeing semantic consistency to ensure clinical responsibility. To address limited training data, we propose a novel report data augmentation method and a data oversampling method, increasing dataset diversity. These enhancements enable our CN-X2RG model as a responsible AI to generate more accurate and comprehensive medical reports for the Chinese domain.

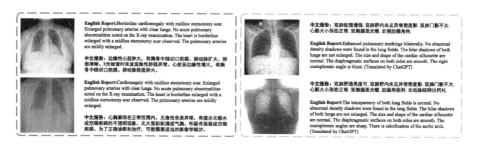

Fig. 1. Illustration of the Chinese(Right)(**The proposed dataset**) and English(Left) reports. The blue box [16] indicates that the original report is in English, and the red indicates that the original report is in Chinese. Using ChatGPT [6] as a translation tool.

3   Datasets

3.1   CN-CXR Dataset

The proposed method is evaluated on our Chinese X-ray reports dataset, CN-CXR, which comprises a total of 46,301 X-ray images along with their corresponding Chinese reports. The dataset was collected from one hospital in China and spans the years 2012 to 2021. In terms of patient demographics, the dataset includes 27,949 male patients, 23,109 female patients, and 923 patients with unknown sex. The age distribution of the patients is reported as 44.18 ± 22.34 years. Table 1 presents the anatomy with lesion extracted using our CN-RadGraph. The table provides an overview of the approximate distribution of some diseases in the dataset. It offers valuable insights into the prevalence and occurrence of various diseases within the extracted anatomical structures. Figure 1 illustrates examples of Chinese reports and their corresponding English translations, as well as English reports and their corresponding Chinese translations. It is evident that the language descriptions and styles differ significantly between the two. Such differences can result in substantial domain shifts, potentially causing a model trained on English reports to fail when generating Chinese reports with translations, and vice versa. Therefore, such a clinically relevant CN-CXR dataset is essential to obtain responsible Chinese MRGMI models.

Table 1. The 48 keywords for *anatomy* and *lesion* selected from the Chinese reports. A *lesion* present on an *anatomy* counts both the *anatomy* and the *lesion* once.

Anatomy Keywords				Lesion Keywords			
	train	valid	test		train	valid	test
Chest	3765	1000	1897	Postoperative	3125	599	1246
Hilum	2803	1309	2271	Gas	783	132	283
Heart	3431	890	1686	Shadow	13911	4210	7798
Diaphragmatic	3096	981	1718	Texture	19774	2578	6082
Costophrenic Angle	5670	1645	3038	Calcification	1431	299	608
Lung	35245	7534	15167	Insert	2375	272	662
Aorta	1888	485	925	No Lung Texture	762	388	676
Rib	2488	299	715	Effusion	743	338	512
Mediastinum	870	311	574	Transparency	1557	606	1067
Pleura	867	327	559	Fracture	131	22	56
Vertebrae	703	239	407	Prominence	1441	361	657
Aortic Knot	2387	534	1038	Side Bend	429	188	299
Aortic Arch	73	13	38	Intubation	132	4	18
Fissures	141	55	89	Deformed	47	25	41
Bone	179	35	73	Drainage	100	29	63
Trachea	313	41	123	Emphysema	62	26	48
Neck	165	29	54	Atelectasis	9	4	6
Horizontal Split	40	24	26	Flame	6	3	4
Bronchi	57	22	36	Torque	953	265	500
Bowel	204	11	36	Blur	265	92	201
Diaphragm	274	90	180	Disappeared	23	12	12
Pulmonary artery	183	79	142	Weaken	123	80	126
Belly	72	10	26	Enhanced	4734	1343	2539
Yessels	6	1	5	Shift	431	153	294

3.2 CN-RadGraph Dataset

To create the CN-RadGraph dataset for our model, we employed a sampling strategy from the CN-CXR dataset. A total of 500 samples were selected based on the length of the reports. The sampling process involved randomly choosing 100 samples, as well as 100 samples from both the top 10% longest reports and the top 10% shortest reports. Additionally, 200 samples were randomly selected from the remaining reports. The resulting 500 samples were then annotated according to the following:

Entities: We define entities as continuous spans of text that can consist of one or more adjacent words. In our schema, entities revolve around two main concepts: Anatomy and Observation. We categorize observations into three types, resulting in four entities in our schema: Anatomy, Disease-Positive-Observation (DPO), Disease-Negative-Observation (DNO), and Neutral-Observation (NO). Anatomy represents anatomical body parts mentioned in the radiology report, such as "lung". Observations encompass words associated with visual features, identifiable pathophysiologic processes, or diagnostic disease classifications. For example, a DPO could be "effusion" or more general phrases like "increased". A DNO could be "normal" or "no abnormality". A NO could be "shadow", which is always connected to DPO and DNO.

Relations: Relations are directed edges connecting two entities in our schema. We utilize two types of relations: Located At and Modify. Located At (Observation, Anatomy) represents a relationship between an Observation entity and an Anatomy entity, indicating that the Observation is related to the Anatomy. Although Located At often refers to location, it can also describe other relations between an Observation and an Anatomy. Modify (Observation, Observation) or (Anatomy, Anatomy) represents a relation between two Observation entities or two Anatomy entities, signifying that the first entity modifies the scope or quantifies the degree of the second entity. Furthermore, to ensure accurate labeling of diseased or non-diseased conditions, the Observation determining the disease appearance is always placed as the outermost node. Supplementary illustrates an example of a report annotated according to our schema, along with the resulting graph representation.

In CN-RadGraph dataset, we annotate 4 types entities and 2 types relations as shown in Table 2. This carefully curated CN-RadGraph dataset serves as the training and evaluation data for our CN-RadGraph model, enabling accurate and context-aware analysis of radiology reports, which ensures the clinical responsibility of our model.

4 Method

We first formulate the problem of MRGMI mathematically. Formally, we have access to labeled dataset contained radiogy images and chinese reports, denoted by $(X, Y) = \{(x_j, y_j)\}_{j=1}^N$, where N is the number of data points. We encode the radiogy images x_j to patch features squence, denoted by $x_{Pj} = \{x_1^{pj}, x_2^{pj}, \ldots, x_K^{pj}\}$, where K is the length of the patch features from vision extractors and embed the corresponding report y_j to the squence, denoted by $y_{Rj} = \{y_1^{rj}, y_2^{rj}, \ldots, y_M^{rj}\}, y_m^{rj} \in \mathbb{T}$, where y_M^{rj} are the generated tokens, M is the length of the generated tokens and $\mathbb{T}$ is the token library which contains all possible tokens. To learn a reports generation model to predict the reports squence of target image sequence x_{pj}, i.e., $\hat{y}_{rj}$, we propose prompt-based vision feature extraction which combine the prompt module with vision encoder and then employ memory-driven Transformer. Note that for simplicity we denote the proposed framework as CN-X2RG, the Chinese X-ray-to-Reports Generation.

The framework of the proposed method is illustrated in Fig. 2. We first extract the radiology images feature by the proposed Prompt-based Vision Feature Extraction which can fuse the features from prompt module and vision encoder and then transfer the extracted feature to patch features for generation. To achieve more accurate and responsible reports, we employ memory-driven Transformer architecture inspired by the work of [3]. To enhance the representation of the feature, we introduce an extra classification task. The details of the

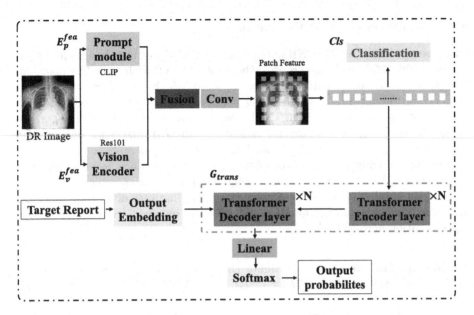

Fig. 2. Overview of the proposed framework, which contains four modules, including prompt module (E_p^{fea}), vision encoder (E_v^{fea}), classification module (Cls) and transformer-based language model (G_{trans}). More specifically, E_p^{fea} and E_v^{fea} are respectively aimed to encoder the learned knowledges and vision features from Xray images. Cls is a auxiliary classification task. G_{trans} performs on a fusion feature space to generate radiology reports.

above, the total loss function and the architecture of proposed network can be found in the supplementary material.

Table 2. Annotation statistics of the CN-RadGraph and statistics of the results obtained by CN-RadGraph on the CN-CXR dataset

Data	Anatomy	DNO	DPO	NO	Locate at	Modify
Annotations (425 training)	5,905	1,433	2,932	674	3,400	4,474
Annotations (75 validation)	1,029	243	515	116	591	772
Results (32,410 training)	366,699	142,411	125,583	57,853	209,731	279,770
Results (4,160 validation)	55,566	14,292	25,980	6,867	30,824	43,180
Results (9,731 testing)	123,142	36,844	52,038	16,584	68,714	94,922

5   Results and Analysis

In this section, we first introduce the dataset, pre-processing and evaluation indicators used for experiments in Sect. 5.1. Then, in Sect. 5.2, we compare the proposed CN-X2RG to other state-of-the-art methods. Finally, we analyze the effectiveness of the modules in the proposed method using two ablation studies which can be found in supplementary material.

5.1   Pre-processing and Evaluation

Pre-processing. For CN-CXR dataset, we resized all training images into resolution of 256×256 pixel, and cropped them into an ROI with 224×224 pixel. All images were normalized with the z-score method, which is conducive to the convergence of the network at the training stage. We folllow the method of R2Gen [3] to split the dataset into train/validation/test set by 7:1:2. Specifically, 32410 images for training, 4160 images for validating and 9731 images for testing. And we used pkuseg [12] and jieba [17] for Chinese word segmentation.

During the training stage, to address the class imbalance issue among keywords, we employed an oversampling technique for positive samples with a keyword count smaller than 5,000. A maximum sampling rate of 10 times was set, and a maximum sampling number of 5,000 was imposed to ensure balanced representation across the classes.

Evaluation Indicators. To evaluate the generation accuracies, we used six metrics, i.e., the $BLEU_1$, $BLEU_2$, $BLEU_3$, $BLEU_4$ [15], $METEOR$ and $ROUGE_L$.

Due to the potential proximity of sentences with opposite semantics when evaluated using $BLEU$ scores, we employ the CN-RadGraph model, which is clinical responsibility due to semantic sensitivity, to extract crucial semantic graph for evaluating model performance. For accurate assessment, we consider true positives when both lesion and anatomy in graphs match between the label and prediction. Conversely, false positives are counted when there are incorrect lesion or anatomy predictions, and false negatives are counted when lesions are missing. Based on this definition, evaluation metrics such as recall, precision, and F1-score can be utilized for assessing lesion and anatomy keywords, as demonstrated in the supplementary material.

5.2   Performance and Comparisons

CN-X2RG Model. We did the comparison study on the CN-CXR dataset for Chinese reports generation. The results are presented in Supplementary. CN-X2RG achieved the best performances in $BLEU_4$, $METEOR$ and $ROUGE_L$ values among all the methods. Specifically, CN-X2RG obtained higher $BLEU_4$, $METEOR$ and $ROUGE_L$ scores than R2GenCMN, with a margin about 1.0%, 0.66% and 0.55% than R2GenCMN, respectively. Compared to R2Gen, R2GenCMN obtained better results. The reason could be that R2GenCMN use cross-modal mapping to facilitate radiology report generation, which was more delicate than R2Gen. However, R2GenCMN consumes a significant amount of graphics memory, which is why we chose R2Gen as the base model.

CN-RadGraph Model. To assess the performance of our CN-RadGraph model, we conducted validation using a subset of the CN-CXR dataset called the CN-RadGraph validation dataset. This dataset comprises 75 Chinese X-ray reports specifically selected for evaluation purposes. We evaluated the model's performance based on mean precision, mean recall, and mean F1-score for affinity and relation. The impressive results obtained from the CN-RadGraph model are presented in Supplementary, highlighting its strong performance in accurately capturing and analyzing the relationships within the radiology reports.

References

1. Alsentzer, E., et al.: Publicly available clinical bert embeddings. arXiv preprint arXiv:1904.03323 (2019)
2. Chen, Z., Shen, Y., Song, Y., Wan, X.: Cross-modal memory networks for radiology report generation. arXiv preprint arXiv:2204.13258 (2022)
3. Chen, Z., Song, Y., Chang, T.H., Wan, X.: Generating radiology reports via memory-driven transformer. arXiv preprint arXiv:2010.16056 (2020)
4. Demner-Fushman, D., et al.: Preparing a collection of radiology examinations for distribution and retrieval. J. Am. Med. Inform. Assoc. **23**(2), 304–310 (2016)
5. Endo, M., Krishnan, R., Krishna, V., Ng, A.Y., Rajpurkar, P.: Retrieval-based chest x-ray report generation using a pre-trained contrastive language-image model. In: Machine Learning for Health, pp. 209–219. PMLR (2021)
6. Floridi, L., Chiriatti, M.: Gpt-3: Its nature, scope, limits, and consequences. Mind. Mach. **30**, 681–694 (2020)
7. Jain, S., et al.: Radgraph: extracting clinical entities and relations from radiology reports. arXiv preprint arXiv:2106.14463 (2021)
8. Jeong, J., et al.: Multimodal image-text matching improves retrieval-based chest x-ray report generation. arXiv preprint arXiv:2303.17579 (2023)
9. Jing, B., Xie, P., Xing, E.: On the automatic generation of medical imaging reports. arXiv preprint arXiv:1711.08195 (2017)
10. Johnson, A.E., et al.: Mimic-cxr, a de-identified publicly available database of chest radiographs with free-text reports. Sci. Data **6**(1), 317 (2019)
11. Li, Y., Liang, X., Hu, Z., Xing, E.P.: Hybrid retrieval-generation reinforced agent for medical image report generation. In: Advances in Neural Information Processing Systems 31 (2018)
12. Luo, R., Xu, J., Zhang, Y., Zhang, Z., Ren, X., Sun, X.: Pkuseg: a toolkit for multi-domain chinese word segmentation. arXiv preprint arXiv:1906.11455 (2019)
13. Miura, Y., Zhang, Y., Tsai, E.B., Langlotz, C.P., Jurafsky, D.: Improving factual completeness and consistency of image-to-text radiology report generation. arXiv preprint arXiv:2010.10042 (2020)
14. Najdenkoska, I., Zhen, X., Worring, M., Shao, L.: Uncertainty-aware report generation for chest x-rays by variational topic inference. Med. Image Anal. **82**, 102603 (2022)
15. Papineni, K., Roukos, S., Ward, T., Zhu, W.J.: Bleu: a method for automatic evaluation of machine translation. In: Proceedings of the 40th annual meeting of the Association for Computational Linguistics. pp. 311–318 (2002)
16. Rongsheng, W., Yaofei, D., Junrong, L., Patrick, P., Tao, T.: Xrayglm: the first chinese medical multimodal model that chest radiographs summarization. https://github.com/WangRongsheng/XrayGLM (2023)
17. Sun, J.: Jieba chinese word segmentation tool (2012)

18. Wang, Z., Tang, M., Wang, L., Li, X., Zhou, L.: A medical semantic-assisted transformer for radiographic report generation. In: Medical Image Computing and Computer Assisted Intervention-MICCAI 2022: 25th International Conference, Singapore, 18–22 September 2022, Proceedings, Part III. pp. 655–664. Springer (2022). https://doi.org/10.1007/978-3-031-16437-8_63

19. Wang, Z., Wu, Z., Agarwal, D., Sun, J.: Medclip: contrastive learning from unpaired medical images and text. arXiv preprint arXiv:2210.10163 (2022)

20. Yan, A., et al.: Weakly supervised contrastive learning for chest x-ray report generation. arXiv preprint arXiv:2109.12242 (2021)

21. Yang, S., Wu, X., Ge, S., Zhou, S.K., Xiao, L.: Knowledge matters: chest radiology report generation with general and specific knowledge. Med. Image Anal. **80**, 102510 (2022)

Gradient Self-alignment in Private Deep Learning

David Bani-Harouni[1]([✉]), Tamara T. Mueller[2,3], Daniel Rueckert[2,4], and Georgios Kaissis[2,3,5]

[1] Computer Aided Medical Procedures, School of Computation, Information and Technology, Technical University of Munich, Garching, Germany
david.bani-harouni@tum.de

[2] Chair for AI in Medicine and Healthcare, School of Computation, Information and Technology and School of Medicine, Technical University of Munich, Munich, Germany

[3] Department of Diagnostic and Interventional Radiology, School of Medicine, Technical University of Munich, Munich, Germany

[4] Department of Computing, Imperial College London, London, UK

[5] Institute for Machine Learning in Biomedical Imaging, Helmholtz-Zentrum Munich, Neuherberg, Germany

Abstract. Differential Privacy (DP) has become a gold-standard to preserve privacy in deep learning. Intuitively speaking, DP ensures that the output of a model is approximately invariant to the inclusion or exclusion of a single individual's data from the training set. There is, however, a trade-off between privacy and utility. DP models tend to perform worse than non-DP models trained on the same data. This is caused by the clipping of per-sample gradients and the addition of noise required for DP guarantees causing an obfuscation of the individual data point's contribution. In this work, we propose a method to reduce this discrepancy by improving the alignment between the per-sample gradients of each individual training sample with its non-DP gradient by increasing their cosine similarity. Optimizing the alignment in only a relevant subset of gradient dimensions, further improves the performance. We evaluate our method on CIFAR-10 and a pediatric pneumonia chest x-ray dataset.

Keywords: Differential Privacy · Private learning · Gradient alignment

1 Introduction

A common mantra in deep learning is that *any model can only be as good as the data it is trained on*. There are, however, many obstacles to the collection of good datasets. Privacy concerns are one major impediment. Especially in the medical domain, there is enormous potential for deep learning solutions to significantly impact patient health and well-being. At the same time, this is also

M. E. Celebi et al. (Eds.): MICCAI 2023 Workshops, LNCS 14393, pp. 89–97, 2023.
https://doi.org/10.1007/978-3-031-47401-9_9

an area where data is especially sensitive. Simply training models on private medical data opens up a multitude of possibilities for adversarial actors to attack the model, e.g. through membership inference attacks [14], an attack aimed at disclosing whether a data record owned by the adversary was part of the training database, to gain information about individuals in the dataset [13].

To this end, Differential Privacy (DP) can be used as a mathematically provable promise to anyone willing to contribute their data to a dataset that they will not experience any substantial additional consequences (adverse or beneficial) relative to the consequences they could expect to experience if their data were not included. This can also be ensured irrespective of any additional information an attacker may have on the individual. Their situation will not worsen due to the inclusion of their data in the dataset. DP methods bound the influence of any individual data point while allowing the extraction of information about general trends in the whole population [3].

DP is achieved in deep learning by changing the magnitude and direction of learning gradients. This intervention is the reason why DP solutions generally perform worse than their non-DP counterparts. The processed gradients lead to impeded convergence and worse weight updates [1]. Towards alleviating the aforementioned problem, we here propose an algorithm for improving the training utility by privately increasing the alignment of the data points' gradients with their non-DP gradient counterparts. The non-DP gradients do not suffer from deviations due to privatization. A thus improved gradient leads to a situation closer to training without DP constraints while still satisfying privacy guarantees. We show that overall alignment is, however, not the most relevant metric to be maximized. In fact, increasing alignment *in specific relevant gradient dimensions* leads to better performance despite overall alignment being worse.

2   Background and Related Work

(ε, δ)-DP [4] is a framework that ensures the privacy of individuals in data analysis. It employs a randomized algorithm $\mathcal{M}$ with the privacy parameters ε and δ to produce an output from a dataset D. The algorithm introduces calibrated random noise, guaranteeing that any individual's data does not significantly affect the outcome of the mechanism. Mathematically, for datasets D and D' differing in a single individual's data, and for any set of possible outputs S, $\mathcal{M}$ satisfies $\Pr[\mathcal{M}(D) \in S] \leq e^{\varepsilon} \cdot \Pr[\mathcal{M}(D') \in S] + \delta$. The parameters ε and δ determine the level of privacy protection, with smaller values of δ providing stronger privacy but potentially increasing the amount of added noise.

For training a deep learning model using DP an adaptation of stochastic gradient descent (SGD) called DP-SGD was developed [1]. The algorithm builds on standard SGD by first clipping the per-sample gradients and then adding Gaussian noise to them before averaging the gradients for the weight update. In contrast to standard DP-SGD which uses all data points of the random sample, our method drops data points from the current update during training based on

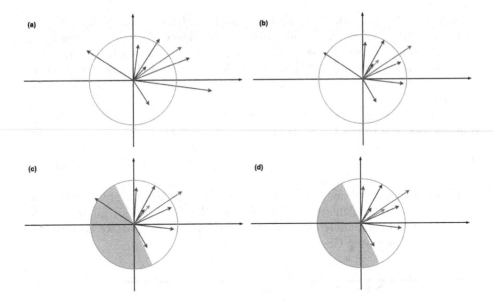

Fig. 1. Schematic showing the steps of our method in a two-dimensional example. The blue arrows represent the per-sample gradients. The green arrow is the non-DP average gradient. The orange arrow shows the current average gradient of the per-sample gradients. (a) The state at the beginning of the algorithm. (b) Per-sample gradients are clipped and noise is added. (c) The cosine similarity with the non-DP gradient is calculated privately and a threshold applied. (d) Gradients outside of this threshold get removed from the weight update step. (Color figure online)

the cosine similarity of that point's gradient with the average non-DP gradient of the randomly sampled group to improve the gradient update direction.

Another DP method that drops specific data points during training is the work by Feldman et al. [5], where the method assigns an individual gradient norm budget to each data point which is then dropped for the remaining training if that budget is spent. While they drop data points completely from the database based on the spent budget to prolong training on other samples, we temporarily drop data points from the current update based on their cosine similarity (CS) with the non-DP gradient to improve training performance under a specific privacy budget. To the best of our knowledge, our work is the first that tries to gain performance improvements by improving the direction of gradients.

3 Methodology

3.1 DP-SGD with a Cosine Similarity Filter

The increase in privacy of DP learning is usually paid for with a decrease in performance. This is caused by the clipping and the noise added to the gradients and therefore a change in the magnitude and direction of the weight update. We hypothesize that reducing the effects of these gradient deviations should lead to better performance under similar privacy guarantees. We achieve a denoising effect by removing per-sample gradients from being included in the averaged gradient of the batch depending on their similarity with the non-DP gradient that would have been used by non-DP training, i.e., if their CS is below some threshold $\psi \in [-1, 1]$.

Our algorithm, is shown schematically in Fig. 1 and explicitly in Algorithm 1. It starts identical to the DP-SGD algorithm [1] with an additional step of computing the average gradient of the batch $\hat{\mathbf{g}}_t$ before privatization. After adding the noise to the per-sample gradients, we use this batch gradient to calculate a CS with all per-sample gradients.

In order to still ensure DP of our method, we can not simply use the non-DP gradient in our calculations and still have the same privacy guarantees, in fact, that would completely eliminate the certification. Instead, we have to also privatize the calculated CS.

Algorithm 1. CS filter for DP learning

Input: Samples $\{x_1, \ldots, x_N\}$, loss function $\mathcal{L}(\theta, x_i)$. Parameters: iterations T, learning rate η_t, noise scale σ, group size L, gradient norm bound C, CS threshold ψ, CS clipping range λ, CS noise scale τ.
Initialize θ_0 randomly
for $t \in [T]$ **do**
    Take a random sample L_t with sampling probability L/N
    Compute per-sample gradients
    For each $i \in L_t$, compute $\mathbf{g}_t(x_i) \leftarrow \nabla_{\theta_t} \mathcal{L}(\theta_t, x_i)$
    Compute average gradient
    $\hat{\mathbf{g}}_t \leftarrow \frac{1}{L} \sum_i \mathbf{g}_t(x_i)$
    Clip gradient
    $\bar{\mathbf{g}}_t(x_i) \leftarrow \mathbf{g}_t(x_i)/\max\left(1, \frac{\|\mathbf{g}_t(x_i)\|_2}{C}\right)$
    Add noise
    $\tilde{\mathbf{g}}_t(x_i) \leftarrow \bar{\mathbf{g}}_t(x_i) + \frac{\mathcal{N}(0, \sigma^2 C^2 \mathbf{I})}{L}$
    Calculate CSs
    For each $i \in L_t$, compute $c_t(x_i) \leftarrow (\hat{\mathbf{g}}_t \cdot \tilde{\mathbf{g}}_t(x_i))/(\|\hat{\mathbf{g}}_t\| \|\tilde{\mathbf{g}}_t(x_i)\|)$
    Privatize CSs
    For each $i \in L_t$, compute $\bar{c}_t(x_i) \leftarrow \min(\psi + \lambda, \max(c_t(x_i), \psi - \lambda))$
    For each $i \in L_t$, compute $\tilde{c}_t(x_i) \leftarrow \bar{c}_t(x_i) + \mathcal{N}(0, \tau^2(2\lambda)^2)$
    Select samples based on CS
    $X_t \leftarrow \{x_i | i \in L_t, \tilde{c}_t(x_i) > \psi\}$
    Average remaining per-sample gradients
    $\tilde{\mathbf{g}}_t \leftarrow \frac{1}{|X_t|} \sum_{x \in X_t} \tilde{\mathbf{g}}_t(x)$
    Descend
    $\theta_{t+1} \leftarrow \theta_t - \eta_t \tilde{\mathbf{g}}_t$
end for
Output: θ_T

Note, that with the hard threshold ψ on the CS, based on which we select the gradients in the next step, we are really only interested in values close to that boundary. We reduce the sensitivity by clipping the CS inside a range close to ψ. Explicitly, we introduce a parameter $\lambda \in [0, 2]$ and clip the CSs into a range of $[\max(-1, \psi - \lambda), \min(\psi + \lambda, 1)]$, thus obtaining the mechanism's sensitivity of 2λ. Together with the CS noise multiplier $\tau \in \mathbb{R}$, we then sample noise from the Gaussian distribution $\mathcal{N}(0, \tau^2(2\lambda)^2)$ and add it to the clipped CSs, thus, privatizing the values. Then we select all samples whose CS with the non-DP gradient is larger than the threshold ψ, i.e., the set $\{x_i | i \in L_t, \tilde{c}_t(x_i) > \psi\}$, where $\tilde{c}_t(x_i)$ is the privatized CS. Using this set, we calculate the average gradient. This improves the alignment of the gradient with the average non-DP gradient of the current sample.

In order to include the CS privatization into the calculation of the spent (ε, δ)-budget, we track the budget with Rényi Differential Privacy (RDP) [10]. Therefore, we are able to add up the Rényi guarantees to the total RDP budget, since composition is additive. Transforming the (α, ρ)-RDP guarantee into an (ε, δ)-DP then can be done using the approach defined by Mironov et al. [2,10]. For more information on RDP, please refer to [10].

3.2   DP-SGD with Dimension-Filtered Cosine Similarity Filter

Rather than calculating the CS between per-sample gradients and the non-DP gradient for all dimensions of the gradient, we found that it can be beneficial to first identify dimensions that have a high value in specific measures, e.g., standard deviation (std) or coefficient of variation (CoV), and then project the gradient vectors into a space spanned by those standard basis vectors that correspond to these identified dimensions. We, thus, limit the dimensions under consideration for the CS calculation.

As can be seen in Algorithm 2, this is done by calculating the vector $\mathbf{s}_t \in \mathbb{R}^F$ that holds the values of the per-sample gradient dimension measure. We then find the γ-th percentile score of the values in $\mathbf{s}_t$, with $\gamma \in [0, 1]$, to identify the threshold $\phi \in \mathbb{R}$ for the values. With this threshold, we can create a set $S_t = \{i | (s_t)^i > \phi\}$ that holds all dimension indices whose values are above this threshold and therefore above the γ-th percentile. As a next step, we truncate both the per-sample gradient vectors and the non-DP gradient to those dimensions present in the set S_t as $\tilde{\mathbf{g}}'_t(x_i) \leftarrow (\tilde{\mathbf{g}}_t(x_i))^{i \in S_t}$ and $\hat{\mathbf{g}}'_t \leftarrow (\hat{\mathbf{g}}_t)^{i \in S_t}$, respectively, essentially projecting the vectors into the identified relevant vector space.

Now, calculating the CSs of the truncated per-sample gradients with the truncated non-DP gradient is ignoring the alignment in dimensions with low standard deviation. Importantly, this process does not improve the overall CS of the batch gradient with the non-DP gradient; on the contrary, it generally makes it worse, as the algorithm only optimizes alignment in a subset of dimensions. Still, we identify an experimental benefit in Sect. 4.

4   Experiments and Discussion

4.1   Experimental Setup

We evaluate our method on the CIFAR-10 [9] and the publicly available Pediatric Pneumonia [7] dataset. CIFAR-10 contains 32×32 color images of ten different classes, e.g. airplanes, cars, or cats. The dataset has 50,000 training images and 10,000 for testing [9]. The Pediatric Pneumonia dataset, published in [7], contains x-ray images of children suffering from bacterial pneumonia or viral pneumonia in addition to a control group. There are 5,163 images for training and 624 for testing.

Algorithm 2. CS filter with dimension filter for DP learning

Input: Samples $\{x_1, \ldots, x_N\}$, loss function $\mathcal{L}(\theta, x_i)$. Parameters: iterations T, learning rate η_t, noise scale σ, group size L, gradient norm bound C, CS threshold ψ, CS clipping range λ, CS noise scale τ, dimension measure s, dimension measure percentile γ, dimension measure threshold ϕ.

Initialize θ_0 randomly

for $t \in [T]$ **do**

    Take a random sample L_t with sampling probability L/N

    Compute per-sample gradients

    For each $i \in L_t$, compute $\mathbf{g}_t(x_i) \leftarrow \nabla_{\theta_t} \mathcal{L}(\theta_t, x_i)$

    Compute average gradient

    $\hat{\mathbf{g}}_t \leftarrow \frac{1}{L} \sum_i \mathbf{g}_t(x_i)$

    Clip gradient

    $\bar{\mathbf{g}}_t(x_i) \leftarrow \mathbf{g}_t(x_i) / \max\left(1, \frac{\|\mathbf{g}_t(x_i)\|_2}{C}\right)$

    Add noise

    $\tilde{\mathbf{g}}_t(x_i) \leftarrow \bar{\mathbf{g}}_t(x_i) + \frac{\mathcal{N}(0, \sigma^2 C^2 \mathbf{I})}{L}$

    Calculate measure of gradient dimensions

    $\mathbf{s}_t \leftarrow s(\tilde{\mathbf{g}}_t)$

    Select gradient dimensions based on measure

    $\phi \leftarrow \text{percentile}(\mathbf{s}_t, \gamma)$

    $S_t \leftarrow \{i | (s_t)^i > \phi\}$

    $\hat{\mathbf{g}}_t' \leftarrow (\hat{\mathbf{g}}_t)^{i \in S_t}$

    For each $i \in L_t$, $\tilde{\mathbf{g}}_t'(x_i) \leftarrow (\tilde{\mathbf{g}}_t(x_i))^{i \in S_t}$

    Calculate CSs

    For each $i \in L_t$, compute $c_t(x_i) \leftarrow (\hat{\mathbf{g}}_t' \cdot \tilde{\mathbf{g}}_t'(x_i))/(\|\hat{\mathbf{g}}_t'\| \|\tilde{\mathbf{g}}_t'(x_i)\|)$

    Privatize CSs

    For each $i \in L_t$, compute $\bar{c}_t(x_i) \leftarrow \min(\psi + \lambda, \max(c_t(x_i), \psi - \lambda))$

    For each $i \in L_t$, compute $\tilde{c}_t(x_i) \leftarrow \bar{c}_t(x_i) + \mathcal{N}(0, \tau^2 (2\lambda)^2)$

    Select samples based on CS

    $X_t \leftarrow \{x_i | i \in L_t, \tilde{c}_t(x_i) > \psi\}$

    Average remaining per-sample gradients

    $\tilde{\mathbf{g}}_t \leftarrow \frac{1}{|X_t|} \sum_{x \in X_t} \tilde{\mathbf{g}}_t(x)$

    Descend

    $\theta_{t+1} \leftarrow \theta_t - \eta_t \tilde{\mathbf{g}}_t$

end for

Output: θ_T

In the following experiments, we use a ResNet9 [6] following Klause et al. [8] starting with two convolutional blocks with 64 and 128 filters, respectively, followed by one residual block with 128 filters, two convolutional blocks with 256 filters and one residual block also with 256 filters. The last two layers are one max pooling layer and one fully connected layer with 1024 nodes. The convolutional blocks all consist of one convolutional layer and after a Mish activation [11] layer, a group normalization layer. Additionally, there is a scale normalization after each residual layer. This network is a strong baseline for DP learning tasks on CIFAR-10.

The experiments minimize the cross-entropy loss. We train for 50 epochs on CIFAR-10 and 20 epochs on Pediatric Pneumonia. The learning rate was set to 0.005 for CIFAR-10 and 0.001 for Pediatric Pneumonia, momentum to 0.1, and group size L to 64, as these parameters show the best results on the baseline method. Accordingly, we set the maximum gradient norm to 1. All images are normalized before they are passed to the model. The source code was implemented in Python using PyTorch [12]. The opacus library [15] was used for their implementation of DP-SGD and privacy accounting.

4.2 Results and Discussion

For our method to be DP, the calculation of the CS of the privatized gradient with the original non-DP gradient has to be privatized as well, as we would leak private information from the non-DP gradient without doing so. However, to clearly see the potential benefit of the method, we first evaluate it without that additional step. From that, we can infer an upper bound of the benefit of the method without the extra difficulty of a noisy CS. In Table 1, we show a comparison of our method's validation scores with a standard DP-SGD baseline. We instantiate our method with three different kinds of dimension measures: magnitude, std, and CoV. The magnitude-filtered CS filter only keeps those dimensions that have a high average magnitude, and the std-filtered and CoV-filtered CS filter keeps only those dimensions that have a high std or CoV, respectively.

Table 1 shows that the improved gradient alignment indeed translates into an improvement in performance. For CIFAR-10, The average cosine similarity of the baseline gradients with the non-DP gradient is 0.02. The CS filter raises this to 0.15 and outperforms the baseline. The performance gain between the baseline and the standard unfiltered CS filter is not necessarily surprising, since the latter uses non-private information in the form of cosine similarities. However, the even more substantial improvement in the performance of the CoV-filtered CS filter is very interesting when considering that the average alignment of 0.1 of the gradient is now actually worse than the alignment when using the unfiltered CS filter. This is the case because we are only optimizing alignment in a subset of dimensions. It follows that the CS is apparently not the only relevant metric by which to measure the value of gradients. One property of the CS is that, while it can be decomposed into the calculation of the alignment of each dimension individually, all dimensions are weighted equally. However, it may be the case

Table 1. Validation scores for different dimension filter choices on CIFAR-10 and Pediatric Pneumonia with a ResNet9. The dimension filter quantile is $\gamma = 0.7$ for CIFAR-10 and $\gamma = 0.5$ for Pediatric Pneumonia. The CS filter threshold is $\psi = 0.1$ for CIFAR-10 and $\psi = 0$ for Pediatric Pneumonia. These results do not use privatized CSs. Methods that are not fully DP are marked with an asterisk.

Method	CIFAR-10		Pediatric Pneumonia	
	Accuracy	AUROC	Accuracy	AUROC
baseline	0.6933	0.9491	0.7019	0.8961
unfiltered CS filter*	0.7096	0.9567	0.7228	**0.8962**
magnitude-filtered CS filter*	0.7041	0.9558	0.6939	0.8929
std-filtered CS filter*	0.7292	0.9601	0.7051	0.8950
CoV-filtered CS filter*	**0.7353**	**0.9613**	**0.7340**	0.8924

that not every dimension is equally important. Treating all dimensions the same may dilute the CS metric with alignment in irrelevant dimensions. Filtering out these dimensions prior to calculating the CS, could improve the alignment in relevant dimensions even if it reduces general alignment. The experiments on the medical pediatric pneumonia dataset largely confirm these findings.

The benefit of our method becomes less clear when deploying it in a fully DP context, i.e., including the privatization of the CSs. On CIFAR-10, the validation accuracy of the CoV-filtered CS filter over three seeds gets reduced to 0.698 ± 0.009 at $\varepsilon = 7.46$ and $\delta = 1 \times 10^{-6}$ while the fully unfiltered baseline reaches 0.696 ± 0.002 at $\varepsilon = 6.97$ and $\delta = 1 \times 10^{-6}$ over the same three seeds. These results are, however, preliminary and could be related to a lack of tuning, as our experiments show that there is value in gradient alignment.

5   Conclusion

In this work, we proposed a method to improve the quality of learning gradients in DP-SGD by reducing the amount of deviation of the private gradient from its non-DP counterpart. This improves the utility of the training at minimal privacy cost. We further experimentally show, that pure cosine similarity alignment is not the only relevant metric to measure the quality of the DP gradients. To that end, we develop a second version of our method, that first identifies a subset of gradient dimensions that qualify as being relevant, determined by the CoV in that dimension, and only computes the cosine similarity over this subset of dimensions. This again improves the performance of our method. Optimizing the method to improve results in a fully DP context is part of ongoing efforts.

This work opens up many different venues for further exploration and evaluation. We find that simply optimizing the cosine similarity of the private gradient with the non-private one, does not always leads to the best performance. While we shed some light on the problem, by showing that alignment in certain dimensions may be more important than alignment in all dimensions, the immediate cause for this effect is not perfectly clear yet. Further research is required to understand the relationship between the cosine similarity of gradients and the utility of the training. We believe that this work can provide valuable insights to further understand the intricacies of deep learning with DP and provide a basis for following research on the effect of gradient alignment and how to best utilize this effect to improve the utility of models trained with DP.

References

1. Abadi, M., et al.: Deep learning with differential privacy. In: Proceedings of the 2016 ACM SIGSAC Conference on Computer and Communications Security (2016)
2. Balle, B., Barthe, G., Gaboardi, M., Hsu, J., Sato, T.: Hypothesis testing interpretations and renyi differential privacy. ArXiv abs/ arXiv: 1905.09982 (2019)
3. Dwork, C., McSherry, F., Nissim, K., Smith, A.D.: Calibrating noise to sensitivity in private data analysis. In: Theory of Cryptography Conference (2006)
4. Dwork, C., Roth, A.: The algorithmic foundations of differential privacy. Found. Trends Theor. Comput. Sci. **9**, 211–407 (2014)
5. Feldman, V., Zrnic, T.: Individual privacy accounting via a renyi filter. In: Neural Information Processing Systems (2020)
6. He, K., Zhang, X., Ren, S., Sun, J.: Deep residual learning for image recognition. In: 2016 IEEE Conference on Computer Vision and Pattern Recognition (CVPR), pp. 770–778 (2015)
7. Kermany, D.S., et al.: Identifying medical diagnoses and treatable diseases by image-based deep learning. Cell **172**, 1122-1131.e9 (2018)
8. Klause, H., Ziller, A., Rueckert, D., Hammernik, K., Kaissis, G.: Differentially private training of residual networks with scale normalisation. ArXiv abs/ arXiv: 2203.00324 (2022)
9. Krizhevsky, A.: Learning multiple layers of features from tiny images (2009)
10. Mironov, I.: Rényi differential privacy. In: 2017 IEEE 30th Computer Security Foundations Symposium (CSF), pp. 263–275 (2017)
11. Misra, D.: Mish: a self regularized non-monotonic activation function. In: British Machine Vision Conference (2020)
12. Paszke, A., et al.: PyTorch: An Imperative Style, High-Performance Deep Learning Library. In: Wallach, H., et al. (eds.) Advances in Neural Information Processing Systems 32, pp. 8024–8035. Curran Associates, Inc. (2019). http://papers.neurips.cc/paper/9015-pytorch-an-imperative-style-high-performance-deep-learning-library.pdf
13. Rigaki, M., García, S.: A survey of privacy attacks in machine learning. ArXiv abs/ arXiv: 2007.07646 (2020)
14. Shokri, R., Stronati, M., Song, C., Shmatikov, V.: Membership inference attacks against machine learning models. In: 2017 IEEE Symposium on Security and Privacy (SP), pp. 3–18. IEEE Computer Society, Los Alamitos, CA, USA (May 2017). https://doi.org/10.1109/SP.2017.41, https://doi.ieeecomputersociety.org/10.1109/SP.2017.41
15. Yousefpour, A., et al.: Opacus: user-friendly differential privacy library in pytorch. ArXiv abs/ arXiv: 2109.12298 (2021)

Cellular Features Based Interpretable Network for Classifying Cell-Of-Origin from Whole Slide Images for Diffuse Large B-cell Lymphoma Patients

Qiangqiang Gu[1], Nazim Shaikh[1], Ping-chang Lin[1], Srinath Jayachandran[1], Prasanna Porwal[1], Xiao Li[2], and Yao Nie[1(✉)]

[1] Roche Diagnostic Solutions, Santa Clara, CA 95050, USA
qiangqiang.gu@contractors.roche.com, {nazim.shaikh,
ping-chang.lin,srinath.jayachandran,prasanna.porwal.pp1,
yao.nie}@roche.com
[2] Genentech, Inc., South San Francisco, CA 94080, USA
lix233@gene.com

Abstract. Diffuse large B-cell lymphoma (DLBCL) is an aggressive and most common type of non-Hodgkin lymphoma. The two major molecular subtypes of DLBCL, i.e. germinal center B-cell-like (GCB) and activated B-cell-like (ABC) types of DLBCL, have different clinical outcomes when treated with combined therapy R-CHOP. Cell-of-origin (COO) is a published prognostic method. Up to now, this classification requires either complex gene expression analysis or multiple immunohistochemistry (IHC) stains requiring expert scoring and assessment. In this paper, we aim to develop an effective and tissue-saving COO classification method based on H&E stained whole slide images (WSIs). Specifically, we develop a new approach named **C**ellular **F**eatures Based **I**nterpretable **Net**work (*CellFiNet*), by leveraging both interpretable cellular features derived from image tiles and attention based multi-instance learning (AMIL) framework to train a WSI classification model. In comparison with the conventional AMIL approach based on image embeddings derived from convolutional neural networks (CNNs), the proposed approach achieved comparable classification accuracy, while being favorable in terms of explainability, as the model behavior can be interpreted through both attention scores and biologically relevant feature importances at whole slide as well as image tile levels.

Keywords: Cellular Feature · SHAP Analysis · Deep Learning · Attention Mechanism · Multi-Instance Learning · Cell of Origin · Diffuse Large B-cell Lymphoma

---

Q. Gu and N. Shaikh — Equal Contribution

M. E. Celebi et al. (Eds.): MICCAI 2023 Workshops, LNCS 14393, pp. 98–106, 2023.
https://doi.org/10.1007/978-3-031-47401-9_10

1   Introduction

Diffuse large B-cell lymphoma (DLBCL), accounting for about 25% to 30% of all the non-Hodgkin lymphomas [1], is an aggressive and the most common type of lymphoma. Although about two-thirds of DLBCL patients can be cured with standard treatment, research has focused on determining which patients have less favorable prognosis so that they can be considered for novel targeted-treatment strategies [2]. Germinal center B-cell-like (GCB) and activated B-cell-like (ABC) are two major biologically distinct molecular subtypes of DLBCL. Patients with the ABC DLBCL generally have worse prognosis than the GCB DLBCL patients [1] when treated with combined therapy R-CHOP. Therefore, cell-of-origin (COO) classification or its surrogates have been incorporated into the clinical practice and clinical trials to help better understand DLBCL biological heterogeneity and enable researchers to develop more accurate therapeutic targeting strategies.

Well-established COO classification algorithm uses gene expression profiling (GEP) [3]. However, as GEP is not widely accessible, researchers and pathologists in clinical practice approximate molecular subtypes using immunohistochemical (IHC) patterns such as the most widely used Hans algorithm, where expert visual assessment of multiple IHC assays are required. Due to the imperfection of IHC in assessing molecular subtype, more precise strategies are under development [4].

In this paper, we aim for standardized and automated COO prediction based on hematoxylin and eosin (H&E) stained whole-slide-images (WSIs), which are readily available from primary diagnosis and thus tissue-saving and potentially more efficient by shortening the turnaround time. Previous study in COO predictions of DLBCL patients using H&E WSIs and deep learning approaches is reported [5], but no insights are shared about the relation between histopathology features and different molecular subtypes. Another recent study conducted by Vrabc et al. [6] indicates that the cellular morphological features are of prognostic importance. However, the cellular features extracted were only limited to the basic geometric features of nuclei.

Inspired by the previous works, in this study, we developed a new approach, named **Cellular Features Based Interpretable Net**work (*CellFiNet*). Specifically, in this approach, nuclei segmentation and classification are first performed to identify each nucleus and classify them into different phenotypes. Then, interpretable cellular features are derived from nuclei in each image tile and used as the tile-level histopathological representation. Lastly, attention based multi-instance learning (AMIL) framework is used to aggregate all tile-level histopathological representations from a WSI to form the slide-level representation and train a WSI classifier. Our work has the following major contributions: 1) A comprehensive, quantifiable and generic cellular feature set that characterizes nuclei morphologies, spatial patterns as well as phenotype compositions. The feature set can be used to train diverse machine learning models for clinical predictions. 2) A weakly-supervised AMIL model to classify the GCB and ABC molecular subtypes of DLBCL with superior or comparable performance as the existing machine/deep learning approaches. 3) A systematic approach to analyze and interpret the trained model through a combination of attention mechanism and SHAP (SHapley Additive exPlanations) [7] analysis at both slide- and tile-level.

2 Methodology

The proposed *CellFiNet* approach has three major steps as illustrated in Fig. 1. As a prerequisite, image tiles are extracted from manually annotated tumor regions of the WSI.

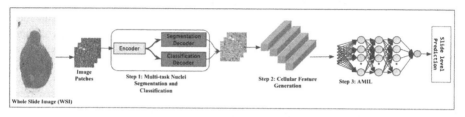

Fig. 1. *CellFiNet* pipeline diagram.

2.1 Nuclei Segmentation and Classification

We first employ an internally trained multi-task semantic segmentation model based on [12] to segment the nuclei in each image tile and classify each nucleus into three phenotypes, namely *"tumor"*, normal *"lymphocyte"* and *"other"* cells. Note that *CellFiNet* can employ other cell segmentation and classification models as long as they facilitate cellular feature extraction as described below.

2.2 Cellular Feature Extraction

Nuclear Level Features. Using the semantic mask generated in the previous step, 210 nuclear morphology features are computed for each nucleus. This includes six categories which are 1) basic geometric features (such as shape, size and circularity) extracted using scikit-image [16], 2) first-order statistics of gray-level intensity inside the nuclei, 3) texture features derived from gray-level co-occurrence matrix, both 2) and 3) extracted using PyRadiomics [17], 4) advanced morphology features for characterizing irregularity, computed internally, 5) chromatin distribution features [13] and 6) nuclear boundary signature and curvature features [14] both computed internally.

Tile Level Features. Nuclear features from cells in each tile are aggregated into tile level features using *median* and *standard deviation* statistics (indicated by "*_med*" and "*_std*" in feature name, respectively in Fig. 3 and 4). Additionally, we implemented spatial distribution features, such as density of each cell phenotype and average distances between cells. Finally, spatial patterns are captured through graph-based methods such as k-nearest neighbor (KNN) graphs using the Igraph library [15].

Feature Pre-processing. Due to general similarity between each nucleus, some cellular features have low variance across cells or high correlations with other cellular features. Such features are excluded by applying predefined variance and correlation thresholds, which results in a 336-dimensional feature representation for each tile. Finally, we apply normalization on the tile-level features before passing them to the network.

2.3 AMIL Model Training

AMIL, first introduced by Ilse et al. [8] consists of two components, an attention mechanism and a multi-instance learning (MIL) classifier. The attention mechanism uses the softmax attention to highlight the individual instance contributions to the entire bag, while the attention weights are learned by the network. This attention mechanism will further supervise the MIL classifier by generating the slide-level feature representation where different instances' (i.e., tile-level features) contributions are no longer considered equally. The AMIL model weighs more on the more relevant instances, thus inherently reduces the impact of noisy samples and improves the prediction performance. *CellFiNet* inherits the state-of-art AMIL model architecture, but uses tile-level cellular feature representations as the input instead of the image embeddings extracted by a pre-trained convolutional neural network model. Based on the cellular feature dimension, the attention module we built is composed of multiple linear layers, each followed by a dropout, 1-dimension batchnorm and Relu activation. The classifier module is a simple multilayer perceptron (MLP) with dropout and Relu activation.

2.4 CellFiNet Interpretability

CellFiNet provides two types of interpretability leveraging the attention mechanism and SHAP analysis [7], a game theoretic approach to interpret AI model predictions. Since the slide-level cellular features is the aggregation of tile-level features, each of the two types of model interpretations can be conducted at the slide-level as well as the tile-level.

The first type of model interpretation is built upon the attention scores, which is the output from the attention module in the *CellFiNet* architecture. The attention scores are used to generate a slide-level attention heatmap to provide a global view of the relevant regions for model prediction, which allows easier localization of regions for inspection in a WSI. In addition, attention score can be used to create a tile-level gallery consisting of the top highest-attended tiles from a given WSI, which enables detailed visual assessment of the relevant tissue morphologies used by the model.

The second type of model interpretation is leveraging SHAP to identify the most contributing cellular features to the model predictions at both the slide- and tile-level through slide- and tile-level feature representations, respectively. In addition to feature importance, SHAP also enables determining if a higher value of a particular feature contributes positively or negatively to the prediction. Thanks to the fact that each individual feature is analytically formulated and biologically relevant, domain experts are enabled to assess the model behavior by accessing individual features against their prior knowledge. The model validity can be further supported beyond good performance metric if identified important features are associated with the expected tissue morphology for the disease. On the other hand, if the important features are found to be correlated with data batch effects, such as datasets variation caused by different data sources, possible model bias can be identified and potentially addressed by simple approaches such as eliminating the feature.

2.5 Benchmark Methods

As a benchmark method, image embeddings generated by a pre-trained model through self-supervised learning [9] on various histopathological images were extracted as the tile-level representations. The pre-trained model uses Resnet50 architecture and outputs embedding with 1024 feature dimensions. Since the pre-trained embeddings were in 1024-dimension, which is significantly greater than the cellular feature dimension, we included more attention layers in the attention module of the CellFiNet framework to capture more complex patterns and potentially allow smoother dimension reduction during learning. As a second benchmark method, a Random Forest (RF) classifier was also trained using the tile-level cellular feature representations to generate prediction for each tile, the average prediction score of all tiles from a WSI is then used to get slide-level prediction.

3 Experiments and Results

3.1 Data

In this study, we used H&E stained WSIs scanned at a magnification of 40X (0.25 um/pixel), from a total of 410 DLBCL patients who participated in the phase 3 GOYA (NCT01287741) or phase 2 CAVALLI (NCT02055820) clinical trials. Among these patients, 142 and 268 slides were labeled as ABC and GCB subtypes, respectively. Out of the 410 WSIs, 356 were designated for cross validation purposes, while the remaining 54 WSIs were dedicated for independent testing. From each WSIs, we extracted non-overlapping tiles of size 1024x1024 pixels. This size was selected such that each tile contains a sufficient number of cells to derive robust cellular feature statistics. To reduce the sample imbalancing due to tumor region size variation, a maximum of K tiles were randomly extracted if there are more than K tiles present in the annotated tumor region. K was empirically chosen taking consideration of the memory and computation requirement, $K = 30$ in our experiments.

To identify the optimal hyperparameter combinations, we generated a 5-fold cross-validation dataset using the afore-mentioned 356 WSIs. Within each fold, we randomly allocated 80% of the WSIs for training, while the remaining 20% served as the validation set. After determining the best hyperparameters, we applied the same split ratio to the 356 WSIs, resulting in 285 WSIs for training and 71 WSIs for validation. This allowed us to retrain the model using the identified optimal hyperparameters. We evaluated the performance of the final model on the independent test dataset consisting of the 54 WSIs as mentioned above.

3.2 Results

We evaluated the proposed *CellFiNet* approach and the two benchmark methods using ROC AUC (see Table 1). The mean and standard deviation were reported for training and validation across the 5-fold cross-validation (CV) datasets. In addition, the performance of the final model on the independent test dataset was also reported. The results showed that *CellFiNet* outperformed RF on both the CV datasets and the independent test dataset.

This demonstrated the benefit of utilizing AMIL architecture to weight each tile based on its relevance to the target prediction, instead of allowing equal contribution from all the tiles by RF. Meanwhile, *CellFiNet* achieved comparable performance as the conventional AMIL approach, with slightly higher mean ROC AUC on the CV datasets and test dataset. This demonstrated the equivalent representation power of the cellular features as compared with the pre-learned image embeddings.

Table 1. Performance Comparison in ROC AUC

Method	Train	Validation	Test
RF	0.713 ± 0.033	0.675 ± 0.045	0.715
Convention AMIL	**0.740 ± 0.005**	0.686 ± 0.025	0.737
CellFiNet	0.716 ± .012	**0.706 ± 0.060**	**0.751**

4 Interpretability

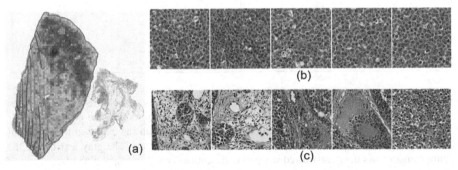

Fig. 2. Visualization of *CellFiNet* attention score based interpretability. (a) Example of slide-level attention heatmap, where high attention regions are highlighted by red colored shade; and examples of top 5 tiles of the (b) highest and (c) lowest attention scores.

CellFiNet offers a dual interpretability approach utilizing attention scores and SHAP. Figure 2 shows the attention heatmap of a sample H&E stained WSI of ABC subtype, which indicates that the model is focusing on the upper part of the annotated tumor region. In addition, the top 5 tiles with the highest and lowest attention scores from the same WSI illustrate how *CellFiNet* model prioritizes dense tumor tiles while assigning lesser importance to tiles depicting open spaces or non-tumor tissue. This emphasizes the model's ability to discern areas of significance within the WSIs.

Figure 3 demonstrates the slide-level cellular feature importance and effect on the training and testing dataset, respectively. As shown, for both the datasets, features related to cell phenotype (***tumor_density, other_density***), tumor cell spatial pattern (***KNN_max_betweeness, KNN_std_betweeness***), nuclear shape (*moment_hu1_med,*

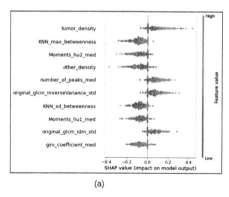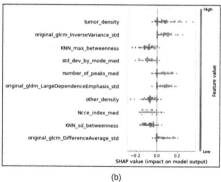

(a)   (b)

Fig. 3. SHAP summary plots for the (a) training dataset and (b) testing dataset. Each dot corresponds to a slide. The top 10 feature importance is ranked along the y-axis. The impact on model output is shown along the x-axis, where positive and negative values indicate moving prediction value towards "1" (i.e., ABC) and "0" (i.e., GCB). Respectively.

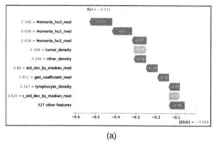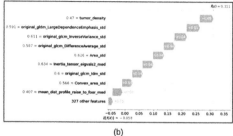

(a)   (b)

Fig. 4. SHAP waterfall plot for an example individual tile which is predicted as a) GCB subtype (f(x) = -0.532) and b) ABC subtype (f(x) = 0.311). Each row shows how the positive (red) or negative (blue) contribution of each feature moves the value from the expected model output (E(f(x)) = -0.058) to the model output for this particular prediction. The gray text before the feature names shows the standardized value of each feature for the corresponding tile.

moment_hu2_med, Ncce_index_med), bournary (**number_of_peaks**, *gini_coefficient_med, std_dev_by_mode_med*), and texture (*original_gldm_LargedependenceEmphasis_std, original_glcm_DifferenceVariance_std,* **original_glcm_InverseVariance_std**) are all contributing to the prediction. Six out of the top 10 features (highlighted in **bold**) are shared by the training and testing datasets, demonstrating the generalizability of these features across different datasets. It is worth noting that *tumor_density* is the most important feature, and higher *tumor_density* value points towards a prediction of "ABC" subtype. Meanwhile, higher variation of the nuclear texture is also associated with the "ABC" subtype. Knowing that ABC DLBCL patients generally have worse prognosis than the GCB DLBCL patients [2], this observation can be linked to the report that within the morphologic spectrum of DLBCL, certain cases of aggressive mature B-cell non-hodgkin lymphoma have some of the morphologic features of burkitt lymphoma but have greater nuclear and cytoplasmic variability [10].

To gain insights about model behavior on a local region, *CellFiNet* classifier can be applied to a tile-level representation and use SHAP waterfall plot to display individual tile prediction explanations. Figure 4 visualizes the contribution of the top 9 features (the remaining 327 features are aggregated in the last row). The top feature differences between Fig. 4 (a) and (b) indicate that the model is adapted to local feature variation and employs different feature importance to derive the prediction. Figure 4 (a) shows that the shape and boundary features are the main determinants for predicting the tile as GCB; while (b) shows that morphological variations are the dominating factors for a ABC prediction; *tumor_density* stays important for both tiles.

5 Conclusion and Discussion

CellFiNet elegantly combines quantified and interpretable cellular features and AMIL network architecture in a simple yet effective way. The notable performance in COO prediction for DLBCL patients demonstrates the descriptive power of the designed cellular features, as well as the effectiveness of attention mechanisms in weighing the relevance of tissue image tiles to the target prediction. The combination also greatly enhances model interpretability through both attention scoring and SHAP analysis, each of which is only applicable to either pure deep neural network based approaches or conventional machine learning approaches alone. As a result, *CellFiNet* allows a holistic interpretation and analysis of model behavior at various levels, covering the entire dataset, whole slide images and individual image tiles. Moreover, the linkage to each individual cellular feature can be established at all levels, enabling more model transparency and trustworthiness and making *CellFiNet* a great biomarker discovery tool for clinical predictions. Future works include using more diverse real-world data for model optimization and verification. Also, using a subset of image tiles from the annotated tumor region due to memory and computation limitation can be suboptimal for model training, which will be addressed in the next phase of development.

Acknowledgements. The authors would like to thank Anil Yuce and Samaneh Abbasi (principal data scientist) for providing the pre-trained model as the benchmark; and Konstanty Korski (senior MD pathologist) for providing the domain consultations; as well as the data team for their diligent work on data sourcing and curation. This study was funded by F. Hoffman-La Roche Ltd. Support with compliance and the paper submission process was provided by PharmaGenesis Cardiff, Cardiff, UK and was funded by F. Hoffman-La Roche Ltd.

References

1. Padala, S.A., Kallam, A.: Diffuse large B-Cell lymphoma. In: StatPearls. StatPearls Publishing (2023)
2. Rutherford, S.C., Leonard, J.P.: DLBCL Cell of origin: what role should it play in care today? Oncol. (Williston Park, N.Y.), **32**(9), 445–449 (2018)
3. Alizadeh, A.A., Eisen, M.B., Davis, R.E., Ma, C., Lossos, I.S., Rosenwald, A., et al.: Distinct types of diffuse large B-cell lymphoma identified by gene expression profiling. Nature **403**(6769), 503–511 (2000)

4. Yan, W.H., et al.: Cell-of-origin subtyping of diffuse large B-Cell lymphoma by using a qPCR-based gene expression assay on formalin-fixed Paraffin-embedded tissues. Front. Oncol. **10**, 803 (2020)

5. Syrykh, C., Schiratti, J.B., Brion, E., et al.: 623MO Machine Learning-based prediction of germinal center, MYC/BCL2 double protein expressor status, and MYC rearrangement from whole slide images in DLBCL patients. Ann. Oncol. **13**(7), S829 (2022)

6. Vrabac, D., Smit, A., Rojansky, R., et al.: DLBCL-Morph: Morphological features computed using deep learning for an annotated digital DLBCL image set. Sci. Data **8**(1), 135 (2021)

7. Lundberg, S.M., Lee, S.I.: A Unified Approach to Interpreting Model Predictions. In: Proceedings of the 31st International Conference on Neural Information Processing Systems, pp. 4765–4774 (2017)

8. Ilse, M., Tomczak, J.M., Welling, M.: Attention-based Deep Multiple Instance Learning. In: Proceedings of the 35th International Conference on Machine Learning, pp. 2127–2136 (2018)

9. Abbasi-Sureshjani, S., et al.: Molecular subtype prediction for breast cancer using H&E specialized backbone. In: MICCAI Workshop on Computational Pathology, pp. 1–9 (2021)

10. Thomas, D.A., et al.: Burkitt lymphoma and atypical Burkitt or Burkitt-like lymphoma: should these be treated as different diseases? Curr. Hematol. Malig. Rep. **6**(1), 58–66 (2011)

11. Alaggio, R., Amador, C., Anagnostopoulos, I., et al.: The 5th edition of the world health organization classification of haematolymphoid tumours: lymphoid neoplasms. Leukemia. **36**(7), 1720–1748 (2022)

12. Chamanzar, A., Nie, Y.: Weakly supervised multi-task learning for cell detection and segmentation. In: 2020 IEEE 17th International Symposium on Biomedical Imaging (ISBI), 513–516 (2020)

13. Young, I.T., Verbeek, P.W., Mayall, B.H.: Characterization of chromatin distribution in cell nuclei. Cytometry **7**(5), 467–474 (1986)

14. Wu, P.H., et al.: Single-cell morphology encodes metastatic potential. Sci. Adv. **6**(4), eaaw6938 (2020)

15. Csardi, G., Nepusz, T.: The igraph software package for complex network research. InterJournal. Complex. Syst. **1695**(5), 1–9 (2006)

16. Van der Walt, S., Sch"onberger, Johannes L, Nunez-Iglesias, J. et al.: scikit-image: image processing in Python. *PeerJ*, **2**, e453 (2014)

17. Van Griethuysen, J.J.M., Fedorov, A., et al.: Computational Radiomics System to Decode the Radiographic Phenotype. Can. Res. **77**, 21 (2017)

Multimodal Learning for Improving Performance and Explainability of Chest X-Ray Classification

Sara Ketabi[1,2], Pranav Agnihotri[3], Hamed Zakeri[1,2], Khashayar Namdar[1,4,7], and Farzad Khalvati[1,2,4,5,6,7]($\boxtimes$)

[1] The Hospital for Sick Children, Toronto, ON, Canada
[2] Department of Mechanical and Industrial Engineering, University of Toronto, Toronto, ON, Canada
farzad.khalvati@utoronto.ca
[3] Engineering Science, University of Toronto, Toronto, ON, Canada
[4] Institute of Medical Science, University of Toronto, Toronto, ON, Canada
[5] Department of Medical Imaging, University of Toronto, Toronto, ON, Canada
[6] Department of Computer Science, University of Toronto, Toronto, ON, Canada
[7] Vector Institute, Toronto, ON, Canada

Abstract. Convolutional Neural Networks (CNNs) applied to medical imaging for disease diagnosis have not yet been widely adopted by radiologists due to the black-box nature of these models, undermining their explainability. A few of the approaches for "opening" the black box include the use of heatmaps to assist with visual interpretation, but these heatmaps remain crude. While it has been shown that utilizing radiologists' attention-related data improves the quality of models' attention maps, its quantitative effect on explainability remains unexplored. Moreover, the impact of combining radiology reports as a separate data modality with medical images on model explainability and performance has not been fully explored. In this work, we use an Eye-Gaze dataset along with radiology reports to exhaustively study the impact of adding radiology reports and Eye-Gaze data to X-ray images on the performance and explainability of CNN-based classification models. Additionally, we introduce an explainability metric to quantitatively evaluate the alignment of model attention with radiologist-specified regions of interest (ROIs). We demonstrate that combining the radiology reports with chest X-ray images improves the CNN's performance significantly (12.85%) in detecting Pneumonia and Congestive Heart Failure. In addition, using Eye-Gaze data as a secondary ground truth alongside the class labels enables the generation of attention maps, as means for model explainability, that have a better attention overlap with the corresponding ROIs compared to the popular model-agnostic GradCAM method. Additionally, the explainability of attention heatmaps generated by Eye-Gaze data as a secondary ground truth improves by approximately 11% when more context via other data modalities, such as radiology reports, is added to the X-ray images. In contrast, the addition of radiology reports has negligible effect on the heatmaps created by GradCAM.

M. E. Celebi et al. (Eds.): MICCAI 2023 Workshops, LNCS 14393, pp. 107–116, 2023.
https://doi.org/10.1007/978-3-031-47401-9_11

Keywords: Explainability · Radiology Report · Chest X-ray · Eye Tracking · Deep Learning

1 Introduction

The rapid success of deep learning (DL) has resulted in its applications in various domains, including medical imaging and radiology. Multiple examples of DL methods have shown great promise in medical imaging, even matching the performance of human practitioners in tasks such as classifying skin lesions, identifying diabetic retinopathy, and detecting hip fractures from medical images [1,12,13]. However, the adoption of DL methods has been slow because of the inability of healthcare professionals to understand the features used in the predictions of these "black-box" models, i.e., lack of explainability [5,11,14]. Moreover, there is a gap in the literature on quantifying performance and explainability gains from adding other data modalities, such as radiologists' Eye-Gaze maps and radiology reports in DL-based disease diagnosis.

The recently created Eye-Gaze dataset [3] provides comprehensive information on a radiologist's Eye-Gaze while performing the diagnosis task, referred to as static Eye-Gaze heatmaps, alongside chest X-ray images and radiology reports. Additionally, this dataset contrasts existing ones in that it provides ground truth for three classification labels, namely Normal, Congestive Heart Failure (CHF), and Pneumonia, which is independent of radiology reports and comes from a group of interdisciplinary clinicians [3]. The Eye-Gaze dataset creators present a baseline framework for multi-class chest X-ray classification using a U-Net architecture [8] trained solely on chest X-ray images [3]. In addition to the baseline model, they propose a method that treats the static heatmaps as a secondary ground truth along with the class labels within a multi-loss architecture [3]. Across the baseline and static heatmap models discussed above, the authors reported an area under the receiver operating characteristic curve (AUC) of 0.87 for both experiments [3]. However, the lack of quantitative evaluation of the generated attention maps is a significant gap in their work. Moreover, while the paper provides a framework for utilizing the Eye-Gaze information, it does not investigate the impact of adding other data modalities, such as the radiology report text, as an input on the performance or explainability of the Convolutional Neural Network (CNN). Finally, as the reported classification performance in [3] was not obtained through cross-validation, a more rigorous set of experiments is required by training the models on different folds of the dataset.

There are other studies that have used similar data modalities to improve model performance and interpretation. Zhu et al. proposed a method called gaze-guided class activation mapping (GG-CAM) [15] that combines human attention with the DL model attention for image classification using the Eye-Gaze dataset. GG-CAM [15] utilizes Eye-Gaze attention maps in the supervised training of class activation mapping (CAM) [4] attention within CNN architectures. However, a significant gap in this work is the lack of investigation into the impact of utilizing all available data modalities as inputs on the model's functionality.

In this paper, we incorporate all available data sources (X-ray images, radiology reports, and Eye-Gaze static heatmap) into a multimodal DL architecture for multi-class classification of Normal, CHF, and Pneumonia. We first uncover how adding free-text radiology reports, even only the indication section, to X-ray images significantly improves multi-class classification performance. Second, we demonstrate how Eye-Gaze information used in a DL architecture as a second ground truth can produce attention heatmaps that outperform the commonly used Explainable Artificial Intelligence Method (XAI) method, namely Gradient-weighted Class Activation Mapping (GradCAM) [7]. We also propose a metric for the quantitative assessment of the explainability of a given heatmap. Finally, we highlight that the quality and accuracy of attention maps generated by utilizing Eye-Gaze data improves by incorporating radiology reports. In contrast, the attention maps derived by GradCAM method are, at best, indifferent to any added context to the initial X-ray images.

2   Method

The MIMIC-CXR database provides a large repository of radiology images and reports [2]. As a subset of this database, the Eye-Gaze dataset [3] offers the following: 1,083 chest X-ray images, the accompanying radiology reports in a free-text format, and the recorded Eye-Gaze information. The dataset also provides ground truth classification labels spanning three classes: Normal (337 data points), CHF (343 data points), and Pneumonia (337 data points). During the initial data processing phase, we excluded 66 chest X-ray images due to incomplete Eye-Gaze information, leading to 1,017 data points being used in this study (Dataset 1). All images were scaled by their maximum values, resized to 224 × 224 pixels using Bilinear interpolation, and normalized by ImageNet mean and standard deviation. The radiology reports consist of several sections: the Exam Indication section, the Findings section, and the Impressions section. The Findings and Impressions sections of a radiology report entail the radiologist's diagnosis. In contrast, the Exam Indication section is a short medical history of patient's symptoms and the reason for the radiology exam.

This study has two primary objectives. First, it aims to measure the impact of different data modalities, specifically radiology reports, on classification performance, which was not investigated by the Eye-Gaze dataset creators in developing their classification model [3] or similar works such as [15]. The second goal is to improve the explainability of the DL classification models by generating attention maps using the static Eye-Gaze data as a second ground truth along with the multi-class classification loss, and the radiology reports as an additional input to the model. We also propose a metric for the quantitative assessment of the model explainability. The attention maps are then compared, both qualitatively and quantitatively, to those created using GradCAM [7], a frequently used XAI method, when applied to the models with only the classification loss.

2.1 Classification Performance Experiments

To improve the classification performance of the baseline framework [3], we first train our model on the images and the indication section of the reports. Then, to evaluate whether the radiologist's findings can help the framework, we use the entire report together with the images in a separate experiment. The dataset was divided into training, validation, and test sets using 5-fold cross-validation, with all three sets rotating through the cross-validation iterations. To maintain the integrity of unique patient IDs across training, validation, and test sets, the cross-validation was based on patient IDs. The primary evaluation metric for this study is the mean AUC and per-class AUC, which have been calculated based on the One-vs-Rest approach. The following paragraphs will outline the methodologies employed for each of the baseline and report-integrated frameworks.

Chest X-Ray (Baseline): The architecture used for performing classification with only the chest X-ray image as input is similar to the one visualized in Fig. 1, with the sole difference that the branch combining the sentence embedding is inactive. This model aligns with the baseline model proposed by the authors of the Eye-Gaze dataset [3]. In this framework, EfficientNet-b0 [16], a CNN architecture pretrained on ImageNet, was used as the image encoder. Our baseline classification framework refers to the model trained on only the X-ray images using this encoder. This model contains a sequence of convolutional layers along with batch normalization and average adaptive pooling. Adam optimizer and Cross-entropy loss were used for our experiments. Also, the values of learning rate and batch size were set to 0.006 and 32, respectively. The network was trained for 20 epochs, and Triangular scheduler [17] was used to adjust the learning rate during the training.

Radiology Report Text and Chest X-Ray: The DL model architecture, shown in Fig. 1, combines radiology report text embedding with the chest X-ray image. Sentence embeddings are created using word embeddings of size 150, which were trained with a Word2Vec Skip-gram scheme [10] on the extracted MIMIC CXR reports, which are not included in the Eye-Gaze dataset. Each input text word is converted to its corresponding word vector, and an average embedding is calculated by taking the mean of the word vectors for all vocabulary words in the model. Out-of-vocabulary words are given the value of the average embedding. The image and sentence embeddings are combined before the final classification layer. This classification model is fed with three input data combinations: Chest X-ray (baseline); Chest X-ray and Exam Indication text; and Chest X-ray and Full Report text.

2.2 Explainability Experiments

To investigate the explainability of our models, we use the attention maps generated by the models to highlight areas in the input chest X-ray image relevant to the

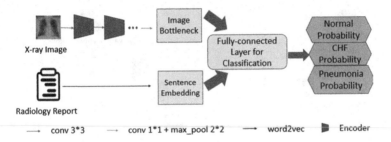

Fig. 1. Classification model architecture: chest X-ray and sentence embedding inputs

final diagnosis. These attention maps are generated in two ways: first, by incorporating the static Eye-Gaze data as a secondary ground truth that enables the U-net decoder to generate attention maps, and second, by applying the GradCAM method to the models in which only the classification loss is used [7].

To generate attention maps using the U-net decoder, we applied a model with the cross-entropy loss of the generated static heatmap compared to the actual Eye-Gaze heatmaps, visualized in Fig. 2 (considered as the baseline for our experiments, similar to [3]) and Fig. 3, depending on whether radiology reports are part of the model's input. In this framework, a multi-task learning approach is conducted to perform Eye-Gaze heatmap generation along with X-ray classification. For integrating radiology reports, we employed Long Short-Term Memory (LSTM) [9], with radiology report word-embedding vectors as the input and image representations as the hidden state. To generate attention maps with GradCAM, this method is applied to the second last layer of the image encoder in Fig. 2 and Fig. 3, with the sole difference that the static heatmap loss branch is inactive and only the classification loss is included. The attention maps generated by these two approaches were compared, quantitatively and qualitatively, for three input data combinations: Chest X-ray (baseline); Chest X-ray and Exam Indication text; and Chest X-ray and Full Report text.

To assess the quality of the generated attention maps by these two methods, the MIMIC-CXR Annotations dataset was used [6]. It consists of 350 chest X-rays diagnosed with Pneumonia and the radiologist-generated bounding boxes (used as the explainability ground truth) highlighting areas of interest (Dataset 2). A radiology report also accompanies each image. The quality of the generated attention map is calculated by measuring the intensity of the attention map within the bounding box(es) if being greater than 100, normalized by the intensity of attention over the rest of the image. The cut-off value of 100 for pixel intensities (ranging 0–255), was set based on the qualitative visual assessment of the attention maps to make our metric more rigorous. This ensures a bare-minimum level of intensity for pixels within bounding boxes of the attention maps that contribute to the metric. As a result, our explainability metric can achieve more robust results compared to others, such as the one proposed in [15].

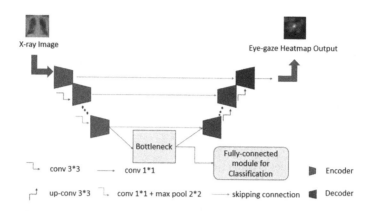

Fig. 2. DL Architecture with static heatmap ground truth and chest X-ray input (baseline)

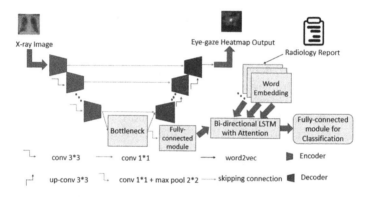

Fig. 3. DL (CNN-RNN) Architecture with static heatmap ground truth as well as chest X-ray plus radiology text (indication section and full report) input

3 Results

In this section, we present the results of the experiments discussed in Sect. 2. First, classification performance based on the average overall AUC and per-class AUC is presented. The results are stated based on 5-fold cross-validation. To prevent the potential bias of spreading a patient ID into different folds, we held the same patient IDs across the folds for all different experiments. Then, we examine the explainability of our DL models via the methods discussed above by showing the mean values of the attention overlap between the generated attention maps and ground-truth bounding boxes.

3.1 Classification Performance Results

The 5-fold cross-validation results for all experiments over Dataset 1 can be found in Table 1. When the indication part of the radiology reports is added to the X-ray images as input, a 6.6% AUC increase (not statistically significant) is observed in model classification performance (0.913 vs. 0.856). The added context from the indication part of the report strengthens the classifications of all three classes, specifically that of the Pneumonia class (0.861 vs. 0.789). Moreover, the added text component only depends on exam indication, which is agnostic to possible radiologist errors and biases reflected in the full report. Nevertheless, adding the full reports to X-rays further improves the average AUC significantly (0.966, p-value = 0.011). The median AUC values further demonstrate the effectiveness of our multimodal approach; as by integrating only the indication section of the report, we achieve superior median AUC compared to that reported in [15] (0.924 vs 0.801).

Table 1. Classification AUC for all experiments

Experiment	Normal AUC	CHF AUC	Pneumonia AUC	Average AUC	Median AUC
X-ray	0.875 (±0.035)	0.904 (±0.053)	0.789 (±0.043)	**0.856** (±0.039)	0.860
X-ray and Report Indication	0.918 (±0.031)	0.962 (±0.015)	0.861 (±0.054)	**0.913** (±0.03)	0.924
X-ray and Full Report	0.987 (±0.007)	0.956 (±0.022)	0.954 (±0.019)	**0.966** (±0.013)	0.959

3.2 Explainability Results

Table 2 shows quantitative explainability analysis based on the mean attention overlap on Dataset 2, and Fig. 4 presents a qualitative analysis of the attention maps generated for a Pneumonia case using the two aforementioned approaches (i.e., Eye-Gaze-based U-net decoder and GradCAM). Also, the bounding box on the image can be an indicator of the radiologist's attention. The quantitative results indicate that incorporating Eye-Gaze information as a secondary ground truth provides higher explainability (31.44% on average) for all three input combinations compared to the GradCAM method applied to the models with only the classification loss. This finding demonstrates that incorporating Eye-Gaze data into the baseline framework improves the model's attention. It is worth mentioning that the enhanced heatmaps produced by the architectures depicted in Fig. 2 and Fig. 3 are accompanied by a slight reduction in the model's classification performance, resulting in an Average AUC decrease of ~1%. This decrease can be attributed to the trade-off between performance and explainability of the classification models. Finding the optimal point where the model can achieve an acceptable level of both performance and explainability should be examined.

The explainability provided via incorporating Eye-Gaze information within the model architecture improves by approximately 10.93% when more context, in this case, radiology reports, is added to the initial input, the X-ray images. In contrast,

Table 2. Attention overlap between the generated attention maps and ground-truth bounding boxes

Input	Mean Attention Overlap: Static Eye-Gaze as Second Ground Truth	Mean Attention Overlap: GradCam
Chest X-ray (Fig. 2)	10.06%	8.30%
Chest X-ray and Exam Indication (Fig. 3)	11.16%	8.29%
Chest X-ray and Full Report (Fig. 3)	11.3%	8.16%

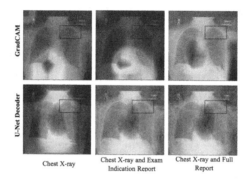

Fig. 4. Attention overlap visualization of our experiments for a Pneumonia case using GradCAM and U-Net decoder (Red areas indicate higher attention.) (Color figure online)

the explainability provided by GradCAM does not improve with the extra context provided by the radiology reports. The indifference of the GradCAM method to varying levels of context is peculiar and should be investigated further to see if it extends to other XAI methods.

4 Conclusion

In this paper, we investigated the impact of different data modalities, specifically radiology reports and radiologists' Eye-Gaze information, on chest X-ray classification. We showed that the information in the radiology reports is highly predictive of the prediction task. This was evident even from the indication part of the radiology report, which does not contain the radiologist's diagnosis.

We also showed Eye-Gaze information could be used as a second ground truth within the DL architecture to explain the model's prediction by generating an attention map, which outperforms attention maps generated by GradCAM. We introduced a quantitative metric to highlight that the attention maps produced via incorporating the Eye-Gaze information improve by an additional level of context, such as a radiology report, and GradCAM is, at best, indifferent to other modalities of additional information. Also, the impact of adding the full report on the mean attention overlap values, both for GradCAM and the decoder outputs, is marginal, meaning that the extra interpretations of radiologists are not notably helpful for improving the model's attention compared to the information available in the indication part of the report. Future work includes comparing the attention overlap of the decoder outputs with other XAI methods, e.g., Layer-wise Relevance Propagation [18], to further validate their quality.

Acknowledgements. This work was supported by VinBrain and Natural Sciences and Engineering Research Council of Canada (NSERC).

References

1. Esteva, A., et al.: Dermatologist-level classification of skin cancer with deep neural networks. Nature **542**(7639), 115–118 (2017)
2. Johnson, A.E.W., et al.: MIMIC-CXR-JPG, a large publicly available database of labeled chest radiographs. arXiv (2019)
3. Karargyris, A., et al.: Creation and validation of a chest X-ray dataset with eye-tracking and report dictation for AI development. Sci. Data **8**(1), 92 (2021)
4. Zhou, B., Khosla, A., Lapedriza, A., Oliva, A., Torralba, A.: Learning deep features for discriminative localization. In: IEEE Conference on Computer Vision and Pattern Recognition (CVPR), vol. 2016, pp. 2921–2929 (2016)
5. Watson, D.S., et al.: Clinical applications of machine learning algorithms: beyond the black box. BMJ **364**, l886 (2019)
6. Tam, L.K., Wang, X., Turkbey, E., Lu, K., Wen, Y., Xu, D.: Weakly supervised one-stage vision and language disease detection using large scale pneumonia and pneumothorax studies. arXiv (2020)
7. Selvaraju, R.R., Cogswell, M., Das, A., Vedantam, R., Parikh, D., Batra, D.: Grad-CAM: visual explanations from deep networks via gradient-based localization. In: IEEE International Conference on Computer Vision (ICCV), vol. 2017, pp. 618–626 (2017)
8. Ronneberger, O., Fischer, P., Brox, T.: U-Net: convolutional networks for biomedical image segmentation. In: Navab, N., Hornegger, J., Wells, W.M., Frangi, A.F. (eds.) MICCAI 2015. LNCS, vol. 9351, pp. 234–241. Springer, Cham (2015). https://doi.org/10.1007/978-3-319-24574-4_28
9. Hochreiter, S., Schmidhuber, J.: Long short-term memory. Neural Comput. **9**, 1735–1780 (1997)
10. Mikolov, T., Sutskever, I., Chen, K., Corrado, G.S., Dean, J.: Distributed representations of words and phrases and their compositionality. In: Advances in Neural Information Processing Systems, vol. 26 (2013)
11. Vayena, E., Blasimme, A., Cohen, I.: Machine learning in medicine: addressing ethical challenges. PLoS Med. **15**, e1002689 (2018)
12. Gulshan, V., et al.: Development and validation of a deep learning algorithm for detection of diabetic retinopathy in retinal fundus photographs. JAMA **316**, 11 (2016)

13. Gale, W., Oakden-Rayner, L., Carneiro, G., Bradley, A., Palmer, L.: Detecting hip fractures with radiologist-level performance using deep neural networks, November 2017

14. Lipton, Z.: The Mythos of model interpretability. In: Machine Learning 'The Concept of Interpretability is Both Important and Slippery', Queue, vol. 16, May 2018

15. Zhu, H., Salcudean, S.E., Rohling, R.: Gaze-guided class activation mapping: leveraging human attention for network attention in chest X-rays classification. arXiv arXiv:2202.07107 (2022)

16. Tan, M., Le, Q.V.: EfficientNet: rethinking model scaling for convolutional neural networks. arXiv arXiv:1905.11946 (2019)

17. Smith, L.N.: Cyclical learning rates for training neural networks. In: 2017 IEEE Winter Conference on Applications of Computer Vision (WACV), pp. 464–472. IEEE (2017)

18. Bach, S., Binder, A., Montavon, G., Klauschen, F., Müller, K.-R., Samek, W.: On pixel-wise explanations for non-linear classifier decisions by layer-wise relevance propagation. PLoS ONE **10**(7), e0130140 (2015)

Proceedings of the First International Workshop on Foundation Models for Medical Artificial General Intelligence (MedAGI 2023)

Cross-Task Attention Network: Improving Multi-task Learning for Medical Imaging Applications

Sangwook Kim[1] , Thomas G. Purdie[1,2,4,8] ,
and Chris McIntosh[1,2,3,5,6,7(✉)]

[1] Department of Medical Biophysics, University of Toronto, Toronto, Canada
{sangwook.kim,tom.purdie,chris.mcintosh}@rmp.uhn.ca
[2] Princess Margaret Cancer Centre, University Health Network, Toronto, Canada
[3] Toronto General Research Institute, University Health Network, Toronto, Canada
[4] Princess Margaret Research Institute, University Health Network, Toronto, Canada
[5] Peter Munk Cardiac Centre, University Health Network, Toronto, Canada
[6] Department of Medical Imaging, University of Toronto, Toronto, Canada
[7] Vector Institute, Toronto, Canada
[8] Department of Radiation Oncology, University of Toronto, Toronto, Canada

Abstract. Multi-task learning (MTL) is a powerful approach in deep learning that leverages the information from multiple tasks during training to improve model performance. In medical imaging, MTL has shown great potential to solve various tasks. However, existing MTL architectures in medical imaging are limited in sharing information across tasks, reducing the potential performance improvements of MTL. In this study, we introduce a novel attention-based MTL framework to better leverage inter-task interactions for various tasks from pixel-level to image-level predictions. Specifically, we propose a Cross-Task Attention Network (CTAN) which utilizes cross-task attention mechanisms to incorporate information by interacting across tasks. We validated CTAN on four medical imaging datasets that span different domains and tasks including: radiation treatment planning prediction using planning CT images of two different target cancers (Prostate, OpenKBP); pigmented skin lesion segmentation and diagnosis using dermatoscopic images (HAM10000); and COVID-19 diagnosis and severity prediction using chest CT scans (STOIC). Our study demonstrates the effectiveness of CTAN in improving the accuracy of medical imaging tasks. Compared to standard single-task learning (STL), CTAN demonstrated a 4.67% improvement in performance and outperformed both widely used MTL baselines: hard parameter sharing (HPS) with an average performance improvement of 3.22%; and multi-task attention network (MTAN) with a relative decrease of 5.38%. These findings highlight the significance of our proposed MTL framework in solving medical imaging tasks and its potential to improve their accuracy across domains.

Supplementary Information The online version contains supplementary material available at https://doi.org/10.1007/978-3-031-47401-9_12.

Keywords: Multi-Task Learning · Cross Attention · Automated Radiotherapy

1   Introduction

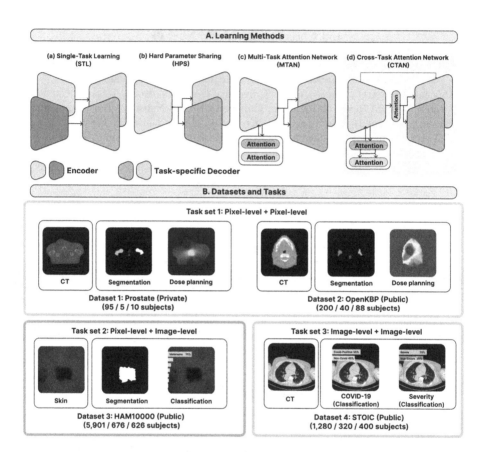

Fig. 1. (Top) Cross-task attention network (CTAN) and other MTL model architectures: hard parameter sharing (HPS) [1] and multi-task learning network (MTAN) [16]. Similar to the concept of one-to-many mappings from HPS and MTAN, CTAN has one shared encoder linked with decoders for each task. MTAN uses encoder features using attention for respective tasks. However, CTAN uses cross-attention in encoder and bottleneck layers to transfer task-specific features to task-specific decoders for better task interaction. (Bottom) Summary of four medical imaging datasets with three different task sets used in this study. **The number of samples of each train, validation, test splits are shown below each dataset.** Test datasets without complete segmentation labels and clinical information were excluded from the original datasets in OpenKBP and HAM10000, respectively.

Multi-task learning (MTL) [5] algorithms train deep learning models for two or more tasks simultaneously using shared parameters between models to encourage beneficial cooperation. MTL provides additional information not by explicitly adding more datasets for model training but by implicitly extracting training signals from multiple related tasks from the existing dataset. The various tasks are thought to regularize shared components of the network, leading to improved model performance and generalization. For example, following [2], it is natural to assume that learning features required to delineate a skin lesion from the background may be relevant in comparing the lesion to its surrounding areas to inform the diagnosis.

Previous studies have demonstrated that learning two relevant tasks can improve model performance using MTL in medical imaging [4,6–8,26,27]. Sainz et al., show the application and improvement of the model performance using MTL in breast cancer screening by training classification and detection of abnormal mammography findings [6]. Chen et al., utilize MTL to improve atrial segmentation and classification using MRI [7]. Weninger et al., propose an MTL framework to improve brain tumour segmentation by jointly training detection of enhancing tumour and image reconstruction using brain MRI [26].

These studies demonstrate the applicability of MTL to improve performance for tasks in medical imaging. However, even though these studies have shown enhanced performance using MTL, most MTL architectures are based on hard-parameter sharing (HPS) [1], which includes a single shared encoder with task-specific decoders in a one-to-many fashion, maximizing encoder regularization between tasks but limiting all tasks to an identical feature set as opposed to some common features.

Introduced by Liu et al., multi-task attention network (MTAN) [16] also employs a one-to-many mapping but adds task-specific independent attention mechanisms that, while they can change the features of the embedding per task, they are not themselves able to share any information. With the introduction of MTAN, there have been studies using attention in MTL for automating binding between task features within the network architectures [17,28]. However, most existing MTL studies using non-medical images focus on scenarios where all tasks are at the pixel-level. This is often impractical in the medical imaging domain, since acquiring pixel-level labels in medical images is impractical and labour-intensive. Thus, we focus on solving multi-task learning in hybrid scenarios including both pixel and image-level tasks by utilizing cross-task attention in MTL using medical imaging datasets.

We hypothesize that by leveraging the shared feature abilities of HPS with the flexibility of MTAN through a novel cross-task attention framework that shares task information across the attention mechanisms, we can better utilize inter-task interaction to improve overall performance using MTL. Additionally, cross-attention of bottleneck features for each task was also employed to provide cross-task dependent information to decoders for each task. We validated our approach using three distinct pairs of tasks from four medical imaging datasets. CTAN shows broad applicability with mixes of tasks at the both the pixel and image-level.

Contributions. We propose a novel Cross-Task Attention Network (CTAN), an MTL framework that leverages cross-task attention modules in the encoder and bottleneck layer to capture inter-task interaction across tasks (see Fig. 2). Our results demonstrate that CTAN is effective in learning three types of vision tasks, including two pixel-level prediction tasks and one image-level task from various domains. As shown in Fig. 1, we experimented with three different task pairs from four datasets. In addition, we showed the performance improvement of CTAN compared to single-task learning (STL), and two widely used MTL baseline architectures, HPS and MTAN.

2   Methods and Materials

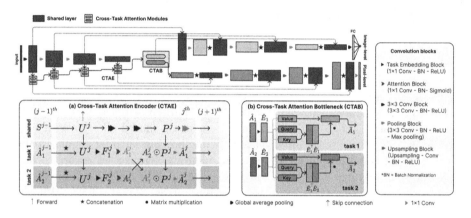

Fig. 2. Overview of architecture of cross-task attention network (CTAN), including the encoder and two decoders for image-level and pixel-level tasks. Convolution blocks are shown on the right, along with the two cross-task attention modules: (a) Cross-task attention encoder (CTAE), and (b) Cross-task attention bottleneck (CTAB).

2.1   Cross-Task Attention Network (CTAN)

CTAN consists of two cross-task attention modules, the cross-task attention encoder (CTAE), and the cross-task attention bottleneck (CTAB) (see Fig. 2). CTAE is employed within the encoder layers by calculating the attentive mask, and uses two pieces of information targeted for each task. CTAE enables the encoder to extract task-specific information in the encoder. It encodes and decodes the input features to highlight and extract significant features. The attention module in CTAE resembles the attention module in [16], wherein for each task Liu et al. calculate attention maps using one attention block per task and multiply with the feature maps during a forward pass with data from that task. However, in CTAE, attention maps are instead multiplied in a cross-direction way, as shown in Fig. 2-a. This helps the model to integrate the shared features by multiplying the cross-task attentive maps with features from the shared block, which enables an inter-task interaction while training. We denote U^j and P^j as features from j^{th} layer of the shared encoder, and t as task index. Note that P^j refers to the output of two convolution blocks using U^j as the input. S^{j-1} denotes the input of jth layer in the shared encoder, which is the output of the shared block in $j - 1^{th}$ layer for $j > 1$. Whereas, when $j = 1$, the input image embedding from the 3×3 Conv block is used (see Fig. 2). The task-specific embedded features, F_t^j, result from the concatenation of U^j and $\hat{A}_t^{j-1}$ for $j > 1$, while U^j for $j = 0$, followed by the task embedding block in Fig. 2. F_t^j is then fed into the task-specific attention block to create attention mask A_t^j. The output of CTAE $\hat{A}_t^j$ is defined as:

$$\hat{A}_t^j = Pool(A_{t'}^j \odot P^j), \ t \in \{1, 2\}, \tag{1}$$

where $Pool$ refers to the pooling block (see Fig. 2), $\odot$ refers to the element-wise multiplication, and t' refers to the task index of the other task trained together. $\hat{A}_t^j$ then serves as the input attention mask for the attention block in the next layer, propagating attention across the decoder ($\hat{A}_t^{j-1}$ is set to all zero for the first layer).

We propose CTAB as shown in Fig. 2-b, in which we calculate and multiply cross-task attention of two task-embedded features to task-specific bottleneck representation. We calculate the cross-task attention mask using a *query* and a *key* and apply the attention mask to a *value*. Herein, *value* and *key* are the same task-embedded features, and *query* is the embedding of the other task. Thus, the output of CTAB $\bar{A}_t$ is defined as:

$$\bar{A}_t = \hat{E}_t \cdot (\hat{E}_{t'}^\top \cdot \hat{E}_t), \ t \in \{1, 2\}, \tag{2}$$

where $\top$ refers to transpose of a matrix, $\cdot$ refers to matrix multiplication, and $\hat{E}_t$ denotes the task-specific embedded features for task t. The output of CTAB, $\bar{A}_t$, is forwarded to task-specific decoders.

Encoder and Decoder. We utilize a ResNet-50 [12] pre-trained with ImageNet [9] as the encoder backbone, with identical architecture across all experiments. However, we implement different decoders for image-level and pixel-level tasks. For pixel-level tasks such as segmentation and dose prediction, we incorporate skip connections [23] between the encoders and decoders, with three up-sampling blocks using bilinear interpolation (as depicted in Fig. 2), followed by a 1×1 convolution layer with output channels equal to the number of segmentation labels, and a single channel for dose prediction. For image-level tasks, we use decoders with skip connections and four down-sampling layers, with a global average pooling layer [11] and a fully-connected layer at the end. Notably, we introduce skip connections in the classifier to balance model training and address asymmetric decoder issues that arise when training MTL to solve both image-level and pixel-level tasks together. Finally, we use a fully-connected layer with a sigmoid activation function for binary classification (STOIC) and a softmax function for multi-class classification (HAM10000) as the final output layer.

2.2 Training Details

We use Adam [14] optimizer with the learning rate of 10^{-4} and the weight decay of 10^{-5}. We use task-specific losses (see Table 1). Dynamic Weight Averaging [16] was utilized to stabilize the combined training losses of all tasks. Batch size of 32 was used for the Prostate dataset, and 8 for the rest. We conducted experiments using PyTorch (ver 1.9.0) [20], with an NVIDIA A100 GPU with 40 GB memory.

Table 1. Summary of loss functions for each task. We use combo loss [18], with the 0.3 and 0.7 for the loss weight of dice loss and cross-entropy loss, respectively.

Task	Loss function	Dataset
Segmentation	Combo Loss [18] (Weighted combination of Dice Loss and Cross-entropy Loss)	Prostate, OpenKBP, HAM10000
Dose prediction	Mean absolute error (MAE) Loss [3]	Prostate, OpenKBP
Classification	Cross-entropy Loss	HAM10000, STOIC

2.3 Evaluation

We used task-specific metrics to evaluate the model performance for each task: dice similarity coefficient for segmentation (%); mean absolute error (Gy) between ground truth and predicted dose distribution maps for dose prediction; accuracy (%) for classification of HAM10000; and the area under the receiver operating characteristic curve (%) for classification of STOIC. Following [15], we define the relative performance of MTL models compared to STL:

$$\Delta_{task}(\%) = 100 * \frac{(-1)^{l_i}(M_{b,i} - M_{m,i})}{M_{b,i}}, \ l \in \{0, 1\}, \tag{3}$$

where i denotes the index of the task, m and b refer to the target MTL model and the baseline STL, respectively. M refers to the task performance metric. l denotes the metric-specific flag, where 1 if the metric is higher the better, and vice versa. We can then calculate the average of the relative difference of all task-specific metrics for each experiment. Positive value of relative performance represents the performance of MTL is better than that of STL.

2.4 Datasets

We validated our approach using four medical imaging datasets with three different task sets (see Fig. 1-B). The first task set consists of two pixel-level tasks: dose prediction and segmentation of organs at risk (OAR) and clinical target volume (CTV) for prostate (Prostate) and head and neck cancer treatment (OpenKBP) (https://www.aapm.org/GrandChallenge/OpenKBP, [3]). Segmentation labels for the Prostate dataset are rectum, bladder, left and right femur, while brain stem, spinal cord, left and right parotid are used in OpenKBP. Patients For the second task set, which contains one image-level and one pixel-level tasks, dermatoscopic images of pigmented skin lesion datasets (HAM10000) (https://doi.org/10.7910/DVN/DBW86T, [24]) are used to segment and diagnose skin lesions. The last set has two image-level tasks: classification of COVID-19 and disease severity using chest CT scans (STOIC) (https://stoic2021.grand-challenge.org, [22]).

3 Experiments and Results

In Table 2, the results showed that CTAN outperformed STL with an average relative difference of 4.67%. For the Prostate and OpenKBP datasets, which have two different pixel-level tasks, CTAN showed an improvement of 2.18% and 1.99%, respectively, over STL. In both datasets, the performance increase for dose prediction task was larger than that of segmentation task. Notably, CTAN improved the performance of dose prediction when the task is trained with segmentation of organs at risk and target volumes, rather than improving the performance of segmentation. For HAM10000, CTAN showed an overall performance improvement with a significant increase in diagnosing skin lesions. However, the performance of segmenting pigmented lesions marginally improved compared to the classification task. For STOIC, CTAN resulted in an average relative difference of 4.67% for both image-level tasks, with a significant increase in diagnosing severe cases but a decrease in diagnosing COVID-19.

As shown in Table 2, CTAN outperformed both HPS and MTAN with an average relative improvement of 3.22% and relative decrease of 5.38%, compared to STL, respectively. Unlike other MTL baselines, CTAN showed performance improvement regardless of task groups combined with different task-levels. However, there were cases where CTAN did not outperform other baselines at the single task level. For instance, for the Prostate datasets' segmentation task, HPS outperformed CTAN with a relative difference of 1.74% while CTAN showed only a 0.54% increase. Nevertheless, overall performance gain using CTAN was higher across datasets and tasks, indicating that the cross-task attention mechanisms in CTAN were effective in learning multiple tasks.

4 Discussion

Our findings suggest that CTAN can improve the MTL performance across three distinct tasks from four distinct medical imaging datasets by 4.67% on average. However, the specific performance improvements on each dataset and task can vary. Compared to other tasks, CTAN only marginally improve performance in segmentation task. This might be due to the faster convergence of segmentation tasks in comparison to others, which may cause them to act more as regularizers

Table 2. Results of task-specific metrics (M_{task}) and their relative difference to STL (Δ_{task}) of STL, HPS, MTAN, and CTAN on four datasets. Higher values are the better for all metrics, except for M_{task2} in the Prostate and OpenKBP datasets. Best and second-best results are bolded and underlined, respectively. Average values are only calculated for relative performance difference of MTL methods.

Dataset	Method	M_{task1}	Δ_{task1} ↑	M_{task2}	Δ_{task2} ↑	Δ_{mean} ↑	Rank
Prostate	STL	81.96		0.93			3
	HPS	**83.28**	**1.74%**	<u>0.91</u>	1.29%	1.51%	2
	MTAN	75.47	−7.92%	0.99	−7.29%	−7.60%	4
	CTAN	<u>82.40</u>	<u>0.54%</u>	**0.89**	**3.82%**	**2.18%**	1
OpenKBP [3]	STL	<u>71.29</u>		<u>0.53</u>			2
	HPS	70.87	−0.52%	<u>0.53</u>	0.31%	−0.10%	3
	MTAN	66.09	−7.30%	0.56	−5.29%	−6.29%	4
	CTAN	**71.59**	**0.42%**	**0.51**	**3.56%**	**1.99%**	1
HAM10000 [24]	STL	<u>92.83</u>		49.24			3
	HPS	92.21	−0.68%	<u>55.49</u>	12.69%	6.01%	2
	MTAN	92.15	−0.73%	47.08	−4.37%	−2.55%	4
	CTAN	**92.91**	**0.09%**	**57.85**	**17.49%**	**8.79%**	1
STOIC [22]	STL	**71.88**		55.83			3
	HPS	63.84	−11.18%	**68.17**	**22.09%**	<u>5.45%</u>	2
	MTAN	57.55	−19.93%	61.30	9.79%	−5.07%	4
	CTAN	<u>68.73</u>	−4.38%	<u>64.66</u>	<u>15.81%</u>	**5.72%**	1
Average	STL			-			3
	HPS	-	−2.66%	-	<u>9.09%</u>	<u>3.22%</u>	2
	MTAN	-	−8.97%	-	−1.79%	−5.38%	4
	CTAN	-	**−0.83%**	-	**10.17%**	**4.67%**	1

with pixel-level prior knowledge providing local contextual information for other tasks [21]. In this regard, results show that CTAN is more effective in utilizing segmentation tasks for learning high-level semantic cues compared to other MTL baselines. In particular, CTAN can implicitly learn to avoid dose exposure to OARs and maximize dose to the CTV by training two clinically relevant tasks. This implies a potential to automate dose planning without the dependence on the contouring information, prior to predicting the dose distribution. This approach can ensure robustness against the variability of human annotators and improve automated planning quality for clinical care [19].

We observed a performance drop in COVID-19 classification in STOIC due to the intricate nature of the task, as diagnosing severity depends on the COVID-19 diagnosis and causes per-task gradient collision during training. However, CTAN proved to be effective in minimizing the performance drop in COVID-19 classification compared to other MTL methods. This implies CTAN can selectively learn cross-task attentive features to improve overall performance. Future work could expand the applications of CTAN to other domains such as videos of natural teeth [13], fundus photography for diagnosing glaucoma [10], or laparoscopic hysterectomy [25], and further investigate what drives the per dataset variations.

In conclusion, we introduce a novel MTL framework, CTAN, that utilizes cross-task attention to improve MTL performance in medical imaging from multiple levels of tasks by 4.67% compared to STL. Results demonstrate that incorporating inter-task interaction in CTAN enhances overall performance of three medical imaging task sets from four distinct datasets, surpassing STL and two widely-used baseline MTL methods. This highlights CTAN's effectiveness and potential to improve MTL performance in the field of medical imaging.

References

1. Andrychowicz, M., et al.: Learning to learn by gradient descent by gradient descent. In: Advances in Neural Information Processing Systems, vol. 29 (2016)
2. Ashraf, H., Waris, A., Ghafoor, M.F., Gilani, S.O., Niazi, I.K.: Melanoma segmentation using deep learning with test-time augmentations and conditional random fields. Sci. Rep. **12**(1), 3948 (2022)
3. Babier, A., et al.: OpenKBP: the open-access knowledge-based planning grand challenge and dataset. Med. Phys. **48**(9), 5549–5561 (2021). https://doi.org/10.1002/mp.14845
4. Boutillon, A., Conze, P.-H., Pons, C., Burdin, V., Borotikar, B.: Multi-task, multi-domain deep segmentation with shared representations and contrastive regularization for sparse pediatric datasets. In: de Bruijne, M., et al. (eds.) MICCAI 2021. LNCS, vol. 12901, pp. 239–249. Springer, Cham (2021). https://doi.org/10.1007/978-3-030-87193-2_23
5. Caruana, R.: Multitask learning. Mach. Learn. **28**, 41–75 (1998). https://doi.org/10.1023/A:1007379606734
6. Sainz de Cea, M.V., Diedrich, K., Bakalo, R., Ness, L., Richmond, D.: Multi-task learning for detection and classification of cancer in screening mammography. In: Martel, A.L., et al. (eds.) MICCAI 2020. LNCS, vol. 12266, pp. 241–250. Springer, Cham (2020). https://doi.org/10.1007/978-3-030-59725-2_24
7. Chen, C., Bai, W., Rueckert, D.: Multi-task learning for left atrial segmentation on GE-MRI. In: Pop, M., et al. (eds.) STACOM 2018. LNCS, vol. 11395, pp. 292–301. Springer, Cham (2019). https://doi.org/10.1007/978-3-030-12029-0_32
8. Chen, S., Bortsova, G., García-Uceda Juárez, A., van Tulder, G., de Bruijne, M.: Multi-task attention-based semi-supervised learning for medical image segmentation. In: Shen, D., et al. (eds.) MICCAI 2019. LNCS, vol. 11766, pp. 457–465. Springer, Cham (2019). https://doi.org/10.1007/978-3-030-32248-9_51
9. Deng, J., Dong, W., Socher, R., Li, L.J., Li, K., Fei-Fei, L.: ImageNet: a large-scale hierarchical image database. In: 2009 IEEE Conference on Computer Vision and Pattern Recognition, pp. 248–255. IEEE (2009)
10. Fang, H., et al.: REFUGE2 challenge: treasure for multi-domain learning in glaucoma assessment. arXiv preprint arXiv:2202.08994 (2022)
11. He, K., Zhang, X., Ren, S., Sun, J.: Delving deep into rectifiers: surpassing human-level performance on ImageNet classification. In: Proceedings of the IEEE International Conference on Computer Vision, pp. 1026–1034 (2015)

12. He, K., Zhang, X., Ren, S., Sun, J.: Deep residual learning for image recognition. In: Proceedings of the IEEE Conference on Computer Vision and Pattern Recognition, pp. 770–778 (2016)
13. Katsaros, E., et al.: Multi-task video enhancement for dental interventions. In: Wang, L., Dou, Q., Fletcher, P.T., Speidel, S., Li, S. (eds.) Medical Image Computing and Computer Assisted Intervention, MICCAI 2022. LNCS, vol. 13437, pp. 177–187. Springer, Cham (2022). https://doi.org/10.1007/978-3-031-16449-1_18
14. Kingma, D.P., Ba, J.: Adam: a method for stochastic optimization. arXiv preprint arXiv:1412.6980 (2014)
15. Liu, B., Liu, X., Jin, X., Stone, P., Liu, Q.: Conflict-averse gradient descent for multi-task learning. Adv. Neural. Inf. Process. Syst. **34**, 18878–18890 (2021)
16. Liu, S., Johns, E., Davison, A.J.: End-to-end multi-task learning with attention. In: Proceedings of the IEEE/CVF Conference on Computer Vision and Pattern Recognition, pp. 1871–1880 (2019)
17. Lopes, I., Vu, T.H., de Charette, R.: Cross-task attention mechanism for dense multi-task learning. In: Proceedings of the IEEE/CVF Winter Conference on Applications of Computer Vision, pp. 2329–2338 (2023)
18. Ma, J., et al.: Loss odyssey in medical image segmentation. Med. Image Anal. **71**, 102035 (2021)
19. McIntosh, C., et al.: Clinical integration of machine learning for curative-intent radiation treatment of patients with prostate cancer. Nat. Med. **27**(6), 999–1005 (2021)
20. Paszke, A., et al.: PyTorch: an imperative style, high-performance deep learning library. In: Advances in Neural Information Processing Systems, vol. 32 (2019)
21. Pinheiro, P.O., Collobert, R.: From image-level to pixel-level labeling with convolutional networks. In: Proceedings of the IEEE Conference on Computer Vision and Pattern Recognition, pp. 1713–1721 (2015)
22. Revel, M.P., et al.: Study of thoracic CT in COVID-19: the STOIC project. Radiology **301**(1), E361–E370 (2021)
23. Ronneberger, O., Fischer, P., Brox, T.: U-Net: convolutional networks for biomedical image segmentation. In: Navab, N., Hornegger, J., Wells, W.M., Frangi, A.F. (eds.) MICCAI 2015. LNCS, vol. 9351, pp. 234–241. Springer, Cham (2015). https://doi.org/10.1007/978-3-319-24574-4_28
24. Tschandl, P., Rosendahl, C., Kittler, H.: The HAM10000 dataset, a large collection of multi-source dermatoscopic images of common pigmented skin lesions. Sci. Data **5**(1), 1–9 (2018)
25. Wang, Z., et al.: AutoLaparo: a new dataset of integrated multi-tasks for image-guided surgical automation in laparoscopic hysterectomy. In: Wang, L., Dou, Q., Fletcher, P.T., Speidel, S., Li, S. (eds.) 25th International Conference on Medical Image Computing and Computer Assisted Intervention, MICCAI 2022, Part VII, Singapore, 18–22 September 2022, pp. 486–496. Springer, Cham (2022). https://doi.org/10.1007/978-3-031-16449-1_46
26. Weninger, L., Liu, Q., Merhof, D.: Multi-task learning for brain tumor segmentation. In: Crimi, A., Bakas, S. (eds.) BrainLes 2019. LNCS, vol. 11992, pp. 327–337. Springer, Cham (2020). https://doi.org/10.1007/978-3-030-46640-4_31
27. Wimmer, M., et al.: Multi-task fusion for improving mammography screening data classification. IEEE Trans. Med. Imaging **41**(4), 937–950 (2021)
28. Zhang, Y., Yang, Q.: A survey on multi-task learning. IEEE Trans. Knowl. Data Eng. **34**(12), 5586–5609 (2021)

Input Augmentation with SAM: Boosting Medical Image Segmentation with Segmentation Foundation Model

Yizhe Zhang[1]([✉]), Tao Zhou[1], Shuo Wang[2,3], Peixian Liang[4], Yejia Zhang[4], and Danny Z. Chen[4]

[1] School of Computer Science and Engineering, Nanjing University of Science and Technology, Nanjing 210094, Jiangsu, China
yizhe.zhang.cs@gmail.com
[2] Digital Medical Research Center, School of Basic Medical Sciences, Fudan University, Shanghai 200032, China
shuowang@fudan.edu.cn
[3] Shanghai Key Laboratory of MICCAI, Shanghai 200032, Shanghai, China
[4] Department of Computer Science and Engineering, University of Notre Dame, Notre Dame, IN 46556, USA
{pliang,yzhang46,dchen}@nd.edu

Abstract. The Segment Anything Model (SAM) is a recently developed large model for general-purpose segmentation for computer vision tasks. SAM was trained using 11 million images with over 1 billion masks and can produce segmentation results for a wide range of objects in natural scene images. SAM can be viewed as a general perception model for segmentation (partitioning images into semantically meaningful regions). Thus, how to utilize such a large foundation model for medical image segmentation is an emerging research target. This paper shows that although SAM does not immediately give high-quality segmentation for medical image data, its generated masks, features, and stability scores are useful for building and training better medical image segmentation models. In particular, we demonstrate how to use SAM to augment image input for commonly-used medical image segmentation models (e.g., U-Net). Experiments on three segmentation tasks show the effectiveness of our proposed SAMAug method.

1 Introduction

The Segment Anything Model (SAM) [10] is a remarkable recent advance in foundation models for computer vision tasks. SAM was trained using 11 million images and over 1 billion masks. Despite its strong capability in producing segmentation for a wide variety of objects, several studies [4,8,28] showed that SAM is not powerful enough for segmentation tasks that require domain expert knowledge (e.g., medical image segmentation).

For a given medical image segmentation task with image and annotation pairs, we aim to build and train a medical image segmentation model, denoted

M. E. Celebi et al. (Eds.): MICCAI 2023 Workshops, LNCS 14393, pp. 129–139, 2023.
https://doi.org/10.1007/978-3-031-47401-9_13

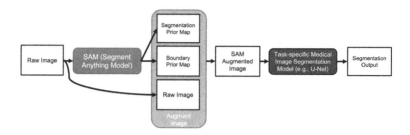

Fig. 1. Input augmentation with SAM for boosting medical image segmentation.

by $\mathcal{M}$, on top of the segmentation foundation model SAM. We propose a new method called SAMAug that directly utilizes the segmentation masks (with stability scores) generated by SAM to augment the raw inputs of the medical image segmentation model $\mathcal{M}$. The input augmentation is performed by a fusion function. The inference process (with SAMAug) for a given image is illustrated in Fig. 1. The task-specific medical image segmentation model $\mathcal{M}$ is trainable using a specific dataset[1] (e.g., MoNuSeg [11]). The parameters of SAM remain fixed, the fusion (augmentation) function is a parameter-free module, and the learning process aims to update the parameters of $\mathcal{M}$ with respect to the given foundation model SAM, the fusion function, and the training data.

Our main contributions can be summarized as follows. (1) We identify that the emerging segmentation foundation model SAM can provide attention (prior) maps for downstream segmentation tasks. (2) With a simple and novel method (SAMAug), we combine segmentation outputs of SAM with raw image inputs, generating SAM-augmented input images for building downstream medical image segmentation models. (3) We conduct comprehensive experiments to demonstrate that our proposed method is effective for both CNN and Transformer segmentation models in three medical image segmentation tasks.

2   Related Work

Data Augmentation. Data augmentation (DA) has been widely used in training medical image segmentation models [3,27]. A main aim of DA is to synthesize new views of existing samples in training data. Our SAMAug can be viewed as a type of DA technique. Unlike previous DA methods which often use hand-designed transformations (e.g., rotation, cropping), SAMAug utilizes a segmentation foundation model to augment raw images, aiming to impose semantically useful structures to the input of a medical image segmentation model.

Image Enhancement. From the image enhancement (IE) view point, SAMAug enhances images by adding semantic structures from a segmentation foundation model. A critical difference between SAMAug and the previous enhancement methods [5,16] is that traditional IE often works at a low level, e.g., deblurring and noise reduction, and the purpose of enhancement is to reconstruct

---

[1] SAMAug performs on all images, including training images and testing images.

and recover. In contrast, SAMAug aims to add high-level structures to raw images, providing better semantics for the subsequent medical image segmentation model.

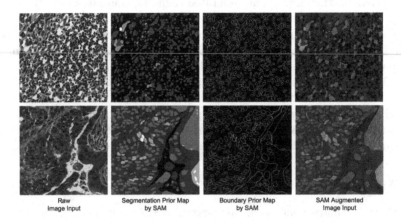

Raw
Image Input   Segmentation Prior Map   Boundary Prior Map   SAM Augmented
                           by SAM   by SAM   Image Input

Fig. 2. Visual examples of a raw input image, its segmentation prior map by SAM, boundary prior map by SAM, and SAM-augmented image input (illustrated in Fig. 1). The image sample is from the MonuSeg dataset [11].

Recent SAM-Related Methods. Since the introduction of SAM, many attempts have been made to understand and utilize SAM for medical image analysis (e.g., [6,12,14,24,25,28]). Recent work has shown that SAM alone, without further fine-tuning and/or adaptation, often delivers unsatisfied results for medical image segmentation tasks [6,28]. In order to utilize SAM more effectively, Ma et al. [12] proposed to fine-tune SAM using labeled images. Wu et al. [24] proposed to add additional layers to adapt SAM for a medical image segmentation task. Compared with these fine-tuning and adaptation methods, our method is more efficient in computation and memory costs during model training. In test time, these fine-tuning, adapting, and augmentation methods all require performing forward propagation of test images through SAM.

3   Methodology

In Sect. 3.1, we describe the two key image representations obtained by applying SAM to a medical image, a segmentation prior map and a boundary prior map. In Sect. 3.2, we show how to augment a medical image using the two obtained prior maps. In Sect. 3.3, we present the details of using augmented images in training a medical image segmentation model. Finally, in Sect. 3.4, we show how to use the trained model in model deployment (model testing).

3.1   Segmentation and Boundary Prior Maps

In the grid prompt setting, SAM uses a grid prompt to generate segmentation masks for a given image. That is, segmentation masks are generated at all plausible locations in the image. The generated segmentation masks are then stored in a list. For each segmentation mask in the list, we draw the mask on a newly created segmentation prior map using the value suggested by the mask's corresponding stability score (generated by SAM). In addition to the segmentation prior map, we further generate a boundary prior map according to the masks provided by SAM. We draw the exterior boundary of each segmentation mask in the mask list and put all the boundaries together to form a boundary prior map. For a given image x, we generate two prior maps, $\text{prior}_{\text{seg}}$ and $\text{prior}_{\text{boundary}}$, using the process discussed above. In Fig. 2 (the second and third columns), we give visual examples of these two prior maps thus generated.

3.2   Augmenting Input Images

With the prior maps generated, our next step is to augment the input image x with the generated prior maps. We choose a simple method for this augmentation: adding the prior maps to the raw image. Note that many medical image segmentation tasks can be reduced to a three-class segmentation task in which the 1st class corresponds to the background, the 2nd class corresponds to the regions of interest (ROIs), and the 3rd class corresponds to the boundaries between the ROIs and background. We add the segmentation prior map to the second channel of the raw image and the boundary prior map to the third channel of the raw image. If the raw image is in gray-scale, we create a 3-channel image with the first channel consisting of the gray-scale raw image, the second channel consisting of its segmentation prior map (only), and the third channel consisting of its boundary prior map (only). For each image x in the training set, we generate its augmented version $x^{aug} = \text{Aug}(\text{prior}_{\text{seg}}, \text{prior}_{\text{boundary}}, x)$. Figure 2 (the fourth column) gives a visual example of the SAM-augmented image input.

3.3   Model Training with SAM-Augmented Images

With the input augmentation on each image sample in the training set, we obtain a new augmented training set $\{(x_1^{aug}, y_1), (x_2^{aug}, y_2), \ldots, (x_n^{aug}, y_n)\}$, where $x_i^{aug} \in \mathbb{R}^{w \times h \times 3}$, $y_i \in \{0, 1\}^{w \times h \times C}$ is the annotation of the input image x_i, and C is the number of classes for the segmentation task. A common medical image segmentation model $\mathcal{M}$ (e.g., a U-Net) can be directly utilized for learning from the augmented training set. A simple way to learn from SAM-augmented images is to use the following learning objective with respect to the parameters of $\mathcal{M}$:

$$\sum_{i=1}^{n} loss(\mathcal{M}(x_i^{aug}), y_i). \tag{1}$$

The above objective only uses SAM-augmented images for model training. Consequently, in model testing, the trained model accepts only images augmented by SAM. In situations where SAM fails to give plausible prior maps, we consider training a segmentation model using both raw images and images with SAM augmentation. The new learning objective is to minimize the following objective with respect to the parameters of $\mathcal{M}$:

$$\sum_{i=1}^{n} \beta loss(\mathcal{M}(x_i), y_i) + \lambda loss(\mathcal{M}(x_i^{aug}), y_i), \tag{2}$$

where β and λ control the importance of the training loss for samples with raw images and samples with augmented images. When setting $\beta = 0$ and $\lambda = 1$, the objective function in Eq. (2) is reduced to Eq. (1). By default, we set both β and λ equal to 1. The spatial cross-entropy loss or Dice loss can be used for constructing the loss function in Eq. (1) and Eq. (2). An SGD-based optimizer (e.g., Adam [9]) can be applied to reduce the values of the loss function.

3.4   Model Deployment with SAM-Augmented Images

When the segmentation model is trained using only SAM-augmented images, the model deployment (testing) requires the input also to be SAM-augmented images. The model deployment can be written as:

$$\hat{y} = \tau(\mathcal{M}(x^{aug})), \tag{3}$$

where τ is an output activation function (e.g., a sigmoid function, a softmax function), and x^{aug} is a SAM-augmented image (as described in Sect. 3.2). When the segmentation model $\mathcal{M}$ is trained using both raw images and SAM-augmented images, we identify new opportunities in inference time to fully realize the potential of the trained model. A simple way of using $\mathcal{M}$ would be to apply sample inference twice for each test sample: The first time inference uses the raw image x as input and the second time inference uses its SAM augmented image as input. The final segmentation output can be generated by the average ensemble of the two outputs. Formally, this inference process can be written as:

$$\hat{y} = \tau(\mathcal{M}(x) + \mathcal{M}(x^{aug})). \tag{4}$$

Another way of utilizing the two output candidates $\mathcal{M}(x)$ and $\mathcal{M}(x^{aug})$ is to select a plausible segmentation output from these two candidates:

$$\hat{y} = \tau(\mathcal{M}(x^*)), \tag{5}$$

where x^* is obtained via solving the following optimization:

$$x^* = \operatorname{argmin}_{x' \in \{x, x^{aug}\}} Entropy(\tau(\mathcal{M}(x'))). \tag{6}$$

Namely, we choose an input version out of the two input candidates (x and x^{aug}) according to the entropy (prediction certainty) of the segmentation output. Segmentation output with a lower entropy means that the model is more certain in its prediction, and a higher certainty in prediction often positively correlates to higher segmentation accuracy [21].

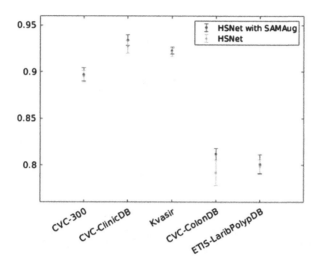

Fig. 3. Polyp segmentation results of the vanilla HSNet and SAMAug-enhanced HSNet.

4   Experiments and Results

4.1   Datasets and Setups

We perform experiments on the Polyp [28], MoNuSeg [11], and GlaS [18] benchmarks to demonstrate the effectiveness of our proposed SAMAug method. For the polyp segmentation experiments, we follow the training setup used in training the state-of-the-art (SOTA) model HSNet [26][2]. For the MoNuSeg and GlaS segmentation, the training of a medical image segmentation model uses the Adam optimizer [9], with batch size = 8, image cropping window size = 256×256, and learning rate = $5e - 4$. The total number of training iterations is 50K. The spatial cross entropy loss is used for the model training.

4.2   Polyp Segmentation on Five Datasets

Automatic polyp segmentation in endoscopic images can help improve the efficiency and accuracy in clinical screenings and tests for gastrointestinal diseases. Many deep learning (DL) based models have been proposed for robust and automatic segmentation of polyps. Here, we utilize the SOTA model HSNet [26] for evaluating our proposed SAMAug method. We use the objective function described in Eq. (2) in model training. In test time, we use the model deployment strategy given in Eq. (6). In Fig. 3, we show the segmentation performance (in Dice score) of the vanilla HSNet and SAMAug-enhanced HSNet on the test

---

[2] https://github.com/baiboat/HSNet.

sets of CVC-300 [20], CVC-ClinicDB [1], Kvasir [7], CVC-ColonDB [19], and ETIS [17]. All the model training sessions were run ten times with different random seeds for reporting the means and standard deviations of the segmentation performance. In Fig. 3, we observe that SAMAug improves HSNet on the CVC-ClinicDB and CVC-ColonDB datasets significantly, and remains at the same level of performance on the other three datasets (all validated by t-test). Furthermore, we give visual result comparisons in Fig. 4.

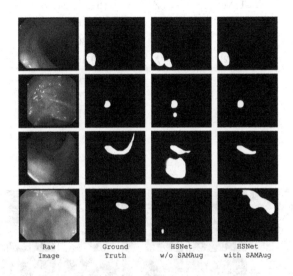

Fig. 4. Visual results of the HSNet and SAMAug-enhanced HSNet in polyp segmentation.

4.3   Cell Segmentation on the MoNuSeg Dataset

The MoNuSeg dataset [11] was constructed using H&E stained tissue images (at 40× magnification) from the TCGA archive [23]. The training set consists of 30 images with about 22000 cell nuclear annotations. The test set contains 14 images with about 7000 cell nuclear annotations. We use the objective function described in Eq. (1) in model training. In test time, we use the model deployment strategy given in Eq. (3). In Table 1, we show clear advantages of our proposed method in improving segmentation results for the U-Net, P-Net, and Attention U-Net models. AJI (Aggregated Jaccard Index) is a standard segmentation evaluation metric[3] used on MoNuSeg which evaluates segmentation performance on the object level. F-score evaluates the cell segmentation performance on the pixel level. In addition, we give visual result comparisons in Fig. 5. Note that, although the segmentation generated by SAM (e.g., see the 3rd column of Fig. 5)

---

[3] https://monuseg.grand-challenge.org/Evaluation/.

does not immediately give accurate cell segmentation, SAM provides a general segmentation perceptual prior for the subsequent DL models to generate much more accurate task-specific segmentation results.

Table 1. Cell segmentation results on the MoNuSeg dataset.

Model	SAMAug	AJI	F-score
Swin-UNet [2]	✗	61.66	80.57
U-Net [15]	✗	58.36	75.70
	✓	64.30	82.36
P-Net [22]	✗	59.46	77.09
	✓	63.98	82.56
Attention UNet [13]	✗	58.76	75.43
	✓	63.15	81.49

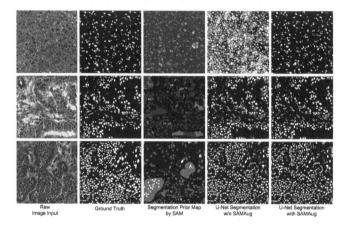

Fig. 5. Visual comparisons of segmentation results on the MoNuSeg dataset.

4.4 Gland Segmentation on the GlaS Dataset

The GlaS dataset [18] has 85 training images (37 benign (BN), 48 malignant (MT)), and 60 test images (33 BN, 27 MT) in part A and 20 test images (4 BN, 16 MT) in part B. We use the official evaluation code[4] for evaluating segmentation performance. For simplicity, we merge test set part A and test set part B, and

---

[4] https://warwick.ac.uk/fac/cross_fac/tia/data/glascontest/evaluation/.

perform segmentation evaluation at once for all the samples in the test set. We use the objective function described in Eq. (1) in model training. In test time, we use the model deployment strategy given in Eq. (3). From Table 2, one can see that U-Net with SAMAug augmentation performs considerably better than that without SAMAug augmentation.

Table 2. Gland segmentation results on the GlaS dataset.

Model	SAMAug	F-score	Object Dice
U-Net [15]	✗	79.33	86.35
	✓	82.50	87.44

5 Conclusions

In this paper, we proposed a new method, SAMAug, for boosting medical image segmentation that uses the Segment Anything Model (SAM) to augment image input for commonly-used medical image segmentation models. Experiments on three segmentation tasks showed the effectiveness of our proposed method. Future work may consider conducting further research on: (1) designing a more robust and advanced augmentation function; (2) improving the efficiency of applying SAM in the SAMAug scheme; (3) utilizing SAMAug for uncertainty estimations and in other clinically-oriented applications.

Acknowledgement. This work was supported in part by National Natural Science Foundation of China (62201263) and Natural Science Foundation of Jiangsu Province (BK20220949). S.W. is supported by Shanghai Sailing Programs of Shanghai Municipal Science and Technology Committee (22YF1409300).

References

1. Bernal, J., Sánchez, F.J., Fernández-Esparrach, G., Gil, D., Rodríguez, C., Vilariño, F.: WM-DOVA maps for accurate polyp highlighting in colonoscopy: validation vs. saliency maps from physicians. Comput. Med. Imaging Graph. **43**, 99–111 (2015)
2. Cao, H., et al.: Swin-Unet: Unet-like pure transformer for medical image segmentation. In: Karlinsky, L., Michaeli, T., Nishino, K. (eds.) Computer Vision, ECCV 2022 Workshops. LNCS, vol. 13803, pp. 205–218. Springer, Cham (2023). https://doi.org/10.1007/978-3-031-25066-8_9
3. Chlap, P., Min, H., Vandenberg, N., Dowling, J., Holloway, L., Haworth, A.: A review of medical image data augmentation techniques for deep learning applications. J. Med. Imaging Radiat. Oncol. **65**(5), 545–563 (2021)
4. Deng, R., et al.: Segment anything model (SAM) for digital pathology: assess zero-shot segmentation on whole slide imaging. arXiv preprint arXiv:2304.04155 (2023)

5. Dinh, P.-H., Giang, N.L.: A new medical image enhancement algorithm using adaptive parameters. Int. J. Imaging Syst. Technol. **32**(6), 2198–2218 (2022)
6. Huang, Y., et al.: Segment Anything Model for medical images? arXiv preprint arXiv:2304.14660 (2023)
7. Jha, D., et al.: Kvasir-SEG: a segmented polyp dataset. In: Ro, Y.M., et al. (eds.) MMM 2020. LNCS, vol. 11962, pp. 451–462. Springer, Cham (2020). https://doi.org/10.1007/978-3-030-37734-2_37
8. Ji, G.-P., Fan, D.-P., Xu, P., Cheng, M.-M., Zhou, B., Van Gool, L.: SAM struggles in concealed scenes-empirical study on "segment anything". arXiv preprint arXiv:2304.06022 (2023)
9. Kingma, D.P., Ba, J.: Adam: a method for stochastic optimization. arXiv preprint arXiv:1412.6980 (2014)
10. Kirillov, A., et al.: Segment anything. arXiv preprint arXiv:2304.02643 (2023)
11. Kumar, N., Verma, R., Sharma, S., Bhargava, S., Vahadane, A., Sethi, A.: A dataset and a technique for generalized nuclear segmentation for computational pathology. IEEE Trans. Med. Imaging **36**(7), 1550–1560 (2017)
12. Ma, J., Wang, B.: Segment anything in medical images. arXiv preprint arXiv:2304.12306 (2023)
13. Oktay, O., et al. Attention U-Net: learning where to look for the pancreas. In: International Conference on Medical Imaging with Deep Learning (2018)
14. Qiao, Y., et al.: Robustness of SAM: segment anything under corruptions and beyond. arXiv preprint arXiv:2306.07713 (2023)
15. Ronneberger, O., Fischer, P., Brox, T.: U-Net: convolutional networks for biomedical image segmentation. In: Navab, N., Hornegger, J., Wells, W.M., Frangi, A.F. (eds.) MICCAI 2015. LNCS, vol. 9351, pp. 234–241. Springer, Cham (2015). https://doi.org/10.1007/978-3-319-24574-4_28
16. Rundo, L., et al.: MedGA: a novel evolutionary method for image enhancement in medical imaging systems. Exp. Syst. Appl. **119**, 387–399 (2019)
17. Silva, J., Histace, A., Romain, O., Dray, X., Granado, B.: Toward embedded detection of polyps in WCE images for early diagnosis of colorectal cancer. Int. J. Comput. Assist. Radiol. Surg. **9**, 283–293 (2014)
18. Sirinukunwattana, K., et al.: Gland segmentation in colon histology images: the GlaS challenge contest. Med. Image Anal. **35**, 489–502 (2017)
19. Tajbakhsh, N., Gurudu, S.R., Liang, J.: Automated polyp detection in colonoscopy videos using shape and context information. IEEE Trans. Med. Imaging **35**(2), 630–644 (2015)
20. Vázquez, D., et al.: A benchmark for endoluminal scene segmentation of colonoscopy images. J. Healthcare Eng. **2017**, 1–9 (2017)
21. Wang, D., Shelhamer, E., Liu, S., Olshausen, B., Darrell, T.: Tent: fully test-time adaptation by entropy minimization. In: International Conference on Learning Representations (2021)
22. Wang, G., et al.: DeepIGeoS: a deep interactive geodesic framework for medical image segmentation. IEEE Trans. Pattern Anal. Mach. Intell. **41**(7), 1559–1572 (2018)
23. Wang, Z., Jensen, M.A., Zenklusen, J.C.: A practical guide to the cancer genome atlas (TCGA). Stat. Genomics Meth. Protoc. **1418**, 111–141 (2016)
24. Wu, J., et al.: Medical SAM adapter: adapting segment anything model for medical image segmentation. arXiv preprint arXiv:2304.12620 (2023)
25. Zhang, C., et al.: A survey on segment anything model (SAM): vision foundation model meets prompt engineering. arXiv preprint arXiv:2306.06211 (2023)

26. Zhang, W., Chong, F., Zheng, Yu., Zhang, F., Zhao, Y., Sham, C.-W.: HSNet: a hybrid semantic network for polyp segmentation. Comput. Biol. Med. **150**, 106173 (2022)

27. Zhao, A., Balakrishnan, G., Durand, F., Guttag, J.V., Dalca, A.V.: Data augmentation using learned transformations for one-shot medical image segmentation. In: Proceedings of the IEEE/CVF Conference on Computer Vision and Pattern Recognition, pp. 8543–8553 (2019)

28. Zhou, T., Zhang, Y., Zhou, Y., Wu, Y., Gong, C.: Can SAM segment polyps? arXiv preprint arXiv:2304.07583 (2023)

Empirical Analysis of a Segmentation Foundation Model in Prostate Imaging

Heejong Kim[1]([✉]), Victor Ion Butoi[3], Adrian V. Dalca[3,4],
and Mert R. Sabuncu[1,2]

[1] Department of Radiology, Weill Cornell Medicine, New York City, USA
hek4004@med.cornell.edu
[2] School of Electrical and Computer Engineering, Cornell University and Cornell Tech, Ithaca, USA
[3] Martinos Center for Biomedical Imaging, Massachusetts General Hospital and Harvard Medical School, Boston, USA
[4] Computer Science and Artificial Intelligence Laboratory, Massachusetts Institute of Technology, Cambridge, USA

Abstract. Most state-of-the-art techniques for medical image segmentation rely on deep-learning models. These models, however, are often trained on narrowly-defined tasks in a supervised fashion, which requires expensive labeled datasets. Recent advances in several machine learning domains, such as natural language generation have demonstrated the feasibility and utility of building foundation models that can be customized for various downstream tasks with little to no labeled data. This likely represents a paradigm shift for medical imaging, where we expect that foundation models may shape the future of the field. In this paper, we consider a recently developed foundation model for medical image segmentation, UniverSeg [6]. We conduct an empirical evaluation study in the context of prostate imaging and compare it against the conventional approach of training a task-specific segmentation model. Our results and discussion highlight several important factors that will likely be important in the development and adoption of foundation models for medical image segmentation.

Keywords: Foundation model · Medical Image Segmentation · Prostate MRI · In-context Learning

1 Introduction

Foundation models (FMs) are general-purpose models trained on extensive amounts of data, typically in a self-supervised fashion [4]. These pre-trained models can serve as the 'foundation' from which to adapt to various downstream

---

Supplementary Information The online version contains supplementary material available at https://doi.org/10.1007/978-3-031-47401-9_14.

M. E. Celebi et al. (Eds.): MICCAI 2023 Workshops, LNCS 14393, pp. 140–150, 2023.
https://doi.org/10.1007/978-3-031-47401-9_14

tasks with minimal or no supervision. From BERT [11] to GPT-4 [25], FMs have fueled ground-breaking advances in natural language tasks. The success of large language models inspired applications to different domains such as speech [1,26], robotics [5,31], and vision [20,37].

Classical methods for medical image segmentation (MIS) implement carefully-customized pipelines (e.g., FreeSurfer [14]). Pipelines might include pre-selecting images that include the region of interest (ROI), preprocessing the images to reduce artifacts and/or noise, and applying image-processing algorithms like thresholding and deformable-templates, with empirically chosen parameters. The introduction of deep learning models simplified and improved the performance of automatic segmentation tools [19,27]. In deep learning, the common approach involves curating a set of labeled images and training a task-specific model on these data. These models can be brittle and not generalize well to new datasets. Moreover, they demand the creation of a relatively large labeled training set for each task. Importantly, training for each task often requires significant computational resources and expertise. Recent studies have proposed data augmentation and synthesis methods to address these problems but they are still early stage [3,34].

Recently, several FMs for image segmentation tasks have been proposed. These include the Segment Anything Model (SAM) and Segment everything everywhere all at once model (SEEM), which demonstrate great performance in a variety of interactive segmentation tasks in natural images [20,37]. Unlike task-specific models, these FMs are trained with prompt inputs like points and boxes that guide the segmentation tasks. Once trained, these methods solve new tasks without updating their weights (Fig. 1). Another recent FM, UniverSeg [6], is specifically designed to generally solve *medical* image segmentation tasks. The "prompt" for UniverSeg is a set of image-label pairs, also called a support set. The support set precisely defines the segmentation task. As one of the first FMs developed for medical image segmentation, UniverSeg demonstrated promising performance using limited number of image-label pairs compared to few-shot baseline methods.

A FM for MIS offers several benefits. This approach can minimize the need for labeled data, which can represent a significant reduction in cost for developing automatic segmentation tools. Since these models leverage commonalities across different annotation tasks, adapting a FM to a new task can be made to be computationally efficient and reduce the computational burden for creating task-specific solutions. Finally, adapting FMs to specific tasks can be made easy and user-friendly, which will help lower barriers for clinical practitioners to build on these technologies.

Although promising, studies have shown the limitations of the SAM FM for MIS tasks [8,10,16–18,23,24,29,35]. The inferior performance of SAM on MIS tasks is often attributed to the fact that SAM was trained with natural images. Some works propose possible remedies, such as prompt-engineering [30,32] and fine-tuning [15,22,33] to improve the performance. In this paper, we report the potential and limitations of an MIS-specific FM, UniverSeg, by evaluating it for prostate MRI segmentation.

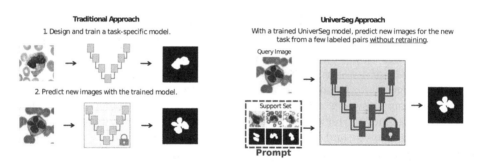

Fig. 1. Traditional Approach vs. Foundational Model Approach. Traditional segmentation models like nnUNet are trained first to predict the new images. FMs like UniverSeg and SAM use a trained model for inference of a new task. Instead of retraining, prompts like support sets are used for UniverSeg and points and masks for SAM (Image modified from [6])

2   Related Works

2.1   UniverSeg

UniverSeg [6] is a FM for MIS tasks that uses support sets of image-label pairs as a prompt to define new tasks. The architecture employs a Cross-Block mechanism leveraging information from the query image and support sets by averaging the feature maps. UniverSeg was built using MegaMedical, which contains 53 open-access medical segmentation datasets comprising over 22,000 scans to achieve strong performance when generalizing to held out datasets used to evaluate UniverSeg on unseen anatomies and tasks.

2.2   Prostate MR Segmentation

Prostate MR scans have been increasingly acquired as an initial diagnostic tool. The ROI labels are manually segmented for the clinical workflow, for example, biopsy guidance, and surgical/treatment planning. High-quality segmentation labels can be beneficial but the label generation is time-consuming and demands expertise. Thus, automatic segmentation tools can have a large clinical impact.

3   Experiments

3.1   Datasets

We consider three anatomical ROIs in the prostate that are defined in two datasets. For each dataset, we created five sets of support/test splits. Since obtaining high-quality ground-truth labels is a significant bottleneck for real-world MIS problems, we focus on the limited sample size scenario. We created support sets with randomly selected N = 1, 2, 5, and 10 cases, while the other cases were used as test set. Since each training case is a 3D volume, we extracted 2D slices from these volumes to create the support or training sets. Unless specified otherwise, we used 2D slices that contained the ROI. All slices are resized to 128×128 and intensities are normalized to $[0, 1]$.

Prostate Gland Segmentation. We used our in-house prostate MRI dataset (Prostate-Gland) for prostate gland segmentation, amounting to 859 anonymized MRI scans. T2-weighted prostate MRI scans are acquired as part of prostate cancer diagnosis.

Transitional and Peripheral Zone Segmentation. We used the publicly available zonal anatomy segmentation labels of 204 patients [9]. The transitional zone (TZ) and peripheral zone (PZ) labels are from the training dataset of the PROSTATEx challenge [21] and annotated by expert radiologists, with rigorous quality assessment [9]. We present two sets of results corresponding to two different labels: PROSTATEx-TZ and PROSTATEx-PZ.

3.2   UniverSeg Inference

One of the crucial limitations of existing FMs for segmentation, including UniverSeg [6], is that they are all trained in 2D. However, most medical image segmentation tasks are in 3D, and the ROIs can be present in a small portion of the entire volume. Thus, many 2D slices will not contain the segmentation label. Regular prompt-based FM's like SAM [20] struggle with this, as they are expected to return a non-zero result for a given query and prompt. Although UniverSeg is trained using 2D slices containing the label, UniverSeg can use images with missing ROIs in the support set, which can be critical for 3D segmentation tasks. Following the original paper, in all our experiments, we set the maximum support set size S to 64 2D image-label pairs. Furthermore, as previously demonstrated, the quality of the result obtained with UniverSeg heavily depends on the quality of the provided support set [6]. In our experiments, we implement different support set selection strategies, described below.

Slice-Index-Aware Support Set Selection. The anatomical field-of-view along the z-axis of prostate MR images is roughly similar across subjects. We leveraged this to implement a support set selection strategy that relies on the slice index Z of the query image. For a given query image I_q, we computed weights for each of the available labeled slices I_t as follows: $1/(|Z_{I_t} - Z_{I_q}| + 1)$, where Z_I denote the slice index in image I. Then we randomly selected S annotated slices with a probability proportional to the pre-computed weights. This is our default support set selection strategy, which was used for the main results.

Random Support Set Selection. As an ablation, we ignore the z-index and randomly draw S support images from available labeled slices, where each of these images has the same (uniform) probability.

These support set selection techniques can be restricted to slices where the ROI is present ("ROI-inclusive"), or can consider all possible slices in the training volumes (i.e., be agnostic to whether the ROI is present or absent in the slice, which we refer to as "ROI-agnostic"). Because UniverSeg was trained with only

"ROI-inclusive" slices, comparing the result with "ROI-agnostic" can serve as a good stress test of the released tool.

3.3 nnUNet

As the baseline, we used the (2D) nnUNet, which trains the model from a random initialization on the given labeled data using heavy data augmentation, automatic network configuration, and ensembling (nnUNet-original) [19]. The nnUNet model is widely considered state-of-the-art for a wide range of task-specific segmentation tasks. For further comparison, we trained and tested the nnUNet model with a smaller network capacity that is similar to the size of the UniverSeg model, which we refer to as nnUNet-small (See Appendix for the details).

3.4 Empirical Evaluation

Because high-performance machines are often unavailable in clinical and medical-research settings, understanding the required computational resources is important to utilize deep learning models for clinical use. As many FMs for segmentation are based on Vision Transformer [13] trained with large datasets, they involve a large number of parameters. Also, compared to classification problems, MIS models often involve higher memory requirements. We performed computational resource analysis on nnUNet and UniverSeg by comparing the number of parameters, training, and inference time.

As the main performance metric, we used the Dice score [12] that quantifies the overlap between an automatic and ground-truth segmentation, and is widely used in the field. We compare UniverSeg with nnUNet models, when different number (N) of training cases are available. We performed ablation studies to understand where the performance improvement occurs for the UniverSeg and nnUNet models. We compute Dice both in 2D and in 3D. The 2D Dice results are presented only for slices that contain the ROI, and aggregated over all slices in the test subjects. For these results, we implemented the ROI-inclusive support set strategy. We also present 3D Dice values, which are computed based on the volumetric overlap in each test subject, which is in turn averaged across subjects.

4 Results

4.1 Computational Resource

Table 1 shows computational resources needed for nnUNet and UniverSeg. UniverSeg has a much smaller number of parameters and faster inference runtime. Importantly, UniverSeg does not require task-specific training – saving substantial computational requirement, and obviating the need for a GPU. This substantial savings makes is more applicable to clinical and clinical-research settings. nnUNet implements five-fold cross-validation, which it in turn uses to ensemble five models. This means that for each nnUNet, we store five models and run five inferences. For nnUNet-orig, the automatic configuration in our experiment yielded models with 20.6M parameters, which is 100 times larger than UniverSeg (1.2M). Our nnUNet-small implementation had 1.3M learnable parameters, yet we emphasize that ensembling over cross-validation runs meant that the memory footprint of nnUNet-small is about five times of UniverSeg. While the inference time for the nnUNet models will not depend on the training set size (N), UniverSeg's will, since we need to ensemble over various support sets when $N > 2$ for better performance. However, the support set size does not affect the number of parameters as the Cross-Block of UniverSeg averages the representations of interaction between query and support sets at each step in the network.

Table 1. Computational resource comparison. The values are averaged across ROIs and calculated for $N = 1$ case for all methods. All models are tested on Nvidia TITAN Xp GPU (12 GB vRAM).

	nnUNet–orig	nnUNet–small	UniverSeg
#Params	20.6 M × 5 folds	1.3 M × 5 folds	**1.2 M**
Training time (ms)	1.6×10^8	1.2×10^8	–
Inference time (ms)	9.7×10^3	7.5×10^3	$\mathbf{6.9 \times 10^2}$

Table 2. 2D Dice scores for UniverSeg and nnUNet models. The scores are averaged across 5 support/test splits.

ROI	Method	$N = 1$	$N = 2$	$N = 5$	$N = 10$
Prostate-Gland	nnUNet-Orig	0.592 ± 0.088	0.714 ± 0.045	0.810 ± 0.007	0.817 ± 0.016
	nnUNet-Small	0.520 ± 0.076	0.698 ± 0.057	0.802 ± 0.008	0.808 ± 0.019
	UniverSeg	$\mathbf{0.711 \pm 0.008}$	$\mathbf{0.769 \pm 0.009}$	0.780 ± 0.003	0.802 ± 0.005
PROSTATEx-TZ	nnUNet-Orig	0.614 ± 0.049	0.764 ± 0.034	0.803 ± 0.006	0.821 ± 0.010
	nnUNet-Small	0.599 ± 0.066	0.759 ± 0.033	0.800 ± 0.006	0.814 ± 0.011
	UniverSeg	$\mathbf{0.632 \pm 0.046}$	0.717 ± 0.010	0.743 ± 0.012	0.754 ± 0.015
PROSTATEx-PZ	nnUNet-Orig	0.368 ± 0.111	0.589 ± 0.041	0.644 ± 0.042	0.706 ± 0.018
	nnUNet-Small	0.333 ± 0.122	0.572 ± 0.048	0.633 ± 0.049	0.699 ± 0.016
	UniverSeg	$\mathbf{0.478 \pm 0.056}$	0.570 ± 0.014	$\mathbf{0.647 \pm 0.018}$	0.673 ± 0.015

4.2   Segmentation Performance

We first analyzed segmentation performance for 2D slices that contain the ROI. Table 2 and Fig. 2 show quantitative and qualitative results. Models perform better when more training images are available. For Prostate-Gland segmentation, UniverSeg showed overall comparable results to the nnUNet models, particularly when compared with the size-matched version (nnUNet-small). Interestingly, UniverSeg achieved good performance given extremely limited annotated data, e.g., $N = 1$, outperforming the nnUNet models for all three tasks. The lower scores in TZ and PZ segmentation have been previously analyzed, and are due to the small size and difficult shape of these ROIs. For example, prior zonal segmentation studies report varying scores ranging between 0.59 to 0.94 showing the difficulty and variability [2, 7, 28, 36]. The nnUNet models outperform UniverSeg in TZ segmentation when $N = 5$ and $N = 10$ annotated examples are available. This difference is smaller for PZ and only becomes significant at $N = 10$. It is important to note that the nnUNet models use test time augmentation, which may improve the UniverSeg performance.

Table 3 shows 3D Dice score values and compares two support set selection methods. We observe that the ROI-agnostic support selection method which includes slices that are missing the ROI, achieves significantly better results. This is because, in 3D, there will be many slices that don't include the ROI and if all support examples include the ROI, then the model will likely produce false positive labels for these slices. This highlights the importance of considering the possibility that the query image might be lacking the ROI.

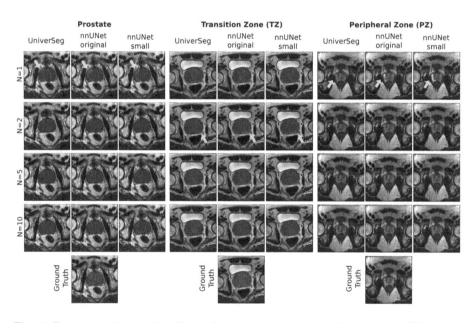

Fig. 2. Representative results. UniverSeg results are comparable to the nnUNet baseline. When existing segmentation labels are limited, e.g., $N = 1$ and $N = 2$, UniverSeg shows superior performance than nnUNet models (highlighted in yellow). (Color figure online)

Ablation. We conducted ablation studies for both UniverSeg and nnUNet models to assess the impact of model configuration choices. The nnUNet with the default configurations includes ensembling and test time augmentation. The prediction results from five cross-validation models are ensembled by averaging softmax probabilities and at test time augmentation is applied by mirroring all axis.

Table 3. 3D Dice scores for UniverSeg models with two different support set selection strategies.

Support Set Selection	N	Prostate	PROSTATEx-TZ	PROSTATEx-PZ
ROI-agnostic	1	0.596 ± 0.047	0.610 ± 0.060	0.428 ± 0.070
	2	0.690 ± 0.035	0.706 ± 0.011	0.510 ± 0.031
	5	0.716 ± 0.006	0.740 ± 0.019	0.593 ± 0.014
	10	0.778 ± 0.006	0.751 ± 0.024	0.621 ± 0.009
ROI-inclusive	1	0.481 ± 0.035	0.579 ± 0.066	0.349 ± 0.042
	2	0.488 ± 0.034	0.665 ± 0.009	0.393 ± 0.009
	5	0.513 ± 0.027	0.685 ± 0.016	0.487 ± 0.013
	10	0.543 ± 0.013	0.707 ± 0.019	0.493 ± 0.027

As the post-processing step did not improve the accuracy on validation sets, we did not post-process the predicted labels. We report the 2D Dice scores of nnUNet models before the ensembling and without the test time augmentation. For UniverSeg, we compared the different slice selection methods.

Table 4 demonstrates the ablation results on prostate gland segmentation. Ensembling gave all models a boost. For nnUNet models, test time augmentation also slightly enhanced the scores. The results of the support set selection methods demonstrate the effect of support set quality. The result of ensembling 5 times with slice-index-aware (z-weighted) selection method showed superior performance than using all images for support sets for both $N = 5$ and $N = 10$. This, again, highlights the importance of the quality of support sets. The ablation for TZ and PZ achieved the similar results (See Appendix Table 1).

Table 4. 2D Dice scores from the ablation study conducted for the prostate segmentation task.

ROI	Method	$N = 1$	$N = 2$	$N = 5$	$N = 10$
nnUNet-Orig	w/o augmentation	0.590 ± 0.085	0.712 ± 0.046	0.809 ± 0.007	0.815 ± 0.016
	fold-1	0.581 ± 0.086	0.681 ± 0.060	0.798 ± 0.011	0.808 ± 0.017
	fold-2	0.564 ± 0.095	0.710 ± 0.039	0.797 ± 0.010	0.798 ± 0.023
	fold-3	0.590 ± 0.092	0.691 ± 0.044	0.795 ± 0.014	0.807 ± 0.025
	fold-4	0.599 ± 0.088	0.708 ± 0.043	0.785 ± 0.006	0.804 ± 0.006
	fold-5	0.553 ± 0.046	0.692 ± 0.046	0.790 ± 0.006	0.810 ± 0.008
	default	$\mathbf{0.592 \pm 0.088}$	$\mathbf{0.714 \pm 0.045}$	$\mathbf{0.810 \pm 0.007}$	$\mathbf{0.817 \pm 0.016}$
nnUNet-Small	w/o augmentation	0.519 ± 0.072	0.696 ± 0.056	0.801 ± 0.007	0.807 ± 0.018
	fold-1	0.537 ± 0.047	0.668 ± 0.074	0.784 ± 0.014	0.801 ± 0.021
	fold-2	0.518 ± 0.068	0.686 ± 0.051	0.793 ± 0.012	0.792 ± 0.023
	fold-3	0.512 ± 0.091	0.689 ± 0.057	0.784 ± 0.011	0.803 ± 0.011
	fold-4	0.508 ± 0.076	0.705 ± 0.046	0.787 ± 0.015	0.792 ± 0.022
	fold-5	0.530 ± 0.089	0.680 ± 0.045	0.782 ± 0.014	0.798 ± 0.020
	default	$\mathbf{0.520 \pm 0.076}$	$\mathbf{0.698 \pm 0.057}$	$\mathbf{0.802 \pm 0.008}$	$\mathbf{0.808 \pm 0.019}$
UniverSeg	all	$\mathbf{0.711 \pm 0.008}$	$\mathbf{0.769 \pm 0.009}$	0.778 ± 0.006	0.799 ± 0.005
	random	–	–	0.777 ± 0.002	0.798 ± 0.005
	random+5 ensemble	–	–	0.779 ± 0.004	0.800 ± 0.006
	z-weighted	–	–	0.777 ± 0.002	0.798 ± 0.005
	z-weighted +5 ensemble	–	–	$\mathbf{0.780 \pm 0.003}$	$\mathbf{0.802 \pm 0.005}$
Average # of images available for support set		14.0 ± 2.1	31.4 ± 6.5	83.4 ± 2.9	148.0 ± 3.7

4.3 Conclusion

Based on the successful employment of FMs in multiple domains, we believe FMs will instigate a paradigm shift for medical imaging. In this paper, we evaluated the FM for MIS, called UniverSeg, and discussed its performance and adaptability to prostate segmentation tasks.

As future directions, we see several limitations and opportunities in a FM for MIS. First, FMs for 3D MIS are needed, and promise to be impactful. Many medical image data is acquired in 3D and the existing FMs are based on 2D slices extracted from the 3D volumes. Previous studies have shown superior performance when designed for 3D compared to 2D data. FMs like UniverSeg, where the model can account for images without ROI labels, should be further studied for 3D tasks. Second, adaptation of FMs should be further studied. Prostate gland and TZ were comparably easier segmentation tasks then the PZ. Different approaches would include but not be limited to ensembling different models, e.g., ensembling nnUNet and UniverSeg results, prompt engineering, and finetuning. Third, clinical practitioners can easily adapt FMs in their workflows, as it obviates the need to fine-tune. For prostate MRI, some practitioners use an automated prostate gland segmentation tool from the software DynaCAD[1]. Even though the segmentation needs to be reviewed and edited, the software saves a lot of time over manual segmentation. An FM like UniverSeg, can be used for various segmentation tasks even when limited labels are available.

Acknowledgements. This work was supported by NIH, United States grant R01AG053949 and 1R01AG064027, the NSF, United States NeuroNex grant 1707312, and the NSF, United States CAREER 1748377 grant.

References

1. Baevski, A., Zhou, Y., Mohamed, A., Auli, M.: wav2vec 2.0: a framework for self-supervised learning of speech representations. In: Advances in Neural Information Processing Systems, vol. 33, pp. 12449–12460 (2020)
2. Bardis, M., Houshyar, R., Chantaduly, C., Tran-Harding, K., Ushinsky, A., et al.: Segmentation of the prostate transition zone and peripheral zone on MR images with deep learning. Radiol. Imaging Cancer **3**(3), e200024 (2021)
3. Billot, B., et al.: A learning strategy for contrast-agnostic MRI segmentation. arXiv preprint arXiv:2003.01995 (2020)
4. Bommasani, R., Hudson, D.A., Adeli, E., Altman, R., Arora, S., et al.: On the opportunities and risks of foundation models. arXiv preprint arXiv:2108.07258 (2021)
5. Brohan, A., Brown, N., Carbajal, J., Chebotar, Y., Dabis, J., et al.: RT-1: robotics transformer for real-world control at scale. arXiv preprint arXiv:2212.06817 (2022)
6. Butoi, V.I., Ortiz, J.J.G., Ma, T., Sabuncu, M.R., Guttag, J., Dalca, A.V.: UniverSeg: universal medical image segmentation. arXiv preprint arXiv:2304.06131 (2023)

---

[1] https://www.usa.philips.com/healthcare/product/HC784029/dynacad-prostate.

7. Chen, C., Qin, C., Ouyang, C., Li, Z., Wang, S., et al.: Enhancing MR image segmentation with realistic adversarial data augmentation. Med. Image Anal. **82**, 102597 (2022)

8. Cheng, D., Qin, Z., Jiang, Z., Zhang, S., Lao, Q., Li, K.: Sam on medical images: a comprehensive study on three prompt modes. arXiv preprint arXiv:2305.00035 (2023)

9. Cuocolo, R., Stanzione, A., Castaldo, A., De Lucia, D.R., Imbriaco, M.: Quality control and whole-gland, zonal and lesion annotations for the PROSTATEx challenge public dataset. Eur. J. Radiol. **138**, 109647 (2021)

10. Deng, R., Cui, C., Liu, Q., Yao, T., Remedios, L.W., et al.: Segment anything model (SAM) for digital pathology: assess zero-shot segmentation on whole slide imaging. arXiv preprint arXiv:2304.04155 (2023)

11. Devlin, J., Chang, M.W., Lee, K., Toutanova, K.: BERT: pre-training of deep bidirectional transformers for language understanding. arXiv preprint arXiv:1810.04805 (2018)

12. Dice, L.R.: Measures of the amount of ecologic association between species. Ecology **26**(3), 297–302 (1945)

13. Dosovitskiy, A., Beyer, L., Kolesnikov, A., Weissenborn, D., Zhai, X., et al.: An image is worth 16×16 words: transformers for image recognition at scale. arXiv preprint arXiv:2010.11929 (2020)

14. Fischl, B.: Freesurfer. Neuroimage **62**(2), 774–781 (2012)

15. Gao, Y., Xia, W., Hu, D., Gao, X.: DeSAM: decoupling segment anything model for generalizable medical image segmentation. arXiv preprint arXiv:2306.00499 (2023)

16. He, S., Bao, R., Li, J., Grant, P.E., Ou, Y.: Accuracy of segment-anything model (SAM) in medical image segmentation tasks. arXiv preprint arXiv:2304.09324 (2023)

17. Hu, M., Li, Y., Yang, X.: SkinSAM: empowering skin cancer segmentation with segment anything model. arXiv preprint arXiv:2304.13973 (2023)

18. Huang, Y., Yang, X., Liu, L., Zhou, H., Chang, A., et al.: Segment anything model for medical images? arXiv preprint arXiv:2304.14660 (2023)

19. Isensee, F., Jaeger, P.F., Kohl, S.A., Petersen, J., Maier-Hein, K.H.: nnU-Net: a self-configuring method for deep learning-based biomedical image segmentation. Nat. Meth. **18**(2), 203–211 (2021)

20. Kirillov, A., Mintun, E., Ravi, N., Mao, H., Rolland, C., et al.: Segment anything. arXiv preprint arXiv:2304.02643 (2023)

21. Litjens, G., Debats, O., Barentsz, J., Karssemeijer, N., Huisman, H.: Computer-aided detection of prostate cancer in MRI. IEEE Trans. Med. Imaging **33**(5), 1083–1092 (2014)

22. Ma, J., Wang, B.: Segment anything in medical images. arXiv preprint arXiv:2304.12306 (2023)

23. Mattjie, C., de Moura, L.V., Ravazio, R.C., Kupssinskü, L.S., Parraga, O., et al.: Exploring the zero-shot capabilities of the segment anything model (SAM) in 2D medical imaging: a comprehensive evaluation and practical guideline. arXiv preprint arXiv:2305.00109 (2023)

24. Mazurowski, M.A., Dong, H., Gu, H., Yang, J., Konz, N., Zhang, Y.: Segment anything model for medical image analysis: an experimental study. arXiv preprint arXiv:2304.10517 (2023)

25. OpenAI: GPT-4 technical report (2023)

26. Radford, A., Kim, J.W., Xu, T., Brockman, G., McLeavey, C., Sutskever, I.: Robust speech recognition via large-scale weak supervision. arXiv preprint arXiv:2212.04356 (2022)

27. Ronneberger, O., Fischer, P., Brox, T.: U-Net: convolutional networks for biomedical image segmentation. In: Navab, N., Hornegger, J., Wells, W.M., Frangi, A.F. (eds.) MICCAI 2015. LNCS, vol. 9351, pp. 234–241. Springer, Cham (2015). https://doi.org/10.1007/978-3-319-24574-4_28

28. Rouvière, O., Moldovan, P.C., Vlachomitrou, A., Gouttard, S., Riche, B., et al.: Combined model-based and deep learning-based automated 3D zonal segmentation of the prostate on T2-weighted MR images: clinical evaluation. Eur. Radiol. **32**, 3248–3259 (2022)

29. Roy, S., Wald, T., Koehler, G., Rokuss, M.R., Disch, N., et al.: SAM.MD: zero-shot medical image segmentation capabilities of the segment anything model. arXiv preprint arXiv:2304.05396 (2023)

30. Shi, P., Qiu, J., Abaxi, S.M.D., Wei, H., Lo, F.P.W., Yuan, W.: Generalist vision foundation models for medical imaging: a case study of segment anything model on zero-shot medical segmentation. Diagnostics **13**(11), 1947 (2023)

31. Stone, A., Xiao, T., Lu, Y., Gopalakrishnan, K., Lee, K.H., et al.: Open-world object manipulation using pre-trained vision-language models. arXiv preprint arXiv:2303.00905 (2023)

32. Wald, T., Roy, S., Koehler, G., Disch, N., Rokuss, M.R., et al.: SAM.MD: zero-shot medical image segmentation capabilities of the segment anything model. In: Medical Imaging with Deep Learning, short paper track (2023)

33. Wu, J., Fu, R., Fang, H., Liu, Y., Wang, Z., et al.: Medical SAM adapter: adapting segment anything model for medical image segmentation. arXiv preprint arXiv:2304.12620 (2023)

34. Zhao, A., Balakrishnan, G., Durand, F., Guttag, J.V., Dalca, A.V.: Data augmentation using learned transformations for one-shot medical image segmentation. In: Proceedings of the IEEE/CVF Conference on Computer Vision and Pattern Recognition, pp. 8543–8553 (2019)

35. Zhou, T., Zhang, Y., Zhou, Y., Wu, Y., Gong, C.: Can SAM segment polyps? arXiv preprint arXiv:2304.07583 (2023)

36. Zhu, Y., Wei, R., Gao, G., Ding, L., Zhang, X., et al.: Fully automatic segmentation on prostate MR images based on cascaded fully convolution network. J. Magn. Reson. Imaging **49**(4), 1149–1156 (2019)

37. Zou, X., Yang, J., Zhang, H., Li, F., Li, L., et al.: Segment everything everywhere all at once. arXiv preprint arXiv:2304.06718 (2023)

GPT4MIA: Utilizing Generative Pre-trained Transformer (GPT-3) as a Plug-and-Play Transductive Model for Medical Image Analysis

Yizhe Zhang[1]([✉]) and Danny Z. Chen[2]

[1] School of Computer Science and Engineering, Nanjing University of Science and Technology, Nanjing 210094, Jiangsu, China
yizhe.zhang.cs@gmail.com
[2] Department of Computer Science and Engineering, University of Notre Dame, Notre Dame, IN 46556, USA
dchen@nd.edu

Abstract. In this paper, we propose a novel approach (called GPT-4MIA) that utilizes Generative Pre-trained Transformer (GPT) as a plug-and-play transductive inference tool for medical image analysis (MIA). We provide theoretical analysis on why a large pre-trained language model such as GPT-3 can be used as a plug-and-play transductive inference model for MIA. At the methodological level, we develop several technical treatments to improve the efficiency and effectiveness of GPT4MIA, including better prompt structure design, sample selection, and prompt ordering of representative samples/features. We present two concrete use cases (with workflow) of GPT4MIA: (1) detecting prediction errors and (2) improving prediction accuracy, working in conjecture with well-established vision-based models for image classification (e.g., ResNet). Experiments validate that our proposed method is effective for these two tasks. We further discuss the opportunities and challenges in utilizing Transformer-based large language models for broader MIA applications.

Keywords: Medical Image Classification · Generative Pre-trained Transformer · GPT-3 · Large Language Models · Transductive Inference

1 Introduction

Modern large language models (LLMs) are built based on the Transformer architecture and are trained to produce a sequence of text output given a sequence of text input such that the output is expected to be semantically **coherent** to the input. For example, for a text completion task, the input text is a sequence of

---

Supplementary Information The online version contains supplementary material available at https://doi.org/10.1007/978-3-031-47401-9_15.

M. E. Celebi et al. (Eds.): MICCAI 2023 Workshops, LNCS 14393, pp. 151–160, 2023.
https://doi.org/10.1007/978-3-031-47401-9_15

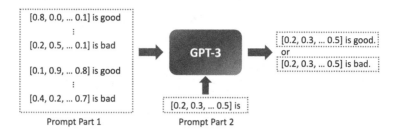

Fig. 1. Illustrating our high-level idea: Using GPT-3 for transductive inference on a binary classification task. Feature texts in Prompt Part 1 are from a set of samples with known labels. Prompt Part 2 contains feature text of a test sample.

text from a text resource, and the model is trained to produce the next character, word, or sentence of the input text. Open AI's GPT-3 has 175 billion parameters, and was trained on hundreds of billions of words. Brown et al. [4] showed that GPT-3 is capable of few-shot learning: Given a few examples/demonstrations to GPT-3, it can generalize considerably well to new samples with similar characteristics. The input and output coherency and the strong generalization capability indicates that pre-trained LLMs such as GPT-3 are potentially capable as general tools for **transductive inference** tasks with limited data.

The notion of transductive inference was first introduced by Vapnik [9]. Given training samples (with labels) and test samples, transductive inference predicts the labels of the test samples using either a parametric model (e.g., a transductive support vector machine (SVM) [7]) or a non-parametric model (e.g., a nearest neighbor based classifier [5]). Different from inductive inference, transductive inference does not aim to induce a prediction function from known samples; instead, its goal is to obtain the labels of test samples via propagating the information from known samples (e.g., training samples).

In this paper, we propose a novel approach, called GPT4MIA, which utilizes GPT-3 as a plug-and-play transductive model to improve medical image analysis (MIA). For an MIA task (e.g., medical image classification), we give information of **known** samples as part of GPT-3's input and ask GPT-3 to infer a new sample's label (see Fig. 1). We expect GPT-3 to infer a test sample's label by using transductive information from the known samples on the test sample. We give theoretical analysis on why this approach is feasible by drawing connections between attention mechanism and nearest neighbor inference. To make this approach more efficient and effective, we optimize the prompt construction, aiming to choose the most representative samples/features and order them in the prompt based on their importance. We present two practical use cases of utilizing our proposed method in medical image classification. We then validate the effectiveness of our method on medical image classification benchmarks.

Our method utilizes a generative pre-trained Transformer for performing transduction from known medical image samples (e.g., training samples) to new test samples. The GPT-3 used in this work has billions of parameters. However, these parameters were pre-trained with language (text) data, and are not being updated during the transduction process for medical image classification. To our best knowledge, this is the first study to utilize a large pre-trained Transformer-based language model for performing transductive inference for image classification tasks (computer vision tasks), which are out of the data domain of the pre-training (language) domain. Our contributions are summarized as follows.

(1) We propose to utilize a large pre-trained language model (e.g., GPT-3) as a plug-and-play transductive inference method for improving MIA. We show that GPT-3 can serve as a general tool for performing transduction with an appropriate setup. Our approach is novel and flexible, suggesting a new direction of research for improving medical AI's accuracy and reliability.

(2) We develop techniques to improve the efficiency, effectiveness, and usability of our proposed GPT4MIA. Two use cases are proposed for GPT4MIA, and strong empirical results validate that GPT4MIA outperforms conventional and state-of-the-art methods in both inductive and transductive method categories.

(3) Our work offers a new way of utilizing a small set of additional labeled data in medical AI: Given a trained deep learning (DL) model and a small set of labeled data (e.g., a validation set), utilizing GPT-3 as a transductive inference method in conjunction with a DL model can achieve better prediction reliability (use case #1) and higher prediction accuracy (use case #2).

2   Approach

In this section, we first provide theoretical analysis on the connection between the attention mechanism and transductive inference mechanism. Then we show details on how to design prompts for using GPT-3 as a transductive inference method. Finally, we present two use cases with workflow to demonstrate how to use GPT-3 as a plug-and-play transductive inference method for MIA.

2.1   Theoretical Analyses

A fundamental component of GPT-3 is the scaled dot-product attention. Typically, three pieces of input are fed to an attention layer: queries Q, keys K, and values V. The scaled dot-product attention can be described as:

$$Attention(Q, K, V) = softmax(\frac{QK^T}{s})V, \tag{1}$$

where s is a scaling factor. Below, we show a special case of Eq. (1) can be viewed as a nearest neighbor (NN) classifier under a cosine distance metric system[1].
Setup 1: Suppose the key component K contains features of a set of m known samples, and each feature is of a unit length. The value component V contains

---

[1] Nearest neighbor classifiers are a typical type of transductive methods for prediction problems.

these m samples' corresponding labels, and each label is a one-hot vector. The query component Q contains a feature vector (of a unit length), which represents a new test sample whose label is yet to be determined.

Proposition 1: When the scaling factor s is approaching 0 (e.g., s is a very small positive number), the attention function in Eq. (1) is approaching an NN classifier in the cosine distance metric system.

The above is not difficult to show. QK^T computes the pair-wise similarities between the test sample's feature and the features in the keys K. A small s would enlarge the numerical gap between similar pairs and dissimilar pairs. This then leads to a one-hot-like result after applying the *softmax* operation. The one-hot-like result is then multiplied with the values V, which chooses the label of a known sample that is most similar to the test sample.

Generative Pre-trained Transformer uses a special type of attention called "self-attention", where the K, V, and Q components are all the same. We will show that in a slightly different setup from Setup 1, the self-attention mechanism can also serve a role as an NN classifier for inferring a new sample's label given known samples' information.

Setup 2: For each known sample, we concatenate its feature vector with the corresponding label vector to form a feature-label vector. We repeat this process for every known sample, and put all the thus-obtained feature-label vectors into K (row by row). In addition, we construct the test sample's feature-label vector by concatenating its feature vector with a label vector containing all zeros. We put this feature-label vector into K as well. Since we are considering the self-attention mechanism, V and Q are constructed in the same way as for K.

Proposition 2: Under Setup 2, self-attention (i.e., Eq. (1) with $K = V = Q$) generates the same label vector as the one that is generated from the attention in Setup 1 for the test sample. With s approaching a small value, self-attention can serve as an NN classifier for inferring the test sample's label.

Since the label vector for the test sample has all zeros at the input, the similarity measures between the test sample and known samples are influenced only by their features. This leads the inference process for the label of the test sample to be essentially the same as shown in Proposition 1. Transformer architecture used in modern large language models, including GPT-3, consists of multiple layers of self-attentions. Below we give more results on stacking self-attentions.

Proposition 3: Under Setup 2, a single layer of self-attention (Eq. (1) with $K = V = Q$) performs one iteration of clustering on feature-label vectors (including those for the known samples and test sample). L layers of self-attention perform L iterations of clustering. There exists a number L^* for the number of layers of self-attention for which the clustering process converges.

Guided by the above theoretical analysis, below we proceed to design the prompt (input) of GPT-3 for transductive inference. We use Setup 2 to guide the prompt construction since GPT-3 uses self-attention: The features and labels of the known samples and the feature of the test sample are put together to feed to GPT-3. According to Proposition 3, stacking self-attentions is functionally more advanced than a nearest neighbor-based classifier. GPT-3 uses not only stacking self-attentions but also numerous pre-trained parameters to augment these attentions. Hence, we expect GPT-3 to be more robust than the conventional methods (e.g., KNN) for transductive inference.

2.2 Prompt Construction

A set of m known samples is provided with their features $F = \{f_1, f_2, \ldots, f_m\}$ and corresponding labels $Y = \{y_1, y_2, \ldots, y_m\}$. A feature vector f_{test} of a test sample is given. The task in this section is to construct a prompt text representation that contains information from F, Y, and f_{test}, which is fed to GPT-3 for inferring the label of the test sample.

Selecting and Ordering Known Samples. As a language model, the original goal of training GPT-3 was to train the model to generate output that is semantically coherent with its input. The data used for training GPT-3 implicitly imposed a prior: The later a text appears in the input prompt (the closer the text to the output text), the larger impact it would impose on the output generation process. Hence, it is essential to put the more representative feature-label texts near the end of the prompt for inferring the test sample's label.

We compute pair-wise similarities between the features in the set F of the known samples and obtain an affinity matrix S, in which each entry $S_{i,j}$ describes the similarity between samples i and j and is computed as $sim(f_i, f_j)$. A cosine similarity function is the default choice for $sim(.,.)$.

For a feature vector $f_i \in F$, we define a simple measure of how well f_i represents the other known samples: $\mathrm{rep}_i = \sum_{j=1}^{m} S_{i,j}$. To select the top k representative samples, one can compute rep_i for each $i = 1, 2, \ldots, m$, and choose the largest k representative samples: **index** $= argsort(\mathrm{rep}_1, \ldots, \mathrm{rep}_m, \text{``}descend\text{''})$, and **index** is represented as **index**$[1, 2, \ldots, k]$. The order of the samples in the prompt for GPT-3 should be in the reverse order of that in the **index** list, where the most representative sample ($f_{index[1]}$) should be put at the end of the prompt in order to give more influence on the output generation. When dealing with imbalanced classification problems, we perform the above process for the samples in each class, and join them in an interleaved fashion.

Converting Features and Labels to Feature-Label Texts. For all the feature vectors f_i where i is in the **index** list computed above, we convert these features to texts in an array-like format. For each feature text thus obtained, we put its corresponding label together with the feature text to form a feature-label text. We then put these feature-label texts together into a long text. More details can be found in the Python-like pseudo-code in Listing 1.1 below.

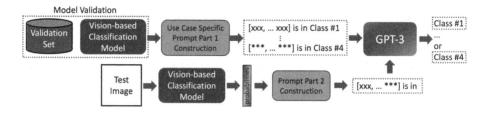

Fig. 2. The workflow of GPT4MIA. A validation set provides references for transductive inference.

```
 1  def Prompt_Construct_Part1(F,Y,selection_ratio=0.25): #only run once
 2      ot1=""; m=len(F); k = selection_ratio * m; rep=np.zeros(m,1)
 3      for i in range(m):
 4          for j in range(m):
 5              rep[i]=rep[i]+cosine_sim(f[i],f[j]))
 6      ind=argsort(rep,"descend"); ind=ind[0:k];
 7      for i in reversed(range(k)):
 8          ot1 = ot1+str(f[ind[i]]) + " is in class "
 9          + str(argmax(y[ind[i]]) + "\n")
10      return ot1
11
12  def Prompt_Construct_Part2(f_test): #for each test sample
13      ot2= str(f_test) + "is in class \n"
14      return ot2
```

Listing 1.1. Generating prompts for GPT4MIA.

2.3 Workflow and Use Cases

In this section, we propose two use cases for improving an already-trained vision-based classification model with our proposed GPT4MIA method. The main workflow is illustrated in Fig. 2.

Use Case #1: Detecting Prediction Errors. The first use case of utilizing GPT-3 as a transductive inference method is for detecting prediction errors by a trained vision-based classifier. Conventionally, a validation set is commonly used for comparing and selecting models. Here, we utilize a validation set to provide known samples for transductive inference. Feature vectors in F are obtained from the output probabilities of the vision-based classification model, and labels in Y are obtained by checking whether the classification model gives the correct prediction on each validation sample.

Use Case #2: Improving Classification Accuracy. The second use case aims to improve an already-trained classifier by directly adjusting its predictions. This is a more challenging scenario in which the method not only seeks to detect wrong predictions but also acts to convert them into correct ones. Feature vectors in F are obtained from the output probabilities of the vision-based classification model, and labels in Y are obtained from the validation set for each validation sample.

3   Experiments

In this section, we empirically validate the effectiveness of our proposed GPT4MIA. Inductive methods (e.g., Linear Regression (LR) [10], Multi-Layer Perception (MLP) [6], and Support Vector Machine (SVM) [2]) and transductive methods (e.g., K-Nearest Neighbor (KNN) [8] and Underbagging KNN (UbKNN) [5]) are applicable to the two use cases presented above. We compare these methods with GPT4MIA in the experiments below.[2]

Configurations: We use the OpenAI API [1] for querying the GPT-3 service for all the experiments related to GPT4MIA. More specifically, the text-Davinci-003 model is used, which can process up to 4000 tokens per request. The hyper-parameter k (for top k) is chosen to be a quarter of the number of the total available known samples (m). Inference for one test sample costs about $0.05 USD (charged by OpenAI). For the compared methods, we test their default settings as well as other hyper-parameter settings to report their best results.

3.1   On Detecting Prediction Errors

We utilize the RetinaMNIST and FractureMNIST3D datasets from the MedM-NIST dataset [11] for these experiments. We apply a ResNet-50 model trained with the training set as the vision-based classifier, for which the weights can be obtained from the official release.[3] We then collect the model's output probabilities for each validation sample and label it based on whether the prediction is correct. An error detection method is then built based on the information from the validations for classifying the predictions into two classes (being correct or incorrect). The error detection model is then evaluated using the test set working with the same prediction model which was used on the validation (ResNet-50 in this case). We compare our proposed GPT4MIA method on this task with a set of well established inductive methods and transductive methods. From Table 1, one can see that GPT4MIA significantly outperforms the known competing methods for detecting prediction errors from a CNN-based classifier.

3.2   On Improving Classification Accuracy

We utilize the RetinaMNIST and FractureMNIST3D datasets from MedM-NIST [11] for these experiments. ResNet-50 is used as the trained vision-based classification model. The model weights are obtained from the MedMNIST official release. In Table 2, we observe that GPT4MIA performs similarly when comparing with the state-of-the-art transductive inference method Underbagging KNN in balanced accuracy. In Tabel 3, we observe that GPT4MIA performs considerably better in balanced accuracy.

---

[2] LR, MLP, SVM, and KNN are conducted using the scikit-learn library at https://scikit-learn.org/, and UbKNN is with our implementation.

[3] The model weights are obtained from https://github.com/MedMNIST/experiments.

3.3 Ablation Studies

We validate the effect of performing sample selection and ordering described in Sect. 2.2. In Table 4 and Table 5, we show the performances for the setting without the step of sample selection and ordering. From these results, it is clear that sample selection and ordering is important for better performance when utilizing GPT-3 as a transductive inference tool.

Table 1. Experiments for Use Case #1: Detecting Prediction Errors.

Method	RetinaMNIST				FractureMNIST3D			
	Precision	Recall	F-score	Bal-Accu	Precision	Recall	F-score	Bal-Accu
LR	**0.617**	0.631	0.624	0.486	0.492	**0.776**	0.604	0.517
MLP	0.616	0.637	0.626	0.488	0.571	0.482	0.523	0.572
SVM	0.607	0.648	0.627	0.489	0.527	0.414	0.464	0.533
KNN	0.608	0.407	0.488	0.458	0.488	0.716	0.580	0.507
UbKNN	0.574	0.859	0.689	0.551	0.673	0.673	0.673	0.564
GPT4MIA	0.581	**0.860**	**0.693**	**0.679**	**0.706**	0.673	**0.689**	**0.603**

Table 2. Experiments for Use Case #2. Dataset: RetinaMNIST.

Method	Class #1	Class #2	Class #3	Class #4	Class #5	Bal-Accu
N/A	0.813	0.063	0.400	0.563	0.0	0.368
LR	0.753	0.0	0.663	0.29	0.0	0.342
MLP	0.736	0.0	0.456	0.50	0.0	0.338
SVM	0.729	0.0	0.369	0.75	0.0	0.370
UbKNN	0.747	0.130	0.478	0.603	0.0	0.392
GPT4MIA	0.672	0.437	0.207	0.529	0.150	**0.399**

Table 3. Experiments for Use Case #2. Dataset: FractureMNIST3D.

Method	Class #1	Class #2	Class #3	Bal-Accu
N/A	0.778	0.375	0.326	0.493
LR	0.600	0.596	0.304	0.500
MLP	0.556	0.673	0.283	0.504
SVM	0.533	0.596	0.391	0.507
UbKNN	0.644	0.394	0.478	0.505
GPT4MIA	0.522	0.510	0.543	**0.525**

Table 4. Ablation study for Use Case #2. Dataset: RetinaMNIST.

Method	Class #1	Class #2	Class #3	Class #4	Class #5	Bal-Accu
w/o Selection & Ordering	0.724	0.086	0.435	0.456	0.1	0.360
GPT4MIA (Full)	0.672	0.437	0.207	0.529	0.150	**0.399**

Table 5. Ablation study for Use Case #2. Dataset: FractureMNIST3D.

Method	Class #1	Class #2	Class #3	Bal-Accu
w/o Selection & Ordering	0.311	0.769	0.283	0.454
GPT4MIA (Full)	0.522	0.510	0.543	**0.525**

4   Discussion and Conclusions

In this paper, we developed a novel method called GPT4MIA that utilizes a pre-trained large language model (e.g., GPT-3) for transductive inference for medical image classification. Our theoretical analysis and technical developments are well-founded, and empirical results demonstrated that our proposed GPT4MIA is practical and effective. Large language models (LLMs) such as GPT-3 and, recently, ChatGPT [3] have shown great capability and potential in many different AI applications. In this work, we showed that GPT-3 can perform transductive inference for medical image classification with better accuracy than conventional and state-of-the-art machine learning methods. LLMs are great new technologies that can push the boundaries of AI research; on the other hand, new concerns are raised in using these generative models. Reliability and privacy are among the top priorities for medical image analysis, and more efforts should be put into this frontier when working with LLMs. In addition, further improving LLMs for medical image analysis, including better robustness and accuracy, lower costs, and more use cases, are all exciting and important future research targets.

Acknowledgement. This work was supported in part by National Natural Science Foundation of China (62201263) and Natural Science Foundation of Jiangsu Province (BK20220949).

References

1. OpenAI API. https://openai.com/api/
2. Chang, C.-C., Lin, C.-J.: LIBSVM: a library for support vector machines. ACM Trans. Intell. Syst. Technol. **2**(3), 1–27 (2011)
3. ChatGPT. https://openai.com/blog/chatgpt/
4. Brown, T., et al.: Language models are few-shot learners. Adv. Neural. Inf. Process. Syst. **33**, 1877–1901 (2020)
5. Hang, H., Cai, Y., Yang, H., Lin, Z.: Under-bagging nearest neighbors for imbalanced classification. J. Mach. Learn. Res. **23**(118), 1–63 (2022)

6. He, K., Zhang, X., Ren, S., Sun, J.: Delving deep into rectifiers: surpassing human-level performance on ImageNet classification. In: Proceedings of the IEEE International Conference on Computer Vision, pp. 1026–1034 (2015)
7. Joachims, T., et al.: Transductive inference for text classification using support vector machines. In: ICML, vol. 99, pp. 200–209 (1999)
8. Peterson, L.E.: K-nearest neighbor. Scholarpedia 4(2), 1883 (2009)
9. Vapnik, V.: Statistical Learning Theory. Wiley (1998)
10. Weisberg, S.: Applied Linear Regression, vol. 528. Wiley (2005)
11. Yang, J., et al.: MedMNIST v2 - a large-scale lightweight benchmark for 2D and 3D biomedical image classification. Sci. Data 10(1), 41 (2023)

SAM-Path: A Segment Anything Model for Semantic Segmentation in Digital Pathology

Jingwei Zhang[1]([✉]), Ke Ma[2], Saarthak Kapse[1], Joel Saltz[1],
Maria Vakalopoulou[3], Prateek Prasanna[1], and Dimitris Samaras[1]

[1] Stony Brook University, New York, USA
{jingwezhang,samaras}@cs.stonybrook.edu,
{saarthak.kapse,prateek.prasanna}@stonybrook.edu,
Joel.Saltz@stonybrookmedicine.edu
[2] Snap Inc., New York, USA
kemma@cs.stonybrook.edu
[3] CentraleSupélec, University of Paris-Saclay, Gif-sur-Yvette, France
maria.vakalopoulou@centralesupelec.fr

Abstract. Semantic segmentations of pathological entities have crucial clinical value in computational pathology workflows. Foundation models, such as the Segment Anything Model (SAM), have been recently proposed for universal use in segmentation tasks. SAM shows remarkable promise in instance segmentation on natural images. However, the applicability of SAM to computational pathology tasks is limited due to the following factors: **(1)** lack of comprehensive pathology datasets used in SAM training and **(2)** the design of SAM is not inherently optimized for semantic segmentation tasks. In this work, we adapt SAM for semantic segmentation by first introducing trainable class prompts, followed by further enhancements through the incorporation of a pathology encoder, specifically a pathology foundation model. Our framework, **SAM-Path** enhances SAM's ability to conduct semantic segmentation in digital pathology without human input prompts. Through extensive experiments on two public pathology datasets, the BCSS and the CRAG datasets, we demonstrate that the fine-tuning with trainable class prompts outperforms vanilla SAM with manual prompts by 27.52% in Dice score and 71.63% in IOU. On these two datasets, the proposed additional pathology foundation model further achieves a relative improvement of 5.07% to 5.12% in Dice score and 4.50% to 8.48% in IOU.

Keywords: Segment anything · Semantic segmentation · Fine-tuning

Supplementary Information The online version contains supplementary material available at https://doi.org/10.1007/978-3-031-47401-9_16.

1 Introduction

Digital pathology has revolutionized histopathological analysis by leveraging sophisticated computational techniques to augment disease diagnosis and prognosis [6,16]. A critical aspect of digital pathology is semantic segmentation, which entails dividing images into discrete regions corresponding to various tissue structures, cell types, or subcellular components [12,17]. Accurate and efficient semantic segmentation is essential for numerous applications, such as tumor detection, grading, and prognostication, in addition to the examination of tissue architecture and cellular interactions [4,13–15]. As a result, the development and optimization of robust segmentation algorithms hold significant importance for the ongoing advancement of digital pathology [8,10,20].

The AI research community is currently experiencing a significant revolution in the development of large foundation models. Among the latest advancements in computer vision is the Segment Anything Model (SAM), which serves as a universal segmentation model [9]. SAM is pretrained on a dataset containing over 1 billion masks across 11 million images. The model is designed to segment objects using various human input prompts, such as dots, bounding boxes, or text. SAM's evaluation highlights its remarkable zero-shot performance, frequently competing with or even surpassing previous fully supervised models across diverse tasks. Considering these capabilities, SAM has the potential to become a valuable tool for enhancing segmentation in digital pathology.

Although SAM has demonstrated considerable potential in computer vision, its direct applicability to digital pathology has two major limitations: 1) The basic design of SAM involves manually inputting prompts, or densely sampled points, to segment instances while it does not have any component for semantic classification. Consequently, it does not intrinsically facilitate semantic segmentation, a crucial component in digital pathology that enables the identification and differentiation of various tissue structures, cell types, and sub-cellular components. 2) The training set of SAM lacks diverse pathology images. This hinders SAM's capacity to effectively address digital pathology tasks without additional enhancements. Deng et al. confirm that the zero-shot SAM does not achieve satisfactory performance in digital pathology tasks, even with 20 prompts (clicks/boxes) per image [3].

In this work, we adpat vanilla SAM for semantic segmentation tasks in computational pathology. Our proposed adaptation involves the incorporation of trainable class prompts, which act as cues for the targeted class of interest. The performance is further enhanced by introducing a pathology foundation model as an additional feature encoder, thereby incorporating domain-specific knowledge. The proposed method enables SAM to perform semantic segmentation without the need for human input prompts. Our primary contributions are summarized as follows:

1. The introduction of a novel trainable prompt approach, enabling SAM to conduct multi-class semantic segmentation.
2. The introduction of a pathology foundation model as an additional pathology encoder to provide domain-specific information.

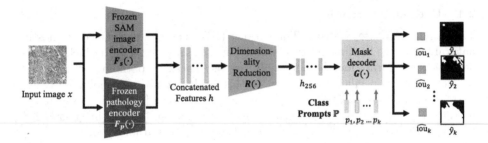

Fig. 1. Overview of SAM-Path. A pathology encoder $F_p(\cdot)$ is added in parallel with the vanilla SAM image encoder $F_s(\cdot)$ to provide more domain knowledge. The concatenated features from both the SAM image encoder and the pathology encoder are then passed to a dimensionality reduction module $R(\cdot)$. For mask prediction, we use class prompts $\mathbb{P}$ consisting of k learnable prompt tokens, in which each token prompts the mask decoder to predict the mask $\hat{y}_i$ of class i.

Through experimentation on two public pathology datasets, BCSS and CRAG, we demonstrate the superiority of our method over vanilla SAM. Here vanilla SAM refers to the classic SAM method with manual dot prompts or densely sampled dot prompts and some post-processing. On the CRAG dataset, the proposed trainable prompts achieve a relative improvement of 27.52% in Dice score and 71.63% in IOU compared to the vanilla SAM with manual prompts. We also demonstrate the benefit of the extra pathology foundation model, which leads to a further relative improvement of 5.07% to 5.12% in Dice score and 4.50% to 8.48% in IOU. Note that our goal is not to achieve SOTA performance on these datasets but to adapt SAM to semantic segmentation in digital pathology and boost its performance. To the best of our knowledge, we are the first to adapt SAM for semantic segmentation tasks in digital pathology without the need of manual prompts. By leveraging the power of SAM, pathology foundation models, and our innovative fine-tuning scheme, we aim to advance digital pathology segmentation and contribute to the ongoing development of AI-assisted diagnostic tools. Our code is available at https://github.com/cvlab-stonybrook/SAMPath.

2 Method

As shown in Fig. 1, our method consist of four modules: a SAM image encoder $F_s(\cdot)$ and a SAM mask decoder $G(\cdot)$ inspired from the vanilla SAM, a pathology encoder to extract domain-specific features $F_p(\cdot)$, and a dimensionality reduction module $R(\cdot)$. We discard the prompt encoder in the vanilla SAM because of the manually labeled prompts are not available in our segmentation tasks. Formally, given an input image x, our task is to predict its corresponding segmentation map y with the same resolution as x. Each pixel in y belongs to one of k predefined classes. We convert y into k segmentation masks $\{y_1, y_2, \ldots, y_k\}$, where y_i represents the segmentation mask of class i.

2.1 Pathology Encoder

The vanilla SAM uses a Vision Transformer (ViT) network pretrained on mostly natural images as the image encoder and thus its generated features lack pathology specific information. In our study, we use an extra pathology encoder to provide domain specific information. In this study, we use a pathology foundation model, the first stage ViT-Small of the HIPT model [2] which is pretrained on the TCGA Pan-cancer dataset [18]. As shown in Fig. 1, input image x is fed into both the vanilla SAM image encoder $F_s(\cdot)$ and the pathology encoder $F_p(\cdot)$. The output features are then concatenated as

$$h = [F_s(x), F_p(x)]. \tag{1}$$

The vanilla SAM contains the dimensionality reduction module within its image encoder, but as the dimensionality of output features h is now increased and not capable with decoder, we move this module $R(\cdot)$ after concatenation and adjust its input dimensionality accordingly.

2.2 Class Prompts

To enable the mask decoder $G(\cdot)$ to conduct semantic segmentation without manually inputting prompts, we use the trainable prompt token [7,19]. As shown in Fig. 1, for a segmentation task with k classes, we provide a set of class prompts. It consists of k trainable tokens $\mathbb{P} = \{p_i | i = 1, 2, \ldots, k\}$, where p_i is the class prompt of class i. Each of these class prompts p_i serve as the prompt to the mask decoder that it should segment class i. Different from the manually annotated dot prompts in the vanilla SAM, our class prompts are trainable and thus do not require human labelling.

For a class prompt p_i, the mask decoder, like that in the vanilla SAM, produces a predicted segmentation map $\hat{y}_i$ of class i and a IOU (Intersection over Union) prediction $\hat{iou}_i$ that predicts the IOU of the predicted segmentation map and the ground truth y_i. The prediction is formulated as follows:

$$G(h_{256}, \mathbb{P}) = \{<\hat{iou}_i, \hat{y}_i> | i = 1, 2, \ldots, k\} \tag{2}$$

Note that we conduct an extra softmax on all y_i for better performance.

2.3 Optimization

The vanilla SAM uses a combination of Dice loss, focal loss and the IOU loss (MSE loss on IOU predictions). We adapt their loss as follows:

$$\mathcal{L} = \sum_{i=1}^{k} [(1 - \alpha)\mathcal{L}_{dice}(\hat{y}_i, y_i) + \alpha\mathcal{L}_{focal}(\hat{y}_i, y_i) + \beta\mathcal{L}_{mse}(\hat{iou}_i, IOU(\hat{y}_i, y_i))] \tag{3}$$

where $\alpha \in [0, 1]$ and β are weight hyper-parameters. $\mathcal{L}_{dice}$ represents the Dice loss function, $\mathcal{L}_{focal}$ represents the focal loss function and $\mathcal{L}_{mse}$ represents the Mean Squared Error (MSE) loss function. We update parameters in the mask decoder $G(\cdot)$, class prompts $\mathbb{P}$ and the dimensionality reduction module $R(\cdot)$ and keep the SAM image encoder $F_s(\cdot)$ and the pathology encoder $F_p(\cdot)$ frozen.

Table 1. Quantitative results of segmentation on the BCSS and CRAG datasests.

Dataset	BCSS		CRAG	
Metric	Dice	IOU	Dice	IOU
Vanilla SAM	/[a]	/	0.5245^{b}	0.3555^{b}
Vanilla SAM with post-processing	/[a]	/	0.6598	0.4924
Fine-tuned SAM (w.o. F_p)	0.7562	0.6080	0.8414	0.8451
SAM-Path w.o F_s	0.7813	0.6411	0.8191	0.8252
SAM-Path	**0.7949**	**0.6596**	**0.8841**	**0.8831**

[a] The vanilla SAM does not work on the BCSS dataset, as it cannot assign semantic labels to the multi-class segmented objects in this dataset.
[b] We assume all the objects that the vanilla SAM segmented are glands.

3   Experiments

3.1   Dataset

In our experiments, we use the BCSS [1] and CRAG [5] datasets for model evaluation. For both datsets, we use their official training and test splits and further split 20% of the training data into an explicit validation set.

BCSS: The Breast Cancer Semantic Segmentation (BCSS) dataset [1] has over 20,000 semantic segmentation annotations of tissue regions sampled from 151 H&E stained breast cancer images at 40× magnification from TCGA-BRCA [11]. The annotations include 21 classes, we use the major 4 classes: Tumor, Stroma, Inflammatory and Necrosis. The rest are grouped into the 'others' class.

CRAG: The Colorectal adenocarcinoma gland (CRAG) dataset [5] has 213 images of the size ≈1536 × 1536 sampled from 38 H&E whole slide images (WSIs) at 20× magnification. The annotations include the instance-level segmentation masks of the adenocarcinoma and benign glands in colon cancer. In our experiments, we convert the instance-level masks to semantics masks.

3.2   Results

For both datasets, we use the Dice score and Inter-section Over Union (IOU) as the main evaluation metrics. Implementation details and hyper-parameters are provided in the supplementary material. We also show the comparison of average prediction time in supplementary Table 1.

Evaluation of the Overall Performance. We mainly compare the proposed method with four baselines: 1) the vanilla SAM, i.e., SAM provided with manual dot prompts of each instance, 2) the vanilla SAM with post-processing, i.e., filtering out from the vanilla SAM output any instance occupying more than half of the image; this is because SAM occasionally erroneously segments the entire image as a single instance, 3) Fine-tuned SAM utilizing our class prompts, equivalent to SAM-Path without the pathology encoder F_p, and 4) SAM-Path without

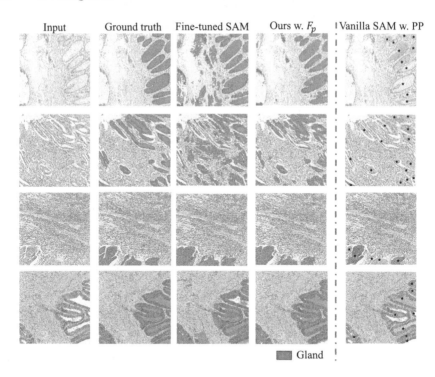

Fig. 2. Qualitative analysis on the CRAG dataset. PP represents post-processing that filters out instances occupying more than half of the image. For vanilla SAM, we provide a dot prompt (black asterisks) for each gland instance and assume all the segmented instances are glands. Our method performs better than the baselines.

the SAM image encoder F_s. Note that the original SAM lacks the capacity to predict semantics; we treat all segmented instances as glands within the context of the CRAG dataset.

As indicated in Table 1, the post-processing step enhances the performance of the original SAM, though the performance remains suboptimal. Compared with the vanilla SAM with post-processing, the fine-tuned SAM on the CRAG dataset achieves a relative improvement of 27.52% in Dice score and 71.63% in IOU, demonstrating the significant enhancement resulting from our fine-tuning scheme. The addition of the pathology encoder F_p (resulting in our proposed SAM-Path) leads to further improvements. Compared with the fine-tuned SAM without F_p, our method achieves a relative improvement of 5.12% in Dice score and 8.48% in IOU on the BCSS dataset, and 5.07% in Dice score and 4.50% in IOU on the CRAG dataset. These results underscore the value of incorporating domain-specific information from the pathology encoder to boost the performance of SAM in digital pathology tasks.

Input	Ground truth	Fine-tuned SAM	Ours w. F_p	Vanilla SAM

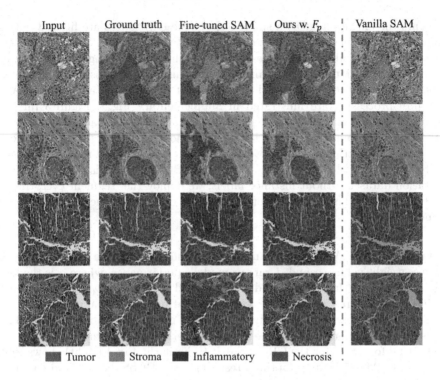

■ Tumor   ■ Stroma   ■ Inflammatory   ■ Necrosis

Fig. 3. Qualitative analysis on the BCSS dataset. The other class "others" and unlabeled regions are not colored. For the vanilla SAM, different colors represent different instances without any semantic meaning. Our method performs better than the baselines.

Also, when the SAM image encoder F_s is excluded, the BCSS dataset shows a relative decrease in performance by 1.71% in Dice score and 2.80% in IOU. For the CRAG dataset, the performance decline is more substantial, with a relative drop by 7.35% in Dice score and 6.56% in IOU. This suggests that the pathology segmentation can benefit from pre-taining of millions of natural images. Intriguingly, Table 1 reveals that SAM-Path without the pathology encoder (line 3) outperforms SAM-Path without the SAM encoder (line 4) on the CRAG dataset. However, the inverse is true for the BCSS dataset. This discrepancy is likely attributed to the fact that BCSS dataset segmentation involves multi-class semantic segmentation and hence benefits more from a domain-specific encoder, in contrast to the single semantic class of the CRAG dataset.

Qualitative Analysis. To qualitatively compare the performance of our method against others, we visualize the segmentation masks. In Fig. 2, we compare our method with vanilla SAM in which the dot prompts for each gland are provided (shown in black asterisks). Without fine-tuning, SAM lacks significant knowledge about the semantics in the pathology images. It frequently segments the entire image as a single object (these instances are filtered out in the figure), or segments the white region within the gland as an object. However, our class prompts allow us to fine-tune SAM, thereby enabling the learning of semantic information from the training data. This leads to substantial improvement in performance. Also, the visualizations of vanilla SAM and vanilla SAM with post-processing are illustrated in Supplementary Fig. 1. Figure 3 further illustrates that in the BCSS dataset, our method with the pathology encoder outperforms its counterpart that lacks the pathology encoder. This is particularly evident in distinguishing between semantic classes like stroma and necrosis. For the vanilla SAM shown in Fig. 3, since the BCSS dataset is a semantic segmentation dataset without instance labels, we deploy the "segment everything" function of SAM. This function densely samples dots within the image to create segment instances.

Ablation Study. We conduct an ablation study to evaluate the influence of two loss weight values, α and β, on our model's performance, where α is the loss weight controlling the dice loss and focal loss and β is the loss weight controlling the IOU loss. Figure 4 presents the results, indicating the optimal values of α and β for the two datasets. Specifically, Fig. 4 (left) reveals that an α value of 0.25 yields the best performance for the BCSS dataset and an α value of 0.125 yields the best performance for the CRAG dataset. Similarly, Fig. 4 (right) shows that a β value of 0.0625 leads to optimal results for the BCSS dataset and the best β value for the CRAG dataset is 0.

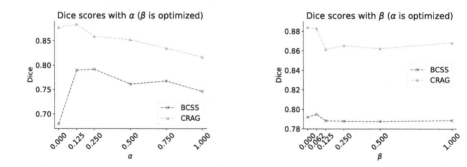

Fig. 4. Ablation study on the choice of two loss weights: α and β

4   Conclusion

In this paper, we introduced a novel fine-tuning approach using trainable class prompts to identify classes in segmentation tasks using SAM. Furthermore, we proposed the integration of a pathology encoder to incorporate more domain-specific knowledge. We evaluated our approach on two pathology segmentation datasets, demonstrating that our method facilitates semantic segmentation without the need for manually inputted prompts and the pathology encoder consistently yielded improvements in Dice and IOU scores. Our approach indicates the promising potential of SAM for pathology semantic segmentation tasks. In future research, we plan to explore its potential in pathology panoptic segmentations.

References

1. Amgad, M., et al.: Structured crowdsourcing enables convolutional segmentation of histology images. Bioinformatics **35**(18), 3461–3467 (2019)
2. Chen, R.J., et al.: Scaling vision transformers to gigapixel images via hierarchical self-supervised learning. In: Proceedings of the IEEE/CVF Conference on Computer Vision and Pattern Recognition (CVPR), June 2022, pp. 16144–16155 (2022)
3. Deng, R., et al.: Segment anything model (SAM) for digital pathology: assess zero-shot segmentation on whole slide imaging. arXiv preprint arXiv:2304.04155 (2023)
4. Ding, R., et al.: Image analysis reveals molecularly distinct patterns of TILs in NSCL associated with treatment outcome. npj Precis. Oncol. **6**(1), 33 (2022)
5. Graham, S., et al.: MILD-Net: minimal information loss dilated network for gland instance segmentation in colon histology images. Med. Image Anal. **52**, 199–211 (2019)
6. Gurcan, M.N., Boucheron, L.E., Can, A., Madabhushi, A., Rajpoot, N.M., Yener, B.: Histopathological image analysis: a review. IEEE Rev. Biomed. Eng. **2**, 147–171 (2009)
7. Jia, M., et al.: Visual prompt tuning. In: Avidan, S., Brostow, G., Cisse, M., Farinella, G.M., Hassner, T. (eds.) Computer Vision, ECCV 2022. LNCS, vol. 13693. Springer, Cham (2022). https://doi.org/10.1007/978-3-031-19827-4_41
8. Kapse, S., Torre-Healy, L., Moffitt, R.A., Gupta, R., Prasanna, P.: Subtype-specific spatial descriptors of tumor-immune microenvironment are prognostic of survival in lung adenocarcinoma. In: 2022 IEEE 19th International Symposium on Biomedical Imaging (ISBI), pp. 1–5. IEEE (2022)
9. Kirillov, A., et al.: Segment anything. arXiv preprint arXiv:2304.02643 (2023)
10. Komura, D., Ishikawa, S.: Machine learning methods for histopathological image analysis. Comput. Struct. Biotechnol. J. **16**, 34–42 (2018)
11. Lingle, W., et al.: Radiology data from the cancer genome atlas breast invasive carcinoma (TCGA-BRCA) collection. Cancer Imaging Arch. **10**, K9 (2016)
12. Litjens, G., et al.: A survey on deep learning in medical image analysis. Med. Image Anal. **42**, 60–88 (2017)
13. Lu, C., et al.: Feature-driven local cell graph (FLocK): new computational pathology-based descriptors for prognosis of lung cancer and HPV status of oropharyngeal cancers. Med. Image Anal. **68**, 101903 (2021)
14. Madabhushi, A., Lee, G.: Image analysis and machine learning in digital pathology: challenges and opportunities. Med. Image Anal. **33**, 170–175 (2016)
15. Niazi, M.K.K., Parwani, A.V., Gurcan, M.N.: Digital pathology and artificial intelligence. Lancet Oncol. **20**(5), e253–e261 (2019)
16. Pantanowitz, L., et al.: Validating whole slide imaging for diagnostic purposes in pathology: guideline from the college of American pathologists pathology and laboratory quality center. Arch. Pathol. Lab. Med. **137**(12), 1710–1722 (2013)
17. Tizhoosh, H.R., Pantanowitz, L.: Artificial intelligence and digital pathology: challenges and opportunities. J. Pathol. Inf. **9**(1), 38 (2018)

18. Weinstein, J.N., et al.: The cancer genome atlas Pan-Cancer analysis project. Nat. Genet. **45**(10), 1113–1120 (2013)
19. Zhang, J., et al.: Prompt-MIL: boosting multi-instance learning schemes via task-specific prompt tuning. arXiv preprint arXiv:2303.12214 (2023)
20. Zhang, J., et al.: Precise location matching improves dense contrastive learning in digital pathology. In: Frangi, A., de Bruijne, M., Wassermann, D., Navab, N. (eds.) Information Processing in Medical Imaging, IPMI 2023. LNCS, vol. 13939, pp. 783–794. Springer, Cham (2023). https://doi.org/10.1007/978-3-031-34048-2_60

Multi-task Cooperative Learning via Searching for Flat Minima

Fuping Wu[1]([✉]), Le Zhang[1], Yang Sun[2], Yuanhan Mo[2], Thomas Nichols[1,2], and Bartłomiej W. Papież[1,2]

[1] Nuffield Department of Population Health, University of Oxford, Oxford, UK
{Fuping.Wu,Le.Zhang}@ndph.ox.ac.uk
[2] Big Data Institute, University of Oxford, Oxford, UK
{yang.sun,thomas.nichols,bartlomiej.papiez}@bdi.ox.ac.uk,
yuanhan.mo@ndm.ox.ac.uk

Abstract. Multi-task learning (MTL) has shown great potential in medical image analysis, improving the generalizability of the learned features and the performance in individual tasks. However, most of the work on MTL focuses on either architecture design or gradient manipulation, while in both scenarios, features are learned in a competitive manner. In this work, we propose to formulate MTL as a multi/bi-level optimization problem, and therefore force features to learn from each task in a cooperative approach. Specifically, we update the sub-model for each task alternatively taking advantage of the learned sub-models of the other tasks. To alleviate the negative transfer problem during the optimization, we search for flat minima for the current objective function with regard to features from other tasks. To demonstrate the effectiveness of the proposed approach, we validate our method on three publicly available datasets. The proposed method shows the advantage of cooperative learning, and yields promising results when compared with the state-of-the-art MTL approaches. *The code will be available online.*

Keywords: Multi-Task · Cooperative Learning · Optimization

1 Introduction

With the development of deep learning, multi-task learning (MTL) has shown great potential to improve performance for individual tasks and to learn more transferable features (better generalizability), whilst reducing the number of the network parameters [16]. MTL has been widely studied in many domains including image classification [14] or image segmentation [9]. The core assumption

Supplementary Information The online version contains supplementary material available at https://doi.org/10.1007/978-3-031-47401-9_17.

behind MTL is that tasks could be correlated and thus provide complementary features for each other [4]. MTL is also applied in medical image analysis tasks [5,6,11,20], where strong associations between multiple tasks commonly exist. For example, the diagnosis of cancer may indicate the extent of disease severity, which can be correlated with the patient's survival, thus diagnosis and prognosis of cancer could be learned simultaneously [18]. In clinical diagnosis, annotations of organs or tissues could support radiologists to grade disease, to mimic this process, Zhou *et al.* [24] studied to simultaneously segment and classify (grade) tumors into benign or malignant class using 3D breast ultrasound images. Similarly, to improve the prediction of lymph node (LN) metastasis [21], Zhang *et al.* proposed a 3D multi-attention guided multi-task learning network for joint gastric tumor segmentation and LN classification [23].

Typically, MTL methods can be broadly categorized into hard and soft parameter-sharing paradigms [16]. The former adopts one backbone as the encoder to extract common features for all tasks, and the latter designs encoders for each task while constraining their associated parameters. To exploit the correlation between tasks, a large amount of work focuses on the architecture design of the network to enable the cross-task interaction [23]. For example, Misra *et al.* designed a cross-stitch model to combine features from multiple networks [12]. Besides network design, many researchers pay more attention to the neural network optimization process to counter the *negative transfer* issue [16]. As tasks could compete with each other for shared resources, the overall performance might be even poorer than those of solving individual tasks. To address this issue, previous works either change the weights of each task objective adaptively using heuristics [2], or manipulate the gradient to be descending direction for each task [10]. However, as those methods formulate MTL in a competitive manner, it is difficult to guarantee that the complementary information is fully utilized by each task. Moreover, most of them are designed for or evaluated on a simple scenario, where only one domain is involved and the tasks are homogeneous, namely all tasks are either dense prediction or image-level classification.

In this work, we propose a novel cooperative MTL framework (MT-COOL), which manages to update the features of one task while taking into account the current state of other features. Specifically, we adopt the soft parameter-sharing strategy and update each sub-model conditioning on the information learned by other tasks in an alternative manner. To avoid the *negative transfer* problem during the training, we further propose to search for flat minima of the current task with regard to others at each iteration. As a proof of concept, we first validate this method on the simple MNIST dataset for classification tasks. To show the advantage of the proposed approach in the medical domain, we use REFUGE2018 dataset for optic cup/disc segmentation and glaucoma classification, and HRF-AV dataset for artery and vein segmentation tasks. The results show a promising perspective of the proposed multi-task cooperative approach, compared to the state-of-the-art methods.

The main contributions of this work are as follows:

- We propose a novel MTL framework, which learns features for each task in a cooperative manner.
- We propose an effective optimization strategy to alleviate convergence issues.
- We validate the proposed method on three MTL scenarios with different task settings. The proposed method delivers promising results in all settings, compared with the state-of-the-art MTL approaches.

2   Method

For a better explanation, here we take two-task learning as an example, which can be generalized to n-task problems easily.

2.1   Bi-Level Optimization for Cooperative Two-Task Learning

Formally, let $x_i \in \mathbb{R}^{W \times H \times C}$ denotes an image with the width W, height H and channel C, $y_i \in \mathbb{R}^{C_0}$ is a label for classification, (or $y_i \in \mathbb{R}^{W \times H \times C_0}$ for segmentation) and C_0 is the number of classes, $F_i(\cdot; \theta_i)$ is a feature extractor, $G_i(\cdot; \phi_i)$ is a prediction function for task $i = 1, \ldots, T$ where T is a number of tasks, and here $T = 2$. θ_i and ϕ_i are corresponding parameters to be learned. Our task is to predict label $\widehat{y}_i = G_i(F_i(x_i))$.

For MTL, instead of using shared backbone, *i.e.*, $F_1 = F_2$, and updating them simultaneously with a single loss ℓ, we propose to optimize them in a cooperative manner, that is learning (F_1, G_1) conditioned on a fixed and informative F_2, and versa vice. Generally, it can be formulated as a bi-level optimization problem:

$$(U) \min_{\theta_1, \phi_1} \mathcal{L}_1(\theta_1, \phi_1, \theta_2) = \ell_1(G_1(\mathcal{M}(F_1(x_1; \theta_1), F_2(x_1; \theta_2)); \phi_1), \widehat{y}_1), \quad (1)$$

$$(L) \min_{\theta_2, \phi_2} \mathcal{L}_2(\theta_2, \phi_2, \theta_1) = \ell_2(G_2(\mathcal{M}(F_1(x_2; \theta_1), F_2(x_2; \theta_2)); \phi_2), \widehat{y}_2), \quad (2)$$

where ℓ_i is the loss function, e.g. cross-entropy loss for classification. $\mathcal{M}$ denotes a feature fusion to facilitate the current task learning by incorporating useful information from other tasks. A common choice for $\mathcal{M}$ is to use a linear combination of features, also known as *cross-stitch* [12] or concatenation operation in multi-layers (which is used in this work due to its simplicity).

To solve the problem Eq. (1)–(2), we propose to update (θ_1, ϕ_1) and (θ_2, ϕ_2) alternatively, as other traditional methods for bi-level optimization problem could be inefficient [1] due to the complexity of deep neural networks. However, without any constraint, this alternative optimization strategy could fail to achieve convergence to an optimal solution. For example, at the t-th iteration, we first optimize $\mathcal{L}_1(\theta_1, \phi_1, \theta_2^{(t-1)})$ to obtain an optimum $(\theta_1^{(t)}, \phi_1^{(t)})$. It is possible that for the second task, $\mathcal{L}_2(\theta_2^{(t-1)}, \phi_2^{(t-1)}, \theta_1^{(t-1)}) < \mathcal{L}_2(\theta_2^{(t-1)}, \phi_2^{(t-1)}, \theta_1^{(t)})$, which means that the update for the first task could increase the prediction risk of the second one, and cancel the gain from optimization of $\mathcal{L}_2$. Here, we also term this issue as *negative transfer*. To alleviate this effect, we propose to search for flat minima for one task with regard to the features from the other task in each iteration.

2.2   Finding Flat Minima via Injecting Noise

As mentioned above, the network optimized for one task could be sensitive to the change of parameters for other tasks, which may cause non-convergent solutions. Hence, at each iteration, for each task, we search for an optimum that is non-sensitive to the update of other parameters within a fixed neighborhood. We term this kind of optima as *flat minima*.

To formally state this idea, assume that noise $\epsilon_i \sim \{\mathcal{U}(-b,b)\}^{d_{\epsilon_i}}$ with $b > 0$, $d_\epsilon = d_{\theta_i}$ and d_{θ_i} the dimension of θ_i. Then for *task 1*, at t-th iteration our target is to minimize the expected loss function with regard to the parameters (θ_1, ϕ_1) and noise ϵ_2, *i.e.*,

$$(U)\ \mathcal{R}_1^{[t]}(\theta_1, \phi_1) = \int_{\mathbb{R}^{d_{\epsilon_2}}} \mathcal{L}_1(\theta_1, \phi_1, \theta_2^{[t-1]} + \epsilon_2)dP(\epsilon_2) = \mathbb{E}[\mathcal{L}_1(\theta_1, \phi_1, \theta_2^{[t-1]} + \epsilon_2)], \tag{3}$$

$$s.t.\ |\theta_1 - \theta_1^{[t-1]}| < b,$$

where $P(\epsilon_2)$ is the noise distribution, and the solution is denoted as $(\theta_1^{[t]}, \phi_1^{[t]})$. Similarly, for *task 2*, the loss function is as follows,

$$(L)\ \mathcal{R}_2^{[t]}(\theta_2, \phi_2) = \int_{\mathbb{R}^{d_{\epsilon_1}}} \mathcal{L}_2(\theta_2, \phi_2, \theta_1^{[t]} + \epsilon_1)dP(\epsilon_1) = \mathbb{E}[\mathcal{L}_2(\theta_2, \phi_2, \theta_1^{[t]} + \epsilon_1)], \tag{4}$$

$$s.t.\ |\theta_2 - \theta_2^{[t-1]}| < b.$$

Note that it is hard to find an ideal flat minimum $(\theta_1^{[t]}, \phi_1^{[t]})$ for Eq. (3), such that $\mathcal{L}_1(\theta_1^{[t]}, \phi_1^{[t]}, \theta_2^{[t-1]} + \epsilon_2^{(j_1)}) = \mathcal{L}_1(\theta_1^{[t]}, \phi_1^{[t]}, \theta_2^{[t-1]} + \epsilon_2^{(j_2)}), \forall \epsilon_2^{(j_1)}, \epsilon_2^{(j_2)} \sim P(\epsilon_2)$, and $\mathcal{L}_1(\theta_1^{[t]}, \phi_1^{[t]}, \theta_2^{[t-1]}) < \mathcal{L}_1(\theta_1^{[t-1]}, \phi_1^{[t-1]}, \theta_2^{[t-1]})$, which satisfies the requirement to avoid the optimization issue (see Sect. 2.1). Hence, our goal is to find an approximately flat minimum to alleviate this issue. A similar idea has been proposed for continual learning [19]. However, our method differs as follows: (1) the flat minimum in [19] is searched for the current task, while in our work, it is searched with regard to other tasks; (2) Once the flat minimum is found for the first task in a continual learning problem, search region for the remaining tasks is fixed, while in our work, the parameters for each task are only constrained in a single iteration, and search region could change during the optimization.

In practice, it is difficult to minimize the expected loss, we instead minimize its empirical loss for Eq. (3) and Eq. (4) as follows,

$$(U)\ L_1^{[t]}(\theta_1, \phi_1) = \frac{1}{M}\sum_{j=1}^{M} \mathcal{L}_1(\theta_1, \phi_1, \theta_2^{[t-1]} + \epsilon_2^{(j)}) + \lambda \cdot KL(\widehat{y}_1^{(j)}, \frac{1}{M}\sum_{n=1}^{M} \widehat{y}_1^{(n)}), \tag{5}$$

$$(L)\ L_2^{[t]}(\theta_2, \phi_2) = \frac{1}{M}\sum_{j=1}^{M} \mathcal{L}_2(\theta_2, \phi_2, \theta_1^{[t]} + \epsilon_1^{(j)}) + \lambda \cdot KL(\widehat{y}_2^{(j)}, \frac{1}{M}\sum_{n=1}^{M} \widehat{y}_2^{(n)}), \tag{6}$$

Algorithm 1: Cooperative Learning via Searching Flat Minima

Input: Images and labels (x_i, y_i) for task $i \in \mathcal{T} = \{1, 2\}$. Network for both tasks with randomly initialized parameters $\psi_i = (\theta_i, \phi_i)$, $\psi = (\psi_1, \psi_2)$. Sampling times M, inner iteration number L, the flat region bound b. The step sizes α, β.

/* Warm up the network to obtain initialized parameters $\psi^{[0]}$ */

1 **for** *iteration* $t = 1, 2, \cdots, T_w$ **do**

2 $\quad$ Sampling $\epsilon_i \sim \{\mathcal{U}(-b, b)\}^{d_{\epsilon_i}}$ with M times for $i = 1, 2$, respectively;

3 $\quad$ Compute $\mathcal{L}_{total}$ in Eq. (7);

4 $\quad$ Update $\psi^{[t]} = \psi^{[t-1]} - \alpha \nabla \mathcal{L}_{total}(\psi)$;

5 **end**

6 Start cooperative learning with $\psi^{[0]} = \psi^{[T_w]}$;

/* Alternative Update ψ_i for task $i = 1, 2$.   */

7 **for** *Outer iteration* $t = 1, 2, \cdots$ **do**

8 $\quad$ **for** *task* $i = 1, 2$ **do**

9 $\quad\quad$ **for** *inner iteration* $l = 1, 2, \cdots, L$ **do**

10 $\quad\quad\quad$ Sampling $\epsilon_i \sim \{\mathcal{U}(-b, b)\}^{d_{\epsilon_i}}$ with M times for task i ;

11 $\quad\quad\quad$ Compute $L_i^{[t]}(\theta_i, \phi_i)$ in Eq. (5) (or Eq. (6)) with fixed $\theta_{\mathcal{T} \setminus \{i\}}^{[t-1]}$;

12 $\quad\quad\quad$ **if** *l=1* **then**

13 $\quad\quad\quad\quad$ Update $\psi_i^{[t]} = \psi_i^{[t-1]} - \beta \nabla L_i^{[t]}(\psi_i)$;

14 $\quad\quad\quad$ **else**

15 $\quad\quad\quad\quad$ Update $\psi_i^{[t]} = \psi_i^{[t]} - \beta \nabla L_i^{[t]}(\psi_i)$;

16 $\quad\quad\quad$ **end**

17 $\quad\quad\quad$ Clamp $\theta_i^{[t]}$ into $[\theta_i^{[t-1]} - b, \theta_i^{[t-1]} + b]$;

18 $\quad\quad$ **end**

19 $\quad$ **end**

20 **end**

Output: Model parameters $(\theta_1, \phi_1, \theta_2, \phi_2)$.

---

where $\epsilon_i^{(j)}$ is a noise vector sampled from $P(\epsilon_i)$, M is the sampling times, and KL is the Kullback-Leibler Divergence. The first term in Eq. (5) or Eq. (6) is designed to find a satisfying minimum for the current task, and the second term enforces this minimum to be flat as desired.

Warm up the Network. To initialize the parameters for Eq. (3) and Eq. (4) with non-sensitive $(\theta_1^{[0]}, \theta_2^{[0]})$, we minimize the following loss function,

$$\mathcal{L}_{total} = \frac{1}{M} \sum_{j=1}^{M} (\mathcal{L}_1(\theta_1 + \epsilon_1^{(j)}, \phi_1, \theta_2 + \epsilon_2^{(j)}) + \mathcal{L}_2(\theta_2 + \epsilon_2^{(j)}, \phi_2, \theta_1 + \epsilon_1^{(j)})). \quad (7)$$

Algorithm. We term the proposed **multi-task coo**perative **learning** method as MT-COOL. The algorithm is described in Algorithm 1. Note that to alleviate the optimization issue discussed in Sect. 2.1, after the update for each task, we clamp the parameters to ensure that they fall within the flat region, as described in Line 17 in Algorithm 1.

Network Configuration. Figure 1 illustrates the framework for two-task cooperative learning. Our framework consists of an encoder and task-specific decoders. The parameters at each layer of the encoder are evenly allocated to each task, and the learned features are then concatenated as the input of the next layer.

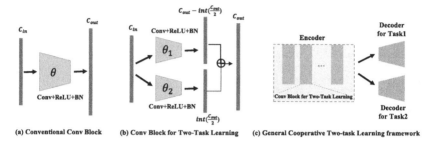

Fig. 1. A general framework for our MTL method. (a) is the conventional convolution block, (b) illustrates the structure of a convolution block for cooperative two-task learning, and (c) shows the general framework for MTL, which contains an encoder and task-specific decoders.

3   Experiments

We validate our MTL framework in three scenarios as follows: (1) classification tasks on different classes with the MNIST dataset [8], (2) one domain for simultaneous segmentation and classification tasks using the REFUGE2018 dataset [13], and (3) one domain for two segmentation tasks with HRF-AV dataset [7]. For our method, we adopt the stochastic gradient descent (SGD) optimizer, and empirically set the bound value $b = 0.05$, the learning rate $\alpha = \beta = 0.1$. To reduce the training time and the memory, we simply set the sampling number $M = 1$. All experiments are implemented using one GTX 1080Ti GPU.

3.1   Dataset

(1) **MNIST.** This dataset contains 50,000 training and 10,000 testing images. To simulate a multi-task learning setting, we divide both the training and test images into two subsets with either even numbers $\{0, 2, 4, 6, 8\}$ (denoted as *Task 1*) or odd numbers $\{1, 3, 5, 7, 9\}$ (denoted as *Task 2*). For the network, we adopt the widely used LeNet architecture for MNIST dataset [8], of which the last layer contains 50 hidden units, followed by a final prediction output. (2) **REFUGE2018.** The REFUGE2018 challenge [13] provides 1200 retinal color fundus photography. The target of this challenge is glaucoma detection and optic disc/cup segmentation. We divide this dataset into 800 samples for training and 400 test subset, where the ratio of the number of glaucomas to non-glaucoma images are both 1 : 9. As discussed in [13], glaucoma is mostly characterized by the optic nerve head area. Hence, we cropped all images around the optic disc

into 512×512. We used the UNet [15] for the segmentation task, with the four down-sampling modules as the shared encoders. The output of segmentation and the features from the bottom layers are taken as the input of the decoder for classification. (3) **HRF-AV.** This dataset [7] contains 45 fundus images with a high resolution of 3504×2336. The tasks for this dataset are the binary vessel segmentation and the artery/vein (A/V) segmentation. We randomly split the dataset into 15 and 30 samples for training and testing. We adopt the U-Net as the backbone with the bottom feature channel being 256. During training, we crop patches with size of 2048×2048 randomly as input.

3.2   Results on MNIST Dataset

Ablation Study. To validate the effectiveness of the two terms in Eq. (5) and Eq. (6), we conduct two experiments: (1) **Vanilla.** We simply optimize the objective of each task alternatively without any constraints or sampling operations. (2) **Ours (*w/o*Reg).** We sample noises during training, and optimize the losses with solely the first term in Eq. (5) and Eq. (6), *i.e.*, without the similarity regularization. We run 5 times for each method, and report their mean and standard deviation values.

As shown in the top four rows of Table 1, compared to the **Independent** approach, the proposed **Vanilla** bi-level optimization method can utilize the features from other tasks and boost the performance of the current one. By introducing noises to find flat minima during training, **Ours (*w/o* Reg)** further achieves higher prediction, particularly for *Task 2*. Finally, by adding similarity regularization, our method obtains the best results.

Table 1. Performance of SOTA MTL methods on MNIST dataset. We set the number of parameters of **Joint** method as the base 1, and the values in the column 'Params' are the ratio of the parameter number of each method to the **Joint**.

Methods	Params	Task 1	Task 2
Independent	≈2	99.41 ± 0.03492	98.77 ± 0.06029
Ours (Vanilla)	1	99.61 ± 0.06210	99.37 ± 0.04494
Ours (*w/o* Reg)	1	99.66 ± 0.03765	99.56 ± 0.07203
MT-COOL (Ours)	1	**99.72 ± 0.03978**	**99.62 ± 0.01576**
Joint	1	99.60 ± 0.03765	99.51 ± 0.06281
CAGrad [10]	1	99.67 ± 0.05293	99.51 ± 0.05229
GradDrop [3]	1	99.65 ± 0.03492	99.53 ± 0.04245
MGDA [17]	1	99.63 ± 0.05883	99.47 ± 0.05078
PCGrad [22]	1	99.66 ± 0.04180	99.51 ± 0.09108

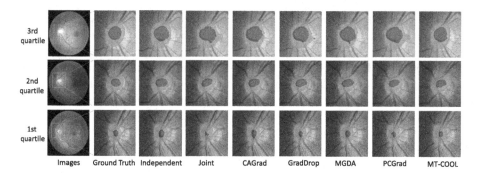

Fig. 2. Visualization results from MTL methods on REFUGE2018 dataset. The selected samples rank the 1st quartile, median and 3rd quartile in terms of the segmentation performance of **Independent**.

Comparison Study. We compare the proposed method with four state-of-the-art (SOTA) MTL approaches, including MGDA [17], PCGrad [22], GradDrop [3] and CAGrad [10]. We also implement the **Joint** method as a baseline, which simply sums the loss of each task as the total loss for training.

As shown in Table 1, all MTL methods improve the performance on each task, compared to **Independent**. Among all the compared methods, our technique performs the best on both tasks.

3.3 Comparison on REFUGE2018 Dataset

For REFUGE2018 dataset, we compare our method with CAGrad, GradDrop, MGDA, PCGrad, and Joint. We run each method three times, and report the *mean ± std* values of Dice score on optic cup and disc for the segmentation task, and accuracy (Acc), Area Under the Receiver Operating Characteristics (AUROC), sensitivity (Sen) and specificity (Spe) for the classification task.

As shown in Table 2, our method achieves comparable results on the segmentation task with the **Independent**, while other MTL methods degrade significantly, particularly on Disc. For the classification task, our method achieves the best performance in terms of all the metrics. Figure 2 provides the visualization results for qualitative comparison. One can see that the proposed method obtains the best prediction shape among all MTL methods.

3.4 Comparison on HRF-AV Dataset

We also conduct a comparison study on HRF-AV dataset. Each method is repeated three times, and the mean results are presented in Table 3. One can see that compared to the **Independent**, all the other MTL methods perform poorly, especially on A/V segmentation task. For example, the best F1 scores on A/V segmentation among the five MTL methods are 0.5127 and 0.5736, respectively, obtained by GradDrop, which are much lower than those from **Independent**.

Table 2. Performance of SOTA MTL methods on REFUGE2018 dataset.

Methods	Params	Segmentation		Classification			
		Cup (Dice%)	Disc (Dice%)	Acc	AUROC	Sen	Spe
Independent	≈2	95.14 ± 0.05110	86.87 ± 005644	0.900 ± 0.00235	0.902 ± 0.0106	0.658 ± 0.0117	0.927 ± 0.00392
Joint	1	91.19 ± 0.7600	77.36 ± 0.5236	0.907 ± 0.0183	0.895 ± 0.0221	0.658 ± 0.0656	0.935 ± 0.0264
CAGrad [10]	1	92.67 ± 0.7702	81.71 ± 0.2874	0.914 ± 0.00513	0.904 ± 0.00562	0.658 ± 0.0235	0.942 ± 0.00796
GradDrop [3]	1	91.70 ± 0.6376	78.91 ± 1.439	0.909 ± 0.00424	0.922 ± 0.0115	0.716 ± 0.0471	0.930 ± 0.00988
MGDA [17]	1	93.87 ± 0.5017	83.87 ± 0.9732	0.895 ± 0.0154	0.914 ± 0.00610	0.633 ± 0.0824	0.924 ± 0.0260
PCGrad [22]	1	91.74 ± 0.5569	79.80 ± 0.8748	0.911 ± 0.00849	0.898 ± 0.0136	0.675 ± 0.0204	0.937 ± 0.00796
MT-COOL (Ours)	1	**94.37 ± 0.1706**	**86.18 ± 0.3046**	**0.937 ± 0.0113**	**0.942 ± 0.0149**	**0.750 ± 0.000**	**0.958 ± 0.0126**

Table 3. Performance of SOTA MTL methods on HRF-AV dataset.

Methods	Params	A/V Segmentation						Binary Segmentation	
		Acc (A)	F1 (A)	Acc (V)	F1 (V)	Acc (AV)	F1 (A/V)	Acc	F1
Independent	≈2	0.9814	0.6999	0.9821	0.7492	0.9692	0.7698	0.9691	0.7831
Joint	1	0.9622	0.3537	0.9661	0.5171	0.9664	0.7360	0.9691	0.7835
CAGrad [10]	1	0.9687	0.4754	0.9696	0.5520	0.9668	0.7364	0.9690	0.7790
GradDrop [3]	1	0.9708	0.5127	0.9716	0.5736	0.9666	0.7343	0.9686	0.7742
MGDA [17]	1	0.9636	0.2343	0.9632	0.5315	0.9660	0.7263	0.9691	0.7793
PCGrad [22]	1	0.9671	0.4262	0.9681	0.5387	0.9667	0.7357	0.9687	0.7763
MT-COOL (Ours)	1	**0.9801**	**0.6671**	**0.9811**	**0.7135**	**0.9674**	**0.7424**	**0.9701**	**0.7912**

On the contrary, our method performs comparably with the **Independent** on A/V segmentation, and even slightly better on binary segmentation. For qualitative comparison, please refer to Fig. 1 in the Supplementary material.

4 Conclusion

In this work, we propose a novel MTL framework via bi-level optimization. Our method learns features for each task in a cooperative manner, instead of competing for resources with each other. We validate our model on three datasets, and the results prove its great potential in MTL. However, there are still some issues that need to be studied in the future. For example, we need to validate our method on large-scale tasks and find a more efficient learning strategy such as using distributed learning. Moreover, how to allocate the parameters to each task automatically and effectively is important for model generalization. For better interpretability, learning features specific to each task should also be studied.

References

1. Biswas, A., Hoyle, C.: A literature review: solving constrained non-linear bi-level optimization problems with classical methods. In: International Design Engineering Technical Conferences and Computers and Information in Engineering Conference, vol. 59193, p. V02BT03A025. American Society of Mechanical Engineers (2019)
2. Chen, Z., Badrinarayanan, V., Lee, C.Y., Rabinovich, A.: GradNorm: gradient normalization for adaptive loss balancing in deep multitask networks. In: International Conference on Machine Learning, pp. 794–803. PMLR (2018)

3. Chen, Z., et al.: Just pick a sign: optimizing deep multitask models with gradient sign dropout. Adv. Neural. Inf. Process. Syst. **33**, 2039–2050 (2020)
4. Crawshaw, M.: Multi-task learning with deep neural networks: a survey. arXiv preprint arXiv:2009.09796 (2020)
5. He, K., et al.: HF-UNet: learning hierarchically inter-task relevance in multi-task U-Net for accurate prostate segmentation in CT images. IEEE Trans. Med. Imaging **40**(8), 2118–2128 (2021)
6. He, T., Hu, J., Song, Y., Guo, J., Yi, Z.: Multi-task learning for the segmentation of organs at risk with label dependence. Med. Image Anal. **61**, 101666 (2020)
7. Hemelings, R., Elen, B., Stalmans, I., Van Keer, K., De Boever, P., Blaschko, M.B.: Artery-vein segmentation in fundus images using a fully convolutional network. Comput. Med. Imaging Graph. **76**, 101636 (2019)
8. LeCun, Y., Bottou, L., Bengio, Y., Haffner, P.: Gradient-based learning applied to document recognition. Proc. IEEE **86**(11), 2278–2324 (1998)
9. Li, W.H., Liu, X., Bilen, H.: Learning multiple dense prediction tasks from partially annotated data. In: Proceedings of the IEEE/CVF Conference on Computer Vision and Pattern Recognition, pp. 18879–18889 (2022)
10. Liu, B., Liu, X., Jin, X., Stone, P., Liu, Q.: Conflict-averse gradient descent for multi-task learning. Adv. Neural. Inf. Process. Syst. **34**, 18878–18890 (2021)
11. Liu, L., Dou, Q., Chen, H., Qin, J., Heng, P.A.: Multi-task deep model with margin ranking loss for lung nodule analysis. IEEE Trans. Med. Imaging **39**(3), 718–728 (2019)
12. Misra, I., Shrivastava, A., Gupta, A., Hebert, M.: Cross-stitch networks for multi-task learning. In: Proceedings of the IEEE Conference on Computer Vision and Pattern Recognition, pp. 3994–4003 (2016)
13. Orlando, J.I., et al.: Refuge challenge: a unified framework for evaluating automated methods for glaucoma assessment from fundus photographs. Med. Image Anal. **59**, 101570 (2020)
14. Requeima, J., Gordon, J., Bronskill, J., Nowozin, S., Turner, R.E.: Fast and flexible multi-task classification using conditional neural adaptive processes. In: Advances in Neural Information Processing Systems, vol. 32 (2019)
15. Ronneberger, O., Fischer, P., Brox, T.: U-Net: convolutional networks for biomedical image segmentation. In: Navab, N., Hornegger, J., Wells, W.M., Frangi, A.F. (eds.) MICCAI 2015, Part III. LNCS, vol. 9351, pp. 234–241. Springer, Cham (2015). https://doi.org/10.1007/978-3-319-24574-4_28
16. Ruder, S.: An overview of multi-task learning in deep neural networks. CoRR, abs/1706.05098 (2017)
17. Sener, O., Koltun, V.: Multi-task learning as multi-objective optimization. In: Advances in Neural Information Processing Systems, vol. 31 (2018)
18. Shao, W., et al.: Multi-task multi-modal learning for joint diagnosis and prognosis of human cancers. Med. Image Anal. **65**, 101795 (2020)
19. Shi, G., Chen, J., Zhang, W., Zhan, L.M., Wu, X.M.: Overcoming catastrophic forgetting in incremental few-shot learning by finding flat minima. Adv. Neural. Inf. Process. Syst. **34**, 6747–6761 (2021)
20. Uslu, F., Varela, M., Boniface, G., Mahenthran, T., Chubb, H., Bharath, A.A.: LA-Net: a multi-task deep network for the segmentation of the left atrium. IEEE Trans. Med. Imaging **41**(2), 456–464 (2021)
21. Wang, Y., et al.: CT radiomics nomogram for the preoperative prediction of lymph node metastasis in gastric cancer. Eur. Radiol. **30**(2), 976–986 (2020)
22. Yu, T., Kumar, S., Gupta, A., Levine, S., Hausman, K., Finn, C.: Gradient surgery for multi-task learning. Adv. Neural. Inf. Process. Syst. **33**, 5824–5836 (2020)

23. Zhang, Y., et al.: 3D multi-attention guided multi-task learning network for auto-matic gastric tumor segmentation and lymph node classification. IEEE Trans. Med. Imaging **40**(6), 1618–1631 (2021)
24. Zhou, Y., et al.: Multi-task learning for segmentation and classification of tumors in 3D automated breast ultrasound images. Med. Image Anal. **70**, 101918 (2021)

MAP: Domain Generalization via M̲eta-Learning on A̲natomy-Consistent P̲seudo-Modalities

Dewei Hu[1], Hao Li[1], Han Liu[2], Xing Yao[2], Jiacheng Wang[2], and Ipek Oguz[1,2(✉)]

[1] Department of Electrical and Computer Engineering, Vanderbilt University, Nashville, USA
dewei.hu@vanderbilt.edu
[2] Department of Computer Science, Vanderbilt University, Nashville, USA
ipek.oguz@vanderbilt.edu

Abstract. Deep models suffer from limited generalization capability to unseen domains, which has severely hindered their clinical applicability. Specifically for the retinal vessel segmentation task, although the model is supposed to learn the anatomy of the target, it can be distracted by confounding factors like intensity and contrast. We propose Meta learning on Anatomy-consistent Pseudo-modalities (MAP), a method that improves model generalizability by learning structural features. We first leverage a feature extraction network to generate three distinct pseudo-modalities that share the vessel structure of the original image. Next, we use the episodic learning paradigm by selecting one of the pseudo-modalities as the meta-train dataset, and perform meta-testing on a continuous augmented image space generated through Dirichlet mixup of the remaining pseudo-modalities. Further, we introduce two loss functions that facilitate the model's focus on shape information by clustering the latent vectors obtained from images featuring identical vasculature. We evaluate our model on seven public datasets of various retinal imaging modalities and we conclude that MAP has substantially better generalizability.

Keywords: domain generalization · vessel segmentation · meta-learning · Dirichlet mixup

1 Introduction

In the absence of a single standardized imaging paradigm, medical images obtained from different devices may exhibit considerable domain variation. Figure 1 demonstrates three types of domain shift among images delineating the retinal vessels. The presence of such distribution mismatch can significantly degrade the performance of deep learning models on unseen datasets, thus impeding their widespread clinical deployment. To address the domain generalization (DG) problem [26], a straightforward idea is to focus on the domain-invariant

© The Author(s), under exclusive license to Springer Nature Switzerland AG 2023
M. E. Celebi et al. (Eds.): MICCAI 2023 Workshops, LNCS 14393, pp. 182–192, 2023.
https://doi.org/10.1007/978-3-031-47401-9_18

MAP   183

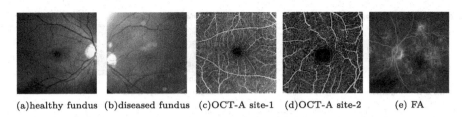

(a)healthy fundus (b)diseased fundus (c)OCT-A site-1 (d)OCT-A site-2   (e) FA

Fig. 1. Domain shift examples. Type I: pathological phenotypes (a vs. b). Type II: cross-site shifts (c vs. d). Type III: cross-modality shifts (a-b vs. c-d vs. e).

patterns for the specific downstream task. For retinal vessel segmentation, the morphology of vessels can be deemed such a domain-invariant pattern. Hence, our hypothesis is that *emphasizing the structural characteristics of the vasculature can enhance the model's DG performance*. Following a similar idea, Hu et al. [9] proposed to explicitly delineate the vessel shape by a Hessian-based vector field. However, the dependency on the image gradient makes this approach vulnerable to low-quality data with poor contrast and/or high noise. In contrast, we instead propose an implicit way of exploiting the morphological features by adopting the meta-learning paradigm on anatomy-consistent pseudo-modalities (MAP).

First, we leverage a structural feature extraction network (Fig. 2(a)) generate three pseudo-modalities, similar to [9]. The network is defined by setting the bottleneck of the U-Net [18] backbone to have the same width and height with the input image. Given its capability to extract interpretable visualization, this architecture is often implemented in representation disentanglement [16] and unsupervised segmentation [8]. Supervised by the binary vessel map, the latent image preserves the vasculature structure while the style exhibits some randomness, as illustrated in Fig. 2(b). Therefore, we refer to these latent images as anatomy-consistent pseudo-modalities.

Meta-learning has recently emerged as a popular technique for addressing the DG problem [4,10]. Following the idea of episodic training presented in MAML [6], researchers split their training data into two subsets, meta-train and meta-test, to mimic the scenario of encountering out-of-distribution (OOD) data during training. Liu et al. [13] proposed to conduct meta-learning in a continuous frequency space created by mixing up [11,23] the amplitude spectrum. They keep the phase spectrum unchanged to preserve the anatomy in the generated images. In contrast, given our pseudo-modalities with identical underlying vasculature, we are able to create a continuous image space via Dirichlet mixup [19] without affecting the vasculature. We regard images in each pseudo-modality as a corner of a tetrahedron, as depicted in Fig. 2(c). The red facet of the tetrahedron is a continuous space created by the convex combination of images from the three pseudo-modalities. We use images in one pseudo-modality (blue node) for meta-train and the mixup space (red facet) for meta-test. An important property of the mixup space is that all the samples share the same vessel structure while

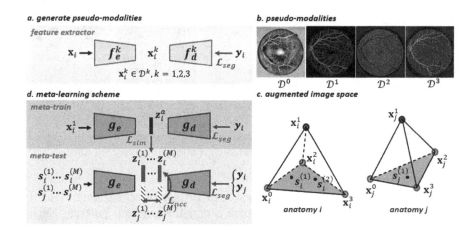

Fig. 2. The key components of MAP, clockwise. **(a)** $f(\cdot)$ is the synthesis network. $\mathbf{x}_i$ is the ith color fundus input and $\mathbf{y}_i$ is its ground truth vessel map. k indexes three different models that generate diverse pseudo-modalities. **(b)** An example image in four pseudo-modalities: $\mathcal{D}^0$ is the histogram equalization of intensity-reversed green channel of input $\mathbf{x}$ and $\mathcal{D}^k$, $k = 1, 2, 3$ are generated by f_e^k. **(c)** The four pseudo-modalities of an input $\mathbf{x}_i$ form the corners of a tetrahedron. The colored facet is a continuous image space created by Dirichlet mixup. $\mathbf{s}_i^{(m)}$ denotes the mth sample from the image space. Anatomy i represents the underlying shape of vasculature in $\mathbf{x}_i$, which is consistent for all samples $\mathbf{s}_i^{(m)}$. **(d)** The meta-learning scheme. $g(\cdot)$ is the segmentation network, M is the number of samples drawn, $\mathbf{z}$ is the latent feature vector. (Color figure online)

the image style may differ drastically. Hence, employing proper constraints on the relationship between features can implicitly encourage the model to learn the shape of vessels. Inspired by [4], we leverage a similarity loss to express the feature consistency between the meta-train and meta-test stages. Additionally, we propose a normalized cross-correlation (NCC) loss to differentiate latent features extracted from images with different anatomy. In the context of contrastive learning, these loss functions cluster positive pairs and separate negative pairs.

In our study, we use seven public datasets including color fundus, OCT angiography (OCT-A) and fluorescein angiography (FA) images. We train MAP on fundus data and test on all modalities. We show that MAP exhibits outstanding generalization ability in most conditions. Our main contributions are:

❖ We generate a continuous space of anatomy-consistent pseudo-modalities with Dirichlet mixup.
❖ We present an episodic learning scheme employed on synthesized images.
❖ We propose a normalized cross-correlation loss function to cluster the feature vectors with regard to the vessel structure.
❖ We conduct extensive experiments on seven public datasets in various modalities which show the superior DG performance of MAP.

MAP   185

2 Methods

2.1 Problem Definition

Given a source domain $\mathcal{S} = \{(\mathbf{x}_i, \mathbf{y}_i)|i \in \{1, \cdots, N\}\}$ that includes N pairs of raw images $\mathbf{x}_i$ and ground truth labels $\mathbf{y}_i$, our goal is to train a segmentation network $g(\cdot)$ that can robustly work on the target domain $\mathcal{T} = \{T^p|p \in \{1, \cdots, P\}\}$ with P unseen datasets. In practice, we include only fundus images in $\mathcal{S}$ since there are many public annotated fundus datasets. For $\mathcal{T}$, data from three different modalities (fundus, OCT-A and FA) are included. We test the model generalization on datasets with three distinct types of domain shift: (I) data with pathological phenotypes, (II) cross-site shifts, (III) cross-modality shifts.

2.2 Pseudo-modality Synthesis

The features in the latent space of a U-Net [18] backbone is usually a low-dimensional representation of the input images. In some applications (e.g., representation disentanglement), it is desirable for the latent features to show visually intuitive structural characteristics. In such scenarios, the bottleneck of the feature extraction network is set to have the same width and height as the input image. We adopt the approach presented in [9] to synthesize pseudo-modalities by exploiting this idea (Fig. 2(a)). Both the encoder f_e and the decoder f_d are residual U-Nets. The input $\mathbf{x}_i \in \mathbb{R}^{3 \times H \times W}$ is a color image while $\mathbf{y}_i$ is the binary vessel map. The model is trained by optimizing a segmentation loss which is the sum of cross-entropy and the Dice loss [14], i.e., $\mathcal{L}_{seg} = \mathcal{L}_{CE} + \mathcal{L}_{Dice}$. Without direct supervision, the latent image $\mathbf{x}_i^k$ can have a different appearance when the model is re-trained. Such randomness is purely introduced by the stochastic gradient descent (SGD) in the optimization process. $k = 1, 2, 3$ indexes three different models and their corresponding synthesized image. For a fair comparison, we use the pre-trained models provided in [9] to generate the three pseudo-modalities ($\mathcal{D}^1$, $\mathcal{D}^2$, and $\mathcal{D}^3$) illustrated in Fig. 2(b).

An essential property of the generated images is that despite significant intensity variations, they consistently maintain the shared anatomical structure of the vasculature. Therefore, the $\mathcal{D}^k$ are termed anatomy-consistent pseudo-modalities. To convert the input color fundus image $\mathbf{x}_i$ to grayscale, we conduct histogram equalization (CLAHE) [17] on the intensity-reversed green channel and denote it as $\mathbf{x}_i^0$. The pseudo-modality of these pre-processed images is $\mathcal{D}^0$.

2.3 Meta-learning on Anatomy Consistent Image Space

Developed from the few-shot learning paradigm, meta-learning seeks to enhance a model's generalizability to unseen data when presented with limited training sets. This is achieved by an episodic training paradigm that consists of two stages: meta-train and meta-test. The source domain $\mathcal{S}$ is split into two subsets $\mathcal{S}_{train}$ and $\mathcal{S}_{test}$ to mimic encountering OOD data during training.

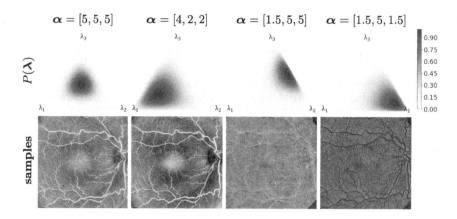

Fig. 3. Examples of Dirichlet distribution and corresponding sample images.

Mixup is a common strategy for data augmentation as it generates new samples via linear interpolation in either image [11] or feature space [21]. Zhang et al. [25] showed Mixup improves model generalization and robustness. In [13], Liu et al. conduct meta-learning on generated images that are synthesized by mixing the amplitude spectrum in frequency domain. They preserve larger structures such as the optic disc by keeping the phase spectrum un-mixed. Given our anatomy-consistent pseudo-modalities, we are able to directly work on the images rather than the frequency domain. We select $\mathcal{D}^1$ as the meta-train data, and we mixup the remaining three pseudo-modalities ($\mathcal{D}^0$, $\mathcal{D}^2$, and $\mathcal{D}^3$) to form a continuous space (red facet in Fig. 2(c)) from which we draw meta-test samples.

In order to mixup three examples, we set a coefficient vector $\boldsymbol{\lambda}$ follow the Dirichlet distribution, i.e., $\boldsymbol{\lambda} \sim \text{Dirichlet}(\boldsymbol{\alpha})$ where $\boldsymbol{\lambda}, \boldsymbol{\alpha} \in \mathbb{R}^3$. The probability density function (PDF) is defined as follows:

$$P(\boldsymbol{\lambda}) = \frac{\Gamma(\alpha_0)}{\Gamma(\alpha_1)\Gamma(\alpha_2)} \prod_{i=1}^{3} \lambda_i^{\alpha_i - 1} \mathbb{1}(\boldsymbol{\lambda} \in H), \tag{1}$$

with $H = \{\boldsymbol{\lambda} \in \mathbb{R}^3 : \lambda_i \geq 0, \sum_{i=1}^{3} \lambda_i = 1\}$ and $\Gamma(\alpha_i) = (\alpha_i - 1)!$. Examples of PDFs with different hyperparameters $\boldsymbol{\alpha}$ are shown in the top row of Fig. 3.

The mixup image $\mathbf{s}_i$ is created by sampling the coefficient vector $\boldsymbol{\lambda}$ from $P(\boldsymbol{\lambda})$, i.e., $\mathbf{s}_i = \lambda_1 \mathbf{x}_i^0 + \lambda_2 \mathbf{x}_i^2 + \lambda_2 \mathbf{x}_i^3$. It is evident from the bottom row of Fig. 1 that the samples drawn from different distributions drastically vary in terms of contrast and vessel intensity. Thus, the Dirichlet mixup can augment the training data with varying styles of images without altering the vessel structure. To thoroughly exploit the continuous image space, we set $\boldsymbol{\alpha} = [1, 1, 1]$ such that $P(\boldsymbol{\lambda})$ is a uniform distribution and all samples are considered equally.

MAP   187

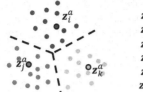 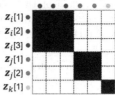

Fig. 4. Left: Feature clusters. Each dot represents a feature vector. Samples representing different anatomies are shown in different colors. The highlighted dots are the latent anchor features extracted from $\mathbf{x}_i^1$, $\mathbf{x}_j^1$ and $\mathbf{x}_k^1$ during meta-training. **Right**: NCC matrix. Each entry of the matrix is the cross-correlation between two feature vectors.

2.4 Structural Correlation Constraints

Next, we design constraints to facilitate the model's concentration on the vessel morphology. We tackle this by delineating the correlation between latent features, as illustrated in Fig. 2(d). For two input images $\mathbf{x}_i$ and $\mathbf{x}_j$ ($i \neq j$), the features $\mathbf{z}_i$ and $\mathbf{z}_j$ are desired to be far apart, as their anatomies differ. In contrast, the M mixup samples $\mathbf{s}_i^{(m)}$ for $m \in \{1, \cdots, M\}$ are all anatomy-consistent, thus the corresponding features $\mathbf{z}_i^{(m)}$ should form subject-specific clusters, as shown in Fig. 4(left). Based on this intuition, we propose two loss functions.

Similarity Loss $\mathcal{L}_{sim}$. As mentioned in Sect. 2.3, we set $\mathcal{S}_{train} = \mathcal{D}^1$. The feature vector extracted during meta-training can be regarded as an anchor in the latent space; we denote it as $\mathbf{z}_i^a$. Then the latent features $\mathbf{z}_i^{(m)}$ from samples $\mathbf{s}_i^{(m)}$, $m \in \{1, \cdots, M\}$, should be close to the anchor $\mathbf{z}_i^a$. Here, we simply use the L1 norm as the similarity loss $\mathcal{L}_{sim} = \sum_{i=1}^{N} \sum_{m=1}^{M} \|\mathbf{z}_i^{(m)} - \mathbf{z}_i^a\|_1$, where N is the number of input images. $\mathcal{L}_{sim}$ is used to reduce the distance between sample features and the anchor within the clusters, as shown in Fig. 4(left).

Normalized Cross-correlation Loss $\mathcal{L}_{ncc}$. In the context of contrastive learning, the Barlow Twins objective function [22] was proposed to minimize the redundant information contained in the embedding vectors. This is realized by computing an empirical cross-correlation matrix of two vectors and bringing it closer to identity such that unmatched entries are not correlated. We extend this idea to a stack of vectors, as illustrated in Fig. 4(right). Feature vectors are color coded in the same way as the left panel of the figure. The normalized cross-correlations (NCC) between each pair of features form a symmetric matrix $\mathcal{C}$. As an example, the NCC of $\mathbf{z}_i^{(3)}$ and $\mathbf{z}_j^{(2)}$:

$$\mathcal{C}_{3,5} = \mathcal{C}_{5,3} = \frac{\mathbf{z}_i^{(3)} \cdot \mathbf{z}_j^{(2)}}{\sqrt{\mathbf{z}_i^{(3)} \cdot \mathbf{z}_i^{(3)}} \sqrt{\mathbf{z}_j^{(2)} \cdot \mathbf{z}_j^{(2)}}} \tag{2}$$

In the ideal ground truth $\mathcal{C}^*$, the entries in the black region are 1, indicating similar features. Conversely, the white region entries are 0, representing dissimilarity. Then the NCC loss can be defined by $\mathcal{L}_{ncc} = \|\mathcal{C}^* - \mathcal{C}\|_F^2$.

Table 1. Datasets. Rows indicating the source domains have a white background while the target domains are shaded according to domain shift type. From top to bottom, (I) pathology: light gray, (II) cross-site: medium gray, (III) cross-modality: dark gray.

dataset	modality	resolution	number	domain
DRIVE [20]	fundus	565×584	20	$\mathcal{S}$
STARE [7]	fundus	700×605	20	$\mathcal{S}$
ARIA[5] healthy	fundus	768×576	61	$\mathcal{S}$
AMD	fundus	768×576	59	$\mathcal{T}$
diabetic	fundus	768×576	23	$\mathcal{T}$
PRIME-FP20 [3]	fundus	4000×4000	15	$\mathcal{T}$
ROSE [15]	OCT-A	304×304	30	$\mathcal{T}$
OCTA-500(6M) [12]	OCT-A	400×400	300	$\mathcal{T}$
RECOVERY-FA19 [2]	FA	3900×3072	8	$\mathcal{T}$

The total loss for the meta-test stage is $\mathcal{L}_{test} = \omega_1 \mathcal{L}_{seg} + \omega_2 \mathcal{L}_{sim} + \omega_3 \mathcal{L}_{ncc}$. Empirically, we set $\omega_1 = \omega_2 = 100$, $\omega_3 = 1$.

2.5   Experimental Settings

Datasets. We use 7 public datasets listed in Table 1. The source domain $\mathcal{S}$ includes three color fundus datasets: DRIVE, STARE and healthy samples in ARIA. By testing on the target domain $\mathcal{T}$, we evaluate the model's ability to generalize across pathological, cross-site, and cross-modality shift conditions.

Implementation Details. The segmentation network $g(\cdot)$ is a 6-layer residual U-Net. If the number of channels n for a layer is denoted as C_n, then the architecture is: $C_8 - C_{32} - C_{32} - C_{64} - C_{64} - C_{16}$. The synthesis model $f(\cdot)$ only functions on color fundus images in $\mathcal{S}$ during training. At test-time, fundus images are converted to grayscale by applying CLAHE on intensity-reversed green channel, while OCT-A and FA images are passed to the segmentation network $g(\cdot)$ directly. $g(\cdot)$ is trained and tested on an NVIDIA RTX 2080TI 11GB GPU. We set the batch size to 10 and train for 30 epochs. We utilize the Adam optimizer with the initial learning rate $\eta_{train} = 1 \times 10^{-3}$ for meta-training and $\eta_{test} = 5 \times 10^{-3}$ meta-testing, both decayed by 0.5 for every 3 epochs.

3   Results

Ablation Study. In Table 2, we investigate the contribution of the three major components of the proposed method: the episodic training paradigm, the similarity loss $\mathcal{L}_{sim}$ and the normalized cross-correlation loss $\mathcal{L}_{ncc}$. Note that $\mathcal{L}_{sim}$ requires the access to the latent anchor and thus is only applicable when using meta-training strategy. Without $\mathcal{L}_{sim}$ and $\mathcal{L}_{ncc}$, the model is trained with only the segmentation loss $\mathcal{L}_{seg}$. Our results show that the introduction of the episodic

MAP   189

Table 2. The ablation study on the main components of MAP on data with three types of distribution shift. Boldface: best result, underline: second-best result.

Episodic	$\mathcal{L}_{sim}$	$\mathcal{L}_{ncc}$	Type I	Type II	Type III	Average
−	−	−	62.93	60.04	63.94	62.95
−	−	✓	64.73	62.48	68.06	66.02
✓	−	−	**67.50**	63.40	64.25	65.19
✓	✓	−	64.75	66.24	68.30	66.77
✓	−	✓	66.10	<u>66.99</u>	<u>69.71</u>	<u>68.05</u>
✓	✓	✓	<u>67.39</u>	**66.99**	**71.60**	**69.43**

training provides noticeable improvement in all types of distribution shift. Both loss functions also contribute positively in general, and the proposed method ranks the best in types II and III, and second best in type I.

Comparison to Competing Methods. There are three major classes of approaches to solve the DG problem: data augmentation, domain alignment, and meta-learning. We compare against a representative algorithm from each: BigAug [24], domain regularization network [1], and MASF [4], respectively. We also compare to VFT [9] as it also focuses on leveraging shape information and pseudo-modalities. Moreover, we train a residual U-Net on $\mathcal{S}$ as a baseline model, and a residual U-Net on each target domain $T^p \in \mathcal{T}$ as an oracle model, to provide an indication of the lower and upper bounds of generalization performance.

Table 3 compares the Dice coefficients (%) of the competing methods. MAP ranks the best in almost all target domains (except RECOVERY, where it ranks second), which proves that the proposed MAP algorithm effectively enhances the robustness of the model under all three domain shift conditions. For some of the datasets such as ROSE and the diabetic subset of ARIA, the MAP's performance approaches the oracle. Compared to the VFT which explicitly models the tubular

Table 3. The Dice values (%) for testing on target domains. Boldface: best result, underline: second best result. ~ : p-value ≥ 0.05, † : p-value $\ll 0.05$ in paired t-test compared to the baseline. The background is encoded the same way as Table 1.

Method	ARIA		PRIME-FP20	OCTA 500	ROSE	RECOVERY
	amd	diabetic				
baseline	63.82	65.19	47.31	73.16	67.41	51.25
Regular [1]	64.89	66.97	55.76	73.54	68.36	55.20
BigAug [24]	<u>65.55</u>	67.27	59.97	76.88	69.32	**63.20**
MASF [4]	65.33	<u>67.75</u>	<u>65.96</u>	77.65	67.25	50.74
VFT [9]	61.81	64.05	54.64	<u>77.91</u>	<u>72.81</u>	48.28
MAP	**66.69**~	**68.08**~	**68.21**†	**78.71**†	**74.25**†	<u>61.85</u>†
oracle	73.34	70.65	77.80	86.57	76.03	74.54

vessel shape, the implicit constraints provide a better guidance for the deep model to learn the structural features.

4   Conclusion

We present MAP, a method that approaches the DG problem by implicitly encouraging the model to learn about the vessel structure, which is considered to be a domain-agnostic feature. This is achieved by providing the model with synthesized images that have consistent vasculature but with significant variations in style. Then by setting constraints with regard to the correlation between latent features, the model is able to focus more on the target vessel structure. Our model's generalization capability is assessed on test data with different sources of domain shift, including data with pathological phenotypes, cross-site shifts, and cross-modality shifts. The results indicate that the proposed method can greatly improve the robustness of the deep learning models across all three domain shift configurations.

Acknowledgements. This work is supported by the NIH grant R01EY033969 and the Vanderbilt University Discovery Grant Program.

References

1. Aslani, S., Murino, V., Dayan, M., Tam, R., Sona, D., Hamarneh, G.: Scanner invariant multiple sclerosis lesion segmentation from MRI. In: 2020 IEEE 17th International Symposium on Biomedical Imaging (ISBI), pp. 781–785. IEEE (2020)
2. Ding, L., Bawany, M.H., Kuriyan, A.E., Ramchandran, R.S., Wykoff, C.C., Sharma, G.: A novel deep learning pipeline for retinal vessel detection in fluorescein angiography. IEEE Trans. Image Process. **29**, 6561–6573 (2020)
3. Ding, L., Kuriyan, A.E., Ramchandran, R.S., Wykoff, C.C., Sharma, G.: Weakly-supervised vessel detection in ultra-widefield fundus photography via iterative multi-modal registration and learning. IEEE Trans. Med. Imaging **40**(10), 2748–2758 (2020)
4. Dou, Q., Coelho de Castro, D., Kamnitsas, K., Glocker, B.: Domain generalization via model-agnostic learning of semantic features. In: Advances in Neural Information Processing Systems, vol. 32 (2019)
5. Farnell, D., et al.: Enhancement of blood vessels in digital fundus photographs via the application of multiscale line operators. J. Franklin Inst. **345**(7), 748–765 (2008)
6. Finn, C., Abbeel, P., Levine, S.: Model-agnostic meta-learning for fast adaptation of deep networks. In: International Conference on Machine Learning, pp. 1126–1135. PMLR (2017)
7. Hoover, A., Kouznetsova, V., Goldbaum, M.: Locating blood vessels in retinal images by piecewise threshold probing of a matched filter response. IEEE TMI **19**(3), 203–210 (2000)

MAP   191

8. Hu, D., Cui, C., Li, H., Larson, K.E., Tao, Y.K., Oguz, I.: LIFE: a generalizable autodidactic pipeline for 3D OCT-a vessel segmentation. In: de Bruijne, M., et al. (eds.) MICCAI 2021. LNCS, vol. 12901, pp. 514–524. Springer, Cham (2021). https://doi.org/10.1007/978-3-030-87193-2_49

9. Hu, D., Li, H., Liu, H., Oguz, I.: Domain generalization for retinal vessel segmentation with vector field transformer. In: International Conference on Medical Imaging with Deep Learning, pp. 552–564. PMLR (2022)

10. Khandelwal, P., Yushkevich, P.: Domain generalizer: a few-shot meta learning framework for domain generalization in medical imaging. In: Albarqouni, S., Xu, Z., et al. (eds.) DART/DCL -2020. LNCS, vol. 12444, pp. 73–84. Springer, Cham (2020). https://doi.org/10.1007/978-3-030-60548-3_8

11. Kim, J.H., Choo, W., Song, H.O.: Puzzle mix: exploiting saliency and local statistics for optimal mixup. In: International Conference on Machine Learning, pp. 5275–5285. PMLR (2020)

12. Li, M., et al.: Image projection network: 3D to 2D image segmentation in OCTA images. IEEE TMI **39**(11), 3343–3354 (2020)

13. Liu, Q., Chen, C., Qin, J., Dou, Q., Heng, P.A.: FedDG: federated domain generalization on medical image segmentation via episodic learning in continuous frequency space. In: Proceedings of the IEEE/CVF Conference on Computer Vision and Pattern Recognition, pp. 1013–1023 (2021)

14. Ma, J., et al.: Loss odyssey in medical image segmentation. Med. Image Anal. **71**, 102035 (2021)

15. Ma, Y., et al.: ROSE: a retinal OCT-angiography vessel segmentation dataset and new model. IEEE TMI **40**(3), 928–939 (2020)

16. Ouyang, J., Adeli, E., Pohl, K.M., Zhao, Q., Zaharchuk, G.: Representation disentanglement for multi-modal brain MRI analysis. In: Feragen, A., Sommer, S., Schnabel, J., Nielsen, M. (eds.) IPMI 2021. LNCS, vol. 12729, pp. 321–333. Springer, Cham (2021). https://doi.org/10.1007/978-3-030-78191-0_25

17. Reza, A.M.: Realization of the contrast limited adaptive histogram equalization (CLAHE) for real-time image enhancement. J. VLSI Signal Process. Syst. Signal Image Video Technol. **38**, 35–44 (2004)

18. Ronneberger, O., Fischer, P., Brox, T.: U-Net: convolutional networks for biomedical image segmentation. In: Navab, N., Hornegger, J., Wells, W.M., Frangi, A.F. (eds.) MICCAI 2015, Part III. LNCS, vol. 9351, pp. 234–241. Springer, Cham (2015). https://doi.org/10.1007/978-3-319-24574-4_28

19. Shu, Y., Cao, Z., Wang, C., Wang, J., Long, M.: Open domain generalization with domain-augmented meta-learning. In: Proceedings of the IEEE/CVF Conference on Computer Vision and Pattern Recognition, pp. 9624–9633 (2021)

20. Staal, J., Abràmoff, M.D., Niemeijer, M., Viergever, M.A., Van Ginneken, B.: Ridge-based vessel segmentation in color images of the retina. IEEE TMI **23**, 501–509 (2004)

21. Verma, V., et al.: Manifold mixup: better representations by interpolating hidden states. In: International Conference on Machine Learning, pp. 6438–6447. PMLR (2019)

22. Zbontar, J., Jing, L., Misra, I., LeCun, Y., Deny, S.: Barlow twins: self-supervised learning via redundancy reduction. In: International Conference on Machine Learning, pp. 12310–12320. PMLR (2021)

23. Zhang, H., Cisse, M., Dauphin, Y.N., Lopez-Paz, D.: mixup: beyond empirical risk minimization. arXiv preprint arXiv:1710.09412 (2017)

24. Zhang, L., et al.: Generalizing deep learning for medical image segmentation to unseen domains via deep stacked transformation. IEEE Trans. Med. Imaging **39**(7), 2531–2540 (2020)
25. Zhang, L., Deng, Z., Kawaguchi, K., Ghorbani, A., Zou, J.: How does mixup help with robustness and generalization? arXiv preprint arXiv:2010.04819 (2020)
26. Zhou, K., Liu, Z., Qiao, Y., Xiang, T., Loy, C.C.: Domain generalization: a survey. IEEE Trans. Pattern Anal. Mach. Intell. **45**, 4396–4415 (2022)

A General Computationally-Efficient 3D Reconstruction Pipeline for Multiple Images with Point Clouds

Qingyang Wu[1]([✉])([iD]), Yiqing Shen[2]([iD]), and Jing Ke[1,3]([iD])

[1] School of Electronic Information and Electrical Engineering, Shanghai Jiao Tong University, Shanghai, China
{alkalisoda,kejing}@sjtu.edu.cn
[2] Department of Computer Science, Johns Hopkins University, Baltimore, USA
yshen92@jhu.edu
[3] School of Computer Science and Engineering, University of New South Wales, Sydney, Australia

Abstract. Histology images are the golden standard for medical diagnostic analysis. However, 2D images can lose some critical information, such as the spatial structure of blood vessels. Therefore, it is necessary to perform 3D reconstruction for the histology images. At the same time, due to the differences between institutions and hospitals, a general 3D reconstruction method is needed. In this work, we propose a 3D reconstruction pipeline that is compatible with Whole Slide Imaging (WSI) and can also be applied to other imaging modalities such as CT images, MRI images, and immunohistochemistry images. Through semantic segmentation, point cloud construction and registration, and 3D rendering, we can reconstruct serialized images into 3D models. By optimizing the pipeline workflow, we can significantly reduce the computation workload required for the 3D reconstruction of high-resolution images and thus save time. In clinical practice, our method helps pathologists triage and evaluate tumor tissues with real-time 3D visualization.

Keywords: Histology Image · Point Clouds · 3D Reconstruction

1 Introduction

Histology images are golden standards for medical diagnosis and analysis, as they contain key information such as the cause and severity of the diseases. With the advancement of deep learning technology, computers are now capable of being applied in the analysis of medical images and in extracting key information. However, traditional 2D images can lose a lot of important information, such as the vascular structure in 3D space. Moreover, due to different task requirements and variations such as machine specifications among hospitals and institutions, there is a need to develop a general 3D reconstruction system. Current 3D reconstruction tasks, especially those involving high-resolution images, require

194   Q. Wu et al.

extensive computational resources and are extremely time-consuming, with the
registration and semantic segmentation tasks as the bottleneck of the real-time
visualization for gigabyte WSIs [1]. In this work, we propose a computational-
efficient method to reconstruct the pathology images for WSI 3D reconstruction
using point clouds, a discrete set of data points in the 3D space. The process
comprises semantic segmentation, point cloud sampling, point cloud registration,
and 3D rendering. This process outperforms the existing reconstruction process
as it combines the sampling and modeling processes by constructing point clouds.
Subsequently, registration is performed, greatly reducing the computational and
time costs required for the process.

2   Related Works

Many approaches have recently been proposed recently for 3D reconstruction.
For example, [2] developed techniques to inspect the surface of organs by reconstruction from endoscope videos. A pipeline named CODA [1] perceives the spatial distribution of tumors such as the pancreas and liver. ITA3D reconstructs
tissues through non-destructive 3D pathology images [3]. Comparative studies
have published to reconstruct 3D organs in the disciplines of ultrasound [4,5],
radiology [6–8] and orthodontic [9,10]. Notably, due to factors such as the quality of the loaded glass slides and manual operation during the preparation of
pathological sections, the three-dimensional reconstruction must perform image
registration, which makes the three-dimensional reconstruction method based
on CT images, as in [11], unsuitable for direct application to WSI. Despite
many AI-powered applications, accuracy and performance are still the dominant
challenges for real-time diagnoses. In the setting of gigabyte pathology images,
cellular-level segmentation and image registration are required to be produced
in a short time to keep up with the high-throughput scanners and minimize the
waiting time for the final confirmation by pathologists.

3   Method

WSI-Level Tissue Segmentation. The medical transformer, namely gated
axial-attention transformer [12,13] employs a position-sensitive axial-attention
mechanism, with a shallow global branch and a deep local branch incorporated.
    Inspired by this design, we trained a network with two branches of gated-
axial transformer and a CNN-transformer hybrid architecture as the backbone to
extract global and local information. The segmentation ground truths are derived
from 2D WSI segmentation maps labeled manually by QuPath [14]. Then the
2D WSIs are cropped to image patches and curated to feed the segmentation
network, as patch-based deep learning networks are currently the mainstream
structures in the discipline of histology image analysis. The raw images and
paired segmentation masks are cropped to 128×128 pixel image patches for
input. The network consists of two branches. The gated-axial transformer aims
to learn global information by capturing feature correlations. The other branch

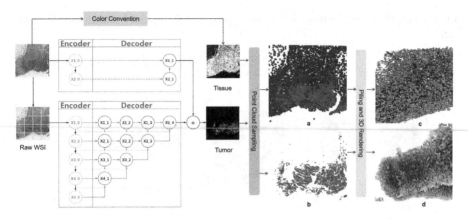

Fig. 1. The 3D visualization pipeline of tumor tissue. For the visualization of tumor volume, the raw WSIs are firstly decoupled to image patches and processed by the binary segmentation network, with the gated axial transformer as the encoder and CNN as the decoder. Then the patches are rejoined to form segmentation maps representing tumor (positive) area. The color convention is applied to WSI binary image to visualize the entire tissue volume. (a) and (b) stand for one layer of point clouds generated from the binary images to represent the density of the tumor (red) and tissue (blue). (c) and (d) are the 3D visualization tissue volume generated from the representative point clouds. (Color figure online)

of CNN-transformer hybrid architecture employs the transformer structure as the encoder and the CNN as the decoder, where the latter is deepened with multiple layers to allow a clear separation of tumor tissue (positive) and dense tissue (negative), as shown in Fig. 1. After the binary segmentation, the output patches are rejoined to form WSI for the later tumor visualization.

Point Clouds. Point clouds are applied for 3D modeling objects such as buildings [15] and human bodies [11,16,17]. This research generates the layered point clouds with down-sampled semantic segmentation results. The pixels of tumor (positive) masks are appended to the layered point cloud. The x and y coordinates of the points are generated from the segmented images, and the z coordinate is the interpolation of the stacked WSI. The computed point clouds are then reconstructed at the three dimensions for WSI registration. Compared with another commonly used 3D reconstruction tool, voxel-based 3D pixel representation using a 3D 0/1 matrix, the point cloud is more suitable for modeling high-resolution images with enormous data volumes thanks to its sparser data. In the current task, point cloud reconstruction also serves the function of extracting feature points. If registering the WSI, even when selecting only a few feature points and calculating simple translation and rotational coordinates, the entire WSI needs to be transformed accordingly, and the model needs to be re-sampled. By building the model first and then applying the transformation to it, only the coordinates of the points in the three-dimensional space need to be transformed, and a model that can be used for subsequent processing can be obtained directly (Fig. 2).

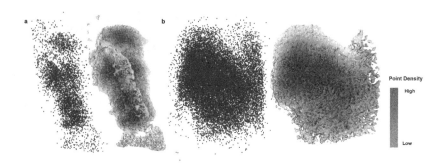

Fig. 2. An example of rendering a point cloud into a model, where darker colors indicate higher point density, which corresponds to potentially tumor tissue in the WSI for this task. Figure a and b correspond to model images generated from two serialized WSI sequences respectively.

Axial Registration. Current registration methods employ Radon transform and cross-correlation, where WSIs are cropped and applied with rigid and elastic registration [1]. This computation workload is often massive and also redundant for unimportant regions. Moreover, elastic segmentation may cause image distortion and inaccuracy in segmentation. By contrast, we optimize the overall framework by bringing forward the segmentation and the point cloud generation before the registration.

Specifically, we incorporate the ICP (Iterative Closest Point) strategy to register for the layered point clouds generated from the segmentation output. As each point cloud for registration uses exclusively one layer, we apply point-to-point strategy [18] without employing the normal vectors. A brief review of the point-to-point strategy is formulated as follows:

$$P_{fix} = RP_{mov} + T \tag{1}$$

P_{fix} and P_{mov} are the fixed and moving point clouds. R and T are the rotation matrix and translation vector.

$$V_{i,fix} = P_{i,fix} - C_{fix} \tag{2}$$

$$V_{i,mov} = P_{i,mov} - C_{mov} \tag{3}$$

$P_{i,fix}$ and $P_{i,mov}$ $(1 \leq i \leq N)$ are the paired-points in the point cloud; C_{fix} and C_{mov} are the center of the two point clouds; and $V_{i,fix}$ and $V_{i,mov}$ are the vectors from point to the center.

$$\mathscr{L}(R,T) = \frac{1}{N} \sum_{i=1}^{N} ||P_{i,fix} - RP_{i,mov} - T||^2 \tag{4}$$

N is the number of points in P_{mov}, and $\mathscr{L}$ is the loss of the registration. Expand the equation and eliminate terms with zero means, $V_{i,fix}$ and $V_{i,mov}$ particularly and we obtain the following formula to calculate the final values of R and T in order to minimize the loss value.

$$R^* = \arg\min(\frac{1}{N-1}\sum_{i=1}^{N-1}||V_{i,fix} - RV_{i,mov}||^2) \tag{5}$$

$$T^* = C_{fix} - R^*C_{mov} \tag{6}$$

where R^* and T^* are the computed rotation matrix and translation vector with minimized loss. The minimum value is achieved through SVD or nonlinear optimization.

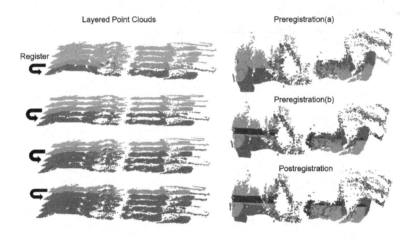

Fig. 3. An example of registration processing. The fixed WSI (pink point clouds) and the corresponding moving WSI (green) are computed in the current iteration, and the registration is iteratively performed from bottom (grey) to top (silver). Our selective algorithm pinpoints the essential points (blue) for matrix computation for the ICP translation speedup. (Color figure online)

Innovatively, to speed up the processing, we select the representative layered point cloud, determined by the spatial density and 2D coordinate, to apply the transformation to the entire layer. In each iteration from bottom to top, we select horizontal and vertical band-shaped areas in the moving point cloud, as shown in Fig. 3. For a consistent spatial presentation of the tumor tissue, interpolation is required upon the different resolutions of x, y, z. In this case study, the z value of the points are multiplied by a factor of 4 to map with the x, y resolution. The point cloud is interpolated based on the nearest layered point cloud. The layered point clouds are then re-registered iteratively in the same manner.

Algorithm 1: The axial registration

Data: WSI image stack $I = \{x^{(i)}\}_{i=1}^n$, band boundary $(u_{min}, u_{max}, v_{min}, v_{max})$, max correspondence point pair distance for point to point ICP d_{max}

Result: PCD(the point cloud generated from the axial-registered layered images)

1 Set band area:
2    $\Psi = \{(u,v,z)\|\, u_{min} < u < u_{max}\ \&\ v_{min} < v < v_{max}\}$
3 Initialization:
4    $PCD, \mathbb{F}, \mathbb{M} \leftarrow \emptyset$;
5 **for** *each image* $x^{(i)} \in I$ **do**
6   **if** $i == 1$ **then**
7   generate layered point cloud $l^{(i)}$ with $x^{(i)}$;
8   store $l^{(i)}$;
9   continue;
10   **end**
11     $\mathbb{F} \leftarrow l^{(i-1)}$;
12   generate $l^{(i)}$ with $x^{(i)}$;
13     $l' \leftarrow l^{(i)}$;
14     $\mathbb{M} \leftarrow l' \cap \Psi$;
15   Matrix calculation:
16     $R, T \leftarrow ICP(\mathbb{M}, \mathbb{F}, d_{max})$;
17     $l' \leftarrow R\, l' + T$;
18   Reset the z value for the moving layer:
19     $l'.z \leftarrow i$;
20     $l^{(i)} \leftarrow l'$;
21 **end**
22 Generate the whole point cloud:
23    $PCD \leftarrow \sum_{i=1}^n l^{(i)}$;

---

4 Implementation

We employ Open3D library [19] to generate point clouds to visualize spatial tissue distribution. The model presents point arrays with x, y, z coordinates, and the functions models produce color point clouds and 3D meshes. The 3D visualization allows the demonstration of comprehensive information interpreted by deep learning structures, including the spatial distribution of tumors and tissues.

5   Quantitative Results

Segmentation. The loss and training time of the segmentation network are demonstrated in Fig. 4. WSIs are cropped to 128×128 image patches to feed the network, then rejoined to generate the layered point clouds, as shown in the segmentation image in Fig. 3.

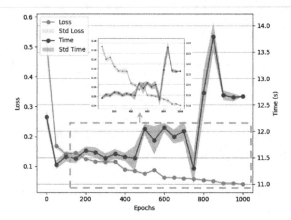

Fig. 4. The loss and time are reported every fifty epochs to train the segmentation network. Observably, our model converges steadily in the loss function. A couple of seconds are required to obtain a reliable segmentation network.

Registration Speedup. Two metrics of speedup and accuracy evaluate the registration performance, and the latter is measured by Root Mean Square Error (RMSE) of the point pairs. For the axial registration example demonstrated in Fig. 5, the representative points are sampled in x value from 2,250 to 2,750, or y value from 6,750 to 7,250 at the bottom layer, about 1/3 of the total points employed for registration. Overall, the axial registration is with smaller RMSE on average, as shown in Fig. 5.

This pipeline attempts a significant decrease in registration computation, with 1.54 s per layer required, which is about 10.94% the time required for the regular ICP registration [18], and is a tremendous advantage compared with WSI-level registration [1] taking about 40 min per image. Overall, processing the WSI stack registration workflow takes only several minutes on average, whereas the state-of-the-art approach requires a couple of hours [1], as shown in Fig. 5. Consequently, the registration processing will not be the bottleneck of the 3D tissue reconstruction.

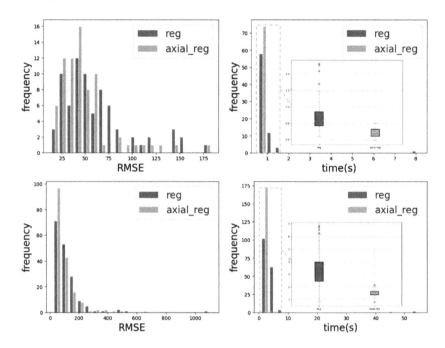

Fig. 5. The experimental results of the two datasets. The left column shows the RMSE-frequency histogram and the right column shows the time-frequency histogram. It is obvious that our method outperforms in both speed and accuracy, with lower average value for each standard.

6   Conclusion and Future Work

In this task, we have optimized and integrated existing 3D reconstruction pipelines for WSI (Whole Slide Imaging) and CT (Computed Tomography), resulting in a more efficient pipeline for 3D reconstruction of high-resolution images. By utilizing point cloud merging and assisted registration processes, this pipeline significantly reduces redundant computations, decreases data volume in comparison to voxel methods, and minimizes time consumption during the registration process. While this pipeline is specifically designed for the unique requirements of Whole Slide Imaging (WSI), it also has the potential to adapt to CT and MRI images through semantic segmentation and point cloud sampling, 3D rendering, and omitting the registration. The 3D reconstruction section in [11,20,21] also utilized a similar method of acquiring layered images, stacking and aligning them to generate a 3D model. Although there were some differences in the specific implementation, it also demonstrated that our method theoretically could be applied to the 3D reconstruction of other medical images, such as immunohistochemistry images. Therefore, as long as there are appropriate training models and data available, this pipeline can be adaptable to 3D reconstruction tasks for different types of images and tissues.

References

1. Kiemen, A.L., Braxton, A.M., Grahn, M.P., et al.: CODA: quantitative 3D reconstruction of large tissues at cellular resolution. Nat. Meth. **19**, 1490–1499 (2022). https://doi.org/10.1038/s41592-022-01650-9

2. Ma, R., Wang, R., Pizer, S., Rosenman, J., McGill, S.K., Frahm, J.-M.: Real-time 3D reconstruction of colonoscopic surfaces for determining missing regions. In: Shen, D., et al. (eds.) MICCAI 2019. LNCS, vol. 11768, pp. 573–582. Springer, Cham (2019). https://doi.org/10.1007/978-3-030-32254-0_64

3. Xie, W., et al.: Prostate cancer risk stratification via nondestructive 3D pathology with deep learning-assisted gland analysis. Cancer Res. **82**(2), 334–345 (2022). https://doi.org/10.1158/0008-5472.CAN-21-2843

4. Chen, C., et al.: Region proposal network with graph prior and IoU-balance loss for landmark detection in 3D ultrasound. In: 2020 IEEE 17th International Symposium on Biomedical Imaging (ISBI), pp. 1–5 (2020). https://doi.org/10.1109/ISBI45749.2020.9098368

5. Wiskin, J., et al.: Full wave 3D inverse scattering transmission ultrasound tomography: breast and whole body imaging. In: 2019 IEEE International Ultrasonics Symposium (IUS), pp. 951–958 (2019). https://doi.org/10.1109/ULTSYM.2019.8925778

6. Kamencay, P., Zachariasova, M., Hudec, R., Benco, M., Radil, R.: 3D image reconstruction from 2D CT slices. In: 2014 3DTV-Conference: The True Vision - Capture, Transmission and Display of 3D Video (3DTV-CON), pp. 1–4 (2014). https://doi.org/10.1109/3DTV.2014.6874742

7. Kermi, A., Djennelbaroud, H.C., Khadir, M.T.: A deep learning-based 3D CNN for automated Covid-19 lung lesions segmentation from 3D chest CT scans. In: 2022 5th International Symposium on Informatics and its Applications (ISIA), pp. 1–5 (2022). https://doi.org/10.1109/ISIA55826.2022.9993505

8. Ueda, D., et al.: Deep learning for MR angiography: automated detection of cerebral aneurysms. Radiology **290**(1), 187–194 (2019). pMID: 30351253. https://doi.org/10.1148/radiol.2018180901

9. Tang, H., Hsung, T.C., Lam, W.Y., Cheng, L.Y.Y., Pow, E.H.: On 2D–3D image feature detections for image-to-geometry registration in virtual dental model. In: 2020 IEEE International Conference on Visual Communications and Image Processing (VCIP), pp. 140–143 (2020). https://doi.org/10.1109/VCIP49819.2020.9301774

10. Zhang, L.z., Shen, K.: A volumetric measurement algorithm of defects in 3D CT image based on spatial intuitionistic fuzzy c-means. In: 2021 IEEE Far East NDT New Technology & Application Forum (FENDT), pp. 78–82 (2021). https://doi.org/10.1109/FENDT54151.2021.9749668

11. Leonardi, V., Vidal, V., Mari, J.L., Daniel, M.: 3D reconstruction from CT-scan volume dataset application to kidney modeling. In: Proceedings of the 27th Spring Conference on Computer Graphics, SCCG 2011, pp. 111–120. Association for Computing Machinery, New York (2011). https://doi.org/10.1145/2461217.2461239

12. Valanarasu, J.M.J., Oza, P., Hacihaliloglu, I., Patel, V.M.: Medical transformer: gated axial-attention for medical image segmentation. In: de Bruijne, M., Cattin, P.C., Cotin, S., Padoy, N., Speidel, S., Zheng, Y., Essert, C. (eds.) MICCAI 2021. LNCS, vol. 12901, pp. 36–46. Springer, Cham (2021). https://doi.org/10.1007/978-3-030-87193-2_4

13. Wang, H., Zhu, Y., Green, B., Adam, H., Yuille, A., Chen, L.-C.: Axial-DeepLab: stand-alone axial-attention for panoptic segmentation. In: Vedaldi, A., Bischof, H., Brox, T., Frahm, J.-M. (eds.) ECCV 2020. LNCS, vol. 12349, pp. 108–126. Springer, Cham (2020). https://doi.org/10.1007/978-3-030-58548-8_7

14. Bankhead, P., et al.: QuPath: open source software for digital pathology image analysis. Sci. Rep. **7**(1), 16878 (2017). https://doi.org/10.1038/s41598-017-17204-5

15. Chauhan, I., Rawat, A., Chauhan, M., Garg, R.: Fusion of low-cost UAV point cloud with TLS point cloud for complete 3D visualisation of a building. In: 2021 IEEE International India Geoscience and Remote Sensing Symposium (InGARSS), pp. 234–237 (2021). https://doi.org/10.1109/InGARSS51564.2021.9792104

16. Chen, M., Miao, Y., Gong, Y., Mao, X.: Convolutional neural network powered identification of the location and orientation of human body via human form point cloud. In: 2021 15th European Conference on Antennas and Propagation (EuCAP), pp. 1–5 (2021). https://doi.org/10.23919/EuCAP51087.2021.9410980

17. Wen, Z., Yan, Y., Cui, H.: Study on segmentation of 3D human body based on point cloud data. In: 2012 Second International Conference on Intelligent System Design and Engineering Application, pp. 657–660 (2012). https://doi.org/10.1109/ISdea.2012.676

18. Arun, K.S., Huang, T.S., Blostein, S.D.: Least-squares fitting of two 3-D point sets. IEEE Trans. Pattern Anal. Mach. Intell. (PAMI) **9**(5), 698–700 (1987). https://doi.org/10.1109/TPAMI.1987.4767965

19. Zhou, Q.Y., Park, J., Koltun, V.: Open3D: a modern library for 3D data processing. arXiv:1801.09847 (2018)

20. Alsaid, B., et al.: Coexistence of adrenergic and cholinergic nerves in the inferior hypogastric plexus: anatomical and immunohistochemical study with 3D reconstruction in human male fetus. J. Anat. **214**(5), 645–654 (2009). https://doi.org/10.1111/j.1469-7580.2009.01071.x. https://onlinelibrary.wiley.com/doi/abs/10.1111/j.1469-7580.2009.01071.x

21. Karam, I., Droupy, S., Abd-Alsamad, I., Uhl, J.F., Benoît, G., Delmas, V.: Innervation of the female human urethral sphincter: 3D reconstruction of immunohistochemical studies in the fetus. Eur. Urol. **47**(5), 627–634 (2005). https://doi.org/10.1016/j.eururo.2005.01.001. https://www.sciencedirect.com/science/article/pii/S0302283805000060

GPC: Generative and General Pathology Image Classifier

Anh Tien Nguyen and Jin Tae Kwak$^{(\boxtimes)}$

School of Electrical Engineering, Korea University, Seoul 02841, Korea
{ngtienanh,jkwak}@korea.ac.kr

Abstract. Deep learning has been increasingly incorporated into various computational pathology applications to improve its efficiency, accuracy, and robustness. Although successful, most previous approaches for image classification have crucial drawbacks. There exist numerous tasks in pathology, but one needs to build a model per task, i.e., a task-specific model, thereby increasing the number of models, training resources, and cost. Moreover, transferring arbitrary task-specific model to another task is still a challenging problem. Herein, we propose a task-agnostic generative and general pathology image classifier, so called GPC, that aims at learning from diverse kinds of pathology images and conducting numerous classification tasks in a unified model. GPC, equipped with a convolutional neural network and a Transformer-based language model, maps pathology images into a high-dimensional feature space and generates pertinent class labels as texts via the image-to-text classification mechanism. We evaluate GPC on six datasets for four different pathology image classification tasks. Experimental results show that GPC holds considerable potential for developing an effective and efficient universal model for pathology image analysis.

Keywords: Computational pathology · Image classification · Generative model · Image-to-Text

1 Introduction

In computational pathology, pathological image classification has been extensively studied [1]. There exist various kinds of image classification tasks such as cancer detection, cancer grading, and tissue typing [2–5]. These tasks are essential in pathology since they are closely related to decision-making in patient care and treatment. In clinics, these routine works suffer from inefficiency, inaccuracy, and variations, particularly with the increase in the workload per pathologist [6]. In recent years, machine learning and artificial intelligence techniques have been increasingly applied to pathology image analysis and shown to be effective in such tasks. Many of such methods adopt convolutional neural networks (CNNs) [2–4] and, more recently, Transformer-based models have been often employed for differing tasks [7,8]. Although both CNN and Transformer-based models have

© The Author(s), under exclusive license to Springer Nature Switzerland AG 2023
M. E. Celebi et al. (Eds.): MICCAI 2023 Workshops, LNCS 14393, pp. 203–212, 2023.
https://doi.org/10.1007/978-3-031-47401-9_20

shown to be promising in analyzing pathology images, there is one drawback with these approaches. There exist numerous tasks in pathology that are closely related to each other; for instance, cancer grading in different types of organs such as the prostate, colon, gastric, and breast. With the current approaches, one needs to develop a separate model per task, which is challenging to transfer a pre-existing model to other related tasks. To tackle such a problem, a unified or general model that can simultaneously process different types of images and conduct multiple tasks on them is needed.

Therefore, we introduce a task-agnostic **G**enerative and general **P**athology image **C**lassifier (GPC) that can process and learn from arbitrary datasets of pathology images and perform multiple image classification tasks in a generative image-to-text fashion. To the best of our knowledge, this is the first attempt to build a generative and general image-to-text classifier for pathology images. GPC exploits the recent developments of CNNs and Transformer-based language models. Given a pathology image x, it produces a high-level feature representation by CNN and generates the pertinent class label as a text by a language model, which is built based upon Transformers. Since GPC utilizes the language model, it can handle different types of images and tasks at the same time. To evaluate the proposed GPC, we integrate four separate pathology classification tasks: colorectal cancer grading, prostate cancer grading, gastric cancer grading, and colorectal tissue typing. By employing pathology images from different types of organs and tasks, we aim to improve the utility of the existing pathology images and task-specific ground truth labels, to learn organ- and task-agnostic representations of pathology images, and to strengthen the predictive power of the pathology image classifier. The experimental results demonstrate that GPC can facilitate a unified and general image classification for pathology images.

2   Methodology

2.1   Problem Formulation

Suppose that we are given M datasets $\{D_1, D_2, ..., D_M\}$, $D_i = \{(x^{i,k}, c^{i,k})\}_{k=1}^{N}$, where $x^{i,k}$ and $c^{i,k}$ denote the k-th pathology image and its ground truth in the i-th dataset, respectively. Since $c^{i,k}$ is a text label such as *benign* and *poorly-differentiated cancer*, we split and pad it into a sequence of tokens $t^{i,k}$ using a tokenizer of a language model $\mathcal{L}$. As a result, each dataset is modeled as $D_i = \{(x^{i,k}, (t_1^{i,k}, t_2^{i,k}, ..., t_T^{i,k})\}_{k=1}^{N}$, where T is the maximum length of the token sequence of all text labels.

Each pathology image $x^{i,k}$ undergoes a feature extractor $\mathcal{F}$ and a projector $\mathcal{P}$ to produce a feature embedding $f^{i,k}$ as follows:

$$f^{i,k} = \mathcal{P}(\mathcal{F}(x^{i,k})) \tag{1}$$

Afterward, the projected embedding $f^{i,k}$ is used as a condition for the language model $\mathcal{L}$ to generate a text label autoregressively, i.e., predicting the next token given the previously generated tokens. Specifically, at each step, the next token is drawn from the probability distribution over the vocabulary that is based on the concatenation of $f^{i,k}$ and the embeddings of the previous tokens. We employ the greedy approach in which the token with the highest probability is selected as the output:

$$\tilde{t}_m^{i,k} = \arg\max_{\hat{t}_m^{i,k}} p(\hat{t}_m^{i,k}|f^{i,k}, \tilde{t}_1^{i,k}, \tilde{t}_2^{i,k}, ..., \tilde{t}_{m-1}^{i,k}) \tag{2}$$

where $\tilde{t}_m^{i,k}$ refers to the m-th predicted token for the k-th pathology image in the i-th dataset. As a result, the objective of our study can be formulated as following:

$$\theta = \arg\max_{\hat{\theta}} \sum_{i=1}^{M} \sum_{k=1}^{N} \sum_{m=1}^{T} \log p_{\hat{\theta}}(\tilde{t}_m^{i,k}|f^{i,k}, \tilde{t}_1^{i,k}, \tilde{t}_2^{i,k}..., \tilde{t}_{m-1}^{i,k}) \tag{3}$$

where θ represents the learnable parameters of GPC.

2.2   Network Architecture

The overview of GPC architecture is illustrated in Fig. 1. GPC consists of three primary components: 1) a feature extractor $\mathcal{F}$, 2) a projector $\mathcal{P}$, and 3) a language model $\mathcal{L}$.

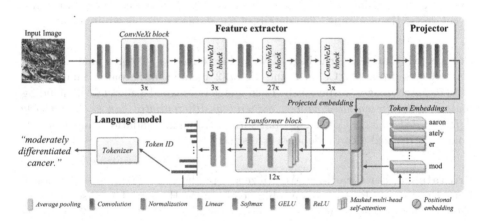

Fig. 1. Overview of GPC.

Feature Extractor. Feature extractor $\mathcal{F}$ is built based upon a CNN to extract high-level representations from input images. We utilize ConvNeXt due to its excellent performance in image classification, comparable to recent Transformer-based approaches while retaining the effectiveness of a simple architecture of CNNs. It employs ResNet-50 [9] as a backbone and transforms the architecture following the design strategies of Transformers by investigating and adopting several design techniques step-by-step, including macro and micro design, ResNeXt [10], inverted bottleneck, and large kernel size.

Projector. Projector $\mathcal{P}$ maps the output features from the space of $\mathcal{F}$ to that of a language model $\mathcal{L}$. It simply utilizes a multilayer perceptron with three fully-connected layers. $\mathcal{P}$ bridges the gap between the image feature domain and the text feature domain in a way that the image feature embeddings of $\mathcal{F}$ guided and adjusted to align with the feature space of $\mathcal{L}$.

Language Model. Language model $\mathcal{L}$ generates the correct pathological text labels for the projected embeddings obtained from $\mathcal{P}$. We select Open Pre-trained Transformer language models (OPT) [11] as $\mathcal{L}$. Since OPT is a decoder-only pre-trained Transformer-based language model, it easily applies to image-to-text generation tasks. We chose the base version of OPT among several variants, including a stack of 12 Transformer layers with 12-head attention layers due to computational complexity and cost.

3   Experiments

3.1   Datasets

We investigate six datasets of four pathology image classification tasks: 1) colorectal cancer grading, 2) prostate cancer grading, 3) gastric cancer grading, and 4) colorectal tissue typing. The details of the datasets are shown in Table 1.

Colorectal Cancer Grading: Two public datasets (Colon-1 and Colon-2) are collected from [3]. Colon-1 and Colon-2 include 9,857 patch images and 110,170 patch images, respectively. Each image is assigned a class label, including *benign, well differentiated cancer, moderately differentiated cancer*, and *poorly differentiated cancer*. Colon-1 is split into a training, validation, and test set. Colon-2 is utilized as an independent test set.

Prostate Cancer Grading: We utilize two public prostate datasets (Prostate-1 and Prostate-2). Prostate-1 was obtained from the Harvard dataverse (https://dataverse.harvard.edu). Prostate-2 was acquired from Gleason2019 challenge (https://gleason2019.grand-challenge.org). Both are annotated with four class labels: *benign, grade 3 cancer, grade 4 cancer*, and *grade 5 cancer*. Prostate-1 contains 22,022 patch images that are split into a training, validation, and test set. Prostate-2 has 17,066 patches that are used as an independent test set.

Gastric Cancer Grading: A single gastric cancer dataset (Gastric) was obtained from a local hospital. It includes 265,066 patch images with four class labels, including *benign, tubular well differentiated cancer, tubular moderately differentiated cancer*, and *tubular poorly differentiated cancer*. The entire dataset is split into a training, validation, and testing set.

Table 1. Details of datasets. TR, VAL, and TS denote training, validation, and test sets, respectively.

Task	Dataset	Mag.	Patch Size	# Patches
Colorectal cancer grading	Colon-1	20×	512 × 512	TR (7,027), VAL (1,242), TS-1 (1,588)
	Colon-2	20×	512 × 512	TS-2 (110,170)
Prostate cancer grading	Prostate-1	40×	750 × 750	TR (15,303), VAL (2,482), TS-1 (4,237)
	Prostate-2	40×	690 × 690	TS-2 (17,066)
Gastric cancer grading	Gastric	40×	512 × 512	TR (233,898), VAL (15,381), TS (15,787)
Colorectal tissue typing	K19	20×	224 × 224	TR (70,000), VAL (15,000), TS (15,000)

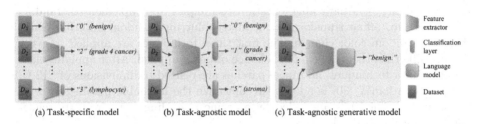

(a) Task-specific model   (b) Task-agnostic model   (c) Task-agnostic generative model

Fig. 2. Three types of classification approaches. (a) Task-specific model, (b) Task-agnostic model, and (c) Task-agnostic generative model.

Colorectal Tissue Typing: A publicly available dataset (K19) was attained from [12]. K19 includes 100,000 images that are categorized into *adipose, background, debris, lymphocyte, normal, stroma, epithelium, muscle,* and *mucus.* K19 is divided into a training, validation, and testing set.

3.2   Comparative Models

We compare three other types of models with GPC. The models include 1) three CNN models: ConvNeXt-L [13], EfficientNetV2-S [14], and ResNet50 [9], 2) three Transformer models: MaxViT [15], SwinV2-B [16], and ViT-B [17], and 3) two generative models: CLIP [18] and GIT-B [19]. GIT-B is an end-to-end Transformer-based model for image captioning that are similar to our approach. Regarding CLIP, we only obtain the pre-trained vision branch of CLIP-ViT-L-14 as an image extractor and integrate OPT-125M as a text decoder.

3.3   Experimental Design

We conduct three settings to assess GPC and competitors (Fig. 2): 1) Task-specific classification (E_{TS}): A model, equipped with a feature extractor and a classifier head, is trained on a training set and tested on the test set(s) per classification task, 2) Task-agnostic classification (E_{TA}): A model contains a feature extractor and four classifier heads, i.e., one classifier head per task. It is trained on all training sets from four classification tasks and assessed on each test set per task using the corresponding classifier, and 3) Task-agnostic generative classification (E_{TAG}): A model includes a feature extractor and a generative classifier. It is trained on all training sets from four classification tasks and evaluated on the entire test sets. Three CNNs and three Transformer models are utilized in E_{TS} and E_{TA}. In E_{TA}, the training loss is only aggregated by the output of the corresponding classification layer. Two generative models and GPC are used in E_{TAG}.

3.4   Training Details

During training, five data augmentation techniques are implemented: random horizontal flip, affine transformation, image blurring, random additive Gaussian, and random color change. The first three techniques are applied to every patch, while the others have a 50% chance of being applied. After applying data augmentation techniques, all image patches are resized to dimensions of 512 Œ 512 pixels. AdamW [20] is adopted to optimize the learnable parameters with a learning rate of 10^{-5} controlled by a cosine annealing warm restarts scheduler [21] during 60 epochs.

3.5   Metrics

To evaluate the performance of GPC and other competitors, we measure several evaluation metrics. For cancer grading, we use accuracy (Acc), cancer grading accuracy (Acc_g), macro-averaged F1 ($F1$), and quadratic weighted kappa (k_w) [22]. Regarding tissue typing, we calculate Acc, $F1$, macro-averaged precision (Pre), and macro-averaged recall (Re).

Table 2. Results of colorectal cancer grading and tissue typing.

Method	Type	Colon-1				Colon-2				K19			
		$Acc(\%)$	$Acc_g(\%)$	$F1$	K_w	$Acc(\%)$	$Acc_g(\%)$	$F1$	K_w	$Acc\ (\%)$	Pre	Re	$F1$
ConvNeXt-L	E_{TS}	87.7	82.8	0.832	0.940	78.1	71.9	0.731	**0.908**	99.6	**0.996**	**0.996**	0.994
EfficientNetV2-S		85.9	80.9	0.819	0.914	76.9	68.4	0.708	0.701	98.0	0.973	0.968	0.985
ResNet50		86.8	82.9	0.838	0.806	79.5	68.2	**0.733**	0.688	98.7	0.988	0.988	0.987
MaxViT		87.9	**84.0**	0.838	0.805	76.3	72.8	0.723	0.895	98.3	0.988	0.991	0.988
SwinV2-B		88.0	82.7	0.829	0.839	77.9	73.7	0.729	0.885	99.4	**0.996**	0.993	0.991
ViT-B		87.5	82.0	0.838	0.838	**79.8**	72.8	0.728	0.899	98.2	0.989	**0.996**	0.988
ConvNeXt-L	E_{TA}	85.9	80.4	0.823	0.933	74.4	66.5	0.698	0.868	98.8	0.986	0.991	0.988
EfficientNetV2-S		83.2	79.2	0.793	0.882	72.5	63.4	0.670	0.722	98.5	0.982	0.982	0.974
ResNet50		84.1	81.0	0.807	0.824	70.1	61.9	0.622	0.671	97.7	0.984	0.983	0.986
MaxViT		86.8	82.6	0.809	0.813	71.3	68.8	0.720	0.888	98.3	0.985	0.991	0.974
SwinV2-B		86.5	81.2	0.822	0.933	70.4	69.0	0.671	0.842	98.4	0.985	0.980	**0.996**
ViT-B		86.0	79.7	0.812	0.831	72.1	67.1	0.701	0.833	98.1	0.985	0.989	0.988
GIT-B	E_{TAG}	85.3	79.7	0.811	0.924	67.9	58.6	0.596	0.839	98.9	0.989	0.988	0.990
CLIP+OPT		82.5	75.6	0.795	0.914	72.7	67.4	0.653	0.791	99.0	0.989	0.992	0.985
GPC (ours)		**88.4**	83.8	**0.848**	**0.944**	79.0	**74.0**	0.722	0.898	99.4	0.995	0.995	**0.996**

Table 3. Results of prostate and gastric cancer grading.

Method	Type	Prostate-1				Prostate-2				Gastric			
		$Acc(\%)$	$Acc_g(\%)$	$F1$	K_w	$Acc(\%)$	$Acc_g(\%)$	$F1$	K_w	$Acc(\%)$	$Acc_g(\%)$	$F1$	K_w
ConvNeXt-L	E_{TS}	70.6	70.1	0.630	0.597	77.8	78.2	0.639	0.696	83.8	68.1	0.760	0.925
EfficientNetV2-S		69.7	66.4	0.582	0.504	74.3	77.3	0.599	0.633	81.3	68.1	0.712	0.890
ResNet50		70.9	67.5	0.643	0.512	**77.3**	78.7	0.608	0.619	82.2	66.9	0.707	0.901
MaxViT		71.6	70.2	**0.652**	**0.649**	75.9	76.7	0.605	0.678	83.2	68.5	0.758	0.926
Swin-V2-B		**71.9**	72.0	0.637	0.639	73.9	75.1	0.623	0.669	83.9	68.5	0.771	**0.935**
ViT-B		**71.9**	**72.2**	0.641	0.643	75.4	75.9	0.608	0.690	**84.4**	69.2	**0.774**	0.930
ConvNeXt-L	E_{TA}	68.5	69.7	0.576	0.578	73.3	76.3	0.562	0.616	83.0	67.2	0.757	0.930
EfficientNetV2-S		65.2	62.1	0.522	0.511	71.9	73.1	0.512	0.589	80.5	63.5	0.701	0.832
ResNet50		69.2	68.1	0.582	0.539	73.6	77.3	0.599	0.601	82.9	64.0	0.713	0.890
MaxViT		67.2	69.2	0.606	0.562	69.2	70.9	0.525	0.631	83.6	65.9	0.749	0.931
Swin-V2-B		65.5	66.9	0.531	0.542	65.8	69.2	0.487	0.553	81.7	65.0	0.739	0.923
ViT-B		67.2	66.4	0.544	0.579	68.8	72.8	0.598	0.629	81.7	64.2	0.710	0.909
GIT-B	E_{TAG}	65.9	67.2	0.538	0.476	68.3	71.7	0.467	0.616	80.7	63.7	0.727	0.867
CLIP+OPT		62.0	63.3	0.598	0.587	63.4	62.2	0.521	0.575	81.6	63.4	0.726	0.912
GPC (ours)		70.4	71.9	0.628	0.612	76.9	**79.0**	**0.641**	**0.700**	83.7	**69.3**	0.768	0.925

4   Results and Discussion

We conduct four classification tasks with six pathology image datasets using GPC and other competitors. The competitors include three CNN models and three Transformer models with two different experimental settings (E_{TS} and E_{TA}) and two generative models, i.e., GPC is compared with 14 different models. Table 2 and 3 demonstrate the experimental results of four classification tasks. For colorectal cancer grading, GPC outperforms all competitors on Colon-1. In terms of Colon-2, it obtains the best Acc_g and ranks top-3 for Acc and Kw. For other metrics, there is no consensus. ViT-B, ResNet50, and ConvNeXt-L in E_{TS} achieved the best Acc, $F1$, and Kw, respectively. In prostate cancer grading, though GPC is sub-optimal for Prostate-1 (top-4 in Acc_g and Kw and top-6 in Acc and $F1$), it outperforms other competitors on three out of four evaluation metrics on Prostate-2. As for gastric cancer grading, GPC is ranked first in Acc_g, third in $F1$, and fourth in Acc. ViT in E_{TS} obtains the best Acc and $F1$. In colorectal tissue typing, GPC achieves the best $F1$ and second best Acc, and is only short by 0.001 for Pre and Re.

In a head-to-head comparison between E_{TS} and E_{TA}, models in E_{TS} generally outperform those in E_{TA}. Two generative models (GIT and CLIP+OPT) are inferior to most of the CNN and Transformer models in both E_{TS} and E_{TA}. It demonstrates the difficulty of fine-tuning a universal model for different classification tasks in pathology images. In the conventional deep learning approaches, a task-specific model is better suited for developing a model per task, which substantially increases the number of models and resources, limiting the scalability of the methods. GPC is not the best model for all classification tasks and datasets. Nonetheless, it achieved the best performance on two datasets (Colon-1 and Prostate-2) and was comparable to the best-performing models on four other datasets. It is also worth noting that there was no consensus on the best performing model for those four datasets. Hence, overall, GPC is the best model across the four classification tasks and six datasets.

| Colon-1 | Colon-2 | K19 | Prostate-1 | Prostate-2 | Gastric |

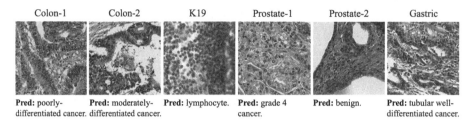

Pred: poorly-differentiated cancer.   **Pred:** moderately-differentiated cancer.   **Pred:** lymphocyte.   **Pred:** grade 4 cancer.   **Pred:** benign.   **Pred:** tubular well-differentiated cancer.

Fig. 3. Examples of correct predictions by GPC. Pred denotes prediction.

| Colon-1 | Colon-2 | K19 | Prostate-1 | Prostate-2 | Gastric |

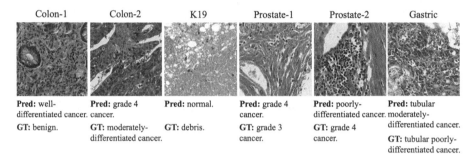

Pred: well-differentiated cancer.
GT: benign.

Pred: grade 4 cancer.
GT: moderately-differentiated cancer.

Pred: normal.
GT: debris.

Pred: grade 4 cancer.
GT: grade 3 cancer.

Pred: poorly-differentiated cancer.
GT: grade 4 cancer.

Pred: tubular moderately-differentiated cancer.
GT: tubular poorly-differentiated cancer.

Fig. 4. Examples of incorrect predictions by GPC. Pred and GT denote a prediction and a ground truth, respectively.

Figure 3 depicts the exemplary samples correctly classified by GPC. Without the information of which organ each image was obtained from, GPC is able to predict and generate the correct class labels for differing cancer and tissue types. Figure 4 shows the incorrect classification examples by GPC. For most such samples, GPC predicts in-domain labels, and cancer samples are classified as cancer, not benign, but of differing grades.

Table 4 demonstrates the model complexity of GPC and other competing models in terms of floating point operations per second (FLOPS), number of parameters (millions), training time (milliseconds per image), and inference time (milliseconds per image) for the four classification tasks. CNN and Transformer models, in general, contain a smaller number of parameters and FLOPS and a shorter amount of time for training and inference. Since GPC and other generative models adopt a visual encoder and a text decoder, they require a substantial amount of resource for training in particular; however, the inference time of GPC and other generative models is still <1 s per image.

Table 4. Model complexity of GPC and other models.

Model	1Type	FLOPS (B)	Parameters (M)	Training (ms/image)	Inference (ms/image)
ConvNeXt-L	E_{TA}	179.6	196.3	924.5	786.7
EfficientNetV2-S		15.0	20.5	204.5	89.9
ResNet50		21.5	24.2	263.1	164.8
MaxViT		27.9	31.9	370.2	129.1
Swin-V2-B		53.4	87.6	477.0	391.0
ViT-B		17.6	86.6	639.3	220.2
GIT	E_{TAG}	211.9	129.2	856.3	592.3
CLIP+OPT		263.8	427.7	1117.2	923.4
GPC (ours)		234.2	332.3	1088.6	870.5

5   Conclusions

In this study, we propose a generative and general pathology image classifier called GPC, which simultaneously learns and conducts multiple classification tasks with a single classification model. The experimental results demonstrate that the generative models, i.e., (pre-trained) language models, hold great potential for pathology image analysis, paving the way for developing a universal model for computational pathology. The future study will entail further development of generative models and extended validation on differing organs and tasks.

Acknowledgements. This work was supported by the grant of the National Research Foundation of Korea (NRF) (No. 2021R1A2C2014557).

References

1. Cui, M., Zhang, D.Y.: Artificial intelligence and computational pathology. Lab. Invest. **101**(4), 412–422 (2021). https://doi.org/10.1038/s41374-020-00514-0
2. Vuong, T.T.L., Song, B., Kim, K., Cho, Y.M., Kwak, J.T.: Multi-scale binary pattern encoding network for cancer classification in pathology images. IEEE J. Biomed. Health Inf. **26**(3), 1152–1163 (2022). https://doi.org/10.1109/JBHI.2021.3099817
3. Vuong, T.T.L., Kim, K., Song, B., Kwak, J.T.: Joint categorical and ordinal learning for cancer grading in pathology images. Med. Image Anal. **73**, 102206 (2021)
4. Vuong, T.T.L., Song, B., Kwak, J.T., Kim, K.: Prediction of epstein-barr virus status in gastric cancer biopsy specimens using a deep learning algorithm. JAMA Netw. Open **5**, e2236408 (2022). https://doi.org/10.1001/jamanetworkopen.2022.36408
5. Vuong, T.T.L., Vu, Q.D., Jahanifar, M., Graham, S., Kwak, J.T., Rajpoot, N.: Impash: a novel domain-shift resistant representation for colorectal cancer tissue classification. In: Karlinsky, L., Michaeli, T., Nishino, K. (eds.) Computer Vision - ECCV 2022 Workshops, pp. 543–555. Springer, Cham (2023). https://doi.org/10.1007/978-3-031-25066-8_31
6. Metter, D., Colgan, T., Leung, S., Timmons, C., Park, J.: Trends in the us and canadian pathologist workforces from 2007 to 2017. JAMA Netw. Open **2**, e194337 (2019). https://doi.org/10.1001/jamanetworkopen.2019.4337

7. Fu, B., Zhang, M., He, J., Cao, Y., Guo, Y., Wang, R.: Stohisnet: A hybrid multi-classification model with cnn and transformer for gastric pathology images. Comput. Methods Programs Biomed. **221**, 106924 (2022). https://doi.org/10.1016/j.cmpb.2022.106924

8. Wang, X., et al.: TransPath: transformer-based self-supervised learning for histopathological image classification. In: de Bruijne, M., et al. (eds.) MICCAI 2021. LNCS, vol. 12908, pp. 186–195. Springer, Cham (2021). https://doi.org/10.1007/978-3-030-87237-3_18

9. He, K., Zhang, X., Ren, S., Sun, J.: Deep residual learning for image recognition. In: 2016 IEEE Conference on Computer Vision and Pattern Recognition (CVPR), pp. 770–778 (2016). https://doi.org/10.1109/CVPR.2016.90

10. Xie, S., Girshick, R., Dollár, P., Tu, Z., He, K.: Aggregated residual transformations for deep neural networks. In: 2017 IEEE Conference on Computer Vision and Pattern Recognition (CVPR), pp. 5987–5995 (2017). https://doi.org/10.1109/CVPR.2017.634

11. Zhang, S., et al.: Opt: open pre-trained transformer language models (2022). https://doi.org/10.48550/arXiv.2205.01068

12. Kather, J.N., Halama, N., Marx, A.: 100,000 histological images of human colorectal cancer and healthy tissue (2018). https://doi.org/10.5281/zenodo.1214456

13. Liu, Z., Mao, H., Wu, C.Y., Feichtenhofer, C., Darrell, T., Xie, S.: A convnet for the 2020s. In: Conference on Computer Vision and Pattern Recognition (2022). https://doi.org/10.48550/arXiv.2201.03545

14. Tan, M., Le, Q.V.: Efficientnetv2: smaller models and faster training. In: International Conference on Machine Learning (2021). https://doi.org/10.48550/arXiv.2104.00298

15. Tu, Z., et al.: Maxvit: multi-axis vision transformer. In: European Conference on Computer Vision (2022). https://doi.org/10.48550/arXiv.2204.01697

16. Liu, Z., et al.: Swin transformer v2: scaling up capacity and resolution. In: 2022 IEEE/CVF Conference on Computer Vision and Pattern Recognition (CVPR), pp. 11999–12009 (2022). https://doi.org/10.1109/CVPR52688.2022.01170

17. Dosovitskiy, A., et al.: An image is worth 16×16 words: transformers for image recognition at scale. In: International Conference on Learning Representations (2021). https://doi.org/10.48550/arXiv.2201.03545

18. Radford, A., et al.: Learning transferable visual models from natural language supervision. In: Meila, M., Zhang, T. (eds.) Proceedings of the 38th International Conference on Machine Learning. Proceedings of Machine Learning Research, vol. 139, pp. 8748–8763. PMLR (2021). https://proceedings.mlr.press/v139/radford21a.html

19. Wang, J., et al.: Git: a generative image-to-text transformer for vision and language. arXiv preprint arXiv:2205.14100 (2022). https://doi.org/10.48550/arXiv.2205.14100

20. Loshchilov, I., Hutter, F.: Decoupled weight decay regularization. In: International Conference on Learning Representations (2019). https://doi.org/10.48550/arXiv.1711.05101

21. Loshchilov, I., Hutter, F.: SGDR: stochastic gradient descent with warm restarts. In: International Conference on Learning Representations (2017). https://doi.org/10.48550/arXiv.1608.03983

22. Cohen, J.: Weighted kappa: nominal scale agreement provision for scaled disagreement or partial credit. Psychol. Bull. **70**(4), 213–220 (1968). https://doi.org/10.1037/h0026256

Towards Foundation Models and Few-Shot Parameter-Efficient Fine-Tuning for Volumetric Organ Segmentation

Julio Silva-Rodríguez[✉], Jose Dolz, and Ismail Ben Ayed

ETS Montreal, Montreal, Canada
julio-jose.silva-rodriguez@etsmtl.ca

Abstract. With the recent raise of foundation models in computer vision and NLP, the *pretrain-and-adapt* strategy, where a large-scale model is fine-tuned on downstream tasks, is gaining popularity. However, traditional fine-tuning approaches may still require significant resources and yield sub-optimal results when the labeled data of the target task is scarce. This is especially the case in clinical settings. To address this challenge, we formalize few-shot efficient fine-tuning (FSEFT), a novel and realistic setting for medical image segmentation. Furthermore, we introduce a novel parameter-efficient fine-tuning strategy tailored to medical image segmentation, with (a) spatial adapter modules that are more appropriate for dense prediction tasks; and (b) a constrained transductive inference, which leverages task-specific prior knowledge. Our comprehensive experiments on a collection of public CT datasets for organ segmentation reveal the limitations of standard fine-tuning methods in few-shot scenarios, point to the potential of vision adapters and transductive inference, and confirm the suitability of foundation models. The project code is available in https://github.com/jusiro/fewshot-finetuning.

Keywords: Efficient fine-tuning · Few-shot adapters · Transduction

1 Introduction

The recent advancements in deep learning have yielded remarkable outcomes in visual recognition tasks. Specifically, under the standard supervised learning paradigm, training on sufficiently large amounts of labeled data could yield excellent performances in medical image segmentation. The success of several recent public challenges, including [1,15,16], attests to this. However, these models are often trained on a specific task and limited numbers of samples, which may lack real-world inter-center variability. As a result, the current literature suggests that general medical image segmentation is hampered by the lack of large, curated datasets for training [8]. This limitation is further exacerbated in volumetric medical image segmentation, where expert knowledge is required for voxel-wise

M. E. Celebi et al. (Eds.): MICCAI 2023 Workshops, LNCS 14393, pp. 213–224, 2023.
https://doi.org/10.1007/978-3-031-47401-9_21

annotations. For example, an experienced clinician would require an average of 10 min to segment a unique structure in a CT scan [34]. Recent literature has examined the potential of large-scale *foundation* models in organ segmentation by integrating multiple publicly available datasets corresponding to various tasks [20]. Models that are trained using a wider variety of centers, acquisition systems, study types, and annotated structures tend to offer better transferability when updated (e.g. fine-tuned) on new tasks and domains. However, since such models are primarily based on public and uncoordinated databases, they may have certain known biases such as long-tail imbalances in the annotated structures or inconsistencies in the annotations [20]. Therefore, identifying efficient and effective learning strategies to adapt these models for new tasks is of high interest in practice.

A popular and widely-adopted approach to adapt a trained model to newly collected data is to fine-tune the whole model on the training images of the novel target task [29]. However, this strategy presents several limitations. First, modern deep-learning models typically have a large number of parameters and require strong hardware requirements for training, which may be unbearable in clinical institutions. Secondly, this approach results in storing a different model for each new domain/task, which might be expensive, especially considering the size of state-of-the-art Transformers-based 3D segmentation networks such as UNETR (#P 555M) [13] or SwinUNETR (#P 371M) [32]. Finally, fine-tuning the entire backbone may lead to suboptimal results, especially when trained on small datasets [21]. An appealing alternative to traditional fine-tuning is parameter-efficient fine-tuning, where only a small subset of parameters are updated during adaptation to new tasks. This family of approaches include, among others, linear probing [23], where only a linear layer staked on top of pre-training features is updated, or adapters [2,17,27], which are trainable, compact feed-forward networks that are inserted between the layers of a fixed pre-trained model.

Nevertheless, even though the *pretrain-and-adapt* paradigm is promising, literature on this subject for medical image segmentation is scarce. Furthermore, these works assume that a large set of labeled samples is accessible for the adaptation to the new task. In the medical context, however, since each institute has limited time, budget, and particular clinical purposes, the number of annotated samples available in clinical practice is usually limited. Therefore, it can be very reasonable to assume that adaptation should only be carried out with a few available samples. This motivates the development of new paradigms that allow for resource-efficient adaptation of foundation models in this field.

Our contributions can be summarized as follows:

- We formalize few-shot efficient fine-tuning (FSEFT), a novel and realistic setting for medical image segmentation. We empirically show that, in this setting, standard fine-tuning methods exhibit significant performance drops.
- We introduce a novel parameter-efficient fine-tuning strategy tailored to medical image segmentation, given a handful of labeled samples in the target task. Specifically, we design (a) spatial adapter modules that are more appropri-

ate for dense predictions; and (b) a constrained transductive inference, which leverages task-specific prior knowledge.
- We report comprehensive experiments on a variety of public datasets. The proposed framework approaches full supervision while requiring significantly fewer annotated samples. These results highlight the potential of our framework in practical clinical settings.

2   Related Work

Fine-tuning (FT) has been the most popular approach in the recent years for transferring knowledge across vision tasks [29]. FT involves updating the weights of a pre-trained model by re-training this model with a supervised dataset corresponding to the target task. Particularly in the medical domain, this technique has become integral in a breadth of applications, from radiology [33] to retinal imaging [9,26]. Despite its popularity in medical imaging, FT presents two main limitations. First, these methods are prone to overfitting when the labeled data of the target task is insufficient. Secondly, FT may require substantial computing resources, as it updates all the network parameters, incurring in long adaptation times, more so when using large pre-training models.

Parameter-efficient fine-tuning (PEFT) tackles these limitations, and has recently emerged as an appealing alternative, mostly studied in computer vision and NLP [14]. The problem amounts to adapt a large pre-trained model on new domains/tasks by updating only a small subset of the existing model parameters and/or adding a new, limited set of parameters (a.k.a *adapters*). A simple solution, commonly referred to as Linear Probing (LP) [23,25], consists of stacking an additional trainable multi-layer perceptron (MLP) layer at the end of the network, whose parameters remain frozen during adaptation. Other strategies include training small auxiliary modules to modify the features extracted by the backbone, such as residual adapters that modify the feature maps [27] or bias parameters [5], batch normalization tuning [24], or side-tuning [36]. More recently, following the popularity of large-scale vision language models, such as CLIP [25], diverse approaches focused on improving their adaption capabilities [11,37]. For instance, [11] proposes CLIP-Adapter, which stacks a small amount of additional learnable bottleneck linear layers to both language and vision branches, while keeping the whole CLIP backbone frozen during adaptation.

Few-shot segmentation (FSS) aims at segmenting novel target classes with just a few labeled samples, where the predominant approach to tackle this problem falls within the meta-learning paradigm. In this scenario, models are trained to learn under few-shot, episodic conditions. In medical image segmentation, the spirit of prototypical networks [30] has been widely adopted, and many mechanisms have been proposed to refine class-wise prototypes. These strategies include, among others, cycle-resemblance attention modules [10], hierarchical attention for time-series consistency [12], iterative refinement through contrastive learning [35] or via local context relationship [31]. However, the meta-learning nature of these approaches hinders the flexible adaptation of foundation models. In particular, their episodic-training procedure implicitly assumes that testing tasks will have a similar structure to the tasks observed during training to reach the best performance [6,7], i.e., the same number of shots during training and testing. Recent empirical evidence on meta-learning-based foundation models for medical imaging attest to this (see [4, Fig. 13]). Furthermore, the complexity of the architectural designs associated with many approaches, coupled with the limitation inherited from episodic learning, presents a significant challenge when attempting to utilize existing FSS methods in a PEFT context.

3 Methodology

An overview of our pretraining-adaptation framework is presented in Fig. 1.

Fig. 1. Pretrain-and-adapt framework. We propose to use a foundation model, trained on extensive domains/tasks (see Eq. 1). Then, spatial adapters are trained for institution tuning on a transductive fashion (see Eq. 3).

Foundation Model. For training a large-scale foundation model, we consider an assembly of M different datasets, which integrate N different volumes in total. Let $X_n \in \mathbb{R}^{\Omega_n}$ denotes a medical imaging volume, with Ω_n representing its spatial domain. Each volume is partially annotated at the voxel level, $Y_n = \{0,1\}^{\Omega_n \times C}$, with C the number of unique categories in the combined dataset. This means that some classes that are considered as foreground in one dataset might be considered as background in another set. Each dataset m presents only partial categories annotated, which are known in the form of a multi-label hot-encoding annotation vector. Thus, each image X_n is associated with the annotation vector corresponding to its dataset. To simplify the notation, we will denote this vector as w_n, which is directly associated with the dataset to which X_n belongs. Thus, the training set is composed of the input volumes, their corresponding partial labels, and annotation vectors: $\mathcal{D}_T = \{(X_n, Y_n, w_n)\}_{n=1}^{N}$. Also, let us define a segmentation model, $\theta = \{\theta_f(\cdot), \theta_c(\cdot)\}$, which is composed of a feature extraction neural network, $\theta_f(\cdot)$, and a classification head, $\theta_c(\cdot)$. Thus, the backbone maps each voxel of the input into a spatial feature representation space, $Z_n = \theta_f(X_n)$, with $Z_n \in \mathbb{R}^{\Omega_n \times D}$ and D the number of channels of the output features. Then, the classification head provides a probability distribution $\hat{Y}_n = \sigma(\theta_c(Z_n))$, with σ a sigmoid activation. Thus, building the pre-training foundation model θ amounts to using the curated assembled dataset by masked backpropagation of partial labels, and optimizing any segmentation loss function, $\mathcal{L}_{SEG}$, using gradient descent:

$$\min_{\theta_f, \theta_c} \frac{1}{\sum_k w_{n,k}} \sum_k w_{n,k} \mathcal{L}_{SEG}(Y_{n,k}, \hat{Y}_{n,k}), \quad n = 1, ..., N \qquad (1)$$

Few-Shot Adapters. Inspired by the recent success of adapters in vision-language models and few-shot image classification [11,37], we introduce a PEFT strategy to adapt a foundation model to new domains in the task of anatomical structure segmentation. Nevertheless, an important difference with respect to existing adapters is that the use of MLP layers is not optimized for dense prediction tasks such as segmentation. Thus, we adopt spatial convolutions in the proposed adapter, which are more suitable for the segmentation problem. Formally, we define a target dataset, $\mathcal{D}^*$, with volumes of an arbitrary study type, X, and a target organ to be segmented, Y. The goal is to adapt the pre-trained foundation model, θ, to the new domain in an efficient way, such as the same backbone, $\theta_f(\cdot)$, is used for different downstream tasks and domains. In addition, we assume that the adaptation should occur using only a few labeled examples (a.k.a the *support set* in the few-shot learning literature [30]), to alleviate the limitation in resources of the target institutions. Thus, a few-shot task includes: (a) A support set of fully-labeled samples, $\mathcal{D}_S = \{(X_k, Y_k)\}_{k=1}^K$, with K the total number of support samples (so-called shots), which usually takes small values, i.e. $K = \{1, 5\}$; and (b) a single query (test) volume X for inference. We aim to use this support supervision to train an adapter module, $\phi = \{\phi_f(\cdot), \phi_c(\cdot)\}$, composed of a vision feature extraction based on a few stacked convolutional layers $\phi_f(\cdot)$, and a new classification head, $\phi_c(\cdot)$. The latter yields sigmoid classification scores for both the query and support voxels: $\forall x \in X, \hat{Y}(x) = \sigma(\phi_c(\phi_f(\theta_f(x))))$ and $\forall x \in X_k, \hat{Y}_k(x) = \sigma(\phi_c(\phi_f(\theta_f(x)))), k \in 1, \ldots K$.

Transductive Inference Leveraging Anatomical Priors from the Support. In image classification, inference is often performed in an *inductive* manner (i.e. one sample at a time). This inductive inference paradigm is common in medical image segmentation, where the task is often seen as a voxel classification. However, segmentation is a *transductive* problem by nature, i.e., one could make joint predictions for all the voxels of the test subject, leveraging available priors on the global structure of the predictions, such the shape of the target organ. Thus, transduction is appealing in our few-shot medical image segmentation setting as the support set could provide such approximate priors. Specifically, we propose to perform inference in a transductive manner, optimizing the cross-entropy loss on the support set while imposing inequality constraints on the size of the target organ in the test subject. Since the volumes are preprocessed to the same resolution, one could estimate an average target-region proportion from the support samples as follows: $S = \frac{1}{K}\sum_k \sum_{x\in\Omega} Y_k(x)$, with Ω denoting the 3D spatial domain. Now, let $\hat{S}$ denotes the predicted size of the target region in the test image, as summation of sigmoid output over the spatial image domain: $\hat{S} = \sum_{x\in\Omega} \hat{Y}(x)$. Thus, we incorporate the following loss during inference, penalizing region proportions that differ from the target by a margin γ:

$$\mathcal{L}_{TI} = \begin{cases} |\hat{S} - (1-\gamma)S|, & \text{if } \hat{S} < (1-\gamma)S \\ |\hat{S} - (1+\gamma)S|, & \text{if } \hat{S} > (1+\gamma)S \\ 0, & \text{otherwise} \end{cases} \tag{2}$$

Finally, we train the adapter by gradient steps, integrating the segmentation loss on the support samples and the transductive anatomical constraints in Eq. 2:

$$\min_{\phi_f,\phi_c} \quad \mathcal{L}_{SEG}(Y_k,\hat{Y}_k) + \lambda\mathcal{L}_{TI}(S,\hat{S}_{query}), \quad k = 1,...,K \tag{3}$$

4 Experiments

Datasets. We use publicly available datasets of partially-labeled CT volumes to build the foundation model and to perform the adaptation experiments. **Foundation model**: a total of 9 datasets with 29 different anatomical structures are assembled. Concretely, BTCV [19], CHAOS [18], LiTS [3], KiTS [15], AbdomenCT-1K [22], AMOS [16], MSD subtasks [1], AbdomenCT-12organ [22] and CT-ORG [28] are gathered to retrieve up to 2022 CT volumes for training. **Adaptation experiments**: We used the TotalSegmentator dataset [34] to evaluate the adaptation of the foundation model, which is composed of 1024 CT volumes with up to 104 anatomical structures, and a wide heterogeneity of scanners and study types. To simulate a real-world use case for adaptation, we retrieved only cases from one of the study types (i.e. CT thorax-abdomen-pelvis) from one institution and selected 9 representative organs present in the foundation model training (i.e. spleen, left kidney, gallbladder, esophagus, liver, pancreas, stomach, duodenum, and aorta). **Pre-processing**: Following previous literature [20], all volumes were standardized and pre-processed to reduce the inter-domain gap. In particular, the orientation of CT volumes was fixed, and isotropic spacing was used to resample the volumes to a voxel size of $1.5 \times 1.5 \times 1.5\,\text{mm}^3$. Finally, the intensity range was clipped to the range $[-175, 250]$, and linearly scaled to $[0, 1]$.

Foundation Model Pre-training. The partial version of SwinUNETR [32] presented in [20] is used as segmentation architecture. The model is trained on the assembly dataset, by optimizing the Dice loss in Eq. 1 using 3 input patches of size $96 \times 96 \times 96$ per volume in each iteration, with a batch size of 2 volumes, during 120 epochs, and using 4 distributed GPUs. We use AdamW with a base learning rate of $1e^{-4}$, and a warm-up cosine scheduler of 10 epochs. Input patches are augmented through intensity shifts and random rotations of $90°$.

Spatial Adapter Training. In order to adapt the foundation model to new target domains, we freeze the weights of the pre-trained model and remove the classifier head. Over the last feature map, we include as the spatial adapter a decoder block of SwinUNETR. Concretely, the module is composed of three stacked convolutions and one skip connection, with a kernel size of 3, Leaky-ReLU activation, and batch normalization. Under the few-shot learning scenario, the module is trained with $k = \{1, 5, 10\}$ support samples for 100 epochs. We use AdamW and an initial learning rate of 0.5 with cosine decay. The model takes as input 6 patches of size $96 \times 96 \times 96$ per volume in each iteration with a batch size of 1 volume. In the transductive inference (TI) setting, the size constraint over the query sample in Eq. 2 is applied for the last 50 epochs, with $\lambda = 1$.

Evaluation. We benchmark the proposed approach against popular approaches for transfer learning. First, we take as baseline the direct application of the foundation model on the target domain, which we refer to as *Generalization* (i.e. no adaptation). Furthermore, we train from scratch the segmentation model (*Scratch*) using all the available samples for training. As standard fine-tuning approaches, we fine-tune the whole network (*FT*), as well as only the last block (*FT-Last*), where the base learning rate is decreased to $1e^{-4}$. Finally, we include a simple Linear Probe classifier [25] over the features of the pre-trained foundation model. The different approaches are evaluated on five randomly selected query samples retrieved from the subset of each target organ. During testing, the predicted probabilities per voxel are thresholded by a fixed value of 0.5, and the binary mask is post-processed to maintain only the largest connected structure, as in [20]. Last, we use the Dice similarity coefficient (DSC) as evaluation metric.

Ablation Experiments. We first assess the effectiveness of the proposed contributions, and motivate our design choices empirically. In particular, Fig. 2a depicts the effect of using the proposed spatial adapters compared to an MLP head, which is the dominant approach in previous literature. To better isolate the impact of the adapters module, we evaluate their performance under the standard inductive inference. Results show that by incorporating spatial information the results consistently improve in $[0.7\%, 2.3\%]$ across the different labeled regimes. Second, Fig. 2b studies the optimum margin for the size regularizer in the transductive setting Results on three representative structures show that a wide range of γ values offer promising results, above the baseline. However, a lower margin value ($\gamma = 0.05$) might degrade the performance, as the target size is estimated just from a few support samples.

Few-Shot Efficient Fine-Tuning. Results obtained with the proposed method and relevant baselines are presented in Table 1. ① *Standard fully-supervised regime.* First, results show that the proposed approach brings substantial improvements compared to training the model from scratch, or to the popular LP strategy. Furthermore, it obtains comparable results to fine-tuning the whole model, while updating 300× less parameters. ② *Low-data regime.* As shown in Table 1, fine-tuning the whole model with only a few labeled samples highly deteriorates the generalization performance. While this effect can be mitigated

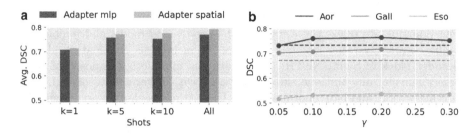

Fig. 2. (a) The role of spatial adapters. (b) Effect of margin γ on the Transductive Inference, with $k = 10$. Dashed lines: no TI. Results using three folds.

by only fine-tuning the last layer, this strategy still underperforms recent PEFT alternatives, such as Linear Probe. We can observe that tuning only the proposed spatial adapter head consistently outperforms relevant approaches, with performance gains ranging from 0.7–1.6% in the low-labeled settings compared to the popular LP method [25]. More interestingly, results suggest that, using only one shot and a spatial adapter module, the model generalizes at the same level as training from scratch on the whole dataset. In addition, if we tune only the last convolutional block, which would present the same computational cost as training the spatial adapter, results are consistently worse across each k-shot scenario. This may be explained by the consequent substitution of the rich features learned on a large-scale foundation model. ③ *Constrained transductive inference.* In addition, results show that by incorporating the proposed constrained transductive inference, which leverages task-specific prior knowledge, we approach standard fine-tuning adaptation with the whole dataset in the 10-shot scenario.

Adapting Publicly Available Pre-trained Models. The core idea of the *pretrain-and-adapt* strategy is to allow the data-efficient adaptation of large-scale publicly available models to new scenarios. However, these models for medical volumetric data are scarce. In the following, we present adaptation experiments using the SwinUNETR with the available weights pre-trained on the BTCV dataset from [32] in Table 2. Results suggest the necessity of introducing large foundation models, since direct generalization using dataset-specific models largely drops the performance. When adapting this model using 5 shots, similar trends to the conclusions drawn in the main experiments are observed.

Qualitative Evaluation. In the following, we introduce in Fig. 3 a qualitative assessment of the performance of the proposed adapter, using the few-shot setting with $k = 5$. The visualizations show the benefits of incorporating anatomical constraints regarding organ proportion during adaptation (*first and second rows*). Also, we observe the segmentation improvement of training a small adapter module on top of the backbone for efficient fine-tuning (*second and third rows*).

Table 1. Few-Shot Efficient Fine-Tuning. Foundation model adaptation results using different baselines and the proposed adapters on five testing folds.

Setting	Methods	Spl	lKid	Gall	Eso	Liv	Pan	Sto	Duo	Aor	Avg.
	Generalization	0.920	0.891	0.768	0.300	0.950	0.782	0.707	0.363	0.628	0.701
	Scratch	0.514	0.896	0.695	0.614	0.902	0.612	0.460	0.552	0.954	0.688
	FT	0.591	0.940	0.654	0.674	0.939	0.853	0.698	0.830	0.926	0.789
	FT-Last	0.954	0.895	0.812	0.423	0.942	0.797	0.784	0.679	0.715	0.777
	Linear Probe [25]	0.948	0.900	0.795	0.422	0.948	0.790	0.773	0.680	0.683	0.771
	Adapter (*Ours*)	0.943	0.904	0.821	0.451	0.948	0.795	0.783	0.669	0.721	**0.781**
10-shot	FT	0.369	0.889	0.249	0.281	0.957	0.454	0.511	0.117	0.917	0.527
	FT-Last	0.960	0.915	0.807	0.425	0.947	0.789	0.723	0.552	0.749	0.763
	Linear Probe [25]	0.942	0.902	0.806	0.452	0.945	0.785	0.786	0.557	0.711	0.765
	Adapter (*Ours*)	0.946	0.900	0.823	0.438	0.945	0.781	0.724	0.704	0.734	0.777
	Adapter + TI (*Ours*)	0.946	0.906	0.821	0.487	0.946	0.785	0.723	0.704	0.735	**0.783**
5-shot	FT	0.553	0.611	0.294	0.586	0.648	0.442	0.164	0.485	0.657	0.493
	FT-Last	0.947	0.712	0.774	0.438	0.952	0.756	0.701	0.619	0.720	0.735
	Linear Probe [25]	0.935	0.887	0.742	0.313	0.960	0.751	0.751	0.525	0.623	0.720
	Adapter (*Ours*)	0.921	0.896	0.822	0.391	0.949	0.752	0.693	0.632	0.680	0.748
	Adapter + TI (*Ours*)	0.928	0.901	0.799	0.442	0.950	0.755	0.712	0.666	0.684	**0.759**
1-shot	FT	0.265	0.255	0.130	0.394	0.519	0.228	0.216	0.162	0.324	0.276
	FT-Last	0.285	0.558	0.366	0.251	0.894	0.585	0.390	0.669	0.394	0.488
	Linear Probe [25]	0.552	0.888	0.671	0.316	0.944	0.488	0.684	0.696	0.679	0.657
	Adapter (*Ours*)	0.549	0.885	0.683	0.351	0.948	0.464	0.703	0.643	0.660	0.654
	Adapter + TI (*Ours*)	0.550	0.888	0.681	0.448	0.947	0.470	0.689	0.631	0.664	**0.663**

#TrainParams: Linear Probe (49) - Adapter/FT-Last (209.6K)

Table 2. Performance using dataset-specific (BTCV), available models.

Setting	Methods	Spl	lKid	Gall	Eso	Liv	Pan	Sto	Aor	Avg.
	Generalization	0.762	0.434	0.398	0.322	0.623	0.458	0.529	0.674	0.524
All train (K=∼ 40)	FT-Last	0.740	0.412	0.419	0.492	0.667	0.510	0.455	0.752	0.555
	Linear Probe [25]	0.576	0.419	0.453	0.327	0.506	0.416	0.458	0.677	0.479
	Adapter (*Ours*)	0.687	0.439	0.522	0.457	0.702	0.532	0.493	0.706	**0.567**
5-shot	FT-Last	0.550	0.405	0.258	0.387	0.722	0.505	0.457	0.732	0.502
	Linear Probe [25]	0.598	0.547	0.078	0.363	0.534	0.352	0.485	0.693	0.456
	Adapter (*Ours*)	0.680	0.496	0.601	0.376	0.585	0.530	0.520	0.676	**0.558**

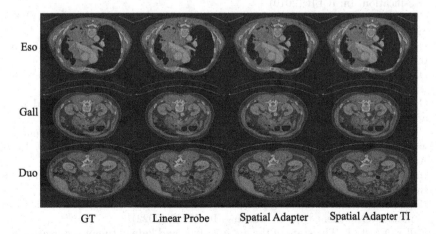

Fig. 3. Qualitative evaluation. The axial view of preprocessed CT scans. The annotation/prediction masks of the target organ are in red. (Color figure online)

5   Conclusions

The results show the promising performance of our fine-tuning strategy tailored to medical image segmentation, under the *pretrain-and-adapt* paradigm. In particular, we have presented a novel and realistic learning scenario, which accommodates practical clinical settings, i.e., adapting efficiently a large pretrained model to a new task/domain with a limited number of labeled samples. Our validation demonstrated that standard fine-tuning approaches substantially degrade the performances under this low-data regime. Thus, our results point to the potential of prior-aware transductive inference and spatial adapters in volumetric medical image segmentation.

Acknowledgments. The work of J. Silva-Rodríguez was partially funded by the *Fonds de recherche du Québec (FRQ)* under the Postdoctoral Merit Scholarship for Foreign Students (PBEEE).

References

1. Antonelli, M., et al.: The medical segmentation decathlon. Nat. Commun. **13**, 1–13 (2022)
2. Bapna, A., Arivazhagan, N., Firat, O.: Simple, scalable adaptation for neural machine translation. In: EMNLP (2019)
3. Bilic, P., et al.: The liver tumor segmentation benchmark (LiTS). Med. Image Anal. **84**, 102680 (2023)
4. Butoi, V.I., Ortiz, J.J.G., Ma, T., Sabuncu, M.R., Guttag, J., Dalca, A.V.: UniverSeg: universal medical image segmentation. In: ICCV (2023)
5. Cai, H., Gan, C., Zhu, L., Han, S.: TinyTL: reduce memory, not parameters for efficient on-device learning. In: NeurIPS (2020)
6. Cao, T., Law, M.T., Fidler, S.: A theoretical analysis of the number of shots in few-shot learning. In: ICLR (2020)
7. Chen, W.Y., Liu, Y.C., Kira, Z., Wang, Y.F., Huang, J.B.: A closer look at few-shot classification. In: ICLR (2019)
8. Chen, X., et al.: Recent advances and clinical applications of deep learning in medical image analysis. Med. Image Anal. **79**, 4 (2022)
9. De Fauw, J., et al.: Clinically applicable deep learning for diagnosis and referral in retinal disease. Nat. Med. **24**(9), 1342–1350 (2018)
10. Ding, H., Sun, C., Tang, H., Cai, D., Yan, Y.: Few-shot medical image segmentation with cycle-resemblance attention. In: WACV (2023)
11. Gao, P., et al.: Clip-adapter: better vision-language models with feature adapters. arXiv Preprint (2021). http://arxiv.org/abs/2110.04544
12. Guo, S., Xu, L., Feng, C., Xiong, H., Gao, Z., Zhang, H.: Multi-level semantic adaptation for few-shot segmentation on cardiac image sequences. Med. Image Anal. **73**, 102170 (2021)
13. Hatamizadeh, A., et al.: UNETR: transformers for 3D medical image segmentation. In: WACV (2022)
14. He, J., Zhou, C., Ma, X., Berg-Kirkpatrick, T., Neubig, G.: Towards a unified view of parameter-efficient transfer learning. In: ICLR (2022)
15. Heller, N., et al.: The state of the art in kidney and kidney tumor segmentation in contrast-enhanced CT imaging: results of the KiTS19 challenge. Med. Image Anal. **67**, 1–16 (2021)

16. Ji, Y., et al.: AMOS: a large-scale abdominal multi-organ benchmark for versatile medical image segmentation. In: NeurIPS (2022)
17. Karimi Mahabadi, R., Henderson, J., Ruder, S.: Compacter: efficient low-rank hypercomplex adapter layers. In: NeurIPS, pp. 1022–1035 (2021)
18. Kavur, A.E., et al.: Chaos challenge - combined (CT-MR) healthy abdominal organ segmentation. Med. Image Anal. **69**, 1–20 (2021)
19. Landman, B., Xu, Z., Igelsias, J., Styner, M., Langerak, T., Klein, A.: MICCAI multi-atlas labeling beyond the cranial vault - workshop and challenge. In: MICCAI Workshop, vol. 5, pp. 1–12. Elsevier B.V. (2015)
20. Liu, J., et al.: CLIP-Driven universal model for organ segmentation and tumor detection. In: ICCV (2023)
21. Long, M., Cao, Y., Wang, J., Jordan, M.I.: Learning transferable features with deep adaptation networks. In: ICML (2015)
22. Ma, J., et al.: AbdomenCT-1K: is abdominal organ segmentation a solved problem? IEEE Trans. Pattern Anal. Mach. Intell. **44**, 6695–6714 (2022)
23. Mahajan, D., et al.: Exploring the limits of weakly supervised pretraining. In: Ferrari, V., Hebert, M., Sminchisescu, C., Weiss, Y. (eds.) ECCV 2018. LNCS, vol. 11206, pp. 185–201. Springer, Cham (2018). https://doi.org/10.1007/978-3-030-01216-8_12
24. Mudrakarta, P.K., Sandler, M., Zhmoginov, A., Howard, A.: K for the price of 1: parameter-efficient multi-task and transfer learning. In: ICLR (2018)
25. Radford, A., et al.: Learning transferable visual models from natural language supervision. In: ICLM, pp. 8748–8763 (2021)
26. Raghu, M., Zhang, C., Kleinberg, J., Bengio, S.: Transfusion: understanding transfer learning for medical imaging. In: NeurIPS (2019)
27. Rebuffi, S.A., Bilen, H., Vedaldi, A.: Learning multiple visual domains with residual adapters. In: NeurIPS (2017)
28. Rister, B., Yi, D., Shivakumar, K., Nobashi, T., Rubin, D.L.: CT-ORG, a new dataset for multiple organ segmentation in computed tomography. Sci. Data **7**, 1–9 (2020)
29. Simonyan, K., Zisserman, A.: Very deep convolutional networks for large-scale image recognition. In: ICLR (2014)
30. Snell, J., Swersky, K., Zemel, R.: Prototypical networks for few-shot learning. In: NeurIPS (2017)
31. Tang, H., Liu, X., Sun, S., Yan, X., Xie, X.: Recurrent mask refinement for few-shot medical image segmentation. In: ICCV (2021)
32. Tang, Y., et al.: Self-supervised pre-training of Swin Transformers for 3D medical image analysis. In: CVPR (2021)
33. Wang, X., Peng, Y., Lu, L., Lu, Z., Bagheri, M., Summers, R.M.: ChestX-ray8: hospital-scale chest x-ray database and benchmarks on weakly-supervised classification and localization of common thorax diseases. In: CVPR (2017)
34. Wasserthal, J., Meyer, M., Breit, H.C., Cyriac, J., Yang, S., Segeroth, M.: TotalSegmentator: robust segmentation of 104 anatomical structures in CT images. Radiol. Artif. Intell. **5** (2023)
35. Wu, H., Xiao, F., Liang, C.: Dual contrastive learning with anatomical auxiliary supervision for few-shot medical image segmentation. In: Avidan, S., Brostow, G., Cissé, M., Farinella, G.M., Hassner, T. (eds.) Computer Vision, ECCV 2022. LNCS, vol. 13680, pp. 417–434. Springer, Cham (2022). https://doi.org/10.1007/978-3-031-20044-1_24

36. Zhang, J.O., Sax, A., Zamir, A., Guibas, L., Malik, J.: Side-tuning: a baseline for network adaptation via additive side networks. In: Vedaldi, A., Bischof, H., Brox, T., Frahm, J.-M. (eds.) ECCV 2020. LNCS, vol. 12348, pp. 698–714. Springer, Cham (2020). https://doi.org/10.1007/978-3-030-58580-8_41

37. Zhang, R., et al.: Tip-adapter: training-free adaption of CLIP for few-shot classification. In: Avidan, S., Brostow, G., Cissé, M., Farinella, G.M., Hassner, T. (eds.) Computer Vision, ECCV 2022. LNCS, vol. 13695, pp. 493–510. Springer, Cham (2022). https://doi.org/10.1007/978-3-031-19833-5_29

Concept Bottleneck with Visual Concept Filtering for Explainable Medical Image Classification

Injae Kim[✉], Jongha Kim, Joonmyung Choi, and Hyunwoo J. Kim

Department of Computer Science and Engineering, Korea University,
Seoul, South Korea
{dna9041,jonghakim,pizard,hyunwoojkim}@korea.ac.kr

Abstract. Interpretability is a crucial factor in building reliable models for various medical applications. Concept Bottleneck Models (CBMs) enable interpretable image classification by utilizing human-understandable concepts as intermediate targets. Unlike conventional methods that require extensive human labor to construct the concept set, recent works leveraging Large Language Models (LLMs) for generating concepts made automatic concept generation possible. However, those methods do not consider whether a concept is *visually* relevant or not, which is an important factor in computing meaningful concept scores. Therefore, we propose a visual activation score that measures whether the concept contains visual cues or not, which can be easily computed with unlabeled image data. Computed visual activation scores are then used to filter out the less visible concepts, thus resulting in a final concept set with visually meaningful concepts. Our experimental results show that adopting the proposed visual activation score for concept filtering consistently boosts performance compared to the baseline. Moreover, qualitative analyses also validate that visually relevant concepts are successfully selected with the visual activation score.

Keywords: Medical Image Classification · Explainable AI · Concept Bottleneck Models · Large Language Models

1 Introduction

Deep Neural Networks (DNNs) have addressed many problems in various fields, including the medical domain [1–4]. For instance, [3] diagnoses breast lesions on dynamic contrast-enhanced MRI with deep learning, and [4] diagnoses hip osteoarthritis using convolutional neural networks (CNNs). Despite the huge success of deep learning based models in the field of medical analysis and diagnosis, such models innately lack a crucial capability required in the medical domain - *interpretability*. Therefore, to tackle the difficulty in interpreting the model

---

I. Kim and J. Kim—Equal contribution.

© The Author(s), under exclusive license to Springer Nature Switzerland AG 2023
M. E. Celebi et al. (Eds.): MICCAI 2023 Workshops, LNCS 14393, pp. 225–233, 2023.
https://doi.org/10.1007/978-3-031-47401-9_22

decision, a series of research have been presented to enhance the interpretability and the explainability of deep learning models.

Concept Bottleneck Models (CBMs) [5] is one of the works that make image classification more interpretable. Instead of directly predicting the target from non-interpretable latent representations, CBMs first predict concept scores, which measure the degree of an image matching to the human-understandable concepts. Then, the final prediction is done based on the predicted concept scores, which makes the prediction process interpretable.

Applying CBMs requires the construction of a set of concepts that well-describe images and are discriminable. Conventional approaches [5,6] try manually defining concepts, which requires extensive labor of skilled expert that is familiar with the target domain. However, such an approach largely hinders the scalability and generalizability of CBMs, since building large-scale concept set manually is costly, especially in the medical domain.

To address the issue, recent works [7,8] propose generating concepts automatically by prompting Large Language Model (LLM) that contains rich information across various subjects to generate the concepts describing target classes. Although such methods remove the need for manual concept generation, LLM turns out to generate non-visual concepts that do not align with images, therefore providing a noisy signal that hinders proper training.

To this end, we propose a *visual activation score*, which measures whether a concept contains visual information or not. By taking account of the visual activation score in the concept filtering phase via a submodular optimization [9], concepts that do not contain any visual cue useful for classifying the image are successfully removed from the initial concept set.

Experimental results demonstrate the effectiveness of the proposed visual activation score with consistent gains in terms of accuracy under multiple experimental settings. Also, further analyses again validate that the visual activation score successfully discriminates the visual and non-visual concepts, therefore helping the model better classify the image with refined concepts.

2   Related Works

2.1   Concept Bottleneck Models

Concept Bottleneck Models (CBMs) [5] aim to make the process of an image classification more interpretable, by implementing a concept bottleneck layer before the final classification layer. A concept bottleneck layer outputs a score of an image corresponding to multiple interpretable concepts. Calculated concept scores are fed into a final linear layer to classify an image. Recent works [7,8] propose leveraging information learned by Large Language Models (LLMs) to automatically extract concepts instead of manually constructing the concept set.

2.2   Large Language Models

Recently, Large Language Models (LLMs) based on Transformer [10] architecture trained with the large-scale text corpus have shown to be effective in various downstream tasks including zero-shot and few-shot learning [11,12], multi-task [13], visual question answering (VQA) [12]. Moreover, leveraging knowledge of LLMs for computer vision tasks, such as generating candidate concepts to classify an image [7,8], is being studied recently (Fig. 1).

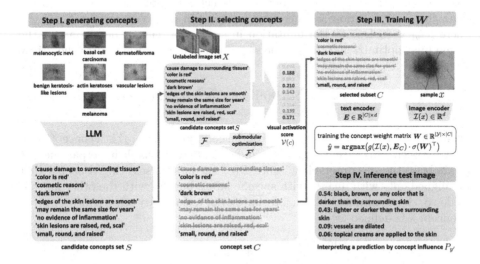

Fig. 1. Method Overview. Step 1: Generate candidate concepts set S by prompting the large language model (LLM); **Step 2**: Select visually relevant concepts via submodular optimization with the score function $\mathcal{F}'$; **Step 3**: Train a concept weight matrix W which projects concept scores into prediction logits; **Step 4**: Interpret inference results with the concept influence $P_{y'}$.

3   Method

3.1   Preliminary

Image classification is the task of predicting the class $y \in \mathcal{Y}$ an input image $x \in \mathcal{X}$ belongs to, where $\mathcal{Y}$ and $\mathcal{X}$ are sets of target classes and images, respectively. In order to make the classification process more interpretable, Concept Bottleneck Models [5,7,8] firstly compute similarities between the image and a concept c in the concept set C, which indicates how well the image and pre-defined concepts are aligned. Computed similarities are then fed into the final classification layer to determine the class an image belongs to.

Generating Candidate Concept Set. We adopt LaBo [8] as the baseline, which constructs the candidate concept set S using GPT-3 [11]. For each class y, LaBo prompts GPT-3 to retrieve sentences that describe the class. 500 sentences per class are retrieved from GPT-3 and split into shorter concepts to form a candidate concept set S_y for each class. Then, the whole concept set S is defined as a union of S_y as below:

$$S = \bigcup_{y \in \mathcal{Y}} S_y \tag{1}$$

Concept Selection via Submodular Optimization. For a concept set S_y, submodular optimization [9] is applied to select concepts with desired property using the score function $\mathcal{F}$, therefore resulting in a concept subset $C_y \subseteq S_y$, where $|C_y| = k$. Due to the limitation in space, we refer to details about the submodular optimization to [8]. The score function $\mathcal{F}$ that evaluates the utility of the subset C_y is defined as:

$$\mathcal{F}(C_y) = \alpha \cdot \sum_{c \in C_y} D(c) + \beta \cdot \sum_{c_1 \in S_y} \max_{c_2 \in C_y} \phi(c_1, c_2), \tag{2}$$

where $D(c)$ is a discriminability score of the concept c, $\phi(c_1, c_2)$ is a concept similarity between two concepts c_1 and c_2, and α, β are controllable hyperparameters. Maximizing the discriminability score $D(c)$ encourages selecting concepts that are aligned only with images with specific labels but not with the other images. To do so, the conditional likelihood $\overline{\mathrm{sim}}(y|c)$ of a similarity score $\mathrm{sim}(y, c)$ given a concept c is defined as:

$$\overline{\mathrm{sim}}(y|c) = \frac{\mathrm{sim}(y, c)}{\sum_{y' \in \mathcal{Y}} \mathrm{sim}(y', c)}, \quad \mathrm{sim}(y, c) = \frac{1}{|\mathcal{X}_y|} \sum_{x \in \mathcal{X}_y} \mathcal{I}(x) \cdot \mathcal{T}(c)^{\top}, \tag{3}$$

where $\mathcal{X}_y$ is training image set labeled with y, and $\mathcal{I}(\cdot)$ and $\mathcal{T}(\cdot)$ are the CLIP [14] image encoder and text encoder, respectively. Finally, $D(c)$ is defined as its negative entropy to maximize:

$$D(c) = \sum_{y' \in \mathcal{Y}} \overline{\mathrm{sim}}(y'|c) \cdot \log\left(\overline{\mathrm{sim}}(y'|c)\right). \tag{4}$$

The second term of Eq. 2 is a coverage score that aims to maximize the minimum similarity between each concept in the subset C_y and the overall set S_y. With the coverage score, the selection of concepts covering a wide range of meanings of a target class is enabled. Then, the whole concept set C is defined as the union of C_y, analogous to the definition of S in Eq. 1.

Optimizing Concept Weight Matrix. After obtaining the concept set C, CLIP text features of concepts are stacked to form a concept embedding matrix $\boldsymbol{E}_C \in \mathbb{R}^{|C| \times d}$, where each row of $\boldsymbol{E}_C$ corresponds to a CLIP text embedding of a concept, $|C|$ is the size of the whole concept set C, and d is a CLIP feature dimension. With $\boldsymbol{E}_C$, a concept score $g(\mathcal{I}(x), \boldsymbol{E}_C) \in \mathbb{R}^{|C|}$ between $\boldsymbol{E}_C$ and an image $x \in \mathcal{X}$ is calculated as:

$$g(\mathcal{I}(x), \boldsymbol{E}_C) = \mathcal{I}(x) \cdot \boldsymbol{E}_C^{\top}. \tag{5}$$

Finally, a concept weight matrix $\boldsymbol{W} \in \mathbb{R}^{|\mathcal{Y}| \times |C|}$ which maps concept scores into the final prediction logit is optimized, where the final prediction $\hat{y}$ is computed as $\mathrm{argmax}\left(g(\mathcal{I}(x), \boldsymbol{E}_C) \cdot \sigma(\boldsymbol{W})^{\top}\right)$. $\sigma(\boldsymbol{W})$ denotes the softmax operation applied along the concept axis, where $\boldsymbol{W}_{y,c} = e^{\boldsymbol{W}_{y,c}} / \sum_{y' \in \mathcal{Y}} e^{\boldsymbol{W}_{y',c}}$. As of the initialization, $\boldsymbol{W}_{y,c}$ is set as 1 if $c \in C_y$ and 0 otherwise, in order to learn the weight $\boldsymbol{W}$ effectively in few-shot settings. Given an image x, the concept influence $P_y \in \mathbb{R}^{|C|}$, which represents how much a concept influences the prediction of the class y can be calculated as below:

$$P_y = g(\mathcal{I}(x), \boldsymbol{E}_c) \odot \sigma(\boldsymbol{W}_{y,*}), \tag{6}$$

where $\odot$ is an element-wise multiplication operation.

3.2 Concept Selection with Visual Activation Score

In order to obtain a reliable concept score in Eq. 5, the concept $c \in C$ must include a *visual cue*, e.g., 'darker in color'. However, the candidate concept set S automatically extracted from LLM includes a lot of *non-visual concepts*, which do not contain any visual cue, e.g., 'most common type of precancerous lesion in the united states'. Those non-visual concepts hinder proper learning of the concept weight matrix $\boldsymbol{W}$ since scores of those concepts provide noisy signals. Therefore, an appropriate criterion to filter out the non-visual concepts is required when constructing the concept subset C via a submodular optimization.

To measure the amount of visual information a concept contains, we define a scalar visual activation score $\mathcal{V}(c)$ of a concept c defined as a standard deviation of CLIP scores between a concept c and images $x \in X$ as below:

$$\mathcal{V}(c) = \text{stdev}(\{\mathcal{T}(c) \cdot \mathcal{I}(x)^{\top}\}_{x \in X}), \tag{7}$$

where X denotes an unlabeled target image set to calculate visual activation scores on, and $\mathcal{T}(c), \mathcal{I}(x) \in \mathbb{R}^d$ are the CLIP text embedding and the image embeddings of a concept c and an image x, respectively. As defined in the equation, the visual activation score of a concept c is calculated as a standard deviation of concept scores among every image in the target image set X. In other words, a concept that is activated differently depending on the image is regarded as a concept containing visual cues, since those concepts sensitively respond to visually distinct samples. Note that an arbitrary dataset can be set as X since it does not require labels. Further analyses regarding the utilization of various datasets as X are provided in Sect. 5.2. Calculated $\mathcal{V}(c)$ is then added to the original score function $\mathcal{F}$ to form a new score function $\mathcal{F}'$ as follows:

$$\mathcal{F}'(C_y) = \alpha \cdot \sum_{c \in C_y} D(c) + \beta \cdot \sum_{c_1 \in S_y} \max_{c_2 \in C_y} \phi(c_1, c_2) + \gamma \cdot \sum_{c \in C_y} \mathcal{V}(c), \tag{8}$$

With the new score function $\mathcal{F}'$, the subset $C_{y'}$ is obtained via a submodular optimization, and the following procedures are done analogously as described in Sect. 3.1.

4   Experiments

We validate the effectiveness of the proposed method by applying the method to
HAM-10000 [15], a skin disease dataset. The dataset consists of 10,015 dermatoscopic images collected from various patients. The target classes $\mathcal{Y}$ consist of 7
types of skin problems, Melanocytic Nevi, Benign Keratosis-like Lesions, Der-
matofibroma, Vascular Lesions, Actinic Keratoses, Basal Cell Carcinoma, and
Melanoma. For all experiments, we follow the experimental settings of LaBo [8]
except for the hyperparameters $\alpha, \beta,$ and γ. All experiments are done with a
single NVIDIA RTX A6000 GPU.

Table 1. Performance on HAM-10000 dataset. "Number of shots" denotes the
number of labeled samples per target class, where 'Full' denotes that the model is
trained with the whole dataset. * denotes reproduced results.

Method	Number of Shots					
	1	2	4	8	16	Full
Linear Probe*	44.4	58.5	44.9	49.0	61.5	82.5
LaBo [8]*	36.5	44.9	44.5	43.0	58.5	80.8
LaBo [8]* + Ours	53.2 (+16.7)	45.4 (+0.5)	47.4 (+2.9)	46.1 (+3.1)	61.4 (+2.9)	81.0(+0.2)

5 concepts with the highest $\mathcal{V}(c)$	5 concepts with the lowest $\mathcal{V}(c)$
- dark brown or black mole with irregular borders - central area of darker pigmentation - small, pearly-white or flesh-colored bump on the skin - dark brown or black lesion with irregular borders - nose, ears, lips, and hands	- others may require medical or surgical treatment - thought to be caused by a combination of genetic and environmental factors - may not become apparent for years - considered to be low-risk - at least one in their lifetime

Fig. 2. Examples of concepts that have the highest and the lowest visual activation
score $\mathcal{V}(c)$ are listed.

4.1   Experimental Results

In Table 1, a consistent gain in accuracy under every single setting compared to
LaBo is reported by applying the visual activation score. In terms of filtering
out non-visual concepts, LaBo's discriminability score $D(c)$ also indirectly refines
non-visual concepts by maximizing the negative entropy of $\overline{\text{sim}}(y|c)$. However,
the fewer label data, the more inaccurate value of $\overline{\text{sim}}(y|c)$ is, and at 1-shot, the
LaBo achieved a low accuracy of 36.7%. By using an unlabeled image set X, the
visual activation score $\mathcal{V}(c)$ encourages to filter non-visual concepts effectively,
therefore outperforming LaBo by 16.5% at 1-shot. Also, while maintaining the
interpretability, in some cases, the proposed method is shown to even outperform
performances of linear probing where the classification process is completely non-
interpretable.

5   Analysis

5.1   Analysis on a Visual Activation Score $\mathcal{V}(c)$

In Fig. 2, five concepts with the highest and the lowest visual activation score $\mathcal{V}(c)$ are listed, respectively. As shown in the figure, concepts with high $\mathcal{V}(c)$ turn out to be visual concepts, such as "dark brown or black mole with irregular borders". On the other hand, concepts with low $\mathcal{V}(c)$ are mostly non-visual or meaningless concepts, including "others may require medical or surgical treatment". Such qualitative examples demonstrate that the visual activation score $\mathcal{V}(c)$ acts as an effective measure to detect non-visual or meaningless concepts.

Table 2. Analysis on the image set X for visual activation score. "Number of shots" denotes the number of labeled samples per target class, where 'Full' denotes that the model is trained with the whole dataset.

Image set X	Number of Shots					
	1	2	4	8	16	Full
w/o $\mathcal{V}(c)$	36.5	44.9	44.5	43.0	58.5	80.8
HAM10000	**53.2**	45.4	47.4	46.1	61.4	**81.0**
ImageNet	48.5	**46.2**	**50.3**	**56.8**	62.1	80.9
COCO	47.7	45.4	48.5	45.7	**62.3**	80.8

5.2   Analysis on Target Image Set X

In Table 2, experimental results with multiple target dataset X to calculate the visual activation score $\mathcal{V}(c)$ in Eq. 7 are provided. We conduct experiments under adopting train splits of HAM-10000 [15], ImageNet [16], and COCO [17] as X. For the ImageNet and COCO datasets, 10,000 images are randomly sampled to match the size of X to that of the HAM-10000 dataset. The result shows that overall performance gains are reported regardless of the target set X. Such results show the effectiveness of the proposed method in that it does not require a domain-specific dataset, but instead can be implemented using an arbitrary dataset. We anticipate that such property could facilitate the application of the proposed method to diverse medical domains, where acquiring large-scale domain-specific target images is expensive.

5.3   Qualitative Examples

In Fig. 3, the final prediction of a model and three concepts with the highest influence P_y in predicting the ground-truth class y are illustrated. As depicted in the figure, the baseline fails correctly classifying the image since the concepts with the highest influences in predicting the ground-truth class are mostly non-visual concepts *e.g.*, "early detection and treatment of skin lesions can help

		baseline	**ours**
	Top 1:	early detection and treatment of skin lesions can help prevent skin cancer	surrounded by **red, inflamed skin**
	Top 2:	more advanced lesions may be **darker**	in some cases, the skin lesions may be **darker in color**
	Top 3:	most common type of precancerous lesion in the united states	a type of skin cancer that typically appears as a **small, pearly-white** or
basal cell carcinoma	**Pred:**	actinic keratoses (X)	**basal cell carcinoma (O)**
	Top 1:	lesions may be associated with other health problems	**waxy or crusted surface**
	Top 2:	lesions may be **surrounded by an inflammatory halo**	**smooth, waxy surface**
	Top 3:	**fluid is clear**	**slightly rough surface**
benign keratosis-like lesions	**Pred:**	vascular lesions (X)	**benign keratosis-like lesions (O)**
	Top 1:	some people with skin lesions may require lifelong treatment	**black, brown, or any color that is darker** than the surrounding skin
	Top 2:	lesions may be associated with other health problems	some nevi may also itch or **bleed**
	Top 3:	lesions may be **surrounded by a halo of lighter skin**	**lighter or darker** than the surrounding skin
melanocytic nevi	**Pred:**	vascular lesions (X)	**melanocytic nevi (O)**

Fig. 3. Qualitative results on HAM-10000 dataset. Several comparisons with the baseline, LaBo, are shown with the top-3 concepts which are ranked by their weights in the linear function. Parts that provide visual cues are colored blue.

prevent skin cancer", "lesions may be associated with other health problems" which does not help classify an image. In contrast, the prediction result on the same image is corrected when applying the proposed method since visually irrelevant concepts are removed from S_y, thus concepts with the highest influences are replaced with concepts with visual cues. The result validates that adding the visual activation score $\mathcal{V}(c)$ to the score function $\mathcal{F}$ helps filter visually irrelevant concepts, therefore contributing to better classification results by providing concepts that are rich in information.

6   Conclusion

In this paper, we propose a method to refine the non-visual concepts generated from large language models (LLMs) which hinder the training of Concept Bottleneck Models (CBMs). In order to filter out non-visual concepts, we propose the visual activation score which measures whether a concept contains visual information or not. With computed visual activation scores of concepts, non-visual concepts are filtered out via a submodular optimization. Quantitative and qualitative analyses demonstrate that the proposed visual activation score contributes to detecting and filtering out non-visual concepts, therefore resulting in consistent improvement in accuracy.

Acknowledgments. This research was supported by the MSIT (Ministry of Science and ICT), Korea, under the ICT Creative Consilience program (IITP-2023-2020-0-01819) supervised by the IITP(Institute for Information & communications Technology Planning & Evaluation).

References

1. Anwar, S.M., Majid, M., Qayyum, A., Awais, M., Alnowami, M., Khan, M.K.: Medical image analysis using convolutional neural networks: a review. J. Med. Syst. **42**, 226 (2018)
2. Chang, K., et al.: Distributed deep learning networks among institutions for medical imaging. J. Am. Med. Inf. Assoc. **25**, 945–954 (2018)
3. Zhou, J., et al.: Diagnosis of benign and malignant breast lesions on DCE-MRI by using radiomics and deep learning with consideration of peritumor tissue. J. Magn. Reson. Imaging **51**, 798–809 (2020)
4. Xue, Y., Zhang, R., Deng, Y., Chen, K., Jiang, T.: A preliminary examination of the diagnostic value of deep learning in hip osteoarthritis. PLOS ONE **12**, e0178992 (2017)
5. Koh, P.W., et al.: Concept bottleneck models. In: ICML (2020)
6. Zarlenga, M.E., et al.: Concept embedding models: beyond the accuracy-explainability trade-off. In: NeurIPS (2022)
7. Oikarinen, T., Das, S., Nguyen, L.M., Weng, T.-W.: Label-free concept bottleneck models. In: ICLR (2023)
8. Yang, Y., Panagopoulou, A., Zhou, S., Jin, D., Callison-Burch, C., Yatskar, M.: Language in a bottle: language model guided concept bottlenecks for interpretable image classification. In: CVPR (2023)
9. Bach, F.: Convex analysis and optimization with submodular functions: a tutorial. arXiv preprint arXiv:1010.4207 (2010)
10. Vaswani, A., et al.: Attention is all you need. In: NeurIPS (2017)
11. Brown, T., et al.: Language models are few-shot learners. In: NeurIPS (2020)
12. Touvron, H., et al.: LLaMA: open and efficient foundation language models. arXiv preprint arXiv:2302.13971 (2023)
13. Radford, A., Jeffrey, W., Child, R., Luan, D., Amodei, D., Sutskever, I., et al.: Language models are unsupervised multitask learners. OpenAI Blog **1**(8), 9 (2019)
14. Radford, A., et al.: Learning transferable visual models from natural language supervision. In: ICML (2021)
15. Tschandl, P., Rosendahl, C., Kittler, H.: The HAM10000 dataset, a large collection of multi-source dermatoscopic images of common pigmented skin lesions. Sci. Data **5**, 180161 (2018). https://doi.org/10.1038/sdata.2018.161
16. Deng, J., Dong, W., Socher, R., Li, L.-J., Li, K., Fei-Fei, L.: ImageNet: a large-scale hierarchical image database. In: CVPR (2009)
17. Lin, T.-Y., et al.: Microsoft COCO: common objects in context. In: Fleet, D., Pajdla, T., Schiele, B., Tuytelaars, T. (eds.) ECCV 2014. LNCS, vol. 8693, pp. 740–755. Springer, Cham (2014). https://doi.org/10.1007/978-3-319-10602-1_48

SAM Meets Robotic Surgery: An Empirical Study on Generalization, Robustness and Adaptation

An Wang[1], Mobarakol Islam[2], Mengya Xu[3], Yang Zhang[4], and Hongliang Ren[1,3(✉)]

[1] Department of Electronic Engineering, Shun Hing Institute of Advanced Engineering (SHIAE), The Chinese University of Hong Kong, Hong Kong SAR, China
wa09@link.cuhk.edu.hk, hlren@ee.cuhk.edu.hk
[2] Department of Medical Physics and Biomedical Engineering, Wellcome/EPSRC Centre for Interventional and Surgical Sciences (WEISS), University College London, London, UK
mobarakol.islam@ucl.ac.uk
[3] Department of Biomedical Engineering, National University of Singapore, Singapore, Singapore
mengya@u.nus.edu
[4] School of Mechanical Engineering, Hubei University of Technology, Wuhan, China
yzhangcst@hbut.edu.cn

Abstract. The Segment Anything Model (SAM) serves as a fundamental model for semantic segmentation and demonstrates remarkable generalization capabilities across a wide range of downstream scenarios. In this empirical study, we examine SAM's robustness and zero-shot generalizability in the field of robotic surgery. We comprehensively explore different scenarios, including prompted and unprompted situations, bounding box and points-based prompt approaches, as well as the ability to generalize under corruptions and perturbations at five severity levels. Additionally, we compare the performance of SAM with state-of-the-art supervised models. We conduct all the experiments with two well-known robotic instrument segmentation datasets from MICCAI EndoVis 2017 and 2018 challenges. Our extensive evaluation results reveal that although SAM shows remarkable zero-shot generalization ability with bounding box prompts, it struggles to segment the whole instrument with point-based prompts and unprompted settings. Furthermore, our qualitative figures demonstrate that the model either failed to predict certain parts of the instrument mask (e.g., jaws, wrist) or predicted parts of the instrument as wrong classes in the scenario of overlapping instruments within the same bounding box or with the point-based prompt. In fact, SAM struggles to identify instruments in complex surgical scenarios characterized by the presence of blood, reflection, blur, and shade. Additionally, SAM is insufficiently robust to maintain high performance when subjected to various forms of data corruption. We also attempt to fine-tune SAM using Low-rank Adaptation (LoRA) and

---

A. Wang and M. Islam—Co-first authors.

© The Author(s), under exclusive license to Springer Nature Switzerland AG 2023
M. E. Celebi et al. (Eds.): MICCAI 2023 Workshops, LNCS 14393, pp. 234–244, 2023.
https://doi.org/10.1007/978-3-031-47401-9_23

propose SurgicalSAM, which shows the capability in class-wise mask prediction without prompt. Therefore, we can argue that, without further domain-specific fine-tuning, SAM is not ready for downstream surgical tasks.

1   Introduction

Segmenting surgical instruments and tissue poses a significant challenge in robotic surgery, as it plays a vital role in instrument tracking and position estimation within surgical scenes. Nonetheless, current deep learning models often have limited generalization capacity as they are tailored to specific surgical sites. Consequently, it is crucial to develop generalist models that can effectively adapt to various surgical scenes and segmentation objectives to advance the field of robotic surgery [18]. Recently, segmentation foundation models have made great progress in the field of natural image segmentation. The segment anything model (SAM) [14], which has been trained on more than one billion masks, exhibits remarkable proficiency in generating precise object masks using various prompts such as bounding boxes and points. SAM stands as the pioneering and most renowned foundation model for segmentation. Whereas, several works have revealed that SAM can fail on common medical image segmentation tasks [4,6,8,16]. This is not surprising or unexpected since SAM's training dataset primarily comprises natural image datasets. Consequently, it raises the question of enhancing SAM's strong feature extraction capability for medical image tasks. Med SAM Adapter [22] utilizes medical-specific domain knowledge to improve the segmentation model through a simple yet effective adaptation technique. SAMed [23] has applied a low-rank-based finetuning strategy to the SAM image encoder, as well as prompt encoder and mask decoder on the medical image segmentation dataset.

However, evaluating the performance of SAM in the context of surgical scenes remains an insufficiently explored area that has the potential for further investigation. This study uses two publicly available robotic surgery datasets to assess SAM's generalizability under different settings, such as bounding box and point-prompted. Moreover, we have examined the possibility of fine-tuning SAM through Low-rank Adaptation (LoRA) to examine its capability to predict masks for different classes without prompts. Additionally, we have analyzed SAM's robustness by assessing its performance on synthetic surgery datasets, which contain various levels of corruption and perturbations.

2   Experimental Settings

Datasets. We have employed two classical datasets in endoscopic surgical instrument segmentation, i.e., EndoVis17 [2] and EndoVis18 [1]. For the EndoVis17 dataset, unlike previous works [5,13,20] which conduct 4-fold cross-validation

Table 1. Quantitative comparison of binary and instrument segmentation on EndoVis17 and EndoVis18 datasets. The best and runner-up results are shown in bold and underlined.

Type	Method	Pub/Year(20-)	Arch.	EndoVis17		EndoVis18	
				Binary IoU	Instrument IoU	Binary IoU	Instrument IoU
Single-Task	Vanilla UNet	MICCAI15	UNet	75.44	15.80	68.89	–
	TernausNet	ICMLA18	UNet	83.60	35.27	–	46.22
	MF-TAPNet	MICCAI19	UNet	87.56	37.35	–	67.87
	Islam et al.	RA-L19	–	84.50	–	–	–
	ISINet	MICCAI21	Res50	–	55.62	–	73.03
	Wang et al.	MICCAI22	UNet	–	–	58.12	–
Multi-Task	ST-MTL	MedIA21	–	83.49	–	–	–
	AP-MTL	ICRA20	–	88.75	–	–	–
	S-MTL	RA-L22	–	–	–	–	43.54
	TraSeTR	ICRA22	Res50 + Trfm	–	60.40	–	76.20
	S3Net	WACV23	Res50	–	72.54	–	75.81
Prompt-based	SAM 1 Point	arxiv23	ViT_h	53.88	55.96*	57.12	54.30*
	SAM Box	arxiv23	ViT_h	89.19	88.20*	89.35	81.09*

*Categorical information directly inherits from associated prompts.

for training and testing on the 8×225-frame released training data, we report SAM's performance directly on all eight sequences (1–8). For the EndoVis18 dataset, we follow the dataset split in ISINet [5], where sequences 2, 5, 9, and 15 are utilized for evaluation.

Prompts. The original EndoVis datasets [1,2] do not have bounding boxes or point annotations. We have labeled the datasets with bounding boxes for each instrument, associated with corresponding class information. Additionally, regarding the single-point prompt, we obtain the center of each instrument mask by simply computing the moments of the mask contour. Since SAM [14] only predicts binary segmentation masks, for instrument-wise segmentation, the output instrument labels are assigned inherited from the input prompts.

Metrics. The IoU and Dice metrics from the EndoVis17 [2] challenge[1] is used. Specifically, only the classes presented in a frame are considered in the calculation for instrument segmentation.

Comparison Methods. We have involved several classical and recent methods, including the vanilla UNet [17], TernausNet [20], MF-TAPNet [13], Islam et al. [10], Wang et al. [21], ST-MTL [11], S-MTL [19], AP-MTL [12], ISINet [5], TraSeTR [24], and S3Net [3] for surgical binary and instrument-wise segmentation. The ViT-H-based SAM [14] is employed in all our investigations except for the finetuning experiments. Note that we cannot provide an absolutely fair comparison because existing methods do not need prompts during inference.

3   Surgical Instruments Segmentation with Prompts

Implementation. With bounding boxes and single points as prompts, we input the images to SAM [14] to get the predicted binary masks for the target objects.

[1] https://github.com/ternaus/robot-surgery-segmentation.

Because SAM [14] can not provide consistent categorical information. We compromise to use the class information from the bounding boxes directly. In this way, we derive instrument-wise segmentation while bypassing the possible errors from misclassifications, an essential factor affecting instrument-wise segmentation accuracy.

Results and Analysis. As shown in Table 1, with bounding boxes as prompts, SAM [14] outperforms previous unprompted supervised methods in binary and instrument-wise segmentation on both datasets. However, with single points as prompts, SAM [14] degrades a lot in performance, indicating its limited ability to segment surgical instruments from weak prompts. This reveals the performance of the SAM closely relies on prompt quality. For complicated surgical scenes, SAM [14] still struggles to produce accurate segmentation results, as shown in columns (a) to (l) of Fig. 1. Typical challenges, including shadows (a), motion blur (d), occlusion (b, g, h), light reflection (c), insufficient light (j, l), over brightness (e), ambiguous suturing thread (f), instrument wrist (i), and irregular instrument pose (k), all lead to unsatisfied segmentation performance.

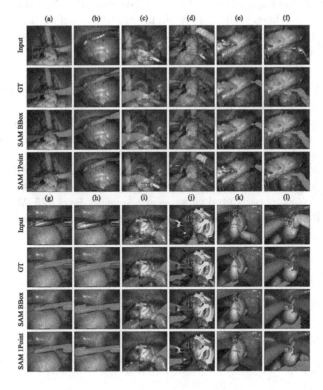

Fig. 1. Qualitative results of SAM on various challenging frames. Red rectangles highlight the typical challenging regions which cause unsatisfactory predictions. (Color figure online)

Table 2. Quantitative results on various corrupted EndoVis18 validation data.

Task	Severity	Noise				Blur					Weather					Digital			
		Gaussian	Shot	Impulse	Speckle	Defocus	Glass	Motion	Zoom	Gaussian	Snow	Frost	Fog	Bright	Spatter	Contrast	Pixel	JPEG	Saturate
Binary	0									89.35									
	1	77.69	80.18	80.43	83.28	82.01	80.53	82.99	80.30	85.40	84.08	83.12	85.38	87.43	86.69	85.76	81.12	58.77	86.64
	2	73.92	76.07	76.15	81.65	80.21	79.20	80.22	77.55	81.69	80.69	80.34	84.65	87.27	84.21	84.90	79.32	56.04	84.85
	3	69.21	71.74	73.02	77.74	76.96	72.64	75.50	75.27	78.31	79.58	78.90	83.62	87.23	82.50	83.36	73.81	56.25	86.84
	4	63.80	65.41	67.29	75.28	73.79	72.38	69.60	73.22	75.23	76.33	78.38	82.28	87.06	83.12	77.12	70.82	57.59	83.21
	5	57.07	60.61	61.61	71.83	69.85	69.59	66.25	71.58	66.96	77.66	76.82	78.84	86.43	79.62	66.58	68.55	56.77	81.26
Instrument	0									81.09									
	1	69.51	71.83	72.25	74.82	73.64	72.13	74.33	71.41	76.79	75.40	74.42	76.82	79.16	78.24	77.17	72.94	54.86	78.27
	2	66.06	68.09	68.53	73.19	71.74	71.02	71.46	68.85	73.15	72.13	71.65	76.14	79.00	75.54	76.22	71.55	52.23	76.61
	3	62.01	64.44	65.89	69.75	68.74	64.97	67.13	67.12	70.08	70.97	70.21	75.01	78.90	73.70	74.67	66.83	51.63	78.39
	4	57.28	59.12	61.03	67.82	65.87	64.87	62.15	65.18	67.23	68.43	69.79	73.73	78.73	74.24	69.48	63.99	51.88	74.91
	5	51.56	55.16	55.86	64.76	62.43	62.23	59.26	63.96	60.60	69.33	68.32	70.45	78.19	70.72	61.14	61.79	51.01	73.35

4   Robustness Under Data Corruption

Implementation. Referring to the robustness evaluation benchmark [7], we have evaluated SAM [14] under 18 types of data corruptions at 5 severity levels following the official implementations[2] with box prompts. Note that the *Elastic Transformation* has been omitted to avoid inconsistency between the input image and associated masks. The adopted data corruption can be allocated into four distinct categories of *Noise, Blue, Weather,* and *Digital.*

Results and Analysis. The severity of data corruption is directly proportional to the degree of performance degradation in SAM [14], as depicted in Table 2. The robustness of SAM [14] may be influenced differently depending on the nature of the corruption present. However, in most scenarios, SAM's performance diminishes significantly. Notably, *JPEG Compression* and *Gaussian Noise* have the greatest impact on segmentation performance, whereas *Brightness* has a negligible effect. Figure 2 presents one exemplar frame in its original state alongside various corrupted versions at a severity level of 5. We can observe that SAM [14] suffers significant performance degradation in most cases.

---

[2] https://github.com/hendrycks/robustness.

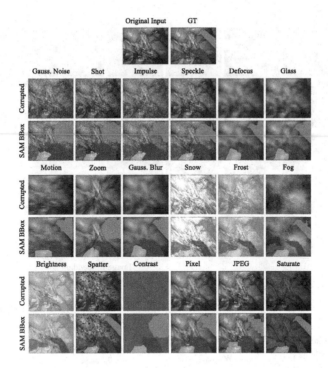

Fig. 2. Qualitative results of SAM under 18 data corruptions of level-5 severity.

5   Automatic Surgical Scene Segmentation

Implementation. Without prompts, SAM [14] can also facilitate automatic mask generation (AMG) for the entire image. For naive investigation of the automatic surgical scene segmentation results, we use the default parameters from the official implementation[3] without further tuning. The colors of each segmented mask are randomly assigned because SAM [14] only generates binary masks for each object.

Results and Analysis. As shown in Fig. 3, in surgical scene segmentation of EndoVis18 [1] data, SAM [14] can produce promising results on simple scenes like columns (a) and (f). But it encounters difficulties when applied to more complicated scenes, as it struggles to differentiate between the entirety of instrument articulating parts accurately and to identify discrete tissue structures as interconnected units. As a foundation model, SAM [14] still lacks comprehensive awareness of objects' semantics, especially in downstream domains like surgical scenes.

---

[3] https://github.com/facebookresearch/segment-anything.

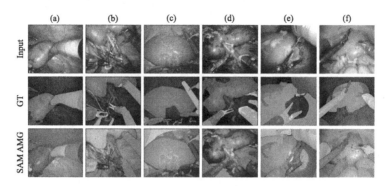

Fig. 3. Unprompted automatic mask generation for surgical scene segmentation.

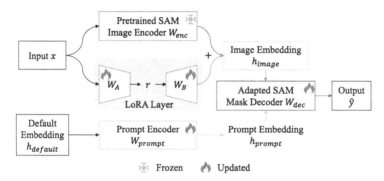

Fig. 4. Overall architecture of our SurgicalSAM.

6 Parameter-Efficient Finetuning with Low-Rank Adaptation

With the rapid emergence of foundational and large AI models, utilizing the pretrained models effectively and efficiently for downstream tasks has attracted increasing research interest. Although SAM [14] has shown decent segmentation performance with prompts and can cluster objects in surgical scenes, we seek to finetune and adapt it to make it capable of traditional unprompted multi-class segmentation pipeline - take one image as input only, and predict its segmentation mask with categorical labels.

Implementation. To efficiently finetune SAM [14] and enable it to support multi-class segmentation without relying on prompts, we consider utilizing the strategy of Low-rank Adaptation (LoRA) [9] and also adapting the original mask decoder to output categorical labels. Taking inspiration from SAMed [23], we implement a modified architecture as shown in Fig. 4, whereby the pretrained SAM image encoder maintains its frozen weights W_{enc} during finetuning while additional light-weight LoRA layers are incorporated for updating purposes. In

Table 3. Quantitative evaluation of SurgicalSAM under data corruption.

Severity	Noise				Blur					Weather					Digital			
	Gaussian	Shot	Impulse	Speckle	Defocus	Glass	Motion	Zoom	Gaussian	Snow	Frost	Fog	Bright	Spatter	Contrast	Pixel	JPEG	Saturate
0	71.38																	
1	24.31	30.68	28.88	45.53	59.50	60.21	61.29	56.32	64.67	57.84	54.80	54.95	66.67	65.74	57.56	64.81	54.30	60.01
2	12.19	15.43	12.77	36.92	53.85	56.48	55.72	52.81	55.54	29.68	36.33	51.32	63.73	62.59	50.89	64.00	49.56	28.92
3	5.84	6.30	7.34	17.26	45.56	43.71	50.97	49.55	47.24	42.20	26.31	44.17	62.22	60.65	36.90	54.99	46.24	64.85
4	4.26	4.15	4.63	10.19	39.23	39.64	43.27	46.38	39.65	30.21	25.80	38.28	60.90	51.22	16.42	40.64	36.69	60.36
5	3.79	3.79	3.92	6.37	32.49	38.05	38.16	43.99	26.67	13.97	20.60	20.92	59.64	40.51	4.95	34.00	24.03	50.50

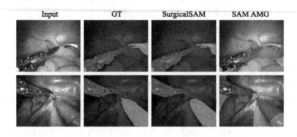

Input   GT   SurgicalSAM   SAM AMG

Fig. 5. Qualitative comparison of our SurgicalSAM with the original SAM.

this way, we can not only leverage the exceptional feature extraction ability of the original SAM encoder, but also gradually capture the surgical data representations and store the domain-specific knowledge in the LoRA layers parameter-efficiently. We denote this modified architecture as "SurgicalSAM". With an input image x, we can derive the image embedding h_{image} following

$$h_{image} = W_{enc}x + \Delta Wx, \tag{1}$$

where ΔW is the weight update matrix of LoRA layers. Then we can decompose ΔW into two smaller matrices: $\Delta W = W_A W_B$, where W_A and W_B are $A \times r$ and $r \times B$ dimensional matrices, respectively. r is a hyper-parameter that specifies the rank of the low-rank adaptation matrices. To maintain a balance between model complexity, adaptability, and the potential for underfitting or overfitting, we empirically set the rank r of W_A and W_B in the LoRA layers to 4.

During the unprompted automatic mask generation (AMG), the original SAM uses fixed default embeddings $h_{default}$ for the prompt encoder with weights W_{prompt}. We adopted this strategy and updated the lightweight prompt encoder during finetuning, as shown in Fig. 4. In addition, we modified the segmentation head of the mask decoder W_{dec} to allow for the production of predictions for each semantic class. In contrast to the binary ambiguity prediction of the original mask decoder of SAM, the modified decoder predicts each semantic class of $\hat{y}$ in a deterministic manner. In other words, it is capable of semantic segmentation beyond binary segmentation (Fig. 5).

We adopt the training split of the Endo18 dataset for finetuning and test with the validation split, as other works reported in Table 1. Following SAMed [23], we adopt the combination of the Cross Entropy loss L_{CE} and Dice loss L_{Dice} which can be expressed as

$$L = \lambda L_{Dice} + (1 - \lambda)L_{CE}, \tag{2}$$

where λ is a weighting coefficient balancing the effects of the two losses. We empirically set λ as 0.8 in our experiments. Due to resource constraints, we utilize the ViT_b version of SAM and finetuning on two RTX3090 GPUs. The maximum epochs are 160, with a batch size 12 and an initial learning rate of 0.001. To stabilize the finetuning process, we apply warmup for the first 250 iterations, followed by exponential learning rate decay. Random flip, rotation, and crop are applied to augment the training images and avoid overfitting. The images are resized to 512×512 as model inputs. Besides, we use AdamW [15] optimizer with a weight decay of 0.1 to update model parameters.

Results and Analysis. After naively finetuning, the SurgicalSAM model can manage the instrument-wise segmentation without reliance on prompts. With further tuning of hyper-parameters like the learning rate, the batch size, and the optimizer, SurgicalSAM can achieve **71.38%** mIoU score on the validation split of the Endo18 dataset, which is on par with the state-of-the-art models in Table 1. Since other methods in Table 1 are utilizing temporal and optical flow information as supplement [5], or conducting multi-task optimization [3, 24], the results of our image-only and single-task architecture SurgicalSAM are promising. Besides, the encoder backbone we finetuned is the smallest ViT_b due to limited computational resources. We believe the largest ViT_h backbone can yield much better performance. Compared with the original SAM, our new architecture is of great practical significance as it can achieve semantic-level automatic segmentation. Moreover, the additionally trained parameters are only **18.28 MB**, suggesting the efficiency of our finetuning strategy.

Furthermore, we have evaluated the robustness of SurgicalSAM in the face of data corruption using the EndoVis18 validation dataset. As shown in Table 3, the model's performance exhibits a significant degradation when subjected to various forms of data corruption, particularly in the case of *Blur* corruption.

7   Conclusion

In this study, we explore the robustness and zero-shot generalizability of the SAM [14] in the field of robotic surgery on two robotic instrument segmentation datasets of MICCAI EndoVis 2017 and 2018 challenges, respectively. Extensive empirical results suggest that SAM [14] is deficient in segmenting the entire instrument with point-based prompts and unprompted settings, as clearly shown in Fig. 1 and Fig. 3. This implies that SAM [14] can not capture the surgical scenes precisely despite yielding surprising zero-shot generalization ability. Besides, it exhibits challenges in accurately predicting certain parts of the instrument mask when there are overlapping instruments or only with a point-based prompt. It also fails to identify instruments in complex surgical scenarios, such as blood, reflection, blur, and shade. Moreover, we extensively evaluate the robustness of SAM [14] with a wide range of data corruptions. As indicated by Table 2 and Fig. 2, SAM [14] encounters significant performance degradation in many scenarios. To shed light on adapting SAM for surgical tasks, we fine-tuned the SAM using LoRA. Our fine-tuned SAM, i.e., SurgicalSAM, demonstrates the capability of class-wise mask prediction without any prompt.

As a foundational segmentation model, SAM [14] shows remarkable generalization capability in robotic surgical segmentation, yet it still suffers performance degradation due to downstream domain shift, data corruptions, perturbations, and complex scenes. To further improve its generalization capability and robustness, a broad spectrum of evaluations and extensions remains to be explored and developed.

Acknowledgements. This work was supported by Hong Kong Research Grants Council (RGC) Collaborative Research Fund (CRF C4063-18G and CRF C4026-21GF), Shun Hing Institute of Advanced Engineering (SHIAE project BME-p1-21) at the Chinese University of Hong Kong (CUHK), General Research Fund (GRF 14203323), Shenzhen-Hong Kong-Macau Technology Research Programme (Type C) STIC Grant SGDX20210823103535014 (202108233000303), and (GRS) #3110167.

References

1. Allan, M., et al.: 2018 robotic scene segmentation challenge. arXiv preprint arXiv:2001.11190 (2020)
2. Allan, M., et al.: 2017 robotic instrument segmentation challenge. arXiv preprint arXiv:1902.06426 (2019)
3. Baby, B., et al.: From forks to forceps: a new framework for instance segmentation of surgical instruments. In: Proceedings of the IEEE/CVF Winter Conference on Applications of Computer Vision, pp. 6191–6201 (2023)
4. Deng, R., et al.: Segment anything model (SAM) for digital pathology: assess zero-shot segmentation on whole slide imaging. arXiv preprint arXiv:2304.04155 (2023)
5. González, C., Bravo-Sánchez, L., Arbelaez, P.: ISINet: an instance-based approach for surgical instrument segmentation. In: Martel, A.L., et al. (eds.) MICCAI 2020, Part III. LNCS, vol. 12263, pp. 595–605. Springer, Cham (2020). https://doi.org/10.1007/978-3-030-59716-0_57
6. He, S., Bao, R., Li, J., Grant, P.E., Ou, Y.: Accuracy of segment-anything model (SAM) in medical image segmentation tasks. arXiv preprint arXiv:2304.09324 (2023)
7. Hendrycks, D., Dietterich, T.: Benchmarking neural network robustness to common corruptions and perturbations. In: International Conference on Learning Representations (2019)
8. Hu, C., Li, X.: When SAM meets medical images: an investigation of segment anything model (SAM) on multi-phase liver tumor segmentation. arXiv preprint arXiv:2304.08506 (2023)
9. Hu, E.J., et al.: LoRA: Low-rank adaptation of large language models. arXiv preprint arXiv:2106.09685 (2021)
10. Islam, M., Atputharuban, D.A., Ramesh, R., Ren, H.: Real-time instrument segmentation in robotic surgery using auxiliary supervised deep adversarial learning. IEEE Robot. Autom. Lett. 4(2), 2188–2195 (2019)
11. Islam, M., Vibashan, V., Lim, C.M., Ren, H.: ST-MTL: spatio-temporal multitask learning model to predict scanpath while tracking instruments in robotic surgery. Med. Image Anal. 67, 101837 (2021)

12. Islam, M., Vibashan, V., Ren, H.: AP-MTL: attention pruned multi-task learning model for real-time instrument detection and segmentation in robot-assisted surgery. In: 2020 IEEE International Conference on Robotics and Automation (ICRA), pp. 8433–8439. IEEE (2020)

13. Jin, Y., Cheng, K., Dou, Q., Heng, P.-A.: Incorporating temporal prior from motion flow for instrument segmentation in minimally invasive surgery video. In: Shen, D., et al. (eds.) MICCAI 2019, Part V. LNCS, vol. 11768, pp. 440–448. Springer, Cham (2019). https://doi.org/10.1007/978-3-030-32254-0_49

14. Kirillov, A., et al.: Segment anything. arXiv preprint arXiv:2304.02643 (2023)

15. Loshchilov, I., Hutter, F.: Decoupled weight decay regularization. arXiv preprint arXiv:1711.05101 (2017)

16. Ma, J., Wang, B.: Segment anything in medical images (2023)

17. Ronneberger, O., Fischer, P., Brox, T.: U-Net: convolutional networks for biomedical image segmentation. In: Navab, N., Hornegger, J., Wells, W.M., Frangi, A.F. (eds.) MICCAI 2015, Part III. LNCS, vol. 9351, pp. 234–241. Springer, Cham (2015). https://doi.org/10.1007/978-3-319-24574-4_28

18. Seenivasan, L., Islam, M., Kannan, G., Ren, H.: SurgicalGPT: end-to-end language-vision GPT for visual question answering in surgery. arXiv preprint arXiv:2304.09974 (2023)

19. Seenivasan, L., Mitheran, S., Islam, M., Ren, H.: Global-reasoned multi-task learning model for surgical scene understanding. IEEE Robot. Autom. Lett. $7(2)$, 3858–3865 (2022)

20. Shvets, A.A., Rakhlin, A., Kalinin, A.A., Iglovikov, V.I.: Automatic instrument segmentation in robot-assisted surgery using deep learning. In: 2018 17th IEEE International Conference on Machine Learning and Applications (ICMLA), pp. 624–628 (2018)

21. Wang, A., Islam, M., Xu, M., Ren, H.: Rethinking surgical instrument segmentation: a background image can be all you need. In: Wang, L., Dou, Q., Fletcher, P.T., Speidel, S., Li, S. (eds.) MICCAI 2022. LNCS, vol. 1343, pp. 355–364. Springer, Cham (2022). https://doi.org/10.1007/978-3-031-16449-1_34

22. Wu, J., et al.: Medical SAM adapter: adapting segment anything model for medical image segmentation. arXiv preprint arXiv:2304.12620 (2023)

23. Zhang, K., Liu, D.: Customized segment anything model for medical image segmentation. arXiv preprint arXiv:2304.13785 (2023)

24. Zhao, Z., Jin, Y., Heng, P.A.: TraSeTR: track-to-segment transformer with contrastive query for instance-level instrument segmentation in robotic surgery. In: 2022 International Conference on Robotics and Automation (ICRA), pp. 11186–11193. IEEE (2022)

Evaluation and Improvement of Segment Anything Model for Interactive Histopathology Image Segmentation

SeungKyu Kim, Hyun-Jic Oh, Seonghui Min, and Won-Ki Jeong[✉]

Korea University, College of Informatics, Department of Computer Science
and Engineering, Seoul, South Korea
wkjeong@korea.ac.kr

Abstract. With the emergence of the Segment Anything Model (SAM) as a foundational model for image segmentation, its application has been extensively studied across various domains, including the medical field. However, its potential in the context of histopathology data, specifically in region segmentation, has received relatively limited attention. In this paper, we evaluate SAM's performance in zero-shot and fine-tuned scenarios on histopathology data, with a focus on interactive segmentation. Additionally, we compare SAM with other state-of-the-art interactive models to assess its practical potential and evaluate its generalization capability with domain adaptability. In the experimental results, SAM exhibits a weakness in segmentation performance compared to other models while demonstrating relative strengths in terms of inference time and generalization capability. To improve SAM's limited local refinement ability and to enhance prompt stability while preserving its core strengths, we propose a modification of SAM's decoder. The experimental results suggest that the proposed modification is effective to make SAM useful for interactive histology image segmentation. The code is available at https://github.com/hvcl/SAM_Interactive_Histopathology

Keywords: Segment Anything Model · Histopathology Image Analysis · Interactive Segmentation · Foundation Models

1 Introduction

Tumor region segmentation in whole slide images (WSIs) is a critical task in digital pathology diagnosis. Numerous segmentation methods have been developed in the computer vision community that perform well on objects with clear edges [1,2,9]. However, as shown in Fig. 1, tumor boundaries in histopathology images are often indistinct and ambiguous. As a result, directly applying conventional image segmentation methods to WSIs tends to yield unsatisfactory results.

Supplementary Information The online version contains supplementary material available at https://doi.org/10.1007/978-3-031-47401-9_24.

M. E. Celebi et al. (Eds.): MICCAI 2023 Workshops, LNCS 14393, pp. 245–255, 2023.
https://doi.org/10.1007/978-3-031-47401-9_24

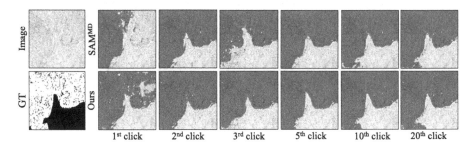

Fig. 1. Comparison between SAM^{MD} and ours. The green and red points represent positive and negative clicks, respectively. Each click is automatically generated on the error region in the previous prediction.

In recent years, deep learning advancements have shown promising outcomes in medical image segmentation [21] when sufficient training labels are available. Nevertheless, even fully-supervised models have room for improvement due to potential disparities between training and inference imaging conditions, making generalization challenging.

Recently, the Segment Anything Model (SAM) [13], a large promptable foundation model that allows user interaction, has gained considerable attention as a general image segmentation model, eliminating the need for task-specific annotation, training, and modeling. Inspired by this, the primary motivation behind our work stems from the notion that a foundation model like SAM holds promise as a general-purpose segmentation model, which can also be applied to histopathology image segmentation without domain-specific training. Several early attempts have been made to employ SAM in medical image segmentation [8,18,22]. However, the exploration of SAM's potential for interactive segmentation has been limited, with only subjective criteria-based prompts being utilized. Another motivation of our work is that supervised training may not generalize well to various target images during inference. Hence, utilizing interactive segmentation to modify the segmentation model's results could prove to be a practical and effective strategy for improving segmentation performance. While numerous interactive segmentation methods exist in computer vision [4,16,24], only a few works have been proposed specifically for interactive histopathology image segmentation [5,20] so far.

In this study, we investigate the potential of SAM for tumor region segmentation in histopathology images using a click-based interactive approach. Our primary objectives are to answer the following questions: 1) Can SAM be directly (zero-shot) applied to interactive histopathology image segmentation tasks? and 2) If not, what is the optimal approach for modifying (or fine-tuning) SAM for interactive histopathology image segmentation? To address these questions, we conducted extensive experiments on two publicly available datasets: PAIP2019 [12] and CAMELYON16 [7]. We investigated SAM mainly with point prompts, using a well-established evaluation protocol by Xu et al. [25] which mimics human click interaction. We conducted a comparison between SAM and other state-of-the-art (SOTA) interactive segmentation methods [4,16,24], both with and without dataset-specific fine-tuning. We also investigated an efficient strategy to harness the potential of SAM through various fine-tuning scenarios. The main contributions of our work are several-fold as follows:

- We assessed SAM's current capability for zero-shot histopathology image segmentation in the context of interactive segmentation by comparing it against SOTA interactive segmentation algorithms.
- We provide insights into the utilization of pretrained weights of SAM by exploring various fine-tuning scenarios. We discovered that SAM requires a prediction refinement strategy for interactive histopathology image segmentation.
- We introduce a modified mask decoder for SAM which enhances performance and reduces the fine-tuning cost while retaining the original SAM's high generalization capability and inference speed. As a result, we achieved an average reduction of 5.19% in the number of clicks required to reach the target IoU.

2   Method

2.1   Overview of Segment Anything Model (SAM)

Introduced by Meta AI, SAM [13] is a promptable foundation model for image segmentation trained with the largest segmentation dataset (SA-1B) over one billion masks and 11 million images. This model demonstrates significant zero-shot performance in natural image domains. SAM consists of three main components: An Image Encoder (IE) is a Vision Transformer (ViT) [6,10]-based encoder to extract image features, a Prompt Encoder (PE) encodes various types of prompts such as points, bounding boxes, masks, and texts, and a lightweight Mask Decoder (MD) maps image embedding and prompt embeddings to segmentation results.

2.2   SAM Fine-Tuning Scenarios

We set up three scenarios for fine-tuning SAM to understand the impact of each component in SAM on the performance and explore an efficient method for utilizing SAM in the interactive segmentation(see Fig. 2 (a) and (b)). First, we train only the lightweight mask decoder (SAM^{MD}) by freezing the pretrained image encoder and prompt encoder. Second, we train IE and MD (SAM^{IE_MD}) to investigate the influence of PE on the model's generalization ability. Third, we train the whole model (SAM^{Whole}) for comparison to other scenarios.

To fully utilize the pretrained weights of SAM's ViT-based image encoder, we resized input patches to a size of 1024 × 1024 and restored the output predictions to match the original input patch size. In the training process, we employed the click guidance scheme by Sofiiuk et al. [24] for automatic point prompts generation. The click guidance scheme uses random sampling for the first iteration

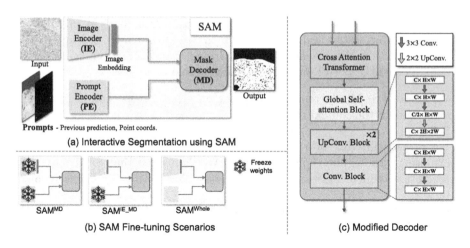

Fig. 2. (a) An illustration of interactive segmentation process using SAM. Image Encoder (IE) extracts features from input patch and Prompt Encoder (PE) encodes prompts which are previous prediction as mask prompt and point coordinates as point prompts. (b) We set up three SAM fine-tuning scenarios. SAM^{MD} freezes IE and PE, training only MD. SAM^{IE-MD} freezes PE and trains IE and MD. SAM^{Whole} trains the entire SAM. (c) Modified mask decoder architecture to improve local refinement capability. Compared to original MD, we exclude dot-product between the final output token and image embedding. Also, we use global self-attention block, and deeper decoder layers.

and samples subsequent clicks from the error regions of the previous predictions, thereby better resembling real-world user interaction. Moreover, we use the previous prediction as a mask prompt to improve the model performance as shown in [19]. We employed the Normalized Focal Loss [24], known for faster convergence and better accuracy compared to Binary Cross-Entropy (BCE) as explained in [4,16,17].

2.3   Decoder Architecture Modification

The graph in Fig. 3 (a), and (b) show the zero-shot and fine-tuned performance with mean Intersection over Union (mIoU) per interaction of SAM and SOTA interactive models on PAIP2019 [12] dataset. SAM demonstrates comparable performance to other models in early iterations, but it struggles in later iterations. As shown in Fig. 4 , SAM without fine-tuning shows weakness in refining predictions locally (i.e., a local modification affects a large area). Considering the architecture of the ViT-based SAM image encoder, training the entire SAM requires a longer time and a higher computational cost. Also, as shown in Table 1 and described in Sect. 4.2, we empirically found that including IE in fine-tuning is not always beneficial.

To address this issue, we modified the lightweight decoder in the original SAM as depicted in Fig. 2 (c) to improve local refinement capability and assign

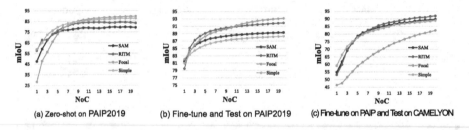

Fig. 3. (a) Zero-shot mIoU scores per click of each model on the PAIP2019 dataset. (b) mIoUs per click after fine-tuning on the PAIP dataset. (c) mIoUs per click on the CAMELYON16 ×10 dataset for models trained on the PAIP dataset.

prompt stability. We add a global self-attention layer to the image embedding after the cross-attention transformer block to enhance the ability to capture the global context across the entire patch. Moreover, we deepen the decoder layers during the upsampling process to increase the representational capacity of the decoder.

The upsampling process is described as follows: We constructed a *UpConvBlock* and *ConvBlock* module. *UpConvBlock* consists of two 3 × 3 convolution layers and a 2 × 2 up-convolution layer and *ConvBlock* consists of two 3 × 3 convolution layers. In the second 3 × 3 convolution layer of both *UpConvBlock* and *ConvBlock*, a channel reduction is performed, reducing the input channel size by half. After global self-attention, the image embedding proceeds through two *UpConvBlock*s and *ConvBlock* sequentially. We integrated instance normalization layers and *GELU* activation functions between each layer. Furthermore, to mitigate information loss, we employed shortcut connections within each Block. After passing through 3 Blocks, features are transformed into a segmentation map through the 1 × 1 convolution layer.

3   Experiments

3.1   Data Description

We utilized two publicly available WSI datasets, namely PAIP2019 [12] and CAMELYON16 [7]. The PAIP2019 WSIs were scaled at a 5× magnification, while for CAMELYON16, we used WSIs scaled at both 10× and 5× magnification. Subsequently, the WSIs were cropped into patches of size 400 × 400 pixels. These patches were then filtered based on the proportion of tumor area, ranging from 20% to 80%, as outlined in [20]. Consequently, for the PAIP2019 dataset, we employed 5190, 576, and 654 patches for training, validation, and testing, respectively. As for CAMELYON16, we utilized 397 patches at 10× magnification and 318 patches at 5× magnification scales for testing.

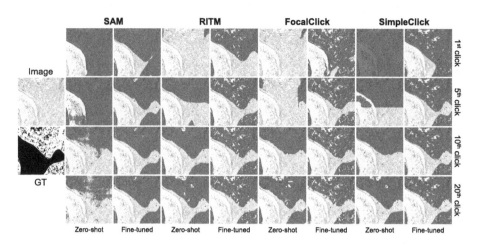

Fig. 4. Qualitative comparison between SAM^{Whole} and SOTA methods. The results show the performance of each method on the PAIP2019 dataset, both in terms of zero-shot and after fine-tuning.

3.2 Implementation Details

We compared SAM to three SOTA interactive segmentation methods: RITM [24], FocalClick [4], and SimpleClick [16]. We fine-tuned the pretrained models in PAIP2019 and validated their generalization capabilities in CAME-LYON16. For a fair comparison, we used the largest pretrained model and the best-performing pretrained weights for each model. For fine-tuning the parameters, we adhered to the default setting of [24], wherein we set the initial learning rate to 5e-4. Additionally, we decreased the learning rate by a factor of 10 at the 20th and 25th epochs out of the total 30 epochs.

To assess the zero-shot transfer ability of each model, we conducted inference without training using WSIs. Additionally, to evaluate the generalization ability and domain adaptability, we performed inference after fine-tuning using WSIs. For a fair comparison, we employed an automatic evaluation method used in the previous work [3,11,14,15,23,25]. Inference per patch continues until it reaches the target IoU (Intersection over Union). We set the maximum number of clicks per patch to 20. As for the evaluation metrics, we used Number of Clicks (NoC), Seconds per Click (SPC), and Number of Fails (NoF). NoC represents the average number of clicks required to reach the target IoU, while SPC measures the average time it takes for the model to perform an inference per click. NoF represents the number of images that failed to reach the target IoU despite the maximum number of clicks. For a more intuitive representation, we divide NoF by the number of testset n. All of evaluations were performed on a single NVDIA RTX A6000 GPU.

Table 1. Quantitative Result of Zero-Shot Performance

Dataset	Method	NoC@			SPC(s)	NoF/n @	
		80	85	90		85	90
PAIP2019	RITM	7.43	10.24	13.00	0.075	0.30	0.47
(×5)	FocalClick	7.37	**9.89**	**12.42**	0.073	**0.28**	**0.43**
	SimpleClick	**7.21**	10.16	13.44	0.189	0.33	0.53
	SAM	9.13	12.10	14.73	**0.052**	0.50	0.66
CAMELYON16	RITM	6.25	7.88	9.98	0.078	0.14	0.24
(×5)	FocalClick	**3.64**	**4.83**	**7.20**	0.085	**0.04**	**0.14**
	SimpleClick	5.26	6.94	9.23	0.187	0.15	0.25
	SAM	5.31	7.45	10.38	**0.053**	0.19	0.36
CAMELYON16	RITM	6.91	8.19	10.07	0.077	0.15	0.22
(×10)	FocalClick	**4.73**	**5.89**	**7.87**	0.076	**0.06**	**0.14**
	SimpleClick	5.20	6.42	8.55	0.187	0.11	0.23
	SAM	6.64	8.49	11.03	**0.053**	0.24	0.37

4 Results

4.1 Zero-Shot Performance

Table 1 presents the zero-shot performance of SAM and state-of-the-art (SOTA) interactive segmentation models. SAM demonstrates lower performance compared to SOTA models across all three different domains. The low NoC and high NoF in the zero-shot setting indicate that SAM lacks the ability to effectively modify the mask to accurately reflect user intent, particularly when faced with challenging images. As depicted in Fig. 4, SAM in the zero-shot setting fails to refine local information. However, SAM exhibits minimal SPC compared to other models due to its feature extraction being performed only once on the input image, resulting in a significantly faster processing time, over three times faster than SimpleClick.

4.2 Fine-Tuned SAM Performance

As introduced in Sect. 2.2, we compare the three scenarios to verify the impact of each SAM component on fine-tuned performance. We fine-tuned the entire SAM (SAM^{Whole}), the IE and MD (SAM$^{\text{IE\_MD}}$), and only the MD (SAM^{MD}) using the PAIP2019 dataset, respectively. Then, we verify the generalization ability of models at two scales of the CAMELYON16 dataset. As shown in Table 2, SAM^{MD} yield lower performance on NoC and NoF compared to IE-trained scenarios on the PAIP2019 dataset. On CAMELYON16, SAM^{MD} exhibited comparable results as IE-trained cases at scale ×5 and better performance at scale ×10. This result demonstrates that the pretrained IE of SAM shows the robustness of feature extraction ability on different data distributions.

Table 2. Quantitative Result of After Fine-tuning on PAIP2019

Dataset	Method	NoC@			SPC(s)	NoF/n @	
		80	85	90		85	90
PAIP2019 (×5)	RITM	2.78	4.93	9.40	0.075	0.12	0.33
	FocalClick	**2.58**	**4.54**	**8.98**	0.071	**0.06**	**0.25**
	SimpleClick	5.11	8.33	12.20	0.189	0.32	0.52
	SAM^{MD}	5.80	8.93	12.09	**0.050**	0.31	0.48
	SAM$^{IE\_MD}$	4.53	7.58	10.86	**0.050**	0.29	0.45
	SAM^{Whole}	4.53	7.50	10.95	0.052	0.28	0.46
	Ours	4.75	7.78	10.85	0.067	0.26	0.42
CAMELYON16 (×5)	RITM	3.74(-2.51)	5.04(-2.84)	7.50(-2.48)	0.081	**0.08**	**0.17**
	FocalClick	4.15(+0.51)	5.57(+0.74)	8.19(+0.99)	0.071	0.10	0.22
	SimpleClick	3.82(-1.44)	5.41(-1.53)	7.94(-1.29)	0.187	0.15	0.25
	SAM^{MD}	4.09(-1.22)	5.84(-1.61)	8.31(-2.07)	**0.050**	0.13	0.24
	SAM$^{IE\_MD}$	4.30(-1.01)	5.64(-1.81)	7.85(-2.53)	0.052	0.15	0.24
	SAM^{Whole}	**3.28**(-2.03)	**4.80**(-2.65)	**7.06**(-3.32)	0.053	0.10	0.20
	Ours	4.27(-1.04)	5.59(-1.86)	8.04(-2.34)	0.066	0.11	0.20
CAMELYON16 (×10)	RITM	6.28(-0.63)	7.65(-0.54)	9.67(-0.31)	0.076	0.13	0.23
	FocalClick	11.82(+7.09)	13.01(+7.12)	14.53(+7.33)	0.076	0.43	0.54
	SimpleClick	6.07(+0.87)	7.44(+1.02)	9.94(+1.39)	0.187	0.18	0.28
	SAM^{MD}	4.88(-1.76)	6.68(-1.81)	9.07(-1.96)	**0.053**	0.13	0.25
	SAM$^{IE\_MD}$	7.63(+0.99)	9.19(+0.7)	11.81(+0.78)	0.049	0.23	0.38
	SAM^{Whole}	6.60(-0.04)	8.10(-0.39)	10.66(-0.37)	0.053	0.20	0.31
	Ours	**4.59**(-2.05)	**5.92**(-2.57)	**8.40**(-2.63)	0.064	**0.11**	**0.20**

4.3 Comparison Between SAM and SOTA Interactive Methods

As shown in Table 2, SAM still exhibits a notable performance gap compared to RITM and FocalClick on the PAIP2019 dataset. SAM requires at least two more NoC compared to RITM and FocalClick. SimpleClick exhibited poorer performance compared to SAM^{Whole} and SAM$^{IE\_MD}$, but similar or slightly better performance compared to SAM^{MD}. On the CAMELYON16 ×5 dataset, SAM^{Whole} exhibited the best performance. The numbers in parentheses in Table 2 represent the changes in the NoC metric compared to the zero-shot performance in Table 1. All models showed a decrease in NoC but an increase in FocalClick, indicating that CAMELYON16 ×5 has similar data distribution with the PAIP2019 dataset. As for the CAMELYON16 ×10 dataset, SAM^{MD} performed second best after SAM with a modified decoder (ours). Furthermore, despite significant differences in data distributions between source and target domain, SAM^{MD} and SAM^{Whole} demonstrated improved performance along with RITM, indicating a higher generalized capability compared to FocalClick and SimpleClick. Note that FocalClick and SimpleClick performed poorly compared to the zero-shot approach with FocalClick's significant performance drop as shown in Fig. 3 (c). These methods utilize local segmentation which refines the prediction locally. As the data distribution changes, more iterations of local segmentation are required, resulting in performance degradation in both NoC and NoF metrics.

4.4 Modified SAM Decoder Performance

As shown in Table 2, our approach exhibits improved performance compared to SAM^{MD} in every dataset. Moreover, it shows comparable performance in PAIP2019 compared to $\text{SAM}^{\text{Whole}}$. Especially on the CAMELYON16 × 10 dataset, our approach demonstrates the best performance among all interactive SOTA models. It shows the highest performance in all of NoC and NoF, highlighting its remarkable generalization capability. However, in PAIP2019, it still shows lower performance compared to SOTA interactive models. Intuitively, Table 2 may not be enough to say that our approach has a clear advantage over other methods. However, when taking into account a comprehensive range of factors including performance, inferencing speed, training cost, and generalization ability, we argue that our approach is sufficiently compelling.

5 Conclusion

In this study, we demonstrate the potential of SAM for interactive pathology segmentation. SAM showed higher generalization capability and notably excelled in terms of inference speed per interaction compared to SOTA interactive models. Additionally, a modified decoder with pretrained encoders of SAM can achieve performance comparable to that of the entire SAM fine-tuning. In this approach, SAM could efficiently capture user intent and precisely refine predictions, which is crucial in interactive segmentation. However, SAM exhibits lower performance compared to state-of-the-art interactive models, especially in achieving high IoU scores. We plan to develop SAM as a foundational interactive model that works well for all histopathology data (different organs, tissues, etc.).

Acknowledgment. This work was partially supported by the National Research Foundation of Korea (NRF-2019M3E5D2A01063819, NRF-2021R1A6A1A 13044830), the Institute for Information & Communications Technology Planning & Evaluation (IITP-2023-2020-0-01819), the Korea Health Industry Development Institute (HI18C0316), the Korea Institute of Science and Technology (KIST) Institutional Program (2E32210 and 2E32211), and a Korea University Grant.

References

1. Boykov, Y., Kolmogorov, V.: An experimental comparison of min-cut/max-flow algorithms for energy minimization in vision. IEEE Trans. Pattern Anal. Mach. Intell. **26**(9), 1124–1137 (2004)
2. Chan, T.F., Vese, L.A.: Active contours without edges. IEEE Trans. Image Process. **10**(2), 266–277 (2001)
3. Chen, X., Zhao, Z., Yu, F., Zhang, Y., Duan, M.: Conditional diffusion for interactive segmentation. In: Proceedings of the IEEE/CVF International Conference on Computer Vision, pp. 7345–7354 (2021)
4. Chen, X., Zhao, Z., Zhang, Y., Duan, M., Qi, D., Zhao, H.: Focalclick: towards practical interactive image segmentation. In: Proceedings of the IEEE/CVF Conference on Computer Vision and Pattern Recognition, pp. 1300–1309 (2022)

5. Cho, S., Jang, H., Tan, J.W., Jeong, W.K.: DeepScribble: interactive pathology image segmentation using deep neural networks with scribbles. In: 2021 IEEE 18th International Symposium on Biomedical Imaging (ISBI), pp. 761–765. IEEE (2021)
6. Dosovitskiy, A., et al.: An image is worth 16x16 words: transformers for image recognition at scale. In: Proceedings of the International Conference on Learning Representations (ICLR) (2021)
7. Ehteshami Bejnordi, B., et al.: The CAMELYON16 Consortium: diagnostic assessment of deep learning algorithms for detection of lymph node metastases in women with breast cancer. JAMA **318**(22), 2199–2210 (12 2017)
8. Gao, Y., Xia, W., Hu, D., Gao, X.: DESAM: decoupling segment anything model for generalizable medical image segmentation. arXiv preprint arXiv:2306.00499 (2023)
9. Grady, L.: Random walks for image segmentation. IEEE Trans. Pattern Anal. Mach. Intell. **28**(11), 1768–1783 (2006)
10. He, K., Chen, X., Xie, S., Li, Y., Dollár, P., Girshick, R.: Masked autoencoders are scalable vision learners. In: Proceedings of the IEEE/CVF Conference on Computer Vision and Pattern Recognition, pp. 16000–16009 (2022)
11. Jang, W.D., Kim, C.S.: Interactive image segmentation via backpropagating refinement scheme. In: Proceedings of the IEEE/CVF Conference on Computer Vision and Pattern Recognition, pp. 5297–5306 (2019)
12. Kim, Y.J., et al.: Paip 2019: liver cancer segmentation challenge. Med. Image Anal. **67**, 101854 (2021)
13. Kirillov, A., et al.: Segment anything. arXiv preprint arXiv:2304.02643 (2023)
14. Li, Z., Chen, Q., Koltun, V.: Interactive image segmentation with latent diversity. In: Proceedings of the IEEE Conference on Computer Vision and Pattern Recognition, pp. 577–585 (2018)
15. Lin, Z., Zhang, Z., Chen, L.Z., Cheng, M.M., Lu, S.P.: Interactive image segmentation with first click attention. In: Proceedings of the IEEE/CVF Conference on Computer Vision and Pattern Recognition, pp. 13339–13348 (2020)
16. Liu, Q., Xu, Z., Bertasius, G., Niethammer, M.: Simpleclick: interactive image segmentation with simple vision transformers (2023)
17. Liu, Q., et al.: PseudoClick: interactive image segmentation with click imitation. In: Avidan, S., Brostow, G., Cissé, M., Farinella, G.M., Hassner, T. (eds.) Computer Vision – ECCV 2022: 17th European Conference, Tel Aviv, Israel, October 23–27, 2022, Proceedings, Part VI, pp. 728–745. Springer, Cham (2022). https://doi.org/10.1007/978-3-031-20068-7_42
18. Ma, J., Wang, B.: Segment anything in medical images. arXiv preprint arXiv:2304.12306 (2023)
19. Mahadevan, S., Voigtlaender, P., Leibe, B.: Iteratively trained interactive segmentation. In: Proceedings of the British Machine Vision Conference (BMVC) (2018)
20. Min, S., Jeong, W.K.: CGAM: click-guided attention module for interactive pathology image segmentation via backpropagating refinement. In: 2023 IEEE 20th International Symposium on Biomedical Imaging (ISBI), pp. 1–5. IEEE (2023)
21. Ronneberger, O., Fischer, P., Brox, T.: U-Net: convolutional networks for biomedical image segmentation. In: Navab, N., Hornegger, J., Wells, W.M., Frangi, A.F. (eds.) Medical Image Computing and Computer-Assisted Intervention – MICCAI 2015: 18th International Conference, Munich, Germany, October 5-9, 2015, Proceedings, Part III, pp. 234–241. Springer, Cham (2015). https://doi.org/10.1007/978-3-319-24574-4_28

22. Shaharabany, T., Dahan, A., Giryes, R., Wolf, L.: AutoSAM: adapting SAM to medical images by overloading the prompt encoder. arXiv preprint arXiv:2306.06370 (2023)

23. Sofiiuk, K., Petrov, I., Barinova, O., Konushin, A.: F-BRS: rethinking backpropagating refinement for interactive segmentation. In: Proceedings of the IEEE/CVF Conference on Computer Vision and Pattern Recognition, pp. 8623–8632 (2020)

24. Sofiiuk, K., Petrov, I.A., Konushin, A.: Reviving iterative training with mask guidance for interactive segmentation. In: 2022 IEEE International Conference on Image Processing (ICIP), pp. 3141–3145. IEEE (2022)

25. Xu, N., Price, B., Cohen, S., Yang, J., Huang, T.S.: Deep interactive object selection. In: Proceedings of the IEEE Conference on Computer Vision and Pattern Recognition, pp. 373–381 (2016)

Task-Driven Prompt Evolution
for Foundation Models

Rachana Sathish, Rahul Venkataramani$^{(\boxtimes)}$, K. S. Shriram,
and Prasad Sudhakar

GE HealthCare, Bangalore, India
rahul.venkataramani@ge.com

Abstract. Promptable foundation models, particularly Segment Anything Model (SAM) [3], have emerged as a promising alternative to the traditional task-specific supervised learning for image segmentation. However, many evaluation studies have found that their performance on medical imaging modalities to be underwhelming compared to conventional deep learning methods. In the world of large pre-trained language and vision-language models, learning prompt from downstream tasks has achieved considerable success in improving performance. In this work, we propose a plug-and-play **Prompt Optimization Technique** for foundation models like **SAM** (SAMPOT) that utilizes the downstream segmentation task to optimize the human-provided prompt to obtain improved performance. We demonstrate the utility of SAMPOT on lung segmentation in chest X-ray images and obtain an improvement on a significant number of cases ($\sim 75\%$) over human-provided initial prompts. We hope this work will lead to further investigations in the nascent field of automatic visual prompt-tuning.

Keywords: foundation models · prompt tuning · segmentation

1 Introduction

The recent release of a foundation model for image segmentation called Segment Anything (SAM) [3] has generated unprecedented excitement about the possibility of realizing artificial general intelligence (AGI) in the field of medical image analysis. SAM is a task-agnostic promptable segmentation model trained on 1 billion masks. This has triggered the possibility of improved zero-shot segmentation performance and obviate the necessity for specialized techniques across medical imaging tasks [4].

Consequently, a number of studies [1,2,6] have evaluated the performance of SAM on a plethora of medical imaging segmentation tasks, and have concluded that while SAM is a promising first step, there exists a significant gap compared to supervised learning algorithms on many datasets. The hypothesized reasons include lack of medical imaging samples in the training database and peculiarities associated with medical images (e.g., scan-cone in Ultrasound, 3D nature of

CT/MR, large intensity variations in X-Ray and higher image resolution compared to natural images).

This sub-optimal performance has prompted researchers to fine-tune the
models to medical imaging modalities using parameter-efficient techniques like
Low-rank adaptation (LoRA) [6,9] and Adapters [8]. However, given the size
of networks, fine-tuning these models also requires access to large scale medical image and label pairs. Obtaining such large scale datasets and availability of
heavy compute is beyond the scope of most small research organizations, thereby
limiting the adoption of SAM.

An alternate direction to improve the performance on downstream tasks is to
learn efficient prompts tailoring for the tasks. A number of works like CoOp [11],
CoCoOp [10] have demonstrated the benefit of learning prompts to adapt CLIP-
like vision-language models for downstream tasks. Prompt learning not only
improves performance over hand-crafted prompts but also reduces manual effort
and expertise required in designing the prompts. While these techniques have
been explored extensively in natural language processing and vision-language
community, their utilization for optimizing prompts for foundation segmentation
models has been conspicuously absent.

In this paper, we present a prompt learning method for segmentation foundation models, and demonstrate it on the task of left-lung segmentation on chest
X-ray images. To demonstrate the challenges involved and motivate the need for
prompt learning, we compute the sensitivity of SAM's output to the choice of
prompt's spatial location.

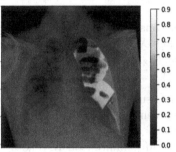

Figure 1 shows the overlay of a
chest X-ray image and the heat-map
of Dice values when the prompt is
placed at different locations of the
lung region. The large diversity of
Dice values (0.2 to 0.9) highlights
that given a click prompt inside the
lung region of an X-ray image, it is
plausible that another location provides a more accurate segmentation.

Fig. 1. Heat-map of Dice values obtained by
placing the prompt at various locations in
the lung.

Since X-ray is a summative
modality, the intensity values under
the lung mask are a result of super-
imposition of soft tissue, ribs, cardiac region, and occasional extrane-
ous objects such as PICC lines. Though visually the lung region may appear
equally dark in X-ray images to the user, it is not homogeneous, and its heterogeneity is further amplified by the presence of pathology.

1.1 Our Approach

To improve the segmentation performance in such confounding settings, we propose a **prompt optimization technique** (SAMPOT) that utilizes the knowledge of

the downstream task to optimally locate the human-provided prompt to obtain a better segmentation output. We design an unsupervised segmentation performance scorer that generates a proxy for the supervised performance metric like the Dice value. At inference, given a test image and prompt, we iteratively maximize this task-based score to *evolve* the location of the prompt to produce superior results compared to utilizing initial prompt location provided by user. Although we develop this method on SAM, SAMPOT can be used in a plug-and-play fashion with any foundation segmentation model.

1.2   Contributions

1. We propose a plug-and-play prompt optimization technique, SAMPOT, for any promptable segmentation algorithm which fine-tunes an input prompt. To the best of our knowledge, this is the first instance of an automatic prompt tuning strategy for foundation segmentation models.
2. We demonstrate the efficacy of SAMPOT on the task of segmenting lungs in chest X-ray images and achieve segmentation gains on $\sim 75\%$ of the test images.

2   Methodology

We shall introduce a few relevant notations before presenting the method.

SAM Model: Let us denote the SAM under consideration by f_{SAM}, a very large deep neural network model that takes an image $X \in \mathbb{R}^{N \times N}$ and a prompt $\boldsymbol{p}$ as input to predict the segmentation mask $\widehat{Y} := f_{\mathsf{SAM}}(X, \boldsymbol{p}) \in \mathbb{R}^{N \times N}$.

Prompt: For segmentation foundation models such as SAM, a prompt can be a point coordinate, bounding box, dense segmentation, or a text input. It is typically accompanied by a label which indicates whether the prompt is in the foreground (1) or otherwise (0). While SAM can simultaneously take a set of heterogeneous prompts, in this work, we consider one single coordinate prompt $\boldsymbol{p} = (x, y, c)^{\mathsf{T}}$, $x, y \in [N] := \{0, 1, \cdots, N-1\}$, $c \in \{0, 1\}$. We assume that the prompt is provided by a human user at the start, and it always lies in the foreground object of interest ($c = 1$). Therefore, without loss of generality, we can consider $\boldsymbol{p}$ to be a two-component vector representing the 2D coordinates.

2.1   Prompt Optimization by Oracle Scoring

Our method is aimed at evolving the location of the prompt and arriving at an optimal prompt $\boldsymbol{p}^*$. Suppose we had access to the ground truth mask Y_{test} for a given input image, we could simply compute the loss $\mathcal{L}_{\text{task}}(\widehat{Y}_{\text{test}}, Y_{\text{test}})$ and choose a $\boldsymbol{p}$ that minimises the loss. However, as that is fallaciously self-fulfilling, we propose to use an oracle $\mathcal{O}$ that acts as a surrogate to the true loss $\mathcal{L}_{\text{task}}$. The scorer takes the input image X_{test} and the predicted mask $\widehat{Y}_{\text{test}}$ and produces a score s. The scorer can be a pre-learnt (and fixed) neural network model that can be used in conjunction with the segmentation model, enabling us to compute the gradients of the score with respect to p. If the scorer is designed to be positively correlated to the performance metric, we can then solve the following maximization problem to achieve our objective:

$$p^* := \arg\max_{p} \mathcal{O}(X_{\text{test}}, \widehat{Y}_{\text{test}}), \text{ where } \widehat{Y}_{\text{test}} := f_{\text{SAM}}(X_{\text{test}}, p). \qquad (1)$$

Note that the gradient of s is computed with respect to p and therefore only p gets updated, while the weights of SAM f_{SAM} and the scorer $\mathcal{O}$ are held fixed.

2.2 Learning to Score

The oracle $\mathcal{O}$ is expected to score the quality of segmentation blindly in the absence of ground truth. To this end, we train a *segmentation regressor* which learns to predict the Dice directly from the input image and the corresponding predicted mask. This segmentation regressor is trained using a small dataset of input images and ground truth masks. For every input image, several candidate masks are synthetically generated by modifying the true segmentation mask, and their corresponding Dice coefficients are computed. This extended set of images, masks and Dice scores are then used to train the regressor. The details of candidate mask generation and segmentation regressor are described in Sect. 3.2. In general, segmentation quality score can be vector valued and along with the described regressor, one can use adversarial loss [5], shape autoencoder [7], etc.

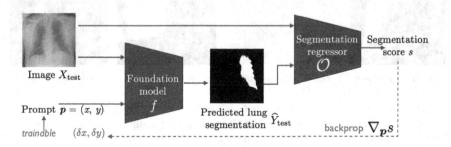

Fig. 2. Schematic of the SAMPOT. The spatial location of the user-provided prompt is updated based on the gradients received from the segmentation score.

Figure 2 shows the schematic of the proposed SAMPOT approach for prompt learning. Starting from an initial location and an input image, the prompt is iteratively evolved by updating its spatial location using the gradient computed from the segmentation score.

3 Experiments and Results

3.1 Dataset Description

In this study, we tapped into a database of X-ray images available within our institution, sourced through data partnerships from US, Africa, and European populations. The datasets were acquired after receiving approval from the relevant Institutional Review Boards. The lung boundaries on the X-ray images were delineated by a team of experienced radiologists. X-ray images from 122 subjects were split into train and test subjects in our experimental setup. This split was used for training and evaluation of the segmentation regressor only. Note that the SAM model is pretrained and is fixed throughout the study. We have evaluated the effectiveness of the prompt optimization technique on the test split of the dataset, thereby ensuring that the results are not biased by the regressor which has been optimized on the train split. The train cohort is further divided into training and validation sets with images from 41 and 28 subjects each. The test set has images from 53 subjects.

3.2 Segmentation Regressor

Data Preparation: We created several synthetic masks for every lung annotation in the dataset and computed the Dice coefficient for these masks as the ground truth segmentation score. We used the level-sets of ground truth annotation to generate under- and over-segmented instances of the lung field as presented in Fig. 3.

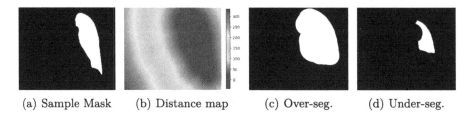

(a) Sample Mask   (b) Distance map   (c) Over-seg.   (d) Under-seg.

Fig. 3. Figure shows (a) sample mask from the dataset, (b) computed distance map, synthetically generated (c) over-segmented mask and (d) sample under-segmented. The dice coefficient for the over-segmented mask is 0.57 and that for under-segmented mask is 0.61.

Additionally, we also included the lung mask predicted by the SAM when given a single positive prompt and the corresponding Dice coefficient. In every image, the lung field was divided into three horizontal bands and the centroid of these regions were chosen as a prompt. We also chose random points outside the three bands, with an offset of 5 pixels as prompts for SAM. Therefore, we obtained predictions corresponding to 6 separate prompts for each image. Thus we had a total of 901 images in the train set, 600 in the val set and 1205 in the test set for learning the regressor.

Training Parameters and Network Architecture: The regressor network consisted of five 2D convolution layers interleaved with Batch normalization and leaky ReLU activation, and sigmoid activation for the final layer. The network was trained for 200 epochs with a batch size of 32 using Adam optimizer and mean squared error (MSE) loss. A constant learning rate of 0.001 was used. We set the stopping criterion as minimal loss on the validation set.

3.3   Prompt Optimization

Under the mild assumption that a human end-user would choose a prompt located centrally within the region of interest, we chose the centroid of the lung mask as the initial prompt to mimic the human user. Subsequently, the optimization of the prompt location was carried out using Adam optimizer. The step size for the prompt update was heuristically chosen as 10 and the weight decay was set to zero. To ensure that the input to the regressor (SAM prediction) is closer to a binary mask, we employed sigmoid activation a with steeper slope. Furthermore, we chose the optimal prompt as the one that maximized the output of the regressor. We have used ViT-B SAM in our experiments.

3.4   Results

Evaluation of Segmentation Regressor: Figure 4(a) is the scatterplot of regressor outputs against true Dice coefficients for all the samples in the test set, including the synthetically generated masks as well as SAM predictions. The high correlation coefficient (0.88) shows that the regressor output can serve as a proxy for Dice coefficient of segmented mask. We also present a similar plot for SAM confidence scores for segmentations when prompted at the centroid of the lung mask. We observe that the confidence scores of SAM have a lower correlation coefficient of 0.67 with Dice compared to our Segmentation Regressor.

Evaluation of Prompt Optimization: An illustration of the prompt optimization process for a sample image, starting from the initial location to the optimal location on the image is presented in Fig. 5. We see how the quality of the predicted lung field mask, measured using Dice coefficient, improves as the prompt traverses through the optimization trajectory.

Figure 6 summarizes the overall performance of the proposed SAMPOT on the test dataset. The scatterplot on the left (initial Dice vs Dice after evolution) shows that 38 of 53 images have improved Dice (points above unit slope line) after prompt evolution. Of them, four images have significant improvements. The scatter plot on the right is a blown-up version of a portion of the scatter plot on the left. The images on the top row contain specific examples where the Dice improved after evolution. On the bottom row, the images contain examples of underperforming cases. For the first two under-performing cases displayed, the segmentation masks after evolution are outside the lung region, even though the initial masks were in the right places. Such catastrophic cases can be handled by employing additional safeguard logic.

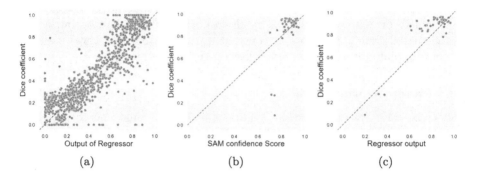

Fig. 4. Comparison of (a) Dice against regressor output for unseen synthetically generated masks (1205 samples); on the test set (53 samples) (b) Dice against SAM confidence score and (c) Dice against regressor output when prompts are placed at the centroid of the lung mask. The correlation coefficient for the regressor on unseen synthetically generated masks is 0.88. On test samples, the correlation coefficient for the regressor is 0.90 in comparison with 0.67 for SAM.

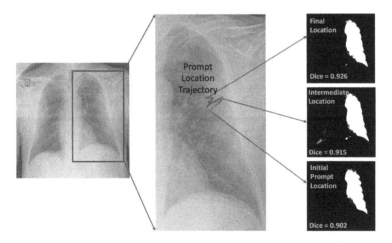

Fig. 5. [Best viewed in color] Figure illustrates the trajectory of the prompt during the optimization process. The initial prompt is set at the centroid of the ground truth lung field annotation. Snapshots of the predicted masks at select locations on the prompt trajectory along with the computed dice score are also shown.

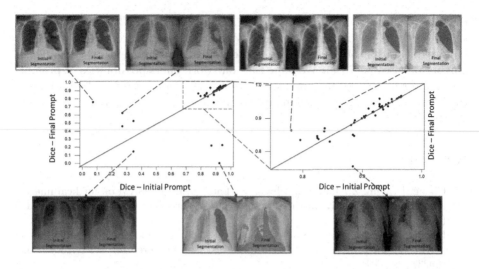

Fig. 6. [Best viewed in color] Scatter plot of Dice coefficients resulting from initial prompts and the final evolved prompts on the test set. 38 of 53 cases have shown improvement in Dice after evolving. Four of them have significant Dice gains. The scatter plot on the right is the blown-up area on the top-right of the scatter plot on the left. The top row shows images that have significantly gained from prompt evolution. On the bottom are some cases which under-performs upon prompt evolution.

4   Discussion

The direct application of foundation models like SAM has shown sub-par performance on a number of different medical image segmentation tasks. Given the relatively modest sizes of datasets available for downstream medical imaging tasks, it may be prohibitive to fine-tune a very large model like SAM. The performance of SAM on the previously unseen problem of lung segmentation on X-ray images is elevated by SAMPOT indicating the possibility of deploying SAM on medical image segmentation problems even with few images. While this work focused only on prompt evolution, the idea of adapting the input to improve the performance of a foundation model is very generic. One can adapt the input image itself, along with the prompt, to meet the desired objective. A future extension to this work can be adaptation to cases where multiple heterogeneous prompts such as bounding boxes, text inputs etc. are optimized. An extensive evaluation of SAMPOT on a multitude of datasets/use-cases will be beneficial as well.

5   Conclusions

On medical images, we observed that the spatial location of the prompt for a general purpose foundation model (SAM) affects the accuracy. Taking a cue from the NLP community, we have presented SAMPOT, a method to optimize the prompt for a foundation model by altering the spatial location to obtain superior results on downstream tasks. We have demonstrated this method on lung segmentation of chest X-rays and obtained improvement on a significant number of cases ($\sim 75\%$). We hope that our work offers possibilities of prompt-learning for extracting maximal value from general purpose foundation models trained on natural images on domain-specific downstream tasks in medical image analysis.

References

1. Cheng, D., Qin, Z., Jiang, Z., Zhang, S., Lao, Q., Li, K.: SAM on medical images: a comprehensive study on three prompt modes. arXiv preprint arXiv:2305.00035 (2023)
2. He, S., Bao, R., Li, J., Grant, P.E., Ou, Y.: Accuracy of segment-anything model (SAM) in medical image segmentation tasks. arXiv preprint arXiv:2304.09324 (2023)
3. Kirillov, A., et al.: Segment anything. arXiv preprint arXiv:2304.02643 (2023)
4. Li, C., et al.: Domain generalization on medical imaging classification using episodic training with task augmentation. Comput. Biol. Med. **141**, 105144 (2022)
5. Luc, P., Couprie, C., Chintala, S., Verbeek, J.: Semantic segmentation using adversarial networks. arXiv preprint arXiv:1611.08408 (2016)
6. Ma, J., Wang, B.: Segment anything in medical images. arXiv preprint arXiv:2304.12306 (2023)
7. Ravishankar, H., Venkataramani, R., Thiruvenkadam, S., Sudhakar, P., Vaidya, V.: Learning and incorporating shape models for semantic segmentation. In: Descoteaux, M., Maier-Hein, L., Franz, A., Jannin, P., Collins, D.L., Duchesne, S. (eds.) MICCAI 2017. LNCS, vol. 10433, pp. 203–211. Springer, Cham (2017). https://doi.org/10.1007/978-3-319-66182-7_24
8. Wu, J., et al.: Medical SAM adapter: adapting segment anything model for medical image segmentation. arXiv preprint arXiv:2304.12620 (2023)
9. Zhang, K., Liu, D.: Customized segment anything model for medical image segmentation. arXiv preprint arXiv:2304.13785 (2023)
10. Zhou, K., Yang, J., Loy, C.C., Liu, Z.: Conditional prompt learning for vision-language models. In: Proceedings of the IEEE/CVF Conference on Computer Vision and Pattern Recognition, pp. 16816–16825 (2022)
11. Zhou, K., Yang, J., Loy, C.C., Liu, Z.: Learning to prompt for vision-language models. Int. J. Comput. Vision **130**(9), 2337–2348 (2022)

Generalizing Across Domains in Diabetic Retinopathy via Variational Autoencoders

Sharon Chokuwa[(✉)] and Muhammad H. Khan

Mohamed Bin Zayed University of Artificial Intelligence, Abu Dhabi, UAE
{sharon.chokuwa,muhammad.haris}@mbzuai.ac.ae

Abstract. Domain generalization for Diabetic Retinopathy (DR) classification allows a model to adeptly classify retinal images from previously unseen domains with various imaging conditions and patient demographics, thereby enhancing its applicability in a wide range of clinical environments. In this study, we explore the inherent capacity of variational autoencoders to disentangle the latent space of fundus images, with an aim to obtain a more robust and adaptable domain-invariant representation that effectively tackles the domain shift encountered in DR datasets. Despite the simplicity of our approach, we explore the efficacy of this classical method and demonstrate its ability to outperform contemporary state-of-the-art approaches for this task using publicly available datasets. Our findings challenge the prevailing assumption that highly sophisticated methods for DR classification are inherently superior for domain generalization. This highlights the importance of considering simple methods and adapting them to the challenging task of generalizing medical images, rather than solely relying on advanced techniques.

Keywords: Domain Generalization · Diabetic Retinopathy · Variational Autoencoder

1 Introduction

Diabetic Retinopathy (DR) is a complication of Diabetes Mellitus (DM) which is characterized by impaired blood vessels in the eye due to elevated glucose levels, leading to swelling, leakage of blood and fluids, and potential ocular damage [6]. With the global population infected with DM projected to reach approximately 700 million by 2045, DR is expected to persist as a prevalent complication of DM, particularly in the Middle East and North Africa as well as the Western Pacific regions [25]. In general, the diagnosis of DR is based on the presence of four types of lesions, namely microaneurysms, hemorrhages, soft and hard exudates, and thus the categorization of DR typically comprises five classes, namely no DR, mild DR, moderate DR, severe DR, and proliferative DR.

The conventional method of diagnosing DR relies on manual examination of retinal images by skilled ophthalmologists. However, this approach is known to

M. E. Celebi et al. (Eds.): MICCAI 2023 Workshops, LNCS 14393, pp. 265–274, 2023.
https://doi.org/10.1007/978-3-031-47401-9_26

involve time-intensive procedures, limited availability of trained professionals, and is susceptible to human error [21,26]. Deep learning methods have emerged as an effective solution for diagnosing DR, addressing the limitations associated with traditional approaches [4,27]. Despite the benefits offered by deep learning models, a major challenge they face is the issue of domain shift [27], which emanates from the oversimplified assumption of independence and identical distribution (i.i.d) between the training and testing data, leading to poor performance when these models are applied to new data from related but unseen distributions [7,12]. The variations in fundus image acquisition procedures and the diverse populations affected by DR result in a substantial domain shift as shown in Fig. 1, which greatly hinders the deployment of large-scale models since a slight variation of the data-generating process often foresees a drastic reduction in model performance [30].

Domain generalization (DG) is a line of research with the goal of handling the domain shift problem [10] under minimal assumptions. It only relies on multiple or seldom single source domain(s) to train a model that can generalize to data from unseen domains, whose distribution can be radically different from source domains. To our knowledge, there exists a rather limited body of literature specifically addressing the problem of domain generalization for DR classification. Therefore, the investigation of DG for deep learning methods holds significant relevance in enhancing the accuracy of DR diagnosis across the various healthcare centers situated in different geographical locations.

In this paper, we propose our Variational Autoencoder for Domain Generalization (VAE-DG), which effectively manipulates the power of classical variational autoencoders (VAEs) [17], whose optimally disentangled latent space [13] enables the model to generalize well to unseen domains in DR classification by effectively capturing essential shared information while selectively disregarding domain-specific variations. Through the acquisition of disentangled representations that separate domain-specific and domain-invariant features, VAE-DG significantly enhances the model's ability to generalize across different domains, leading to improved performance and robustness. Our main contributions in this work are as follows:

1. We aim to inspire researchers to explore and leverage a wider spectrum of techniques, particularly simpler methods, in their pursuit of effective solutions for the challenging task of robustifying the DR classification problem.
2. To our knowledge, we are the first to explore the potential of harnessing VAEs for learning cross-domain generalizable models for the Diabetic Retinopathy classification task. Our extensive analysis reveals compelling evidence of its superiority over the state-of-the-art techniques for the DG approaches in the DR classification task.
3. We report our results using the training-domain validation criterion for model selection, which is an appropriate and widely-adopted model selection method for DG [10], thereby rectifying the existing work's [5] important limitations. To this end, we encourage future studies to conduct fair comparisons with

our methodology, establishing a standard for evaluating advancements in DG for DR classification task.

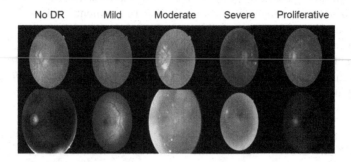

Fig. 1. A sample of fundus images from MESSIDOR-2 (top row) and EyePACS (bottom row) datasets. For an untrained expert, it is challenging to sometimes visually see the differences between the different grades, making the DR classification task challenging. Each dataset exhibits a diverse range of variations in the presentation of fundus images and furthermore, the provided sample from the two domains clearly demonstrates a significant domain shift.

2   Related Works

DG for DR Classification: DRGen [5] could be considered as the first work that tackles the DG challenge in DR classification, by combining the Stochastic Weight Averaging Densely (SWAD) [9] and Fishr [24] techniques. SWAD is a DG technique that promotes flatter minima and reduces gradient variance, while Fishr is a regularization method that aligns gradient variances across different source domains based on the relationship between gradient covariance, Hessian of the loss, and Fisher information. While the work by [5] played a pivotal role in bringing attention to this problem task, it should be noted that the results presented by the authors were based on target-domain-validation, which does not align with the established protocols of evaluating DG methods, as outlined by the widely recognized DomainBed framework [10]. We rectify this limitation by adopting the appropriate model selection strategy of source-domain validation, in accordance with accepted practices in the field of DG research.

DG Using Feature Disentanglement: DG approaches based on feature disentanglement aim to disentangle the feature representation into distinct components, including a domain-shared or invariant feature and a domain-specific feature [29]. Methods like [14,19] focus on disentangling multiple factors of variation, such as domain information, category information, or style; while this can be beneficial for certain applications, this may lead to limited interpretability and difficulties in finding an optimal balance between the different disentangled factors causing complex training procedures. In contrast, our method provides a more holistic approach to feature disentanglement, and with appropriate regularization techniques, it can achieve stable training and straightforward optimization. [22, 23, 31] used fine-grained domain disentanglement, Unified Feature Disentanglement Network, and semantic-variational disentanglement, respectively, which introduces additional complexity to the model architecture, and often leads to increased computational costs during training and inference. On the contrary, our methodology which is both effective and simpler offers a more direct and efficient approach.

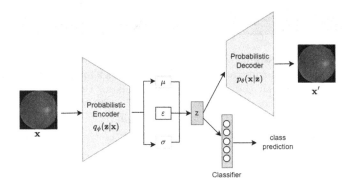

Fig. 2. Overview of our proposed method VAE-DG for domain generalization with a variational autoencoder by manipulating the disentangled fundus image representations to achieve a domain generalization objective.

3   Method

Overview: In this section, we describe in detail on how we exploit conventional variational autoencoders to tackle the challenge of domain generalization by revisiting their operational principles and integrating them into our VAE-DG approach. This showcases their effectiveness in disentangling intricate DR datasets, within which we hypothesize that the optimally disentangled latent space contains domain-shared features, thereby yielding a substantial performance boost compared to existing domain generalization state-of-the-art methods. Our overall pipeline is shown in Fig. 2

Problem Settings: Domain generalization for DR classification is defined within a framework that involves a collection of source domains denoted as $\{S_d\}_{d=1}^N$, where N is the number of source domains. Each source domain $S_d = \{(x_i{}^d, y_i{}^d)\}_{i=1}^n$ comprises i.i.d data points, sampled from a probability distribution $p(X_d, Y_d)$. Y_d is the target random variable corresponding to the progression of DR, while X_d is the input fundus image random variable, with each data point $(x_i{}^d, y_i{}^d)$ representing an observation from its respective domain. The primary objective in domain generalization thus becomes acquiring a predictor that exhibits robust performance on an unseen target domain T_d [10].

Proposed Method (VAE-DG): To achieve domain generalization using our VAE-DG, we manipulate two variables (from the pooled source domains $\{S_d\}_{d=1}^N$) which are the input fundus image X_d and the latent variable Z_d. When we consider only singular data points, z_i is drawn from the distribution $z_i \sim p(z)$ and x_i is drawn from $x_i \sim p(x|z)$, and their joint distribution is given by $p(x, z) = p(x|z)p(z)$. The main goal of this probabilistic model becomes an inference problem of learning a distribution $p(z|x)$ of some latent variables from which we can then sample to generate new fundus images which we will denote as x'. We know that this posterior distribution $p(z|x)$ can be obtained using Bayes Theorem [15].

However, we utilize a 256-dimensional fundus latent vector whose marginal $p(x)$ requires exponential computational time and hence becomes intractable, therefore, instead of directly calculating $p_\theta(z|x)$, we resort to Variational Inference [8] such that we approximate this posterior with a tractable distribution $q_\phi(z|x)$ which has a functional form. We use the Gaussian distribution as the approximation such that the problem decomposes to learning the parameters $\phi = (\mu, \sigma^2)$ instead of θ. By incorporating this Gaussian prior as a constraint on the learned latent variables, our VAE-DG is coerced into disentangling the underlying factors of variation in the data. We can then use Kullback-Leibler (KL) divergence, to measure how well the approximation is close to the true distribution. By minimizing the KL divergence, we simultaneously approximate $p_\theta(z|x)$ and the manipulation of the KL divergence expression (the complete derivation of which is beyond the scope of this discussion but can be found in [20]), we obtain Eq. 1:

$$\log p_\theta(x) - D_{\mathrm{KL}}\left(q_\phi(z|x)||p_\theta(x)\right) = \mathbb{E}_z\left[\log p_\theta(x|z)\right] - D_{\mathrm{KL}}\left(q_\phi(z|x)||p(z)\right) \quad (1)$$

where; $\mathbb{E}_z\left[\log p_\theta(x|z)\right] - D_{\mathrm{KL}}\left(q_\phi(z|x)||p_\theta(z)\right)$ is known as the Evidence Lower Bound (ELBO), the former term thus becomes the lower bound on the log evidence. Subsequently, if we maximize the ELBO we thus indirectly minimize $D_{\mathrm{KL}}\left(q_\phi(z|x)||p_\theta(x)\right)$. Therefore, the objective function of a classical variational autoencoder can be expressed as:

$$\mathcal{L}(\theta, \phi; x) = -\mathbb{E}_{q_\phi(z|x)}\left[\log p_\theta(x|z)\right] + D_{\mathrm{KL}}\left(q_\phi(z|x)||p(z)\right) \quad (2)$$

where the objective function is with respect to θ and ϕ which are the learnable parameters of the generative and inference models, respectively [16,17].

For our VAE-DG we couple the classical variational autoencoder objective $\mathcal{L}(\theta, \phi; x)$ with empirical risk minimization $\sum_{i=1}^n \ell(f(x_i), y_i)$ [28] to ensure the optimization of the original target task as illustrated in Eq. 3, while simultaneously manipulating the domain-invariant latent variables acquired from the probabilistic encoder. Our final objective function consists of three distinct terms;

the first term, denoted by $-\mathbb{E}_{q_\phi(z|x)}\left[\log p_\theta(x|z)\right]$, serves as the reconstruction term, which quantifies the difference between the original fundus image x_i and the reconstructed $x_i{}'$. The second term, $\beta D_{\mathrm{KL}}\left(q_\phi(z|x)||p(z)\right)$, is the regularizer term that minimizes the KL divergence between the encoder distribution $q_\phi(z|x)$ and the prior distribution $p(z)$, thereby promoting the learned latent representation z_i to follow the prior distribution. The strength of this regularization is controlled by the hyperparameter β. The third term, $\sum_{i=1}^{n}\ell(f(x_i),y_i)$, assesses the difference between the true class labels y_i and the predicted class labels $f(x_i)$, subsequently, the parameter α serves as a weight for this term.

$$\mathcal{L} = -\mathbb{E}_{q_\phi(z|x)}\left[\log p_\theta(x|z)\right] + \beta D_{\mathrm{KL}}\left(q_\phi(z|x)||p(z)\right) - \alpha \sum_{i=1}^{n}\ell(f(x_i),y_i) \qquad (3)$$

To optimize $\mathcal{L}$ we use stochastic gradient descent with an incorporation of the alternate optimization trick [17] since we need to learn the parameters for both θ and ϕ.

3.1   Experiments

Datasets: We utilized four openly accessible datasets, namely EyePACS [3], APTOS [1], Messidor [2], and Messidor-2 [2] which according to their sources were obtained from different locations and populations, resulting in a notable domain shift due to variations in instruments, conditions, settings, and environmental contexts across datasets. Each dataset comprises of five distinct classes with the exception of Messidor, which lacks class 5 images. The dataset distribution for these sources is 88702, 3657, 1200, and 1744, respectively. The original images vary in size but are standardized to 224×224 pixels. Due to the inherent characteristics of real-world datasets, there exists an imbalance in class representation across all datasets with class 0 being the most dominant and class 4 the rarest.

Implementation and Evaluation Criteria: Our choice for the encoder architecture involves the Imagenet pretrained ResNet-50 [11] as the backbone. This is substantiated by existing literature [18], wherein the employment of transfer learning, despite the domain gap, has been demonstrated to accelerate the process of developing effective models even in medical imaging. We jointly trained on three source domains, with 0.2 of the source domains as the validation set, and finally evaluate on the unseen target domain using the best training-domain-validation model, this way we truly evaluate the domain generalizability of our model. The model is trained for 15,000 steps, with Adam optimizer, a learning rate of 0.0001, 256 dimensional z latent vector, and a batch size of 66 from the three source domains. To combat class imbalance we utilize resampling. β and α are set as 50,000 to achieve a similar weighting with the magnitude of the reconstruction term. Accuracy is used as the evaluation metric in line with the established DG benchmarks [10]. All our experiments were run on 24 GB Quadro RTX 6000 GPU. Our code is available at https://github.com/sharonchokuwa/VAE-DG.

Baselines: We compare our method with the naive Empirical Risk Minimization (ERM) [10,28] and with state-of-the-art domain generalization methods for this problem task mainly DRGen [5] and Fishr [24]. To ensure a fair comparison, we adopt the same backbone and learning rate for all methods, except for DRGen; where we reproduce it using the original proposed learning rate of 0.0005, as the performance decreased when using 0.0001. The other method-specific hyperparameters were kept constant as proposed in the respective works.

Table 1. Comparison between our proposed method with domain generalization methods for DR classification. Each experiment was repeated thrice, employing distinct random seeds (0, 1, 2), and the average accuracy (Avg.) and corresponding standard deviation are reported for each target domain.

Method	Aptos	EyePACS	Messidor	Messidor-2	Avg.
ERM	63.75 ± 5.5	70.22 ± 1.6	$\mathbf{66.11 \pm 0.8}$	67.38 ± 1.0	66.86 ± 2.2
DRGen	57.06 ± 0.9	72.52 ± 1.3	61.25 ± 4.2	49.16 ± 16.3	60.00 ± 5.7
Fishr	62.89 ± 5.0	71.92 ± 1.3	65.69 ± 1.1	63.54 ± 3.8	66.01 ± 2.8
VAE-DG	$\mathbf{66.14 \pm 1.1}$	$\mathbf{72.74 \pm 1.0}$	65.90 ± 0.7	$\mathbf{67.67 \pm 2.0}$	$\mathbf{68.11 \pm 1.2}$
Oracle Results					
VAE-DG	68.54 ± 2.5	74.30 ± 0.2	66.39 ± 1.3	70.27 ± 1.2	69.87 ± 1.3

Results and Discussion: Table 1 indicates that VAE-DG exhibits the highest average accuracy of 68.11 ± 1.2%, which represents an 8.11% improvement over DRGen, 2.1% over Fishr, and 1.3% over ERM. Furthermore, VAE-DG demonstrates superior performance across most domains (APTOS, EyePACS, and Messidor-2) and exhibits the lowest standard error of 1.2%, indicating its relative robustness compared to the other methods. VAE-DG's enhanced performance solidifies the advantageous characteristics of this simpler approach whose latent space facilitates the explicit disentangling of domain-specific and domain-invariant features, ultimately improving target domain generalization. The oracle results [10] of VAE-DG are presented as a reference for the upper bound of the method, rather than for direct comparison, indicating that our proposed method achieves a 1.8% reduction compared to the upper bound.

ERM outperforms more sophisticated methods (DRGen and Fishr) because it is a simple approach and does not make strong assumptions about source-target domain relationships; it focuses on optimizing performance on available source domains and leveraging multiple domains to capture a wider range of variations, showcasing its ability to generalize to unseen target domains (if the domain shift is small [10]).

Overall, the relatively poor performances of DRGen and Fishr methods which attain 60.00% and 66.01% average accuracies respectively can be attributed to the fact that these methods often impose specific constraints or assumptions about the domain shift, which could limit their performance in scenarios that deviate from those assumptions. The lack of robustness of such methods with variations in the data is also vindicated by the large standard error (16.3%) for DRGen's Messidor-2 domain performance.

In contrast to the findings of [5], our extended analysis presented in Table 2 reveals a significant decline in model performance by 23.14% when incorporating SWAD, aligning with [9]'s observation that SWAD is not a perfect or theoretically guaranteed solver for flat minima. We explored the influence of a larger network architecture (ResNet-152) and the obtained results indicate that a larger network architecture can improve image reconstruction quality but has a negative impact on the primary DG objective, as evidenced by the 1.5% drop.

Table 2. Analysis and ablation studies. Average accuracy (Avg.) values represent the mean accuracy obtained from three independent trials. The "Diff." column indicates the performance variation compared to our main experiments shown in Table 1. A decrease in performance is denoted by ($\downarrow$), while an increase is denoted by ($\uparrow$).

	APTOS	EyePACS	Messidor	Messidor-2	Avg.	Diff.
Extended Analysis						
VAE-DG ResNet-152	61.45 ± 8.2	71.44 ± 3.1	65.94 ± 1.0	67.81 ± 2.6	66.66 ± 3.7	$1.45(\downarrow)$
VAE-DG + SWAD	55.66 ± 8.8	73.52 ± 0.0	34.24 ± 12.2	16.48 ± 12.0	44.97 ± 8.3	$23.14(\downarrow)$
ERM + SWAD	54.93 ± 0.6	71.35 ± 0.5	64.76 ± 0.7	58.48 ± 3.1	62.38 ± 1.2	$4.5(\downarrow)$
Ablations Studies						
Latent-dim 64	62.15 ± 3.1	73.80 ± 0.4	66.42 ± 2.1	68.98 ± 3.0	67.84 ± 2.2	$0.27(\downarrow)$
Latent-dim 128	62.61 ± 3.5	73.64 ± 0.6	66.60 ± 1.9	66.09 ± 2.2	67.23 ± 2.0	$0.88(\downarrow)$
Fixed latent space	63.87 ± 0.6	73.44 ± 0.8	66.46 ± 0.6	69.39 ± 0.8	68.29 ± 0.7	$0.18(\uparrow)$
$\beta, \alpha = 10,000$	64.38 ± 1.8	73.17 ± 0.5	65.42 ± 0.4	69.27 ± 4.0	68.06 ± 1.7	$0.05(\downarrow)$
$\beta, \alpha = 100,000$	62.50 ± 3.5	72.30 ± 1.6	66.56 ± 1.3	67.88 ± 1.0	67.31 ± 1.8	$0.80(\downarrow)$
No Recon Loss	63.44 ± 3.9	70.62 ± 0.8	66.25 ± 0.8	65.21 ± 1.4	66.38 ± 1.7	$1.73(\downarrow)$
No KL Divergence	68.29 ± 2.3	69.98 ± 4.3	66.60 ± 1.1	66.93 ± 1.6	67.95 ± 2.3	$0.17(\downarrow)$

Ablation Studies: In order to comprehensively assess the individual contributions of each component towards our DG objective, we conducted ablation studies, as summarized in Table 2. Our investigation encompassed the following aspects: (i) Latent-Dim: varying the size of the latent dimension [64, 128, 256], (ii) Fixed latent space: evaluating the impact of a fixed latent dimension, (ii) determining the impact of the weighting for the KL divergence and classification terms (β and α), (iii) assessing the effect of the reconstruction term, and (iv) examining the influence of the KL divergence term.

We noticed that a larger latent dimension of 256 leads to higher results, potentially due to its ability to effectively bottleneck information while preserving essential features. The performance difference between a fixed latent vector and a randomly sampled one is not very large, although using a fixed latent space reduces the standard error by nearly half, suggesting that randomly sampled vectors introduce additional variability that hinders the disentanglement of domain-invariant features. Notably, removing the reconstruction and KL divergence terms in the model's objective leads to a decrease in performance, emphasizing the importance of incorporating these regularizations. Furthermore, experimentation with β and α values within the range of $[10{,}000, 50{,}000, 100{,}000]$ reveals that excessively high or low values are suboptimal.

4   Conclusion

In this paper, we explored the potential of classical variational autoencoders for domain generalization in Diabetic Retinopathy classification. We demonstrate that this simple approach provides effective results and outperforms contemporary state-of-the-art methods. By strictly following the established evaluation protocols of DG, we also addressed the important limitations in the evaluations of the existing method. Our study encourages the medical imaging community to consider simpler methods in order to realize robust models.

References

1. Aptos 2019 Blindness Detection. https://www.kaggle.com/c/aptos2019-blindness-detection/data
2. Feedback on a Publicly Distributed Image Database: The MESSI-DOR Database. https://www.ias-iss.org/ojs/IAS/article/view/1155, https://doi.org/10.5566/ias.1155
3. Kaggle: Diabetic Retinopathy Detection - EYEPACS Dataset. https://www.kaggle.com/c/diabetic-retinopathy-detection
4. Abràmoff, M.D., et al.: Automated and computer-assisted detection, classification, and diagnosis of diabetic retinopathy. Telemed. e-Health 26(4), 544–550 (2020)
5. Atwany, M., Yaqub, M.: DRGen: domain generalization in diabetic retinopathy classification. In: Wang, L., Dou, Q., Fletcher, P.T., Speidel, S., Li, S. (eds.) Medical Image Computing and Computer Assisted Intervention-MICCAI 2022: 25th International Conference, Singapore, 18–22 September 2022, Proceedings, Part II, pp. 635–644. Springer, Cham (2022). https://doi.org/10.1007/978-3-031-16434-7_61
6. Atwany, M.Z., Sahyoun, A.H., Yaqub, M.: Deep learning techniques for diabetic retinopathy classification: a survey. IEEE Access 10, 28642–28655 (2022)
7. Blanchard, G., Deshmukh, A.A., Dogan, U., Lee, G., Scott, C.: Domain generalization by marginal transfer learning. J. Mach. Learn. Res. 22(2), 1–55 (2021). http://jmlr.org/papers/v22/17-679.html
8. Blei, D.M., Kucukelbir, A., McAuliffe, J.D.: Variational inference: a review for statisticians. J. Am. Stat. Assoc. 112(518), 859–877 (2017)
9. Cha, J., et al.: SWAD: domain generalization by seeking flat minima (2021)
10. Gulrajani, I., Lopez-Paz, D.: In search of lost domain generalization. arXiv preprint arXiv:2007.01434 (2020)
11. He, K., Zhang, X., Ren, S., Sun, J.: Deep residual learning for image recognition. In: Proceedings of the IEEE Conference on Computer Vision and Pattern Recognition, pp. 770–778 (2016)

12. Hendrycks, D., Dietterich, T.: Benchmarking neural network robustness to common corruptions and perturbations. arXiv preprint arXiv:1903.12261 (2019)
13. Higgins, I., et al.: beta-VAE: learning basic visual concepts with a constrained variational framework. In: International Conference on Learning Representations (2016)
14. Ilse, M., Tomczak, J.M., Louizos, C., Welling, M.: DIVA: domain invariant variational autoencoders. In: Medical Imaging with Deep Learning, pp. 322–348. PMLR (2020)
15. Joyce, J.: Bayes' theorem (2003)
16. Kingma, D.P., Welling, M.: Auto-encoding variational Bayes. arXiv preprint arXiv:1312.6114 (2013)
17. Kingma, D.P., Welling, M.: An introduction to variational autoencoders. Found. Trends® Mach. Learn. **12**(4), 307–392 (2019). https://doi.org/10.1561/2200000056
18. Matsoukas, C., Haslum, J.F., Sorkhei, M., Söderberg, M., Smith, K.: What makes transfer learning work for medical images: feature reuse & other factors (2022)
19. Nam, H., Lee, H., Park, J., Yoon, W., Yoo, D.: Reducing domain gap by reducing style bias. In: Proceedings of the IEEE/CVF Conference on Computer Vision and Pattern Recognition, pp. 8690–8699 (2021)
20. Odaibo, S.: Tutorial: deriving the standard variational autoencoder (VAE) loss function. arXiv preprint arXiv:1907.08956 (2019)
21. Paisan, R., et al.: Deep learning versus human graders for classifying diabetic retinopathy severity in a nationwide screening program. NPJ Digit. Med. **2**(1), 25 (2019)
22. Peng, X., Huang, Z., Sun, X., Saenko, K.: Domain agnostic learning with disentangled representations. In: International Conference on Machine Learning, pp. 5102–5112. PMLR (2019)
23. Qiao, F., Zhao, L., Peng, X.: Learning to learn single domain generalization. In: Proceedings of the IEEE/CVF Conference on Computer Vision and Pattern Recognition, pp. 12556–12565 (2020)
24. Rame, A., Dancette, C., Cord, M.: Fishr: invariant gradient variances for out-of-distribution generalization (2022)
25. Teo, Z.L., et al.: Global prevalence of diabetic retinopathy and projection of burden through 2045: systematic review and meta-analysis. Ophthalmology **128**(11), 1580–1591 (2021)
26. Ting, D.S.W., Cheung, G.C.M., Wong, T.Y.: Diabetic retinopathy: global prevalence, major risk factors, screening practices and public health challenges: a review. Clin. Exp. Ophthalmol. **44**(4), 260–277 (2016)
27. Ting, D.S.W., et al.: Artificial intelligence and deep learning in ophthalmology. Br. J. Ophthalmol. **103**(2), 167–175 (2019)
28. Vapnik, V.N.: An overview of statistical learning theory. IEEE Trans. Neural Networks **10**(5), 988–999 (1999)
29. Wang, J., Lan, C., Liu, C., Ouyang, Y., Qin, T., Lu, W., Chen, Y., Zeng, W., Yu, P.: Generalizing to unseen domains: A survey on domain generalization. IEEE Transactions on Knowledge and Data Engineering (2022)
30. Yang, J., Zhou, K., Li, Y., Liu, Z.: Generalized out-of-distribution detection: a survey. arXiv preprint arXiv:2110.11334 (2021)
31. Zhang, H., Zhang, Y.F., Liu, W., Weller, A., Schölkopf, B., Xing, E.P.: Towards principled disentanglement for domain generalization. In: Proceedings of the IEEE/CVF Conference on Computer Vision and Pattern Recognition, pp. 8024–8034 (2022)

CEmb-SAM: Segment Anything Model with Condition Embedding for Joint Learning from Heterogeneous Datasets

Dongik Shin[1], Beomsuk Kim, M.D.[2], and Seungjun Baek[1(✉)]

[1] Department of Computer Science, Korea University, Seoul, Republic of Korea
{sdimivy014,sjbaek}@korea.ac.kr
[2] Department of Physical and Rehabilitation Medicine, Chung-Ang University
College of Medicine, Seoul, Republic of Korea
grit@cau.ac.kr

Abstract. Automated segmentation of ultrasound images can assist medical experts with diagnostic and therapeutic procedures. Although using the common modality of ultrasound, one typically needs separate datasets in order to segment, for example, different anatomical structures or lesions with different levels of malignancy. In this paper, we consider the problem of jointly learning from heterogeneous datasets so that the model can improve generalization abilities by leveraging the inherent variability among datasets. We merge the heterogeneous datasets into one dataset and refer to each component dataset as a subgroup. We propose to train a single segmentation model so that the model can adapt to each sub-group. For robust segmentation, we leverage recently proposed *Segment Anything model* (SAM) in order to incorporate sub-group information into the model. We propose SAM with Condition Embedding block (CEmb-SAM) which encodes sub-group conditions and combines them with image embeddings from SAM. The conditional embedding block effectively adapts SAM to each image sub-group by incorporating dataset properties through learnable parameters for normalization. Experiments show that CEmb-SAM outperforms the baseline methods on ultrasound image segmentation for peripheral nerves and breast cancer. The experiments highlight the effectiveness of CEmb-SAM in learning from heterogeneous datasets in medical image segmentation tasks. The code is publicly available at https://github.com/DongDong500/CEmb-SAM

Keywords: Breast Ultrasound · Nerve Ultrasound · Segmentation. · Segment Anything Model

1 Introduction

Image segmentation is an important task in medical ultrasound imaging. For example, peripheral nerves are often detected and screened by ultrasound, which

M. E. Celebi et al. (Eds.): MICCAI 2023 Workshops, LNCS 14393, pp. 275–284, 2023.
https://doi.org/10.1007/978-3-031-47401-9_27

has become a convention modality for computer-aided diagnosis (CAD) [20]. As entrapment neuropathies are considered to be accurately screened and diagnosed by ultrasound [2,3,25], the segmentation of peripheral nerves helps experts identify anatomic structures, measure nerve parameters and provide real-time guidance for therapeutic purposes. In addition, Breast ultrasound images (BUSI) can guide experts to localize and characterize breast tumors, which is also one of the key procedures in CAD [27].

The advancements in deep learning enable an automatic segmentation of ultrasound images, though they still require large, high-quality datasets. The scarcity of the labeled data motivated several studies to propose learning from limited supervision, such as transfer learning [24], supervised domain adaptation [19,22] and unsupervised domain adaptation [6,12,17]. In practice, separate datasets are needed to train a model to segment different anatomical structures or lesions with different levels of malignancy. For example, peripheral nerves can be detected and identified across different human anatomic structures, such as peroneal (located below the knee) and ulnar (located inside the elbow) nerves. Typically, the annotated datasets for peroneal and ulnar nerves are separately constructed, and models are separately trained. However, since the models perform a similar task, i.e., segmenting nerve structures from ultrasound images, one may use a *single* model to be jointly trained with peroneal and ulnar nerves in order to leverage the variability in heterogeneous datasets and improve generalization abilities. A similar argument can be applied to breast ultrasound. A breast tumor is categorized into two types, benign and malignant, and we examine the effectiveness of a single model handling the segmentation of both types of lesions. While a simple approach would be incorporating multiple datasets for training, the characteristics of imaging vary among datasets, and it is challenging to train models which deal with distribution shift and generalize well for the entire heterogeneous datasets [4,26,28].

In this paper, we consider methods to train a single model with heterogeneous datasets jointly. We combine the heterogeneous datasets into one dataset and call each component dataset as a *subgroup*. We consider a model which can adapt to domain shifts among sub-groups and improve segmentation performances. We leverage recently proposed *Segment Anything model* (SAM) which has shown great success in natural image segmentation [14]. However, several studies have shown that SAM could fail on medical image segmentation tasks [5,9,10,16,29]. We adapt SAM to distribution shifts across sub-groups using a novel method for condition embedding, which is called SAM with Condition Embedding block (CEmb-SAM). In CEmb-SAM, we encode sub-group conditions and combine them with image embeddings. Through experiments, we show that the sub-group conditioning guides SAM to adapt to each sub-group effectively. Experiments demonstrate that, compared with SAM [14] and MedSAM [16], CEmb-SAM shows consistent improvements in the segmentation tasks for both peripheral nerves and breast lesions. Our main contributions are as follows:

- We propose CEmb-SAM, which jointly trains a model over heterogeneous datasets leveraging *Segment Anything model* for robust segmentation performances.
- We propose a conditional embedding module to combine sub-group representations with image embeddings, which effectively adapts the Segment Anything Model to sub-group conditions.
- Experiments on the peripheral nerve and the breast cancer datasets demonstrate that CEmb-SAM significantly outperforms the baseline models.

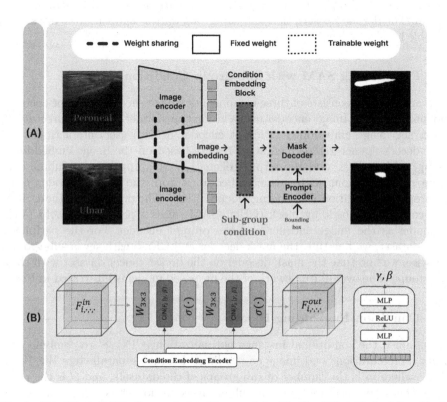

Fig. 1. (A) CEmb-SAM: *Segment Anything model* with Condition Embedding block. Input images come from heterogeneous datasets, i.e., the datasets of peroneal and ulnar nerves, and the model is jointly trained to segment both types of nerves. The sub-group condition is fed into Condition Embedding block and encoded into sub-group representations. Next, the image embeddings are combined with sub-group representations. The image and prompt encoders are frozen during the fine-tuning of Condition Embedding block and mask decoder. (B) Detailed description of Condition Embedding Block. The sub-group condition is encoded into learnable parameters γ and β, and the input feature F^{in} is scaled and shifted using those parameters.

2   Method

The training dataset is a mixture of m heterogeneous datasets or sub-groups. The training dataset with m mutually exclusive sub-groups $\mathcal{D} = \mathbf{g}_1 \cup \mathbf{g}_2 \cup \cdots \cup \mathbf{g}_m$ consists of N samples $\mathcal{D} = \{(x_i, y_i, y_i^a)_{i=1}^N\}$ where x_i is an input image, y_i is a corresponding ground-truth mask. The sub-group condition $y_i^a \in \{0, \ldots, m-1\}$ represents the index of the sub-group the data belongs to. The peripheral nerve dataset consists of seven sub-groups, six different regions at the peroneal nerve (located below the knee) and a region at the ulnar nerve (located inside the elbow). The BUSI dataset consists of three sub-groups: benign, malignant, and normal. The detailed description and sub-group indices and variables are shown in Table 1.

2.1   Fine-Tuning SAM with Sub-group Condition

SAM architecture consists of three components: image encoder, prompt encoder, and mask decoder. Image encoder uses a vision transformer-based architecture [7] to extract image embeddings. Prompt encoder utilizes user interactions, and mask decoder generates segmentation results based on the image embeddings, prompt embeddings, and its output token [14]. We propose to combine sub-group representations with image embeddings from the image encoder using the proposed Condition Embedding block (CEmb). The proposed method, SAM with condition embedding block (CEmb-SAM), uses a pre-trained SAM (ViT-B) model as the image encoder and the prompt encoder. For the peripheral nerve dataset, we fine-tune the mask decoder and CEmb with seven sub-groups. Likewise, we fine-tune the mask decoder on the breast cancer dataset with three sub-groups. The overall framework of the proposed model is illustrated in Fig. 1.

2.2   Condition Embedding Block

We modified the conditional instance normalization (CIN) [8] to combine sub-group representations and image embeddings. Learnable parameters $W_\gamma, W_\beta \in \mathbb{R}^{C \times m}$ where m is the number of sub-groups of the datasets, and C is the number of the output feature maps. A sub-group condition y^a is converted to one-hot vectors, x_γ^a and x_β^a which are fed into Condition Embedding encoder and transformed into sub-group representation parameters γ and β using two fully connected layers (FCNs). Specifically,

$$\gamma = W_2 \cdot \sigma(W_1 \cdot W_\gamma \cdot x_\gamma^a), \ \beta = W_2 \cdot \sigma(W_1 \cdot W_\beta \cdot x_\beta^a) \tag{1}$$

where $W_1, W_2 \in \mathbb{R}^{C \times C}$ are FCN weights, and $\sigma(\cdot)$ represents ReLU activation function.

The image embedding x is transformed into the final representation z using the condition embedding as follows. The image embedding is normalized with mini-batch $\mathcal{B} = \{x_i, y_i^a\}_{i=1}^{N_n}$ of N_n examples as follows:

Table 1. Summary of the predefined sub-group conditions of peripheral nerve and BUSI datasets. FH: fibular head, FN: fibular neuropathy. FN + α represents the measured site is α cm away from the fibular head. m represents the total number of sub-groups.

Study	Region	Sub-group	$m = 7$	Study	Region	Sub-group	$m = 3$
Nerve	Peroneal	FH	0				
		FN	1			Benign	0
		FN+1	2	BUSI	Breast		
		FN+2	3			Malignant	1
		FN+3	4			Normal	2
		FN+4	5				
	Ulnar	Ulnar	6				

$$\text{CIN}(x_i|\gamma, \beta) = \gamma \frac{x_i - \text{E}[x_i]}{\sqrt{\text{Var}[x_i] + \epsilon}} + \beta \tag{2}$$

where $\text{E}[x_i]$ and $\text{Var}[x_i]$ are the instance mean and variance, and γ and β are given by Condition Embedding encoder. The proposed CEmb consists of two independent consecutive CIN layers with convolutional layers given by:

$$F^{\text{mid}} = \sigma(\text{CIN}(W_{3\times3} \cdot x_i|\gamma_1, \beta_1)) \tag{3}$$

$$z = \sigma(\text{CIN}(W_{3\times3} \cdot F^{\text{mid}}|\gamma_2, \beta_2)) \tag{4}$$

where $F \in \mathbb{R}^{c\times h\times w}$ represents an intermediate feature map, $W_{3\times3}$ denotes convolution kernel size with 3×3. Figure 1 (B) illustrates the Condition Embedding block.

Table 2. Sample distribution of peripheral nerve and BUSI datasets. FH: fibular head, FN: fibular neuropathy. FN + α represents that the measured site is α cm away from the fibular head.

Dataset	Region	Sub-group	#of samples	Dataset	Region	Sub-group	#of samples
Nerve	Peroneal	FH	91				
		FN	106			Benign	437
		FN+1	77				
		FN+2	58	BUSI	Breast	Malignant	210
		FN+3	49			Normal	133
		FN+4	29				
	Ulnar	Ulnar	1234				
Total			1644	Total			780

Table 3. Performance comparison between U-net, SAM, MedSAM and CEmb-SAM on BUSI and Peripheral nerve datasets.

Study	Region	DSC (%)				PA (%)			
		U-net	SAM	MedSAM	Ours	U-net	SAM	MedSAM	Ours
BUSI	Breast	64.87	61.42	85.95	**89.35**	90.72	87.19	90.89	**92.86**
Nerve	Peroneal	69.91	61.72	78.87	**85.02**	92.59	90.58	91.81	**93.90**
	Ulnar	77.04	59.56	83.98	**88.21**	96.49	94.89	96.66	**97.72**

3   Experiments

3.1   Dataset Description

We evaluate our method on two datasets: (i) a public benchmark dataset, Breast Ultrasound images (BUSI) [1]; (ii) the peripheral nerve ultrasound images collected in our institution. Ultrasound images in the public BUSI dataset are measured from an identical site. The dataset is categorized into three sub-groups: benign, malignant, and normal. The shape of a breast lesion varies according to its type. The benign lesion possesses a relatively round and convex shape. On the other hand, the malignant lesion possesses a rough and uneven spherical shape. The BUSI dataset consists of 780 images. The average image size of the dataset is 500×500 pixels.

The peripheral nerve dataset was created at the Department of Physical Medicine and Rehabilitation, Korea University Guro Hospital. The dataset consists of ultrasound images of two different anatomical structures, the peroneal nerve and the ulnar nerve. The peroneal nerve, on the outer side of the calf of the leg, contains 410 images with an average size of 494×441 pixels. The peroneal nerve images are collected from six different anatomical structures where the nerve stem comes from the adjacent fibular head. FH represents the fibular head, and FN represents fibular neuropathy. FN+α represents that the measured site is α cm away from the fibular head. The ulnar nerve is located along the inner side of the arm and passing close to the surface of the skin near the elbow. The ulnar nerve dataset contains 1234 images with an average size of 477×435 pixels. Table 2 describes the sample distribution of datasets. This study was approved by the Institutional Review Board at Korea University (IRB number: 2020AN0410).

3.2   Experimental Setup

Each dataset was randomly split at a ratio of 80:20 for training and testing. Each training set was also randomly split into 80:20 for training and validation. SAM comes with three segmentation modes: segmenting everything in a fully automatic way, bounding box mode, and point mode. However, in the case of applying SAM for medical image segmentation, it seems that the segment everything mode is prone to erroneous region partitions. The point-based mode empirically requires multiple iterations of prediction correction. The bounding box-based mode can clearly specify the ROI and obtain good segmentation results without multiple trials and errors [16]. Therefore, we choose the bounding box prompts as input to the prompt encoder for SAM, MedSAM, and CEmb-SAM. In the training phase, the bounding box coordinates were generated from the ground-truth targets with a random perturbation of 0–10 pixels.

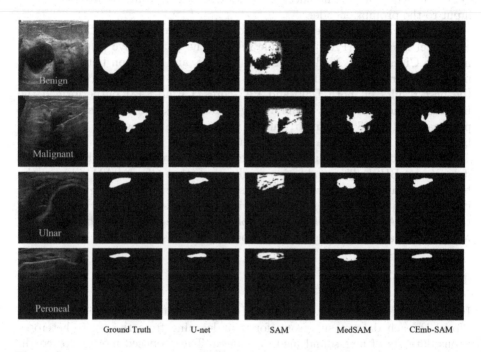

Ground Truth   U-net   SAM   MedSAM   CEmb-SAM

Fig. 2. Segmentation results on BUSI (1st and 2nd rows) and peripheral nerve dataset (3rd and 4th rows).

The input image's intensity values were normalized using Min-Max normalization [21] and resized to $3 \times 256 \times 256$. We used the pre-trained SAM (ViT-B) model as an image encoder. An unweighted sum between Dice loss and cross-entropy loss is used as the loss function [11,15]. Adam optimizer [13] was chosen to train our proposed method and baseline models using NVIDIA RTX 3090 GPUs. The initial learning rate of our model is 3e-4.

3.3   Results

To evaluate the effectiveness of our method, we compare CEmb-SAM with the U-net [23], SAM [14], and MedSAM [16]. The U-net is trained from scratch on BUSI and peripheral nerve datasets, respectively. The SAM is used with the bounding box mode. The pre-trained SAM (ViT-B) weights are used as image encoder and prompt encoder. During inference, the bounding box coordinates are used as the input to the prompt encoder. Likewise, the pre-trained SAM (ViT-B) weights are used as image encoder and prompt encoder in the MedSAM. The mask decoder of MedSAM is fine-tuned on BUSI and peripheral nerve datasets. CEmb-SAM also uses the pre-trained SAM (ViT-B) model as an image encoder and prompt encoder, and fine-tunes the mask decoder on BUSI and peripheral nerve datasets. During inference, the bounding box coordinates are used as the input to the prompt encoder.

For the performance metrics, we used the Dice Similarity Coefficient (DSC) and Pixel Accuracy (PA) [18]. Table 3 shows the quantitative results comparing with CEmb-SAM, MedSAM, SAM (ViT-B), and U-net on both BUSI and peripheral nerve datasets. From Table 3, we observe that our method achieves the best results on both DSC and PA scores. CEmb-SAM outperformed the baseline methods in terms of the average DSC by 18.61% in breast, 14.85% in peroneal, and 14.68% in ulnar, and in terms of the average PA by 3.26% in breast, 2.24% in peroneal and 1.71% in ulnar.

Figure 2 shows the visualization of segmentation results on peripheral nerve dataset and BUSI. The qualitative results show that CEmb-SAM achieves the best segmentation results with fewer missed and false detections in the segmentation of both the breast lesions and peripheral nerves. The results demonstrate that CEmb-SAM is more effective and robust in the segmentation through learning from domain shifts caused by heterogeneous datasets.

4   Conclusion

In this study, we propose CEmb-SAM which adapts the Segment Anything Model to each dataset sub-group for joint learning from the entire heterogeneous datasets of ultrasound medical images. The proposed module for conditional instance normalization was able to guide the model to effectively combine image embeddings with subgroup conditions for both the BUSI and peripheral nerve datasets. The proposed module helped the model deal with distribution shifts among sub-groups. Experiments showed that CEmb-SAM achieved the highest score in DSC and PA on both the public BUSI dataset and peripheral nerve datasets. As future work, we plan to extend our work for improved domain adaptation in which the model is robust and effective under higher degrees of anatomical heterogeneity among datasets.

Acknowledgements. This work was supported by the Korea Medical Device Development Fund grant funded by the Korea Government (the Ministry of Science and ICT, the Ministry of Trade, Industry and Energy, the Ministry of Health & Welfare, the Ministry of Food and Drug Safety) (Project Number: 1711195279, RS-2021-KD000009); the National Research Foundation of Korea (NRF) Grant through the Ministry of Science and ICT (MSIT), Korea Government, under Grant 2022R1A5A1027646; the National Research Foundation of Korea(NRF) grant funded by the Korea government (MSIT) (No.2021R1A2C1007215); the MSIT(Ministry of Science and ICT), Korea, under the ICT Creative Consilience program(IITP-2023-2020-0-01819) supervised by the IITP(Institute for Information & communications Technology Planning & Evaluation)

References

1. Al-Dhabyani, W., Gomaa, M., Khaled, H., Fahmy, A.: Dataset of breast ultrasound images. Data Brief **28**, 104863 (2020)
2. Beekman, R., Visser, L.H.: Sonography in the diagnosis of carpal tunnel syndrome: a critical review of the literature. Muscle Nerve Official J. Am. Assoc. Electrodiagnostic Med. **27**(1), 26–33 (2003)
3. Cartwright, M.S., Walker, F.O.: Neuromuscular ultrasound in common entrapment neuropathies. Muscle Nerve **48**(5), 696–704 (2013)
4. Davatzikos, C.: Machine learning in neuroimaging: progress and challenges. Neuroimage **197**, 652 (2019)
5. Deng, R., et al.: Segment anything model (SAM) for digital pathology: Assess zero-shot segmentation on whole slide imaging. arXiv preprint arXiv:2304.04155 (2023)
6. Dong, N., Kampffmeyer, M., Liang, X., Wang, Z., Dai, W., Xing, E.: Unsupervised domain adaptation for automatic estimation of cardiothoracic ratio. In: Frangi, A.F., Schnabel, J.A., Davatzikos, C., Alberola-López, C., Fichtinger, G. (eds.) MICCAI 2018. LNCS, vol. 11071, pp. 544–552. Springer, Cham (2018). https://doi.org/10.1007/978-3-030-00934-2_61
7. Dosovitskiy, A., et al.: An image is worth 16×16 words: transformers for image recognition at scale. arXiv preprint arXiv:2010.11929 (2020)
8. Dumoulin, V., Shlens, J., Kudlur, M.: A learned representation for artistic style. arXiv preprint arXiv:1610.07629 (2016)
9. He, S., Bao, R., Li, J., Grant, P.E., Ou, Y.: Accuracy of segment-anything model (SAM) in medical image segmentation tasks. arXiv preprint arXiv:2304.09324 (2023)
10. Hu, C., Li, X.: When SAM meets medical images: An investigation of segment anything model (SAM) on multi-phase liver tumor segmentation. arXiv preprint arXiv:2304.08506 (2023)
11. Isensee, F., Jaeger, P.F., Kohl, S.A., Petersen, J., Maier-Hein, K.H.: nnU-net: a self-configuring method for deep learning-based biomedical image segmentation. Nat. Methods **18**(2), 203–211 (2021). https://doi.org/10.1038/s41592-020-01008-z
12. Kamnitsas, K., et al.: Unsupervised domain adaptation in brain lesion segmentation with adversarial networks. In: Niethammer, M., et al. (eds.) IPMI 2017. LNCS, vol. 10265, pp. 597–609. Springer, Cham (2017). https://doi.org/10.1007/978-3-319-59050-9_47
13. Kingma, D.P., Ba, J.: Adam: a method for stochastic optimization. arXiv preprint arXiv:1412.6980 (2014)
14. Kirillov, A., et al.: Segment anything. arXiv preprint arXiv:2304.02643 (2023)
15. Ma, J., et al.: Loss odyssey in medical image segmentation. Med. Image Anal. **71**, 102035 (2021)
16. Ma, J., Wang, B.: Segment anything in medical images. arXiv preprint arXiv:2304.12306 (2023)
17. Mahmood, F., Chen, R., Durr, N.J.: Unsupervised reverse domain adaptation for synthetic medical images via adversarial training. IEEE Trans. Med. Imaging **37**(12), 2572–2581 (2018)

18. Maier-Hein, L., Menze, B., et al.: Metrics reloaded: Pitfalls and recommendations for image analysis validation. arXiv:2206.01653 (2022)
19. Motiian, S., Piccirilli, M., Adjeroh, D.A., Doretto, G.: Unified deep supervised domain adaptation and generalization. In: Proceedings of the IEEE International Conference on Computer Vision, pp. 5715–5725 (2017)
20. Noble, J.A., Boukerroui, D.: Ultrasound image segmentation: a survey. IEEE Trans. Med. Imaging **25**(8), 987–1010 (2006)
21. Patro, S., Sahu, K.K.: Normalization: a preprocessing stage. arXiv preprint arXiv:1503.06462 (2015)
22. Redko, I., Morvant, E., Habrard, A., Sebban, M., Bennani, Y.: A survey on domain adaptation theory: learning bounds and theoretical guarantees. arXiv preprint arXiv:2004.11829 (2020)
23. Ronneberger, O., Fischer, P., Brox, T.: U-Net: convolutional networks for biomedical image segmentation. In: Navab, N., Hornegger, J., Wells, W.M., Frangi, A.F. (eds.) MICCAI 2015. LNCS, vol. 9351, pp. 234–241. Springer, Cham (2015). https://doi.org/10.1007/978-3-319-24574-4_28
24. Shin, H.C., et al.: Deep convolutional neural networks for computer-aided detection: CNN architectures, dataset characteristics and transfer learning. IEEE Trans. Med. Imaging **35**(5), 1285–1298 (2016)
25. Walker, F.O., et al.: Indications for neuromuscular ultrasound: expert opinion and review of the literature. Clin. Neurophysiol. **129**(12), 2658–2679 (2018)
26. Wang, R., Chaudhari, P., Davatzikos, C.: Embracing the disharmony in medical imaging: a simple and effective framework for domain adaptation. Med. Image Anal. **76**, 102309 (2022)
27. Xian, M., Zhang, Y., Cheng, H.D., Xu, F., Zhang, B., Ding, J.: Automatic breast ultrasound image segmentation: a survey. Pattern Recogn. **79**, 340–355 (2018)
28. Zhou, S.K., et al.: A review of deep learning in medical imaging: imaging traits, technology trends, case studies with progress highlights, and future promises. Proc. IEEE **109**(5), 820–838 (2021)
29. Zhou, T., Zhang, Y., Zhou, Y., Wu, Y., Gong, C.: Can SAM segment polyps? arXiv preprint arXiv:2304.07583 (2023)

Histopathological Image Analysis with Style-Augmented Feature Domain Mixing for Improved Generalization

Vaibhav Khamankar, Sutanu Bera$^{(\boxtimes)}$, Saumik Bhattacharya, Debashis Sen, and Prabir Kumar Biswas

Department of Electronics and Electrical Communication Engineering, Indian Institute of Technology Kharagpur, Kharagpur, India
`sutanu.bera@iitkgp.ac.in`

Abstract. Histopathological images are essential for medical diagnosis and treatment planning, but interpreting them accurately using machine learning can be challenging due to variations in tissue preparation, staining and imaging protocols. Domain generalization aims to address such limitations by enabling the learning models to generalize to new datasets or populations. Style transfer-based data augmentation is an emerging technique that can be used to improve the generalizability of machine learning models for histopathological images. However, existing style transfer-based methods can be computationally expensive, and they rely on artistic styles, which may negatively impact model accuracy. In this study, we propose a feature domain style mixing technique that uses adaptive instance normalization to estimate style-mixed versions of image features. We compare our proposed method with existing style transfer-based data augmentation methods and found that it performs similarly or better, despite requiring lower computation. Our results demonstrate the potential of feature domain statistics mixing in the generalization of learning models for histopathological image analysis.

Keywords: Domain Shift · Domain Generalization · Mitotic Figure · Style Mixing · Feature Domain Augmentation · Histopathological Image

1 Introduction

Histopathological images play a critical role in medical diagnosis and treatment planning, allowing healthcare providers to visualize the microscopic structures of tissues and organs. However, accurately interpreting these images can be challenging due to variations in tissue preparation, staining and imaging protocols.

V. Khamankar and S. Bera—Contributed equally to this work and share the first authorship

---

Supplementary Information The online version contains supplementary material available at https://doi.org/10.1007/978-3-031-47401-9_28.

These variations can result in significant differences in image quality, tissue morphology and staining intensity, making it difficult to develop machine learning models for analysis that generalize well to new datasets or populations. Domain generalization is a field of machine learning that seeks to address this limitation by enabling models to generalize to new domains or datasets. In the context of histopathological images, domain generalization methods aim to improve the generalizability of machine learning models by reducing the effects of dataset bias and increasing the robustness of the model to variations in tissue preparation, staining, and imaging protocols. Recently, there has been a growing interest in using style transfer-based data augmentation for learning visual representations that are independent of specific domains for histopathological images viz., [7,13,18]. This technique involves transferring the style or texture of one image to another while maintaining the original content. By generating new images with different styles or textures, this technique can be used to augment the training data and improve the model's generalization performance [18]. Although the style transfer based method achieves good results in domain generalization for histopathological images, it takes a considerable amount of time to generate the augmented data. Further, the collinearity between the various artistic styles used for the style transfer may have a negative impact on the model's accuracy. Unlike the existing methods, in this work, we propose to apply feature domain style mixing for the style transfer. Specifically, we use adaptive instance normalization [6] to mix the feature statistics of the different images to generate a style-augmented version of an image. Feature statistics mixing helps to save a lot of time and computation power as data augmentation is not required, and the dependency on the artistic style is also alleviated. We compare the proposed method with the current state-of-the-art style transfer-based data augmentation methods, on two image classification tasks and one object detection task. We find that the proposed method performs similarly or better than the image domain mixing-based methods, despite having low computation requirements.

2   Related Work

In the field of digital pathology, researchers have developed several deep learning approaches to address challenges related to domain generalization such as normalization and style transfer. One example is StainNet [7], which is designed for stain normalization in digital pathology images. StainNet removes variations in tissue staining across different samples, making it easier to compare and analyze images in a consistent manner. Another approach, STRAP [18], uses a deep neural network to extract features from histopathology images and proposes a style transfer augmentation technique to reduce the domain-specific information in these features. This technique generates a new set of images that have the same content as the original images but in different styles. Domain Adversarial RetinaNet [16], a modified version of the RetinaNet object detection model, has been developed that includes domain adversarial training. The idea is to train in both source and target domain data to address domain generalization challenges.

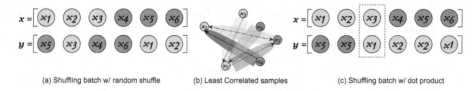

(a) Shuffling batch w/ random shuffle   (b) Least Correlated samples   (c) Shuffling batch w/ dot product

Fig. 1. A graphical illustration of FuseStyle. The shaded areas in (b) are the simulated points for augmentation. The domain label of each sample is colour-coded. There can be cases where the dot product (correlation) is the least within the domain as highlighted in the dotted rectangle in (c).

3   Proposed Method

3.1   Background

Huang et al. [6] introduced Adaptive Instance Normalization (AdaIN) for style transfer based on Instance normalization [15]. AdaIN aims to align the means and variances of instances of the content features (c) with those of the style features (s). It computes the mean $(\mu(s))$ and variance $(\sigma(s))$ parameters from instances of the style input and achieves the style transfer as $AdaIN(c) = \sigma(s)\frac{x-\mu(c)}{\sigma(c)} + \mu(s)$, where $\mu(c)$ and $\sigma(c)$ are respectively the corresponding instance mean and standard deviation of a given content feature tensor. The above parameter adaption allows for arbitrary style transfer, enabling the mixing of the content and style features in a way that produces a new output with the parameters of the style.

3.2   FuseStyle: Proposed Feature Domain Style Mixing

Our feature domain style mixing approach, FuseStyle, is inspired by AdaIN. FuseStyle avoids the use of an image generating network that is usually associated with style transfer based domain generalization. Instead, it regularizes the training of the neural network at hand (for performing a required task) by perturbing the style information of the training instances. It can be easily implemented as a plug-and-play module inserted between the layers of the neural network. So, the need to explicitly create a new style image does not arise.

FuseStyle, depicted in Fig. 1, combines the feature statistics of two instances from the same /different domains as a convex sum using random weights to simulate new styles. As shown in Fig. 1, for an input training batch, x, a reference batch y is generated by shuffling x across the batch dimension. We then compute the means (μ) and variances (σ) of the corresponding instances in x and y, and use them to compute the combined feature statistics as:

$$\gamma_i = \lambda_i\sigma(x_i) + (1 - \lambda_i)\sigma(y_i), \qquad \beta_i = \lambda_i\mu(x_i) + (1 - \lambda_i)\mu(y_i) \qquad (1)$$

where i denotes the ith instance and $\lambda_i \sim \text{Beta}(\alpha, \alpha)$ is computed from a Beta distribution having both its shape parameters as α. A style-modified training instance $\tilde{x}_i$ is then computed as:

$$\tilde{x}_i = \gamma_i \frac{x_i - \mu(x_i)}{\sigma(x_i)} + \beta_i \tag{2}$$

where the batch size of $\tilde{x}$ is the same as that of x and y. x is then randomly (binomial-$B(0,.5)$) replaced by $\tilde{x}$ as the training batch for domain generalization.

Generating the reference batch y is crucial for achieving better generalization to unseen domains. While previous studies [20] have used a random sample selection method for creating the reference batch, a recent study [18] in histopathological image domain generalization has shown that mixing medically irrelevant images, such as artistic paintings, with whole slide images (WSI) results in improved performance. This suggests that using the least correlated image in the reference batch could result in a better generalization than using a meaningful stylized image. With this motivation, we propose a new method of generating the reference batch that allows the mixing of the features of a sample with the features of another sample in the batch that is least correlated to the former. This method has inherent advantages over existing methods. For example, when we combine the parameters of two furthest samples linearly, the interpolated parameter values are more likely to represent a simulated sample that is far from the both the original samples than when we combine two close samples (which may happen during random reference batch generation). This allows us to explore more regions in the feature space and simulate a wider variety of augmented domains, as illustrated in Fig. 1b. Consider that FuseStyle is applied between a layer, f_l, and f_{l+1}, and the output feature of the layer f_l is $z_l \in \mathbb{R}^{B \times C \times W \times H}$ (B - batch dimension). Then, the correlation ($\rho \in \mathbb{R}^{B \times B}$) between different samples of the current batch can be computed by:

$$\rho = \hat{z}_l \odot \hat{z}_l^T \tag{3}$$

where $\odot$ represents the matrix multiplication, $\hat{z}_l \in \mathbb{R}^{B \times CWH}$ is the vectorized version of the z_l and T represents the transpose operation. Next, we set i^{th} sample of the reference batch, that is, y_i to be x_j, where $j = \arg\min_j \rho_i$, and $\rho_i \in \mathbb{R}^B$ is the ith row of the matrix ρ. Then, the ith sample of the batch x is mixed with i^{th} sample of the batch y as mentioned in Eq.(2) to get $\tilde{x}_i$. We set α of the Beta distribution to 0.3 to generate all the results reported in this paper. During the learning phase of the neural network model, the probability of using the FuseStyle method is set at 0.5, but it is not applied during the test phase.

Table 1. Comparison of FuseStyle with SoTA methods on Camelyon17-WILDS.

Methods	STRAP	FuseStyle	LISA	Fish	ERM	V-REx	DomainMix	IB-IRM	GroupDRO
Test Accuracy	93.7%	90.49%	77.1%	74.7%	70.3%	71.5%	69.7%	68.9%	68.4%

Table 2. Classification using FuseStyle and STRAP on $MIDOG'21$ Dataset.

Networks{Train,Test}	STRAP Test Accuracy(%)			FuseStyle Test Accuracy(%)		
	XR	S360	CS	XR	S360	CS
{S360+CS,XR}	67.33	87.99	84.67	**77.56**	**91.07**	**90.46**
{XR+CS, S360}	88.35	**76.78**	91.14	**90.06**	75.16	**92.16**
{XR+S360,CS}	**88.92**	**92.70**	**74.28**	86.65	88.96	74.10

4 Experimental Details

4.1 Datasets and Task

In our study, we compared our proposed method with the recent state-of-the-art histopathological domain generalization using two datasets. 1. The MIDOG'21 Challenge dataset [3] consisted of 200 samples of human breast cancer tissue stained with Haematoxylin and Eosin (H&E). Four scanning systems were used to digitize the samples: Leica GT450, Aperio CS2 (CS), Hamamatsu XR (XR), and Hamamatsu S360 (S360), resulting in 50 WSIs from each system. 2. The Camelyon17-WILDS [9] dataset comprised 1,000 histopathology images distributed across six domains, representing different combinations of medical centres and scanners. In our study, we focused on three tasks: classification between mitotic figures and non-mitotic figures using the MIDOG'21 dataset, tumour classification using the Camelyon17 dataset, and detection of mitotic and non-mitotic figures using the MIDOG'21 dataset. TFor the mitotic figure detection task, the details regarding dataset preparation can be found in the supplementary material of our study. For the Camelyon17 WILDS dataset, we used the default settings and train test split as given on the challenge website. For the classification task on MIDOG'21, we cropped patches of size 64 × 64 around the mitotic and non-mitotic figure, and we then performed an 80–20 train-test split on the cropped patches keeping the patches from each domain separate.

4.2 Model Architecture, Training and Methods

Classification: Here, we employ ResNet50 [5] CNN architecture and integrate FuseStyle after layers 1 and 4 of the network for 15 epochs. We use Binary Cross Entropy (BCE) Loss for training, while Adam Optimizer [8] with a learning rate of 1e-4 is utilized. To facilitate smooth training, a scheduler is used, that is, when no improvement is seen during model training after 2 epochs, the learning rate is reduced by a factor of 0.01. The batch size is set to 256 for both Camelyon17-WILDS [9] and MIDOG'21 Challenge datasets [3]. Recent studies on style transfer indicate that style information can be modified by altering the instance-level feature statistics in the lower layers of a Convolutional Neural Network (CNN) while preserving the image's semantic content representation [4,6], and hence, we consider layers 1 and 4 of the ResNet to use FuseStyle.

Mitotic Figure Detection: For mitotic figure detection, we utilize RetinaNet [11] with ResNet50 as the backbone architecture and incorporate FuseStyle on layers 1 and 4 of the backbone. We use Focal Loss and train the network for 100 epochs on the MIDOG'21 Challenge dataset with a batch size of 6. Adam Optimizer [8] is used with a learning rate of 1e-4. We use the adaptive learning rate decay scheduler, that is, when no improvement is seen in model training after two epochs, the learning rate is reduced by factor of 0.1 for stable training.

Methods: To assess the effectiveness of our proposed approach, we compare it to eight state-of-the-art domain generalization methods, namely STRAP [18], LISA [19], Fish [14], ERM [9], V-REx [10], DomainMix [17], IB-IRM [1], and GroupDRO [12] for classification task on the Camelyon17-WILDS dataset, where we evaluate the classification accuracy. The best existing approach STRAP [18] based on the performance data on Camelyon17-WILDS dataset is used further for comparison with the proposed approach on the MIDOG'21 Challenge dataset, where both classification and mitotic figure detection are considered. We implemented the networks using the PyTorch library in Python and utilized a GeForce GTX 2080Ti GPU for efficient processing.

(a) GT   (b) RetinaNet   (c) STRAP   (d) FuseStyle

Fig. 2. Mitotic figure detection by different methods in S360 image with model trained on XR & CS, where Red box→Mitotic and Blue box→Non-Mitotic. (Color figure online)

5   Results and Discussion

Classification Task Results: We evaluate the state-of-the-art (SOTA) methods along with ours based on their classification performance in out-of-distribution domains, and we use accuracy as the performance metric. Our approach is first compared to the other methods in Table 1, where the Camelyon17 dataset is used for both training and testing (out-of-distribution). The results presented in Table 1 demonstrate that our approach outperforms all the methods except STRAP [18].

One should note regarding STRAP that its performance heavily relies on the generated stylized dataset used for training. The time required to generate the stylized data for the Camelyon17- WILDS is around 300 h in our set up and for the MIDOG'21 Challenge dataset, it is around 75 h. On the other hand, there is no data generation involved with our FuseStyle. Further, the main operation in FuseStyle is a dot product, which is computationally cheap, and the complexity of our feature mixing strategy is negligible compared to existing augmentation techniques.

Due to the substantial dependence of STRAP on the generated stylized augmentation, careful selection of style images for every dataset becomes fundamental to reproduce its similar performance on different datasets. Therefore, to further investigate the performance of FuseStyle and STRAP, we conduct a classification experiment on the MIDOG'21 Challenge Dataset, the results of which are presented in Table 2. As seen, if the network is trained on S360 and CS, and tested on XR, there is a 10.23% advantage in test accuracy for FuseStyle over STRAP. Furthermore, the accuracy improves by 5.79% and 3.08% for S360 and CS, which are the seen domains, respectively. In the other cases of Table 2, the approaches outperform each other almost equal number of times, but most importantly, the differences in their accuracies are relatively low. This shows that FuseStyle is at par with STRAP in these cases in spite of it being significantly less complex. We also infer from the table that FuseStyle produces consistent performance irrespective of the training and testing domains.

Mitotic Figure Detection Task Results: We conduct an experiment on this task using three different models: Our FuseStyle, STRAP and RetinaNet [11]. All these models use ResNet50 as their backbone architecture, but Retinanet does not involve any domain generalization. We provide Precision, Recall and F1 score as the performance metrics of detection in Table 3. Here the models are trained using training data from XR and CS scanners. As a result, the images from S360 represent an out-of-distribution scenario. As can be seen, FuseStyle outperforms both STRAP [18] and RetinaNet in most cases in terms of F1 score that incorporates both precision and recall. FuseStyle's superiority over RetinaNet demonstrates the usefulness of our way of domain generalization.

Table 3. Mitotic Figure Detection Analysis on $MIDOG'21$ Challenge Dataset.

Network	Precision			Recall			F1 Score		
	XR	S360	CS	XR	S360	CS	XR	S360	CS
RetinaNet	0.91	0.93	0.93	0.76	0.3	0.76	0.83	0.45	0.84
STRAP	0.85	0.91	0.88	0.88	0.70	0.95	0.87	0.79	0.92
FuseStyle	0.82	0.92	0.90	0.92	0.76	0.90	0.87	0.83	0.90

Table 4. Objective evaluation on $MIDOG'21$ Challenge Dataset.

Network	Methods	XR	S360	CS	Time/epoch (sec)
Train: S360 & CS Test: XR	M1	76.42	89.45	88.76	08
	RA	**77.56**	**91.07**	**90.46**	08
	M2	67.05	88.64	90.29	08
	M3	74.43	87.18	88.76	111
Train: XR & CS Test: S360	M1	84.09	71.59	85.18	08
	RA	90.06	75.16	**92.16**	08
	M2	**90.34**	75.65	91.65	08
	M3	83.07	**78.90**	89.95	111
Train: XR & S360 Test: CS	M1	**88.64**	89.45	72.40	08
	RA	86.65	88.96	74.10	08
	M2	87.78	**90.91**	76.32	08
	M3	86.34	87.34	**78.02**	111

Table 5. Objective evaluation on $MIDOG'22$ Challenge Dataset.

Network	Methods	XR	S360	CS	Time/epoch (sec)
Train: S360 & CS Test: XR	M1	75.10	81.16	80.58	28
	RA	74.27	**83.59**	79.74	28
	M2	76.78	75.68	68.80	28
	M3	**78.74**	83.28	**81.24**	331
Train: XR & CS Test: S360	M1	77.06	80.24	78.89	28
	RA	80.84	80.24	**81.62**	28
	M2	75.94	**81.76**	81.53	28
	M3	**81.26**	**81.76**	79.26	331
Train: XR & S360 Test: CS	M1	81.12	81.46	82.28	28
	RA	**81.34**	**84.19**	**82.75**	28
	M2	73.71	76.60	73.42	28
	M3	80.14	83.89	74.08	331

A visual result of mitotic figure detection using FuseStyle, STRAP and RetinaNet is shown in Fig. 2a along with the ground truth. As we can see from the figure, the use of FuseStyle, unlike the use of the other two, results in accurate detection and classification of all mitotic and non-mitotic figures present. While the use of RetinaNet results in an unsuccessful classification of a mitotic figure, the use of STRAP results in detection failure.

Design Analysis of Our Approach: Our investigation has revealed that combining distant features can lead to the extraction of domain-invariant features. To achieve this, we had proposed using the dot product method, but other techniques for generating a reference batch exist. To explore this further, we conduct an empirical investigation using four different methods: M1: Mixing with Random Shuffle, Reference Approach (RA): Mixing with Least Dot Product (FuseStyle), M2: Mixing with Maximum Euclidean Distance, and M3: Mixing with Maximum KL Divergence. We study the Euclidean distance based approach and also experiment with an advanced approach based on KL divergence. To evaluate the robustness of the proposed approach, we train the ResNet50 model on two scanner datasets and tested it on the third scanner. The comparison of the results obtained from the study are presented in Tables 4 & 5. The comparison is based on the test accuracy (in percentage) of different scanners and the time required for training. The obtained results reveal the effectiveness of the proposed approach of sample selection for mixing. The detailed analysis of the findings is provided in the table, demonstrating the superiority of the proposed method over the other methods.

Based on the results presented in Table 4, it can be observed that the Dot Product method is the most consistent in terms of network performance across different domains. In contrast, the Random Shuffle method (M1) fails to perform well in the second case, and the Euclidean Distance method (M2) fails in the first case for the out-of-distribution domain. The KL Divergence method (M3) does not perform well in the in-distribution domain, as observed in the second case for the XR scanner, and it also requires a significantly longer computational time compared to the other methods. Therefore, the experimental studies suggest that FuseStyle (RA) provides the most consistent results as well as takes less time compared to KL divergence method (M3) on the MIDOG'21 Challenge dataset. For further analysis of our method, we conduct additional experiments on the MIDOG'22 Challenge dataset [2] as shown in Table 5, using the same reference batch generation methods. The results demonstrate that the FuseStyle (RA) performs well for both in-distribution and out-of-distribution domains.

6   Conclusion

We present, FuseStyle, a novel method that computes generalized features by mixing them in the feature space to address domain shift issues related to histopathological images. It uses a new approach of feature mixing based on correlation computation. FuseStyle has lower computational requirements, with dot product being the main operation in it. We have shown that the performance of our method in classification and detection tasks is at par or better than the state-of-the-art on various datasets. We also find from experimental results that the proposed feature-mixing method has strong domain generalization capabilities. In summary, our method is simple, effective and consistent, and it has the potential to enhance the out-of-distribution performance of any existing machine learning method.

References

1. Ahuja, K., et al.: Invariance principle meets information bottleneck for out-of-distribution generalization. Adv. Neural. Inf. Process. Syst. **34**, 3438–3450 (2021)
2. Aubreville, M., Bertram, C., Breininger, K., Jabari, S., Stathonikos, N., Veta, M.: Mitosis domain generalization challenge 2022 (2022). https://doi.org/10.5281/zenodo.6362337
3. Aubreville, M., et al.: Mitosis domain generalization in histopathology images-the midog challenge. Med. Image Anal. **84**, 102699 (2023)
4. Dumoulin, V., Shlens, J., Kudlur, M.: A learned representation for artistic style. arXiv preprint arXiv:1610.07629 (2016)
5. He, K., Zhang, X., Ren, S., Sun, J.: Deep residual learning for image recognition. In: Proceedings of the IEEE Conference on Computer Vision and Pattern Recognition, pp. 770–778 (2016)
6. Huang, X., Belongie, S.: Arbitrary style transfer in real-time with adaptive instance normalization. In: Proceedings of the IEEE International Conference on Computer Vision, pp. 1501–1510 (2017)
7. Kang, H., et al.: Stainnet: a fast and robust stain normalization network. Front. Med. **8**, 746307 (2021)

8. Kingma, D.P., Ba, J.: Adam: a method for stochastic optimization. arXiv preprint arXiv:1412.6980 (2014)

9. Koh, P.W., et al.: WILDS: A benchmark of in-the-wild distribution shifts. In: International Conference on Machine Learning (ICML) (2021)

10. Krueger, D., et al.: Out-of-distribution generalization via risk extrapolation (rex). In: International Conference on Machine Learning, pp. 5815–5826. PMLR (2021)

11. Lin, T.Y., Goyal, P., Girshick, R., He, K., Dollár, P.: Focal loss for dense object detection. In: Proceedings of the IEEE International Conference on Computer Vision, pp. 2980–2988 (2017)

12. Sagawa, S., Koh, P.W., Hashimoto, T.B., Liang, P.: Distributionally robust neural networks for group shifts: On the importance of regularization for worst-case generalization. arXiv preprint arXiv:1911.08731 (2019)

13. Shaban, M.T., Baur, C., Navab, N., Albarqouni, S.: Staingan: Stain style transfer for digital histological images. In: 2019 IEEE 16th International Symposium On Biomedical Imaging (ISBI 2019), pp. 953–956. IEEE (2019)

14. Shi, Y., Seely, J., Torr, P.H., Siddharth, N., Hannun, A., Usunier, N., Synnaeve, G.: Gradient matching for domain generalization. arXiv preprint arXiv:2104.09937 (2021)

15. Ulyanov, D., Vedaldi, A., Lempitsky, V.: Instance normalization: The missing ingredient for fast stylization. arXiv preprint arXiv:1607.08022 (2016)

16. Wilm, F., Marzahl, C., Breininger, K., Aubreville, M.: Domain adversarial retinanet as a reference algorithm for the mitosis domain generalization challenge. In: Aubreville, M., Zimmerer, D., Heinrich, M. (eds.) MICCAI 2021. LNCS, vol. 13166, pp. 5–13. Springer, Cham (2022). https://doi.org/10.1007/978-3-030-97281-3_1

17. Xu, M., et al.: Adversarial domain adaptation with domain mixup. In: Proceedings of the AAAI Conference on Artificial Intelligence. vol. 34, pp. 6502–6509 (2020)

18. Yamashita, R., Long, J., Banda, S., Shen, J., Rubin, D.L.: Learning domain-agnostic visual representation for computational pathology using medically-irrelevant style transfer augmentation. IEEE Trans. Med. Imaging 40(12), 3945–3954 (2021). https://doi.org/10.1109/TMI.2021.3101985

19. Yao, H., et al.: Improving out-of-distribution robustness via selective augmentation. In: International Conference on Machine Learning, pp. 25407–25437. PMLR (2022)

20. Zhou, K., Yang, Y., Qiao, Y., Xiang, T.: Domain generalization with mixstyle. arXiv preprint arXiv:2104.02008 (2021)

Proceedings of the Fourth Workshop on Distributed, Collaborative and Federated Learning (DeCaF 2023)

DISBELIEVE: Distance Between Client Models Is Very Essential for Effective Local Model Poisoning Attacks

Indu Joshi[1]([✉]), Priyank Upadhya[1], Gaurav Kumar Nayak[2], Peter Schüffler[1], and Nassir Navab[1]

[1] Technical University of Munich, Boltzmannstraße 15, 85748, Garching Bei München, Germany
{indu.joshi,priyank.upadhya,peter.schueffler,nassir.navab}@tum.de
[2] Center for Research in Computer Vision, University of Central Florida, Orlando, FL 32816, USA
gauravkumar.nayak@ucf.edu

Abstract. Federated learning is a promising direction to tackle the privacy issues related to sharing patients' sensitive data. Often, federated systems in the medical image analysis domain assume that the participating local clients are *honest*. Several studies report mechanisms through which a set of malicious clients can be introduced that can poison the federated setup, hampering the performance of the global model. To overcome this, robust aggregation methods have been proposed that defend against those attacks. We observe that most of the state-of-the-art robust aggregation methods are heavily dependent on the distance between the parameters or gradients of malicious clients and benign clients, which makes them prone to local model poisoning attacks when the parameters or gradients of malicious and benign clients are close. Leveraging this, we introduce DISBELIEVE, a local model poisoning attack that creates malicious parameters or gradients such that their distance to benign clients' parameters or gradients is low respectively but at the same time their adverse effect on the global model's performance is high. Experiments on three publicly available medical image datasets demonstrate the efficacy of the proposed DISBELIEVE attack as it significantly lowers the performance of the state-of-the-art *robust aggregation* methods for medical image analysis. Furthermore, compared to state-of-the-art local model poisoning attacks, DISBELIEVE attack is also effective on natural images where we observe a severe drop in classification performance of the global model for multi-class classification on benchmark dataset CIFAR-10.

Keywords: Federated Learning · Model Poisoning Attacks · Deep Learning

---

I. Joshi and P. Upadhya—These authors contributed equally to this work.

M. E. Celebi et al. (Eds.): MICCAI 2023 Workshops, LNCS 14393, pp. 297–310, 2023.
https://doi.org/10.1007/978-3-031-47401-9_29

1   Introduction

The success of deep models for medical image analysis [13] greatly depends on sufficient training data availability. Strict privacy protocols and limited availability of time and resources pose challenges in collecting sizeable medical image datasets [12]. Although different medical institutions may be willing to collaborate, strict privacy protocols governing patients' information restrict data sharing. Federated learning (FL) offers a promising solution that allows different institutions to share information about these models without revealing personal information about the patients [6,18,20]. Federated Learning is a machine learning paradigm that learns a single shared global model by collaboratively learning from different local models on distributed systems without sharing the data.

A federated learning setup involves multiple clients and a global server [18]. The global server initializes the global model and sends the parameters back to the clients. The clients then train their local models on the data present locally. Once the local models are trained, the parameters are sent to the global model for aggregation. The global model then uses an *aggregation algorithm* to aggregate all the parameter updates and transmits the updated parameters back to the clients, and the cycle repeats until convergence. The federated learning setup allows the clients to preserve the privacy of their data. The success of a federated learning system is majorly dependent on the use of an aggregation algorithm. For example, *Federated Averaging* [18] is an aggregation algorithm in which all the parameters accumulated at the global server from different clients are averaged. However, not all clients would act truthfully in real-world scenarios, and there may be some *byzantine* clients. A client is said to be a byzantine client if it acts malicious intentionally due to the presence of an adversary or unintentionally due to faulty equipment or hardware issues [26]. Studies report that even a single byzantine worker can seriously threaten the FL systems [4].

A malicious byzantine worker with an adversary who knows the client's data and model parameters can induce *local poisoning attacks* to degrade the performance of the global model in an FL system. A local poisoning attack in an FL system is a process through which the training of the global model is adversely affected due to either data perturbation or perturbation in model parameters (or gradients) at the local client's side. These attacks are termed as *local data poisoning attacks* or *local model poisoning attacks*, respectively. Several studies indicate that state-of-the-art aggregation methods, for instance, using federated averaging in the presence of a byzantine client, will reduce the performance of the global server. Therefore, to defend against attacks by byzantine clients, the global server uses *robust aggregation algorithms* [25,26]. This research studies the efficacy of state-of-the-art robust aggregation methods for FL systems for medical image analysis and highlights their vulnerability to local model poisoning attacks. We observe that the state-of-the-art robust aggregation methods heavily rely on the distance between malicious and benign client model parameters (or gradients). We argue that some model poisoning attacks can exist when the parameters or gradients of malicious clients are close in Euclidean space to those of benign clients that circumvent the existing state-of-the-art robust aggregation methods.

Research Contribution: We introduce the DISBELIEVE attack that demonstrates the limitation of state-of-the-art robust aggregation methods for FL on medical images in defending against local model poisoning attacks. The novelty of the proposed attack lies in the fact that it maximizes the objective loss function while ensuring that the Euclidean distance between the malicious parameters and benign parameters is kept marginal. As a result, the attacker can optimally reduce the global model's performance without being detected by the aggregation algorithms. Experiments on three publicly available datasets of different medical image modalities confirm the efficacy of DISBELIEVE attack in significantly reducing the classification performance of the global model (by up to 28%). We also benchmark two current state-of-the-art local model poisoning attack methods and demonstrate that the proposed DISBELIEVE attack is stronger, leading to higher performance degradation. Lastly, we demonstrate that DISBELIEVE attack also effectively works on natural images, as similar trends are reported on the CIFAR-10 dataset.

2   Related Work

2.1   Robust Aggregation Algorithms

Robust aggregation algorithms are defense methods that prevent malicious clients from significantly affecting parameter updates and global model performance. KRUM [3] is among the earliest methods for robust aggregation and proposes that for each communication round, only one of the clients is selected as an honest participant, and updates from the other clients are discarded. The client that is chosen as honest is the one whose parameters are closer in Euclidean space to a chosen number of its neighbors. On the other hand, Trimmed Mean [26] assumes malicious clients to have extreme values of parameters and proposes to avoid malicious clients by selecting parameters around the median. Recently, the Distance-based Outlier Suppression (DOS) [1] algorithm was proposed to defend against byzantine attacks in FL systems for medical image analysis. DOS proposes to detect malicious clients using COPOD, a state-of-the-art outlier detection algorithm [15]. Subsequently, it assigns less weight to the parameters from those malicious clients. Specifically, it uses Euclidean and cosine distances between parameters from different clients and computes an outlier score for each client. Later, these scores are converted to weights by normalizing them using a softmax function. We note that all these state-of-the-art robust aggregation algorithms assume that malicious clients' parameters (or gradients) are significantly different from benign clients' parameters (or gradients). However, we hypothesize that an attack can be introduced such that parameters (or gradients) of malicious and benign clients are only marginally different, while it can still severely degrade the global model's performance.

2.2 Attacks in Federated Learning

There are various kinds of attacks in a federated learning paradigm, such as *inference attacks, reconstruction attacks, poisoning attacks* [5,11,16]. In inference attacks, the attacker can extract sensitive information about the training data from the learned features or parameters of the model, thus causing privacy issues. Reconstruction attacks, on the other hand, try to generate the training samples using the leaked model parameters [5]. GAN's [7] have successfully extracted private information about the client's data even when model parameters are unclear due to the use of differential privacy [9]. Poisoning attacks in a federated learning paradigm can be categorized as *data poisoning attacks* or *model poisoning attacks*. Both these attacks are designed to alter the behavior of the malicious client's model [17]. In data poisoning attacks, the attacker tries manipulating the training data by changing the ground truth labels or carefully poisoning the existing data [23]. In model poisoning attacks, the attacker aims to alter the model parameters or gradients before sending them to the global server [17].

In this research, we design a model poisoning attack that can bypass state-of-the-art robust aggregation algorithms such as DOS, Trimmed Mean, and KRUM. We evaluate the performance of existing state-of-the-art model poi-

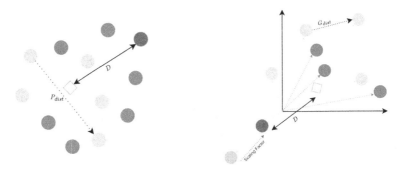

(a) Model Poisoning Attack on Parameters   (b) Model Poisoning Attack on Gradient

Fig. 1. Intuition behind our proposed local model poisoning attack: (a) Green nodes represent the parameters of benign clients, Pink node represent the parameters of malicious clients, Yellow node represents the mean of malicious clients parameters (i.e. average of parameters of Pink nodes), Red node represents the malicious parameters (of model M). We ensure that the shift in parameters of model M from mean is less than the threshold P_{dist} where P_{dist} is the maximum distance between any two attacked clients parameters. (b) Green nodes represent gradients of benign clients, Pink nodes represent the malicious clients gradients, Yellow node represents the mean of malicious clients gradients (i.e. average gradients of Pink nodes), Blue node represents gradient of trained malicious model M, Red node represents gradient of malicious model M after scaling. We ensure that after scaling gradients the distance from mean of gradients is less than threshold G_{dist} where G_{dist} is the minimum distance between any two attacked clients gradients.

Algorithm 1. DISBELIEVE Attack on Parameters

1: Calculate mean of parameters:

$$\mu^{param} = \frac{1}{f}\sum_{i=1}^{f} W_i^{mal}$$

2: Set the threshold value:

$$P_{dist} = Max_{i,k\in f\ i\neq k}||W_i^{mal} - W_k^{mal}||_2^2$$

3: Combine all the training data from malicious clients
4: Initialize the malicious model M with parameters μ^{param}
5: Train M with $Loss = -Loss_{class}$ until:

$$||W_{model}^{mal} - \mu^{param}||_2^2 \leq P_{dist}$$

6: Return W_{model}^{mal}

Algorithm 2. DISBELIEVE Attack on Gradients

1: Calculate the mean of parameters and gradients:

$$\mu^{param} = \frac{1}{f}\sum_{i=1}^{f} W_i^{mal} \qquad \mu^{grad} = \frac{1}{f}\sum_{i=1}^{f} Grad_i^{mal}$$

2: Set the threshold value:

$$G_{dist} = Min_{i,k\in f\ i\neq k}||Grads_i^{mal} - Grads_k^{mal}||_2^2$$

3: Combine all the training data from malicious clients
4: Initialize the malicious model M with parameters μ^{param}
5: Train M with $Loss = -Loss_{class}$
6: $Grads_{model}^{mal} \leftarrow Gradients\ of\ M$
7: $start \leftarrow 0.001, end \leftarrow 1000$
8: **while** $|start - end| > 0.01$ **do**
9: $\quad sf \leftarrow (start + end)/2$
10: $\quad Grads_{new}^{mal} = sf * \frac{Grads_{model}^{mal}}{||Grads_{model}^{mal}||}$
11: $\quad diff = ||Grads_{new}^{mal} - \mu^{grad}||_2^2$
12: $\quad$ **if** $diff > G_{dist}$ **then** $start = sf$ **else** $end = sf$
13: **end while**
14: Return the $Grads_{new}^{mal}$

---

soning attacks such as LIE attack [2] and Min-Max attack [19]. We note that the LIE attack forces the malicious parameters (or gradients) to be bounded in a range $(\mu - z\sigma, \mu + z\sigma)$ where μ and σ are the mean and standard deviation along parameters of the malicious clients, and z is a parameter that sets the lower and upper bounds for deviation around the mean [2]. On the other hand, Min-Max adds deviation to parameters or gradients and then scales them such that their distance from any other non-malicious parameter is less than the maximum distance between two benign updates. However, instead of relying on standard deviation to approximate the range across which malicious clients' parameters (or gradients) can be manipulated, the proposed attack computes the malicious parameters (or gradients) by maximizing the classification loss (as opposed to minimizing it) to degrade the global model's performance. Additionally, we propose to approximate the range across which the parameters (or gradients) can be perturbed by evaluating the distance between the malicious clients' parameters (or gradients) in Euclidean space.

3   Proposed Method

Formally, we assume a total of n federated learning clients out of which f clients $(1 < f < n/2)$ have been compromised such that rather than improving global models' accuracy, the compromised clients work towards decreasing the performance of the global model. We further assume that all the attackers corresponding to different malicious clients are working together or that a single attacker controls all the malicious clients. The attacker thus has access to all the malicious client's model parameters and training data. Our goal is to create malicious parameters or gradients that can bypass the robust aggregation algorithms and reduce the performance of the global model. In this direction, this research introduces a model poisoning attack (DISBELIEVE attack) that creates a single malicious model (M) with access to parameters, gradients, and training data of all the f clients. M serves as a proxy for f clients and aims towards pushing the output of the global model away from the distribution of the ground truth labels.

To be specific, the malicious model (M) is trained to generate malicious parameters or gradients by minimizing the loss $L_{model} = -L_{class}$ as opposed to benign clients where the loss given by $L_{model} = L_{class}$ is minimized. Here L_{class} refers to cross-entropy loss. Once the malicious parameters (or gradients) are computed, M forwards these malicious values to all the f clients, which then transmit these values to the global model. Note that all the f clients receive the same malicious parameters (or gradients) from M. Our work leverages the shortcomings of robust federated learning aggregation algorithms such as KRUM [3] and DOS [1], which are based on the assumption that malicious parameters or gradients are significantly different from the parameters or gradients of benign clients in euclidean space respectively. Therefore, to reduce the defense capabilities of these aggregation algorithms, it is essential to perturb the parameters (or gradients) so that their Euclidean distance from benign clients' parameters (or gradients) does not become significant. This can be ensured if the Euclidean distance between the malicious parameters (or gradients) and the mean of benign clients' parameters (or gradients) remains bounded. Due to the normal distribution of data, it is safe to assume that the mean of parameters (or gradients) of clients controlled by the attacker is closer to the mean of benign clients parameters (or gradients) respectively in the Euclidean space [2].

The local model poisoning attack can be introduced on model parameters or gradients [1,2]. However, the critical difference between parameters and gradients is that gradients have direction and magnitude, whereas parameters only have magnitude. Hence, we propose different attacks on parameters and gradients. Details on the strategy for attacking parameters or the gradients are provided in Sect. 3.1 and Sect. 3.2, respectively. The attacker initially chooses the clients it wants to attack and accumulates the chosen clients' model parameters, gradients, and training data. Subsequently, the attacker computes the mean of chosen (attacked) clients' model parameters (μ^{param}) and gradients (μ^{grad}) and initializes a new malicious model M with these mean values.

$$\mu^{param} = \frac{1}{f} \sum_{i=1}^{f} W_i^{mal} \qquad \mu^{grad} = \frac{1}{f} \sum_{i=1}^{f} Grad_i^{mal}$$

Here, W_i^{mal} and $Grad_i^{mal}$ refer to the model parameters or gradients of the ith malicious client respectively.

3.1   DISBELIEVE Attack on Parameters

The initialized malicious model, M, is trained on the accumulated training data for minimizing the loss function $L_{model} = -L_{class}$ until the Euclidean distance between the malicious model's (M) parameters and the mean values is less than the maximum distance between any two attacked client's parameters.

$$||W_{model}^{mal} - \mu^{param}||_2^2 \leq P_{dist} \quad where, \quad P_{dist} = Max_{i,k \in f \ i \neq k}||W_i^{mal} - W_k^{mal}||_2^2$$

Here, W_{model}^{mal} refers to the malicious parameters after training of the malicious model M, and P_{dist} refers to a threshold. The threshold P_{dist} is critical to ensure a successful attack as it controls how far the malicious parameters can be from the mean of parameters in Euclidean space. Through the proposed attack, we suggest setting this value to the maximum Euclidean distance between any two malicious client parameters. Intuitively this is a reliable value within an upper bound on the malicious parameters by which they can deviate within a fixed bounded Euclidean space around the mean (see Fig. 1a). The pseudo-code for the attack is given in Algorithm 1.

3.2   DISBELIEVE Attack on Gradients

For attacking gradients, as described in Algorithm 2, we train the malicious model M with the similar loss function, $Loss = -Loss_{class}$, however, without any thresholding. Once the model M is trained, we accumulate the malicious gradients ($Grads_{model}^{mal}$) and scale them by a scaling factor sf to make sure that their distance from the mean of gradients of malicious clients (μ^{grad}) is smaller than the minimum distance between any two malicious client's gradients (G_{dist}) (see Fig. 1b).

$$G_{dist} = Min_{i,k \in f \ i \neq k}||Grads_i^{mal} - Grads_k^{mal}||_2^2$$

304 I. Joshi et al.

To find the optimum scaling factor (sf), we use a popular search algorithm known as binary search [19]. We initialize a start value of 0.001 and an end value of 1000. An optimal sf is computed using the divide and conquer binary search algorithm in between these values, which makes sure that after scaling the unit gradient vector, its distance to the mean of gradients (μ^{grad}) is less than G_{dist}

$$||sf * \frac{Grads^{mal}_{model}}{||Grads^{mal}_{model}||} - \mu^{grad}||^2_2 \leq G_{dist}$$

For calculating gradients, the minimum distance (G_{dist}) is preferred over the maximum distance (P_{dist}) when attacking parameters. This preference arises because maximizing the objective loss function results in gradients pointing in the opposite direction compared to the direction of benign gradients. By using the minimum distance, we can prevent malicious gradients from becoming outliers.

4 Experiments

4.1 Datasets

CheXpert-Small: CheXpert [10] is a large publicly available dataset containing over 200,000 chest X-ray images for 65,240 patients. However, consistent with the experimental protocol used by state-of-the-art DOS [1], we use the smaller version of CheXpert, also known as CheXpert-small, that contains 191,456 X-Ray images of the chest. The dataset contains 13 pathological categories. A single observation from the dataset can have multiple pathological labels. Each sample's pathological label is classified as either negative or positive. Consistent with the state-of-the-art aggregation method DOS [1], we preprocess all the images by rescaling them to 224×224 pixels using the torchxrayvision library.

Ham10000: Ham10000 [24] or HAM10k is a publicly available benchmark dataset containing dermatoscopic images of common pigmented skin lesions. It is a multi-class dataset with seven diagnostic categories and 10000 image samples. As suggested in [1], we use this dataset to evaluate the model performance in non-iid settings where each image is resized to 128×128.

Breakhis: The breakhis dataset [22] is a public breast cancer histopathological database that contains microscopic images of breast cancer tissues. The dataset contains 9109 images from 82 different patients. The images are available in magnifying scales such as 40X, 100X, 200X, and 400X. Each image is a 700 × 460 pixels sized image, and we rescale each image to 32 × 32 for our classification task. We use this dataset for binary classification of 400X magnified microscopic images where we classify cancer present in images as either benign or malignant.

CIFAR-10: The Cifar-10 [14] is a popular computer vision dataset that contains 60000 natural images of size 32 × 32. The dataset contains ten classes, and each class has 6000 images. 50000 images are reserved for training, and 10000 images are used for testing.

4.2 Experimental Setup and Implementation Details

The experimental setup used in this research is consistent with the experimental protocols suggested in [1]. Subsequently, we use Chexpert-Small [10] and Ham10k datasets [24] for parameter-based attacks. Likewise, the CheXpert-small dataset is used to train the Resnet-18 [8] model with a batch size of 16 for 40 communication rounds, and the number of local epochs is set to 1, whereas the Ham10k dataset is trained on a custom model with two convolutional layers and three fully connected layers with a batch size of 890 for 120 communication rounds and the number of local epochs were set to 3. For both datasets, the number of clients is fixed at 10, the number of attackers is fixed at 4, and the learning rate is set to 0.01.

For preserving the privacy of clients and their data, federated learning setups usually share gradients instead of model parameters. Hence, we also evaluate our attack for gradient aggregation on the Breakhis [22]. Furthermore, to assess the generalization ability of the proposed DISBELIEVE attack on natural images, we evaluate the proposed DISBELIEVE attack on the CIFAR-10 dataset with a gradient aggregation strategy at the global server. For experiments on Breakhis dataset, VGG-11 [21] model is trained for binary classification. Training occurs for 200 communication rounds with a batch size of 128 and a learning rate 0.0001. For the CIFAR-10 dataset, we use the VGG-11 [21] model with ten output classes

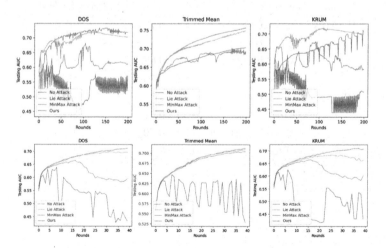

Fig. 2. Performance of different attacks on Ham10k (top-row) and CheXpert (bottom-row) datasets under different parameter aggregation methods. Left to right (in order): AUC scores when attacks are made on DOS, Trimmed Mean and Krum.

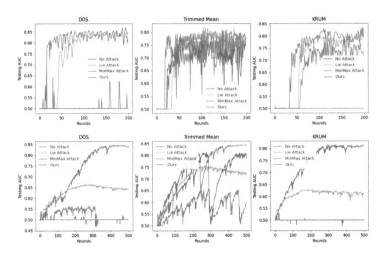

Fig. 3. Performance of different attacks on Breakhis (top-row) and CIFAR-10 (bottom-row) datasets under different gradient aggregation methods. Left to right (in order): AUC scores when attacks are made on DOS, Trimmed Mean and Krum.

for 500 communication rounds with a batch size of 1000 and a learning rate of 0.001. Adam optimizer was used for both datasets. The total number of clients and attackers for both datasets is fixed at 10 and 3, respectively.

Table 1. Area Under the Receiver Operating Characteristic Curve (AUC) scores with different types of poisoning attack on model parameters

Dataset	Attack	DOS	Trimmed Mean	KRUM
Ham10k	No Attack	0.72	0.75	0.70
	LIE Attack	0.70	0.74	0.70
	Min-Max Attack	0.61	0.68	0.58
	Ours	0.52	0.70	0.51
CheXpert	No Attack	0.71	0.71	0.70
	LIE Attack	0.69	0.71	0.65
	Min-Max Attack	0.59	0.70	0.59
	Ours	0.44	0.52	0.43

Table 2. Area Under the Receiver Operating Characteristic Curve (AUC) scores with different types of poisoning attack on model gradients

Dataset	Attack	DOS	Trimmed Mean	KRUM
Breakhis	No Attack	0.81	0.78	0.83
	LIE Attack	0.84	0.77	0.79
	Min-Max Attack	0.50	0.74	0.72
	Ours	0.50	0.75	0.50
CIFAR-10	No Attack	0.83	0.84	0.81
	LIE Attack	0.64	0.71	0.60
	Min-Max Attack	0.50	0.60	0.50
	Ours	0.50	0.78	0.50

5   Results and Discussions

5.1   Baselines

The DISBELIEVE attack is evaluated against three state-of-the-art defense methods: DOS [1], Trimmed Mean [26], and KRUM [3]. Comparisons are also made with prominent attacks, including LIE [2] and Min-Max [19], under different defense methods. Under any defense, AUC scores are highest in the absence of attacks. The LIE attack slightly reduces AUC scores while remaining relatively weaker due to parameter bounding. Conversely, introducing noise and scaling parameters makes the Min-Max attack more potent, consistently reducing AUC scores more significantly across various aggregation methods.

5.2   Vulnerability of State-of-the-Art Defense Methods

The proposed DISBELIEVE attack reveals the vulnerability of the current state-of-the-art robust aggregation algorithms (Trimmed Mean [26], KRUM [3], and DOS [1]) over local model poisoning attacks. We empirically validate that our proposed local model poisoning attack (DISBELIEVE attack) can successfully circumvent all three state-of-the-art robust aggregation algorithms (refer Figs. 2, 3). For both parameters and gradient aggregation, DISBELIEVE attack consistently reduces the global model's area under the curve (AUC) scores on all three benchmark medical image datasets. Furthermore, to assess the effectiveness of the proposed DISBELIEVE attack on natural images apart from the specialized medical images, we additionally conduct DISBELIEVE attack on a popular computer vision dataset, CIFAR-10. For natural images, we also find (refer Fig. 3) that the DISBELIEVE attack reduces the global model's AUC score for different state-of-the-art aggregation algorithms DOS, Trimmed Mean, and KRUM. Tables 1 and 2 show that when subjected to DISBELIEVE attack, the AUC scores fall drastically for all datasets compared to the AUC scores in case of no attack. Therefore, these results demonstrate the vulnerability of state-of-the-art robust aggregation methods to the proposed local model poisoning attack.

5.3   Superiority of DISBELIEVE Attack over State-of-the-art Local Model Poisoning Attacks

The state-of-the-art robust aggregation algorithm for medical images DOS is only evaluated against additive Gaussian noise, scaled parameter attacks, and label flipping attacks. We additionally benchmark the performance of two state-of-the-art model poisoning attacks, namely Min-Max [19] and LIE [2] on all the three medical image datasets (refer Figs. 2 and 3). Results establish the superiority of the proposed DISBELIEVE attack over state-of-the-art model poisoning attacks on different medical image datasets. While using DOS and KRUM aggregation, the DISBELIEVE attack reduces the global model's AUC score by a more significant margin than both Min-Max and LIE for all the datasets. In the case of trimmed mean, the results of DISBELIEVE attack are comparable on Ham10k (parameter aggregation) and Breakhis (gradient aggregation) datasets with the Min-Max attack and better on CheXpert (parameter aggregation) dataset when compared to the Min-Max and LIE attacks. To compare the effectiveness of DISBELIEVE attack with state-of-the-art model poisoning attacks on the natural image dataset (CIFAR-10), we observe that DISBELIEVE attack performs better than LIE and Min-Max on DOS and KRUM defenses. Tables 1 and 2 compare state-of-the-art model poisoning attacks and the proposed DISBELIEVE attack under different state-of-the-art robust aggregation algorithms for parameter and gradient aggregation, respectively.

6   Conclusion and Future Work

This research highlights the vulnerability of state-of-the-art robust aggregation methods for federated learning on medical images. Results obtained on three public medical datasets reveal that distance-based defenses fail once the attack is designed to ensure that the distance between malicious clients and honest clients' parameters or gradients is bounded by the maximum or minimum distance between parameters or gradients of any two attacked clients, respectively. Moreover, we also demonstrate that the proposed DISBELIEVE attack proves its efficacy on natural images besides domain-specific medical images. In the future, we plan to design a robust aggregation algorithm for federated learning in medical images that can withstand the proposed local model poisoning attack.

Acknowledgment. This work was done as a part of the IMI BigPicture project (IMI945358).

References

1. Alkhunaizi, N., Kamzolov, D., Takáč, M., Nandakumar, K.: Suppressing poisoning attacks on federated learning for medical imaging. In: Wang, L., Dou, Q., Fletcher, P.T., Speidel, S., Li, S. (eds.) Medical Image Computing and Computer Assisted Intervention-MICCAI 2022: 25th International Conference, Singapore, September 18–22, 2022, Proceedings, Part VIII, vol. 13438, pp. 673–683. Springer (2022). https://doi.org/10.1007/978-3-031-16452-1_64

2. Baruch, M., Baruch, G., Goldberg, Y.: A little is enough: circumventing defenses for distributed learning (2019)
3. Blanchard, P., El Mhamdi, E.M., Guerraoui, R., Stainer, J.: Machine learning with adversaries: byzantine tolerant gradient descent. In: Guyon, I., et al. (eds.) Advances in Neural Information Processing Systems, vol. 30. Curran Associates, Inc. (2017)
4. Blanchard, P., Mhamdi, E.M.E., Guerraoui, R., Stainer, J.: Byzantine-tolerant machine learning (2017)
5. Chen, Y., Gui, Y., Lin, H., Gan, W., Wu, Y.: Federated learning attacks and defenses: a survey (2022)
6. Dayan, I., et al.: Federated learning for predicting clinical outcomes in patients with COVID-19. Nat. Med. **27**(10), 1735–1743 (2021)
7. Goodfellow, I.J., et al.: Generative adversarial networks (2014)
8. He, K., Zhang, X., Ren, S., Sun, J.: Deep residual learning for image recognition (2015)
9. Hitaj, B., Ateniese, G., Perez-Cruz, F.: Deep models under the GAN: information leakage from collaborative deep learning (2017)
10. Irvin, J., et al.: CheXpert: a large chest radiograph dataset with uncertainty labels and expert comparison (2019)
11. Jere, M.S., Farnan, T., Koushanfar, F.: A taxonomy of attacks on federated learning. IEEE Secur. Priv. **19**(2), 20–28 (2021). https://doi.org/10.1109/MSEC.2020.3039941
12. Joshi, I., Kumar, S., Figueiredo, I.N.: Bag of visual words approach for bleeding detection in wireless capsule endoscopy images. In: Campilho, A., Karray, F. (eds.) Image Analysis and Recognition, pp. 575–582. Springer, Cham (2016)
13. Joshi, I., Mondal, A.K., Navab, N.: Chromosome cluster type identification using a Swin transformer. Appl. Sci. **13**(14), 8007 (2023). https://doi.org/10.3390/app13148007, https://www.mdpi.com/2076-3417/13/14/8007
14. Krizhevsky, A., et al.: Learning multiple layers of features from tiny images (2009)
15. Li, Z., Zhao, Y., Botta, N., Ionescu, C., Hu, X.: COPOD: Copula-based outlier detection. In: 2020 IEEE International Conference on Data Mining (ICDM). IEEE (2020). https://doi.org/10.1109/icdm50108.2020.00135
16. Lyu, L., Yu, H., Yang, Q.: Threats to federated learning: a survey (2020)
17. Lyu, L., Yu, H., Zhao, J., Yang, Q.: Threats to Federated Learning, pp. 3–16 (2020)
18. McMahan, H.B., Moore, E., Ramage, D., Hampson, S., Arcas, B.A.: Communication-efficient learning of deep networks from decentralized data (2023)
19. Shejwalkar, V., Houmansadr, A.: Manipulating the byzantine: optimizing model poisoning attacks and defenses for federated learning. In: NDSS (2021)
20. Sheller, M.J., et al.: Federated learning in medicine: facilitating multi-institutional collaborations without sharing patient data. Sci. Rep. **10**(1), 1–12 (2020)
21. Simonyan, K., Zisserman, A.: Very deep convolutional networks for large-scale image recognition (2015)
22. Spanhol, F.A., Oliveira, L.S., Petitjean, C., Heutte, L.: A dataset for breast cancer histopathological image classification. IEEE Trans. Biomed. Eng. **63**(7), 1455–1462 (2016). https://doi.org/10.1109/TBME.2015.2496264
23. Tolpegin, V., Truex, S., Gursoy, M.E., Liu, L.: Data poisoning attacks against federated learning systems. In: Chen, L., Li, N., Liang, K., Schneider, S. (eds.) Computer Security - ESORICS 2020, pp. 480–501. Springer, Cham (2020)
24. Tschandl, P., Rosendahl, C., Kittler, H.: The HAM10000 dataset, a large collection of multi-source dermatoscopic images of common pigmented skin lesions. Sci. Data **5**(1) (2018). https://doi.org/10.1038/sdata.2018.161, https://doi.org/10.1038

25. Xie, C., Koyejo, O., Gupta, I.: Generalized byzantine-tolerant SGD (2018)
26. Yin, D., Chen, Y., Ramchandran, K., Bartlett, P.: Byzantine-robust distributed learning: towards optimal statistical rates (2021)

ConDistFL: Conditional Distillation for Federated Learning from Partially Annotated Data

Pochuan Wang[1], Chen Shen[2], Weichung Wang[1], Masahiro Oda[2], Chiou-Shann Fuh[1], Kensaku Mori[2], and Holger R. Roth[3(✉)]

[1] National Taiwan University, Taipei City, Taiwan
[2] Nagoya University, Nagoya, Japan
[3] NVIDIA Corporation, Santa Clara, USA
hroth@nvidia.com

Abstract. Developing a generalized segmentation model capable of simultaneously delineating multiple organs and diseases is highly desirable. Federated learning (FL) is a key technology enabling the collaborative development of a model without exchanging training data. However, the limited access to fully annotated training data poses a major challenge to training generalizable models. We propose "ConDistFL", a framework to solve this problem by combining FL with knowledge distillation. Local models can extract the knowledge of unlabeled organs and tumors from partially annotated data from the global model with an adequately designed conditional probability representation. We validate our framework on four distinct partially annotated abdominal CT datasets from the MSD and KiTS19 challenges. The experimental results show that the proposed framework significantly outperforms FedAvg and FedOpt baselines. Moreover, the performance on an external test dataset demonstrates superior generalizability compared to models trained on each dataset separately. Our ablation study suggests that ConDistFL can perform well without frequent aggregation, reducing the communication cost of FL. Our implementation will be available at https://github.com/NVIDIA/NVFlare/tree/main/research/condist-fl.

Keywords: Federated learning · Partially labeled datasets · Multi-organ and tumor segmentation · Abdominal CT

1 Introduction

Accurately segmenting abdominal organs and malignancies from computed tomography (CT) scans is crucial for clinical applications such as computer-aided diagnosis and therapy planning. While significant research has focused on segmenting individual organs [1,7] and multiple classes of organs without malignancies [4,6], a generalized model capable of handling multiple organs and diseases simultaneously is desirable in real-world healthcare scenarios. Traditional supervised learning methods, on the other hand, rely on the amount and quality of the training data. Regrettably, the cost of high-quality medical image data contributed to a paucity of training data. For many anatomies, only trained professionals can produce accurate annotations on medical images. On top of this, even experts often only have specialized knowledge for a specific task, making it challenging to annotate the organs and corresponding malignancies of various anatomies and imaging modalities.

The lack of sufficient annotated datasets for multiple organs and tumors poses a significant challenge in developing generalized segmentation models. To address this issue, several studies have explored partially annotated datasets, where only a subset of targeted organs and malignancies are annotated in each image, to build generalized segmentation models [5,10,11,21,23]. However, sharing private medical datasets among institutions raises privacy and regulatory concerns. To overcome these challenges, federated learning (FL) was introduced [16]. FL enables collaborative training of a shared (or "global") model across multiple institutions without centralizing the data in one location.

FL has emerged as a promising technology to enhance the efficiency of medical image segmentation [19,24,25]. In FL, each client trains a local model using its data and resources while only sending model updates to the server. The server then combines these updates into a global model using "FedAvg" [16]. Recent studies have utilized FL to develop unified multi-organ segmentation models using partially annotated abdominal datasets [15,26] as illustrated in Fig. 1. However, these approaches often neglect lesion areas. Only a few studies attempt to generate to segment the various organs and their cancers simultaneously [20,29]. The model aggregation in FL is a major hurdle because of the data heterogeneity problem brought on by data diversity [30]. Merging models from different sources with non-IID data can lead to performance degradation. This issue is further exacerbated when clients use data annotated for different tasks, introducing more domain shifts in the label space. Additionally, unbalanced dataset sizes among clients may affect the global model's performance on tasks with limited data.

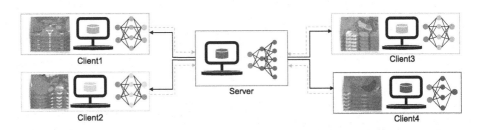

Fig. 1. An illustration of the ConDistFL framework for multi-organ and tumor segmentation from partial labels. Each client has only a subset of the targeted organs and malignancies annotated in their local datasets.

In this work, we suggest a framework to tackle data heterogeneity in FL for multi-class organ and tumor segmentation from partially annotated abdominal CT images. The main contributions of this work are as follows:

1. Our proposed conditional distillation federated learning (ConDistFL) framework enables joint multi-task segmentation of abdominal organs and malignancies without additional fully annotated datasets.
2. The proposed framework exhibits stability and performance with long local training steps and a limited number of aggregations, reducing data traffic and training time in real-world FL scenarios.
3. We further validate our models on an unseen fully annotated public dataset AMOS22 [13]. The robustness of our approach is supported by both the qualitative and quantitative evaluation results.

2   Method

ConDistFL extends the horizontal FL paradigm [27] to handle partially annotated datasets distributed across clients. An illustration of our ConDistFL framework for multi-organ and tumor segmentation from partial labels is shown in Fig. 1. In the client training of ConDistFL, we combine supervised learning on ground truth labels and knowledge distillation learning [9] using the global model's predictions. During supervised learning, we adopt the design of marginal loss [21] to avoid knowledge conflicts caused by missing labels. To improve the knowledge distillation in FL settings, we proposed a conditional distillation loss to maximize the agreement between the global model and local model predictions on unlabeled voxels.

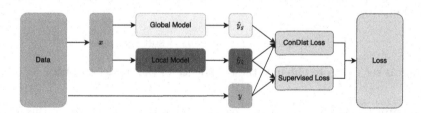

Fig. 2. ConDistFL data flow diagram for client k; x is a batch of image patches from the local dataset; y is the corresponding label; $\hat{y}_g$ is the output of global model; and $\hat{y}_k$ is the output of the local model.

2.1   Conditional Distillation for Federated Learning

In ConDistFL, the client keeps the latest global model as the teacher model for knowledge distillation and uses the local model as the student model. Figure 2 illustrates the training data flow in client k and the relationship between the global, local, and loss functions.

2.2   Supervised Loss

We adopt the design of marginal loss [21] for the supervised loss $\mathcal{L}_{sup}$. Let N be the total number of classes across all datasets, F_k be a collection of foreground classes on client k, B_k be the background class, and all unlabeled classes on client k, and $\hat{y}_{k,i}$ be the output logits of client k's model for class i. By applying softmax normalization on the output logits $\hat{y}_{k,i}$ for each $i \in N$, we can derive the output probability $\hat{p}_{k,i}$ for each class i as

$$\hat{p}_{k,i} = \frac{e^{\hat{y}_{k,i}}}{\sum_{j=0}^{N} e^{\hat{y}_{k,j}}} \text{ for } i = 0, \ 1, \ 2, \ \ldots, \ N-1. \tag{1}$$

Similar to the marginal loss, all probabilities in the background B_k are merged into one for a new non-foreground class. The probabilities remain the same as $\hat{p}_{k,i}$ for all $i \in F_k$. Then we apply Dice loss [17] with cross-entropy loss [28] (DiceCELoss) for supervised learning of the segmentation model. The final loss term $\mathcal{L}_{sup}$ is defined as

$$\mathcal{L}_{sup} = \text{DiceCELoss}(\hat{p}'_k, y'), \tag{2}$$

where the background merged probability is $\hat{p}'_k$, and the corresponding one-hot label is y'.

2.3   ConDist Loss

For the conditional distillation (ConDist) loss $\mathcal{L}_{ConDist}$, we normalize the output logits of both the global and the local model using softmax with temperature τ. The normalized logits from the global model $\hat{p}_g^\tau$ and the k-th client's local model $\hat{p}_k^\tau$ is defined as

$$\hat{p}_k^\tau = \text{softmax}(\hat{y}_k/\tau) \quad \text{and} \quad \hat{p}_g^\tau = \text{softmax}(\hat{y}_g/\tau), \tag{3}$$

where τ is set to 0.5 to enhance the confidence of the model output.

Foreground Merging and Background Grouping. Contrary to the supervised loss, we merge the probabilities for class i for all $i \in F_k$ in $\hat{p}_k^\tau$ and $\hat{p}_g^\tau$. Then we define

$$\hat{p}_{k,F_k} = \sum_{i \in F_k} \hat{p}_{k,i}^\tau \quad \text{and} \quad \hat{p}_{g,F_k} = \sum_{i \in F_k} \hat{p}_{g,i}^\tau, \tag{4}$$

where the $\hat{p}_{k,i}^\tau$ and $\hat{p}_{g,i}^\tau$ are the probabilities for class i in $\hat{p}_k^\tau$ and $\hat{p}_g^\tau$, respectively. Moreover, we group the background classes in client k by the organs in the background B_k. Let M_k be the number of unlabeled organs in client k, and $\mathcal{O}_k = \{G_0, G_1, G_2, \ldots G_{M_k}\}$. G_0 is the set containing the global background class. The probability for each background group can be calculated as

$$\hat{p}_{k,G_i} = \sum_{j \in G_i} \hat{p}^\tau_{k,j} \quad \text{and} \quad \hat{p}_{g,G_i} = \sum_{j \in G_i} \hat{p}^\tau_{g,j} \quad \text{for} \quad i = 0, 1, \ldots, M_k, \quad (5)$$

where G_i is a set containing the class of the healthy part of unlabeled organ i and all the classes of associated lesions to the organ i.

Conditional Probability for Background Organs. We define conditional probabilities $\hat{p}_{k,\mathcal{O}_k|B_k}$ and $\hat{p}_{g,\mathcal{O}_k|B_k}$ as

$$\hat{p}_{k,\mathcal{O}_k|B_k} = \left(\frac{\hat{p}_{k,G_0}}{1 - \hat{p}_{k,F_k}}, \frac{\hat{p}_{k,G_1}}{1 - \hat{p}_{k,F_k}}, \ldots, \frac{\hat{p}_{k,G_{M_k}}}{1 - \hat{p}_{k,F_k}} \right), \quad (6)$$

$$\hat{p}_{g,\mathcal{O}_k|B_k} = \left(\frac{\hat{p}_{g,G_0}}{1 - \hat{p}_{g,F_k}}, \frac{\hat{p}_{g,G_1}}{1 - \hat{p}_{g,F_k}}, \ldots, \frac{\hat{p}_{g,G_{M_k}}}{1 - \hat{p}_{g,F_k}} \right), \quad (7)$$

where $1 - \hat{p}_{k,F_k}$ and $1 - \hat{p}_{g,F_k}$ are the total probabilities of all classes in B_k with respect to $\hat{p}^\tau_k$ and $\hat{p}^\tau_g$. The conditional probability $\hat{p}_{k,\mathcal{O}_k|B_k}$ and $\hat{p}_{g,\mathcal{O}_k|B_k}$ are the probabilities given that the prediction is only in B_k.

Foreground Filtering. To avoid learning from incorrect predictions and reduce the potential conflict with the supervised loss, we filter off undesired voxels with a mask operation $\mathcal{M}$, which removes the union of foreground area in ground truth label y and all the area in $\hat{y}_g$ where the predictions are in F_k.

Segmentation ConDist Loss. Combining the conditional probability $\hat{p}_{k,\mathcal{O}_k|B_k}$, $\hat{p}_{g,\mathcal{O}_k|B_k}$, and the foreground filtering mask $\mathcal{M}$, we define the ConDist loss $\mathcal{L}_{ConDist}$ for segmentation task by applying soft Dice loss as

$$\mathcal{L}_{ConDist} = DiceLoss(\mathcal{M}(\hat{p}_{k,\mathcal{O}_k|B_k}), \mathcal{M}(\hat{p}_{g,\mathcal{O}_k|B_k})). \quad (8)$$

To handle meaningless global model predictions in the initial FL rounds, we incorporate an adjustable weight w for the ConDist loss, gradually increasing it as the FL round number increments. The total loss $\mathcal{L}$ for ConDistFL is defined as

$$\mathcal{L} = \mathcal{L}_{sup} + w * \mathcal{L}_{ConDist}. \quad (9)$$

In practice, we schedule the weight w from 0.01 to 1.0 linearly.

3   Experiments

We conducted our experiments on the Medical Segmentation Decathlon (MSD) [22] and the KiTS19 Challenge [8] datasets. In the MSD dataset, we only used the liver, pancreas, and spleen subsets. Except for the spleen dataset, each above dataset includes annotations for the organs and tumors. We split the dataset into training, validation, and testing subsets by 60%, 20%, and 20%, respectively. For the non-FL standalone training, each model only uses a single dataset. For FL training, we distributed the four datasets to four independent clients. In addition, we evaluated our models on the multi-modality Abdominal Multi-Organ Segmentation Challenge 2022 (AMOS22) dataset [13], which consists of 300 CT volumes with 15 abdominal organ annotations. To accommodate the labeling format of AMOS22, where healthy organs and lesions are not distinguished, we merged the tumor predictions with associated organs from our model output before computing the metrics using ground truth labels.

The nnU-Net [12] data preprocessing pipeline was adopted with minor modifications. We first resampled the images to a median spacing of $[1.44, 1.44, 2.87]$ millimeters and clipped the intensity to the range $[-54, 258]$. Then we applied z-score normalization by assuming the mean intensity under ROI to be 100 and its standard deviation to be 50 since the complete multi-organ ROI is unavailable. We set the input patch size to $[224, 224, 64]$ and the training batch size to 4.

Our neural network backbone was built using the 3D DynU-Net from MONAI [3], an effective and flexible U-Net implementation. Deep supervision was also enabled to speed up the training process and enhance model performance. The deep supervision loss is identical to the supervised loss with an extra exponential weight decay. We trained our models using stochastic gradient descent (SGD) and cosine annealing schedule. The initial learning rate was set to 10^{-2} and decreased gradually to 10^{-7}.

The loss function for the non-FL standalone baselines is Dice loss with cross-entropy. For the FL experiments, we evaluated FedAvg [16], FedOpt [2], Fed-Prox [14], and ConDistFL. To assess the effectiveness of the marginal loss in Sect. 2.2, we trained two sets of FedAvg models: one using the standard Dice loss and the other employing the marginal loss. The FedProx model was trained with the FedAvg aggregator and $\mu = 0.01$. For FedOpt and ConDistFL, we utilized the Federated Optimization (FedOpt) aggregation method, with an additional SGD optimizer with momentum $m = 0.6$ implemented on the server.

We employed a single NVIDIA V100 GPU for each standalone experiment and FL client. The FL experiments were implemented using NVIDIA FLARE [18].

4   Results and Discussion

Our experiments encompass standalone baselines using a single dataset, an ablation study of standard Dice loss on FedAvg (FedAvg*), marginal loss on FedAvg, FedProx, and FedOpt, and the combined marginal loss and ConDist loss on ConDistFL. To establish a fair comparison between related works, we trained a ConDistFL (Union) model with the same learning targets as [15,26], i.e., only to segment the union of the organs and tumors. Additionally, we evaluated the proposed method on the unseen AMOS22 dataset to demonstrate its generalizability.

Table 1 compares the average Dice score of each task between standalone baseline models and the best performance server models for FedAvg, FedProx, FedOpt, and ConDistFL. All the models are trained for a total of 120, 000 steps to allow for a fair comparison. For the best FedAvg*, FedAvg, and ConDistFL models, we utilized 60 FL aggregation rounds with 2000 local steps per round. As for the FedProx and FedOpt best model, we conducted 120 FL rounds and 1000 local steps per round.

The results of FedAvg* and FedAvg demonstrate that the marginal loss effectively resolves conflicts between inconsistent labels and yields reasonable performance. ConDistFL stands out as the top-performing method among all experiments utilizing the marginal loss. FedAvg, FedProx, and FedOpt show similar performance overall, with FedAvg and FedOpt delivering acceptable results for most tasks, except for the pancreas and tumor. In contrast, FedProx performs well for the pancreas and tumor, but there is a notable drop in performance on other tasks. This suggests that although the FedProx loss can regularize the models for heterogeneous clients like the proposed ConDist loss, its task-agnostic nature harms the performance when training on multiple tasks with different partial labels.

Table 1. Comparison between non-FL results and each FL result. The average Dice score of each organ for the standalone model is computed separately from four distinct models. FedAvg* indicates the model trained with FedAvg and standard Dice loss.

	Kidney	Tumor	Liver	Tumor	Pancreas	Tumor	Spleen	Average
Standalone	0.9563	0.8117	0.9525	0.7071	0.7974	0.5012	0.9632	0.8102
FedAvg*	0.7707	0.4894	0.4937	0.3202	0.5403	0.1396	0.0000	0.3934
FedAvg	0.9419	0.6690	0.9381	0.6500	0.6933	0.2985	0.9059	0.7281
FedProx	0.9247	0.6799	0.8972	0.6244	0.7419	**0.4033**	0.7060	0.7111
FedOpt	0.9473	0.7212	0.9386	0.6087	0.6734	0.2390	0.9394	0.7239
ConDistFL	**0.9477**	**0.7333**	**0.9446**	**0.6944**	**0.7478**	0.3660	**0.9562**	**0.7700**

The ablation study in Fig. 3 investigates the impact of the number of local training steps on the global model performance. Increasing the number of local training steps from 100 to 1000 for all tested methods improved performance. However, when more local training steps were used, both FedAvg and FedOpt encountered model divergence issues, with FedAvg experiencing a more significant performance drop than FedOpt. In contrast, ConDistFL consistently delivered better performance across different local step experiments. This can be attributed to ConDistFL providing a common task, preventing model divergence in FL, and the inherent complexity of tumor segmentation requiring more local training steps. By maintaining consistent representations of unknown classes, ConDistFL allows for the use of larger local step sizes to learn the tumor segmentation task effectively.

Table 2 compares the average Dice scores of standalone baselines, ConDistFL, and ConDistFL (Union) on the unseen AMOS22 dataset. ConDistFL demon-

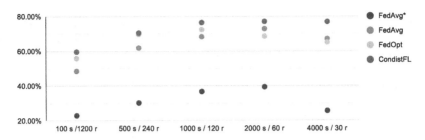

Fig. 3. The ablation study results on the test set. The x-axis is the number of local training steps (s) and rounds numbers (r), while the y-axis is the average Dice score of all organs and tumors.

strates significant generalizability improvements over the standalone baselines, while ConDistFL (Union) further enhances performance. This highlights the challenge of segmenting tumors and organs together compared to considering them a single class.

Table 2. External test results for AMOS22 dataset in average Dice scores.

	Kidney	Liver	Pancreas	Spleen	Average
Standalone	0.5916	0.9419	0.5944	0.8388	0.7417
FedAvg	0.5032	0.8718	0.4637	0.5768	0.6039
FedProx	0.4698	0.6994	0.5185	0.7120	0.5999
FedOpt	0.5171	0.6740	0.4113	0.6418	0.5611
ConDistFL	0.7218	0.9191	0.6188	0.8556	0.7788
ConDistFL (Union)	**0.8746**	**0.9471**	**0.7401**	**0.9079**	**0.8674**

Table 3 compares ConDistFL (Union) and the reported performance of FL PSMOS and MENU-Net on the MSD test set. FL PSMOS utilizes a fully annotated dataset for model pre-training, while MENU-Net introduces a fifth client with a fully annotated dataset. The results demonstrate that ConDistFL achieves comparable performance without needing fully annotated data. Additionally, ConDistFL significantly reduces the number of aggregation rounds, leading to substantial savings in data traffic and synchronization overheads.

Figure 4 showcases 3D visualizations of our proposed ConDistFL, demonstrating effective and simultaneous segmentation of multiple organs and tumors without ensembling. Compared to FedAvg and FedOpt, ConDistFL achieves smoother and more continuous segmentations. The comparison with the ground truth of AMOS22 validates the generalizability of our FL framework.

Table 3. Comparing the average Dice scores of ConDistFL to reported performance of related works. "Rounds" is the number of FL aggregation rounds.

	Rounds	Kidney	Liver	Pancreas	Spleen	Average
FL PSMOS [15]	2,000	**0.966**	0.938	0.788	**0.965**	0.9143
MENU-Net [26]	400	0.9594	0.9407	0.8005	0.9465	0.9118
ConDistFL (Union)	120	0.9657	**0.9619**	**0.8210**	0.9626	**0.9278**

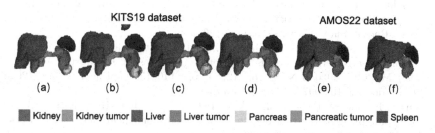

Fig. 4. 3D renderings of segmentation on the best performed FL server model using (a) FedAvg, (b) FedOpt, (c) FedProx, (d) ConDistFL on KITS19 data, and (e) ground truth and (f) the external segmentation using ConDistFL on AMOS22 data.

5   Conclusion

This work offers a promising FL approach for generalized segmentation models from partially annotated abdominal organs and tumors, reducing annotation costs and speeding up model development. Moreover, the proposed method requires less frequent aggregation, making it suitable for real-world FL scenarios with limited communication bandwidth.

References

1. Altini, N., et al.: Liver, kidney and spleen segmentation from CT scans and MRI with deep learning: a survey. Neurocomputing **490**, 30–53 (2022)
2. Asad, M., Moustafa, A., Ito, T.: FedOpt: towards communication efficiency and privacy preservation in federated learning. Appl. Sci. **10**(8), 2864 (2020)
3. Cardoso, M.J., et al.: MONAI: an open-source framework for deep learning in healthcare. arXiv preprint arXiv:2211.02701 (2022)
4. Cerrolaza, J.J., et al.: Computational anatomy for multi-organ analysis in medical imaging: a review. Med. Image Anal.**56**, 44–67 (2019). https://doi.org/10.1016/j.media.2019.04.002, https://linkinghub.elsevier.com/retrieve/pii/S1361841518306273
5. Fang, X., Yan, P.: Multi-organ segmentation over partially labeled datasets with multi-scale feature abstraction. IEEE Trans. Med. Imaging **39**(11), 3619–3629 (2020)
6. Fu, Y., Lei, Y., Wang, T., Curran, W.J., Liu, T., Yang, X.: A review of deep learning based methods for medical image multi-organ segmentation. Physica Med. **85**, 107–122 (2021)

7. Gul, S., Khan, M.S., Bibi, A., Khandakar, A., Ayari, M.A., Chowdhury, M.E.: Deep learning techniques for liver and liver tumor segmentation: a review. Comput. Biol. Med. **157**, 105620 (2022)

8. Heller, N., et al.: The KiTs19 challenge data: 300 kidney tumor cases with clinical context, CT semantic segmentations, and surgical outcomes. https://doi.org/10.48550/ARXIV.1904.00445, https://arxiv.org/abs/1904.00445 (2019)

9. Hinton, G., Vinyals, O., Dean, J.: Distilling the knowledge in a neural network (2015)

10. Hongdong, M., et al.: Multi-scale organs image segmentation method improved by squeeze-and-attention based on partially supervised learning. Int. J. Comput. Assist. Radiol. Surg. **17**(6), 1135–1142 (2022)

11. Huang, R., Zheng, Y., Hu, Z., Zhang, S., Li, H.: Multi-organ segmentation via co-training weight-averaged models from few-organ datasets. In: Martel, A.L., et al. (eds.) MICCAI 2020. LNCS, vol. 12264, pp. 146–155. Springer, Cham (2020). https://doi.org/10.1007/978-3-030-59719-1_15

12. Isensee, F., Jaeger, P.F., Kohl, S.A.A., Petersen, J., Maier-Hein, K.H.: nnU-Net: a self-configuring method for deep learning-based biomedical image segmentation. Nat. Methods **18**(2), 203–211 (2021)

13. Ji, Y., et al.: AMOS: a large-scale abdominal multi-organ benchmark for versatile medical image segmentation. arXiv preprint arXiv:2206.08023 (2022)

14. Li, T., Sahu, A.K., Zaheer, M., Sanjabi, M., Talwalkar, A., Smith, V.: Federated optimization in heterogeneous networks. Proc. Mach. learn. Syst. **2**, 429–450 (2020)

15. Liu, P., Sun, M., Zhou, S.K.: Multi-site organ segmentation with federated partial supervision and site adaptation (2023). http://arxiv.org/abs/2302.03911

16. McMahan, H.B., Moore, E., Ramage, D., Hampson, S., y Arcas, B.A.: Communication-efficient learning of deep networks from decentralized data. In: AISTATS (2017)

17. Milletari, F., Navab, N., Ahmadi, S.A.: V-Net: fully convolutional neural networks for volumetric medical image segmentation. In: 2016 Fourth International Conference on 3d Vision (3DV), pp. 565–571. IEEE (2016)

18. Roth, H.R., et al.: NVIDIA FLARE: Federated learning from simulation to Real-World. (2022)

19. Sheller, M.J., et al.: Federated learning in medicine: facilitating multi-institutional collaborations without sharing patient data. Sci. Rep. **10**(1), 1–12 (2020)

20. Shen, C., et al.: Joint multi organ and tumor segmentation from partial labels using federated learning. In: Albarqouni, S., et al. Distributed, Collaborative, and Federated Learning, and Affordable AI and Healthcare for Resource Diverse Global Health, pp. 58–67. Springer Nature, Switzerland (2022). https://doi.org/10.1007/978-3-031-18523-6_6

21. Shi, G., Xiao, L., Chen, Y., Kevin Zhou, S.: Marginal loss and exclusion loss for partially supervised multi-organ segmentation (2020)

22. Simpson, A.L., et al.: A large annotated medical image dataset for the development and evaluation of segmentation algorithms. CoRR abs/1902.09063. http://arxiv.org/abs/1902.09063 (2019)

23. Tajbakhsh, N., Jeyaseelan, L., Li, Q., Chiang, J.N., Wu, Z., Ding, X.: Embracing imperfect datasets: a review of deep learning solutions for medical image segmentation. Med. Image Anal. **63**, 101693 (2020)

24. Tajbakhsh, N., Roth, H., Terzopoulos, D., Liang, J.: Guest editorial annotation-efficient deep learning: the holy grail of medical imaging. IEEE Trans. Med. Imaging **40**(10), 2526–2533 (2021)

25. Xu, J., Glicksberg, B.S., Su, C., Walker, P., Bian, J., Wang, F.: Federated learning for healthcare informatics. J. Healthc. Inf. Res. **5**, 1–19 (2021)
26. Xu, X., Yan, P.: Federated multi-organ segmentation with partially labeled data. arXiv preprint arXiv:2206.07156 (2022)
27. Yang, Q., Liu, Y., Chen, T., Tong, Y.: Federated machine learning: concept and applications. ACM Trans. Intell. Syst. Technol. (TIST) **10**(2), 1–19 (2019)
28. Yi-de, M., Qing, L., Zhi-Bai, Q.: Automated image segmentation using improved PCNN model based on cross-entropy. In: Proceedings of 2004 International Symposium on Intelligent Multimedia, Video and Speech Processing, 2004, pp. 743–746. IEEE (2004)
29. Zhang, J., Xie, Y., Xia, Y., Shen, C.: DoDNet: learning to segment multi-organ and tumors from multiple partially labeled datasets. In: Proceedings of the IEEE/CVF Conference on Computer Vision and Pattern Recognition (CVPR), pp. 1195–1204 (2021)
30. Zhao, Y., Li, M., Lai, L., Suda, N., Civin, D., Chandra, V.: Federated learning with Non-IID data. arXiv preprint arXiv:1806.00582 (2018)

Validation of Federated Unlearning on Collaborative Prostate Segmentation

Yann Fraboni[1,2(✉)], Lucia Innocenti[1,3], Michela Antonelli[3], Richard Vidal[2], Laetitia Kameni[2], Sebastien Ourselin[3], and Marco Lorenzi[1]

[1] Epione Research Group, Inria Sophia Antipolis, Université Côte D'Azur, Nice, France
`yann.fraboni@inria.fr`
[2] Accenture Labs, Sophia Antipolis, France
[3] King's College London, School of Biomedical Engineering and Imaging Sciences, London, UK

Abstract. Machine Unlearning (MU) is an emerging discipline studying methods to remove the effect of a data instance on the parameters of a trained model. Federated Unlearning (FU) extends MU to unlearn the contribution of a dataset provided by a client wishing to drop from a federated learning study. Due to the emerging nature of FU, a practical assessment of the effectiveness of the currently available approaches in complex medical imaging tasks has not been studied so far. In this work, we propose the first in-depth study of FU in medical imaging, with a focus on collaborative prostate segmentation from multi-centric MRI dataset. We first verify the unlearning capabilities of a panel of FU methods from the state-of-the-art, including approaches based on model adaptation, differential privacy, and adaptive retraining. For each method, we quantify their unlearning effectiveness and computational cost as compared to the baseline retraining of a model from scratch after client dropout. Our work highlights a new perspective for the practical implementation of data regulations in collaborative medical imaging applications.

Keywords: federated unlearning · segmentation · prostate cancer

1 Introduction

With the emergence of new data regulations [1,2], the storage and processing of sensitive personal data is often subject of strict constraints and restrictions. In particular, the "right to be forgotten" states that personal data must be erased upon request, with subsequent potential implications on machine learning models trained by using this data. Machine Unlearning (MU) is an emerging discipline that studies methods to remove the contribution of a given data instance used to train a machine learning model [3].

M. E. Celebi et al. (Eds.): MICCAI 2023 Workshops, LNCS 14393, pp. 322–333, 2023.
https://doi.org/10.1007/978-3-031-47401-9_31

Motivated by data governance and confidentiality concerns, federated learning (FL) has gained popularity in the last years to allow data owners to collaboratively learn a model without sharing their respective data. FL is particularly suited for Machine Learning applications in domains where data security is critical, such as in healthcare [4,5]. With the current deployments of FL in the real-world, it is of crucial importance to extend MU approaches to *federated unlearning* (FU), to guarantee the unlearning of data instances from clients wishing to opt-out from a collaborative training routine. This is not straightforward, since current MU schemes have been proposed essentially for centralized learning, and cannot be seamlessly applied to the federated one without breaking the data governance and privacy setting of FL. Recent FU methods have been proposed in the machine learning literature [6–9], with their effectiveness being demonstrated on typical machine learning benchmarks [10–12]. Nevertheless, these benchmarks mostly focus on cross-device scenarios, with partitioning based on heuristics which often do not reflect the complex variability of real-world data analysis problems, such as the cross-site image biases and heterogeneity typical of collaborative medical imaging studies. The translation of FU in medical imaging applications requires the investigation of unlearning through the setup of realistic cross-silo benchmarks.

This work provides the first study of the effectiveness of existing FU approaches in a real-world collaborative medical imaging setup, focusing on federated prostate segmentation. To this end, we develop a benchmark composed by large publicly available prostate segmentation dataset, and define a realistic cross-silo FL scenario with heterogeneity depending on acquisition protocol and scanner. We introduce novel criteria to quantitatively compare the FU methods, assessing the 1) utility of the model after unlearning, 2) unlearning capability, and 3) efficiency of the unlearning procedure. Our results identify critical aspects of current unlearning methods, and show that paradigms based on adaptive retraining are the only effective FU approaches from the state-of-the-art.

This manuscript is structured as follows. In Sect. 2, we provide formal definitions for FL and the different existing FU schemes. We also introduce the metrics used to measure the effectiveness of an unlearning scheme. In Sect. 3, we introduce the federated dataset for prostate segmentation used in this work and verify the effectiveness of all the FU schemes.

2   Methodology

After providing in Sect. 2.1 the formalism of FL, we introduce FU in Sect. 2.2. We explain the limitations of MU methods for the federated setting in Sect. 2.3 and detail the existing FU schemes investigated in this paper in Sect. 2.4.

2.1   Federated Learning

FL consists in optimizing the average of local loss functions $\mathcal{L}_i$ across a set I of clients, weighted by their importance p_i such that $\sum_{i \in I} p_i = 1$, i.e.

$$\mathcal{L}(\boldsymbol{\theta}, I) = \sum_{i \in I} p_i \mathcal{L}_i(\boldsymbol{\theta}), \tag{1}$$

where $\boldsymbol{\theta}$ represents the parameters to be optimized. The weight p_i can be interpreted as the importance given by the server to client i in the federated optimization problem which, without loss of generality, can be considered identical for every client, i.e. $p_i = 1/n$ where $n = |I|$. We define $\boldsymbol{\theta}^*$ the parameters minimizing the federated problem (1), i.e. $\boldsymbol{\theta}^* := \arg\min_{\boldsymbol{\theta}} \mathcal{L}(\boldsymbol{\theta}, I)$.

To estimate the global optimum $\boldsymbol{\theta}^*$, FEDAVG [13] is an iterative training strategy based on the aggregation of local model parameters. At each iteration step t, the server sends the current global model parameters $\boldsymbol{\theta}^t$ to the clients. Each client updates the model by minimizing the local cost function $\mathcal{L}_i$ through a fixed amount of SGD initialized with $\boldsymbol{\theta}^t$. Subsequently each client returns the updated local parameters $\boldsymbol{\theta}_i^{t+1}$ to the server. The global model parameters $\boldsymbol{\theta}^{t+1}$ at the iteration step $t+1$ are then estimated as a weighted average, i.e.

$$\boldsymbol{\theta}^{t+1} = \sum_{i \in I} p_i \boldsymbol{\theta}_i^{t+1}. \tag{2}$$

We define $\tilde{\boldsymbol{\theta}}$ the parameters vector obtained after performing FL over T server aggregations, i.e. $\tilde{\boldsymbol{\theta}} = \boldsymbol{\theta}^{T+1}$. When the clients' local loss functions $\mathcal{L}_i$ are convex, [14,15] show that $\tilde{\boldsymbol{\theta}}$ converges to $\boldsymbol{\theta}^*$ as T goes to infinity.

2.2   Federated Unlearning

Removing a client c from the set of clients I modifies the federated problem (1), which becomes $\mathcal{L}(\boldsymbol{\theta}, I \setminus c)$. We define $\boldsymbol{\theta}_{-c}^* = \arg\min_{\boldsymbol{\theta}} \mathcal{L}(\boldsymbol{\theta}, I \setminus c)$ as the optimum of this new optimization problem. An FU scheme can be formalized as a function h taking as input $\tilde{\boldsymbol{\theta}}$, the model trained with every client in I, including c, to return parameters $h(\tilde{\boldsymbol{\theta}}, c)$ ideally equivalent to $\boldsymbol{\theta}_{-c}^*$. In practice, due to the non-convexity and stochasticity characterizing the optimization problems of typical medical imaging tasks, it is challenging to assess the proximity between the model $h(\tilde{\boldsymbol{\theta}}, c)$ and the ideal target $\boldsymbol{\theta}_{-c}^*$ in terms of pre-defined metrics in the parameters space. For this reason, in this work we quantify the quality of FU by introducing a series of criteria motivated by the ideal requirements that an unlearning scheme should satisfy.

To this end, we first notice that the baseline FU approach, here named SCRATCH, achieves unlearning by performing a new FEDAVG training from scratch on the remaining clients $I \setminus c$. We define $\tilde{\boldsymbol{\theta}}_{-c}$ the parameters vectors obtained with SCRATCH which, by construction, provide perfect unlearning of client c. We note however that this procedure wastes the contribution of the other clients which was already available from the training of $\tilde{\boldsymbol{\theta}}$, i.e. the set of parameters $\{\boldsymbol{\theta}_i^t\}_{i \in I \setminus c, t \in \{1,...,T\}}$ gathered during federated optimization. Therefore, an effective FU methods should be more efficient than SCRATCH in optimizing $h(\tilde{\boldsymbol{\theta}}, c)$. These considerations motivate the following criteria to assess the unlearning quality of FU scheme:

- **Utility.** The predictive capability of the model with parameters $h(\tilde{\boldsymbol{\theta}}, c)$ on the testing sets of the available clients $I \setminus c$ should be equal or superior to the one of SCRATCH for the FU scheme considered. This criterion shows that the model resulting from FU maintains high predictive performances on the available clients data.
- **Unlearning.** Unlearning of client c implies the loss of predictive capabilities of the model $h(\tilde{\boldsymbol{\theta}}, c)$ on the training set of this client. If the performance of the model after unlearning is superior to the one of SCRATCH, we deduce that FU was ineffective in removing the information from client c.
- **Time.** The amount of server aggregations needed to complete the unlearning of client c should be inferior to the ones achieved by SCRATCH.

2.3 Machine Unlearning vs Federated Unlearning

Several MU methods have been proposed in the centralized learning setting [3]. Most MU approaches consists in defining h as a Newton step based on the Hessian H and gradients G estimated on all the remaining data points from the current model $\tilde{\boldsymbol{\theta}}$, i.e. $h(\tilde{\boldsymbol{\theta}}, c) = \tilde{\boldsymbol{\theta}} - H(\tilde{\boldsymbol{\theta}}, I \setminus c)^{-1} G(\tilde{\boldsymbol{\theta}}, I \setminus c)$ [16–21]. The main drawback behind the use of this approach in the federated setting is that it requires clients to compute and share gradients and Hessians of the local loss function. This operation should be avoided in FL, as these quantities are known to potentially leak information about the training data [22]. Other approaches to MU consist in applying zero-mean Gaussian perturbations to the model parameters, with magnitude of the standard deviation σ depending on the properties of the data on which unlearning has to be operated [16,23,24]. This approach is also not practical in a federated setting, as the estimation of the noise amplitude requires the access to potentially sensitive clients information.

2.4 Federated Unlearning Schemes

To meet the practical requirements of real-world use of FL, we consider FU methods compatible with the following criteria: 1) no additional work has to be performed by the clients withdrawing the study, 2) no additional information beyond model parameters must be exchanged between clients and server, 3) no modification of data is allowed at client side. Following this consideration, we identified 4 state-of-the-art FU approaches for our benchmark [6–9], and excluded a number of methods not satisfying the criteria [25–28]. We provide a brief description of the selected approaches, and refer to the related publications for additional details.

Fine-tuning. Fine-tuning of model parameters after excluding client c is a standard FU baseline [16,18]. Nevertheless, although fine-tuning can be shown to satisfy the utility criterion, it does not formally guarantee unlearning [9].

FedAccum [6]. FEDACCUM implements an heuristic based on the removal of the contribution of the parameters $\{\theta_c^t\}_{t=1}^T$ provided by client during FL optimization. Similarly to SCRATCH, the server performs the training procedure of equation (2), while however integrating in the optimization routine the existing contributions of the remaining clients $\{\theta_i^t\}_{i \in I \setminus c, t \in \{1,...,T\}}$.

FedEraser [6]. This approach performs a retraining from scratch, by however scaling the new contributions by the norm of the ones computed to obtain $\tilde{\theta}$, i.e. $\tilde{p}_i = p_i \|\theta_i^t\| / \|\tilde{\theta}_i^t\|$, every Δt aggregation rounds. FEDERASER is faster than SCRATCH by requiring a smaller amount of local work from the remaining clients, and less aggregations.

Unlearning with Knowledge Distribution (UKD) [7]. UKD consists in subtracting to $\tilde{\theta}$, the model trained with every client in I, all the contributions of client c, i.e. $h(\tilde{\theta}, c) = \tilde{\theta} - p_i \sum_{t=1}^T \theta_c^t$. The server subsequently applied fine-tuning to optimize the similarity of the predictions $\tilde{\theta}$ and $h(\tilde{\theta}, c)$ on a control dataset owned by the server. With UKD, no client needs to participate to the unlearning phase, while it is required the use of a dataset owned by the server.

Projected Gradient Ascent (PGA) [8]. This FU scheme unlearns client c by performing a succession of projected gradient ascents (PGA) on $\tilde{\theta}$ to achieve low performance of $h(\tilde{\theta}, c)$ on the dataset of client c. While PGA requires the dataset of client c to unlearn it, we consider this FU scheme to show that minimizing the performances of client c is not sufficient to unlearn it.

Informed Federated Unlearning (IFU) [9]. IFU consists in tracing back the history of global models $\{\theta^t\}_{t=1}^T$ and restart FL from a specific round t^*, which is identified by fixing a cutoff on the magnitude of the contributions of client c, measured as $\sum_{t < t^*} \|\theta_c^{t+1} - \theta^t\|$. Prior to retraining, the global model θ^{t^*-1} is perturbed with Gaussian noise according to a given unlearning budget (ϵ, δ), with an analogy to randomized mechanisms in differential privacy [29].

3   Experiments

We introduce the federated dataset used for prostate segmentation in Sect. 3.1, and verify in Sect. 3.2 the efficiency of the FU schemes introduced in Sect. 2.4, based on the criteria introduced in Sect. 2.2. The code for the experiments is publicly available[1].

3.1   Federated Dataset for Prostate Segmentation

Our benchmark consists of a FL application on prostate segmentation from a large collection of magnetic resonance images (MRIs) dataset. We consider three publicly available image segmentation benchmarks (Decathlon [30], Promise12 [31], and ProstateX [32]) to create a cross-silo federated partitioning composed by four centers ($C1$ to $C4$), where data split are based on specific image acquisition properties, as summarized in Table 1.

---

[1] https://github.com/Accenture/Labs-Federated-Learning/tree/FU_prostate_segmentation.

Table 1. Description of the four centers used for FL and the respective training and testing DSC, obtained with the model trained with the four of them.

ID	Samples	Dataset	Description	DSC Train	DSC Test
C_1	32	Decathlon	Full Dataset	91.8(0.37)	87.4(1.4)
C_2	23	Promise12	With Endorectal Coil	96.3(0.15)	81.8(2.7)
C_3	27	Promise12	W o Endorectal Coil	95.8(0.14)	84.1(5.7)
C_4	184	ProstateX	With Scanner Skyra	96.1(0.22)	84.4(5.8)

Decathlon [30] is a dataset composed of medical images of ten different organs including prostate. We allocate to C_1 the 32 publicly available Decathlon MRIs of prostate segmentation acquired with different scanners. We merge the masks of the peripheral and transition zone to define the prostate mask.

Promise12 [31] was created for the Prostate MRI Segmentation challenge of 2012. We partition the 50 published training data samples based on the acquisition method: images acquired with and without endorectal coil (respectively allocated to C_2 and C_3).

ProstateX [32] is a collection of MRIs from different medical studies acquired with two different scanners (Skyra and Triotim, both from Siemens) and segmentation masks provided for 189 of them [33]. We ignore the five data points obtained with Triotim and allocate the remaining 184 images to C_4.

We note that the images in C_2 are the only ones acquired by using the endorectal coil, thus introducing a specific bias for this center. Prostate MRIs were resized to a resolution of $320 \times 320 \times 16$. For each center, we randomly select 80% of its data samples to create a training set and allocate the remaining 20% to a testing set. FEDAVG was used to optimized the federated training problem by optimizing a UNET [34] to maximise the dice score (DSC). To ensure generality of the results, we consider 5 random federated splits of the data and 5 different model initialization for the FL process. Hence, mean and standard error of the results reported in this section are estimated across 25 learning and unlearning scenarios. We detail in Appendix A the tuning of the hyperparameters for dropout value, learning rate, and amount of local work. We also detail the implementation of each FU scheme.

The model obtained when training with FL and the four centers has the performances summarized in Table 1. As expected, C_2 is associated with the lowest testing DSC, reflecting the specific heterogeneity of the data in C_2.

3.2   FU Benchmark

The unlearning benchmark here considered consists in unlearning the contributions of center C_2, the only center with MRIs acquired with endorectal coil. We provide in Table 2 a quantification of the impact of the FU schemes on utility and unlearning criteria, when the server performs 500 server aggregations to unlearn center C_2 with each FU scheme. The utility of our FU application is the average testing DSC of the remaining centers (C_1, C_3, and C_4), while the unlearning capability is quantified by the DSC on the training data of center C_2.

Table 2. Unlearning center C_2: FU utility and unlearning criteria described in Sect. 2.2. We note that only FEDERASER and IFU are able to unlearn center C_2, while keeping high utility on the remaining ones.

FU Scheme	SCRATCH	FINE-TUN.	FEDACCUM	FEDERASER	UKD	PGA	IFU
Utility	84.7(3.4)	85.0(3.6)	84.9(3.6)	84.6(3.6)	34.5(3.6)	85.1(3.7)	84.6(3.3)
Unlearning	62.2(3.5)	84.5(1.2)	84.4(1.4)	60.5(4.4)	24.0(2.9)	83.5(1.4)	58.3(4.2)

As discussed in Sect. 2.2, an optimal FU scheme should lead to a model with utility and unlearning capabilities as close as possible to the ones obtained with SCRATCH. Based on the results of Table 2, we note that not all the FU schemes provide acceptable unlearning and utility properties. In particular:

1. FINE-TUNING and FEDACCUM have high utility on the remaining centers but their unlearning criterion is more than 20% higher than SCRATCH. Figure 1 illustrates this result, where the predictive mask of the model obtained with FINE-TUNING is almost identical to the ground truth (similar qualitative results are obtained for FEDACCUM, and are illustrated in Appendix A).
2. UKD has utility and unlearning performances respectively 50% and 30 % different from SCRATCH, which shows that the predictive accuracy of the model obtained with UKD is degraded on every center. Figure 1 shows that this method provides poor segmentation results for images from both C_2 (to be unlearnt) and C_3 (to be preserved).
3. FEDERASER and IFU have identical utility to SCRATCH, while having only up to a 4% difference in unlearning capability. We see in Fig. 1 that while the segmentation performance in C_3 is still of good quality, the correct unlearning of C_2 leads to poor segmentation results, similar to those obtained with SCRATCH. The slight difference between unlearning performances for IFU, FEDERASER, and SCRATCH is likely due to the variability between model parameters as a result of the associated optimization routine.

The ensemble of results shown in Table 2, Fig. 1, and Appendix A, show that only FU schemes based on adaptive retraining (FEDERASER and IFU) provide satisfactory unlearning capabilities. On the contrary, the other approaches are either too conservative, thus leading to overly degraded models, or not effective, thus leading to poor unlearning properties. Concerning time efficiency, we report for IFU the amount of server aggregations needed for the resulting model to perform identically to SCRATCH after 500 server aggregations. For FEDERASER, we vary the frequency Δt at which the server requires contributions from the remaining centers. Table 3 shows that both IFU and FEDERASER achieve the desired utility and unlearning in a fraction of iterations needed by SCRATCH (resp. 2× and 1.9× faster). In addition of being able to unlearn center C_2,

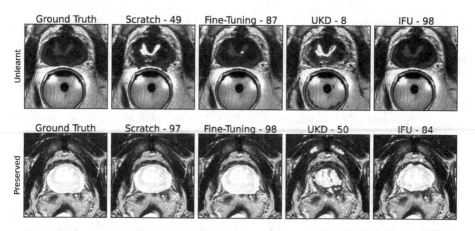

Fig. 1. Prediction Mask on a slice of a sample MRI from center C_2 (in blue) and from center C_3 (red), where FU is applied to the data of C_2. Additional results for all the FU schemes in Fig. 2 and 3 are available in the appendix.

IFU provides statistical guarantees for the unlearning of the center C_2. We also provide in Table 6 of Appendix A the impact of the unlearning budget (ϵ, δ) associated to IFU on utility and unlearning. These results show that regardless of the unlearning budget, IFU reaches almost identical utility to SCRATCH, while with the increase in budget ϵ and/or δ, the model is associated with worse unlearning capabilities.

Table 3. Optimization rounds when unlearning center C_2 with IFU for varying unlearning budget (3a) or with FEDERASER (3b). SCRATCH requires 500 rounds.

	$\delta = 0.01$	$\delta = 0.025$	$\delta = 0.1$
$\epsilon = 0.1$	276(13)	271(15)	271(14)
$\epsilon = 1$	298(18)	295(16)	298(15)
$\epsilon = 10$	259(18)	251(18)	228(17)

(a) FL iterations (mean, std) required by IFU to unlearn center C_2 for varying unlearning budget parameters (ϵ, δ).

Δt	Utility	Unlearning	FL iter.
1	84.6(3.6)	60.5(4.4)	500(0)
2	84.7(3.3)	61.8(4.1)	250(0)

(b) Utility, unlearning, and FL iterations (mean, std) for FEDERASER to unlearn center C_2 for varying frequency Δt.

4 Conclusion

We provide in this work an investigation of FU in a practical collaborative segmentation task on prostate imaging data. We first define a benchmark from a collection of large available public dataset, to create a realistic scenario of data heterogeneity in cross-silo applications. We show that FU methods based on adaptive retraining (FEDERASER and IFU) lead to optimal results in terms of trade-off between model utility, unlearning, and efficiency.

This study highlights a new perspective for the practical implementation of new data regulations in collaborative medical imaging applications. Future extensions of this work will be devoted to the investigation of FU in general medical applications, and to the assessment of the unlearning properties of the proposed methods, especially related to the definition of unlearning budget and parameters. In particular, since FEDERASER does not come with specific guarantees on the effectiveness of the unlearning, we believe that further assessment of the unlearning capabilities of this approaches are needed (Tables 4 and 5)..

A Additional Experiments and Experimental Details

Table 4. Hyperparameters fine-tuned to maximise the testing DSC when training with the four centers on a 5 folds cross-validation scenario, and then used for all our learning and unlearning scenario.

Description	Range	Best Value
Amount of Local Work	1 to 100	5
Amount of Server Aggregations	–	500
Batch Size	–	8
Local learning rate	0.0001 to 0.1	0.001
Dropout value	0 to 0.5	0.2

Table 5. Hyperparameters values for the different unlearning schemes.

Description	FU scheme	Range	Best Value
Unlearning budget parameter ϵ	IFU	$\{0.1, 1, 10\}$	1
Unlearning budget parameter δ	IFU	$\{0.01, 0.025, 0.1\}$	0.025
Amount of unlearning SGDs	PGA	–	100
Upper bound on the training DSC of C_2	PGA	–	0.12
Amount of local work for remaining clients	FEDERASER	–	5

Table 6. Impact of the unlearning budget (ϵ, δ) on the difference in utility and unlearning obtained with IFU and SCRATCH, when unlearning center C_2.

	$\delta = 0.01$	$\delta = 0.025$	$\delta = 0.1$
$\epsilon = 0.1$	.54(.13)	.54(.14)	.54(.13)
$\epsilon = 1$	.29(.19)	.31(.18)	.28(.17)
$\epsilon = 10$	.42(.15)	.46(.15)	.55(.15)

(a) Utility

	$\delta = 0.01$	$\delta = 0.025$	$\delta = 0.1$
$\epsilon = 0.1$	$-4.2(4.6)$	$-3.7(4.7)$	$-3.9(4.5)$
$\epsilon = 1$	$-4.6(3.8)$	$-3.9(3.7)$	$-2.9(3.5)$
$\epsilon = 10$	$2.5(5.2)$	$3.9(4.7)$	$6.0(4.3)$

(b) Unlearning

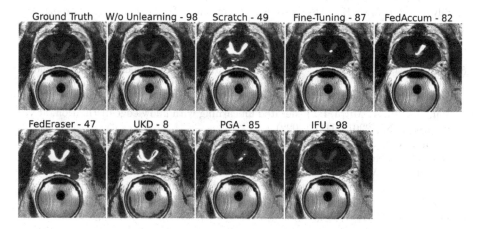

Fig. 2. Prediction Mask on a slice of a sample MRI from center C_2, where FU is applied to the data of C_2.

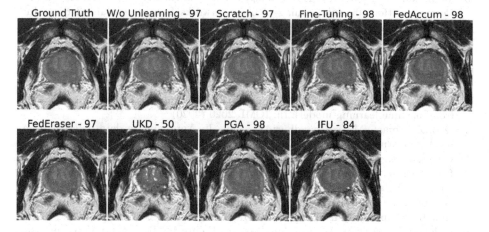

Fig. 3. Prediction Mask on a slice of a sample MRI from center C_3, where FU is applied to the data of C_2.

References

1. Voigt, P., von dem Bussche, A.: The EU General Data Protection Regulation (GDPR). Springer, Cham (2017). https://doi.org/10.1007/978-3-319-57959-7
2. Harding, E.L., Vanto, J.J., Clark, R., Hannah Ji, L., Ainsworth, S.C.: Understanding the scope and impact of the California consumer privacy act of 2018. J. Data Protect. Priv. **2**(3), 234–253 (2019)
3. Nguyen, T.T., et al.: A survey of machine unlearning. arXiv (2022)
4. Brisimi, T.S., Chen, R., Mela, T., Olshevsky, A., Paschalidis, I.C., Shi, W.: Federated learning of predictive models from federated electronic health records. Int. J. Med. Inf. **112**, 59–67 (2018)
5. Silva, S., Gutman, B.A., Romero, E., Thompson, P.M., Altmann, A., Lorenzi, M.: Federated learning in distributed medical databases: meta-analysis of large-scale subcortical brain data. In: 2019 IEEE 16th International Symposium on Biomedical Imaging, IEEE (2019)
6. Liu, G., Ma, X., Yang, Y., Wang, C., Liu, J.: Federaser: enabling efficient client-level data removal from federated learning models. In: 2021 International Symposium on Quality of Service (2021)
7. Wu, C., Zhu, S., Mitra, P.: Federated unlearning with knowledge distillation. arXiv preprint arXiv:2201.09441 (2022)
8. Halimi, A., Kadhe, S., Rawat, A., Baracaldo, N.: Federated unlearning: how to efficiently erase a client in FL? arXiv (2022)
9. Fraboni, Y., Vidal, R., Kameni, L., Lorenzi, M.: Efficient and provable client unlearning in federated optimization, Sequential informed federated unlearning (2022)
10. LeCun, Y., Bottou, L., Bengio, Y., Ha, P.: LeNet. In: Proceedings of the IEEE (1998)
11. Krizhevsky, A.: Learning multiple layers of features from tiny images (2009)
12. Liu, Z., Luo, P., Wang, X., Tang, X.: Deep learning face attributes in the wild. In: Proceedings of ICCV 2015 (2015)
13. McMahan, B., Moore, E., Ramage, D., Hampson, S., y Arcas, B.A.: Communication-efficient learning of deep networks from decentralized data. In: ICML 2017 (2017)
14. Li, X., Huang, K., Yang, W., Wang, S., Zhang, Z.: On the convergence of FedAvg on Non-IID data. In: ICLR 2020 (2020)
15. Khaled, A., Mishchenko, K., Richtárik, P.: Tighter theory for local SGD on identical and heterogeneous data. In: AISTATS 2020 (2020)
16. Guo, C., Goldstein, T., Hannun, A., Van Der Maaten, L.: Certified data removal from machine learning models. In: ICML 2020 (2020)
17. Izzo, Z., Smart, M.A., Chaudhuri, K., Zou, J.: Approximate data deletion from machine learning models. In: AISTATS 2021 (2021)
18. Golatkar, A., Achille, A., Soatto, S.: Eternal sunshine of the spotless net: selective forgetting in deep networks. In: Proceedings of the IEEE Conference on Computer Vision and Pattern Recognition (2020)
19. Golatkar, A., Achille, A., Soatto, S.: Scrubbing deep networks of information accessible from input-output observations, Forgetting outside the box (2020)
20. Golatkar, A., Achille, A., Ravichandran, A., Polito, M., Soatto, S.: Mixed-privacy forgetting in deep networks. In: Proceedings of the IEEE Conference on Computer Vision and Pattern Recognition (CVPR) (2021)

21. Mahadevan, A., Mathioudakis, M.: Certifiable machine unlearning for linear models. CoRR, abs/2106.15093 (2021)
22. Zhu, L., Liu, Z., Han, S.: Deep leakage from gradients. In: NeurIPS 2019 (2019)
23. Neel, S., Roth, A., Sharifi-Malvajerdi, S.: Descent-to-delete: Gradient-based methods for machine unlearning. In: Proceedings of the 32nd International Conference on Algorithmic Learning Theory, PMLR (2021)
24. Gupta, V., Jung, C., Neel, S., Roth, A., Sharifi-Malvajerdi, S., Waites, C.: Adaptive machine unlearning. In: Advances in Neural Information Processing Systems. Curran Associates Inc (2021)
25. Liu, Y., Xu, L., Yuan, X., Wang, C., Li, B.: The right to be forgotten in federated learning: an efficient realization with rapid retraining. In: IEEE INFOCOM 2022-IEEE Conference on Computer Communications (2022)
26. Wang, J., Guo, S., Xie, X., Qi, H.: Federated unlearning via class-discriminative pruning. In: Proceedings of the ACM Web Conference 2022 (2021)
27. Gao, X., et al.: Towards verifiable federated unlearning. arXiv, Verifi (2022)
28. Leijie, W., Guo, S., Wang, J., Hong, Z., Zhang, J., Ding, Y.: Federated unlearning: guarantee the right of clients to forget. IEEE Network **36**(5), 129–135 (2022)
29. Dwork, C., Roth, A.: The algorithmic foundations of differential privacy. Found. Trends Theor. Comput. Sci. **9**(3–4), 211–407 (2014)
30. Antonelli, M., et al.: The medical segmentation decathlon. Nat. Commun. **13**(1), 4128 (2022)
31. Koshkin, V.S., et al.: Promise: a real-world clinical-genomic database to address knowledge gaps in prostate cancer. Prostate cancer and prostatic diseases (2022)
32. Armato, S.G., III., et al.: Prostatex challenges for computerized classification of prostate lesions from multiparametric magnetic resonance images. J. Med. Imaging **5**(4), 044501–044501 (2018)
33. Cuocolo, R., Stanzione, A., Castaldo, A., Lucia, D.R.D., Imbriaco, M.: Quality control and whole-gland, zonal and lesion annotations for the prostatex challenge public dataset. Eur. J. Radiol. **138**, 109647 (2021)
34. Ronneberger, O., Fischer, P., Brox, T.: U-net: convolutional networks for biomedical image segmentation. In: Navab, N., Hornegger, J., Wells, W.M., Frangi, A.F. (eds.) MICCAI 2015. LNCS, vol. 9351, pp. 234–241. Springer, Cham (2015). https://doi.org/10.1007/978-3-319-24574-4_28

Federated Model Aggregation via Self-supervised Priors for Highly Imbalanced Medical Image Classification

Marawan Elbatel[1,2]([envelope]), Hualiang Wang[1], Robert Mart[2], Huazhu Fu[3], and Xiaomeng Li[1]

[1] The Hong Kong University of Science and Technology, Hong Kong, People's Republic of China
mkfmelbatel@connect.ust.hk
[2] Computer Vision and Robotics Institute, University of Girona, Girona, Spain
[3] Institute of High Performance Computing (IHPC), Agency for Science, Technology and Research (A*STAR), Singapore, Singapore

Abstract. In the medical field, federated learning commonly deals with highly imbalanced datasets, including skin lesions and gastrointestinal images. Existing federated methods under highly imbalanced datasets primarily focus on optimizing a global model without incorporating the intra-class variations that can arise in medical imaging due to different populations, findings, and scanners. In this paper, we study the inter-client intra-class variations with publicly available self-supervised auxiliary networks. Specifically, we find that employing a shared auxiliary pre-trained model, like MoCo-V2, locally on every client yields consistent divergence measurements. Based on these findings, we derive a dynamic balanced model aggregation via self-supervised priors (MAS) to guide the global model optimization. Fed-MAS can be utilized with different local learning methods for effective model aggregation toward a highly robust and unbiased global model. Our code is available at https://github.com/xmed-lab/Fed-MAS.

1 Introduction

Federated learning (FL) has emerged as a way to train models with decentralized data while preserving privacy. Due to the inherent nature of data heterogeneity in medical imaging, training in a decentralized manner exhibits performance degradation compared to centralized training. With FedAvg [23] as the main baseline, multiple works proposed to improve the model's generic performance under data decentralization [19,20,24]. These methods have been successful in achieving positive results, assuming a balanced global data distribution. However, they struggle to address extreme data heterogeneity, especially in highly imbalanced medical datasets. There have been some methods proposed to address the imbalanced setting [21,25]. Nevertheless, these methods shared local features among clients, which may raise privacy concerns.

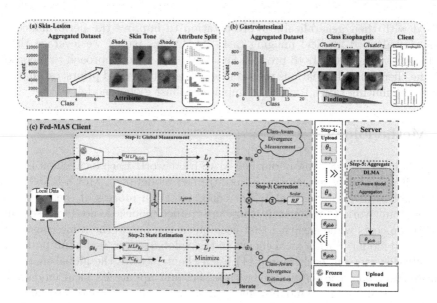

Fig. 1. (a) Skin lesion attribute imbalance, (b) Gastrointestinal findings imbalance (Ex: tracheleriazation, varices, leukoplakia). (c) Fed-MAS framework.

Label distribution skewness has been studied in the context of FL [33]. FedLC [33], inspired by LDAM [3], showed promising results by adjusting the local client class distribution. Additionally, multiple works proposed to tackle the issue of highly skewed label distribution (i.e. long-tailed) by decoupling the classifier and the feature extractor [5,29,32]. The rationale behind these methods is rooted in the understanding that the classifier is the bottleneck for majority class bias [18]. For instance, CReFF [29] retrained a balanced classifier on the server by leveraging federated features. A notable limitation of classifier re-training is its inability to address the intra-class attribute imbalance. Recently, [30] showed that training with imaging data with high attribute imbalance impedes representation learning by exacerbating the intra-class variations. In FL, the issue of intra-class imbalance is critical when dealing with highly imbalanced medical imaging datasets. As depicted in Fig. 1 (a), different skin tones can arise across different clients for the same class [1]. For gastrointestinal recognition depicted in Fig. 1 (b), different findings can arise in different clients for the same class [2]. Hence, the challenge of an unbiased robust global model that takes into account both the attribute and class imbalance still remains. More recently, FedCE [16] showed promising results by calculating a fair client contribution estimation in gradient and data space for medical image segmentation; Nevertheless, it relies on local validation samples, which may not adequately represent attribute imbalance and rare diseases in highly imbalanced medical image datasets.

Publicly available pre-trained models, such as MoCo-V2 [12] that were trained without any labels using a large set of naturals images, have been utilized with their batch statistics in calculating image priors [11] and have been utilized with their generalizable representation to improve the performance in highly imbalanced medical imaging tasks [8]. In this paper, we leverage these pre-trained models locally to propose Fed-MAS as a novel approach to incorporate the client's local variations with consistent self-supervised priors, estimating client contributing ratios toward an unbiased robust global model.

2 Methodology

Figure 1 shows the overview of our Fed-MAS framework. Each local client is provided with a publicly self-supervised pre-trained model (e.g., MoCo-RN50 [12]) that is not involved in the training or communication process of the federated learning framework. Consequently, these pre-trained models do not increase communication costs while ensuring that each client can access the same consistent pre-trained model. With n local clients and one global server, Fed-MAS performs the following steps in each round: (1) Each client receives the global model to measure its global class-aware divergence, w_k, and update its local model; (2) Each client trains its local model while estimating its class-aware divergence, $\hat{w}_k$; (3) Each client corrects $\hat{w}_k$ with w_k to generate a rescue scalar, RF; (4) Client uploads the parameters of its local model and RF to the server; (5) The server applies our proposed MAS to aggregate a new model from the parameters of the received client models, weighted by RF;

2.1 Class Aware Global Observation via Self-supervised Priors

In highly imbalanced medical image datasets, both extreme class imbalance and inter-client intra-class variations can lead to client drift. Due to the decentralization of data, estimating the global intra-class attribute distribution in medical imaging within the FL framework is a challenge that is yet to be explored.

At the beginning of each round in the FL process, each client receives the model from the global server θ_{global}. We study locally the distance between the distribution of the self-supervised pre-trained model, f_ξ, and θ_{glob} over each client's local data.

Given an input image x, we feed x to the local feature encoder g to generate a representation $z = g_\theta(x)$. This representation is then fed to an MLP projector to generate a projection $y = MLP_\theta(z)$ in a space comparable with the self-supervised model. From the same discriminative pre-trained model in all clients, we can get a target representation $y' = f_\xi(x)$, where both y and y' are L2 normalized. We can measure the distribution difference using mean squared error as:

$$\mathcal{L}_f^\theta = 2 - 2 \cdot \langle y, y' \rangle. \tag{1}$$

From Eq. 1, we can generate a class-aware distance for class k with M_k total samples as:

$$\mathcal{L}_k^\theta = \frac{1}{M_k} \sum_{i=1}^{M_k} \mathcal{L}_f^\theta(x_{k,i}). \tag{2}$$

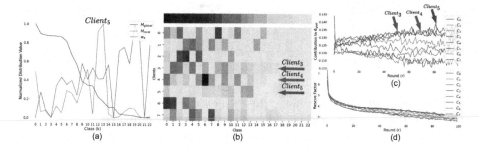

Fig. 2. Analysis of MAS on HyperKvasir: (a) The globally aggregated class counts, M_{global}, client local count, M_{local}, and w_k in one round. (b) HyperKvasir non-IID setting, (c) Client's Contribution to θ_{glob} throughout rounds, (d) Rescue Factor (RF) on different clients throughout rounds

We define $w_k = \mathcal{L}_k^{\theta_{glob}}$. The factor w_k can help to capture the distance in distribution between the global server and the self-supervised model on each client's local data. This divergence can provide insights into the sensitivity of the global model, θ_{glob}, in effectively capturing the specific class attribute in each client's local data. A high w_k indicates the failure of θ_{glob} in capturing a local class k. In Fig. 2 (a), we can see that w_k is inversely proportional to the global class distribution, even if the local client distribution is not necessarily the same.

2.2   State Estimation via Knowledge Distillation

While w_k provides class-aware global divergence measurement with the same consistent local frozen self-supervised model, a client receives the global model, θ_{glob}, and takes subsequent optimization steps for E local epochs with uncertainty to generate θ_c'. Hence, the client's drift from the global model is hideous after its uncertain optimization.

With a running average, a client can provide a class-aware divergence likelihood $\hat{w}_k$, where $\hat{w}_k = \sum_{e=1}^{E} \mathcal{L}_k^{\theta_c'}$. The factor $\hat{w}_k$ can help to capture how far the client drifted from f_ξ since the global measurement, w_k, was taken. A client can then correct this estimation, $\hat{w}_k$, with the global observation, w_k, to generate a posterior rescue factor, RF, in every round.

$$RF = \sum_{k=1}^{K} w_k \hat{w}_k. \qquad (3)$$

A higher RF indicates that the client has information that the global model has not appropriately captured.

To train the projector $MLP_\theta(\cdot)$, we propose to minimize Eq. 1 along with the local balanced risk minimization [28] to minimize a total loss $\mathcal{L}_{total}$ concerning θ only as:

$$\mathcal{L}_{total} = \mathcal{L}_{sup} + \lambda_f \, \mathcal{L}_f, \qquad (4)$$

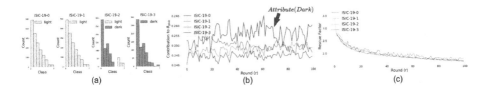

Fig. 3. (a) ISIC-FL Attribute Split, (b) Client's Contribution to θ_{glob} throughout rounds, (c) Rescue Factor (RF) on different clients throughout rounds

where $\mathcal{L}_{sup}$ refers to the original supervised loss and λ_f as a weighting factor. This can be seen as restricting the client optimization direction. However, the self-supervised model ensures clients align with a common reference distribution and possess implicit regularization capabilities for minority classes through generalizable features [9].

2.3   Model Aggregation via Self-supervised Posteriors

Inspired by the fact that client-specific models should contribute more to the global server to capture local variance, we propose a novel model aggregation via the corrected self-supervised posteriors (MAS) . We use our proposed RF to indicate client-specific models that should contribute more to the global model than client-generic models to capture their attribute-class variations. While our proposed RF can be used for biased client selection [15], we use it to aggregate a global model. Instead of aggregating based on the weighted samples as in FedAvg [23], we propose to weight the global model, θ_{glob}, based on the RF value as follows:

$$\bar{RF}_c = \frac{RF_c}{\sum_j RF_j} \text{ , and } \theta_{glob}^{r+1} = \sum_{c=1}^{C} \bar{RF}_c \theta_c'. \tag{5}$$

For instance, Client 3,4,5 in Fig. 2 (b) have mostly minority classes and contribute the most to θ_{glob} in Fig. 2 (c). Morever, in Fig. 3 (a) Client ISIC-3 have mostly underrepresented attribute and contributes the most in Fig. 3 (b). Additionally, we show in Figs. 2 (d) and 3 (c) that the rescue factor for all clients is decreasing throughout rounds. This highlights the ability of MAS to accommodate different clients. (See Algorithm 1 in Appendix).

3   Experiments

Dataset. HyperKvasir [2] is a long-tailed (LT) dataset of 10,662 gastrointestinal tract images with 23 classes from different anatomical and pathological landmarks and findings. We divide the 23 classes into Head (> 700 images per class), Medium ($70 \sim 700$ images per class), and Tail (< 70 images per class) with respect to their class counts. Additionally, we partition the data across eight clients with IID (similar label distributions) and non-IID (heterogeneous partition with Dirichlet distribution). **ISIC** [7] is a highly imbalanced dataset of skin

Table 1. Comparison with other methods on HyperKvasir Dataset. All clients are initialized with ImageNet pre-trained weights; each result is averaged over five runs.

Methods	IID					non-IID $Dir(\alpha = 0.5)$				
	Head	Medium	Tail	All	B-acc	Head	Medium	Tail	All	B-acc
Federated Learning Methods (FL-Methods)										
FedAvg [23]	94.1 ± 1.3	72.9 ± 1.3	3.1 ± 0.9	56.69 ± 0.6	58.1 ± 0.6	86.2 ± 2.7	70.3 ± 0.5	8.0 ± 1.2	54.83 ± 1.0	56.17 ± 0.9
FedProx [20]	94.6 ± 0.4	72.1 ± 0.2	3.0 ± 1.2	56.58 ± 0.4	57.93 ± 0.4	88.1 ± 2.2	73.1 ± 2.7	3.6 ± 2.5	54.93 ± 1.3	56.51 ± 1.3
MOON [19]	94.7 ± 0.7	74.6 ± 0.4	4.0 ± 1.8	57.77 ± 0.6	59.23 ± 0.6	84.4 ± 3.6	73.1 ± 1.6	5.5 ± 2.1	54.3 ± 1.2	55.93 ± 1.1
LT-integerated FL Methods										
LDAM-FL [3]	95.4 ± 0.5	72.2 ± 1.1	5.7 ± 3.9	57.77 ± 1.4	59.03 ± 1.3	86.9 ± 2.8	70.9 ± 1.2	4.7 ± 4.6	54.16 ± 1.4	55.61 ± 1.4
BSM-FL [28]	93.2 ± 1.5	74.6 ± 2.6	9.1 ± 3.7	58.92 ± 0.6	60.28 ± 0.7	89.6 ± 3.9	68.7 ± 3.0	16.4 ± 5.4	58.24 ± 1.2	59.15 ± 1.3
Label-Skew FL Methods										
CReFF [29]	95.1 ± 0.8	72.0 ± 1.5	2.6 ± 1.8	56.53 ± 1.4	57.88 ± 1.4	89.3 ± 0.7	70.1 ± 1.6	9.0 ± 4.5	56.12 ± 1.3	57.34 ± 1.2
FedLC [33]	96.5 ± 0.4	75.3 ± 2.5	7.4 ± 5.5	59.73 ± 1.8	61.08 ± 1.7	95.8 ± 0.6	73.1 ± 2.4	6.6 ± 4.1	58.51 ± 1.5	59.78 ± 1.5
Fed-Mas (ours)	94.3 ± 1.2	72.9 ± 1.0	15.9 ± 2.7	**61.05 ± 0.3**	**62.08 ± 0.2**	93.0 ± 0.9	72.5 ± 2.6	16.2 ± 1.3	**60.57 ± 1.1**	**61.61 ± 1.0**

lesion images with 8 classes that exhibits skin-tone attribute imbalance [1]. For instance, melanoma incidence is lower in quantity and higher in mortality rates in black patients than in others [6]. We partition the dataset on four clients based on two attributes, light and dark skin tones, with [1] labeling. Additionally, we split the data between the four clients for training, validation, and testing with 70%, 15%, and 15%, respectively. We also benchmark Fed-MAS over Flamby-ISIC split [31] with six different hospitals with stratified 5-fold cross-validation.

Implementation Details. For both datasets, we use resnet-18 [13] as the local target model. For the long-tailed HyperKvasir dataset, we employ an SGD optimizer and a cosine annealing scheduler [22] with a maximum learning rate of 0.1. For ISIC, we employ Adam optimizer with the 3e−4 learning rate. Additionally, we employ balanced risk minimization [28] and train methods for 200 communication rounds with 10 local epochs. We set λ_f to 3 and provide an ablation in Table 4 in Appendix.

Evaluation Metrics. We evaluate the model performance of the global model in this paper. To assess the unequal treatment of each class in HyperKvasir, we report the top-1 accuracy on shot-based division (head, medium, tail) and their average results denoted as "All" as existing works [17]. Following prior work [10,14,27], we also report the Balanced Accuracy "B-Acc", which calculates the average per-class accuracy and is resistant to class imbalance. As the test set of HyperKvasir contains only 12 classes, we follow previous work [10] to assess the model performance with a stratified 5-fold cross-validation. To evaluate the performance of attributes in ISIC-FL, we report the "B-Acc" separately for each attribute ("Light", "Dark") and the average of these scores "Avg". Additionally, we report the overall "B-Acc" across all attributes and distributions.

3.1 Performance on the HyperKvasir

We compare our methods with FL-methods [19,20,23], LT-integrated FL methods [3,28], and label-skew FL methods [29,33]

FL-Methods [19,20,23]. One simple solution for federated learning with highly imbalanced medical data is to apply existing FL methods to our setting directly.

To this end, we compare our methods with state-of-the-art FL methods, including FedAvg [23], FedProx [20], and MOON [19], under the same setting. As shown in Table 1, we find that our method outperforms the best existing FL method MOON by 2.85% and 5.68% on "B-acc" in both IID and non-IID settings, respectively. Notably, our Fed-MAS achieves similar results with MOON [19] on the "Head" while reaching large improvements on the "Tail" (11.9% on iid and 10.71% on non-iid), showing that our Fed-MAS can tackle LT distribution under FL more effectively. The limited results could be attributed to the use of local empirical risk minimization in MOON [19]. However, even when we applied a balanced risk minimization [28] in MOON, our method still outperformed it (60.69% vs. 62.08% on "B-acc" for IID); see results in Table 6 in Appendix.

LT integrated FL Methods [3,28]. To design FL methods for local clients with long-tailed distribution, a straightforward idea is to directly use LT methods in each local client and then use an FL framework such as FedAvg to obtain the final results. In this regard, we implement LDAM-DRW [3] and BSM [28] into the FedAvg framework and rename them as LDAM-FL and BSM-FL respectively. From Table 1, we can notice the LT methods utilizing an FL framework have produced limited results on "Tail" primarily due to the extreme client drifting phenomenon. Please note that Fed-MAS does not focus on designing any specific long-tailed training for each local client. Instead, MAS enables the global server to effectively aggregate the model parameters from long-tailed distributed local clients. As a result, our Fed-MAS can successfully capture the "Tail" with a 6.84% accuracy gain on IID with lower variance than the best-performing LT method BSM-FL [28]. Notably, our method consistently outperforms the best-performing LT method on the "B-acc" with a lower variance (improvement of 1.8% on IID and 2.46% on non-IID).

Label-Skew FL. We compare our method with the state-of-the-art label-skew FL method, FedLC [33], and the highly labeled skew (i.e. long-tailed) FL method, CReFF [29]. CReFF, as proposed by [29], involves a method of re-training the classifier by utilizing learnable features on the server at each communication round, holding an equal treatment of all clients' models. However, this technique fails to accommodate inter-client intra-class variations which could arise. From Table 1, we can notice that FedAvg with local LT such as BSM-FL [28] can outperform CReFF [29] on the HyperKvasir dataset in both IID and non-IDD by 2.4% and 1.8% on "B-acc", respectively. Our comparative analysis illustrates that Fed-MAS consistently outperforms CReFF in both IID and non-IID by 4.2% and 4.27% on "B-acc", respectively, by incorporating the client's local variations with MAS. FedLC [33] proposes a loss function to address label distribution skewness by locally calibrating logits and reducing local bias in learning. Their modification yields compelling performance. Nevertheless, our method surpasses them in both IID and non-IID, achieving improvements of 1.0% and 1.83% on "B-Acc", respectively. Remarkably, our method effectively captures the tail classes with reduced variance in both IID and non-IID, exhibiting improvements of 8.5% and 9.6%, respectively, while experiencing only a minor drop in performance for the head classes (96.5% vs 94.3% for IID and 95.8% vs 93.0% for non-IID).

Table 2. Ablation of minimizing Eq. 1 (KD) and MAS on HyperKvasir non-IID

	KD	MAS	Metrics		
			All (%)	B-acc (%)	p-value
BSM-FL [28] (Baseline)	×	×	58.24 ± 1.2	59.15 ± 1.3	—
[28] w/ KD	✓	×	59.26 ± 1.2	60.19 ± 1.1	<0.001
Fed-MAS	✓	✓	**60.57 ± 1.1**	**61.61 ± 1.0**	<0.001

Table 3. Experimental Results on ISIC-FL. Results are averaged over 5 folds.

Method	Attribute Setting (ours)				Flamby-ISIC [31]
	Light	Dark	Avg	B-Acc	B-Acc
	With ImageNet Weight Initialization				
FedLC [33]	71.11 ± 1.8	73.64 ± 6.6	72.38 ± 2.9	71.63 ± 1.6	76.54 ± 2.6
BSM-FL [28] (Baseline)	73.88 ± 1.4	74.78 ± 5.4	74.33 ± 2.5	74.49 ± 1.4	78.19 ± 1.8
[28] w/ KD	73.87 ± 1.6	72.44 ± 5.9	73.16 ± 3.0	74.09 ± 1.5	79.17 ± 2.1
Fed-Mas (ours)	73.43 ± 1.6	77.0 ± 6.6	**75.21 ± 2.9**	**74.61 ± 1.4**	**80.87 ± 2.2**

Effectiveness of KD and MAS. As shown in Table 2, minimizing Eq. 1 (KD) can enhance the "All" and "B-Acc" via 1.02% and 1.04% due to the implicit regularization of MoCo-V2 on the tail classes for extreme imbalance datasets. With both KD and MAS, the performance is further improved to the best via 2.33% and 2.46% on "All" and "B-Acc", respectively. MAS utilizes unbiased frozen generalizable representations to incorporate the inter-client intra-class characteristics in FL and combine them with the drifting belief. This combination helps in capturing client-specific models in the aggregation step.

3.2   Performance on ISIC-FL

We evaluate the best-performing and competitive methods with the ISIC-FL dataset to shorten the benchmark. While previous studies neglect weight initialization to provide better convergence analysis as pre-trained weights are architecture dependent. Recently, [26] and [4] studied the impact of pre-training initialization on reducing the data and system heterogeneity in FL. We present in Table 3 the results of the most competitive methods with weight initialization on the ISIC-FL attribute setting. FedLC [33] demonstrates compelling performance to address label skewness in Hyperkvasir-FL. Nevertheless, it falls short in accommodating attribute heterogeneity in ISIC-FL due to its local learning focus. Our method consistently outperforms FedLC [33] with a notable improvement of 2.8% and 3.0% in terms of the averaged balanced accuracies "Avg" and balanced accuracy "B-acc" respectively. Compared to the baseline [28], Fed-MAS notably captured the underrepresented attribute with 2.2% on the "B-acc" of the "Dark Attribute" with a minimal drop of 0.5% on the "B-acc" of the "Light Attribute", balancing the intra-class attribute characteristics in FL. On the highly heterogeneous Flamby-ISIC split resembling six hospitals,

Fed-MAS outperform FedLC and the baseline on the "B-acc" with 4.33% and 2.68%, respectively.

3.3 Privacy Concerns

Similarly to traditional FL methods [19,20,23], Fed-MAS shares the model weights with an additional scalar, RF, which protects data privacy by not revealing input data or label distribution. The *scalar*, RF, is calculated in the output feature space, safeguarding the input data distribution. Moreover, RF poses uncertainty in approximating the client's label distribution as it can be influenced by diverse attributes in the majority class or a common attribute in the minority class.

4 Conclusion

Highly Imbalanced datasets are present in most medical image classifications. This work presents Fed-MAS to deal with this problem. We show that publicly available self-supervised models benefit the FL training procedure more than restricting the optimization direction by incorporating the global attribute imbalance. Future work can explore delayed re-weighting to unleash non-vanishing terms and explore MAS with different local learning strategies in FL settings (Tables 4, 5, 7, 8 and Figs. 4, 5).

Acknowledgement. M.E is partially funded by the EACEA Erasmus Mundus grant. RM is partially funded by the research project PID2021-123390OB-C21 funded by the Spanish Science and Innovation Ministry. This work was supported by the Hong Kong Innovation and Technology Fund under Projects PRP/041/22FX and ITS/030/21, as well as by grants from Foshan HKUST Projects under Grants FSUST21-HKUST10E and FSUST21-HKUST11E.

A Appendix for Fed-MAS

Table 4. HyperKvasir λ_f ablation.

Method	IID			non-IID		
	$\lambda_f = 0$	$\lambda_f = 1$	$\lambda_f = 3$	$\lambda_f = 0$	$\lambda_f = 1$	$\lambda_f = 3$
Fed-MAS	60.28	61.43	**62.08**	59.15	61.08	**61.61**

Table 5. HyperKvasir f_ξ ablation non-IID. Note that features of f_ξ can be pre-computed.

f_ξ	All	B-Acc
CLIP-ViTB/32	60.34	61.39±2.1
MoCo-RN50	60.57	61.61±1.0

Table 6. HyperKvasir FL methods with local BRM [28].

Method	All		B-Acc	
	IID	non-IID	IID	non-IID2
FedAvg	58.92	58.24	60.28±0.6	59.15±1.3
FedProx	59.37	58.86	60.47±1.3	59.64±2.0
Moon	59.45	58.72	60.69±0.9	59.66±0.8
Ours	**61.05**	**60.57**	**62.08±0.2**	**61.61±1.4**

Table 7. Using a plug-in cRT [18] on HyperKvasir on non-IID.

Method + cRT	All	B-Acc
Decoupling [18]	54.21	55.6
BSM-FL [28]	62.67	63.11
Ours	**65.05**	**65.11**

Table 8. Flamby-ISIC [31] results on the first fold with the global model (gFL) and the local models (pFL) with ImageNet Weight Initialization. MOON [19] and FedProx [20] are reported with local BRM [28].

Method	Metric		Method	Metric	
	gFL	pFL		gFL	pFL
MOON ($\mu = 0.01$)	72.13	80.03	FedProx ($\mu = 0.1$)	72.47	79.82
MOON ($\mu = 0.1$)	72.45	79.64	FedProx ($\mu = 0.01$)	73.25	79.82
MOON ($\mu = 1$)	73.12	79.46	FedProx ($\mu = 0.001$)	73.52	79.70
FedLC [33]	68.07	78.60	BSM-FL [28]	72.83	79.79
[28] w/ KD ($\lambda_f=1$)	72.26	79.66	[28] w/ KD ($\lambda_f=3$)	72.85	80.06
Fed-MAS ($\lambda_f=1$)	72.94	82.73	Fed-MAS ($\lambda_f=3$)	**74.12**	**83.28**

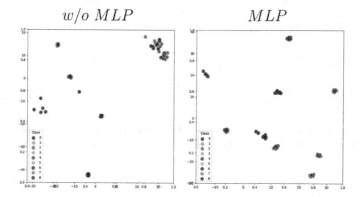

Fig. 4. Feature representation with and without the learnable projector MLP_θ. We sample a subset of head (0,1,2), medium (3,4,5), and tail (6,7,8) classes for feature visualization across different clients. Each point represents the mean feature output for each class (color) in each client (point).

Algorithm 1. Pseudocode for Fed-MAS.

1:   **Notations** total number of clients (C), server (S), total communication rounds (R), local epochs (E), learning rate (η), and a set of client's data sliced into batches of size B ($\mathcal{B}$).

2:   **ServerExecution:**

3:   Init θ^1_{glob}

4:   **for** *each round* $r = 1, ..., R$ **do**

5:     **for** *client* $c \in C$ *in parallel* **do**

6:        $\theta_c, RF_c \leftarrow$ **LocalUpdate**(θ^r_{glob});

7:        $\theta^{r+1}_{glob} \leftarrow$ **DLMA**$(RF_c, \theta'_c, c = 1$ to C$)$; // Eq. 5

8:   **Return** θ^R_{glob}

9:   **LocalUpdate** (θ_{glob}):

10:   Init $\hat{w}_k = 0$;

11:   Init $w_k = \mathcal{L}^{\theta_{glob}}_k$;

12:   **for** *each local epoch* $e = 1, ..., E$ **do**

13:     **for** *each batch* $b \in \mathcal{B}$ **do**

14:        $\mathcal{L}_{total} = \mathcal{L}_{sup} + \lambda_f \mathcal{L}_f$; // Eq. 4

15:        $\theta' \leftarrow \theta' - \eta \nabla \mathcal{L}_{total}$;

16:        $\hat{w}_k \leftarrow \hat{w}_k + \mathcal{L}_f(b_k)$; // running distillation loss mean for each class k

17:   $RF = \sum\limits_{k=1}^{K} w_k \hat{w}_k$;   // RF $\uparrow \approx$ divergence $\theta_{glob}, f_\xi \uparrow$

18:   **Return** θ', RF

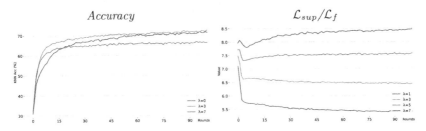

Fig. 5. Higher Value of λ_f ($\lambda_f = 7$) causes task deviation. $\lambda = 3$ show faster convergence (Acc.), and make L_{sup}/L_f ratio consistent on a toy dataset (CIFAR-100 non-iid).

References

1. Bevan, P.J., Atapour-Abarghouei, A.: Detecting melanoma fairly: skin tone detection and debiasing for skin lesion classification. In: Kamnitsas, K., et al. (eds.) Domain Adaptation and Representation Transfer, pp. 1–11. Springer Nature Switzerland, Cham (2022). https://doi.org/10.1007/978-3-031-16852-9_1

2. Borgli, H., et al.: Hyperkvasir, a comprehensive multi-class image and video dataset for gastrointestinal endoscopy. Sci. Data **7**(1), 283 (2019)

3. Cao, K., Wei, C., Gaidon, A., Arechiga, N., Ma, T.: Learning imbalanced datasets with label-distribution-aware margin loss. In: NeurIPS (2019)

4. Chen, H.Y., Tu, C.H., Li, Z., Shen, H.W., Chao, W.L.: On the importance and applicability of pre-training for federated learning. In: ICLR (2023)

5. Chen, Z., Liu, S., Wang, H., Yang, H.H., Quek, T.Q.S., Liu, Z.: Towards federated long-tailed learning. ArXiv abs/2206.14988 (2022)
6. Collins, K.K., Fields, R.C., Baptiste, D.F., Liu, Y., Moley, J.F., Jeffe, D.B.: Racial differences in survival after surgical treatment for melanoma. Ann. Surg. Oncol. **18**, 2925–2936 (2011)
7. Combalia, M., et al.: Bcn20000: Dermoscopic lesions in the wild. ArXiv abs/1908.02288 (2019)
8. Ding, X., Liu, Z., Li, X.: Free lunch for surgical video understanding by distilling self-supervisions. In: Wang, L., Dou, Q., Fletcher, P.T., Speidel, S., Li, S. (eds.) MICCAI 2022. LNCS, vol. 13437, pp. 365–375. Springer, Cham (2022). https://doi.org/10.1007/978-3-031-16449-1_35
9. Elbatel, M., Martí, R., Li, X.: FoPro-KD: fourier prompted effective knowledge distillation for long-tailed medical image recognition. ArXiv abs/2305.17421 (2023)
10. Galdran, A., Carneiro, G., González Ballester, M.A.: Balanced-mixup for highly imbalanced medical image classification. In: de Bruijne, M., et al. (eds.) Medical Image Computing and Computer Assisted Intervention - MICCAI 2021, pp. 323–333. Springer International Publishing, Cham (2021). https://doi.org/10.1007/978-3-030-87240-3_31
11. Hatamizadeh, A., et al.: GradViT: gradient inversion of vision transformers. In: 2022 IEEE/CVF Conference on Computer Vision and Pattern Recognition (CVPR), pp. 10011–10020 (2022)
12. He, K., Fan, H., Wu, Y., Xie, S., Girshick, R.B.: Momentum contrast for unsupervised visual representation learning. In: CVPR, pp. 9726–9735 (2020)
13. He, K., Zhang, X., Ren, S., Sun, J.: Deep residual learning for image recognition. In: CVPR, pp. 770–778 (2016)
14. Holste, G., Wang, S., Jiang, Z., Shen, T.C., Shih, G., Summers, R.M., Peng, Y., Wang, Z.: Long-tailed classification of thorax diseases on chest x-ray: a new benchmark study. In: Nguyen, H.V., Huang, S.X., Xue, Y. (eds.) Data Augmentation, Labelling, and Imperfections, pp. 22–32. Springer Nature Switzerland, Cham (2022). https://doi.org/10.1007/978-3-031-17027-0_3
15. Jee Cho, Y., Wang, J., Joshi, G.: Towards understanding biased client selection in federated learning. In: Camps-Valls, G., Ruiz, F.J.R., Valera, I. (eds.) Proceedings of The 25th International Conference on Artificial Intelligence and Statistics. Proceedings of Machine Learning Research, vol. 151, pp. 10351–10375. PMLR, 28–30 March 2022
16. Jiang, M., et al.: Fair federated medical image segmentation via client contribution estimation. In: CVPR (2023)
17. Ju, L., et al.: Flexible sampling for long-tailed skin lesion classification. In: Wang, L., Dou, Q., Fletcher, P.T., Speidel, S., Li, S. (eds.) MICCAI 2022, pp. 462–471. Springer Nature Switzerland, Cham (2022). https://doi.org/10.1007/978-3-031-16437-8_44
18. Kang, B., et al.: Decoupling representation and classifier for long-tailed recognition. In: ICLR (2020)
19. Li, Q., He, B., Song, D.: Model-contrastive federated learning. In: CVPR (2021)
20. Li, T., Sahu, A.K., Zaheer, M., Sanjabi, M., Talwalkar, A., Smith, V.: Federated optimization in heterogeneous networks. In: Dhillon, I., Papailiopoulos, D., Sze, V. (eds.) Proceedings of Machine Learning and Systems, vol. 2, pp. 429–450 (2020)
21. Liu, Q., Yang, H., Dou, Q., Heng, P.-A.: Federated semi-supervised medical image classification via inter-client relation matching. In: de Bruijne, M., et al. (eds.) MICCAI 2021. LNCS, vol. 12903, pp. 325–335. Springer, Cham (2021). https://doi.org/10.1007/978-3-030-87199-4_31

22. Loshchilov, I., Hutter, F.: SGDR: stochastic gradient descent with warm restarts. In: ICLR (2017)
23. McMahan, H.B., Moore, E., Ramage, D., Hampson, S., y Arcas, B.A.: Communication-efficient learning of deep networks from decentralized data. In: AISTATS (2017)
24. Mendieta, M., Yang, T., Wang, P., et al.: Local learning matters: rethinking data heterogeneity in federated learning. In: CVPR, pp. 8397–8406 (2022)
25. Mu, X., et al.: FedProc: prototypical contrastive federated learning on non-IID data. Future Gener. Comput. Syst. **143**, 93–104 (2021)
26. Nguyen, J., Wang, J., Malik, K., Sanjabi, M., Rabbat, M.: Where to begin? on the impact of pre-training and initialization in federated learning. In: ICLR (2023)
27. Reinke, A., Christodoulou, E., Glocker, B., et al.: Metrics reloaded - a new recommendation framework for biomedical image analysis validation. In: Medical Imaging with Deep Learning (2022)
28. Ren, J., et al.: Balanced meta-softmax for long-tailed visual recognition. In: Proceedings of Neural Information Processing Systems (NeurIPS), December 2020
29. Shang, X., Lu, Y., Huang, G., Wang, H.: Federated learning on heterogeneous and long-tailed data via classifier re-training with federated features. In: Raedt, L.D. (ed.) IJCAI, pp. 2218–2224, July 2022
30. Tang, K., Tao, M., Qi, J., Liu, Z., Zhang, H.: Invariant feature learning for generalized long-tailed classification. In: ECCV, p. 709–726 (2022)
31. Ogier du Terrail, J., Ayed, S.S., et al.: FLamby: datasets and benchmarks for cross-silo federated learning in realistic healthcare settings. In: NeurIPS. vol. 35, pp. 5315–5334, Curran Associates, Inc. (2022)
32. Wicaksana, J., Yan, Z., Cheng, K.T.: FCA: taming long-tailed federated medical image classification by classifier anchoring. ArXiv abs/2305.00738 (2023)
33. Zhang, J., Li, Z., et al.: Federated learning with label distribution skew via logits calibration, vol. 162, pp. 26311–26329. Proceedings of Machine Learning Research, 17–23 July 2022

FedAutoMRI: Federated Neural Architecture Search for MR Image Reconstruction

Ruoyou Wu[1,2,3], Cheng Li[1], Juan Zou[1,4], and Shanshan Wang[1,2(✉)]

[1] Paul C. Lauterbur Research Center for Biomedical Imaging, Shenzhen Institute of Advanced Technology, Chinese Academy of Sciences, Shenzhen 518055, China
[2] Peng Cheng Laboratory, Shenzhen 518055, China
ss.wang@siat.ac.cn
[3] University of Chinese Academy of Sciences, Beijing 100049, China
[4] School of Physics and Optoelectronics, Xiangtan University, Xiangtan 411105, China

Abstract. Centralized training methods have shown promising results in MR image reconstruction, but privacy concerns arise when gathering data from multiple institutions. Federated learning, a distributed collaborative training scheme, can utilize multi-center data without the need to transfer data between institutions. However, existing federated learning MR image reconstruction methods rely on manually designed models which have extensive parameters and suffer from performance degradation when facing heterogeneous data distributions. To this end, this paper proposes a novel FederAted neUral archiTecture search approach fOr MR Image reconstruction (FedAutoMRI). The proposed method utilizes differentiable architecture search to automatically find the optimal network architecture. In addition, an exponential moving average method is introduced to improve the robustness of the client model to address the data heterogeneity issue. To the best of our knowledge, this is the first work to use federated neural architecture search for MR image reconstruction. Experimental results demonstrate that our proposed FedAutoMRI can achieve promising performances while utilizing a lightweight model with only a small number of model parameters compared to the classical federated learning methods.

Keywords: Magnetic resonance imaging (MRI) · Federated learning · Neural architecture search

1 Introduction

Magnetic resonance imaging (MRI) plays a crucial role in clinical diagnosis and scientific research as a non-invasive imaging modality that can provide multi-contrast images. However, acquiring fully-sampled k-space data is usually time-consuming due to the physical limitations of the scanning device [18]. To address

M. E. Celebi et al. (Eds.): MICCAI 2023 Workshops, LNCS 14393, pp. 347–356, 2023.
https://doi.org/10.1007/978-3-031-47401-9_33

this issue, different methods have been introduced to accelerate MRI data acquisition. K-space data undersampling followed by high-quality MR image reconstruction is one of the most common techniques in the field [25]. Recently, deep learning-based methods have shown outstanding performance in accelerating MR image reconstruction. These methods can capture rich prior information from large amounts of data [1,9,20,23,24,28]. Deep learning-based MR image reconstruction methods can be broadly classified into data-driven [20,23,24,28] and model-driven approaches [1,9]. Data-driven approaches typically rely on large amounts of data and learn mapping relationships from undersampled data to fully-sampled data. Instead, model-driven approaches unroll the traditional optimization algorithm to the network to achieve end-to-end reconstruction. Although these methods have facilitated the development of MR image reconstruction to some extent, they need to collect large amounts of data for centralized training. For some institutions, it is difficult to collect adequate data due to the expensive acquisition cost. On the other hand, aggregating data from multiple institutions raises a serious problem—data privacy leakage, which may become infeasible in a realistic healthcare scenario [13].

Federated learning (FL), a distributed training paradigm, allows for collaborative learning across multiple institutions while protecting privacy [15–17,21]. The basic training processes of federated learning are as follows: 1) the server sends the initialized model to each client; 2) each client uses local computational resources and private data to train the model and sends the trained model to the server; 3) the server aggregates the models sent by the clients and broadcasts the aggregated model to the clients; 4) each client uses the aggregated model to update the local model and tests the performance of the updated model. After multiple interactive training between the clients and the server, a better global model can be obtained eventually. FedAvg [21] is the most classical federated learning framework that implements aggregation by averaging the model parameters of each client. Several researchers have attempted to solve the MR image reconstruction problem using federated learning [3,5–8]. For example, FL-MRCM [8] is the first attempt of employing federated learning method in MR image reconstruction. It alleviates the problem of domain shift by continuously aligning the latent features of source and target domains. In addition, FedMRI [6] achieves client-specific reconstruction by decomposing the reconstruction model into a global-shared encoder and local-personalized decoder. Although existing federated learning MR reconstruction methods have achieved promising performance, their reconstruction models are manually designed by experts, which may suffer from performance degradation when facing heterogeneous data distributions. In addition, the model parameters may be intentionally increased to improve the reconstruction performance, which undoubtedly increases the consumption of computational resources and may also result in parameter redundancy.

Neural Architecture Search (NAS) [4] can achieve better performance with fewer computational resources through automated architecture design. NAS methods can be roughly divided into three categories: evolutionary algorithm-based [27]; reinforcement learning-based [2,22] and gradient-based methods [11,19]. The first two methods demand heavy computational resources, while the gradient-based method can effectively save computational resources. There have been applications of NAS for MR image reconstruction [12,26]. To the best of our knowledge, neural architecture search methods have not been explored for federated MR image reconstruction. In order to improve the performance of the federated learning MR image reconstruction model, we propose a federated neural architecture search algorithm to improve the learning ability of the model and improve the performance of MR image reconstruction. We adopt a gradient-based NAS (differentiable architecture search) algorithm, which is more efficient and requires fewer computational resources [11]. Among different gradient-based NAS algorithms, DARTS [19] is the most classical one, but its search efficiency is not high enough. Following DARTS, MiLeNAS [11] is proposed, which achieves better search performance with mixed-level optimization. Our method adopts the MiLeNAS framework, and we improve the search space according to the demand for the number of model parameters and representation ability to make it suitable for the federated MR image reconstruction task. Our main contributions can be summarized as follows: (1) To the best of our knowledge, this is the first work to study federated neural architecture search techniques for MR image reconstruction. (2) We design a new search space according to the number of parameters, feature extraction, and representation capabilities of the model to make it more suitable for the federated MR image reconstruction task. (3) We introduce an exponential moving average method into the parameter update process of the client to increase the robustness of the client model. (4) Qualitative and quantitative experimental results demonstrate the effectiveness of our method.

2   Proposed Method

2.1   DL-Based MR Image Reconstruction

The aim of MR image reconstruction is to reconstruct a fully-sampled image $\mathbf{x} \in \mathbb{C}^N (M < N)$ from undersampled k-space data $\mathbf{k} \in \mathbb{C}^M$, such that:

$$\mathbf{k} = \mathbf{Ax} + \epsilon \tag{1}$$

where $\mathbf{A} \in \mathbb{C}^{M \times N}$ is the undersampling encoding matrix, and $\epsilon \in \mathbb{C}^M$ is the measurement noise. The process of solving $\mathbf{x}$ can be transformed into the following unconstrained optimization problem:

$$arg \min_{\mathbf{x}} \frac{1}{2} \|\mathbf{k} - \mathbf{Ax}\|_2^2 + \lambda R(\mathbf{x}) \tag{2}$$

where $R(\mathbf{x})$ denotes the regularization term in the image domain, and λ denotes the regularization coefficient. According to [1], Eq. (2) can be transformed into the following alternating optimization process:

$$\begin{cases} \mathbf{r}^j = D_\omega\left(\mathbf{x}^j\right) \\ \mathbf{x}^{j+1} = \left(\mathbf{A}^H\mathbf{A} + \lambda\mathbf{I}\right)^{-1}\left(\mathbf{A}^H\mathbf{k} + \lambda\mathbf{r}^j\right) \end{cases} \tag{3}$$

where $D_\omega(\cdot)$ represents a neural network for denoising, and $\mathbf{A}^H$ denotes the conjugate operator of $\mathbf{A}$. The regularization parameter λ can also be learned by the neural network. In this work, we mainly search the internal cell structure of $D_\omega(\cdot)$, and then stack the cell to form our denoising network. The structure is shown in Fig. 1.

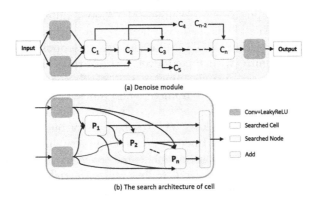

(a) Denoise module

(b) The search architecture of cell

Fig. 1. The overall structure of search space. (a) The structure of denoiser module $D_\omega(\cdot)$ in our reconstruction network. The searched cells are stacked to form our basic architecture, with each cell connected to the two consecutive cells that follow it. (b) The search architecture of the cell. P_n denotes the node in the cell.

2.2   FedAutoMRI: FederAted NeUral ArchiTecture Search for MR Image Reconstruction

Problem Definition. In the federated neural architecture search setting, it is assumed that there are C clients/hospitals, each of which has a private dataset $D_c = (x_c^i, k_c^i), i = 1, ..., N_c$. The corresponding objective function is defined as:

$$arg\min_{\theta,\alpha} \sum_{c=1}^{C} \frac{N_c}{N} \cdot \{\mathbb{E}_{(x_c,k_c)\sim D_c}[\|f_c(\mathbf{A}^H\mathbf{k}_c; \theta_c, \alpha_c) - \mathbf{x}_c\|_2]\} \tag{4}$$

where α_c and θ_c denote the architecture parameters and the corresponding model parameters of the cth client, respectively.

A typical NAS approach consists of three components: search space, search strategy, and performance evaluation [4]. We designed our candidate operation set $\mathcal{O}$ based on the number of parameters and representation capabilities of the target model. The set includes (1) Standard convolution, which extracts multi-scale information through convolution kernels of different sizes:

$std\_conv\_3 \times 3$, $std\_conv\_5 \times 5$ and $std\_conv\_7 \times 7$; (2) Dilated convolution, enlarging receptive field and reducing the number of parameters: $dil\_2\_conv\_3 \times 3$ and $dil\_3\_conv\_3 \times 3$; (3) Depthwise separable convolution, reducing parameters and computation while improving feature extraction and representation ability: $sep\_conv\_3 \times 3$, $sep\_conv\_5 \times 5$ and $sep\_conv\_7 \times 7$. An edge between two nodes in Fig. 1(b) represents one of these candidate operations. Inside the cell, to make the search space continuous by relaxing the categorical candidate operations between two nodes, mixed operations using $softmax$ over all candidate operations are performed [19]:

$$\bar{\varrho}^{(j,k)}(x) = \sum_{o=1}^{|\mathcal{O}|} \frac{exp(\alpha_o^{(j,k)})}{\sum_{o'=1}^{|\mathcal{O}|} exp(\alpha_{o'}^{(j,k)})} \varrho_o(x) \tag{5}$$

where $\bar{\varrho}^{(j,k)}(x)$ denotes the mixed operation for a pair of nodes (j,k), $|\mathcal{O}|$ denotes the number of candidate operations, $\alpha_o^{(j,k)}$ denotes the weight of the oth operation for a pair of node (j,k), and $\varrho_o(x)$ denotes the oth operation for a pair of node (j,k). The aim of architecture search is to learn the encoding $\alpha = \{\alpha^{(j,k)}\}$ of the architecture.

Searching Phase. In DARTS [19], the architecture parameters are optimized using only the loss of the validation set, which may not be optimal. To this end, He et al., [11] proposed a mixed optimization framework MiLeNAS that exploits both training and validation losses. Specifically, Eq. (4) is solved by optimizing ω and α during the local search process:

$$\begin{cases} \omega_c^{t,z+1} = \omega_c^{t,z} - \eta_\omega \nabla_\omega \mathcal{L}_{tr}(\mathbf{x}_c; \omega_c^{t,z}, \alpha_c^{t,z}) \\ \alpha_c^{t,z+1} = \alpha_c^{t,z} - \eta_\alpha \{\nabla_\alpha \mathcal{L}_{tr}(\mathbf{x}_c; \omega_c^{t,z}, \alpha_c^{t,z}) + \\ \qquad \beta \nabla_\alpha \mathcal{L}_{val}(\mathbf{x}_c; \omega_c^{t,z}, \alpha_c^{t,z})\} \end{cases} \tag{6}$$

where t and z denote global communication rounds and local training epochs, respectively. β denotes a non-negative regularization parameter that balances the importance of training and validation loss for α. η_ω and η_α represent the learning rates for updating ω and α, respectively. After the local search, all clients send the updated α and ω to the server, and the central server aggregates all parameters. We use a similar aggregation scheme as in [10], namely the average aggregation approach. Then, the server broadcasts the aggregated ω and α to all clients, and each client updates the local parameters for the next communication round.

Training Phase. After the model architecture search, the operations with the top two weights are selected as the operations in our final model for each pair of nodes (j,k). Considering the limitation of computational resources, there are only three nodes in the cell. In the training phase, in order to improve the robustness of the local client model, we introduce an exponential moving average method, which can be used to estimate the local mean of the variable. The corresponding formula is:

$$\omega_c^t = \frac{\gamma \cdot \omega_c^{t-1} + (1 - \gamma) \cdot \omega^t}{1 - \gamma^t} \tag{7}$$

where ω_c^t represents the weight of the cth client at the tth communication, ω^t represents the aggregated weight of the server at the tth communication, and γ represents the weighting coefficient.

3   Experiments and Results

3.1   Experimental Settings

Dataset. We search and train our proposed framework on three public datasets. Details of the datasets are provided as follows: 1) **fastMRI** [14]: A large public dataset of 1.5T and 3T data, from which we utilized T1 brain data of 1140 subjects; 2) **MoDL-Brain**[1]: A total of 524 slices are provided and the matrix size is cropped to 256×256; 3) **CC359**[2]: A total of 35 subjects are provided. The fastMRI dataset is used in the searching phase, which is equally divided into four clients, each containing 285 objects. All datasets are divided into training, validation and testing sets with a ratio of 7: 1: 2.

Implementation Details. All the networks were trained using the PyTorch framework with one NVIDIA RTX A6000 GPU (with 48 GB memory). In the searching phase, the Adam optimizer with a learning rate of 3e−3 is used to update architecture parameters and the weight decay is set to 1e−3. Besides, the Adam optimizer with a learning rate of 1e−3 is used to update local model parameters. Networks are trained for 50 global communication rounds with 5 local epochs. In the training phase, the AdamW optimizer with the initial learning rate of 1e−3 is adopted. Networks are trained for 150 global communication rounds with 5 local epochs. Figure 2 illustrates the evaluation metric corresponding to the searching and training phases.

3.2   Comparison with State-of-the-Art Methods

To demonstrate the effectiveness of our proposed method, we compare it with various state-of-the-art (SOTA) methods: 1) **Centralized**: centralized training using searched model; 2) **Non-Fed**: each client is individually trained using their private data without federated learning; 3) **FedAvg** [21]: a global model is obtained by using the average aggregation method; 4) **FedProx** [16]: a global model is obtained by adding a regularization term to the loss function of the client; 5) **FedMRI** [6]: personalized model is learned by adding a weighted contrastive regularization term to each client.

---

[1] https://github.com/hkaggarwal/modl.

[2] https://sites.google.com/view/calgary-campinas-dataset/mr-reconstruction-challenge.

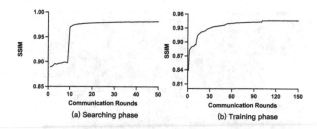

Fig. 2. evaluation metric corresponding to the searching and training phases. (a) Searching phase. (b) Training phase.

Table 1 lists the quantitative results of different methods. Overall, our proposed FedAutoMRI achieves a better reconstruction performance when compared to the SOTA methods. Due to the small amount of data provided by the MoDL-Brain dataset, the results of the comparison methods are worse on this dataset. By introducing the exponential moving average method, the robustness of our model is improved. Thus, it obtains satisfactory performance on this dataset. In addition, the number of parameters of our model is 0.016M, much fewer than the comparison methods. In other words, our proposed FedAutoMRI achieves better performance compared to the other methods except centralized method by using a very lightweight network architecture, which proves that our model is more efficient. In addition to the quantitative results, qualitative results are plotted in Fig. 3, and similar conclusions can be made that FedAutoMRI can reconstruct higher-quality MR images with smaller errors.

Table 1. Quantitative results of different methods on the three datasets. Bold numbers indicate our results.

Method	PSNR/dB			SSIM			Param/M
	fastMRI	CC359	MoDL-Brain	fastMRI	CC359	MoDL-Brain	
Centralized	39.9151	35.6296	33.0772	0.9792	0.9552	0.9131	0.016
Non-Fed	35.2427	31.5358	29.7220	0.9488	0.8990	0.8084	7.76
FedAvg [21]	35.4097	31.6159	29.5923	0.9519	0.9053	0.8040	7.76
FedProx [16]	35.6159	31.8033	29.8534	0.9529	0.9052	0.8148	7.76
FedMRI [6]	36.4179	32.0351	29.8061	0.9594	0.9105	0.8114	7.76
FedAutoMRI	**39.6817**	**35.2123**	**31.3378**	**0.9782**	**0.9515**	**0.8639**	**0.016**

3.3 Ablation Study

In this section, we analyze the effectiveness of the exponential moving average method and the efficiency of the model obtained by searching. Table 2 gives the corresponding results. According to these quantitative metrics, the performance of the model is improved after adding the exponential moving average, which verifies the effectiveness of this module. In addition, in order to compare the model

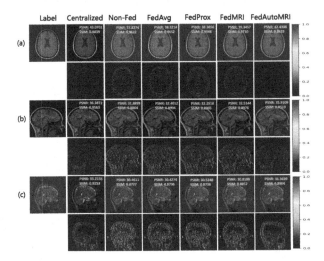

Fig. 3. Qualitative reconstruction results of different methods on the three datasets ((a) fastMRI, (b) CC359, (c) MoDL-Brain). From left to right, the seven images corresponding to the reference image, and the reconstructed images of Centralized, Non-Fed, FedAvg, FedProx, FedMRI and our FedAutoMRI, respectively. The second, fourth and six rows plot the corresponding error maps.

performance with the manually designed model, we list the number of parameters and computational complexity corresponding to a single model. Compared with the baseline model, our model only needs about 6.1% of the parameters and 5.7% of the computation, which proves the efficiency of our searched model.

Table 2. Results from ablation studies. Bold numbers indicate the best results.

Method	PSNR/dB			SSIM			Param/M	FLOPs/G
	fastMRI	CC359	MoDL-Brain	fastMRI	CC359	MoDL-Brain		
baseline	37.0153	33.6756	30.1359	0.9611	0.9297	0.8417	0.26	85.65
ema(w/o)	39.6064	35.1756	31.0704	0.9776	0.9499	0.8546	0.016	4.92
ema(w)	**39.6817**	**35.2123**	**31.3378**	**0.9782**	**0.9515**	**0.8639**	-	-

4   Conclusions

In this work, we proposed a federated neural architecture search framework for MR image reconstruction. We designed the search space to capture the heterogeneous data distributions, and we utilized differentiable architecture search methods to find the optimal architecture. In addition, to improve the robustness of the client model, we introduced an exponential moving average method. Experimental results validated that our method can better learn the prior knowledge from the data and obtain enhanced reconstruction performance on the three datasets. Results from ablation studies further verified the efficiency and effectiveness of our model.

Acknowledgment. This research was partly supported by the National Natural Science Foundation of China (62222118, U22A2040), Guangdong Provincial Key Laboratory of Artificial Intelligence in Medical Image Analysis and Application (2022B1212010011), Shenzhen Science and Technology Program (RCYX20210706092104034, JCYJ20220531100213029), and Key Laboratory for Magnetic Resonance and Multimodality Imaging of Guangdong Province (2020B 1212060051).

References

1. Aggarwal, H.K., Mani, M.P., Jacob, M.: MoDL: model-based deep learning architecture for inverse problems. IEEE Trans. Med. Imaging **38**(2), 394–405 (2018)
2. Bello, I., Zoph, B., Vasudevan, V., Le, Q.V.: Neural optimizer search with reinforcement learning. In: International Conference on Machine Learning, pp. 459–468. PMLR (2017)
3. Elmas, G., et al.: Federated learning of generative image priors for MRI reconstruction. IEEE Trans. Med. Imaging (2022)
4. Elsken, T., Metzen, J.H., Hutter, F.: Neural architecture search: a survey. J. Mach. Learn. Res. **20**(1), 1997–2017 (2019)
5. Feng, C.M., Li, B., Xu, X., Liu, Y., Fu, H., Zuo, W.: Learning federated visual prompt in null space for MRI reconstruction. In: Proceedings of the IEEE/CVF Conference on Computer Vision and Pattern Recognition, pp. 8064–8073 (2023)
6. Feng, C.M., Yan, Y., Wang, S., Xu, Y., Shao, L., Fu, H.: Specificity-preserving federated learning for MR image reconstruction. IEEE Trans. Med. Imaging (2022)
7. Gong, X., et al.: Federated learning with privacy-preserving ensemble attention distillation. IEEE Trans. Med. Imaging (2022)
8. Guo, P., Wang, P., Zhou, J., Jiang, S., Patel, V.M.: Multi-institutional collaborations for improving deep learning-based magnetic resonance image reconstruction using federated learning. In: Proceedings of the IEEE/CVF Conference on Computer Vision and Pattern Recognition, pp. 2423–2432 (2021)
9. Hammernik, K., et al.: Learning a variational network for reconstruction of accelerated MRI data. Magn. Reson. Med. **79**(6), 3055–3071 (2018)
10. He, C., Annavaram, M., Avestimehr, S.: Towards non-IID and invisible data with fedNAS: federated deep learning via neural architecture search. arXiv preprint arXiv:2004.08546 (2020)
11. He, C., Ye, H., Shen, L., Zhang, T.: MiLeNAS: efficient neural architecture search via mixed-level reformulation. In: Proceedings of the IEEE/CVF Conference on Computer Vision and Pattern Recognition, pp. 11993–12002 (2020)
12. Huang, Q., et al.: Enhanced MRI reconstruction network using neural architecture search. In: Liu, M., Yan, P., Lian, C., Cao, X. (eds.) MLMI 2020. LNCS, vol. 12436, pp. 634–643. Springer, Cham (2020). https://doi.org/10.1007/978-3-030-59861-7_64
13. Kaissis, G., et al.: End-to-end privacy preserving deep learning on multi-institutional medical imaging. Nat. Mach. Intell. **3**(6), 473–484 (2021)

14. Knoll, F., et al.: fastMRI: a publicly available raw K-space and DICOM dataset of knee images for accelerated MR image reconstruction using machine learning. Radiol. Artif. Intell. **2**(1), e190007 (2020)
15. Li, T., Sahu, A.K., Talwalkar, A., Smith, V.: Federated learning: challenges, methods, and future directions. IEEE Signal Process. Mag. **37**(3), 50–60 (2020)
16. Li, T., Sahu, A.K., Zaheer, M., Sanjabi, M., Talwalkar, A., Smith, V.: Federated optimization in heterogeneous networks. Proc. Mach. Learn. Syst. **2**, 429–450 (2020)
17. Li, X., Jiang, M., Zhang, X., Kamp, M., Dou, Q.: FedBN: federated learning on non-IID features via local batch normalization. arXiv preprint arXiv:2102.07623 (2021)
18. Liang, Z.P., Lauterbur, P.C.: Principles of Magnetic Resonance Imaging. SPIE Optical Engineering Press, Bellingham (2000)
19. Liu, H., Simonyan, K., Yang, Y.: DARTS: differentiable architecture search. arXiv preprint arXiv:1806.09055 (2018)
20. Mardani, M., et al.: Deep generative adversarial neural networks for compressive sensing MRI. IEEE Trans. Med. Imaging **38**(1), 167–179 (2018)
21. McMahan, B., Moore, E., Ramage, D., Hampson, S., Arcas, B.A.: Communication-efficient learning of deep networks from decentralized data. In: Artificial Intelligence and Statistics, pp. 1273–1282. PMLR (2017)
22. Pham, H., Guan, M., Zoph, B., Le, Q., Dean, J.: Efficient neural architecture search via parameters sharing. In: International Conference on Machine Learning, pp. 4095–4104. PMLR (2018)
23. Schlemper, J., Caballero, J., Hajnal, J.V., Price, A., Rueckert, D.: A deep cascade of convolutional neural networks for MR image reconstruction. In: Niethammer, M., et al. (eds.) IPMI 2017. LNCS, vol. 10265, pp. 647–658. Springer, Cham (2017). https://doi.org/10.1007/978-3-319-59050-9_51
24. Wang, S., et al.: Accelerating magnetic resonance imaging via deep learning. In: 2016 IEEE 13th International Symposium on Biomedical Imaging (ISBI), pp. 514–517. IEEE (2016)
25. Wang, S., Xiao, T., Liu, Q., Zheng, H.: Deep learning for fast MR imaging: a review for learning reconstruction from incomplete k-space data. Biomed. Signal Process. Control **68**, 102579 (2021)
26. Yan, J., Chen, S., Zhang, Y., Li, X.: Neural architecture search for compressed sensing magnetic resonance image reconstruction. Comput. Med. Imaging Graph. **85**, 101784 (2020)
27. Yang, Z., et al.: CARS: continuous evolution for efficient neural architecture search. In: Proceedings of the IEEE/CVF Conference on Computer Vision and Pattern Recognition, pp. 1829–1838 (2020)
28. Zhu, B., Liu, J.Z., Cauley, S.F., Rosen, B.R., Rosen, M.S.: Image reconstruction by domain-transform manifold learning. Nature **555**(7697), 487–492 (2018)

Fed-CoT: Co-teachers for Federated Semi-supervised MS Lesion Segmentation

Geng Zhan[1,2], Jiajun Deng[2], Mariano Cabezas[2], Wanli Ouyang[3], Michael Barnett[1,2], and Chenyu Wang[1,2(✉)]

[1] Sydney Neuroimaging Analysis Centre, Sydney, Australia
chenyu.wang@sydney.edu.au
[2] The University of Sydney, Sydney, Australia
[3] Shanghai Artificial Intelligence Lab, Shanghai, China

Abstract. Federated learning (FL) is an emerging technique for obtaining a global model while ensuring the data privacy of each client, which is particularly significant in protecting the patients' privacy when conducting medical image analysis. However, previous FL methods for medical images typically assume a fully supervised setting where each client's data is fully annotated, disregarding the fact that obtaining such extensive annotations may present significant obstacles due to the need for specialized expertise and the associated overhead costs. In this work, we focus on lesion segmentation for brain MRI images and propose a federated semi-supervised framework to address this problem. Formally, we introduce a Federated Co-Teachers algorithm (Fed-CoT) that extends the prevalent Mean Teacher algorithm into the federated learning framework, and demonstrate its effectiveness. Particularly, in Fed-CoT, two teacher models, namely sync-teacher and async-teacher, which capitalize on different weight updating schemes are leveraged to provide informative consistency regularization and to avoid overfitting to the noise of targets generated by a single teacher model. Our experimental results validate the merits of our proposed method and suggest that the federated learning model can benefit from extra data even without annotations. This approach relaxes the requirement for client participation in federated learning, making it easier to deploy in real applications.

Keywords: Federated learning · Medical Image Segmentation · Semi-supervised learning

1 Introduction

Medical image segmentation, which aims to identify regions of interest in medical images by taking advantage of computer assistance, exhibits its great potential in medical applications, such as early diagnosis, disease course tracking [8,20],

---

G. Zhan and J. Deng—Contributed equally to this work.

M. E. Celebi et al. (Eds.): MICCAI 2023 Workshops, LNCS 14393, pp. 357–366, 2023.
https://doi.org/10.1007/978-3-031-47401-9_34

and surgical treatment [6,17]. Brain lesion segmentation, as one of the critical topics aiming to identify lesions in brain medical images, has attracted a surge of research interest. However, there are two typical obstacles that prevent to-date brain lesion segmentation approaches to be applicable. For one thing, the advances in brain lesion segmentation heavily rely on large-scale and centralized datasets, which are challenging to be collected together due to data privacy concerns [15]. For another, most of the algorithms are developed on well-annotation data, but the medical expertise for distinguishing lesion regions together with the time costs make it hard to obtain full annotations.

To this end, federated learning and semi-supervised medical image segmentation have been employed to tackle the challenges of data privacy and annotation difficulties, respectively. Regarding the literature, these two steam techniques are developed independently. In federated learning [10], multiple clients collaborate to train the model under the scheduling of the server. This approach ensures that the raw medical data is kept private while enabling the training of a robust and accurate global model. In recent studies, federated learning was investigated in various segmentation tasks, where multiple hospitals collaborated to train a machine learning model [11,14]. The models achieved comparable performance to those trained on centralized data, demonstrating the potential of federated learning in medical applications [13]. In parallel with federated learning, semi-supervised algorithms are developed to make use of the combination of labeled and unlabeld data. In the literature, various semi-supervised frameworks have been proposed for medical image analysis [1,2,12]. Particularly, semi-supervised medical image segmentation learns the segmentation head from a small number of labeled data, and learns the effective representation from a large quantity of unlabeled data. Despite their efficacy, these two domains have been developed in isolation, resulting in a lack of exploration of the federated semi-supervised setting - a more relevant framework for real-world scenarios.

In this study, we devote our main efforts to developing a federated semi-supervised framework to address the problem of brain lesion segmentation. Formally, we introduce Federated Co-Teachers (Fed-CoT) algorithms, facilitating learning from abundant unlabeled and privacy-sensitive data sources. Specifically, we first generalize the idea of Mean Teacher in previous semi-supervised learning studies [7,16] from the centralized data to the distributed data in federated learning. Unlike previous methods where there is only a single teacher network, we keep two teacher networks at the training stage, namely sync-teacher and async-teacher. Despite both being a running weighted average of the student network at each iteration, the sync-teacher periodically synchronizes across clients and aggregates information from other clients, while the async-teacher does not interact with teacher models of other clients and therefore preserves the information on the local data. In this way, the student model learns the knowledge of unlabeled target data from intra-client async-teacher by encouraging prediction consistency, as well as obtaining generalization ability in unlabeled source data from inter-client sync-teacher. Under the supervision of different teacher models, the student model can also avoid overfitting the noise in the target generated by every single model. Moreover, we also extend the CutMix augmentation [19] to LeisionCutMix by taking into account the unique characteristics of brain lesions *i.e.*, the lesions volumes only occupy a small fraction of the brain and are scattered across the brain image. Consequently, the student model can effectively exploit the information from all data resources of different clients and achieve improved performance. Note that our proposed Fed-CoT can be incorporated into the federated learning framework seamlessly by leveraging common weighting average techniques (EMA [7] and FedAvg [10]).

2   Problem Formulation

2.1   Preliminary

Federated Learning. Given a set of distributed clients with their own local data, federated learning targets to collaboratively train a shared model without exchanging the private data of each client. This technique is particularly useful in applications such as medical image analysis, where patient privacy is of paramount importance to each clinic.

Semi-supervised Lesion Segmentation. Given a dataset of medical images, some of which are labeled with the locations of lesions and some of which are unlabeled, the task of semi-supervised lesion segmentation is to develop a segmentation algorithm that can accurately and efficiently identify the locations and boundaries of lesions in the images. The algorithm should be trained on both the labeled and unlabeled images, using the labeled images to guide the segmentation process and the unlabeled images to learn patterns and features that can improve segmentation performance.

2.2   Federated Semi-supervised Lesion Segmentation

Suppose there are K clients (*i.e.*, clinics) in our federated learning system, where each client C_k provides a set of labeled samples $\mathcal{L}_k = \{x_k^i, m_k^i\}_{i=1}^{L_k}$ and a set of unlabeled samples $\mathcal{U}_k = \{u_k^j\}_{j=1}^{U_k}$. Here x_k^i and u_k^j are the input MRI images, and m_k^i is the ground-truth mask of MRI image x_k^i. Note that the value of each pixel in m_k^i is either "0" or "1" since we only consider whether the lesion exists or not at each location. Under the federated learning framework, we have a global model G and a set of local models G_k. At the beginning of each communication round r, the local model is initialized with the same weights from G, and then optimized with local data independently. At the end of each round, the weights of all local models are aggregated to update the weights of the global model G.

3   Method

3.1   Mean Teacher

Our method is based on Mean Teacher framework [7,16], which is previously devised for centralized data. In Mean Teacher algorithm, A student model and a

---

Algorithm 1. *Federated-CoT.* The K clients are indexed by k. B is the local batch size. E is the number of local epochs. I is the number of iterations. T is the total number of rounds. η is the learning rate. The student model, sync-teacher model, async-teacher model are denoted as w, $\hat{w}$, and $\tilde{w}$, respectively. Steps that are particular for Fed-co-teacher and not in regular federated learning are highlighted in blue.

1: **procedure** *Server executes:*
2:      initialize the student model $\{w_0^k\}_{k=1}^K$ of each client with the same parameters
3:      initialize the sync-teacher of each client as $\hat{w}_0^k = w_0^k$
4:      initialize the async-teacher of each client as $\tilde{w}_0^k = w_0^k$
5:      **for** each round $t = 1, 2, ...T$ **do**
6:          **for** each client k **do**
7:              $w_{t+1}^k \leftarrow ClientUpdate(k, w_t, \hat{w}_t, \tilde{w}_t)$
8:          $w_{t+1} \leftarrow \frac{1}{K}\sum_{k=1}^K w_{t+1}^k$
9:          $\hat{w}_{t+1} \leftarrow \frac{1}{K}\sum_{k=1}^K \hat{w}_{t+1}^k$

10:
11: **procedure** *ClientUpdate*$(k, w, \hat{w}, \tilde{w})$:
12:      $\tilde{w} \leftarrow EMA(\tilde{w}, w, \alpha_2)$
13:      **for** each local epoch $e = 1, 2, ..., E$ **do**
14:          **for** each iteration $i = 1, 2, ..., I$ **do**
15:              $w \leftarrow w - \eta \bigtriangledown L$ // Loss function in Eqn. 3
16:              $\hat{w} \leftarrow EMA(\hat{w}, w, \alpha_1)$ // Eqn. 1
17:              $\tilde{w} \leftarrow EMA(\tilde{w}, w, \alpha_1)$ // Eqn. 1
         return $w, \hat{w}$ to server

---

teacher model are kept during the training phase. The parameters of the student model are optimized through back-propagation, while those of the teacher model are not trainable. In each iteration, the student model gets supervision from the ground-truth label on the labeled data. Meanwhile, the teacher model provides targets in the form of soft logits to the student model on the unlabeled data. Particularly, the teacher model is a slow-moving ensemble of the student model, which is initialized with the same parameters as the student model, and then updated with Exponential Moving Average (EMA) algorithm:

$$\hat{w}_t = \alpha \hat{w}_{t-1} + (1 - \alpha)w_t, \tag{1}$$

where α is the decay factor that controls the weight of the teacher's parameter $\hat{w}_{t-1}$ at the last step, and w_t is the current parameter of the student model.

3.2 Fed-CoT

The overview of our Fed-CoT pipeline is presented in Algorithm 1. Particularly, Fed-CoT includes a student model and two teacher models, namely sync-teacher and async-teacher. The sync-teacher periodically synchronizes across clients, while the async-teacher does not interact with teacher models from other clients and only interacts with the local model. These two teacher models work together to enable the student model to benefit from inter-client consistency while also preserving intra-client local information. Note that at the beginning of training, both sync-teacher and async-teacher models are initialized with the same parameters as the student model. However, at the end of each round, only the sync-teacher operates by synchronizing among multiple teachers from other clients, whereas the async-teacher operates independently of other clients' teacher models and thus maintains the local information.

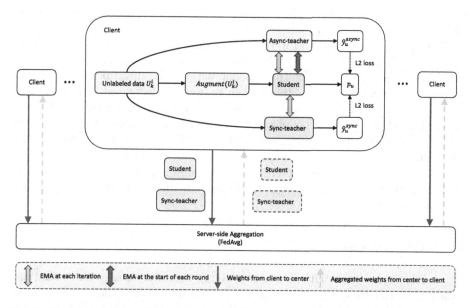

Fig. 1. Illustration for our Fed-CoT. In this figure, '$\rightarrow$' means forward operation, while '$--\rightarrow$' indicates providing supervision.

At each iteration i, a client randomly samples a mini batch of labeled data $\mathcal{L}_k^i = \{x_k^i, m_k^i\}_{i=1}^B \subset \mathcal{L}_k$ and another mini batch of unlabeled data $\mathcal{U}_k^i = \{u_k^j\}_{j=1}^B \subset \mathcal{U}_k$, where B is the mini batch size. The inputs to the student model consist of $\mathcal{L}_k^i$ and $Augment(\mathcal{U}_k^i)$, where the $Augment(\mathcal{U}_k^i)$ is the unlabeled data processed by our extended LeisionCutMix. In contrast to the original CutMix [19] that cuts a large patch and pastes to another image, our LesionCutMix randomly samples multiple small volumes. These volumes are from 8^3 voxels to 16^3 voxels, which and are similar to the size of lesions. The predictions of the student model for $\mathcal{L}_k^i$ and $Augment(\mathcal{U}_k^i)$ are denoted as p_l and p_u respectively. The input to the sync-teacher and async-teacher models is only $\mathcal{U}_k^i = \{u_k^j\}_{j=1}^B \subset \mathcal{U}_k$, and their predictions are denoted as $\hat{y}_u^{sync}$ and $\hat{y}_u^{async}$. For the labeled data, the training objective L_l is calculated as the binary cross entropy (BCE) Loss between the prediction p_l and the label y_l. For the unlabeled data, the training objective is a combination of the Euclidean distance between the outputs of sync/async-teacher and the student, which is as follows:

$$L_u = \frac{1}{2}(\|p_u - \hat{y}_u^{sync}\|^2 + \|p_u - \hat{y}_u^{async}\|^2). \tag{2}$$

By taking the training objectives of labeled and unlabeled data together, we get:

$$L = L_l + \lambda L_u, \tag{3}$$

where λ is a scaling factor. The overview of this forward process on unlabeled data is illustrated in Fig. 1.

During each iteration, both teacher models are updated by EMA algorithm after the student is updated. Different from the previous centralized setting where the parameters of the student network is only updated by backpropagation in each iteration, the student network in federated learning is also updated by weight aggregation at the end of each round during federated training. To keep the property of being a slow-moving ensemble of the student network for the teacher network, our async teacher model is additionally updated by the EMA immediately after the student gets updated by weight aggregation. Our sync teacher is additionally updated by the same aggregation method of the student network, where the sync teacher model of each client is averaged as the new sync teacher model.

4   Experiments

This section commences with an introduction to the datasets used for evaluation, namely MSSEG-16 and the in-house Clinic MS dataset, in Sect. 4.1. Following this, Sect. 4.2 provides the implementation details of Fed-CoT. Subsequently, the experimental results on two datasets are presented and analyzed in Sect. 4.3.

4.1   Dataset

MSSEG-16. This dataset is publicly available and is used for the MICCAI 2016 lesion segmentation challenge [4,5]. It comprises of 53 patients acquired from 4 distinct scanners, with each scanner being considered as a center in our experiments. For each center, we adopt a 50-50 data split, with 50% of the data being utilized for training the model, and the remaining 50% for testing. In accordance with the default configuration, we randomly select 1/4 of the training data as groundtruth data, while the remaining 3/4 are utilized as raw data without groundtruth.

Clinical MS Dataset. In order to further validate the efficacy of our approach in a clinical setting, we perform experiments utilizing the Clinical MS dataset, an in-house multi-scanner dataset for MS lesion segmentation. The dataset consists of 109 MS patients. The data is divided into three centers, denoted as C1, C2, and C3, where the data from each center is obtained using identical scanners. All lesion masks in the dataset are manually annotated by at least two experienced neuroimaging analysts. For each center, we adopt a 60-40 data split, with 60% of the data utilized for training the model and the remaining 40% for testing. As per the default configuration, we randomly select 1/4 of the training data as groundtruth data, while the remaining 3/4 are utilized as raw data without groundtruth.

4.2 Implementation Details

The student and two teacher networks in our study are constructed using the 3D U-Net architecture [3] with GroupNorm [18]. Unless otherwise specified, we set the local batch size $B = 16$, the local epochs $E = 1$, the iterations per epoch $I = 300$, the total number of rounds $T = 10$, and the learning rate $\eta = 0.00025$. Additionally, we employ the Adam optimizer for our experiments. We use the FLAIR image as the input and use input intensity normalization at the pre-processing step. Model training is conducted on a Nvidia DGX Station, with four V100 GPU.

Table 1. Experimental results on MSSEG-16 dataset. All the performances are reported in subject-wise DICE score.

Training data site				Use unlabled data	Method	Results				
C1	C2	C3	C4			C1	C2	C3	C4	All
✓					Single Client	0.078	0.520	0.638	0.616	0.080
	✓				Single Client	0.487	0.540	0.471	0.397	0.490
		✓			Single Client	0.108	0.136	0.085	0.049	0.090
			✓		Single Client	0.333	0.428	0.378	0.440	0.391
✓	✓	✓	✓		Centralized	0.478	0.598	0.462	0.583	0.522
✓	✓	✓	✓	✓	FL	0.495	0.544	0.416	0.567	0.501
✓	✓	✓	✓	✓	FL + PL	0.578	0.599	0.567	0.576	0.569
✓	✓	✓	✓	✓	FL+MT	0.368	0.492	0.391	0.457	0.430
✓	✓	✓	✓	✓	Fed-CoT	**0.607**	**0.600**	**0.614**	**0.598**	**0.605**

4.3 Experimental Results

MSSEG-16. We first perform comparison experiments on the MSSEG-16 dataset. We incorporate the following methods in FL setting into the comparison: supervised segmentation utilizing only labeled data, semi-supervised segmentation with pseudo-label (PL) [9], and semi-supervised segmentation with mean-teacher (MT) [7]. Moreover, we report the performance of supervised learning utilizing only labeled data for each individual center. The results are presented in Table 1.

The FL baseline model ($DICE = 0.501$ for testing data from all centers) utilizing labeled data from all centers demonstrates superiority over results obtained using only labeled data from a single client. Moreover, the results illustrate that training on a limited number of labeled data from a single client, i.e., C1

($DICE = 0.08$) or C2 ($DICE = 0.09$), can be unfeasible. These results high-light the effectiveness of general federated learning. Our proposed Fed-CoT out-performs the FL baseline by 0.104 in DICE score by utilizing unlabeled data. It also exhibits better results than the other two semi-supervised learning methods, Pseudo Labeling and Mean-teacher. While both Fed-CoT and Pseudo Labeling improve the FL baseline, the Mean-teacher method performs worse than the FL baseline. A plausible explanation for this inferior performance of the Mean-teacher method in FL is that the Mean-teacher model is not explicitly designed for the FL setting. In FL, the weight aggregation step of the student model may prevent the teacher model from updating properly, which is not a concern in centralized learning. This can lead to less effective guidance from the teacher model, resulting in sub-optimal segmentation performance.

Clinical MS Data. We validate the generalization ability of our method on a different dataset, the Clinical MS. The results are presented in Table 2. It is worth noting that Clinical MS is a larger dataset compared to the MSSEG-16 dataset. We observed that both Pseudo Labeling and Mean Teacher methods achieved inferior results compared to the baseline. This observation implies that designs that are not specifically tailored for the FL setting may lack the necessary adaptability and robustness to effectively address the unique challenges of FL. In contrast, our Fed-CoT, which is specifically designed for this setting, consistently outperformed the other methods on every client, demonstrating its efficacy and robustness in various scenarios.

Table 2. Experimental results on in-house Clinical MS dataset. All the performances are reported in subject-wise DICE score.

Method	Results			
	C1	C2	C3	All
FL baseline	0.540	0.605	0.444	0.526
FL + PL	0.516	0.583	0.419	0.502
FL + MT	0.522	0.594	0.431	0.510
Fed-CoT	**0.556**	**0.616**	**0.482**	**0.547**

5 Conclusion

In this study, we propose Fed-CoT, a semi-supervised lesion segmentation method in a federated learning framework. Fed-CoT utilizes two teacher net-works, namely, sync-teacher and async-teacher, to apply regularization consis-tency to the student network. The sync-teacher network aggregates inter-client information, while the async-teacher preserves more intra-client client-specific knowledge. We evaluate the proposed method on both public and in-house brain lesion datasets and demonstrate its superiority over other semi-supervised learning methods in the federated learning framework. Our findings suggest that Fed-CoT has the potential in relaxing the requirement for client participation, thereby facilitating the deployment of federated learning.

References

1. Bai, W., et al.: Semi-supervised learning for network-based cardiac MR image segmentation. In: Descoteaux, M., Maier-Hein, L., Franz, A., Jannin, P., Collins, D.L., Duchesne, S. (eds.) MICCAI 2017. LNCS, vol. 10434, pp. 253–260. Springer, Cham (2017). https://doi.org/10.1007/978-3-319-66185-8_29

2. Bortsova, G., Dubost, F., Hogeweg, L., Katramados, I., de Bruijne, M.: Semi-supervised medical image segmentation via learning consistency under transformations. In: Shen, D., et al. (eds.) MICCAI 2019. LNCS, vol. 11769, pp. 810–818. Springer, Cham (2019). https://doi.org/10.1007/978-3-030-32226-7_90

3. Çiçek, Ö., Abdulkadir, A., Lienkamp, S.S., Brox, T., Ronneberger, O.: 3D U-Net: learning dense volumetric segmentation from sparse annotation. In: Ourselin, S., Joskowicz, L., Sabuncu, M.R., Unal, G., Wells, W. (eds.) MICCAI 2016. LNCS, vol. 9901, pp. 424–432. Springer, Cham (2016). https://doi.org/10.1007/978-3-319-46723-8_49

4. Commowick, O., et al.: Objective evaluation of multiple sclerosis lesion segmentation using a data management and processing infrastructure. Sci. Rep. **8**(1), 13650 (2018)

5. Commowick, O., et al.: Multiple sclerosis lesions segmentation from multiple experts: the MICCAI 2016 challenge dataset. Neuroimage **244**, 118589 (2021)

6. De Bruijne, M.: Machine learning approaches in medical image analysis: from detection to diagnosis (2016)

7. French, G., Laine, S., Aila, T., Mackiewicz, M., Finlayson, G.: Semi-supervised semantic segmentation needs strong, varied perturbations. arXiv preprint arXiv:1906.01916 (2019)

8. Hesamian, M.H., Jia, W., He, X., Kennedy, P.: Deep learning techniques for medical image segmentation: achievements and challenges. J. Digit. Imaging **32**, 582–596 (2019)

9. Lee, D.H., et al.: Pseudo-label: the simple and efficient semi-supervised learning method for deep neural networks. In: Workshop on Challenges in Representation Learning, ICML, vol. 3, p. 896 (2013)

10. Li, T., Sahu, A.K., Talwalkar, A., Smith, V.: Federated learning: challenges, methods, and future directions. IEEE Signal Process. Mag. **37**(3), 50–60 (2020)

11. Li, W., et al.: Privacy-preserving federated brain tumour segmentation. In: Suk, H.-I., Liu, M., Yan, P., Lian, C. (eds.) MLMI 2019. LNCS, vol. 11861, pp. 133–141. Springer, Cham (2019). https://doi.org/10.1007/978-3-030-32692-0_16

12. Nie, D., Gao, Y., Wang, L., Shen, D.: ASDNet: attention based semi-supervised deep networks for medical image segmentation. In: Frangi, A.F., Schnabel, J.A., Davatzikos, C., Alberola-López, C., Fichtinger, G. (eds.) MICCAI 2018. LNCS, vol. 11073, pp. 370–378. Springer, Cham (2018). https://doi.org/10.1007/978-3-030-00937-3_43

13. Qi, X., Yang, G., He, Y., Liu, W., Islam, A., Li, S.: Contrastive re-localization and history distillation in federated CMR segmentation. In: Wang, L., Dou, Q., Fletcher, P.T., Speidel, S., Li, S. (eds.) Medical Image Computing and Computer Assisted Intervention-MICCAI 2022: 25th International Conference, Singapore, 18–22 September 2022, Proceedings, Part V, pp. 256–265. Springer, Cham (2022). https://doi.org/10.1007/978-3-031-16443-9_25

14. Rieke, N., et al.: The future of digital health with federated learning. NPJ Digit. Med. **3**(1), 119 (2020)

15. Tajbakhsh, N., Jeyaseelan, L., Li, Q., Chiang, J.N., Wu, Z., Ding, X.: Embracing imperfect datasets: a review of deep learning solutions for medical image segmentation. Med. Image Anal. **63**, 101693 (2020)

16. Tarvainen, A., Valpola, H.: Mean teachers are better role models: weight-averaged consistency targets improve semi-supervised deep learning results. In: Advances in Neural Information Processing Systems, vol. 30 (2017)

17. Treadaway, K., et al.: Factors that influence adherence with disease-modifying therapy in MS. J. Neurol. **256**, 568–576 (2009)

18. Wu, Y., He, K.: Group normalization. In: Ferrari, V., Hebert, M., Sminchisescu, C., Weiss, Y. (eds.) ECCV 2018. LNCS, vol. 11217, pp. 3–19. Springer, Cham (2018). https://doi.org/10.1007/978-3-030-01261-8_1

19. Yun, S., Han, D., Oh, S.J., Chun, S., Choe, J., Yoo, Y.: CutMix: regularization strategy to train strong classifiers with localizable features. In: Proceedings of the IEEE/CVF International Conference on Computer Vision, pp. 6023–6032 (2019)

20. Zhang, H., Oguz, I.: Multiple sclerosis lesion segmentation - a survey of supervised CNN-based methods. In: Crimi, A., Bakas, S. (eds.) BrainLes 2020. LNCS, vol. 12658, pp. 11–29. Springer, Cham (2021). https://doi.org/10.1007/978-3-030-72084-1_2

SplitFed Resilience to Packet Loss: Where to Split, that is the Question

Chamani Shiranthika[✉][ID], Zahra Hafezi Kafshgari[ID], Parvaneh Saeedi[ID], and Ivan V. Bajić[ID]

School of Engineering Science, Simon Fraser University, Burnaby, BC, Canada
{csj5,zha72,psaeedi,ibajic}@sfu.ca

Abstract. Decentralized machine learning has broadened its scope recently with the invention of Federated Learning (FL), Split Learning (SL), and their hybrids like Split Federated Learning (SplitFed or SFL). The goal of SFL is to reduce the computational power required by each client in FL and parallelize SL while maintaining privacy. This paper investigates the robustness of SFL against packet loss on communication links. The performance of various SFL aggregation strategies is examined by splitting the model at two points – shallow split and deep split – and testing whether the split point makes a statistically significant difference to the accuracy of the final model. Experiments are carried out on a segmentation model for human embryo images and indicate the statistically significant advantage of a deeper split point.

Keywords: SplitFed Learning · packet loss · human embryo image segmentation

1 Introduction

Federated learning (FL) [14] enables the training of machine learning models by multiple clients without sharing data. FL holds great promise for healthcare because of privacy constraints regarding medical data. In FL, clients train their local models and send them to the server for aggregation, after which the aggregated global model is sent back to the clients. Although FL addresses privacy concerns, it requires all clients to train local models that are usually of the same size as the global model. Since clients might not have the necessary computing resources (comparable to the server), this presents a challenge, especially for training large models.

Split Learning (SL) [7, 22] was developed to overcome this client-server processing disparity. In SL, a model is split into several parts that can reside in various locations and/or devices. Typically, the front-end of the model (usually the first few layers) is located on a client device, and the more computationally demanding back-end is located on a server. During model training, features

---

Supported in part by the Natural Sciences and Engineering Research Council (NSERC) of Canada under the grants RGPIN-2021-02485 and RGPAS-2021-00038.

M. E. Celebi et al. (Eds.): MICCAI 2023 Workshops, LNCS 14393, pp. 367–377, 2023.
https://doi.org/10.1007/978-3-031-47401-9_35

are sent from the front-end to the back-end, while gradients are sent from the back-end to the front-end. Thus, SL can solve the existing computational imbalance between the client(s) and the server in FL. However, SL on its own does not enable clients to collaborate in model training. Hence, recent research has blended FL and SL, resulting in hybrid Split-Federated Learning (SFL) [17,20], which combines the best of both worlds. SFL allows privacy preservation and collaboration between clients (like FL) while balancing computational resources between the client(s) and the server (like SL).

Error resilience is a critical challenge in distributed learning. The robustness of SFL to annotation errors has recently been studied in [9], while the issue of noisy communication links was tackled in [8]. Packet loss is another frequent transmission error in real-world communication networks, which occurs when one or more data packets fail to reach their destination. Several attempts have been made to address packet loss in the FL literature.

Authors in [18] modeled the link between the clients and the server in FL as a packet erasure channel and experimentally studied the model convergence with and without packet loss. Loss tolerant FL (LT-FL) was explored in [24] in terms of aggregation, fairness, and personalization. Authors used ThrowRight-Away (TRA) to accelerate the data uploading for low bandwidth devices by intentionally ignoring some packet losses. In SL, packet loss happens at model split points. Therefore, the question of *where to split* directly impacts the loss resilience. The optimal choice of split points [11,21] and loss resilience [1,3,5] have been active, but thus far separate, research topics in *split inference* (SI) or *colloborative intelligence* (CI) [2,10]. However, to the best of our knowledge, there appear to be no existing studies of the impact of the choice of split points on loss resilience in SL, let alone the more recent SFL paradigm.

This study investigates the impact of model split points on the loss resilience of SFL. We examine five parameter aggregation algorithms under various conditions such as different numbers of clients facing packet loss and different loss rates. Section 2 describes the system model and the aggregation methods examined. Section 3 describes the experiments and provides an analysis of the results. Conclusions and suggestions for future work are given in Sect. 4.

2   System Model

Figure 1 shows a SplitFed U-Net model for human embryo component segmentation on which our experiments are conducted. The U-Net consists of four downsampling blocks between the input and the bottleneck, and four upsampling blocks between the bottleneck and the output. Each block contains two convolutional layers with 3×3 kernels, a batch normalization layer, and ReLU activation. Each downsampling block starts with the aforementioned two convolutional layers followed by a 2×2 max-pooling layer. The number of filters in the four downsampling blocks increases as 32, 64, 128, and 256, from input towards the bottleneck. The bottleneck consists of two convolutional layers with 512 filters. Each upsampling block starts with a 2×2 upsampling layer followed by a transpose convolutional layer. The number of filters in the four upsampling blocks increases to 256, 128, 64, and 32 toward the output. The final upsampling block is followed by a convolutional layer with the **argmax** function.

We examine two ways of splitting the model: *shallow split* and *deep split*, indicated in Fig. 1. In shallow split, the first convolutional layer (front-end, FE), and the last two convolutional layers together with the output argmax layer (back-end, BE) are located on the client side, while the rest of the model is on the server. In deep split, the first two convolutional layers and the first max-pooling layer (front-end, FE), and the last three convolutional layers together with the final upsampling layer (back-end, BE) are located on the client side, while the rest of the model resides on the server.

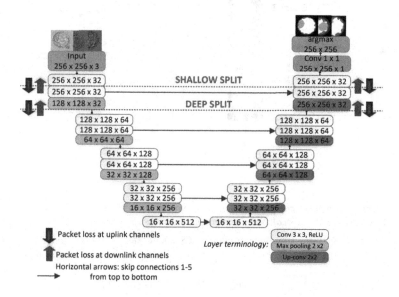

Fig. 1. Split U-Net architecture

The training process is as follows. First, initial copies of FE and BE are sent to each client, and the server makes a separate copy of its own model for each client. Each client then trains its local FE and BE in collaboration with its own copy of the server model for a certain number of local epochs. After that, each client sends its FE and BE models to the server, and aggregation is applied to all clients' FEs, BEs, and copies of the server model. The new aggregated global model consists of FE, server model, and BE. The server sends global FE and BE to each client to perform local validation. This completes one global epoch. During the forward pass, the features produced by the FE are sent from the client to the server. The server processes them through its own model and sends the resulting features back to the client to be processed by the BE. Client-side BE produces the prediction, computes the loss, and starts the back-propagation.

Gradient updates from the client-side BE are sent to the server, back-propagated through the server model, and then sent to the client-side FE. Figure 2 shows the adopted splitFed architecture of the U-Net model.

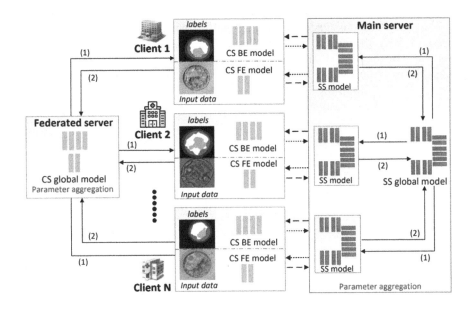

(1) Transmission of the current global model from the federated server or the main server
(2) Transmission of the local model parameters from the clients

     − −▶   Features/ smashed data flow   *CS: Client side*   *FE: Front End*
     ·······▶   Error gradients flow   *SS: Server side*   *BE: Back End*

Fig. 2. SplitFed U-Net architecture [17]

We implemented five well-known parameter aggregation algorithms: naïve averaging [14], federated averaging (FedAvg) [14], auto-FedAvg [23], fed-NCL_V2 [12], and fed-NCL_V4 [12]. In naïve averaging, parameter aggregation is based on the number of clients, while FedAvg considers the client's data distribution. Auto-FedAvg considers client's current training progress with their data distribution. In Fed-NCL_V2, each layer gets the same weight, while in Fed-NCL_V4, layer weights are proportional to their divergence from the global model. In both cases, parameter aggregation is based on the client's data distribution and local model divergence from the aggregated global model, while fed-NCL_V2 additionally considers training loss of local training data on the aggregated global model.

3   Experiments

3.1   Experimental Setup

The dataset consists of 781 human embryo images [13], each with ground-truth segmentation masks for five components: Background, Zona Pellucida (ZP), Tro-phectoderm (TE), Inner Cell Mass (ICM), and Blastocoel (BL). Of these, 70 images are saved as the test set, and the rest are used for training. Data are distributed among 5 clients - 240, 120, 85, 179, 87. Each client reserves 85% of its data for training and 15% for validation. During training, the input images are resized to 256 × 256. Augmentation is performed using horizontal and ver-tical flipping. *Soft Dice* loss [19] is chosen as the loss function. Adam optimizer is used with the initial learning rate of 10^{-4}. *Mean Jaccard index* (MJI) [4] without background is taken as the performance metric. The system is trained for 12 local and 15 global epochs. As in [3], each packet is assumed to be one row of a feature map. Data from the lost packets are assumed to be zero (i.e., no sophisticated packet loss concealment is deployed), so packet loss results in zeroing out some rows in the feature maps and gradient maps at split points. Figure 3 shows an example of a feature map in the forward pass and a gradient map in the back-propagation pass in the first epoch of SFL, both subject to 10% packet loss.

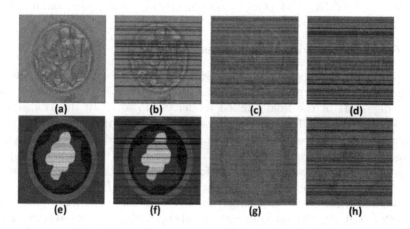

Fig. 3. A feature map (top row) and gradient map (bottom row) subject to 10% packet loss. Missing data is indicated by black horizontal lines. (a) Client FE feature map output before loss; (b) Server input after loss; (c) Server output feature map; (d) Client BE input after loss; (e) Client BE output gradient map; (f) Server input after loss; (g) Server output gradient map; (h) Client FE input after loss.

3.2   Baseline Experiments Without Packet Loss

First, we verify the performance of our core U-Net model by comparing it with BLAST-NET [15], a state-of-the-art network for human embryo image segmentation. We trained our U-Net model without splits, in a centralized manner[1] on the same dataset [16] of 235 images that BLAST-NET was trained on. The MJI of our U-Net was 81.70%, while the MJI of BLAST-NET [15] is 79.88%. Hence, our model compares favorably against BLAST-NET. Instead of achieving the new best embryo segmentation result, the aim of this experiment was simply to show that our U-Net model is a reasonable one.

Next, we verify the performance of our model in a split-federated scenario without packet loss. We test the performance of all five aggregation methods over 10 runs. Average MJI were 82.78%, 82.57%, 82.99%, 83.02%, and 82.95% for naïve avg, FedAvg, auto-FedAvg, fed-NCL_V2 and fed-NCL_V4, respectively.

We performed pairwise statistical significance testing for the difference in these average MJIs. Specifically, if J_{method1} and J_{method2} are MJI's of two parameter aggregation methods, the two-tail t-test is

$$
\begin{aligned}
H_0 &: J_{\text{method1}} = J_{\text{method2}} \\
H_1 &: J_{\text{method1}} \neq J_{\text{method2}}
\end{aligned}
\tag{1}
$$

When the p-value [6] is less than 0.05, the null hypothesis H_0 can be rejected (at the significance level of 0.05) to conclude that the difference is significant.

Most of the MJI differences were not statistically significant ($p \geq 0.05$), except that FedAvg had a significantly lower MJI than auto-FedAvg, fed-NCL_V2, and fed-NCL_V4. This is not surprising, as all three methods were developed to improve over FedAvg.

3.3 Experiments with Packet Loss

In our experiments, packet loss is assumed to be independent and identically distributed (iid) with probability $P_L \in \{0.1, 0.3, 0.5, 0.7, 0.9\}$. Figure 4 shows the average MJI of the final trained model vs. P_L over 10 runs for shallow- and deep-split models. In each case, six curves are shown: baseline performance without packet loss (green horizontal line) and the curves for $m/5$ clients experiencing packet loss, where $m \in \{1, 2, ..., 5\}$. For $P_L \in \{0.1, 0.3, 0.5\}$, deep and shallow split curves are close to the performance without packet loss, regardless of how many clients are experiencing packet loss. When $P_L = 0.7$, MJI starts to decrease, and more so when a larger number of clients experience packet loss. When $P_L = 0.9$, the shallow-split model ends up with near-zero MJI, regardless of how many clients experience packet loss. Meanwhile, the deep-split model can still be trained close to its no-loss performance when only a single client is experiencing packet loss, but in all cases ends up with higher MJI values than the shallow-split model.

Based on Fig. 4, it appears that the deep-split model can be trained to a higher MJI than the shallow-split model under all conditions. To test this, we performed 125 pairwise t-tests comparing shallow vs. deep split, for each unique combination of P_L and the number of clients experiencing packet loss. Table 1

---

[1] That is, without distributing data across the clients.

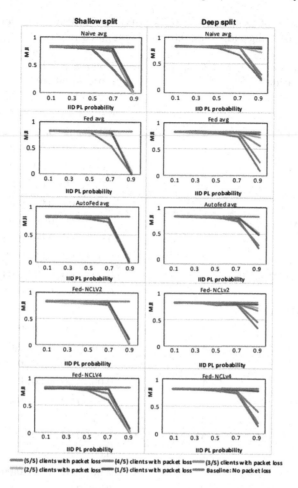

Fig. 4. MJI vs. P_L for shallow split (left) and deep split (right), with various numbers of clients experiencing packet loss.

shows the p-values of the corresponding one-tailed t-test comparing the MJI with deep and shallow splits, J_{deep} and J_{shallow}, respectively:

$$H_0 : J_{\text{deep}} \leq J_{\text{shallow}}$$
$$H_1 : J_{\text{deep}} > J_{\text{shallow}} \tag{2}$$

As seen in the table, in all cases we have $p < 0.05$, so one can reject the null-hypothesis H_0 and conclude that deep split produces a higher MJI than shallow split at the significance level of 0.05. Moreover, table cells highlighted in green indicate the cases where $p < 0.01$, and in all these cases, we can conclude that deep split is better than shallow split at a stronger significance level of 0.01. Hence, *in SFL over lossy links, the split point has a significant influence on the final model performance, and a deeper split is better.*

Table 1. Summary of the pairwise t-tests **between shallow and deep split** under various conditions. Values less than 0.01 are highlighted in green.

Parameter aggregation algorithm	# clients w/loss	One-tail p-value rounded off to 2nd decimal place				
P_L		0.1	0.3	0.5	0.7	0.9
Nave avg.	5	0.01	0.02	0.02	0.02	0.02
	4	0.00	0.00	0.00	0.00	0.00
	3	0.00	0.03	0.00	0.02	0.00
	2	0.00	0.00	0.02	0.02	0.00
	1	0.00	0.00	0.02	0.03	0.00
Fed avg.	5	0.00	0.00	0.00	0.02	0.03
	4	0.00	0.00	0.00	0.02	0.02
	3	0.01	0.03	0.00	0.00	0.00
	2	0.00	0.00	0.01	0.03	0.00
	1	0.00	0.00	0.00	0.00	0.00
Auto-Fedavg.	5	0.02	0.01	0.00	0.00	0.00
	4	0.00	0.00	0.00	0.00	0.00
	3	0.00	0.00	0.00	0.00	0.00
	2	0.02	0.00	0.00	0.00	0.00
	1	0.00	0.00	0.00	0.03	0.00
Fed-NCL_V2	5	0.00	0.00	0.01	0.00	0.00
	4	0.01	0.02	0.02	0.00	0.00
	3	0.00	0.00	0.00	0.00	0.00
	2	0.00	0.01	0.00	0.01	0.00
	1	0.00	0.01	0.02	0.00	0.00
Fed-NCL_V4	5	0.00	0.02	0.00	0.00	0.00
	4	0.00	0.00	0.00	0.00	0.00
	3	0.00	0.00	0.00	0.00	0.00
	2	0.00	0.00	0.00	0.00	0.00
	1	0.00	0.00	0.00	0.00	0.00

Finally, we examined whether any aggregation methods perform significantly better than others under the packet loss scenario for the deep-split model. With five aggregation methods, $\binom{5}{4} = 10$ pairwise comparisons can be made for five values of P_L and five numbers of clients experiencing packet loss; hence $10 \times 5 \times 5 = 250$ comparisons. We performed a t-test for each of the 250 cases. Some methods performed (significantly) better than others in certain cases, but we did not notice any pattern that would allow us to conclude that a certain method is better than others across the board. The full results can be found at https://drive.google.com/drive/u/0/folders/140f6OGYLRhjqcNQe2aLbnfy1dA7dYt60.

4 Conclusions and Future Work

In this paper, we examined the effects of model split points in split-federated learning (SFL) under packet loss. Experiments with five state-of-the-art aggregation methods showed that the split point has a statistically significant impact on the final model performance and that a deeper split is better. The reason for this is twofold: (1) the deep-split model has more layers available in the client-side back-end to learn how to recover the lost data, and (2) in our deep-split U-Net model, the first skip connection was fully located at the client and was able to transfer some features without packet loss.

It was also observed that SFL with our U-Net model was fairly robust to packet loss of up to 50%, with both shallow and deep split. This can be due to two reasons. The first reason is the use of ReLU activations in our split U-Net. It was reported in [3] that models with ReLU activations tend to be fairly robust to packet loss, because ReLU activations produce a lot of zeros in their output. Hence, when a missing feature value is replaced with a zero, much of the time, the zero value is the actual value that was lost. On the other hand, many high-performance models for applications in medical image analysis and computer vision use other activation functions, and such models could be more sensitive to packet loss. The second reason is that packet loss can act as a regularization technique, similar to dropout. To test this, we compared the MJI of models trained under packet loss with $P_L \in \{0.1, 0.3, 0.5, 0.7, 0.9\}$ and models trained with dropout rates that match these values. A split U-Net model was trained on all training samples ten times for each P_L and a matching dropout rate at the split points. At the significance level of 0.01, there were no statistically significant differences between the MJI of the models trained with packet loss and dropout of $P_L \in \{0.1, 0.3, 0.5\}$. For higher loss rates, models trained under packet loss had significantly lower MJI than those trained with the dropout. Hence, for low to moderate loss rates, the effect of packet loss is similar to dropout and will not negatively affect the MJI of trained models.

Other avenues for future work include testing the effectiveness of SFL with multiple application scenarios that apply diverse semantic segmentation networks across multiple split points, studying SFL with more realistic packet loss models, such as bursty loss or real packet traces, as well as developing more robust parameter aggregation algorithms for SFL and methods for packet loss recovery. Some work on missing data recovery in feature maps has been done in the context of collaborative inference [1,3,5]. However, in SFL, a loss is observed not only in feature maps but also in gradient maps, creating a new challenge. As the first study on the effects of packet loss in SFL, we hope that this paper will stimulate further work on that topic.

References

1. Bajić, I.V.: Latent space inpainting for loss-resilient collaborative object detection. In: Proceedings of IEEE International Conference Communication, pp. 1–6 (2021)

2. Bajić, I.V., Lin, W., Tian, Y.: Collaborative intelligence: challenges and opportunities. In: Proceedings of IEEE ICASSP, pp. 8493–8497 (2021)
3. Bragilevsky, L., Bajić, I.V.: Tensor completion methods for collaborative intelligence. IEEE Access **8**, 41162–41174 (2020)
4. Cox, M.A.A., Cox, T.F.: Multidimensional Scaling, pp. 315–347. Springer, Heidelberg (2008)
5. Dhondea, A., Cohen, R.A., Bajić, I.V.: CALTeC: content-adaptive linear tensor completion for collaborative intelligence. In: Proceedings of IEEE ICIP, pp. 2179–2183. IEEE (2021)
6. Fisher, R.A.: Statistical methods for research workers. In: Kotz, S., Johnson, N.L. (eds.) Breakthroughs in Statistics. Springer Series in Statistic, pp. 66–70. Springer, New York (1992). https://doi.org/10.1007/978-1-4612-4380-9_6
7. Gupta, O., Raskar, R.: Distributed learning of deep neural network over multiple agents. J. Netw. Comput. **116**, 1–8 (2018)
8. Kafshgari, Z.H., Bajić, I.V., Saeedi, P.: Smart split-federated learning over noisy channels for embryo image segmentation. In: ICASSP 2023–2023 IEEE International Conference on Acoustics, Speech and Signal Processing (ICASSP), pp. 1–5 (2023)
9. Kafshgari, Z.H., Shiranthika, C., Saeedi, P., Bajić, I.V.: Quality-adaptive split-federated learning for segmenting medical images with inaccurate annotations. arXiv preprint arXiv:2304.14976 (2023)
10. Kang, Y., et al.: Neurosurgeon: collaborative intelligence between the cloud and mobile edge. ACM SIGARCH Comput. Arch. News **45**(1), 615–629 (2017)
11. Kim, J., Park, Y., Kim, G., Hwang, S.J.: Splitnet: learning to semantically split deep networks for parameter reduction and model parallelization. In: Proceedings of Machine Learning and Research, pp. 1866–1874. PMLR (2017)
12. Li, L., Gao, L., Fu, H., Han, B., Xu, C.Z., Shao, L.: Federated noisy client learning (2021). arXiv:2106.13239 [cs]
13. Lockhart, L., Saeedi, P., Au, J., Havelock, J.: Multi-label classification for automatic human blastocyst grading with severely imbalanced data. In: 2019 IEEE 21st International Workshop on Multimedia Signal Processing (MMSP), Kuala Lumpur, Malaysia, pp. 1–6 (2019)
14. McMahan, B., Moore, E., Ramage, D., Hampson, S., Arcas, B.A.: Communication-efficient learning of deep networks from decentralized data. In: Artificial Intelligence and Statistics, pp. 1273–1282. PMLR (2017)
15. Rad, R.M., Saeedi, P., Au, J., Havelock, J.: BLAST-NET: semantic segmentation of human blastocyst components via cascaded atrous pyramid and dense progressive upsampling. In: Proceedings of IEEE ICIP, pp. 1865–1869 (2019)
16. Saeedi, P., Yee, D., Au, J., Havelock, J.: Automatic identification of human blastocyst components via texture. IEEE Trans. Biomed. Eng. **64**(12), 2968–2978 (2017)
17. Shiranthika, C., Saeedi, P., Bajić, I.V.: Decentralized learning in healthcare: a review of emerging techniques. IEEE Access **11**, 54188–54209 (2023)
18. Shirvanimoghaddam, M., Salari, A., Gao, Y., Guha, A.: Federated learning with erroneous communication links. IEEE Commun. Lett. **26**(6), 1293–1297 (2022)
19. Sudre, C.H., Li, W., Vercauteren, T., Ourselin, S., Jorge Cardoso, M.: Generalised dice overlap as a deep learning loss function for highly unbalanced segmentations. In: Cardoso, M.J., et al. (eds.) DLMIA/ML-CDS -2017. LNCS, vol. 10553, pp. 240–248. Springer, Cham (2017). https://doi.org/10.1007/978-3-319-67558-9_28
20. Thapa, C., Arachchige, P.C.M., Camtepe, S., Sun, L.: SplitFed: when federated learning meets split learning. In: Proceedings of AAAI, vol. 36, pp. 8485–8493 (2022)

21. Tuli, S., Casale, G., Jennings, N.R.: SplitPlace: AI augmented splitting and placement of large-scale neural networks in mobile edge environments (2022). arXiv:2205.10635 [cs]

22. Vepakomma, P., Gupta, O., Swedish, T., Raskar, R.: Split learning for health: distributed deep learning without sharing raw patient data (2018). arXiv:1812.00564 [cs, stat]

23. Xia, Y., et al.: Auto-FedAvg: learnable federated averaging for multi-institutional medical image segmentation (2021). arXiv:2104.10195 [cs, eess]

24. Zhou, P., Fang, P., Hui, P.: Loss tolerant federated learning. arXiv preprint arXiv:2105.03591 (2021). arXiv:2105.03591 [cs.LG]

Author Index

M. E. Celebi et al. (Eds.): MICCAI 2023 Workshops, LNCS 14393, pp. 379–381, 2023.
https://doi.org/10.1007/978-3-031-47401-9

Printed in the United States
by Baker & Taylor Publisher Services

Printed in the United States
by Baker & Taylor Publisher Services